Artificial Intelligence
and
Molecular Biology

Artificial Intelligence

and

Molecular Biology

Edited by

Lawrence Hunter

AAAI Press / The MIT Press
Menlo Park, California
Cambridge, Massachusetts
London, England

Copublished and distributed by

The MIT Press
Massachusetts Institute of Technology
Cambridge, Massachusetts, and London, England.

ISBN 0-262-58115-9

Manufactured in the United States of America

This book was typeset on an Apple Macintosh IIfx computer, with
Quark Xpress 3.1. The cover was designed by Lawrence Hunter and
Becky Cagle, using MacMolecule1.0 and Canvas 3.0.

Contents

Foreward ix
Joshua Lederberg
The Rockerfeller University

1. Molecular Biology for Computer Scientists 1
Lawrence Hunter,
National Library of Medicine

2. The Computational Linguistics of Biological Sequences 47
David B. Searls
University of Pennsylvania School of Medicine

3. Neural Networks, Adaptive Optimization, and RNA
Secondary Structure Prediction 121
Evan W. Steeg
University of Toronto

4. Predicting Protein Structural Features With Artificial
Neural Networks 161
Stephen R. Holbrook, Steven M. Muskal and Sung-Hou Kim
Lawrence Berkeley Laboratory

5. Developing Hierarchical Representations for Protein
Structures: An Incremental Approach 195
Xiru Zhang and David Waltz
Thinking Machines Corporation

6. Integrating AI with Sequence Analysis 210
Richard H. Lathrop, Teresa A. Webster, Randall F. Smith,
Patrick H. Winston and Temple F. Smith
MIT AI Lab, Arris Pharmaceutical Corporation,
Baylor College of Medicine and Boston University

7. Planning to Learn about Protein Structure 259
Lawrence Hunter

8. A Qualitative Biochemistry and its Application to the
   Regulation of the Tryptophan Operon   289
   Peter D. Karp
   SRI International

9. Identification of Qualitatively Feasible Metabolic Pathways   325
   Michael L. Mavrovouniotis
   University of Maryland, College Park

10. Knowledge-Based Simulation of DNA Metabolism:
    Prediction of Action and Envisionment of Pathways   365
    Adam R. Galper, Douglas L. Brutlag and David H. Millis
    Stanford University

11. An AI Approach to the Interpretation of the NMR
    Spectra of Proteins   396
    Peter Edwards, Derek Sleeman, Gordon C.K. Roberts
    and Lu Yun Lian
    University of Aberdeen

12. Molecular Scene Analysis: Crystal Structure Determination
    Through Imagery   433
    Janice I. Glasgow, Suzanne Fortier and Frank H. Allen
    Queen's University and Cambridge University

    Afterword: The Anti-Expert System—Thirteen Hypotheses
    an AI Program Should Have Seen Through   459
    Joshua Lederberg

    Index   464

Acknowledgements

This book has been a long time in coming, probably because I asked too few people for help. Nevertheless, I managed to accrue quite a few debts of gratitude along the way. In particular, the chapter authors have been great; they waited patiently for me to get my act together, and then responded quickly and graciously when I was suddenly in a hurry. Their warm collegiality was much appreciated. David Searls deserves special mention for driving his new MR2 down to Bethesda to spend a beautiful weekend inside, retypesetting his own chapter, fueled on little more than soda and potato chips. And Evan Steeg's remark that organization and good planning are just crutches for people who can't handle stress and caffeine will stay with me always.

The American Association for Artificial Intelligence has been supportive in several ways. They sponsored the 1990 Spring Symposium on AI and Molecular Biology, which was the meeting that eventually led to this book. The AAAI Press, particularly in the person of Mike Hamilton, have expressed unwavering enthusiasm for the book, and have been very generous.

The National Library of Medicine has also been supportive of my efforts, both on this book and in developing the field generally. NLM is a wonderful place to work, thanks to people like David States, Nomi Harris, Charles McMath, Fred Bowell, Ruth Lay, Debby Bennett, Steve Johnson-Leva, Jim Ostell, May Cheh, Jules Aronson, Susanne Humphrey, Bill Hole, Peter Clepper, Milton Corn and many others, including my "chain of command," Larry Kingsland, Dan Masys and Donald Lindberg.

I was first shown the potent synergy of AI & MolBio by Harold Morowitz, and through the BioMatrix workshops he organized. Although I missed the first one, the 1989 meeting introduced me to the amazing diversity of AI-interesting possibilities inherent in the field, and to valued colleagues like Kimberle Koile, Lindley Darden, Rick Lathrop and Chris Overton.

My wife, Kalí Tal, was my inspiration for this book. Her dedication, hard work and creative ability to understand and explain almost anything make her one of the most productive scholars I have ever known. I do my best to follow her example. Since she also singlehandedly publishes an academic journal and several books a year, I thought I would try my hand at typesetting this book myself. I emerge from the process all the more respectful of her accomplishments, and ready to admit that not just anyone who can use a Macintosh can produce a good looking book. Thanks for the inspiration, the help and the love, Kalí.

Larry Hunter

To Shirley, Michael, and Joan

Foreward

Joshua Lederberg

Historically rich in novel, subtle, often controversial ideas, Molecular Biology has lately become heir to a huge legacy of standardized data in the form of polynucleotide and polypeptide sequences. Fred Sanger received two, well deserved Nobel Prizes for his seminal role in developing the basic technology needed for this reduction of core biological information to one linear dimension. With the explosion of recorded information, biochemists for the first time found it necessary to familiarize themselves with databases and the algorithms needed to extract the correlations of records, and in turn have put these to good use in the exploration of phylogenetic relationships, and in the applied tasks of hunting genes and their often valuable products. The formalization of this research challenge in the Human Genome Project has generated a new impetus in datasets to be analyzed and the funds to support that research.

There are, then, good reasons why the management of DNA sequence databases has been the main attractive force to computer science relating to molecular biology. Beyond the pragmatic virtues of access to enormous data, the sequences present few complications of representation; and the knowledge-acquisition task requires hardly more than the enforcement of agreed standards of deposit of sequence information in centralized, network-linked archives.

The cell's interpretation of sequences is embedded in a far more intricate context than string-matching. It must be conceded that the rules of base-complementarity in the canonical DNA double-helix, and the matching of codons to the amino acid sequence of the protein, are far more digital in their flavor than anyone could have fantasized 50 years ago (at the dawn of both molecular biology and modern computer science.) There is far more intricate knowledge to be acquired, and the representations will be more problematic, when we contemplate the pathways by which a nucleotide change can perturb the shape of organic development or the song of a bird.

The current volume is an effort to bridge just that range of exploration, from nucleotide to abstract concept, in contemporary AI/MB research. That bridge must also join computer scientists with laboratory biochemists—my afterword outlines some of the hazards of taking biologists's last word as the settled truth, and therefore the imperative of mutual understanding about how imputed knowledge will be used. A variety of target problems, andperhaps a hand-crafted representation for each, is embraced in the roster. There is obvious detriment to premature standardization; but it is daunting to see the difficulties of merging the hardwon insights, the cumulative world knowledge, that comes from each of these efforts. The symposium had also included some discussion of AI for bibliographic retrieval, an interface we must learn how to cultivate if we are ever to access where most of that knowledge is now deposited, namely the published literature. Those papers were, however, unavailable for the printed publication.

It ends up being easy to sympathize with the majority of MB computer scientists who have concentrated on the published sequence data. Many are even willing to rely on neural-network approaches that ignore, may even defeat, insights into causal relationships. But it will not be too long before the complete sequences of a variety of organisms, eventually the human too, will be in our hands; and then we will have to face up to making real sense of them in the context of a broader frame of biological facts and theory. This book will be recalled as a pivotal beginning of that enterprise as an issue for collective focus and mutual inspiration.

Molecular Biology for Computer Scientists

Lawrence Hunter

"Computers are to biology what mathematics is to physics."

— Harold Morowitz

One of the major challenges for computer scientists who wish to work in the domain of molecular biology is becoming conversant with the daunting intricacies of existing biological knowledge and its extensive technical vocabulary. Questions about the origin, function, and structure of living systems have been pursued by nearly all cultures throughout history, and the work of the last two generations has been particularly fruitful. The knowledge of living systems resulting from this research is far too detailed and complex for any one human to comprehend. An entire scientific career can be based in the study of a single biomolecule. Nevertheless, in the following pages, I attempt to provide enough background for a computer scientist to understand much of the biology discussed in this book. This chapter provides the briefest of overviews; I can only begin to convey the depth, variety, complexity and stunning beauty of the universe of living things.

Much of what follows is not about *molecular* biology per se. In order to explain what the molecules are doing, it is often necessary to use concepts involving, for example, cells, embryological development, or evolution. Biology is frustratingly holistic. Events at one level can effect and be affected by events at very different levels of scale or time. Digesting a survey of the basic background material is a prerequisite for understanding the significance of the molecular biology that is described elsewhere in the book. In life, as in cognition, context is very important.

Do keep one rule in the back of your mind as you read this: for every generalization I make about biology, there may well be thousands of exceptions. There are a lot of living things in the world, and precious few generalizations hold true for all of them. I will try to cover the principles; try to keep the existence of exceptions in mind as you read. Another thing to remember is that an important part of understanding biology is learning its language. Biologists, like many scientists, use technical terms in order to be precise about reference. Getting a grasp on this terminology makes a great deal of the biological literature accessible to the non-specialist. The notes contain information about terminology and other basic matters. With that, let's begin at the beginning.

1 What Is Life?

No simple definition of what it is to be a living thing captures our intuitions about what is alive and what is not. The central feature of life is its ability to reproduce itself. Reproductive ability alone is not enough; computer programs can create endless copies of themselves—that does not make them alive. Crystals influence the matter around them to create structures similar to themselves but they're not alive, either. Most living things take in materials from their environment and capture forms of energy they can use to transform those materials into components of themselves or their offspring. Viruses, however, do not do that; they are nearly pure genetic material, wrapped in a protective coating. The cell that a virus infects does all the synthetic work involved in creating new viruses. Are viruses a form of life? Many people would say so.

Another approach to defining "life" is to recognize its fundamental interrelatedness. All living things are related to each other. Any pair of organisms, no matter how different, have a common ancestor sometime in the distant past. Organisms came to differ from each other, and to reach modern levels of complexity through *evolution*. Evolution has three components: inheritance, the passing of characteristics from parents to offspring; variation, the processes that make offspring other than exact copies of their parents; and selection, the process that differentially favors the reproduction of some organisms, and hence their characteristics, over others. These three factors define an evolutionary process. Perhaps the best definition of life is that it is the result of the evolutionary process taking place on Earth. Evolution is the key not only to defining what counts as life but also to understanding how living systems function.

Evolution is a cumulative process. *Inheritance* is the determinant of almost all of the structure and function of organisms; the amount of variation from one generation to the next is quite small. Some aspects of organisms, such as the molecules that carry energy or genetic information, have changed very little since that original common ancestor several billion of years ago. Inheritance alone, however, is not sufficient for evolution to occur; perfect inheritance would lead to populations of entirely identical organisms, all exactly like the first one.

In order to evolve, there must be a source of *variation* in the inheritance. In biology, there are several sources of variation. Mutation, or random changes in inherited material, is only one source of change; sexual recombination and various other kinds of genetic rearrangements also lead to variations; even viruses can get into the act, leaving a permanent trace in the genes of their hosts. All of these sources of variation modify the message that is passed from parent to offspring; in effect, exploring a very large space of possible characteristics. It is an evolutionary truism that almost all variations are neutral or deleterious. As computer programmers well know, small changes in a complex system often lead to far-reaching and destructive consequences (And computer programmers make those small changes by design, and with the hope of improving the code!). However, given enough time, the search of that space has produced many viable organisms.

Living things have managed to adapt to a breathtaking array of challenges, and continue to thrive. *Selection* is the process by which it is determined which variants will persist, and therefore also which parts of the space of possible variations will be explored. Natural selection is based on the reproductive fitness of each individual. Reproductive fitness is a measure of how many surviving offspring an organism can produce; the better adapted an organism is to its environment, the more successful offspring it will create. Because of competition for limited resources, only organisms with high fitness will survive; organisms less well adapted to their environment than competing organisms will simply die out.

I have likened evolution to a search through a very large space of possible organism characteristics. That space can be defined quite precisely. All of an organism's inherited characteristics are contained in a single messenger molecule: deoxyribonucleic acid, or DNA. The characteristics are represented in a simple, linear, four-element code. The translation of this code into all the inherited characteristics of an organism (e.g. its body plan, or the wiring of its nervous system) is complex. The particular genetic encoding for an organism is called its *genotype*. The resulting physical characteristics of an organism is called its *phenotype*. In the search space metaphor, every point in the space is a genotype. Evolutionary variation (such as mutation, sexual recombination and genetic rearrangements) identifies the legal moves in this space. Selection is an evaluation function that determines how many other points a point can generate, and how long each point persists. The difference between genotype and phenotype is important because allowable (i.e. small) steps in genotype space can have large consequences in phenotype space. It is also worth noting that search happens in genotype space, but selection occurs on phenotypes. Although it is hard to characterize the size of phenotype space, an organism with a large amount of genetic material (like, e.g., that of the flower Lily) has about 10^{11} elements taken from a four letter alphabet, meaning that there are roughly $10^{70,000,000,000}$ possible genotypes of that size or less. A vast space indeed! Moves (reproductive events) occur asynchronously, both with each other and with the selection process. There are many non-deterministic elements; for example, in which of many possible moves is taken, or in the application of the selection function. Imagine this search process running for billions of iterations, examining trillions of points in this space in parallel at each iteration. Perhaps it is not such a surprise that evolution is responsible for the wondrous abilities of living things, and for their tremendous diversity.[*]

1.1 The Unity and the Diversity of Living Things

Life is extraordinarily varied. The differences between a tiny archebacterium living in a superheated sulphur vent at the bottom of the ocean and a two-ton polar bear roaming the arctic circle span orders of magnitude in many dimensions. Many organisms consist of a single cell; a Sperm Whale has more than 10^{15} cells. Although very acidic, very alkaline or very salty environments are generally deadly, living things can be found in all of them. Hot or cold, wet or dry, oxygen-rich or anaerobic, nearly every niche on the planet has been invaded by life. The diversity of approaches to gathering nutrients, detecting danger, moving around, finding mates (or other forms of reproduction), raising offspring and dozens of other activities of living creatures is truly awesome. Although our understanding of the molecular level of life is less detailed, it appears that this diversity is echoed there. For example, proteins with very similar shapes and identical functions can have radically different chemical compositions. And organisms that look quite similar to each other may have very different genetic blueprints. All of the genetic material in an organism is called its *genome*. Genetic material is discrete and hence has a particular size, although the size of the genome is not directly related to the complexity of the organism. The size of genomes varies from about 5,000 elements in a very simple organism (e.g. the viruses SV40 or ϕx) to more than 10^{11} elements

---

[*]Evolution has also become an inspiration to a group of researchers interested in designing computer algorithms, e.g. Langton (1989).

in some higher plants; people have about 3×10^9 elements in their genome.

Despite this incredible diversity, nearly all of the same basic mechanisms are present in all organisms. All living things are made of cells[*]: membrane-enclosed sacks of chemicals carrying out finely tuned sequences of reactions. The thousand or so substances that make up the basic reactions going on inside the cell (the core *metabolic pathways*) are remarkably similar across all living things. Every species has some variations, but the same basic materials are found from bacteria to human. The genetic material that codes for all of these substances is written in more or less the same molecular language in every organism. The developmental pathways for nearly all multicellular organisms unfold in very similar ways. It is this underlying unity that offers the hope of developing predictive models of biological activity. It is the process of evolution that is responsible both for the diversity of living things and for their underlying similarities. The unity arises through inheritance from common ancestors; the diversity from the power of variation and selection to search a vast space of possible living forms.

1.2 Prokaryotes & Eukaryotes, Yeasts & People

Non-biologists often fail to appreciate the tremendous number of different kinds of organisms in the world. Although no one really knows, estimates of the number of currently extant species range from 5 million to 50 million (May, 1988).[†] There are at least 300,000 different kinds of beetles alone, and probably 50,000 species of tropical trees. Familiar kinds of plants and animals make up a relatively small proportion of the kinds of living things, perhaps only 20%. Vertebrates (animals with backbones: fish, reptiles, amphibians, birds, mammals) make up only about 3% of the species in the world.

Since Aristotle, scholars have tried to group these myriad species into meaningful classes. This pursuit remains active, and the classifications are, to some degree, still controversial. Traditionally, these classifications have been based on the *morphology* of organisms. Literally, morphology means shape, but it is generally taken to include internal structure as well. Morhpology is only part of phenotype, however; other parts include physiology, or the functioning of living structures, and development. Structure, development and function all influence each other, so the dividing lines are not entirely clear.

In recent years, these traditional taxonomies have been shaken by information gained from analyzing genes directly, as well as by the discovery of an entirely new class of organisms that live in hot, sulphurous environments in the deep sea.

---

[*]A virus is arguably alive, and is not a cell, but it depends on infecting a cell in order to reproduce.

[†]May also notes that it is possible that half the extant species on the planet may become extinct in the next 50 to 100 years.

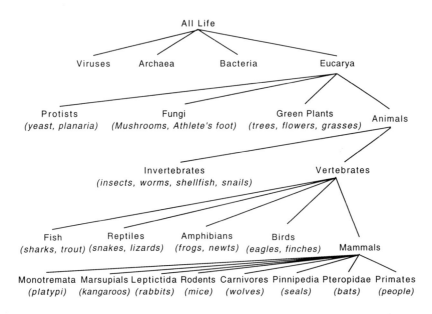

Figure 1. A very incomplete and informal taxonomic tree. Items in italics are common names of representative organisms or classes. Most of the elided taxa are Bacteria; Vertebrates make up only about 3% of known species.

Here I will follow Woese, Kandler & Wheelis (1990), although some aspects of their taxonomy are controversial. They developed their classification of organisms by using distances based on sequence divergence in a ubiquitous piece of genetic sequence As shown in Figure 1, there are three most basic divisions: the Archaea, the Bacteria and the Eucarya. Eucarya (also called eucaryotes) are the creatures we are most familiar with. They have cells that contain nuclei, a specialized area in the cell that holds the genetic material. Eucaryotic cells also have other specialized cellular areas, called organelles. An example of organelles are mitochondria and chloroplasts. Mitochondria are where respiration takes place, the process by which cells use oxygen to improve their efficiency at turning food into useful energy. Chloroplasts are organelles found in plants that capture energy from sunlight. All multicellular organisms, (e.g. people, mosquitos and maple trees) are Eucarya, as are many single celled organisms, such as yeasts and paramecia.

Even within Eucarya, there are more kinds of creatures than many non-biologists expect. Within the domain of the eucaryotes, there are generally held to be at least four kingdoms: animals, green plants, fungi and protists. From a genetic viewpoint, the protists, usually defined as single celled organisms other than fungi, appear to be a series of kingdoms, including at least the ciliates (cells with many external hairs, or cillia), the flagellates (cells with a single, long external fiber) and the microsporidia. The taxonomic tree continues down about a dozen levels, ending with particular species at the leaves. All of these many eucaryotic life forms have a great deal in common with human beings, which is the reason we can learn so much about ourselves by studying them.

Bacteria (sometimes also called eubacteria, or prokaryotes) are ubiquitous single-celled organisms. And ubiquitous is the word; there are millions of them everywhere — on this page, in the air you are breathing, and in your gut, for example. The membranes that enclose these cells are typically made of a different kind of material than the ones that surround eucarya, and they have no nuclei or other organelles (they do have ribosomes, which are sometimes considered organelles; see below). Almost all bacteria do is to make more bacteria; it appears that when food is abundant, the survival of the fittest in bacteria means the survival of those that can divide the fastest (Alberts, et al., 1989). Bacteria include not only the disease causing "germs," but many kinds of algae, and a wide variety of symbiotic organisms, including soil bacteria that fix nitrogen for plants and Escherichia coli, a bacterium that lives in human intestines and is required for normal digestion. E. coli is ubiquitous in laboratories because it is easy to grow and very well studied.

Archaea are a recently discovered class of organism so completely unlike both bacteria and eucarya, both genetically and morphologically, that they have upset a decades old dichotomy. Archaea live in superheated sulphur vents in the deep sea, or in hot acid springs, briny bogs and other seemingly inhospitable places. They are sometimes called *archebacteria* even though they bear little resemblence to bacteria. Their cell membranes are unlike either Bacteria or Eucarya. Although they have no nuclei or organelles, at a genetic level, they are a bit more like Eucarya than like Bacteria. These organisms are a relatively recent discovery, and any biological theories have yet to include Archaea, or consider them simply another kind of procaryote. Archaea will probably have a significant effect on theories about the early history of life, and their unusual biochemistry has already turned out to be scientifically and commercially important (e.g. see the discussion of PCR in the last section of this chapter).

Viruses form another important category of living forms. They are *obligatory parasites* meaning that they rely on the biochemical machinery of their host cell to survive and reproduce. Viruses consist of just a small amount of genetic material surrounded by a protein coat. A small virus, such as ϕX, which infects bacteria, can have as few as 5000 elements in its genetic material. (Viruses that infect bactieria are called *bacteriophages*, or just *phages*.) Their simplicity and their role in human disease make viruses an active area of study. They also play a crucial role in the technology of molecular biology, as is described in the last section in this chapter.

1.3 Evolutionary Time and Relatedness

There are so many different kinds of life, and they live in so many different ways. It is amazing that their underlying functioning is so similar. The reason that there is unity within all of that diversity is that all organisms appear to have evolved from a common ancestor. This fundamental claim underpins nearly all biological theorizing, and there is substantial evidence for it.

All evolutionary theories hold that the diversity of life arose by inherited variation through an unbroken line of descent. This common tree of descent is the basis for the taxonomy described above, and pervades the character of all biological explanation. There is a great deal of argument over the detailed functioning of evolution (e.g. whether it happens continuously or in bursts), but practically every biologist agrees with that basic idea.

There are a variety of ways to estimate how long ago two organisms diverged; that is, the last time they had a common ancestor. The more related two species are, the more recently they diverged. To the degree that phenotypic similarity indicates genotypic similarity, organisms can be classified on the basis of their structure, which is the traditional method. Growing knowledge of the DNA sequences of many genes in many organisms makes possible estimates of the time of genetic divergence directly, by comparing their genetic sequences. If the rate of change can be quantified, and standards set, these differences can be translated into a "molecular clock;" Li & Graur, (1991) is a good introduction to this method. The underlying and somewhat controversial assumption is that in some parts of the genome, the rate of mutation is fairly constant. There are various methods for trying to find these areas, estimate the rate of change, and hence calibrate the clock. The technique has mostly confirmed estimates made with other methods, and is widely considered to be potentially reliable, if not quite yet so. Most of the dates I will use below were derived from traditional (archaeological) dating.

In order to get a rough idea of the degrees of relatedness among creatures, it is helpful to know the basic timeline of life on Earth. The oldest known fossils, stromalites found in Australia, indicate that life began at least 3.8 billion years ago. Geological evidence indicates that a major meteor impact about 4 billion years ago vaporized all of the oceans, effectively destroying any life that may have existed before that. In effect, life on earth began almost as soon as it could have. Early life forms probably resembled modern bacteria in some important ways. They were simple, single celled organisms, without nuclei or other organelles. Life remained like that for nearly 2 billion years. Then, about halfway through the history of life, a radical change occurred: Eucarya came into being. There is evidence that eucarya began as symbiotic collections of simpler cells which were eventually assimilated and became organelles (see, e.g. Margolis (1981)). The advantages of these specialized cellular organelles made early eucarya very successful. Single-celled

Eucarya become very complex, for example, developing mechanisms for moving around, detecting prey, paralyzing it and engulfing it.

The next major change in the history of life was the invention of sex. Evolution, as you recall, is a mechanism based on the inheritance of variation. Where do these variations come from? Before the advent of sex, variations arose solely through individual, random changes in genetic material. A mutation might arise, changing one element in the genome, or a longer piece of a genome might be duplicated or moved. If the changed organism had an advantage, the change would propagate itself through the population. Most mutations are neutral or deleterious, and evolutionary change by mutation is a very slow, random search of a vast space. The ability of two successful organisms to combine bits of their genomes into an offspring produced variants with a much higher probability of success. Those moves in the search space are more likely to produce an advantageous variation than random ones. Although you wouldn't necessarily recognize it as sex when looking under a microscope, even some Bacteria exchange genetic material. How and when sexual recombination first evolved is not clear, but it is quite ancient. Some have argued that sexual reproduction was a necessary precursor to the development of multicellular organisms with specialized cells (Buss, 1987). The advent of sex dramatically changed the course of evolution. The new mechanism for the generation of variation focused nature's search through the space of possible genomes, leading to an increase in the proportion of advantageous variations, and an increase in the rate of evolutionary change.

This is probably a good place to correct a common misperception, namely that some organisms are more "primitive" than others. Every existing organism has, tautologically, made it into the modern era. *Simple modern organisms are not primitive.* The environment of the modern world is completely unlike that of earth when life began, and even the simplest existing creatures have evolved to survive in the present. It is possible to use groups of very distantly related creatures (e.g. people and bacteria) to make inferences about ancient organisms; whatever people and bacteria have in common are characteristics that were most likely shared by their last common ancestor, many eons ago. Aspects of bacteria which are not shared with people may have evolved as recently as any human characteristic not shared with bacteria. This applies to the relation between people and apes, too: apes are not any more like ancestral primates than we are. It is what we have *in common* with other organisms that tells us what our ancestors were like; the differences between us and other organisms are much less informative.

Whether or not it occurred as a result of the advent of sexual recombination, the origin of multicellular organisms led to a tremendous explosion in the kinds of organisms and in their complexity. This event occurred only about a billion years ago, about three quarters of the way through the history of life.

Of course, nearly all of the organisms people can see are multicellular (although the blue-green algae in ponds and swimming pools are a kind of bacteria). Multicellular organisms gain their main evolutionary advantage through cellular specialization. Creatures with specialized cells have the ability to occupy environmental niches that single-celled organisms cannot take advantage of. In multicellular organisms, cells quite distant from each other can exchange matter, energy or information for their mutual benefit. For example, cells in the roots of a higher plant exist in a quite different environment than the cells in the leaves, and each supplies the other with matter or energy not available in the local environment.

An important difference between multicellular organisms and a colony of unicellular organisms (e.g. coral) is that multicellular organisms have separated germ line (reproductive) cells from somatic (all the other) cells. Sperm and eggs are germ cells; all the other kinds of cells in the body are somatic. Both kinds of cells divide and make new cells, but only germ cells make new organisms. Somatic cells are usually specialized for a particular task; they are skin cells, or nerve cells, or blood cells. Although these cells divide, when they divide, they create more of the same kind of cell. The division of somatic cells and single celled organisms is a four stage process that ends with *mitosis,* resulting in the production of two identical *daughter cells.* The process as a whole is referred to as the *cell cycle.*

Only changes in germ cells are inherited from an organism to its offspring. A variation that arises in a somatic cell will affect all of the cell's descendents, but it will not affect any of the organism's descendents. Germ cells divide in a process called *meiosis;* part of this process is the production of sperm and egg cells, each of which have only half the usual genetic material. The advent of this distinction involved a complex and intricate balance between somatic cells becoming an evolutionary deadends and the improved competitive ability of a symbiotic collection of closely related cells.

Multicellular organisms all begin their lives from a single cell, a fertilized egg. From that single cell, all of the specialized cells arise through a process called cellular differentiation. The process of development from fertilized egg to full adult is extremely complex. It involves not only cellular differentiation, but the migration and arrangement of cells with respect to each other, orchestrated changes in which genes are used and which are not at any given moment, and even the programmed death of certain groups of cells that act as a kind of scaffolding during development. The transition from single-celled organism to multicellular creature required many dramatic innovations. It was a fundamental shift of the level of selection: away from the individual cell and to a collection of cells as a whole. The reproductive success of a single cell line within a multicellular individual may not correlate with the success of the individual.* Embryology and development are complex and important topics, but are touched on only briefly in this chapter.

Most of the discussion so far has focused on organisms that seem very simple and only distantly related to people. On a biochemical level, however, people are much like other eucaryotes, especially multicellular ones. Genetic and biochemical distance doesn't always correlate very well with morphological differences. For example, two rather similar looking species of frogs may be much more genetically distant from each other than are, say, people and cows (Cherty, Case & Wilson, 1978). A great deal of human biochemistry was already set by the time multicellular organisms appeared on the Earth. We can learn a lot about human biology by understanding how yeasts work.

We've now covered, very briefly, the diversity of living things, and some of the key events in the evolution of life up to the origin of multicellular organisms. In the next section, we'll take a closer look at how these complex organisms work, and cover the parts of eucaryotic cells in a bit more detail.

2 Living Parts: Tissues, Cells, Compartments and Organelles

The main advantage multicellular organisms possess over their single-celled competitors is cell specialization. Not every cell in a larger organism has to be able to extract nutrients, protect itself, sense the environment, move itself around, reproduce itself and so on. These complex tasks can be divided up, so that many different classes of cells can work together, accomplishing feats that single cells cannot. Groups of cells specialized for a particular function are *tissues*, and their cells are said to have *differentiated*. Differentiated cells (except reproductive cells) cannot reproduce an entire organism.

In people (and most other multicellular animals) there are fourteen major tissue types. There are many texts with illustrations and descriptions of the various cell types and tissue, e.g. Kessel and Kardon (1979) which is full of beautiful electron micrographs. Some of these tissue types are familiar: bones, muscles, cardiovascular tissue, nerves, and connective tissue (like tendons and ligaments). Other tissues are the constituents of the digestive, respiratory, urinary and reproductive systems. Skin and blood are both distinctive tissue types, made of highly specialized cells. Lymphatic tissue, such as the spleen and the lymph nodes make up the immune system. Endocrine tissue comprises a network of hormone-producing glands (for example, the adrenal gland, source of adrenaline) that exert global control over various aspects of the body as a whole. Finally, epithelium, the most basic tissue type, lines all of the body's cavities, secreting materials such as mucus, and, in the in-

---

*Cancer is an example where a single cell line within a multicellular organism reproduces to the detriment of the whole.

testines, absorbing water and nutrients.

There are more than 200 different specialized cell types in a typical verte-brate. Some are large, some small; for example, a single nerve cell connects your foot to your spinal cord, and a drop of blood has more than 10,000 cells in it. Some divide rapidly, others do not divide at all; bone marrow cells divide every few hours, and adult nerve cells can live 100 years without dividing. Once differentiated, a cell cannot change from one type to another. Yet despite all of this variation, all of the cells in a multicellular organism have exactly the same genetic code. The differences between them come from differences in *gene expression*, that is, whether or not a the product a gene codes for is produced, and how much is produced. Control of gene expression is an elaborate dance with many participants. Thousands of biological substances bind to DNA, or bind to other biomolecules that bind to DNA. Genes code for products that turn on and off other genes, which in turn regulate other genes, and so on. One of the key research areas in biology is development: how the intricate, densely interrelated genetic regulatory process is managed, and how cells "know" what to differentiate into, and when and where they do it. A prelude to these more complex topics is a discussion of what cells are made of, and what they do.

2.1 The Composition of Cells

Despite their differences, most cells have a great deal in common with each other. Every cell, whether a Archaea at the bottom of the ocean or a cell in a hair follicle on the top of your head has certain basic qualities: they contain cytoplasm and genetic material, are enclosed in a membrane and have the basic mechanisms for translating genetic messages into the main type of biological molecule, the protein. All eucaryotic cells share additional components. Each of these basic parts of a cell is described briefly below:

Membranes are the boundaries between the cell and the outside world. Although there is no one moment that one can say life came into being, the origin of the first cell membrane is a reasonable starting point. At that moment, self-reproducing systems of molecules were individuated, and cells came into being. All present day cells have a *phospholipid* cell membrane. Phospholipids are *lipids* (oils or fats) with a phosphate group attached. The end with the phosphate group is *hydrophillic (*attracted to water) and the lipid end is *hydrophobic* (repelled by water). Cell membranes consist of two layers of these molecules, with the hydrophobic ends facing in, and the hydrophillic ends facing out. This keeps water and other materials from getting through the membrane, except through special pores or channels.

A lot of the action in cells happens at the membrane. For single celled organisms, the membrane contains molecules that sense the environment, and in some cells it can surround and engulf food, or attach and detach parts of itself in order to move. In Bacteria and Archaea, the membrane plays a crucial role in energy production by maintaining a large acidity difference between the inside and the outside of the cell. In multicellular organisms, the membranes contain all sorts of signal transduction mechanisms, adhesion molecules, and other machinery for working together with other cells.

Proteins are the molecules that accomplish most of the functions of the living cell. The number of different structures and functions that proteins take on in a single organism is staggering. They make possible all of the chemical reactions in the cell by acting as *enzymes* that promote specific chemical reactions, which would otherwise occur only so slowly as to be otherwise negligible. The action of promoting chemical reactions is called *catalysis*, and enzymes are sometimes refered to as *catalysts*, which is a more general term. Proteins also provide structural support, and are the keys to how the immune system distinguishes self from invaders. They provide the mechanism for acquiring and transforming energy, as well as translating it into physical work in the muscles. They underlie sensors and the transmission of information as well.

All proteins are constructed from linear sequences of smaller molecules called amino acids. There are twenty naturally occurring amino acids. Long proteins may contain as many as 4500 amino acids, so the space of possible proteins is very large: 20^{4500} or 10^{5850}. Proteins also fold up to form particular three dimensional shapes, which give them their specific chemical functionality. Although it is easily demonstrable that the linear amino acid sequence completely specifies the three dimensional structure of most proteins, the details of that mapping is one of the most important open questions of biology. In addition a protein's three dimensional structure is not fixed; many proteins move and flex in constrained ways, and that can have a significant role in their biochemical function. Also, some proteins bind to other groups of atoms that are required for them to function. These other structures are called *prosthetic groups.* An example of a prosthetic group is *heme,* which binds oxygen in the protein hemoglobin. I will discuss proteins in more detail again below.

Genetic material codes for all the other constituents of the the cell. This information is generally stored in long strands of DNA. In Bacteria, the DNA is generally circular. In Eucaryotes, it is linear. During cell division Eucaryotic DNA is grouped into X shaped structures called chromosomes. Some viruses (like the AIDS virus) store their genetic material in RNA. This genetic material contains the blueprint for all the proteins the cell can produce. I'll have much more to say about DNA below.

Nuclei are the defining feature of Eucaryotic cells. The nucleus contains the genetic material of the cell in the form of *chromatin.* Chromatin contains long stretches of DNA in a variety of conformations,[*] surrounded by *nuclear proteins.* The nucleus is separated from the rest of the cell by a *nuclear membrane.* Nuclei show up quite clearly under the light microscope; they are perhaps the most visible feature of most cells.

Cytoplasm is the name for the gel-like collection of substances inside the cell. All cells have cytoplasm. The cytoplasm contains a wide variety of different substances and structures. In Bacteria and Archaea, the cytoplasm contains all of the materials in the cell. In Eucarya, the genetic material is segregated into the cell nucleus.

Ribosomes are large molecular complexes, composed of several proteins and RNA molecules. The function of ribosomes is to assemble proteins. All cells, including Bacteria and Archaea have ribosomes. The process of translating genetic information into proteins is described in detail below. Ribosomes are where that process occurs, and are a key part of the mechanism for accomplishing that most basic of tasks.

Mitochondria and Chroloplasts are cellular organelles involved in the production the energy that powers the cell. Mitochondria are found in all eucaryotic cells, and their job is respiration: using oxygen to efficiently turn food into energy the cell can use. Some bacteria and archaea get their energy by a process called *glycolysis*, from glyco- (sugar) and -lysis (cleavage or destruction). This process creates two energy-carrying molecules for every molecule of sugar consumed. As oxygen became more abundant[†], some organisms found a method for using it (called *oxidative phosphorylation*) to make an order of magnitude increase in their ability to extract energy from food, getting 36 energy-carrying molecules for every sugar.

These originally free living organisms were engulfed by early eucaryotes. This symbiosis gradually became obligatory as eucaryotes came to depend on their mitochondria for energy, and the mitochondria came to depend on the surrounding cell for many vital functions and materials. Mitochondria still have their own genetic material however, and, in sexually reproducing organisms, are inherited only via the cytoplasm of the egg cell. As a consequence, all mitochondria are maternally inherited.

Like the mitochondria, chloroplasts appear to have originated as free-living bacteria that eventually became obligatory symbionts, and then parts of eucaryotic plant cells. Their task is to convert sunlight into energy-carrying molecules.

Other Parts of Cells. There are other organelles found in eucaryotic

---

Conformation means shape, connoting one of several possible shapes. DNA conformations include the traditional double helix, a *supercoiled* state where certain parts of the molecule are deeply hidden, a reverse coiled state called Z-DNA, and several others.

†There was very little oxygen in the early atmosphere. Oxygen is a waste product of glycolysis, and it eventually became a significant component of the atmosphere. Although many modern organisms depend on oxygen to live, it is a very corrosive substance, and living systems had to evolve quite complex biochemical processes for dealing with it.

cells. The *endoplasmic reticulum* (there are two kinds, rough and smooth) is involved in the production of the cell membrane itself, as well as in the production of materials that will eventually be exported from the cell. The *Golgi apparatus* are elongated sacs that are involved in the packaging of materials that will be exported from the cell, as well as segregating materials in the cell into the correct intracellular compartment. *Lysosomes* contain substances that are used to digest proteins; they are kept separate to prevent damage to other cellular components. Some cells have other structures, such as *vacuoles* of lipids for storage (like the ones often found around the abdomen of middle-aged men).

Now that you have a sense of the different components of the cell, we can proceed to examine the activities of these components. Life is a dynamical system, far from equilibrium. Biology is not only the study of living things, but living actions.

3 Life as a Biochemical Process

Beginning with the highest levels of taxonomy, we have taken a quick tour of the varieties of organisms, and have briefly seen some of their important parts. So far, this account has been entirely descriptive. Because of the tremendous diversity of living systems, descriptive accounts are a crucial underpinning to any more explanatory theories. In order to understand how biological systems work, one has to know what they are.

Knowledge of cells and tissues makes possible the functional accounts of physiology. For example, knowing that the cells in the bicep and in the heart are both kinds of muscle helps explain how the blood circulates. However, at this level of description, the work that individual cells are able to do remains mysterious. The revolution in biology over the last three decades resulted from the understanding cells in terms of their chemistry. These insights began with descriptions of the molecules involved in living processes, and now increasingly provides an understanding of the molecular structures and functions that are the fundamental objects and actions of living material.

More and more of the functions of life (e.g. cell division, immune reaction, neural transmission) are coming to be understood as the interactions of complicated, self-regulating networks of chemical reactions. The substances that carry out and regulate these activities are generally referred to as biomolecules. Biomolecules include proteins, carbohydrates, lipids—all called *macromolecules* because they are relatively large—and a variety of small molecules. The genetic material of the cell specifies how to create proteins, as well as when and how much to create. These proteins, in turn, control the flow of energy and materials through the cell, including the creation and transformation of carbohydrates, lipids and other molecules, ultimately accomplishing all of the functions that the cell carries out. The genetic material itself is also now known to be a particular macromolecule: DNA.

In even the simplest cell, there are more than a thousand kinds of biomolecules interacting with each other; in human beings there are likely to be more than 100,000 different kinds of proteins specified in the genome (it is unlikely that all of them are present in any particular cell). Both the amount of each molecule and its concentration in various compartments of the cell determines what influence it will have. These concentrations vary over time, on scales of seconds to decades. Interactions among biomolecules are highly non-linear, as are the interactions between biomolecules and other molecules from outside the cell. All of these interactions take place in parallel among large numbers of instances of each particular type. Despite this daunting complexity, insights into the structure and function of these molecules, and into their interactions are emerging very rapidly.

One of the reasons for that progress is the conception of life as a kind of information processing. The processes that transform matter and energy in living systems do so under the direction of a set of symbolically encoded instructions. The "machine" language that describes the objects and processes of living systems contains four letters, and the text that describes a person has about as many characters as three years' worth of the *New York Times* (about 3×10^9). In the next section, we will delve more deeply into the the chemistry of living systems.

4 The Molecular Building Blocks of Life

Living systems process matter, energy and information. The basic principle of life, reproduction, is the transformation of materials found in the environment of an organism into another organism. Raw materials from the local environment are broken down, and then reassembled following the instructions in the genome. The offspring will contain instructions similar to the parent. The matter, energy and information processing abilities of living systems are very general; one of the hallmarks of life is its adaptability to changing circumstances. Some aspects of living systems have, however, stayed the same over the years. Despite nearly 4 billion years of evolution, the basic molecular objects for carrying matter, energy and information have changed very little. The basic units of matter are proteins, which subserve all of the structural and many of the functional roles in the cell; the basic unit of energy is a phosphate bond in the molecule adenosine triphosphate (ATP); and the units of information are four nucleotides, which are assembled together into DNA and RNA.

The chemical composition of living things is fairly constant across the entire range of life forms. About 70% of any cell is water. About 4% are small molecules like sugars and inorganic *ions*[*]. One of these small molecules is ATP, the energy carrier. Proteins make up between 15% and 20% of the cell;

DNA and RNA range from 2% to 7% of the weight. The cell membranes, lipids and other, similar molecules make up the remaining 4% to 7% (Alberts, et al., 1989).

4.1 Energy

Living things obey all the laws of chemistry and physics, including the second law of thermodynamics, which states that the amount of entropy (disorder) in the universe is always increasing. The consumption of energy is the only way to create order in the face of entropy. Life doesn't violate the second law; living things capture energy in a variety of forms, use it to create internal order, and then transfer energy back to the environment as heat. An increase in organization within a cell is coupled with a greater increase in disorder outside the cell.

Living things must capture energy, either from sunlight through photosynthesis or from nutrients by respiration. The variety of chemicals that can be oxidized by various species to obtain energy through respiration is immense, ranging from simple sugars to complex oils and even sulfur compounds from deep sea vents (in the case of Archaea).

In many cases, the energy is first available to the cell as an electrochemical gradient across the cell membrane. The cell can tap into electrochemical gradient by coupling the energy that results from moving electrons across the membrane to other processes. There are many constraints on the flow of energy through a living system. Most of the chemical reactions that organisms need to survive require an input of a minimum amount of energy to take place at a reasonable rates; efficient use of energy dictates that this must be delivered in a quanta exceeding the minimum requirement only slightly.

The energy provided for biochemical reactions has to be useable by many different processes. It must be possible to provide energy where it is needed, and to store it until it is consumed. The uses of energy throughout living systems are very diverse. It is needed to synthesize and transport biomolecules, to create mechanical action through the muscle proteins actin and myosin, and to create and maintain electrical gradients, such as the ones that neurons use to communicate and compute.

Storing and transporting energy in complex biochemical systems runs the

---

*An inorganic ion is a charged atom, or a charged small group of atoms, not involving carbon. These substances, like iron and zinc, play small but vital role. For example, changing the balance of calcium and sodium ions across a cell membrane is the basic method for exciting of neurons.

The individual building blocks of the larger molecules, i.e. amino acids and nucleic acids, are also considered small molecules when not part of a larger structure. Some of these molecules play roles in the cell other than as components of large molecules. For example, the nucleic acid adenine is at the core of the energy carrying molecule adenosine triphosphate (ATP).

risk of disrupting chemical bonds other than the target ones, so the unit of energy has to be small enough not to do harm, but large enough to be useful. The most common carrier of energy for storage and transport is the outermost phosphate bond in the molecule *adenosine triphosphate, or ATP.* This molecule plays a central role in every living system: it is the carrier of energy. Energy is taken out of ATP by the process of *hydrolysis*, which removes the outermost phosphate group, producing the molecule adenosine diphosphate (ADP). This process generates about 12 kcal per mole* of ATP, a quantity appropriate for performing many cellular tasks. The energy "charge" of a cell is expressed in the ratio of ATP/ADP and the electrochemical difference between the inside and the outside of the cell (which is called the *transmembrane potential*). If ATP is depleted, the movement of ions caused by the transmembrane potential will result in the synthesis of additional ATP. If the transmembrane potential has been reduced (for example, after a neuron fires), ATP will be consumed to pump ions back across the gradient and restore the potential.

ATP is involved in most cellular processes, so it is sometimes called a *currency* metabolite. ATP can also be converted to other high energy phosphate compounds such as *creatine phosphate*, or other nucleotide triphosphates. In turn, these molecules provide the higher levels of energy necessary to transcribe genes and replicate chromosomes. Energy can also be stored in different chemical forms. Carbohydrates like glycogen provide a moderate density, moderately accessible form of energy storage. Fats have very high energy storage density, but the energy stored in them takes longer to retrieve.

4.2 Proteins

Proteins are the primary components of living things, and they play many roles. Proteins provide structural support and the infrastructure that holds a creature together; they are enzymes that make the chemical reactions necessary for life possible; they are the switches that control whether genes are turned on or off; they are the sensors that see and taste and smell, and the effectors that make muscles move; they are the detectors that distinguish self from nonself and create an immune response. Finding the proteins that make up a creature and understanding their function is the foundation of explanation in molecular biology.

Despite their radical differences in function, all proteins are made of the same basic constituents: the amino acids. Each amino acid shares a basic structure, consisting of a central carbon atom (C), an *amino* group (NH_3) at

---

*kcal is an abbreviation for kilocalorie, the amount of energy necessary to raise a liter of water one degree centigrade at standard temperature and pressure. It is equivalent to 1 dieter's calorie. A mole is an amount of a substance, measured in terms of the number of molecules, rather than by its mass. One mole is 6×10^{23} molecules.

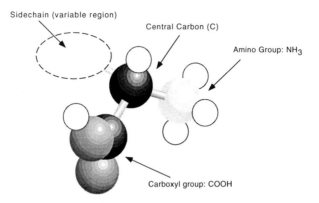

Sidechain (variable region)

Central Carbon (C)

Amino Group: NH₃

Carboxyl group: COOH

Figure 2: The basic chemical structure of an amino acid. Carbon atoms are black, Oxygen is dark grey, Nitrogen light grey, and hydrogen white.

one end, a *carboxyl* group (COOH) at the other, and a variable sidechain (R), as shown in Figure 2. These chemical groups determine how the molecule functions, as Mavrovouniotis's chapter in this volume explains. For example, under biological conditions the amino end of the molecule is positively charged, and the carboxyl end is negatively charged. Chains of amino acids are assembled by a reaction that occurs between the nitrogen atom at the amino end of one amino acid and the carbon atom at the carboxyl end of another, bonding the two amino acids and releasing a molecule of water. The linkage is called a *peptide bond*, and long chains of amino acids can be strung together into polymers[*], called *polypeptides*, in this manner. All proteins are polypeptides, although the term polypeptide generally refers to chains that are shorter than whole proteins.

When a peptide bond is formed, the amino acid is changed (losing two hydrogen atoms and an oxygen atom), so the portion of the original molecule integrated into the polypeptide is often called a *residue*. The sequence of amino acid residues that make up a protein is called the protein's *primary structure*. The primary structure is directly coded for in the genetic material: The individual elements of a DNA molecule form triples which unambiguously specify an amino acid. A genetic sequence maps directly into a sequence of amino acids. This process is discussed in greater detail below.

It is interesting to note that only a small proportion of the very many possible polypeptide chains are naturally occurring proteins. Computationally, this is unsurprising. Many proteins contain more than 100 amino acids (some

---

[*]Polymers are long strings of similar elements; -mer means "element," as in monomer, dimer, etc. Homopolymer is a term that refers to polymers made up of all the same element; heteropolymers are made of several different units. Proteins and DNA are both heteropolymers. Glycogen, a substance used for the medium-term storage of excess energy, is an example of a homopolymer.

have more than 4000). The number of possible polypeptide chains of length 100 is 20^{100} or more than 10^{130}. Even if we take the high estimates of the number of species (5×10^7) and assume that they all have as many different proteins as there are in the most complex organism ($< 10^7$) and that no two organisms share a single protein, the ratio of actual proteins to possible polypeptides is much less than $1:10^{100}$—a very small proportion, indeed.

The twenty naturally occuring amino acids all have the common elements shown in Figure 2. The varying parts are called *sidechains*; the two carbons and the nitrogen in the core are sometimes called the *backbone*. Peptide bonds link together the backbones of a sequence of amino acids. That link can be characterized as having two degrees of rotational freedom, the phi (ϕ) and psi (ψ) angles (although from the point of view of physics this is a drastic simplification, in most biological contexts it is valid). The conformation of a protein backbone (i.e. its shape when folded) can be adequately described as a series of ϕ/ψ angles, although it is also possible to represent the shape using the Cartesian coordinates of the central backbone atom (the alpha carbon, written Cα), or using various other representational schemes (see, e.g., Hunter or Zhang & Waltz in this volume).

The dimensions along which amino acids vary are quite important for a number of reasons. One of the major unsolved problems in molecular biology is to be able to predict the structure and function of a protein from its amino acid sequence. It was demonstrated more than two decades ago that the amino acid sequence of a protein determines ultimate conformation and, therefore, its biological activity and function. Exactly how the properties of the amino acids in the primary structure of a protein interact to determine the protein's ultimate conformation remains unknown. The chemical properties of the individual amino acids, however, are known with great precision. These properties form the basis for many representations of amino acids, e.g. in programs attempting to predict structure from sequence. Here is a brief summary of some of them.

Glycine is the simplest amino acid; its sidechain is a single hydrogen atom. It is nonpolar, and does not ionize easily. The *polarity* of a molecule refers to the degree that its electrons are distributed asymmetrically. A nonpolar molecule has a relatively even distribution of charge. *Ionization* is the process that causes a molecule to gain or lose an electron, and hence become charged overall. The distribution of charge has a strong effect on the behavior of a molecule (e.g. like charges repel). Another important characteristic of glycine is that as a result of having no heavy (i.e. non-hydrogen) atoms in its sidechain, it is very flexible. That flexibility can give rise to unusual kinks in the folded protein.

Alanine is also small and simple; its sidechain is just a *methyl* group (consisting of a carbon and three hydrogen atoms). Alanine is one of the most commonly appearing amino acids. Glycine and alanine's sidechains are *aliphatic*, which means that they are straight chains (no loops) containing only carbon and hydrogen atoms. There are three other aliphatic amino acids: *valine, leucine* and *isoleucine*. The longer aliphatic sidechains are hydrophobic. Hydrophobicity is one of the key factors that determines how the chain of amino acids will fold up into an active protein. Hydrophobic residues tend to come together to form compact core that exclude water. Because the environment inside cells is *aqueous* (primarily water), these hydrophobic residues will tend to be on the inside of a protein, rather than on its surface.

In contrast to alanine and glycine, the sidechains of amino acids *phenylalanine, tyrosine* and *tryptophan* are quite large. Size matters in protein folding because atoms resist being too close to one another, so it is hard to pack many large sidechains closely. These sidechains are also *aromatic*, meaning that they form closed rings of carbon atoms with alternating double bonds (like the simple molecule benzene). These rings are large and inflexible. Phenylalanine and tryptophan are also hydrophobic. Tyrosine has a *hydroxyl* group (an OH at the end of the ring), and is therefore more reactive than the other sidechains mentioned so far, and less hydrophobic. These large amino acids appear less often than would be expected ifproteins were composed randomly. *Serine* and *threonine* also contain hydroxyl groups, but do not have rings.

Another feature of importance in amino acids is whether they ionize to form charged groups. Residues that ionize are characterized by their *pK*, which indicates at what *pH* (level of acidity) half of the molecules of that amino acid will have ionized. *Arginine* and *lysine* have high pK's (that is, they ionize in basic environments) and *histidine, gluatmic acid* and *aspartic acid* have low pK's (they ionize in acidic ones). Since like charges repel and opposites attract, charge is an important feature in predicting protein conformation. Most of the charged residues in a protein will be found at its surface, although some will form bonds with each other on the inside of the molecule (called *salt-bridges*) which can provide strong constraints on the ultimate folded form.

Cysteine and *methionine* have hydrophobic sidechains that contain a sulphur atom, and each plays an important role in protein structure. The sulphurs make the amino acids' sidechains very reactive. Cysteines can form *disulphide* bonds with each other; disulphide bonds often hold distant parts of a polypeptide chain near each other, constraining the folded conformation like salt bridges. For that reason, cysteines have a special role in determining the three dimensional structure of proteins. The chapter by Holbrook, Muskal and Kim in this volume discusses the prediction of this and other folding constraints. Methionine is also important because all eucaryotic proteins, when originally synthesized in the ribosome, start with a methionine. It is a kind of "start" signal in the genetic code. This methionine is generally removed before the protein is released into the cell, however.

Histidine is a relatively rare amino acid, but often appears in the *active site* of an enzyme. The active site is the small portion of an enzyme that effects the target reaction, and it is the key to understanding the chemistry involved. The rest of the enzyme provides the necessary scaffolding to bring the active site to bear in the right place, and to keep it away from bonds that it might do harm to. Other regions of enzymes can also act as a switch, turning the active site on and off in a process called *allosteric* control. Because histidine's pK is near the typical pH of a cell, it is possible for small, local changes in the chemical environment to flip it back and forth between being charged and not charged. This ability to flip between states makes it useful for catalyzing chemical reactions. Other charged residues also sometimes play a similar role in catalysis.

With this background, it is now possible to understand the basics of the protein folding problem which is the target of many of the AI methods applied in this volume. The genetic code specifies only the amino acid sequence of a protein. As a new protein comes off the ribosome, it folds up into the shape that gives it its biochemical function, sometimes called its *active conformation* (the same protein unfolded into some other shape is said to be *denatured*, which is what happens, e.g. to the white of an egg when you cook it). In the cell, this process takes a few seconds, which is a very long time for a chemical reaction. The complex structure of the ribosome may play a role in protein folding, and a few proteins need helper molecules, termed *chaperones* to fold properly. However, these few seconds are a very short time compared to how long it takes people to figure out how a protein will fold. In raw terms, the folding problem involves finding the mapping from primary sequence (a sequence of from dozens to several thousand symbols, drawn from a 20 letter alphabet) to the real-numbered locations of the thousands of constituent atoms in three space.

Although all of the above features of amino acids play some role in protein folding, there are few absolute rules. The conformation a protein finally assumes will minimize the total "free" energy of the molecule. Going against the tendencies described above (e.g. packing several large sidechains near each other) increases the local free energy, but may reduce the energy elsewhere in the molecule. Each one of the tendencies described can be traded off against some other contribution to the total free energy of the folded protein. Given any conformation of atoms, it is possible in principle to compute its free energy. Ideally, one could examine all the possible conformations of a protein, calculate the free energy by applying quantum mechanical rules, and select the minimum energy conformation as a prediction of the folded structure. Unfortunately, there are very many possible conformations to test, and each energy calculation itself is prohibitively complex. A wide variety of approaches have been taken to making this problem tractable, and, given a few hours of supercomputer time, it is currently possible to evaluate several thousand possible conformations. These techniques are well surveyed in Karplus & Petsko (1990). An alternative to the pure physical simulations are the various AI approaches which a significant portion of this volume is dedicated to describing.

The position of the atoms in a folded protein is called its *tertiary* structure. The *primary* structure is the amino acid sequence. *Secondary* structure refers to local arrangements of a few to a few dozen amino acid residues that take on particular conformations that are seen repeatedly in many different proteins. These shapes are stabilized by *hydrogen bonds* (a hydrogen bond is a relatively weak bond that also plays a role in holding the two strands of the DNA molecule together). There are two main kinds of secondary structure: corkscrew-shaped conformations where the amino acids are packed tightly together, called *α-helices*, and long flat sheets made up of two or more adjacent strands of the molecule, extended so that the amino acids are stretched out as far from each other as they can be. Each extended chain is called a *β-strand*, and two or more β-strands held together by hydrogen bonds are called a *β-sheet*. β-sheets can be composed of strands running in the same direction (called a *parallel* β-sheet) or running in the opposite direction (*antiparallel*). Other kinds of secondary structure include structures that are even more tightly packed than α-helices called *3-10 helices*, and a variety of small structures that link other structures, called *β-turns*. Some local combinations of secondary structures have been observed in a variety of different proteins. For example, two α-helices linked by a turn with an approximately 60° angle have been observed in a variety of proteins that bind to DNA. This pattern is called the *helix-turn-helix* motif, and is an example of what is known as *super-secondary* structure. Finally, some proteins only become functional when assembled with other molecules. Some proteins bind to copies of themselves; for example, some DNA-binding proteins only function as dimers (linked pairs). Other proteins require prostehtic groups such as heme or chlorophyl. Additions necessary to make the folded protein active are termed the protein's *quaternary* structure.

4.3 Nucleic Acids

If proteins are the workhorses of the biochemical world, nucleic acids are their drivers; they control the action. All of the genetic information in any living creature is stored in deoxyribonucleic acid (DNA) and ribonucleic acid (RNA), which are polymers of four simple nucleic acid units, called *nucleotides*. There are four nucleotides found in DNA. Each nucleotide consists of three parts: one of two base molecules (a *purine* or a *pyrimidine*), plus a sugar (ribose in RNA and deoxyribose DNA), and one or more phosphate groups. The purine nucleotides are *adenine* (A) and *guanine* (G), and the pyrimidines are *cytosine* (C) and *thymine* (T). Nucleotides are sometimes called bases, and, since DNA consists of two complementary strands bonded together, these units are often called base-pairs. The length of a DNA sequences is often measured in thousands of bases, abbreviated kb. Nucleotides are generally abbreviated by their first letter, and appended into sequences, written, e.g., CCTATAG. The nucleotides are linked to each other in the polymer by phosphodiester bonds. This bond is directional, a strand of DNA has a head (called the *5' end*) and a tail (the *3' end*).

One well known fact about DNA is that it forms a double helix; that is, two *helical* (spiral-shaped) strands of the polypeptide, running in opposite directions, held together by hydrogen bonds. Adenines bond exclusively with the thymines (A-T) and guanines bond exclusively with cytosines (G-C). Although the sequence in one strand of DNA is completely unrestricted, because of these bonding rules the sequence in the complementary strand is completely determined. It is this feature that makes it possible to make high fidelity copies of the information stored in the DNA. It is also exploited when DNA is transcribed into complementary strands of RNA, which direct the synthesis of protein. The only difference is that in RNA, uracil (U) takes the place of thymine; that is, it bonds to adenine.

DNA molecules take a variety of conformations (shapes) in living systems. In most biological circumstances, the DNA forms a classic double helix, called B-DNA; in certain circumstances, however, it can become supercoiled or even reverse the direction of its twist (this form is called Z-DNA). These alternative forms may play a role in turning particular genes on and off (see below). There is some evidence that the geometry of the B-DNA form (e.g for example, differing twist angles between adjacent base pairs) may also be exploited by cell mechanisms. The fact that the conformation of the DNA can have a biological effect over and above the sequence it encodes highlights an important lesson for computer scientists: *there is more information available to a cell than appears in the sequence databases.* This lesson also applies to protein sequences, as we will see in the discussion of post-translational modification.

Now that we have covered the basic structure and function of proteins and nucleic acids, we can begin to put together a picture of the molecular processing that goes on in every cell.

5 Genetic Expression: From Blueprint to Finished Product

5.1 Genes, the Genome and the Genetic Code

The genetic information of an organism can be stored in one or more distinct DNA molecules; each is called a *chromosome*. In some sexually reproducing organisms, called *diploids*, each chromosome contains two similar DNA molecules physically bound together, one from each parent. Sexually reproducing organisms with single DNA molecules in their chromosomes are

called haploid. Human beings are diploid with 23 pairs of linear chromosomes. In Bacteria, it is common for the ends of the DNA molecule to bind
together, forming a circular chromosome. All of the genetic information of
an organism, taken together as a whole, is refered to as its *genome*.

The primary role of nucleic acids is to carry the encoding of the primary
structure of proteins. Each non-overlapping triplet of nucleotides, called a
codon, corresponds to a particular amino acid (see table 1). Four nucleotides
can form $4^3 = 64$ possible triplets, which is more than the 20 needed to code
for each amino acid (pairs would provide only 16 codons). Three of these
codons are used to designate the end of a protein sequence, and are called
stop codons. The others all code for a particular amino acid. That means that
most amino acids are encoded by more than one codon. For example, alanine
is represented in DNA by the codons GCT, GCC, GCA and GCG. Notice
that the first two nucleotides of these codons are all identical, and that the
third is redundant. Although this is not true for all of the amino acids, most
codon synonyms differ only in the last nucleotide. This phenomenon is
called the *degeneracy* of the code. Whether it is an artifact of the evolution,
or serves a purpose such as allowing general changes in the global composition of DNA (e.g. increasing the proportion of purines) without changing the
coded amino acids is still unknown.

There are some small variations in the translation of codons into amino
acids from organism to organism. Since the code is so central to the functioning of the cell, it is very strongly conserved over evolution. However, there
are a few systems that use a slightly different code. An important example is
found in mitochondria. Mitochondria have their own DNA, and probably
represent previously free living organisms that were enveloped by eucaryotes. Mitochondrial DNA is translated using a slightly different code, which
is more degenerate (has less information in the third nucleotide) than the
standard code. Other organisms that diverged very early in evolution, such as
the ciliates, also use different codes.

The basic process of synthesizing proteins maps from a sequence of
codons to a sequence of amino acids. However, there are a variety of important complications. Since codons come in triples, there are three possible
places to start parsing a segment of DNA. For example, the chain
...AATGCGATAAG... could be read ...AAT-GCG-ATA... or ...ATG-CGA-
TAA... or ...TGC-GAT-AAG.... This problem is similar to decoding an asynchronous serial bit stream into bytes. Each of these parsings is called a *reading frame*. A parsing with a long enough string of codons with no intervening
stop codons is called an *open reading frame*, or *ORF*; and could be translated
into a protein. Organisms sometimes code different proteins with overlapping reading frames, so that if the reading process shifts by one character, a
completely different, but still functional protein results! More often, frame
shifts, which can be introduced by insertions and deletions in the DNA se-

quence or transcriptional "stuttering," produce nonsense.

Not only are there three possible reading frames in a DNA sequence, it is possible to read off either strand of the double helix. Recall that the second strand is the complement of the first, so that our example above (AATGC-GATAAG) can also be read inverted and in the opposite direction, e.g. CT-TATCGCATT. This is sometimes called reading from the *antisense* or *complementary* strand. An antisense message can also be parsed three ways, making a total of 6 possible reading frames for every DNA sequence. There are known examples of DNA sequences that code for proteins in both directions with several overlapping reading frames: quite a feat of compact encoding.

And there's more. DNA sequences coding for a single protein in most eucaryotes have noncoding sequences, called *introns*, inserted into them. These introns are spliced out before the sequence is mapped into amino acids. Different eucaryotes have a variety of different systems for recognizing and removing these introns. Most bacteria don't have introns. It is not known whether introns evolved only after the origin of eucaryotes, or whether selective pressure has caused bacteria to lose theirs. The segments of DNA that actually end up coding for a protein are called *exons*. You can keep these straight by remembering that **in**trons are **in**sertions, and that **ex**ons are **ex**pressed.

DNA contains a large amount of information in addition to the coding sequences of proteins. Every cell in the body has the same DNA, but each cell type has to generate a different set of proteins, and even within a single cell type, its needs change throughout its life. An increasing number of DNA signals that appear to play a role in the control of expression are being characterized. There are a variety of signals identifying where proteins begin and end, where splices should occur, and an exquisitely detailed set of mechanisms for controlling which proteins should be synthesized and in what quantities. Large scale features of a DNA molecule, such as a region rich in Cs and Gs can play a biologically important role, too.

Finally, some exceptions to the rules I mentioned above should be noted. DNA is sometimes found in single strands, particularly in some viruses. Viruses also play other tricks with nucleic acids, such as transcribing RNA into DNA, going against the normal flow of information in the cell. Even non-standard base-pairings sometimes play an important role, such as in the structure of transfer RNA (see below).

5.2 RNA: Transcription, Translation, Splicing & RNA Structure

The process of mapping from DNA sequence to folded protein in eucaryotes involves many steps (see Figure 3). The first step is the *transcription* of a portion of DNA into an RNA molecule, called a messenger RNA (mRNA). This process begins with the binding of a molecule called RNA polymerase to a location on the DNA molecule. Exactly where that polymerase binds determines which strand of the DNA will be read and in which direction. Parts of the DNA near the beginning of a protein coding region contain signals which can be recognized by the polymerase; these regions are called *promoters*. (Promoters and other control signals are discussed further below.) The polymerase catalyzes a reaction which causes the DNA to be used as a template to create a complementary strand of RNA, called the *primary transcript*. This transcript contains introns as well as exons. At the end of the transcript, 250 or more extra adenosines, called a *poly-A tail*, are often added to the RNA. The role of these nucleotides is not known, but the distinctive signature is sometimes used to detect the presence of mRNAs.

The next step is the *splicing* the exons together. This operation takes takes place in a ribosome-like assembly called a *spliceosome*. The RNA remaining after the introns have been spliced out is called a *mature* mRNA. It is then transported out of the nucleus to the cytoplasm, where it then binds to a ribosome.

A ribosome is a very complex combination of RNA and protein, and its operation has yet to be completely understood. It is at the ribosome that the mRNA is used as a blueprint for the production of a protein; this process is called *translation*. The reading frame that the translation will use is determined by the ribosome. The translation process depends on the presence of molecules which make the mapping from codons in the mRNA to amino acids; these molecules are called *transfer-RNA* or *tRNAs*. tRNAs have an anti-codon (that binds to its corresponding codon) near one end and the corresponding amino acid on the other end. The anti-codon end of the tRNAs bind to the mRNA, bringing the amino acids corresponding the mRNA sequence into physical proximity, where they form peptide bonds with each other. How the tRNAs find only the correct amino acid was a mystery until quite recently. This process depends on the three dimensional structure of the RNA molecule, which is discussed in Steeg's chapter of this volume. As the protein comes off the ribosome, it folds up into its native conformation. This process may involve help from the ribosome itself or from chaperone molecules, as was described above.

Once the protein has folded, other transformations can occur. Various kinds of chemical groups can be bound to different places on the proteins, including sugars, phosphate, actyl or methyl groups. These additions can change the hyrogen bonding proclivity or shape of the protein, and may be necessary to make the protein active, or may keep it from having an effect before it is needed. The general term for these transformations is *post-translational modifications*. Once this process is complete, the protein is then transported to the part of the cell where it will accomplish its function. The transport process may be merely passive diffusion through the cytoplasm, or there may be an active transport mechanism that moves the protein across

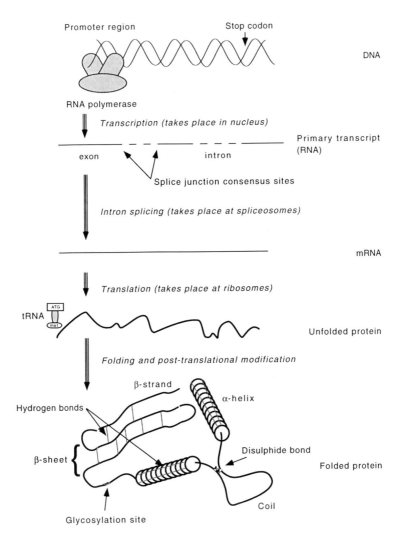

Figure 3. A schematic drawing of the entire process of protein synthesis. An RNA Polymerase binds to a promoter region of DNA, and begins the transcription process, which continues until a stop codon is reached. The product is an RNA molecule called the primary transcript, which contains regions that code for proteins (exons) and regions which do not (introns). The introns are spliced out at splicosomes, and the joined exons are transported to a ribosome. There, transfer RNAs match amino acids to the appropriate codons in the RNA; the amino acids form peptide bonds and become an unfolded protein. The protein then folds into local formations like helices and sheets, and forms internal bonds across longer distances. Post-translational processing can add additional substance; e.g., glycosylation adds sugar molecules to the protein.

membranes or into the appropriate cellular compartment.

5.3 Genetic Regulation

Every cell has the same DNA. Yet the DNA in some cells codes for the proteins needed to function as, say, a muscle, and other code for the proteins to make the lens of the eye. The difference lies in the regulation of the genetic machinery. At any particular time, a particular cell is producing only a small fraction of the proteins coded for in its DNA. And the amount of each protein produced must be precisely regulated in order for the cell to function properly. The cell will change the proteins it synthesizes in response to the environment or other cues. The mechanisms that regulate this process constitute a finely tuned, highly parallel system with extensive multifactoral feedback and elaborate control structure. It is also not yet well understood.

Genes are generally said to be on or off (or *expressed/not expressed*), although the amount of protein produced is also important. The production process is controlled by a complex collection of proteins in the nucleus of eucaryotic cells that influence which genes are expressed. Perhaps the most important of these proteins are the *histones*, which are tightly bound to the DNA in the chromosomes of eucaryotes. Histones are some of the most conserved proteins in all of life. There are almost no differences in the sequence of plant and mammalian histones, despite more than a billion years of divergence in their evolution. Other proteins swarm around the DNA, some influencing the production of a single gene (either encouraging or inhibiting it), while others can influence the production of large numbers of genes at once. An important group of these proteins are called *topoisomerases*; they rearrange and untangle the DNA in various ways, and are the next most prevalent proteins in the chromosome.

Many regulatory proteins recognize and bind to very specific sequences in the DNA. The sequences that these proteins recognize tend to border the protein coding regions of genes, and are known generally as *control regions*. Sequences that occur just upstream (towards the 5' end) of the coding region that encourage the production of the protein are called *promoters*. Similar regions either downstream of the coding region or relatively far upstream are called *enhancers*. Sequences that tend to prevent the production of a protein are called *repressors*. Karp's chapter in this volume discusses how this complex set of interactions can be modeled in knowledge-based systems.

Cells need to turn entire suites of genes on and off in response to many different events, ranging from normal development to trying to repair damage to the cell. The control mechanisms are responsive to the level of a product already in the cell (for homeostatic control) as well as to a tremendous variety of extracellular signals. Perhaps the most amazing activities in gene regulation occur during development; not only are genes turned on and off with precise timing, but the control can extend to producing alternative splicings of the nascent primary transcripts (as is the case in the transition from fetal to normal hemoglobin).

5.4 Catalysis & Metabolic Pathways

The translation of genes into proteins, crucial as it is, is only a small portion of the biochemical activity in a cell. Proteins do most of the work of managing the flow of energy, synthesizing, degrading and transporting materials, sending and receiving signals, exerting forces on the world, and providing structural support. Systems of interacting proteins form the basis for nearly every process of living things, from moving around and digesting food to thinking and reproducing. Somewhat surprisingly, a large proportion of the chemical processes that underlie all of these activities are shared across a very wide range of organisms. These shared processes are collectively referred to as *intermediary metabolism.* These include the *catabolic* processes for breaking down proteins, fats and carbohydrates (such as those found in food) and the *anabolic* processes for building new materials. Similar collections of reactions that are more specialized to particular organisms are called *secondary metabolism.* The substances that these reactions produce and consume are called *metabolites.*

The biochemical processes in intermediary metabolism are almost all *catalyzed reactions.* That is, these reactions would barely take place at all at normal temperatures and pressures; they require special compounds that facilitate the reaction — these compounds are called *catalysts* or *enzymes.* (It is only partially in jest that many biochemistry courses open with the professor saying that the reactions that take place in living systems are ones you were taught were impossible in organic chemistry.) Catalysts are usually named after the reaction they facilitate, usually with the added suffix *-ase.* For example, alcohol dehydrogenase is the enzyme that turns ethyl alcohol into acetaldehyde by removing two hydrogen atoms. Common classes of enzymes include *dehydrogenases, synthetases, proteases* (for breaking down proteins), *decarboxylases* (removing carbon atoms), *transferases* (moving a chemical group from one place to another), *kinases, phosphatases* (adding or removing phosphate groups, respectively) and so on. The materials transformed by catalysts are called *substrates.* Unlike the substrates, catalysts themselves are not changed by the reactions they participate in. A final point to note about enzymatic reactions is that in many cases the reactions can proceed in either direction. That is, and enzyme that transforms substance A into substance B can often also facilitate the transformation of B into A. The direction of the transformation depends on the concentrations of the substrates and on the energetics of the reaction (see Mavrovouniotis' chapter in this volume for further discussion of this topic).

Even the basic transformations of intermediary metabolism can involve dozens or hundreds of catalyzed reactions. These combinations of reactions, which accomplish tasks like turning foods into useable energy or compounds are called metabolic *pathways*. Because of the many steps in these pathways and the widespread presence of direct and indirect feedback loops, they can exhibit many counterintuitive behaviors. Also, all of these chemical reactions are going on in parallel. Mavrovouniotis's chapter in this volume describes an efficient system for making inferences about these complex systems.

In addition to the feedback loops among the substrates in the pathways, the presence or absence of substrates can affect the behavior of the enzymes themselves, through what is called *allosteric* regulation. These interactions occur when a substance binds to an enzyme someplace other than its usual *active site* (the atoms in the molecule that have the enzymatic effect). Binding at this other site changes the shape of the enzyme, thereby changing its activity. Another method of controlling enzymes is called *competitive inhibition*. In this form of regulation, substance other than the usual substrate of the enzyme binds to the active site of the enzyme, preventing it from having an effect on its substrate.

These are the basic mechanisms underlying eucaryotic cells (and much of this applies to bacterial and archaeal ones as well). Of course, each particular activity of a living system, from the capture of energy to immune response, has its own complex network of biochemical reactions that provides the mechanism underlying the function. Some of these mechanisms, such as the *secondary messenger system* involving cyclic adenosine monophosphate (cAMP) are widely shared by many different systems. Others are exquisitely specialized for a particular task in a single species: my favorite example of this is the evidence that perfect pitch in humans (being able to identify musical notes absolutely, rather than relative to each other) is mediated by a single protein. The functioning of these biochemical networks is being unravelled at an ever increasing rate, and the need for sophisticated methods to analyze relevant data and build suitable models is growing rapidly.

5.5 Genetic Mechanisms of Evolution

In the beginning of this chapter, I discussed the central role that evolution plays in understanding living systems. The mechanisms of evolution at the molecular level are increasingly well understood. The similarities and differences among molecules that are closely related provide important information about the structure and function of those molecules. Molecules (or their sequences) which are related to one another are said to be *homologous*. Although genes or proteins that have similar sequences are often assumed to be homologous, there are well known counterexamples due to *convergent evolution*. In these cases, aspects of very distantly related organisms come to resemble one another through very different evolutionary pathways. Unless there is evidence to the contrary, it is usually safe to assume that macromolecular sequences that are similar to each other are homologous.

The sources of variation at the molecular level are very important to understanding how molecules come to differ from each other (or *diverge*). Perhaps the best known mechanism of molecular evolution is the *point mutation,* or the change of a single nucleotide in a genetic sequence. The change can be to *insert* a new nucleotide, to *delete* an existing one, or to change one nucleotide into another. Other mechanisms include large scale chromosomal rearrangements and inversions. An important kind of rearrangement is the *gene duplication*; in which additional copies of a gene are inserted into the genome. These copies can then diverge, so that, for example, the original functionality may be preserved at the same time as related new genes evolve. These duplication events can lead to the presence of *pseudogenes*, which are quite similar to actual genes, but are not expressed. These pseudogenes present challenges for gene recognition algorithms, such as the one proposed in Searls chapter in this volume. Sexual reproduction adds another dimension to the exchange of genetic material. DNA from the two parents of a sexually reproducing organism undergoes a process called *crossover,* which forms a kind of mosaic that is passed on to the offspring.

Most mutations have relatively little effect. Mutations in the middle of introns generally have no effect at all (although mutations at the ends of an intron can affect the splicing process). Mutations in the third position of most codons have little effect at the protein level because of the redundancy of the genetic code. Even mutations that cause changes in the sequence of a protein are often neutral, as demonstrated by Sauer, *et al* (1989). Their experimental method involved *saturation mutagenesis* which explores are relatively large proportion of the space of possible mutations in parallel. Neutral mutations are the basis of genetic drift, which is the phenomena that accounts for the differences between the DNA that codes for functionally identical proteins in different organisms. This drift is also the basis for the molecular clock, described above. Of course, some point mutations are lethal, and others lead to diseases such as cystic fibrosis. Very rarely, a mutation will be advantageous; it will then rapidly get fixed in the population, as the organisms with the conferred advantage out reproduce the ones without it. Diploid sexually reproducing organisms have two copies of each gene (one from each parent), resulting in an added layer of complexity in the effect of mutations. Sometimes the extra copy can compensate (or partially compensate) for a mutation.

Molecular evolution also involves issues of selection and inheritance. Inheritance requires that the genes from the parent be passed to the offspring. DNA itself is replicated by splitting the double helix into two complimentary strands and then extending a primer by attaching complementary nucleotides. This process is modelled in detail Brutlag, *et al*'s chapter in this volume. The molecular mechanisms underlying the whole complex process of cell division (i.e. the cell cycle) are strikingly conserved in eucaryotes, and knowledge about this process is growing rapidly (see, e.g., Hartwell (1991) for a review). Selection also occurs on factors that are only apparent on the molecular level, such as the efficiency of certain reaction pathways (see, e.g. Hochachka & Somero [1984]).

6 Sources of Biological Knowledge

The information in this chapter has been presented textbook style, with little discussion of how the knowledge arose, or where errors might have crept in. The purpose of this section is to describe some of the basic experimental methods of molecular biology. These methods are important not only in understanding the source of possible errors in the data, but also because computational methods for managing laboratory activities and analyzing raw data are another area where AI can play a role (see the chapters by Edwards, *et al* and Glasgow, *et al*, in this volume). I will also describe some of the many online information resources relevant to computational molecular biology that are available.

6.1 Model Organisms: Germs, Worms, Weeds, Bugs & Rodents

The investigation of the workings of even a single organism is so complex as to take many dedicated scientists many careers worth of time. Trying to study all organisms in great depth is simply beyond the abilities of modern biology. Furthermore, the techniques of biological experimentation are often complex, time consuming and difficult. Some of the most valuable methods in biological research are invasive, or require organisms to be sacrificed, or require many generations of observation, or observations on large populations. Much of this work is impractical or unethical to carry out on humans. For these reasons, biologists have selected a variety of model organisms for experimentation. These creatures have qualities that make possible controlled laboratory experiments at reasonable cost and difficulty with results that can often be extrapolated to people or other organisms of interest.

Of course, research involving humans can be done ethically, and in some areas of biomedical research, such as final drug testing, it is obligatory. Other research methods involve kinds of human cells can be grown successfully in the laboratory. Not many human cell types thrive outside of the body. Some kinds of human cancer cells do grow well in the laboratory, and these cells are an important vehicle for research.

Sometimes the selection of a new model organism can lead to great advances in a field. For example, the use of a particular kind of squid made possible the understanding of the functioning of neurons because it contained a motor neuron that is more than 10 times the size of most neural cells, and hence easy to find and use in experiments. There are experimentally useful correlates of nearly every aspect of human biology found in some organism or another, but the following six organisms form the main collection of models used in molecular biology:

E. coli The ubiquitous intestinal bacterium *Escherichia coli* is a workhorse in biological laboratories. Because it is a relatively simple organism with fast reproduction time and is safe and easy to work with, *E. coli* has been the focus of a great deal of research in genetics and molecular biology of the cell. Although it is a Bacterium, many of the basic biochemical mechanisms of *E. coli* are shared by humans. For example, the first understanding of how genes can be turned on and off came from the study of a virus that infects these bacteria (Ptashne, 1987). *E. coli* is a common target for genetic engineering, where genes from other organisms are inserted into the bacterial genome then produced in quantity. *E. coli* is now the basis of the international biotechnology industry, churning out buckets full of human insulin, the heart attack drug TPA, and a wide variety of other substances.

Saccharomyces *Saccharomyces cervesiae* is better known as brewer's yeast, and it is another safe, easy to grow, short generation time organism. Other yeasts, such as *Schizosaccharomyces pombe,* are also used extensively. Surprisingly, yeasts are very much like people in many ways. Unlike the bacterium *E. coli,* yeasts are eucaryotes, with a cell nucleus, mitochondria, a eucaryotic cell membrane, and many of the other cellular components and processes found in most other eucaryotes, including people. Because these yeasts are so easy to grow and manipulate, and because they are so biochemically similar to people, many insights about the molecular processes involved in metabolism, biosynthesis, cell division, and other crucial areas of biology have come from the investigation of *Saccharomyces* (Saccharomyces is a genus name, which, when used alone, refers to all species that are within that genus). Yeasts play another important role in molecular biology. One of the crucial steps in sequencing large amounts of DNA is to be able to prepare many copies of moderate sized pieces of DNA. An widely used method for doing this is the *yeast artificial chromosome* (or YAC), which is discussed below.

Arabidopsis The most important application of increased biological understanding is generally thought to be in medicine, and increased understanding of human biology has indeed led to dramatic improvements in health care. However, in terms of effect on human life, agriculture is just as significant. A great deal of research into genetics and biochemistry has been motivated by the desire to better understand various aspects of plant biology. An important model organism for plants is *Arabidopsis thaliana*, a common weed. *Arabidopsis* makes a good model because it undergoes the same processes of growth, development, flowering and reproduction as most higher plants, but it's genome has 30 times less DNA than corn, and very little repetitive DNA. It also produces lots of seeds, and takes only about six weeks to grow to maturity. There are several other model organisms used to investigate botanical questions, including tomatoes, tobacco, carrots and corn.

C. elegans One of the most exciting model organisms to emerge recently has been the nematode worm *Caenorhabditis elegans*. This tiny creature, thousands of which can be found in a spadeful of dirt, has already been used to generate tremendous insight about cellular development and physiology. The adult organism has exactly 959 cells, and every normal worm consists of exactly the same collection of cells in the same places doing the same thing. It is one of the simplest creatures with a nervous system (which involves about a third of its cells). Not only is the complete anatomy of the organism known, but a complete cell fate map has been generated, tracing the developmental lineage of each of each cell throughout the lifespan of the organism. This map allows researchers to relate behaviors to particular cells, to trace the effects of genetic mutations very specifically, and perhaps to gain insight into the mechanisms of aging as well as development. A large, highly integrated picture and text database of information about the cell fates, genetic maps and sequences, mutation effects and other relevant information about *C. elegans* is currently under construction at the University of Arizona.

D. melanogaster *Drosophila melanogaster,* a common fruit fly, has long been a staple of classical genetics research. These flies have short generation times, and many different genetically determined morphological characteristics (e.g. eye color) that can readily be determined by visual inspection. *Drosophila* were used for decades in exploring patterns of inheritance; now that molecular methods can be applied, they have proven invaluable for a variety of studies of genetic expression and control. An important class of genetic elements that regulate many other genes, in effect, specifying complex genetic programs, were first discovered in *Drosophila*; these areas are called *homeoboxes*. Molecular genetics in *Drosophila* is also providing great insights into how complex body plans are generated.

M. musculus *Mus musculus* is the basic laboratory mouse. Mice are mammals, and, as far as biochemistry is concerned, are practically identical to people. Many questions about physiology, reproduction, functioning of the immune and nervous systems and other areas of interest can only be addressed by examining creatures that are very similar to humans; mice nearly always fit the bill. The similarities between mice and people mean also that the mouse is a very complicated creature; it has a relatively large, complex genome, and mouse development and physiology is not as regular or consistent as that of *C. elegans* or *Drosophila*. Although our depth of understanding of the mouse will lag behind understanding of simpler organisms, the comparison of mouse genome to human is likely to be a key step, both in understanding their vast commonalities, and in seeing the aspects of our genes that make us uniquely human.

7 Experimental Methods

Molecular biologists have developed a tremendous variety of tools to address questions of biological function. This chapter can only touch briefly on a few of the most widely used methods, but the terminology and a sense of the kinds of efforts required to produce the data used by computer scientists can be important for understanding the strengths and limitations of various sources of data.

Imaging. The first understanding of the cellular nature of life came shortly after the invention of the light microscope, and microscopy remains central to research in biology The tools for creating images have expanded tremendously. Not only are there computer controled light microscopes with a wide variety of imaging modalities, but there are now many other methods of generating images of the very small. The electon microscope offers extremely high resolution, although it requires exposing the imaged sample to high vacuum and other harsh treatments. New technologies including the Atomic Force Microscope (AFM) and the Scanning Tunnelling Microscope (STM) offer the potential to create images of individual molecules. Biologists use these tools extensively.

Gel Electrophoresis. A charged molecule, when placed in an electric field, will be accelerated; positively charged molecules will move toward negative electrodes and vice versa. By placing a mixture of molecules of interest in a medium and subjecting them to an electric charge, the molecules will migrate through the medium and separate from each other. How fast the molecules will move depends on their charge and their size—bigger molecules see more resistance from the medium. The procedure, called *electrophoresis* involves putting a spot of the mixture to be analyzed at the top of a polyacrylamide or agarose gel, and applying an electric field for a period of time. Then the gel is stained so that the molecules become visible; the stains appear as stripes along the gel, and are called *bands*. The location of the bands on the gel are proportional to the charge and size of the molecules in the mixture (see Figure 4 for an example). The intensity of the stain is an indication of the amount of a particular molecule in the mixture. If the molecules are all the same charge, or have charge proportional to their size (as, for example, DNA does) then electrophoresis separates them purely by size.

Often, several mixtures are run simultaneously on a single gel. This allows for easy calibration to standards, or comparison of the contents of different mixtures, showing, for example, the absence of a particular molecular component in one. The adjacent, parallel runs are sometimes called *lanes*. A variation on this technique allows the sorting of molecules by a chemical property called the *isoelectric point*, which is related to its pK. A combination of the two methods, called *2D electrophoresis* is capable of very fine

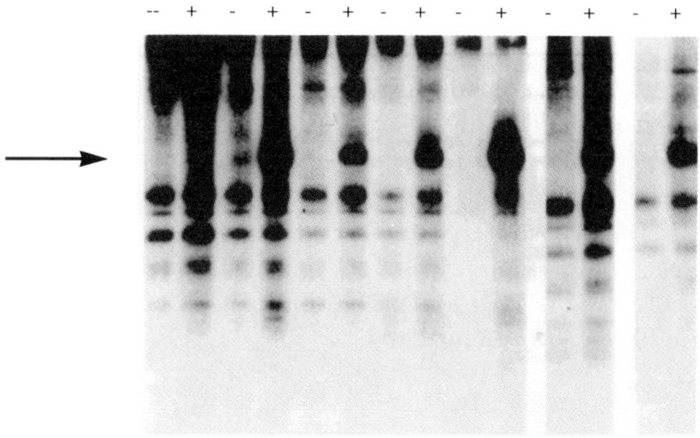

Figure 4. This is an example of a gel electrophoresis run.. Each column was loaded with a different mixture. The mixtures are then separated vertically by their charge and size. The gel is then stained, producing dark bands where a molecule of a given size or charge is present in a mixture. In this gel, the columns marked with a - are a control group. The band marked with an arrow is filled only in the + columns.

distinctions, for example, mapping each protein in a cell to a unique *spot* in two-space, the size of the spot indicating the amount of the protein. Although there are still some difficulties in calibration and repeatability, this method is potentially a very powerful tool for monitoring the activities of large bio-chemical systems. In addition, if a desired molecule can be separated from the mixture this way, individual spots or bands can be removed from the gel for further processing, in a procedure called *blotting*.

Cloning. A group of cells with identical genomes are said to be *clones* of one another. Unless there are mutations, a single cell that reproduces asexu-ally will produce identical offspring; these clones are sometimes called a *cell line*, and certain standardized cell lines, for example the HeLa cell line, play an important role in biological research.

This concept has been generalize to cloning individual genes. In this case, a piece of DNA containing a gene of interest is inserted into the genome of a target cell line, and the cells are screened so that all of the resulting cells have an identical copy of the desired genetic sequence. The DNA in these cells is said to be *recombinant,* and the cell will produce the protein coded for by the inserted gene.

Cloning a gene requires some sophisticated technology. In order for a cloned gene to be expressed, it must contain the appropriate transcription sig-nals for the target cell line. One way biologists ensure that this will happen is to put the new gene into a bacteriophage (a virus that infects bacteria), or a plasmid (a circular piece of DNA found outside of the chromosome of bacte-ria that replicates independently of the bacteria's chromosomal DNA). These devices for inserting foreign DNA into cells are called *vectors*.

In order to cut and paste desired DNA fragments into vectors, biologists use *restriction enzymes*, which cut DNA at precisely specified points. These enzymes are produced naturally by bacteria as a way of attacking foreign DNA. For example, the commonly used enzyme *EcoRI* (from *E. coli)* cuts DNA between the G and the A in the sequence GAATTC; these target sequences are called *restriction sites*. Everywhere a restriction site occurs in a DNA molecule treated with *EcoRI*, the DNA will be broken. Restriction enzymes play many roles in biology in addition to making gene cloning possible; a few others will be described below.

Both the insertion of the desired gene into the vector and the uptake of the vector by the target cells are effective only a fraction of the time. Fortunately, cells and vectors are small and it is relatively easy to grow a lot of them. The process is applied to a population of target cells, and then the resulting population is screened to identify the cells where the gene was successfully inserted. This can be difficult, so many vectors are designed to facilitate screening. One popular vector, *pBR322*, contains a naturally occurring transcription start signal and some antibiotic resistance genes, designed with conveniently placed restriction sites. If this vector is taken up by the target cells, it will confer resistance to certain antibiotics to them. By applying the anitbiotic to the whole colony, the researcher can kill all the cells that did not get the cloned gene. More sophisticated manipulations involving multiple antibiotic resistances and carefully placed restriction sites can also be used to ensure that the gene was correctly taken up by the vector.

There are many variations on these techniques for inserting foreign genes. It is now possible to use simple bacteria to produce large amounts of almost any isolated protein, including, for example, human insulin. Although it is a more complex process, it is also possible to insert foreign genes into plants and animals, even people. A variety of efforts are underway to use these techniques to engineer organisms for agriculture, medicine and other applications. Not all of these applications are benign. One of the most successful early efforts was to increase the resistance of tobacco plants to pesticides, and there are clear military applications. On the other hand, these methods also promise new approaches to producing important rare biological compounds inexpensively (e.g. for novel cancer treatments or cleaning up toxic waste) and improving the nutritional value or hardiness of agricultural products. The entire field of genetic engineering is controversial, and there are a variety of controls on what experiments can be done and how they can be done.

Hybridization and Immunological Staining. Biological compounds can show remarkable specificity, for example, binding very selectively only to one particular compound. This ability plays an important role in the laboratory, where researchers can identify the presence or absence of a particular molecule (or even a region of a molecule) in vanishingly small amounts.

Antibodies are the molecules that the immune system uses to identify and fight off invaders. Antibodies are extremely specific, recognizing and binding to only one kind of molecule. Dyes can be attached to the antibody, forming a very specific system for identifying the presence (and possibly quantifying the amount) of a target molecule that is present in a system.

There is a conceptually related method for identifying very specifically the presence of a particular nucleotide sequence in a macromolecule. The complement to a single-stranded DNA sequence will bind quite specifically to that sequence. One technique measures how similar two related DNA sequences are by testing how strongly the single-stranded versions of the molecules stick to each other, or *hybridize*. The more easily they come apart, the more differences there are between their sequences. It is also possible to attach a dye or other marker to a specific piece of DNA (called a *probe*) and then hybridize it to a longer strand of DNA. The location along the strand that is complementary to the probe will then be marked. There are many variations on hybridization and immunological staining that are customized to the needs of a particular experiment.

Gene Mapping and Sequencing. The Human Genome Project is the effort to produce a map and then the sequence of the human genome. The purpose of a genetic map is to identify the location and size of all of the genes of an organism on its chromosomes. This information is important for a variety of reasons. First, because crossover is an important component of inheritance in sexually reproducing organisms, genes that are near each other on the chromosome will tend to be inherited together. In fact, this forms the basis for *linkage analysis*, which is a technique that looks at the relationships between genes (or phenotypes) in large numbers of matings (in this context, often called *crosses*) to identify which genes tend to be inherited together, and are therefore likely to be near each other. Second, it is possible to clone genes of known locations, opening up a wide range of possible experimental manipulations. Finally, it is currently possible to determine the sequence of moderate size pieces of DNA, so if an important gene has been mapped, it is possible to find the sequence of that area, and discover the protein that is responsible for the genetic characteristic. This is especially important for understanding the basis of inherited diseases.

The existence of several different kinds of restriction enzymes makes possible a molecular method of creating genetic maps. The application of each restriction enzyme (the process is called a *digest*) creates a different collection of *restriction fragments* (the cut up pieces of DNA). By using gel electrophoresis, it is possible to determine the size of these fragments. Using multiple enzymes, together and separately, results in sets of fragments which can be (partially) ordered with respect to each other, resulting in a genetic map. AI techniques for reasoning about partial orders have been effectively applied to the problem of assembling the fragments into a map (Letovsky &

Berlyn, 1992). These *physical maps* divide a large piece of DNA (like a chromosome) into parts, and and there is an associated method for obtaining any desired part.

Restriction fragment mapping becomes problematic when applied to large stretches of DNA, because the enzymes can produce many pieces of about the same size, making the map ambiguous. The use of different enzymes can help address this problem to a limited degree, but a variety of other techniques are now also used.

Being able to divide the genome into moderate sized chunks is a prerequisite to determining its sequence. Although there are several clever methods for determining the sequence of DNA molecule, all of them are limited to a resolution of well under a thousand basepairs at a time. In order to take this sequencing ability and determine the sequence of large pieces of DNA, many different overlapping chunks must be sequenced, and then these sequences must be assembled. In order to accomplish this task, it is necessary to break the DNA in an entire genome down into a set of more manageable sized pieces. The ordering of these pieces must be known (so they can be reassembled into a complete sequence), taken together the pieces must cover the entire genome, and the same set of pieces must be accessible to many different laboratories. This process is usually accomplished in several stages. The first stage generates relatively large pieces called *contigs*. Contigs are maintained in cloned cell lines so that they can be reproduced and distributed. Often, these pieces of DNA are made into *Yeast artificial chromosomes,* or *YACs*, which can hold up to about a million basepairs of sequence each, requiring on the order of 10,000 clones to adequately cover the entire human genome. Each of these is then broken down into sets of smaller pieces, often in the form of *cosmids*. A cosmid is a particular kind of bacteriophage (a virus that infects bacteria) that is capable of accepting inserts of 30,000 or so basepairs. The difficulties in generating and maintaining collections of clones that large have led to alternative technologies for large scale sequencing.

One alternative involves a new technology based on the *polymerase chain reaction,* or *PCR*. This mechanism was revolutionary becauase it made it possible to rapidly produce huge amounts of a specific region of DNA, simply by knowing a little bit of the sequence around the desired region. PCR exponentially *amplifies* (makes copies of) a segment of a DNA molecule, given a unique pair of sequences that bracket the desired piece. First, short sequences of DNA (called *oligonucleotides*, or *oligos*) complementary to

---

*There are many interesting uses of this technology. For example, it gives law enforcement the ability to generate enough DNA for identification from vanishing small samples of tissue. A more amusing application is the rumored use of PCR to spy on what academic competitors are doing in their research. Almost any correspondence from a competitor's lab will contain traces of DNA which can be amplified by PCR to identify the specific clones the lab is working with.

each of the bracketing sequences are synthesized. Creating short pieces of DNA with a specific sequence is routine technology, now often performed by laboratory robots. These pieces are called *primers*. The primers, the target DNA and the enzyme DNA polymerase are then combined. The mixture is heated, so that the hydrogen bonds in the DNA break and the molecule splits into two single strands. When the mixture cools sufficiently, the primers bond to the regions around the area of interest, and the DNA polymerase replicates the DNA downstream of the primers. By using a heat resistant polymerase from an Archaea species that lives at high temperatures, it is possible to rapidly cycle this process, doubling the amount of desired segment of DNA each time. This technology makes possible the exponential amplification of entire DNA molecules or any specific region of DNA for which bracketing primers can be generated.[*]

In order to use PCR for genome mapping and sequencing, a collection of unique (short) sequences spread throughout the genome must be identified for use as primers. The sequences must be unique in the genome so that the source of amplified DNA is unambiguous, and they have to be relatively short so that they are easy to synthesize. The sites in the genome that correspond to these sequences are called *sequence tagged sites* or *STSs*. The more STSs that are known, the finer grained the map of the genome they provide. Finding short, unique sequences even in 3×10^9 bp of DNA is not that difficult; a simple calculation shows that most sequences of length 16 or so can reasonably be expected to be unique in a genome of that size. An early goal of the Human Genome Project is to generate a list of STSs spaced at approximately 100kbp intervals over the entire human genome. If it is possible to find STSs that adequately cover the genome, it will not be necessary to build and maintain libraries of 10,000 YACs and ten times as many cosmids. Any region of DNA of interest can be identified by two STSs that bracket it. Instead of having to maintain large clone collections, these STSs can be stored in a database, and any researcher who needs a particular section of DNA can synthesize the appropriate primers and use PCR to produce many copies of just of that section.

Another issue that has been raised about the project to sequence the genome is the need to know the sequences of all of the introns and other noncoding regions of DNA. One way to address this issue is to target only coding regions for sequencing. The ability to find the sequences that a particular cell is using to produce proteins at a particular point in time is also useful in a variety of other areas as well. This information can be gleaned by gathering the mRNAs present in the cytoplasm of the cell, and sequencing them. Instead of sequencing the mRNAs directly, biologists use an enzyme called *reverse transcriptase* to make DNA molecules complementary to the mRNAs (called *cDNAs*) and then sequence that DNA. Using PCR and other technology, it is possible to capture at least portions of most of the mRNAs a cell is producing. By sequencing these cDNAs, researchers can focus their attention on just the parts of the genome that code for expressed proteins.

Large scale attempts to sequence at least part of all of the cDNAs that can be produced from brain tissue have resulted in partial sequences for more than 2500 new proteins in a very short period of time (Adams, *et al,* 1992). These sequences called ESTs, for *expressed sequence tags* can be used as PCR primers for future, more detailed experiments. This work has created controversy because of the ensuing attempt by the National Institutes of Health to patent the EST sequences.

Crystallography and NMR. Until the relationship between protein sequence and structure is more fully understood, the sequences produced by genome projects will provide only part of the biochemical story. Additional information about protein structure is necessary to understand how the proteins function. This structural information is at the present primarily gathered by *X-ray crystallography.* In order to determine the structure of a protein in this manner, a very large, pure crystal of the protein must be grown (this process can take years, and may never succeed for certain proteins). Then the X-ray diffraction pattern of the crystal is measured, and this information can be used indirectly to determine the positions of the atoms in the molecule. Glasgow, *et al's* chapter in this volume describes this process in more detail. Because of the difficulties in crystallography, relatively few structures are known, but the number of new structures is growing exponentially, with a doubling time of a bit over two years.

A promising alternative to crystallography for determining protein structure is multi-dimensional *nuclear magnetic resonance*, or *NMR.* Although this process does not require the crystallization of the protein, there are technical difficulties in analyzing the data associated with large molecules like proteins. *Edwards, et al's* chapter in this volume describes some of the challenges. Both crystallography and NMR techniques result in static protein structures, which are to some degree misleading. Proteins are flexible, and the patterns of their movement are likely to play an important role in their function. Although NMR has the potential to provide information about this facet of protein activity, there is very little data available currently.

7.1 Computational Biology

In the last five years, biologists have come to understand that sharing the results of experiments now takes more than simple journal publication. In the 1980s, many journals were overwhelmed with papers reporting novel sequences and other biological data. Paper publications of sequences are hard to analyze, prone to typographical errors, and take up valuable journal space.

*Researchers without internet access can contact NCBI by writing to NCBI/National Library of Medicine/Bethesda, MD 20894 USA or calling +1 (301) 496-2475.

Databases were established, journals began to require deposition into the databases before publication, and various tools began to appear for managing and analyzing the databases.

When Doolittle, et al (1983) used the nascent genetic sequence database to prove that a cancer causing gene was a close relative of a normal growth factor, molecular biology labs all over the world began installing computers or linking up to networks to do database searches. Since then, a bewildering variety of computational resources for biology have arisen. These databases and other resources are a valuable service not only to the biological community, but also to the computer scientist in search of domain information.

There is a database of databases, listing these resources which is maintained at Los Alamos National Laboratory. It is called LiMB(Lawton, Burks & Martinez, 1989), and contains descriptions, contacts and access methods for more than 100 molecular biology related databases. It is a very valuable tool for tracking down information. Another general source for databases and information about them is the National Center for Biotechnology Information (NCBI), which is part of the National Library of Medicine. Many databases are available via anonymous ftp from the NCBI server, ncbi.nlm.nih.gov.*

A few of the databases that may be of particular interest to computer scientists are described here. There are several databases that maintain genetic sequences, and they are increasingly coordinated. They are Genbank (Moore, Benton & Burks, 1990), the European Molecular Biology Laboratory nucleotide sequence database (EMBL) (Hamm & Cameron, 1986), and the DNA Database, Japan (DDBJ) (Miyazawa, 1990). NCBI will also provide a sequence database beginning in 1992. The main protein sequence database is the Protein Identification Resource (PIR) (George, Barker & Hunt, 1986). NCBI also provides a non-redundant combination of protein sequences from various sources (including translations of genetic sequences) in its NRDB.

Several databases contain information about three dimensional structures of molecules. The Protein Data Bank (PDB) maintained by Brookhaven National Laboratory, contains protein structure data, primarily from crystallographic data. BioMagRes (BMR) is a database of NMR derived data about proteins, including three dimensional coordinates, that is maintained at the University of Wisconsin, Madison (Ulrich, Markley & Kyogoku, 1989). CARBBANK, contains structural information for complex carbohydrates (Doubet, Bock, Smith, Albersheim & Darvill, 1989). Chemical Abstracts Service (CAS) Online Registry File is a commercial database that contains more than 10 million chemical substances, many with three dimensional coordinates and other useful information. The Cambridge Structural Database contains small molecule structures, and is available to researchers at moderate charge.

Genetic map databases (GDB), as well as a database of inherited human diseases and characteristics (OMIM) are maintained at the Welch Medical

Library at Johns Hopkins University. To get access to these databases, send email to help@welch.jhu.edu. Other genetic map databases are available for many of the model organisms listed above; consult LiMB for more information about them.

There is a database of information about compounds involved in intermediary metabolism called CompoundKB, developed by Peter Karp that is available from NCBI. This database is available in KEE knowledge base form as well as several others, and there is associated LISP code which makes it attractive for artificial intelligence researchers; see Karp's and Mavrovouniotis's chapters in this volume for possible applications of the knowledge base.

Finally, one of the most important computer-based assets for a computer scientist interested in molecular biology information is the bulletin board system called *bionet*. This bboard is available through usenet as well as by electronic mail. The discussion groups include computational biology, information theory and software, as well as more than 40 other areas. Bionet is an excellent source for information and contacts with computationally sophisticated biologists.

8 Conclusion

AI researchers have often had unusual relationships with their collaborators. "Experts" are somehow "knowledge engineered" so that what they know can be put into programs. Biology has a long history of collaborative research, and it does not match this AI model. Computer scientists and biologists often have differing expectations about collaboration, education, conferences and many other seemingly mundane aspects of research. In order to work with biologists, AI researchers must understand a good deal about the domain and find ways to bridge the gap between these rather different scientific cultures.

This brief survey of biology is intended to help the computer scientist get oriented and understand some of the commonly used terms in the domain. Many more detailed, but still accessible books are listed in the references. I find this material fascinating. Not only is it interesting as a domain for AI research, but it provides a rich set of metaphors for thinking about intelligence: genetic algorithms, neural networks and Darwinian automata are but a few of the computational approaches to behavior based on biological ideas. There will, no doubt, be many more.

Acknowledgements

This chapter was written at the instigation of Harold Morowitz, who understood long before I did that such an introduction could indeed be accomplished in less than 1000 pages. He also taught the biochemistry course that I finally took, two years *after* finishing my Ph.D. David J. States deserves much of the credit as well. In the three years we have been working together, he greatly extended my understanding of not only what biologists know, but how they think. He has read several drafts of this chapter and made helpful suggestions. David Landsman, Mark Boguski, Kalí Tal and Jill Shirmer have also read the chapter and made suggestions. Angel Lee graciously supplied the gel used in Figure 4. Of course, all remaining mistakes are my responsibility.

References

Adams, M. D., Dubnick, M., Kerlavage, A. R., Moreno, R., Kelley, J. M., Utterback, T. R., Nagle, J. W., Fields, C. & Venter, J. C. (1992). Sequence Identification of 2,375 Brain Genes. *Nature, 355*(6361), 632-4.

Alberts, B., Bray, D., Lewis, J., Raff, M., Roberts, K. & Watson, J. (1989). *The Molecular Biology of the Cell* (2nd. ed. ed.). New York, NY: Garland Publishing.

Buss, L. (1987). *The Evolution of Individuality*. Princeton, NJ: Princeton University Press.

Cherty, L. M., Case, S. M. & Wilson, A. C. (1978). Frog Perspectives on the Morphological difference between Humans and Chimpanzees. *Science, 200*, 209-211.

Doolittle, R. F., Hunkapiller, M. W., Hood, L. E., Devare, S. G., Robbins, K. C., Aaronson, S. A., & Antoniades, H. N. (1983). Simian Sarcoma *Onc* Gene, *v-sis,* Is Derived from the Gene (or Genes) Encoding Platelet Derived Growth Factor. *Science*, 221, 275-277.

Doubet, S., Bock, K., Smith, D., Albersheim, P. & Darvill, A. (1989). The Complex Carbohydrate Structure Database. *Trends in Biochemical Sciences, 14*, 475.

George, D., Barker, W. & Hunt, L. (1986). The Protein Identification Resource. *Nucleic Acids Research, 14*, 11-15.

Hamm, G. & Cameron, G. (1986). The EMBL Data Library. *Nucleic Acids Research, 14*, 5-9.

Hartwell, L. (1991). Twenty-five Years of Cell Cycle Genetics. *Genetics, 129*(4), 975-980.

Hochachka, P. W. & Somero, G. N. (1984). *Biochemical Adaptation*. Princeton, NJ: Princeton University Press.

Karplus, M. & Petsko, G. A. (1990). Molecular Dynamics Simulations in Biology. *Nature, 347*(October), 631-639.

Kessel, R. G. & Kardon, R. H. (1979). *Tissues and Organs: A Text-Atlas of Scanning electron Microscopy*. San Francisco, CA: W.H. Freeman and Company.

Langton, C., eds. (1989). *Artificial Life* (VI.). Redwood City, CA: Addison Wesley.

Lawton, J., Burks, C. & Martinez, F. (1989). Overview of the LiMB Database. *Nucleic Acids Research, 17*, 5885-5899.

Letovsky, S. & Berlyn, M. (1992). CPROP: A Rule-based Program for Constructing a Genetic Map. *Genomics, 12*, 435-446.

Li, W.-H. & Graur, D. (1991). *Fundamentals of Molecular Evolution*. Sunderland, MA: Sinauer Associates, Inc.

Margolis, L. (1981). *Symbiosis and Cell Evolution*. San Francisco: Freeman.

May, R. M. (1988). How Many Species Are There on Earth? *Science, 241*(September 16), 1441-1450.

Miyazawa, S. (1990). DNA Data Bank of Japan: Present Status and Future Plans. *Computers and DNA, 7,* 47-61.

Moore, J., Benton, D. & Burks, C. (1990). The GenBank Nucleic Acid Data Bank. *Focus, 11*(4), 69-72.

Ptashne, M. (1987). *A Genetic Switch: Gene Control and the Phage Lambda.* Palo Alto, CA: Blackwell Scientific Publications.

Sauer, R. T. (1989). Genetic Analysis of Protein Stability and Function. *Annual Review of Genetics, 23,* 289-310.

Ulrich, E., Markley, J. & Kyogoku, Y. (1989). Creation of Nuclear Magnetic Resonance Data Repository and Literature Base. *Protein Sequence and Data Analysis, 2,* 23-37.

Woese, C. R., Kandler, O. & Wheelis, M. L. (1990). Towards a Natural System of Organisms: Proposal for the Domains Archaia, Bacteria, and Eucarya. (June), 4576-4579.

2

The Computational Linguistics
of Biological Sequences

David B. Searls

1 Introduction

Shortly after Watson and Crick's discovery of the structure of DNA, and at about the same time that the genetic code and the essential facts of gene expression were being elucidated, the field of linguistics was being similarly revolutionized by the work of Noam Chomsky [Chomsky, 1955, 1957, 1959, 1963, 1965]. Observing that a seemingly infinite variety of language was available to individual human beings based on clearly finite resources and experience, he proposed a formal representation of the rules or *syntax* of language, called generative grammar, that could provide finite—indeed, concise—characterizations of such infinite languages. Just as the breakthroughs in molecular biology in that era served to anchor genetic concepts in physical structures and opened up entirely novel experimental paradigms, so did Chomsky's insight serve to energize the field of linguistics, with putative correlates of cognitive processes that could for the first time be reasoned about

axiomatically as well as phenomenologically. While Chomsky and his follow-
ers built extensively upon this foundation in the field of linguistics, generative
grammars were also soon integrated into the framework of the theory of computation, and in addition now form the basis for efforts of computational linguists to automate the processing and understanding of human language.

Since it is quite commonly asserted that DNA is a richly-expressive *language* for specifying the structures and processes of life, also with the potential for a seemingly infinite variety, it is surprising that relatively little has
been done to apply to biological sequences the extensive results and methods
developed over the intervening decades in the field of formal language theory.
While such an approach has been proposed [Brendel and Busse, 1984], most
investigations along these lines have used grammar formalisms as tools for
what are essentially information-theoretic studies [Ebeling and Jimenez-Montano, 1980; Jimenez-Montano, 1984], or have involved statistical analyses at
the level of vocabularies (reflecting a more traditional notion of comparative
linguistics) [Brendel et al., 1986; Pevzner et al., 1989a,b; Pietrokovski et al.,
1990]. Only very recently have generative grammars for their own sake been
viewed as models of biological phenomena such as gene regulation [Collado-
Vides, 1989a,b, 1991a], gene structure and expression [Searls, 1988], recombination [Head, 1987] and other forms of mutation and rearrangement [Searls,
1989a], conformation of macromolecules [Searls, 1989a], and in particular as
the basis for computational analysis of sequence data [Searls, 1989b; Searls
and Liebowitz, 1990; Searls and Noordewier, 1991].

Nevertheless, there is an increasing trend throughout the field of computational biology toward abstracted, hierarchical views of biological sequences,
which is very much in the spirit of computational linguistics. At the same
time, there has been a proliferation of software to perform various kinds of
pattern-matching search and other forms of analysis, which could well
benefit from the formal underpinnings that language theory offers to such en-
terprises. With the advent of very large scale sequencing projects, and the resulting flood of sequence data, such a foundation may in fact prove essential.

This article is intended as a prolegomenon to a formally-based computational linguistics of biological sequences, presenting an introduction to the
field of mathematical linguistics and its applications, and reviewing and extending some basic results regarding structural and functional phenomena in
DNA and protein sequences. Implementation schemes will also be offered,
largely deriving from logic grammar formalisms, with a view toward practical tools for sequence analysis.

2 Formal Language Theory

This section will provide a compact but reasonably complete introduction
to the major results of formal language theory, that should allow for a basic

understanding of the subsequent sections by those with no background in mathematical linguistics. Proofs will be omitted in this section; some will be offered later as regards biological sequences, and will use a range of proof techniques sufficient to demonstrate the basic methodologies of the field, but by and large these will be simple and by mathematical standards "semi-formal." Readers interested in further studies along these lines are encouraged to consult textbooks such as [Sudkamp, 1988; Hopcroft and Ullman, 1979; Harrison, 1978] (in order of increasing difficulty). Those already familiar with the subject area should skip this section.

2.1 The Formal Specification of Languages

Formally, a *language* is simply a set of *strings* of characters drawn from some *alphabet*, where the alphabet is a set of symbols usually denoted by Σ. One such language would be simply the set of *all* strings over an alphabet $\Sigma = \{0,1\}$; this "maximal" language is indicated by the use of an asterisk, e.g.

$$\Sigma^* = \{0,1\}^* = \Big\{ \ \varepsilon, 0, 1, 00, 01, 10, 11, 000, 001, \cdots \ \Big\} \qquad (1)$$

Here, the ε represents the *empty string* or string of length zero; the set containing ε, however, should not be confused with the empty set $\varnothing$. The challenge of computational linguistics is to find concise ways of specifying a given (possibly infinite) language $L \subseteq \Sigma^*$, preferably in a way that reflects some underlying model of the "source" of that language. We can use informal descriptions that make use of natural language, such as in the following example:

$$L_a = \Big\{ \ w \in \{0,1\}^* \ \Big| \ w \text{ begins with a 0 and contains at least one 1} \ \Big\} \qquad (2)$$

(The vertical bar notation is used to define a set in terms of its properties; this specification would be read "the set of all strings w of 0's and 1's *such that* each w begins with a 0 and . . .") However, properties expressed in natural language are typically neither precise enough to allow for easy mathematical analysis, nor in a form that invites the use of computational support in dealing with them. On the other hand, simply exhaustively enumerating languages such as the example in (2) is also clearly ineffective—in fact, impossible:

$$L_a = \Big\{ \ 01, 001, 010, 011, 0001, 0010, 0011, 0100, \cdots \ \Big\} \qquad (3)$$

The remainder of this section will examine formal methods that have been used to provide finite specifications of such languages.

2.1.1 Regular Expressions and Languages. A widely-used method of specifying languages is by way of *regular expressions,* which in their mathematically pure form use only three basic operations. These operations are given below, using a notation in which a regular expression is given in bold type, and the language "generated" by that expression is derived by the application of a function L (defined recursively in the obvious way):

(i) **concatenation**, denoted by an infix operator '·', or more often by simply writing symbols in juxtaposition, e.g. $L(\textbf{01}) = \{ 01 \}$;

(ii) **disjunction** (or logical OR), denoted in this case by the infix operator '+', e.g. $L(\textbf{0+1}) = \{ 0,1 \}$; and

(iii) **Kleene star**, denoted by a postfix superscript '*', represents the set containing zero or more concatenated instances of its argument, e.g. $L(\textbf{0*}) = \{ \varepsilon, 0, 00, 000, 0000, \cdots \}$.

The latter operation is also known as the *closure* of concatenation. Note the connection between the definition of Kleene star and our previous use of the asterisk:

$$\Sigma^* = L((\textbf{0+1})^*) \qquad \text{for } \Sigma = \{ 0,1 \} \tag{4}$$

One additional non-primitive operator, a postfix superscript '+', is used to specify one or more occurrences of its argument. This is the *positive closure* of concatenation, defined in terms of concatenation and Kleene star as

$$L(\textbf{0}^+) = L(\textbf{00*}) = \{ 0, 00, 000, 0000, \cdots \} \tag{5}$$

The language from our running example of (2) can now be described using any of several regular expressions, including

$$L_a = L(\textbf{00*1(0+1)*}) \tag{6}$$

From this point, we will dispense with the $L(\ )$ notation and let the regular expression standing alone denote the corresponding language. Any such language, that can be described by a regular expression, will be called a *regular language* (RL)[*].

2.1.2 Grammars. Such regular expressions have not only found wide use in various kinds of simple search operations, but are also still the mainstay of many biological sequence search programs. However, it is a fact that many important languages simply cannot be specified as regular expressions, e.g.

$$\{ 0^n 1^n \mid n \geq 1 \} \tag{7}$$

where the superscript integers denote that number of concatenated symbols, so that (7) is the set of all strings beginning with any non-zero number of 0's followed by an equal number of 1's. This shortcoming of regular expressions for language specification can be remedied through the use of more powerful representations, called *grammars*. Besides a finite alphabet Σ of *terminal* symbols, grammars have a finite set of "temporary" *nonterminal* symbols (including a special *start* symbol, typically S), and a finite set of *rules* or *productions*; the latter use an infix '$\rightarrow$' notation to specify how strings containing nonterminals may be rewritten by expanding those embedded nonterminals (given on the left-hand side of the arrow) to new substrings (given on the right-hand side). For instance, a grammar specifying the language L_a of (2) can be written:

$$
\begin{array}{ll}
S \to 0A & B \to 0B \\
A \to 0A & B \to 1B \\
A \to 1B & B \to \varepsilon
\end{array}
\qquad (8)
$$

Note that nonterminals are traditionally designated by capital letters. A *derivation*, denoted by an infix '$\Rightarrow$', is a rewriting of a string using the rules of the grammar. By a series of derivations from S to strings containing only terminals, an element of the language is specified, e.g.

$$ S \Rightarrow 0A \Rightarrow 00A \Rightarrow 001B \Rightarrow 0010B \Rightarrow 00101B \Rightarrow 00101 \qquad (9) $$

Often there will be multiple nonterminals in a string being derived, and so there will be a choice as to which nonterminal to expand; when we choose the leftmost nonterminal in every case, we say that the series is a *leftmost derivation*.

2.1.3 Context-Free Languages. Grammars such as that of (8), whose rules have only single nonterminals on their left-hand sides, are called *context-free*. The corresponding languages, i.e. those that can be generated by any such grammar, are called *context-free languages* (CFLs); it happens that they include the RLs and much more. For example, the language of (7) is specified by a grammar containing the following productions:

$$
\begin{array}{lll}
S \to 0A & A \to 0A1 & A \to 1
\end{array}
\qquad (10)
$$

Many other grammars can be used to describe this language, but no regular expression suffices. Another classic context-free (and not regular) language is that of *palindromes*, which in this case refer to "true" palindromes—strings that read the same forward and backward—rather than the biological use of this word to describe dyad symmetry (see section 2.4.1). We can denote such a language (for the case of even-length strings over any alphabet) as

$$ \left\{ ww^R \mid w \in \Sigma^* \right\} \qquad (11) $$

for any given Σ, where the superscript R denotes reversal of its immediately preceding string argument. Such languages can be specified by context-free grammars like the following, for $\Sigma = \{0,1\}$:

$$ S \to 0S0 \mid 1S1 \mid \varepsilon \qquad (12) $$

(Note the use of the vertical bar to more economically denote rule disjunction, i.e. multiple rules with the same left-hand side.) Thus, context-free grammars are said to be "more powerful" than regular expressions—that is, the RLs are a proper subset of the CFLs.

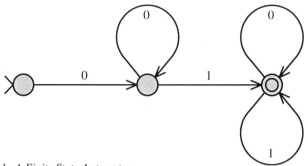

Figure 1. A Finite State Automaton

2.1.4 Automata. Grammars are intimately related to conceptual *machines* or *automata* which can serve as language recognizers or generators. For example, regular languages are recognized and generated by *finite state automata* (FSAs), which are represented as simple directed graphs, with distinguished starting and final nodes, and directed arcs labelled with terminal symbols that are consumed (if the machine is acting as a recognizer) or produced (if the machine is being used to generate a language) as the arc is traversed.

Figure 1 shows an FSA which again expresses the language L_a of (2). The starting node is at the left, and a final node is at the right. It can be seen that it corresponds closely to the "operation" of the regular expression given in (6). In fact, any such regular expression can be expressed as an FSA with a finite number of nodes or *states*, and vice versa, so that the languages recognized by FSAs correspond exactly to the regular languages.

More sophisticated machines are associated with more powerful languages. For example, by adding a limited memory capability in the form of a *stack* or simple pushdown store, we can create *pushdown automata* (PDA) that recognize context-free languages. Figure 2 shows a PDA which recognizes the language of (7). After consuming a 0, the machine enters a loop in which it pushes some symbol (typically drawn from a separate alphabet) on the stack for each additional 0 it consumes. As soon as a 1 is recognized, it makes a transition to another state in which those symbols are popped off the stack as each additional 1 is consumed. The stack is required to be empty in a final state, guaranteeing equal numbers of 0's and 1's. (As before, it is instructive to note how the PDA compares to the grammar of (10).) Once again, it can be shown that PDAs recognize all and only the CFLs.

More elaborate memory schemes can certainly be used in such machines, leading us to ask whether they can be made to recognize additional languages,

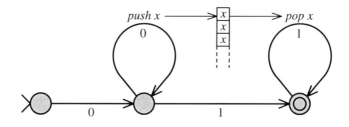

Figure 2. A Pushdown Automaton

and whether there are correspondingly more powerful grammar formalisms.

2.1.5 Context-Sensitive Languages. Indeed, even CFLs do not include some apparently simple languages, such as:

$$\{\, 0^n 1^n 2^n \mid n \geq 1 \,\} \qquad \{\, 0^i 1^j 2^i 3^j \mid i,j \geq 1 \,\} \qquad (13)$$

Note the similarity of these languages to (7), which *is* a CFL. We can intuit why a PDA could not recognize (13a), for instance, by noting that the stack would have to be emptied in the course of recognizing the string of 1's, leaving no way to "count" the 2's. Another well-known class of non-context-free languages are the *copy languages*:

$$\{\, ww \mid w \in \Sigma^* \,\} \qquad (14)$$

However, by relaxing our restriction and allowing more than one symbol on the left-hand sides of grammar rules (but always including at least one nonterminal), all these languages are encompassed. Such a grammar will be called *context-sensitive* if the left-hand side of each rule is not longer than its right-hand side. Note that this effectively excludes languages containing ε (such as (14)), since any rule deriving ε would necessarily have a right-hand side shorter than its left-hand side; we will often supplement the languages specified by such grammars by allowing ε, for purposes of comparison. The corresponding context-sensitive languages (CSLs), augmented where necessary with ε, properly contain the CFLs as well as the examples in (13) and (14). For instance, a grammar specifying (13a) is as follows:

$$
\begin{array}{lll}
S \to 0SBC & 0B \to 01 & CB \to BC \\
S \to 0BC & 1B \to 11 & C \to 2
\end{array} \qquad (15)
$$

This grammar specifies (13a) via sequences of derivations like the following. Note how in the second line the context-sensitive rule allows B's to traverse C's leftward to their final destinations:

$$S \Rightarrow 0SBC \Rightarrow 00SBCBC \Rightarrow 000BCBCBC \Rightarrow 0001CBCBC$$
$$\Rightarrow 0001BCCBC \Rightarrow 00011CCBC \Rightarrow 00011CBCC \Rightarrow 00011BCCC \quad (16)$$
$$\Rightarrow 000111CCC \Rightarrow 0001112CC \Rightarrow 00011122C \Rightarrow 000111222$$

The machines associated with CSLs are called *linear-bounded automata,* which can move in *either* direction on the input, and whose memory scheme consists of the ability to overwrite symbols on the input (but not beyond it). The requirement that each rule's right-hand side be at least as long as its left-hand side ensures that strings produced by successive derivations never grow longer than the final terminal string, and thus exceed the memory available to the automaton.

2.2 The Chomsky Hierarchy and Subdivisions

If there is no constraint on the number of symbols on the left hand sides of rules, the grammar is called *unrestricted,* and the corresponding languages, called *recursively enumerable,* contain the CSLs and much more. The automaton corresponding to recursively enumerable languages is, in fact, the Turing machine itself, which establishes an important link to general algorithmic programming.

This completes the basic *Chomsky hierarchy* of language families, which are related by set inclusion (ignoring ε) as follows:

$$\text{regular} \subset \text{context-free} \subset \text{context-sensitive} \subset \text{unrestricted} \quad (17)$$

Care must be taken in interpreting these set inclusions. While the *set* of RLs is a subset of the CFLs, since any RL can be expressed with a context-free grammar, it is also the case that any CFL (or indeed any language at all) is a subset of an RL, namely Σ^*. That is, by ascending the hierarchy we are augmenting the range of languages we can express by actually *constraining* Σ^* in an ever wider variety of ways.

The Chomsky hierarchy has been subdivided and otherwise elaborated upon in many ways. A few of the important distinctions will be described.

2.2.1 Linear Languages. Within the CFLs, we can distinguish the *linear* CFLs, which include examples (7) and (11) given above. The linear CFLs are those that can be expressed by grammars that never spawn more than one nonterminal, i.e. those in which every rule is of the form

$$A \rightarrow uBv \qquad \text{or} \qquad A \rightarrow w \qquad (18)$$

where A and B are any nonterminal and $u,v,w \in \Sigma^*$. The machines corresponding to linear CFLs are *one-turn PDAs,* which are restricted so that in effect nothing can be pushed on the stack once anything has been popped.

If either u or v is always empty in each rule of the form (18a), the resulting grammars and languages are called *left-linear* or *right-linear,* respectively, and the corresponding languages are RLs. For example, the language L_a

of (2), which was first specified by regular expressions and is thus regular, is also described by the right-linear grammar of (8). In one sense, then, the linear CFLs can be thought of as the simplest CFLs that are not regular.

2.2.2 Deterministic and Nondeterministic Languages. Other classifications depend on the nature of derivations and the behavior of the automata that produce or recognize languages. One such distinction is that between *deterministic* and *nondeterministic* languages and automata. Essentially, a deterministic automaton is one for which any acceptable input in any given state of the automaton will always uniquely determine the succeeding state. A deterministic language, in turn, is one that can be recognized by some deterministic machine. The FSA of Figure 1 is deterministic, since no node has more than one arc leaving it with the same label. In a nondeterministic FSA, there might be more than one arc labelled "0" leaving a node, for instance, and then a choice would have to be made; in attempting to recognize a given input, that choice might later prove to be the wrong one, in which case a recognizer would somehow have to backtrack and try the alternatives.

The PDA of Figure 2 is also deterministic, and thus the language of (7) is a deterministic CFL. This can be seen from the fact that the automaton merely has to read 0's until it encounters its first 1, at which point it begins popping its stack until it finishes; it need never "guess" where to make the switch. However, the palindromic language of (11) is a nondeterministic CFL, since the automaton has to guess whether it has encountered the center of the palindrome at any point, and can begin popping the stack.

Any nondeterministic FSA may be converted to a deterministic FSA, though obviously the same cannot be said of PDAs. Thus, the deterministic subset of CFLs properly contains the RLs.

2.2.3 Ambiguity. Another useful distinction within the CFLs concerns the notion of *ambiguity*. Formally, we say that a grammar is ambiguous if there is some string for which more than one leftmost derivation is possible. As it happens all of the example grammars we have given are unambiguous, but it is easy to specify ambiguous grammars, e.g.

$$S \rightarrow S0S \mid 1 \tag{19}$$

for which it can be seen that the string '10101' has two leftmost derivations:

$$
\begin{aligned}
S &\Rightarrow S0S \Rightarrow 10S \Rightarrow 10S0S \Rightarrow 1010S \Rightarrow 10101 \\
S &\Rightarrow S0S \Rightarrow S0S0S \Rightarrow 10S0S \Rightarrow 1010S \Rightarrow 10101
\end{aligned}
\tag{20}
$$

However, the language specified by this grammar,

$$\{ (10)^n 1 \mid n \geq 0 \} \tag{21}$$

can in fact also be specified by a different grammar that is unambiguous:

$$S \rightarrow 10S \mid 1 \tag{22}$$

Can all languages be specified by some unambiguous grammar? The answer is no, and languages that cannot be generated by any such grammar are called *inherently ambiguous*. An example is the following CFL (not to be confused with the CSL of (13a)):

$$\left\{ 0^i 1^j 2^k \mid i{=}j \text{ or } j{=}k, \text{ where } i,j,k{\geq}1 \right\} \tag{23}$$

Intuitively, it can be seen that this language will contain strings, e.g. those for which $i{=}j{=}k$, that can be parsed in more than one way, satisfying one or the other of the grammar elements that impose constraints on the superscripts. Inherently ambiguous languages are necessarily nondeterministic; a PDA recognizing (23), for instance, would have to guess ahead of time whether to push and pop the stack on the 0's and 1's, respectively, or on the 1's and 2's.

2.2.4 Indexed Languages. The CSLs can also be subdivided. We choose only one such subdivision to illustrate, that of the *indexed languages* (ILs), which contain the CFLs and are in turn properly contained within the CSLs, except that ILs may contain ε. They are specified by indexed grammars, which can be viewed as context-free grammars augmented with indices drawn from a special set of symbols, strings of which can be appended to nonterminals (which we will indicate using superscripts). Rules will then be of the forms

$$A \rightarrow \alpha \qquad \text{or} \qquad A \rightarrow B^x \qquad \text{or} \qquad A^x \rightarrow \alpha \tag{24}$$

where α is any string of terminals and nonterminals, and x is a single index symbol. Now, whenever a rule of form (24a) is applied to expand a nonterminal A in the string being derived, all the indices currently attached to A in that input string are carried through and attached to each of the nonterminals (but not terminals) in α when it is inserted in place of A in the input string. For rules of form (24b), when A is expanded to B, x is added to the front of the string of indices on B in the terminal string being derived. Finally, for rules of form (24c), the index x at the head of the indices following A is removed, before the remainder of the indices on A are distributed over the nonterminals in α, as before.

This rather complicated arrangement may be clarified somewhat with an example. The following indexed grammar specifies the language of (13a):

$$
\begin{array}{lll}
S \rightarrow T^s & A^t \rightarrow 0A & A^s \rightarrow 0 \\
T \rightarrow T^t & B^t \rightarrow 1B & B^s \rightarrow 1 \\
T \rightarrow ABC & C^t \rightarrow 2C & C^s \rightarrow 2
\end{array} \tag{25}
$$

Note that, but for the indices, this grammar is in a context-free form, though (13a) is not a CFL. Under this scheme, indices behave as if they were on stacks attached to nonterminals, as may be seen in the following sample derivation (compare (16)):

$$S \Rightarrow T^{s} \Rightarrow T^{ts} \Rightarrow T^{tts} \Rightarrow A^{tts}B^{tts}C^{tts} \Rightarrow 0A^{ts}B^{tts}C^{tts}$$

$$\Rightarrow 00A^{s}B^{tts}C^{tts} \Rightarrow 000B^{tts}C^{tts} \Rightarrow 0001B^{ts}C^{tts} \Rightarrow 00011B^{s}C^{tts} \quad (26)$$

$$\Rightarrow 000111C^{tts} \Rightarrow 0001112C^{ts} \Rightarrow 00011122C^{s} \Rightarrow 000111222$$

Several types of machines are associated with ILs, including *nested stack automata*, whose name suggests a view of ILs as allowing stacks within stacks.

2.3 Lindenmayer Systems

Not all research in formal linguistics falls within the traditions of the Chomsky hierarchy and grammars in the form we have presented. One other important area will be described here, that of *Lindenmayer systems* or *L-systems*. These differ from the grammars above in that they have no nonterminals, and instead a derivation is accomplished by rewriting *every* terminal in a string simultaneously, according to production rules which of course have single terminals on the left and strings of terminals on the right. Actually, this describes the simplest, context-free form of these grammars, called a 0L-system, an example of which would be the following:

$$0 \to 1 \qquad\qquad 1 \to 01 \qquad\qquad (27)$$

Beginning with a single 0, this produces a series of derivations as follows:

$$0 \Rightarrow 1 \Rightarrow 01 \Rightarrow 101 \Rightarrow 01101 \Rightarrow 10101101 \Rightarrow 0110110101101 \Rightarrow \cdots \quad (28)$$

The language of an L-system, called an *L-language*, is the set of all strings appearing in such a derivation chain. In this case, the language specified contains strings whose lengths are Fibonacci numbers, since in fact each string is simply the concatenation of the two previous strings in the series.

The 0L-languages, as it happens, are contained within the ILs, and thus within the CSLs (with ε), though they contain neither CFLs nor RLs in their entirety. Context-sensitive L-languages, on the other hand, contain the RLs but are only contained within the recursively enumerable languages [Prusinkiewicz and Hanan, 1989].

2.4 Properties of Language Families

Much of the content of formal language theory is concerned with examining the properties of families of languages—how they behave when various operations are performed on them, and what kinds of questions can be effectively answered about them. This section will give an overview of these properties.

2.4.1 Closure Properties. One such area of investigation is that of *closure* properties of families of languages, that is, whether applying various operations to languages leaves the resulting language at the same level in the Chomsky hierarchy. For example, all four of the language families in the hierarchy, and the ILs as well, are *closed under union*, which means that, for instance, the union of any CFL with any other CFL will always yield another CFL. Note, however, that the deterministic CFLS are not closed under union; consider the following two languages:

$$\{\, 0^i 1^j 2^j \mid i,j \geq 1 \,\} \qquad\qquad \{\, 0^i 1^i 2^j \mid i,j \geq 1 \,\} \qquad\qquad (29)$$

Both these languages are deterministic, by reasoning similar to that given in a previous section for the language of (7). However, their union can be seen to be equivalent to the language of (23), which is inherently ambiguous and thus nondeterministic (though it is still a CFL).

The RLs, CFLs, ILs, CSLs, and recursively enumerable languages are all closed under concatenation (that is, the concatenation of each string in one language to each string in another, denoted $L_1 \cdot L_2$), as well as under the closures of concatenation (denoted L^* and L^+, the only difference being that the former contains ε whether or not L does). All are closed under intersection with any RL, e.g. the set of all strings occurring in both a given CFL and a given RL will always be a CFL. This fact will prove to be an important tool in proofs given below. CFLs, however, are not closed under intersection with each other, as can be seen from the fact that intersecting the two CFLs of (29) produces the CSL of (13a). The same is true of ILs, though CSLs and recursively enumerable languages *are* closed under intersection.

Another operation that will prove important in many proofs is that of *homomorphism*. A homomorphism in this case is a function mapping strings to strings, that is built upon a function mapping an alphabet to strings over a (possibly different) alphabet, by just transforming each element of a string, in place, by the latter function. For a function h on an alphabet Σ to extend to a homomorphism on strings over that alphabet, it is only necessary that it *preserve concatenation*, that is, that it satisfy

$$h(u) \cdot h(v) = h(uv) \quad \text{for } u,v \in \Sigma^*, \quad\text{and}\quad h(\varepsilon) = \varepsilon \qquad (30)$$

For instance, given a homomorphism φ based on the functions $\varphi(0) = \varepsilon$, $\varphi(1) = 00$, and $\varphi(2) = \varphi(3) = 1$, we would have $\varphi(123031200) = 00111001$. All four language families in the Chomsky hierarchy (and ILs as well) are closed under homomorphisms applied to each of the strings in a language, except that if the homomorphism maps any alphabetic elements to ε, the CSLs are no longer closed. Perhaps more surprising is the finding that they are all also closed under *inverse* homomorphisms, including those which thus map ε back to alphabetic elements. Since h need not be one-to-one (φ, for example, is not), h^{-1} may not be a unique function; thus inverse homomorphisms must map strings to sets of strings, and in fact both homomorphisms and inverse homomorphisms are notationally extended to themselves apply to languages, e.g. $h(L)$. Note that, since ε is a substring of any string at any point in that string, one can use the inverse of a homomorphism mapping letters to ε as a means to insert any number of letters randomly into strings of a language, e.g. $\varphi^{-1}(001)=\{$ 12, 13, 012, 102, 120, 0102, $\cdots$ $\}$; yet, by the closure property, languages thus enlarged (even CSLs) remain at the same level in the Chomsky hierarchy.

We can employ an even more flexible means for substituting elements in languages, based on FSAs. A *generalized sequential machine* (GSM) is an FSA whose arcs are labelled, not only with symbols from the alphabet which are expected on the input, but also with corresponding *output* symbols to which the input symbols are converted by the action of the automaton. Thus, a GSM arc might be labelled "0/1" to indicate that a 0 read on the input produces a 1 on the output. (A useful example of a GSM will be encountered in section 2.5.3.) All four Chomsky hierarchy language families and ILs as well are closed under both GSM and inverse GSM mappings, though again the CSLs are not closed for GSMs with arcs that have ε as their output.

We note in passing that 0L-systems, in keeping with their other distinctions from the Chomsky hierarchy, are closed under none of the operations described thus far. However, being ILs, we know that, for instance, the union of two 0L-languages will be an IL, and the intersection will be a CSL (excepting ε).

2.4.2 Decidability Properties. There are many questions that may be asked about languages, not all of which can be answered in the most general case by any algorithmic method—that is, there are certain *undecidable* problems related to languages. For example, we noted above that the intersection of two CFLs need not be a CFL, but of course it *may* be; it happens that determining whether it is or not for arbitrary CFLs is undecidable. It is undecidable whether one language is a subset of another, or even equal to another, for languages that are beyond regular; the same is the case for determining if two languages are pairwise disjoint (i.e. non-overlapping). Surprisingly, even the question of whether a language is empty is decidable only up through the ILs.

Perhaps the most basic question we can ask about languages is whether a given string is a member of a given language. Luckily, this question is decidable for all but the recursively enumerable languages, i.e. those specified by unrestricted grammars. This latter should not be too surprising, since in general Turing machines cannot be guaranteed to halt on arbitrary input.

Closure properties, and even more so decidability properties, suggest a motivation for studying languages in these terms, and wherever possible for using grammars to specify them that are as low on the Chomsky hierarchy as possible. Simply put, there is a marked tradeoff between the expressive power required for languages and their general "manageability." Nowhere is this more obvious than in the task of determining membership of a given string in a given language, which, though decidable, may yet be intractable. This task of recognition is the subject of the next section.

2.5 Parsing

While automata can be used for recognition, these theoretical machines may not lead to practical implementations. The algorithmic aspect of computational linguistics is the search for efficient recognizers or *parsers* which take as input a grammar G and a string w, and return an answer as to whether w belongs to $L(G)$, the language generated by G. Many such parsers have been designed and implemented; we will mention a few of the most important.

The regular languages can be parsed in time which is O(n) on the length of the input string, and in fact it is easy to see how to implement a parser based on regular expression specifications. It is also the case that the deterministic subset of CFLs can be parsed in linear time, using a class of parsers typified by the LR(k) parsers [Sudkamp, 1988]. For CFLs in general, the Cocke-Kasami-Younger (CKY) parser uses a *dynamic programming* technique to save results concerning already-parsed substrings, preventing their being reparsed multiple times. The CKY algorithm can parse any CFL in time that is O(n^3) on the length of the input, though for linear CFLs it is O(n^2) [Hopcroft and Ullman, 1979]. The Earley algorithm is a context-free parser with similar worst-case time complexity, but it is O(n^2) for unambiguous grammars and in practice is nearly linear for many real applications [Harrison, 1978]. Modifications of the CKY and Earley parsers are often useful in proving the complexity of parsing with novel grammar formalisms.

For grammars beyond context-free, parsing is greatly complicated, and in fact we have already seen that no fully general parser is possible for unrestricted grammars, membership being undecidable. In all cases, it must be emphasized, it may be possible to write special purpose parsers that very efficiently recognize strings belonging to a specific language, even ones beyond the CFLs. The results given here are important when no restrictions are to be placed on languages, other than their membership in these broad families. This is in keeping with a philosophy that grammars should be declarative rather than "hard-wired" into an algorithm, and by the same token parsers should be general-purpose procedural recognizers. Nevertheless, some types of parsers may be better suited to a domain than others, just as backward-chaining inferencing (which corresponds to a parsing style known as *top-down*) may be better in some applications than forward-chaining (which corresponds to *bottom-up* parsing), or vice-versa.

A related field in computational linguistics, that of *grammatical inference,* attempts to develop algorithms that *induce* grammars by learning from exam-

sentence → noun_phrase verb_phrase

noun_phrase → article modified_noun | modified_noun

modified_noun → adjective modified_noun |
      modified_noun prepositional_phrase | noun

verb_phrase → verb_phrase noun_phrase |
      verb_phrase prepositional_phrase | verb

prepositional_phrase → preposition noun_phrase

noun → **man** | **boats** | **harbor**

verb → **watched**   adjective → **old** | **kind**

article → **the**   preposition → **in**

Figure 3. A Simple Natural Language Grammar

ple input strings, both positive and negative [Fu, 1982]. While some such approaches have been developed for RLs, no great practical success has been achieved as yet for CFLs or above, again reflecting the decreasing manageability of languages as the Chomsky hierarchy is ascended.

3 Computational Applications of Language Theory

In this section we will first briefly review the major arenas in which formal language theory has been applied computationally, and then present in more detail an application of a specific grammar formalism and parsing system to the problem of specifying and recognizing genes in DNA sequences. This will serve to motivate the remainder of our investigations.

3.1 Natural Language

Consider the natural language sentence *"The kind old man watched the boats in the harbor."* A highly simplified grammar that can specify this sentence (among many others) is given in Figure 3. Here, the top-level rule says that a sentence consists of a noun phrase followed by a verb phrase. Following this are the phrase-level rules, and finally the lexical entries—the tokens in this case being English words—given according to their parts of speech.

The study of human language has led to the creation of much more complex and specialized grammar formalisms, and parsers to deal with them. It is far beyond the scope of this work to review the rich literature that has resulted; for this the reader is referred to textbooks such as [Allen, 1987]. We will note, however, some basic results concerning the formal status of natural language. One straightforward observation is that natural language is ambiguous at many levels [Shanon, 1978], including a structural or syntactic level. For

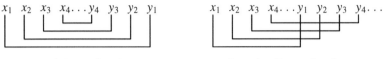

Nested Dependencies   *Crossing Dependencies*

Figure 4. Dependencies

example, if I say *"I was given the paper by Watson and Crick,"* alternative valid parses could attach the prepositional phrase to the noun phrase *the paper* (e.g. to mean that someone gave me a paper written by Watson and Crick), or to the verb phrase *was given the paper* (to mean that Watson and Crick gave me some paper). Somewhat more controversial is the notion that natural language is nondeterministic, based in part on the evidence of "garden path" sentences like *"The old man the boats."* Most persons first parse *man* as a noun modified by *old*, then must backtrack upon "unexpectedly" encountering the end of the sentence, to reparse *old* as a noun and *man* as a verb. (Many, however, consider such phenomena to be jarring exceptions that prove the rule, that the human "parser" is ordinarily deterministic.)

There has been much debate on the subject of where natural language lies on the Chomsky hierarchy, but there is little doubt that it is not regular, given the apparent capacity of all human languages to form arbitrarily large sets of *nested dependencies*, as illustrated in Figure 4. An exaggerated example of such a construction would be *"The reaction the enzyme the gene the promoter controlled encoded catalyzed stopped."* Using the symbols from Figure 4, we can understand the nested relative clauses of this sentence to indicate that there is a certain promoter (x_4) that controls (y_4) some gene (x_3) that encodes (y_3) an enzyme (x_2) that catalyzes (y_2) a reaction (x_1) that has stopped (y_1). However difficult to decrypt (particularly in the absence of relative pronouns), this is a syntactically valid English sentence, and many more reasonable examples of extensive nesting can be found; these require a "stack," and thus a context-free grammar, to express. Moreover, a consensus appears to have formed that natural language is in fact greater than context-free [Schieber, 1985]; this is largely because of the existence of *crossing dependencies* in certain languages, also schematized in Figure 4, which are not suited to pushdown automata for reasons that should by now be apparent. In Dutch, for example, phrases similar to the one above have a different word order that crosses the dependencies [Bresnan et al., 1982]. Evidence that English is greater than context-free, which is generally less straightforward, is perhaps typified by the sentence (from [Postal and Langendoen, 1984]) *"Some bourbon hater lover was nominated, which bourbon hater lover*

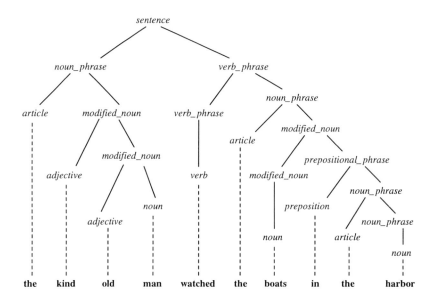

Figure 5. A Natural Language Parse Tree

fainted." Here, the instances of *hater* and *lover* form crossing dependencies, and these can theoretically be propagated indefinitely into forms such as *"bourbon hater lover lover hater . . ."* which must be duplicated in a sentence of this type, in effect forming a copy language.

3.2 Computer Languages and Pattern Recognition

Artificial languages such as computer languages are designed (whether consciously or not) to inhabit the lower reaches of the Chomsky hierarchy, for reasons of clarity and especially efficiency. The standard Backus-Naur Form (BNF) for specifying computer language syntax is, in fact, essentially a context-free grammar formalism. (A typical BNF, describing a domain-specific computer language for performing various operations on DNA, can be found in [Schroeder and Blattner, 1982].) That such languages should be unambiguous is obviously highly desirable, and they are usually deterministic CFLs as well so as to allow for fast parsing by compilers. Wherever possible, special-purpose languages such as string matchers in word processors, operating system utilities like *grep*, etc., are designed to be regular for even better performance in recognition, and overall simplicity.

Pattern recognition applications are not limited to RLs, however. The field of *syntactic pattern recognition* makes use of linguistic tools and techniques in discriminating complex patterns in signals or even images, in a manner

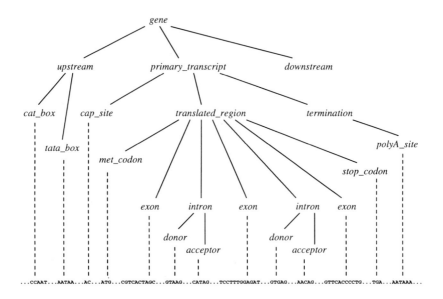

Figure 6. A Gene Parse Tree

that is more model-based and structurally oriented than traditional decision-theoretic approaches [Fu, 1982]. Specifying two-dimensional images appears to require greater than context-free power; among the formalisms used in the field for this purpose are indexed grammars [Fu, 1982; Searls and Liebowitz, 1990].

3.3 Developmental Grammars

The L-systems were in fact originally developed as a foundation for an axiomatic theory of biological development [Lindenmayer, 1968]. The process of rewriting terminals was meant to model cell division, with various elaborations on the 0L-systems allowing for developmental stage-specific variations and (in the case of context-sensitive rules) for intercellular communication. Since that time, formal linguists have explored the mathematical properties of L-systems exhaustively, while theoretical biologists have extended their application to such topics as form in plants. Quite convincing three-dimensional images of ferns, trees, and other plants, even specific species, can be generated by L-systems; these are reviewed in [Prusinkiewicz and Hanan, 1989], which also discusses the intriguing relationship of L-systems to fractals.

```
gene --> upstream, xscript, downstream.
upstream --> cat_box, 40...50, tata_box, 19...27.
xscript --> cap_site,..., xlate,..., polyA_site.

cat_box --> pyrimidine, "caat".
tata_box --> "tata", base, "a".
cap_site --> "ac".

base --> purine, pyrimidine.
purine --> "g" | "a".  pyrimidine --> "t" | "c".

xlate([met|RestAAs]) --> codon(met).
    rest_xlate(RestAAs), stop_codon.
rest_xlate(AAs) --> exon(AAs).
rest_xlate(AAs) --> exon(X1), intron,
    rest_xlate(Xn), {append(X1,Xn,AAs)}.

exon([]) --> [].
exon([AA|Rest]) --> codon(AA), exon(Rest).

intron --> splice.
intron, [B1] --> [B1], splice.
intron, [B1,B2] --> [B1,B2], splice.

splice --> donor, ..., acceptor.
donor --> "gt".            acceptor --> "ag".

stop_codon --> "tga" | "ta", purine.
codon(met) --> "atg".
codon(phe) --> "tt", pyrimidine.
codon(ser) --> "tc", base.            % etc...
```

Figure 7. A Simple Gene DCG

3.4 Gene Grammars

One of the useful byproducts of any practical parsing algorithm is a *parse tree*, illustrated for the example above in Figure 5. This is a tree-structured depiction of the expansion of the grammar rules in the course of a derivation—a *structural* representation of the syntactic information used in recognition. In practice, a parse tree or some other form of information about the parse is essential to further interpretation, e.g. for semantic analysis in the case of natural language, since otherwise a recognizer simply returns "yes" or "no."

It is the premise of this article that DNA, being a language, should be amenable to the same sort of structural depiction and analysis; indeed, the parse tree shown in Figure 6 would appear to any biologist to be a reasonable representation of the hierarchical construction of a typical gene. This being the case, we can fairly ask what the nature of a grammar determining such a parse tree might be, and to what extent a grammar-based approach could be usefully generalized.

To further explore this question at a pragmatic level, we have implemented such grammars using the logic-based formalism of *definite clause grammars* (DCGs). These are grammars closely associated with the Prolog programming language, and in fact are directly compiled into Prolog code which constitutes a top-down, left-to-right parser for the given grammar. The simplified gene grammar shown in Figure 7 illustrates a range of features.

The top-level rule for `gene` in this grammar is an uncluttered context-free statement at a highly abstract level. The immediately succeeding rules show how the grammar can be "broken out" into its components in a clear hierarchical fashion, with detail always presented at its appropriate level. The rules for `cat_box`, `tata_box`, and `cap_site` specify double-quoted lists of terminals (i.e., nucleotide bases), sometimes combined with nonterminal atoms like `pyrimidine`. The "gap" infix operator ('. . .') simply consumes input, either indefinitely, as in `xscript`, or within bounds, as in `up-stream`.

DCGs use *difference lists*, hidden parameter pairs attached to nonterminals, to maintain the input list and to express the span of an element on it [Pereira and Warren, 1980]. For notational convenience, we will refer to *spans* on the input list using an infix operator '/' whose arguments will represent the difference lists; that is, we will write *S0/S* where *S0* is the input list at some point, and *S* is the remainder after consuming some span. We will also use an infix derivation operator '==>' whose left argument will be a nonterminal or sequence of nonterminals, and whose right argument will be either a list or a span to be parsed. Note that this actually represents the reflexive, transitive closure of the formal derivation operator described above. Top-level calls might appear as follows:

```
tata_box ==> "tataaa".
tata_box ==> "tatatagcg"/S.
```
(31)

Both these calls would succeed, with the latter leaving S bound to "gcg".

Features of DCGs that potentially raise them beyond context-free power include (1) *parameter-passing,* used here to build the list of amino acids in the transcript. The `exon` rule assembles sublists recursively, after which `xlate` and `xlate1` combine them to form a complete polypeptide by means of (2) *procedural attachment* in the form of a curly-bracketed call to the Prolog built-in `append`. This feature of DCGs allows arbitrary Prolog code (or other languages) to be invoked within rule bodies, extending to simple utilities, more complex search heuristics, entire expert systems, dynamic programming algorithms, or even calls to special-purpose hardware.

```
| ?- (...,gene,...):Parse ==> mushba.
[loading /sun/mn2/dbs/dna/mushba.db...]
[mushba.db loaded 0.933 sec 1,442 bases]

Parse =
...
gene:
  upstream$0:
    cat_box:282/"ccaat"
      ...
    tata_box:343/"tataa"
      ...
    cap_site:371/"ac"
      ...
  xscript:
      codon(met):
        405/"atg"
      exon:(405/501)
      intron:
        donor$2:500/"gtgaga"
          ...
        acceptor$0:606/"tctctccttctcccag"
      exon:(623/827)
      intron:
        donor$2:827/"gtatgc"
          ...
        acceptor$1:945/"cactttgtctccgcag"
      exon:(961/1087)
      stop_codon:1087/"taa"
      ...
    polyA_site$0:1163/"aataaa"
...
```

Figure 8. A Gene DCG Parse

DCGs also allow for (3) *terminals on the left-hand side* of a rule, trailing the nonterminal; they are added onto the front of the input string after such a rule parses. This feature is used by `intron` in such a way that a new codon is created when the reading frame straddles the splice site [Searls, 1988]. Rules in this form are not context-free. We can also see that procedural attachment gives the grammar Turing power, so that it can specify recursively enumerable languages, and in fact the same is true of unrestricted parameter-passing.

For large-scale search we have abandoned the built-in Prolog list structure for the input string, which is instead implemented as a global data structure in an external 'C' array. (Thus, numerical indexing replaces the DCG difference lists.) In conjunction with this, intermediate results are saved in a *well-formed substring table* (similar in principle to a CKY parser) that also prevents repeated scanning for features across large gaps. Other additions include a large number of extra hidden DCG parameters to help manage the parse, including one which builds and returns a parse tree. We have also implemented specialized operators to manage the parse at a meta level, to arbitrarily control position on the input string, and to allow for imperfect matching. In the terminal session shown in Figure 8 a search is performed on the GenBank entry "MUSHBA" containing the mouse α-globin sequence. The top level derivation operator is extended to allow calls of the form sentence:Parse ==> input, where the input may be specified as (among other things) a file containing sequence data, and where a parse tree may be returned via the variable Parse.

The grammar used was derived from that of Figure 7, but with the additional control elements described above, and much more complex rules for splice junctions that use simulated weight matrices for donors and detection of branch points and pyrimidine-rich regions for acceptors, in addition to the invariant dinucleotides. The resulting grammar, with considerable tuning, has been successful in recognizing not only mouse but human α-like globins, while ignoring pseudogenes (e.g., in the human α gene cluster "HUMHBA4"). We have also tested it against the whole 73,000+ base pair human β-globin gene region ("HUMHBB"), and were able to collect the entire cluster of five genes on a single pass that required 4.7 CPU-minutes on a Sun 3/60. A pseudogene as well as large intergenic stretches were passed over.

By "relaxing" the specifications in various ways (allowing in-frame stop codons within exons and an out-of-frame final stop codon, and loosening constraints on the splice donor weight matrix), we have also been able to study aberrant splicing that would otherwise produce untranslatable message [Searls and Noordewier, 1991]. By duplicating known β-thalassemia mutations, additional cryptic donors were recognized, most of which are observed in nature in aberrant splicing. The alternative transcription products seen experimentally were also produced by the DCG parser because of backtracking, which may also be useful for modeling the alternative transcription start sites and splicing seen in certain viruses, as well as in experiment planning applications [Searls, 1988].

The weakest links in the gene grammars developed to date are the signals for splice junctions. In a practical implementation, it may be preferable to incorporate other specialized algorithms (e.g. neural net recognizers) directly into the grammar, and procedural attachment in DCGs makes this relatively easy. The grammar still provides a very useful organizing framework, which can serve to place such algorithms in an overall hierarchical context that captures the complex orderings and relationships among such features.

The gene grammars used for the investigations described above are written without great regard for the linguistic status of the features being parsed, and we have seen that the power of DCGs is such that the languages defined potentially may reside at any level of the Chomsky hierarchy. Nevertheless, this does not prove that the language of nucleic acids is beyond regular, and indeed most of the features specified above can be rewritten as regular expressions, however awkward they may be. The grammar form is preferable if for no other reason than that it promotes an abstracted, hierarchical view of the domain. Regular grammars have been written describing much simpler genes [Brendel and Busse, 1984], and at least one author [Shanon, 1978] has argued that the genetic language is no more than context-free, and in fact that a syntactic approach is not even necessary given its lack of structure in the usual linguistic sense. However, these arguments are based on a very limited view of biological phenomena, confined to the amino acid code itself. On the contrary, in succeeding sections it will be seen that biological sequences are rich with structural themes, both literal and linguistic.

4 Structural Linguistics of Nucleic Acids

We now proceed to consider exactly how much linguistic power is actually required to encompass various phenomena observed in nucleic acids that are literally *structural*—that is, depending on the physical nature of DNA and RNA, rather than any information encoded. The informational structure, which we will refer to as *functional* linguistics, will be discussed later. Only a minimal knowledge of the molecular biology of nucleic acids is required for this section, though a wider range of biological phenomena is cited elsewhere which is beyond the scope of this work to review; for background, readers are referred to standard textbooks such as [Watson et al., 1987; Lewin, 1987].

4.1 Properties of Reverse Complementarity

Before beginning, we will establish a notation and some basic properties of nucleic acid complementarity. We will uniformly adopt the alphabet of DNA

$$\Sigma_{DNA} = \left\{ g, c, a, t \right\} \tag{32}$$

and let a bar notation represent an operation corresponding to simple base complementarity, i.e. indicating bases that are able to physically and informationally *base-pair* between strands of double-helical DNA:

$$\overline{g} = c, \qquad \overline{c} = g, \qquad \overline{a} = t, \qquad \text{and} \qquad \overline{t} = a \tag{33}$$

While much of the work to follow will apply primarily to RNA structure, we will assume that features of interest are actually being examined on the DNA which encodes them. Clearly this operation can be extended over strings and constitutes a homomorphism, since we can say that

$$\bar{u} \cdot \bar{v} = \overline{(uv)} \qquad \text{for } u,v \in \Sigma^*_{\text{DNA}} \qquad (34)$$

We will abbreviate (34a) as $\overline{uv}$. We can also see that this homomorphism and string reversal have the following properties:

$$\overline{(\bar{w})} = w, \qquad (w^R)^R = w, \qquad \text{and} \qquad \overline{(w^R)} = (\bar{w})^R \qquad (35)$$

The composition of complementarity and reversal in (35c), which will be written as $\bar{w}^R$, is of course the "opposite strand" of a string w of DNA, since not only are the strands of a double helix complementary but they are oriented in opposite directions. Care must be taken not to treat this operation as a homomorphism, since it does not itself preserve concatenation in general:

$$\bar{u}^R \cdot \bar{v}^R \neq \overline{(uv)}^R = \bar{v}^R \cdot \bar{u}^R \qquad \text{where } |u| \neq |v| \qquad (36)$$

Rather, such a string function is an *involution* [Head, 1987]. We can easily derive from the lemmas of (35) the familiar property that in essence allows nucleic acids to be replicated from opposite strands:

$$\overline{(\overline{w}^R)}^R = \overline{(\bar{w}^R)^R} \;=\; \overline{(\bar{w})} \;=\; w \qquad (37)$$

We will demonstrate one other fundamental property (also noted by [Head, 1987]), concerning the special case of strings that are identical to their opposite strands, i.e. those in the language

$$L_e = \left\{ \; w \in \Sigma^*_{\text{DNA}} \;\middle|\; w = \bar{w}^R \; \right\} \qquad (38)$$

We note first that any such w must be of even length, or else it would have a centermost base not identical to the centermost base of its opposite strand, since they are required to be complementary. Thus, we can divide w into two equal halves, and also conclude that

$$w = uv = \bar{w}^R = \bar{v}^R \bar{u}^R = u\bar{u}^R \qquad \text{where } |u| = |v| \qquad (39)$$

(where the bar notation is now used to denote the lengths of the strings). Thus we see that L_e is in fact the language

$$L_e = \left\{ \; u\bar{u}^R \;\middle|\; w \in \Sigma^*_{\text{DNA}} \; \right\} \qquad (40)$$

The equivalence of the languages (38) and (40) will come as no surprise to any molecular biologist, since it is simply a linguistic expression of the basic notion of *dyad symmetry*. The language L_e will become important in the following section.

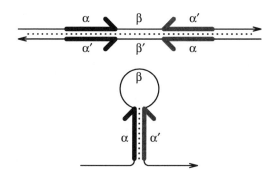

Figure 9. An Inverted Repeat

4.2 Nucleic Acids Are not Regular

Inverted repeats are prevalent features of nucleic acids, which in the case of DNA result whenever a substring on one strand is also found nearby on the opposite strand, as shown at the top of Figure 9. This implies that the substring and its reverse complement are both to be found on the same strand, which can thus fold back to base-pair with itself and form a stem-and-loop structure, as shown at the bottom.

Such base-pairing within the same strand is called *secondary structure*. It would seem that we could specify such structures with the following context-free grammar:

$$S \rightarrow bS\overline{b} \mid A \qquad A \rightarrow bA \mid \varepsilon \qquad \text{where } b \in \Sigma_{\text{DNA}} \qquad (41)$$

The first rule sets up the complementary base pairings of the stem, while the second rule makes the loop. Note that disjuncts using b, here and in all subsequent grammars, are actually abbreviations that expand to four disjuncts, e.g. allowing in the first rule above every possible alphabetic substitution that maintains the required complementarity. These complementary bases establish nested dependencies between respective positions along the stem.

However, the A rule for the loop in (41) is an obstacle to further analysis, since it can specify any string and thus the resulting language is simply Σ_{DNA}^*, making it trivially regular. We will return to this issue in a moment, but in order to study the essential aspects of this language, we will first focus on the base-pairing stems and drop the A rule from (41), thusly:

$$S \rightarrow bS\overline{b} \mid \varepsilon \qquad (42)$$

The resulting language may be thought of as that of idealized, gapless biological "palindromes," able to form secondary structure extending through entire strings with no loops (i.e., we imagine them having no steric hindrance to prevent complete base-pairing to the ends of the stems, whereas in reality there is a minimal loop necessary). In fact, this is simply the language L_e of (40) representing sequences concatenated to their own reverse complements. This equivalence can be shown by simple inductions on the length of strings in (40) and the number of derivation steps used in (42); we leave this to the reader, though proofs along the same lines will be given below.

We will, however, show that L_e cannot be an RL, by proving that no FSA can recognize it. Such an FSA would, for instance, be required to accept $g^i c^i$ for all $i \geq 1$ and reject $g^j c^i$ for all $i \neq j$. Let q_n denote the node or state in which the FSA arrives after having processed a string g^n. Then we know that $q_i \neq q_j$ for all $i \neq j$, since starting from the state q_i and consuming the string c^i leads to a final node, while from q_j, consuming the same string c^i must *not* lead to a final node. Thus the FSA must have distinct states q_i and q_j for all $i \neq j$ and, since any length input is allowed, it must therefore have an infinite number of states. Since an FSA must by definition be finite, there can be no such FSA recognizing L_e, and thus L_e cannot be regular.

4.3 Non-Ideal Secondary Structure

Let us call a string *ideal* whenever, for each base type, its complement is present in the string in equal number. Languages having only ideal strings, or grammars that specify them, will also be called ideal. The grammar (42) is ideal, since any time a base is added to the terminal string, so is its complement. However, the grammar (41) is non-ideal, due to its loop rule.

In addition, (41) is inadequate as a model because in fact it accepts *any* string of any size via the loop disjunct, and can bypass the more meaningful stem disjunct entirely. One practical solution to this problem is to place constraints on the extents of these subcomponents, for instance requiring a minimum length p for the stem and a maximum length q for the loop. This reflects biological reality to the extent that inverted repeats that are too small or too far separated in a nucleic acid molecule can be expected to base-pair less readily. For a given fixed p and q, this gives rise to the language

$$L_n = \left\{ uv\bar{u}^R \mid u,v \in \Sigma^*_{DNA}, |u| \geq p, \text{ and } |v| \leq q \right\} \tag{43}$$

That this is still a CFL is demonstrated by our ability to specify it as a context-free grammar, as follows:

$$
\begin{aligned}
S &\to A_0 \\
A_i &\to bA_{i+1}\bar{b} & \text{for } 0 \leq i < p \\
A_p &\to bA_p\bar{b} \mid B_0 & (44) \\
B_j &\to bA_{j+1} \mid \varepsilon & \text{for } 0 \leq j < q \\
B_q &\to \varepsilon
\end{aligned}
$$

Here, subscripted rules are meant to be expanded into multiple rules according to p and q. The A rules account for the stem, with each distinct rule "counting" the base pairs up to the minimum required, then permitting any number of additional base pairs; similarly, the B rules count the unpaired bases of the loop, but in this case impose a maximum. We will prove that this language L_n is not regular, by contradiction. Suppose that it were indeed regular, and let us derive a new language from it:

$$L'_n = \phi\big(\mathbf{gc} \cup \mathbf{ggcc} \cup \mathbf{gggccc} \cup \cdots \cup \mathbf{g}^{p\text{-}1}\mathbf{c}^{p\text{-}1} \cup (L_n \cap \mathbf{g^*a}^q\mathbf{c^*})\big) \quad (45)$$

where ϕ is the homomorphism based on $\phi(g)=0$, $\phi(c)=1$, and $\phi(a)=\phi(t)=\varepsilon$. We see that for fixed p and q each of the expressions in L'_n is regular, and furthermore we know that the RLs are closed under each of the operations used, i.e. intersection, union, and homomorphism. Thus L'_n itself must also be regular. Now let us simplify the expression (45), first examining the intersection of L_n with the regular expression on the right. Of all the strings generated by L_n, this regular expression "selects" ones that have exactly q consecutive a's, flanked by any number of g's on the left and c's on the right, and no t's at all. Since the a's thus have nothing with which to base-pair, they must all be in the loop portion, and in fact because there are q of them they must constitute the entire loop. The flanking g's and c's thus base-pair to form the stem, and being base-paired they must be present in equal numbers, greater than or equal to p. Similarly the sub-expressions on the left are a finite union of RLs containing equal numbers (less than p) of g's followed by c's. The homomorphism ϕ serves to convert g's and c's to a different alphabet and to discard the a's, leaving the language

$$L'_n = \phi\big(\{ g^j c^j \mid 1 \leq j < p \} \cup \{ g^i a^q c^i \mid i \geq p \}\big) = \{ 0^n 1^n \mid n \geq 1 \} \quad (46)$$

But this language is the same as (7), which is known not to be regular (as can be demonstrated using essentially the same proof as in the previous section). Thus our assumption that L_n is regular must be false, and we may extend this result to a conjecture that secondary structure with any suitable limits placed on its non-ideal components will not be regular. (In particular, relating the non-ideal to the ideal regions, e.g. allowing them to be proportional in size, would appear to raise the resulting languages even beyond context-free.)

4.4 Nucleic Acids are neither Deterministic nor Linear

As was noted above, the nondeterministic parser inherent in DCGs is useful in dealing with empirical nondeterminism in biological systems, such as alternative splicing and other transcriptional variants. But besides this observed nondeterminism, we can now see that the structure of nucleic acids, in particular that associated with inverted repeats, is nondeterministic by its na-

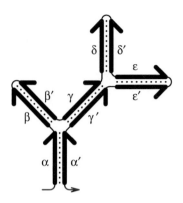

Figure 10. Recursive Secondary Structure

ture. By reasoning similar to that given above for (11), any recognizer for such structures would have to guess at the center point of the inverted repeat. The presence of a loop does not alter this result.

The grammar (42) for inverted repeats is linear; however, many more elaborate forms of secondary structure are possible, and anything with more than a single stem structure would not be linear. For example, a grammar specifying any number of consecutive inverted repeats would be simply

$$S \to AS \mid \varepsilon \qquad A \to bA\bar{b} \mid \varepsilon \qquad\qquad (47)$$

Clearly this, or any other grammar specifying multiple inverted repeats, would exceed the capabilities of a one-turn PDA. Even this is not a "most general" form for ideal secondary structure, however, because it does not allow for structure within structure, which is quite common in RNA in configurations like that of Figure 10. We can propose a formal description of all such secondary structure by recursively building a set of strings of this nature.

Let us define an *orthodox* string as either ε, or a string derived from an orthodox string by inserting an adjacent complementary pair, $b\bar{b}$, at any position. The intuition behind this definition is that adding such pairs to a secondary structure will either extend the tip of a stem, or cause a new stem to "bud off" the side of a stem, and these are the only operations required to create arbitrary such secondary structure. Clearly every orthodox string is ideal. Moreover, we can specify the set of all orthodox strings, L_O, with a grammar that merely adds to (42) a disjunct that duplicates the start symbol:

$$S_O \to bS_O\bar{b} \mid S_OS_O \mid \varepsilon \qquad\qquad (48)$$

That this specifies exactly the orthodox strings is shown by induction on the length of the string. The empty string ε is both orthodox and derivable from (48). Assuming that any and all orthodox strings of length $2n$ (only even-length strings being allowed) are derivable from (48), we must show that the same is true for orthodox strings of length $2(n+1)$. For the longer string to be orthodox, it must be built on some orthodox string w of length $2n$ that, we know by the inductive hypothesis, is derivable from (48). Without loss of generality, we can assume that the derivation of w delays all ε rule applications to the end. Note also that, for every derivation step applying the first disjunct of (48) to derive the substring $bS_0\bar{b}$, we can substitute a derivation producing the substring $S_0 b S_0 \bar{b} S_0$ instead, since

$$S_0 \Rightarrow S_0 S_0 \Rightarrow S_0 S_0 S_0 \Rightarrow S_0 b S_0 \bar{b} S_0 \Rightarrow b S_0 \bar{b} S_0 \Rightarrow b S_0 \bar{b} \tag{49}$$

Therefore, we can ensure that in the intermediate string just before the ε rules are applied in the derivation of w, there will be S_0's flanking every terminal base, in every possible position where the next $b\bar{b}$ might be added to create the orthodox string of length $2(n+1)$. Since $b\bar{b}$ is derivable from such S_0's, this same derivation can be easily extended to produce any and all such strings, completing the inductive proof.

4.5 Nucleic Acids Are Ambiguous

We have seen that non-ideal secondary structure grammars such as (41) are ambiguous, in a way that can subvert the implicit biological meaning (since bases which rightfully could base-pair in the stem via the first disjunct can also be attributed to the loop by the second rule). We can observe a much more interesting form of ambiguity in the grammar of (48) that relates biologically to the underlying language of orthodox secondary structure, L_0. Consider the sublanguage of L_0 consisting of concatenated inverted repeats:

$$L_e^2 = L_e \cdot L_e = \left\{\, u\bar{u}^R \, v\bar{v}^R \mid u, v \in \Sigma_{DNA}^* \,\right\} \tag{50}$$

This in turn contains the set of ideal double inverted repeats, i.e.

$$L_d = \left\{\, u\bar{u}^R \, u\bar{u}^R \mid u \in \Sigma_{DNA}^* \,\right\} \tag{51}$$

Any such string can clearly be derived from S_0 as two side-by-side inverted repeats, but it follows from the equivalence of (38) and (40) that the entire string can also be parsed as a single inverted repeat, e.g. the following two leftmost derivations from the grammar (48):

$$S_0 \Rightarrow S_0 S_0 \Rightarrow g S_0 c S_0 \Rightarrow g a S_0 t c S_0 \Rightarrow g a t c S_0$$
$$\Rightarrow g a t c g S_0 c \Rightarrow g a t c g a S_0 t c \Rightarrow g a t c g a t c \tag{52}$$

$$S_0 \Rightarrow g S_0 c \Rightarrow g a S_0 t c \Rightarrow g a t S_0 a t c \Rightarrow g a t c S_0 g a t c \Rightarrow g a t c g a t c$$

Note that these two derivations correspond to two alternative secondary structures available to the input string, as illustrated in Figure 11. The first derivation of (52), which spawns two S_0's, in effect describes the so-called "dumbbell" structure shown at the left, in which the two inverted repeats

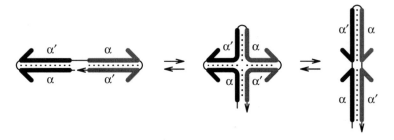

Figure 11. Dumbbell, Cloverleaf, and Hairpin Structures

base-pair separately; the second derivation, which uses a single S_0 through-out, describes the uniform "hairpin" structure shown at the right. Such double inverted repeats are indeed thought to assume both structures alternative-ly in certain biological situations (e.g. RNAs specifically replicated by the bacteriophage T7 DNA-dependent RNA polymerase [Konarska and Sharp, 1990]), as well as intermediate "cloverleaf" structures, as shown in the center of Figure 11. In fact it can be seen that for ideal double inverted repeats of this form, a continuous series of such intermediate structures are available, base pair by base pair, between the two extremes. It is gratifying that each such secondary structure corresponds to a different partition on the set of leftmost derivations, interpreted in this manner, e.g. the following cloverleaf version of the input from (52):

$$S_0 \Rightarrow gS_0c \Rightarrow gS_0S_0c \Rightarrow gS_0S_0S_0c \Rightarrow gaS_0tS_0S_0c$$
$$\Rightarrow gatS_0S_0c \Rightarrow gatcS_0gS_0c \Rightarrow gatcgS_0c \Rightarrow gatcgaS_0tc \Rightarrow gatcgatc \tag{53}$$

This suggests a strong analogy between derivations and physical sec-ondary structures—in fact, parse trees from these grammars can be seen as actually depicting such structure. (The extent to which alternative structures are allowed is related to the language-theoretic notion of *degree of ambiguity*.)

Of course, having found an ambiguous grammar for such features does not imply that the language containing them is *inherently* ambiguous; that would require proving that no unambiguous grammar suffices. Surprisingly, the language L_0 of generalized orthodox secondary structure appears not to be inherently ambiguous, since it falls in a class of languages (the full or two-sided Dyck languages—see section 2.7.5) for which unambiguous gram-mars are possible [Harrison, 1978, p. 322]. However, there may well exist sublanguages of L_0 which are inherently ambiguous (perhaps the language L_e^2 of (50), which is similar to the inherently ambiguous language of concate-nated pairs of ordinary palindromes [Harrison, 1978, p. 240]). In any case,

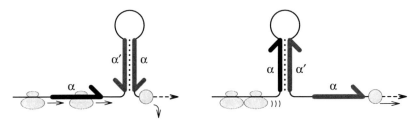

Figure 12. Attenuator Structure

we might actually prefer an ambiguous grammar that models an underlying biological ambiguity, such as alternative secondary structure, particulary when that ambiguity has functional significance.

Attenuators, for example, are bacterial regulatory elements that depend on alternative secondary structure in their corresponding mRNA to control their own expression [Searls, 1989a]; a simplified representation of their structure is shown in Figure 12. An attenuator has the capability to form alternative secondary structure in its nascent mRNA, under the influence of certain exogenous elements depicted in the figure, to establish a kind of binary switch controlling expression of a downstream gene [Lewin, 1987]. If we model an attenuator as either of two alternative languages corresponding to these states,

$$L_{\text{off}} = \left\{ uv\bar{v}^R \mid u,v \in \Sigma^*_{\text{DNA}} \right\} \qquad L_{\text{on}} = \left\{ u\bar{u}^R v \mid u,v \in \Sigma^*_{\text{DNA}} \right\} \qquad (54)$$

then the relationship of these languages to those of (29), and of their *union* to the inherently ambiguous language of (23), is apparent. Nevertheless, this is still not a formal proof, and in fact it can be argued that L_{off} and L_{on} should actually be *intersected*, since both conditions are required to be present in the same language to produce the function described (see section 2.7.2).

Again, while we leave open the question of the formal status of nucleic acids vis-à-vis inherent ambiguity, we note that a contrived unambiguous grammar for any given secondary structure may be inferior as a model, if it fails to capture alternatives in the secondary structure. Moreover, the definitional requirement for a *leftmost* derivation may itself be irrelevant to the physics of folding, which presumably can occur simultaneously along the length of the molecule. An interesting exception to this would be the folding of nascent RNA that occurs as it is synthesized, which of course is leftmost.

Another functional theme in nature involving alternative secondary structure is *self-priming* of certain DNA molecules, such as parvoviruses [Watson et al., 1987] where the ends of double-stranded molecules are able to refold into T-shaped configurations that can "bootstrap" the synthesis of a new copy of the entire viral genome. In this case, the most fundamental process of

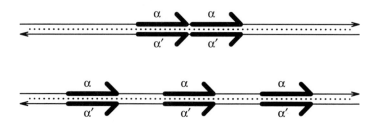

Figure 13. Tandem and Direct Repeats

replication of an organism may be viewed as depending on a kind of ambiguity in the language containing its genome (see section 2.7). We will shortly see how replication might itself result in inherent ambiguity (see section 2.5.1).

The nondeterminism of secondary structure rules out linear-time parsing, and its nonlinearity and possible inherent ambiguity would also preclude certain quadratic-time simplifications of well-known parsers. Any of the structural elements given so far could be parsed in cubic time at worst (or, indeed, recognized more efficiently by less general algorithms), but we will now offer evidence for non-context-free features that may create further complications.

4.6 Nucleic Acids Are not Context-Free

The presence (and importance) of tandem repeats and direct repeats of many varieties in DNA, as depicted in Figure 13, indicate the need to further upgrade the language of nucleic acids; these are clearly examples of copy languages, as specified in (14), which are known to require CSLs for their expression. Direct repeats entail crossing dependencies, where each dependency is in fact simply equality of the bases.

While there is thus strong empirical evidence for any general language of nucleic acids being greater than context-free, we may yet ask if there is any structural correlate, as is the case for context-free secondary structure. Several possibilities are shown in Figure 14. The illustration on the left suggests that a string of direct repeats extending infinitely in either direction could shift an arbitrary number of times, and still maintain base-paired structure with its reverse complementary string through alternative "hybridization." In practice, of course, only a few direct repeats might suffice, and in fact such misalignment in highly repetitive sequences is postulated to occur in mechanisms of change involving unequal crossing over [Lewin, 1987]. The illustration on the right of Figure 14 shows how a circular molecule could be formed by alternative base pairing between a simple tandem repeat and its

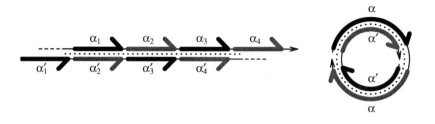

Figure 14. Structural Correlates for Direct Repeats

reverse complement. (Circular molecules, which we will have occasion to deal with again, are in fact quite important in biology; they have been suggested as a motivation to extend formal language theory to circular strings [Head, 1987].)

Are there, however, mechanisms whereby a *single* strand can form secondary structure that is not encompassed by the grammar of (48), and is thus perhaps greater than context-free? In fact, recent evidence points to "non-orthodox" forms of secondary structure, called *pseudoknots,* in many RNA species [Pleij, 1990]. Such a structure is shown in Figure 15. While each base-paired region only creates nested dependencies, the combination of the two necessitates crossing those dependencies.

To formally illustrate the consequences of this, consider an ideal pseudoknot language (i.e. one without unpaired gaps, etc.), which can be represented as follows:

$$L_k = \left\{ \; uv\bar{u}^R\bar{v}^R \mid u,v \in \Sigma^*_{\text{DNA}} \; \right\} \tag{55}$$

We will prove that this language is not context-free, again by contradiction. If L_k were indeed a CFL, then since CFLs are closed under intersection with RLs, the language

$$L'_k = L_k \cap \mathbf{g^+a^+c^+t^+} \tag{56}$$

would also be a CFL. We can see that any choice of the substring u from (55) must exactly cover the initial g's selected by the regular expression, while v must exactly cover the a's, etc. Otherwise, some substring from (55) would have to contain the boundary pairs 'ga', 'ac', and/or 'ct'; this cannot be, because each substring's reverse complement is present, and therefore so would be the pairs 'tc', 'gt', and/or 'ag', respectively, all of which are forbidden by the regular expression. We know that the length of u and thus the number of g's is equal to the length of $\bar{u}^R$ and the number of c's, and similarly for v and $\bar{v}^R$ so that in fact

$$L'_k = \left\{ \; \mathbf{g}^i\mathbf{a}^j\mathbf{t}^i\mathbf{c}^j \mid i,j \geq 1 \; \right\} \tag{57}$$

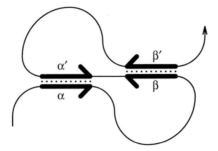

Figure 15. Pseudoknot Structure

which is related by a trivial homomorphism (under which CFLs are also closed) to the language (13b), known to be greater than context-free. Hence, L_k cannot be context-free.

The pseudoknot language L_k of (55) is clearly ideal, but cannot be orthodox because it contains strings, such as those in L'_k, that have no adjacent complementary bases. Thus, there exist ideal but non-orthodox secondary structure languages which are greater than context-free. We can, however, show that the most general ideal language, i.e. the set of all ideal strings (orthodox or not) L_i, is a CSL with ε since it is specified by the following essentially context-sensitive grammar:

$$S_i \rightarrow B_b b S_i \mid \varepsilon$$
$$B_b \rightarrow \bar{b} \qquad \text{for each } b, d \in \Sigma^*_{DNA} \qquad (58)$$
$$d B_b \rightarrow B_b d$$

This grammar can only generate ideal strings, since every b derived is accompanied by a B_b which must eventually produce exactly one $\bar{b}$. The proof that (58) generates every ideal string is by induction on the lengths of such strings. The ideal string ε derives from (58); we assume that any ideal string of length $2n$ does also, and attempt to show this for any ideal string w of length $2(n+1)$. It must be the case that $w = u\bar{b}vb$ for some $u, v \in \Sigma^*_{DNA}$, and furthermore the ideal string uv of length $2n$ must derive from (58) by the inductive hypothesis. It can be seen that S_i can only appear once in any intermediate string of this derivation, and always at the end; thus, in a leftmost derivation the final step must be an application of the ε rule to the string uvS_i, in which case we can adapt this derivation to produce

$$S_i \Rightarrow \cdots \Rightarrow uvS_i \Rightarrow uvB_b b S_i \Rightarrow uvB_b b \Rightarrow^m u B_b vb \Rightarrow u\bar{b}vb \qquad (59)$$

where the penultimate derivation steps comprise sufficient applications of the final, context-sensitive rule of (58) to allow B_b to traverse v leftwards to its final position—that is, $m=|v|$. This completes the induction, as well as the proof that the grammar of (58) generates exactly L_i, the set of all ideal strings.

From the results thus far concerning secondary structure, we may make the informal generalization that orthodox structure is inherently context-free, and ideal non-orthodox structure is greater than context-free. Care must be taken in extending these intuitions to specific cases, though, since subsets of languages may be either higher or lower in the Chomsky hierarchy than the original language. For example, the language generated by **(gact)*** is ideal and non-orthodox, but obviously regular, while the language of double inverted repeats, L_d of (51), is orthodox but not a CFL, since it also specifies direct repeats. We also note in passing, without proof, the interesting observation that for a complementary alphabet of less than four letters (e.g. if only g's and c's are used) there can be no non-orthodox ideal strings.

4.7 Nucleic Acids as Indexed Languages

The features described thus far are all encompassed by CSLs with ε, and in fact can be described by indexed grammars, which specify the IL subset of CSLs. The following indexed grammar defines the copy language of DNA (i.e., tandem repeats):

$$S \rightarrow bS^b \mid A \qquad A^b \rightarrow A\,b \qquad A \rightarrow \varepsilon \qquad (60)$$

(It may be noted that this simplified grammar does not strictly correspond to the formal definition of an indexed grammar, but there is an easy transformation to one that does, e.g. using stack end markers, etc.) The first rule serves to record in the indices all of the bases encountered, while the A rule "plays back" the bases in the proper order. A sample derivation from this grammar would be

$$\begin{aligned} S &\Rightarrow gS^g \Rightarrow gcS^{cg} \Rightarrow gcaS^{acg} \Rightarrow gcaA^{acg} \\ &\Rightarrow gcaA^{cg}a \Rightarrow gcaA^gca \Rightarrow gcaAgca \Rightarrow gcagca \end{aligned} \qquad (61)$$

Note that we can easily specify inverted repeats as well, which is not surprising since the ILs contain the CFLs. We just substitute in the grammar (60) a different rule for A:

$$S \rightarrow bS^b \mid A \qquad A^b \rightarrow \bar{b}A \qquad A \rightarrow \varepsilon \qquad (62)$$

Then, following the same course as the last example derivation (61), we have

$$\begin{aligned} S &\Rightarrow gS^g \Rightarrow gcS^{cg} \Rightarrow gcaS^{acg} \Rightarrow gcaA^{acg} \\ &\Rightarrow gcatA^{cg} \Rightarrow gcatgA^g \Rightarrow gcatgcA \Rightarrow gcatgc \end{aligned} \qquad (63)$$

ILs can contain an unbounded number of repeats (or inverted repeats, or combinations thereof), by simply interposing an additional recursive rule in the grammar (60). We can also specify "interleaved" repeats, as in the following grammar specifying the pseudoknot language L_k of (55):

$$S \to bS^b \mid A \qquad A^b \to bA\overline{b} \mid B \qquad B \to \overline{b}B \qquad B \to \varepsilon \qquad (64)$$

With this facility for handling both crossing and nested dependencies, it is tempting to speculate that the phenomena observed in biological sequences may be contained within the ILs. It has been suggested that ILs suffice for natural language [Gazdar, 1985], and it is also interesting to recall that 0L-systems, which have been so widely used to specify biological form, are contained within the ILs [Prusinkiewicz and Hanan, 1989].

5   Closure Properties for Nucleic Acids

Viewed as a kind of *abstract datatype,* nucleic acids could be usefully defined by the range of biological operations that can be performed on them. Viewed as language, it thus becomes important to understand their linguistic behavior under those operations. In this section we examine a number of known closure properties of languages under various operations that are relevant to nucleic acids, as well as some derived operations that are specific to the domain.

5.1   Closure under Replication

Consider the operation devised on strings $w \in \Sigma^*_{DNA}$ to denote the reverse complementary string, $\overline{w}^R$. Are the language families of interest closed under this operation? In other words, if we decide that some phenomenon in DNA falls within the CFLs (for example), can we be assured that the *opposite strand* will not be greater than context-free?

Recall that the bar operation is an "ε-free" homomorphism. Of the language families we have described, the RLs, CFLs, ILs, CSLs, and recursively enumerable languages are all closed under such homomorphisms; as it happens, they are also all closed under string reversal, and thus we can be confident that opposite strands will maintain the same general linguistic status. This being the case, we can design an operation on sets of strings that will *replicate* them in the sense of creating and adding to the set all their opposite strands:

$$REP(L) = \left\{ w, \overline{w}^R \mid w \in L \right\} = L \cup \overline{L}^R \qquad \text{for } L \subseteq \Sigma^*_{DNA} \qquad (65)$$

Since we have closure under union for all these language families as well, they are still closed under this replicational operation. Note that the definition of (65) accords well with the biological fact of *semi-conservative replication,* in which there is a "union" of each original string with its newly-synthesized opposite strand. Indeed, we can extend this operation to its own closure (i.e., allowing any number of applications of it), denoted as usual by an asterisk, and observe a much stronger, biologically-relevant result:

$$REP^*(L) = REP(L) \tag{66}$$

This follows from (37), and is simply a linguistic statement of the fact that, once REP has been applied to any population of strings and they are thus "double-stranded," the same strings will recur for any number of replications.

It should be noted, however, that the deterministic CFLs are not closed under either homomorphism or string reversal, so that a context-free feature that parses deterministically on one strand may be nondeterministic (though still context-free) on the opposite strand. The following suggests why:

$$L_D = \left\{ \, ag^i c^i g^j \mid i,j \geq 1 \, \right\} \cup \left\{ \, tg^i c^j g^j \mid i,j \geq 1 \, \right\} \tag{67}$$

Were it not for the initial 'a' or 't' on every string in this CFL, it would be nondeterministic for reasons described in relation to the languages of (23) and (29). However, the 'a' and 't' act as "markers" that tip off the recognizer as to what elements it should use the stack to count, making L_D deterministic. Note, therefore, that any homomorphism that mapped 'a' and 't' to the same element would negate the effects of the markers and leave a nondeterministic language. More to the point, string reversal moves the marker bases to the opposite ends of the strings where the recognizer will not encounter them until the end. Thus,

$$\overline{L}_D^R = \left\{ \, c^i g^i c^j a \mid i,j \geq 1 \, \right\} \cup \left\{ \, c^i g^j c^j t \mid i,j \geq 1 \, \right\} \tag{68}$$

would be recognized (in a leftmost fashion) nondeterministically. (A more formal grounding for this nonclosure proof may be found in [Harrison, 1978]). One practical consequence of this is that there may be situations where it is better to parse a string in one direction than another, particularly with a top-down backtracking parser like that of DCGs; for example, one would want to establish the presence of the invariant dinucleotides in a splice junction before searching for the much more difficult flanking signals.

Since replication as we have defined it constitutes a union of a language with its reverse complementary language, it is easy to show that unambiguous CFLs are not closed under this operation, since there may be strings in "double-stranded" sets such that we cannot know *a priori* from which strand they came. For example, the language

$$L_U = \left\{ \, g^i c^i g^j \mid i,j \geq 1 \, \right\} \tag{69}$$

is a deterministic (and thus unambiguous) CFL, since a PDA could simply push the stack on the first set of g's and pop on the c's, with no guesswork required. However, when replicated this language becomes

$$REP(L_U) = \left\{ \, g^i c^j g^k \mid i=j \text{ or } j=k \, \right\} \tag{70}$$

which is essentially the inherently ambiguous language of (23), necessarily having multiple leftmost derivations whenever $i=j=k$.

5.2 Closure under Recombination

Other "operations" that are performed on nucleic acid molecules include recombinatory events. For simplicity, we will confine ourselves here to primitive manipulations like scission and ligation. The latter is ostensibly straightforward, for, if we define ligation and the "closure" of ligation (i.e. the ligation of any non-zero number of strings from a language) as follows

$$\text{LIG}(L) = \left\{ xy \mid x,y \in L \right\} = L \cdot L$$
$$\text{LIG}^*(L) = \left\{ x_1 x_2 \cdots x_n \mid n \geq 1 \text{ and } x_i \in L \text{ for } 1 \leq i \leq n \right\} = L^+ \tag{71}$$

then we can see that these correspond to concatenation and its positive closure over languages, and it is the case that RLs, CFLs, ILs, CSLs, and recursively enumerable languages are all closed under these operations.

It must be emphasized that this simple definition has inherent in it an important assumption regarding the modelling of biological ligation. Viewing nucleic acids as literal strings in solution, one might think that there is no *a priori* reason they should not ligate head-to-head and tail-to-tail, as well as head-to-tail as is implicit in the usual mathematical operation of concatenation. It happens, though, that these strings are not only directional, but that ligation is only chemically permitted in the head-to-tail configuration; in this instance, life mimics mathematics. As a practical matter, however, ligation generally occurs in populations of double-stranded molecules, so we must take account of the fact that in this case the strings from L in the definitions (71) will also ligate head-to-tail as reverse *complements*. Indeed we see that

$$\text{LIG}(\text{REP}(L)) = \text{LIG}(L \cup \overline{L}^R)$$
$$= (L \cdot L) \cup (L \cdot \overline{L}^R) \cup (\overline{L}^R \cdot L) \cup (\overline{L}^R \cdot \overline{L}^R) \tag{72}$$

gives all the required combinations, and uses only operations that preserve our stated closure results.

In the case of scission, we take advantage of the fact that the language families listed above, with the sole exception of the CSLs, are closed under the operations of selecting all prefixes or all suffixes of a language, i.e. under

$$\text{PRE}(L) = \left\{ x \mid xy \in L \right\} \qquad \text{SUF}(L) = \left\{ y \mid xy \in L \right\} \tag{73}$$

This being the case, we can prove closure under scission for either a single cut or for any number of cuts, by combinations of these operations:

$$\text{CUT}(L) = \left\{ x,y \mid xy \in L \right\} = \text{PRE}(L) \cup \text{SUF}(L)$$
$$\text{CUT}^*(L) = \left\{ u \mid xuy \in L \right\} = \text{PRE}(\text{SUF}(L)) \tag{74}$$

The latter operation, in fact, is just the set of all substrings of L. Once again, it is interesting to note that, within the CFLs, neither deterministic nor unambiguous languages are closed under these operations, even though CFLs overall are closed.

Ligation offers one further complication, based on the fact that it may occur so as to form *circular* molecules. We will denote this variation LIG○, but we are left at a loss as to how to represent it linguistically, since the strings have no beginnings. However, we *can* define the results of scission of languages formed by this operation. Assuming in the simplest case that we perform a circular ligation of each individual string in L and then cut each circle once at every possible position, we arrive at the language

$$\text{CUT}(\text{LIG}○(L)) = \{ vu \mid uv \in L \} = \text{CYC}(L) \qquad (75)$$

which is the set of circular permutations of each string. As it happens, all of the language families in the Chomsky hierarchy are closed under this operation (though, again, deterministic CFLs are not); a constructive proof of this for CFLs is given in [Hopcroft and Ullman, 1979]. Closure of LIG○ really only amounts to circular ligation of repeated linear ligations, i.e. LIG○(LIG*(L)), since a string can only be circularized once. Thus, our closure results still hold for this extension.

Biologists can manipulate DNA molecules by cutting them at specific sites using *restriction enzymes*, and then ligating the resulting fragments (also in a sequence-specific manner). The closure of so-called *splicing systems* under these domain-specific operations has been studied using formal language theory [Head, 1987]. Natural recombination, as between homologous chromosomes during meiosis, is an exceedingly important biological phenomenon that bears some resemblance to *shuffle* operations on languages [Hopcroft and Ullman, 1979].

5.3 Closure under Evolution

Consider the following linguistic formulations of several known modes of rearrangement at a genomic level that occur in evolution—duplication, inversion, transposition, and deletion:

$$
\begin{aligned}
\text{DUP}(L) &= \{ xuuy \mid xuy \in L \} \\
\text{INV}(L) &= \{ x\bar{u}^R y \mid xuy \in L \} \qquad \text{where } x, y, u, v \in \Sigma^*_{\text{DNA}} \\
\text{XPOS}(L) &= \{ xvuy \mid xuvy \in L \} \qquad \text{and } L \subseteq \Sigma^*_{\text{DNA}} \\
\text{DEL}(L) &= \{ xy \mid xuy \in L \}
\end{aligned} \qquad (76)
$$

We see immediately that CFLs (and RLs, for that matter) could not be closed under DUP since this operation creates direct repeats of arbitrary length, as in (14), which are greater than context-free. What is somewhat more surprising, given the results of the previous section, is that the CFLs are also not closed under either INV or XPOS. This can be seen by the effects of the operations on inverted repeats, from which INV can make direct repeats and XPOS can make pseudoknot patterns; formal proofs of this follow. Consider the CFL selected from among the inverted repeats—that is, from the language L_e of (40) – by intersection with a regular expression:

$$L_{C1} = L_e \cap (\mathbf{g+c})^*\mathbf{at}(\mathbf{g+c})^* = \{\, x\mathrm{at}\bar{x}^R \mid x \in \{g,c\}^* \,\} \tag{77}$$

We can use intersection with a different RL to examine only the inversions of this language that occur over suffixes of L_{C1} (i.e. for which $y=\varepsilon$ in (76b)):

$$\mathrm{INV}(L_{C1}) \cap (\mathbf{g+c})^*\mathbf{at} = \{\, xx\mathrm{at} \mid x \in \{g,c\}^* \,\} \tag{78}$$

The 'at' can only arrive at the end of the string as the result of inversions of the suffix starting just before the 'at' in each string of L_{C1}. We can then use a homomorphism mapping 'a' and 't' to ε, such as ϕ given for (45), to get rid of the final at's and leave a simple copy language as in (14). Since we have arrived at a non-CFL, and every other operation used preserves CFLs, it must be the case that CFLs are not closed under inversion, and the specific case of inverted repeats yields direct repeats.

Transposition is dealt with by a similar route, first selecting a different subset of inverted repeats as our test CFL:

$$L_{C2} = L_e \cap \mathbf{g^+a^+t^+c^+} = \{\, g^i a^j t^j c^i \mid i,j \geq 1 \,\} \tag{79}$$

We now force transpositions that again occur over suffixes of strings in L_{C2}, such that x in (76c) covers the g's and a's, u covers the t's, v covers the c's, and $y=\varepsilon$:

$$\mathrm{XPOS}(L_{C2}) \cap \mathbf{g^*a^*c^*t^*} = \{\, g^i a^j c^i t^j \mid i,j \geq 1 \,\} \tag{80}$$

But this is a pseudoknot language—in fact, L'_k of (56), which we have already seen is greater than context-free. We conclude that CFLs are also not closed under transposition.

Among the evolutionary operators, CFLs are closed only under deletion. To show this, let us temporarily supplement Σ^*_{DNA} with the character §, and design a homomorphism for which $\phi(b)=b$ for $b \in \Sigma^*_{\mathrm{DNA}}-$§, and $\phi(§)=\varepsilon$. We will also set up a GSM G with transitions as given in Figure 16. Then, we see that the deletion operator can be defined as

$$\mathrm{DEL}(L) = G(\phi^{-1}(L)) \tag{81}$$

The inverse homomorphism will distribute any number of §'s in every possible position in every string of L, so we can use the first two such §'s in each resulting string as end markers for deletions, and be assured of arriving at every possible deletion, as in DEL. We accomplish those deletions with G (which also disposes of the §'s), as the reader may confirm. Since CFLs are closed under inverse homomorphism and the action of GSMs, we know that DEL(L) will be a CFL. Similar results hold for RLs, ILs, and recursively enumerable languages, though it happens that CSLs need not be closed under DEL because G is not ε-free.

Note that minor variations of G can be used to prove the closure proper-

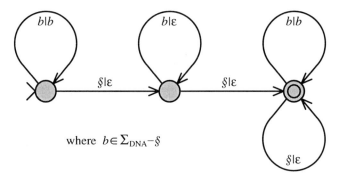

where $b \in \Sigma_{\text{DNA}} - \S$

Figure 16. The Generalized Sequential Machine G

ties of the prefix and suffix operations given in (73), and in fact those results can be used to demonstrate the closure properties of the deleted fragments themselves, whether linear or circular. In addition, the definitions of G and ϕ may be modified to reflect other, domain-specific models in order to take advantage of the same proof methodology. For example, $\phi(\S)$ can be defined to be a recognition sequence that delimits "directed" deletions (see section 2.8.2). Using a combination of two bracketing deletion markers, we might model the splicing that occurs in RNA processing (see section 2.3.4), or indeed even the inverse operation of inserting languages (at least RLs) into existing languages at designated points; this suggests that the evolution of interrupted genes may not in itself have contributed to their linguistic complexity.

6 Structural Grammars for Nucleic Acids

As noted, the DCG gene grammar presented previously was largely created without regard for the linguistic status of DNA, but rather as a rapidly-prototyped, reasonably efficient recognizer for "real-world" search applications. This section details our efforts to adapt logic grammars to a wider variety of biological phenomena, with formally-based conventions suitable to the domain.

6.1 Context-Free and Indexed Grammars

Base complementarity, as defined in (33), is easily implemented within DCGs by creating a special prefix tilde operator as follows:

$$\sim"\text{g}" \; --> \; "\text{c}" . \qquad \sim"\text{c}" \; --> \; "\text{g}" .$$
$$\sim"\text{a}" \; --> \; "\text{t}" . \qquad \sim"\text{t}" \; --> \; "\text{a}" . \tag{82}$$

Then, creating a DCG version of the formal grammar (41) specifying

Figure 17. An n-*leaf Clover (n=3)*

stem-and-loop structures is straightforward:

```
inverted_repeat --> [X], inverted_repeat, ~[X]
inverted_repeat --> ... .
```
(83)

Here, the Prolog variables within square-bracketed lists indicate terminals. The gap rule represents the loop, corresponding to the rule for the nonterminal *A* in the formal grammar. We have noted that this non-ideal specification is insufficient as a model, and it is also impractical in actual parsing; however, we can implement the constrained version of (44) with little extra trouble, using parameters and embedded code to create a concise and workable (though inefficient) DCG for inverted repeats with specified minimum-length stems and maximum-length loops:

```
inverted_repeat(Stem,Loop) --> {Stem=<0},
     0...Loop.
inverted_repeat(Stem,Loop) --> {Next is Stem-1},
     [X], inverted_repeat(Next,Loop), ~[X].
```
(84)

It is just as easy to transcribe other formal grammars, e.g. that of (48) representing generalized orthodox secondary structure, to their DCG equivalents. Again, a practical implementation of the DCG form would allow us to add length constraints, gaps, and other conditions to take account of "real-world" factors. We can also write grammars for more distinctive (that is, less general) features, such as structures in the nature of "*n*-leaf clovers" like the one illustrated in Figure 17:

```
cloverleaf --> [X], cloverleaf, ~[X] | leaves.
leaves --> leaf, leaves | [].
leaf --> [Y], leaf, ~[Y] | [].
```
(85)

As was noted above, indexed grammars can be thought of as context-free grammars that are extended by the addition of a stack feature to nonterminal elements; thus they are easily implemented in DCGs, by just attaching parameters in the form of Prolog lists to nonterminals. A DCG-based indexed grammar corresponding to (60) would be

```
tandem_repeat(Stack) --> [X],
     tandem_repeat([X|Stack]).
tandem_repeat(Stack) --> repeat(Stack).
repeat([]) --> [].                                    (86)
repeat([H|T]) --> repeat(T), [H].
```

while, to make the `repeat` rule instead play back the reverse complement of the sequence stored on the stack, we could substitute the rule corresponding to (62) as follows:

```
complement([]) --> [].
complement([H|T]) --> ~[H], complement(T).            (87)
```

Calling the top-level rule with an empty stack gives the desired results. An indexed grammar expressing the n-leaf clover of (85) would be

```
cloverleaf(Stack) --> [X], cloverleaf([X|Stack]).
cloverleaf(Stack) --> leaves([]), complement(Stack).
leaves([]) --> [].                                    (88)
leaves(Stack) --> [X], leaves([X|Stack]).
leaves(Stack) --> complement(Stack), leaves([]).
```

Compared with the context-free DCG of (85), this notation becomes somewhat clumsy, a problem we will address in the next section.

6.2 String Variable Grammars

We have developed a domain-specific formalism called *string variable grammar* (SVG) which appears to handle secondary structure phenomena with significantly greater perspicuity than indexed grammars [Searls, 1989a]. SVGs allow *string variables* on the right-hand sides of otherwise context-free rules, which stand for substrings of unbounded length. An example of an SVG implemented within an extended DCG formalism would be:

```
tandem_repeat --> X, X.                               (89)
```

This requires only some minor modification to the DCG translator to recognize such variables as what amounts to indexed grammar nonterminals, with the Prolog variable itself representing the nested stack [Searls, 1989a]. The variables, on their first occurrence, are bound nondeterministically to arbitrary substrings, after which they require the identical substring on the input whenever they recur. We can also generalize our rules for single base complements, to recognize the reverse complement of an arbitrary string. This allows rules of the form

```
inverted_repeat --> X, _, ~X.                          (90)
```

Here we have used an anonymous string variable to denote the gap, since it is the case that . . . --> _ . Now, the rules for direct and inverted repeats—features that intuitively share a similar status in this domain—can also assume a very similar grammatical structure.

Returning to our example of the n-leaf clover of the grammars (85) and (88), we can now write a much more concise grammar in the form of an SVG:

```
cloverleaf --> X, leaves, ~X.
leaves --> [] | Y, ~Y, leaves.                         (91)
```

We also offer economical SVG representations of the attenuator structure of Figure 12 and the pseudoknot structure of Figure 15:

```
attenuator --> A, _, ~A, _, A.
pseudoknot --> A, _, B, _, ~A, _, ~B.                  (92)
```

The use of string variables can be augmented in various ways. For instance, by allowing them to be passed as parameters, we can specify an unbounded number of direct repeats:

```
direct_repeats(X) --> X, _, direct_repeats(X).
direct_repeats(X) --> X.                               (93)
```

Then, by defining compositions of string variables (e.g. ~(~X) --> X.), we can do such things as specify any number of strictly alternating inverted repeats:

```
inverted_repeats(X) --> X, _, inverted_repeats(~X).
inverted_repeats(X) --> [].                            (94)
```

We have recently shown that SVGs used in the manner described up to this point specify languages that are formally contained within the ILs, contain the CFLs, and furthermore can be parsed in $O(n^3)$ time using a variation on the Earley parser [Searls, manuscript in preparation].

6.3 Structural Grammar Examples

The SVG formalism makes it possible to describe and recognize much more complex patterns of secondary structure, such as the following specification of the 3' (right-hand) end of tobacco mosaic virus RNA, covering 177 nucleotides of which two thirds are base paired [Pleij, 1990]:

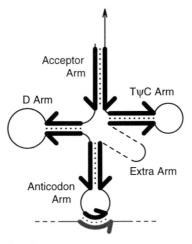

Figure 18. tRNA Secondary Structure

```
tmv_3prime --> A, _, B, ~A, _, ~B,
        C, _, D, ~C, _, ~D, E, _, F, ~E, _, ~F, _,
        G, _, H, I, _, J, _, ~J, ~I, ~G, _, ~H,        (95)
        K, _, ~K, L, _, M, ~L, _, ~M, _.
```

This pattern consists of three consecutive, contiguous pseudoknots (corresponding to the variable sets *A/B*, *C/D*, and *E/F*), another pseudoknot *(G/H)* whose gap contains an inverted repeat with a bulge *(I/J)*, followed by another inverted repeat *(K)* and a final pseudoknot *(L/M)*. Another example, adapted from [Gautheret et al., 1990], is the following grammar describing a consensus secondary structure for a class of autocatalytic introns:

```
group_I_intron --> _, A, _, B, ~A, _, C, _,
        E, _, F, _, ~F, _, ~E, G, _, ~G, _,
        D, _, ~C, _, H, _, ~H, _, ~D, _,        (96)
        I, _, ~I, _, ~B, _.
```

This structure contains two pseudoknot patterns; one *(A/B)* spans the entire sequence and in fact brackets the cleavage sites *in vivo*, while the other *(C/D)* is embedded in a series of stem-and-loop structures and variants.

These rules could obviously be written more hierarchically, using the appropriate rules for "phrases" (such as `inverted_repeat` from (90), `pseudoknot` from (92b), and others), but even as they stand they are significantly more readable than other grammar formalisms would be. Nevertheless, they do lack the necessary length constraints to make them practi-

```
tRNA(AA) --> Stem@7, "t", base, d_arm, base,
    anticodon_arm(AA), extra_arm, t_psi_arm,
    ~Stem$1, acceptor_arm.

d_arm --> Stem@4, "a", purine, 1...3, "gg",
    1...3, "a", 0...1, ~Stem$1.

anticodon_arm(AA) --> Stem@5, pyrimidine, "t",
    anticodon(AA), purine, base, ~Stem$1.

extra_arm --> 3...20, pyrimidine.

t_psi_c_arm --> Stem@4, "gttc", purine, "a",
    base, pyrimidine, "c", ~Stem$1.

acceptor_arm --> base, "cca".

anticodon(AA) --> ~[X,Y,Z],
    {codon(AA)==>[X,Y,Z], ! ; AA=suppressor}.
```

Figure 19. A tRNA SVG

cal. In order to demonstrate a real parsing application, we will use a slightly simpler case, that of transfer RNA, which is illustrated in Figure 18 and whose typical cloverleaf structure is represented abstractly by the following SVG:

```
tRNA(Codon) --> AcceptorArm, _, DArm, _, ~DArm, _,
    AnticodonArm, _, ~Codon, _, ~AnticodonArm,   (97)
    _, TpsiCArm, _, ~TpsiCArm, ~AcceptorArm, _.
```

Here, a parameter is used to return the codon identity of the tRNA, which is the reverse complement of the *anticodon* by which it recognizes the triplet on the mRNA specifying a particular amino acid.

The *E. coli* tRNA SVG listed in Figure 19 is a more practical version [Searls and Liebowitz, 1990], again using string variables for the secondary structure, but now combined with grammar features specifying known conserved bases or base classes. Despite these lexical constraints, most of the information available has to do with the folded structure of the tRNA, which causes nested dependencies to be evolutionarily conserved even where primary sequence is not. We have here used an infix control operator '@' to specify the length of the *Stem* string variables. The reverse complementary stretch uses the '$' operator to constrain the *cost* of the match, and here indicates that up to one mismatch is allowed in the stem. The grammar now returns a parameter AA indicating the actual amino acid the tRNA will carry;

```
|  ?-test_tRNA(Codon,Start,End).
```

Parsing Arg-tRNA-1 (76bp)...   Parsing NKV region (730bp)...
Parse succeeded in 16 ms: Parse succeeded in 583 ms:
Codon = arg,   Codon = lys,
Start = 1,   Start = 272,
End = 76 ;   End = 347 ;

Parsing Asn-tRNA-1 (76bp)...   Parse succeeded in 434 ms:
Parse succeeded in 16 ms: Codon = val,
Codon = arg,   Start = 480,
Start = 1,   End = 555 ;
End = 76 ;

                                  Parse succeeded in 434 ms:
                                  Codon = suppressor,
             ...   Start = 558,
                                  End = 633

Figure 20. Parses of tRNAs (left) and Genomic DNA (right)

this is determined in the anticodon rule using *recursive derivation* [Searls, 1989a], i.e. by parsing the triplet inside curly braces in the body of the rule. This will fail on a stop codon, as occurs in bacterial *suppressor* mutations, in which case the latter fact is returned.

This grammar was actually created from the ground up in a few hours, using 17 known bacterial tRNA sequences in isolation as a "training set." Starting with an overly constrained model based on the idealized textbook representation, the bounded gaps and cost parameters were adjusted until the entire set parsed. This is shown through the use of a higher-level Prolog rule which retrieves successive database entries, measures their length, and applies the derivation operator, keeping track of CPU time, as shown at the left in Figure 20. The grammar was then tested on genomic sequences containing tRNA gene clusters, as shown at the right of Figure 20. In this and one other gene region, all seven known genes parsed on the first try. In each case the codon was identified correctly, including a suppressor mutation [Searls and Liebowitz, 1990].

An approach similar to this one is currently being pursued in the laboratory of Dr. Ross Overbeek at Argonne National Laboratory [R. Taylor, personal communication], in the domain of ribosomal RNA molecules. These are much larger and more complex than tRNA, with dozens of stem-and-loop structures and several pseudoknots. The specialized parser being developed there will assist in the classification of new molecules, using a grammar derived from an alignment that takes account of "covariances" or dependencies preserved over evolution. We are currently investigating parsing strategies

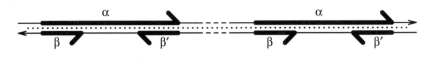

Figure 21. A Transposable Element

that would make generalized SVG parsing practical [Cheever et al., 1991].

6.4 Superpositional Grammars

Transposable elements such as *copia* typically have long terminal repeats that have "superimposed" on them terminal inverted repeats, as illustrated in Figure 21. An SVG that specifies this case would be

```
transposon --> X, Y, ~X, _, X, Y, ~X.                    (98)
```

However, a better representation is as follows:

```
transposon --> W, _, W, {(X, _, ~X) ==> W}.              (99)
```

This description uses the recursive derivation to "subordinate" the inverted repeats to the more dominant terminal direct repeats—a better reflection of the semantics of the domain, since the direct repeats are typically much larger and better matches, and in fact the inverted repeats are not even always present. Other SVGs given previously can be similarly restated using recursive derivation to suggest different interpretations. For example, pseudoknots may occur in a form illustrated in Figure 22, where there is a *coaxial stacking* of the two base-pairing regions to form a quasi-continuous double helix [Pleij, 1990]. The following rule for this form of pseudoknot, it may be argued, tends to emphasize the continuity of the central stretch, and its relationship to the flanking complementary regions:

```
pseudoknot --> A, _, ~AB, _, B, {(A, B) ==> AB}. (100)
```

We have previously presented similar sorts of "reinterpretations" of attenuator structure [Searls, 1989a], which are better at capturing the dual nature of these sequences, in that they use a recursive derivation to specify the alternative secondary structure separately.

Recursive derivation, used in this way, allows substrings to be parsed more than once within a single overall parse. We can generalize this to a notion of *superposition* of grammar elements, by defining an appropriate operator '&' (after [Pereira and Shieber, 1987]) as follows:

```
X & Y --> W, {X ==> W}, {Y ==> W}.                       (101)
```

This superposition operator, which requires its operands to exactly coincide on the input, allows for some novel views on structures discussed before:

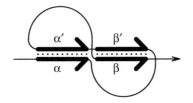

Figure 22. Coaxial Stacking in a Pseudoknot

```
tandem_inverted_repeat  --> W & ~W.                    (102)
double_inverted_repeat  --> (X, ~X) & (Y, Y).
```

The first rule expresses the fact that the superposition of a sequence with its own reverse complement is an ideal inverted repeat, per the language L_e of (38). The second rule shows how an ideal double inverted repeat, as in L_d of (51), may be specified as the superposition of an inverted repeat with a direct repeat.

Superposition in effect acts to "disconnect" elements of the grammar from the usual strict consecutivity, as do gaps. In combination, these two features permit, for instance, specifying a promoter that has a stretch of Z-DNA (a change in the twist of the double helix that can occur where there are alternating purines and pyrimidines) occurring anywhere within it, even in superposition to other important lexical elements – which in fact is likely to be the case:

```
promoter & (_, zDNA, _)                                (103)
```

Thus, superposition may prove to be an important element of functional grammars, which we will examine in the next section. For example, Z-DNA is actually most often associated with enhancers, which are even more "loosely connected" in that they can occur anywhere in the general vicinity of gene promoters, in either orientation, sometimes as direct repeats. Promoters themselves, in fact, can overlap the transcription units they control (cf. RNA polymerase III promoters), and even coding regions can coincide in certain phage [Lewin, 1987]. This suggests a need for a general capability to specify arbitrary relations between the spans of different features, similar to Allen's interval calculus [Allen, 1983]. In fact, the superposition and gap operators suffice. We can, for instance, combine them to create a subsumption ordering of alternative interpretations for an element X "preceding" an element Y:

$$(X, Y) \quad \preceq \quad (X, \_, Y) \quad \preceq \quad ((X, \_) \& (\_, Y)) \quad (104)$$

The first case, in which Y begins immediately after X ends, is subsumed

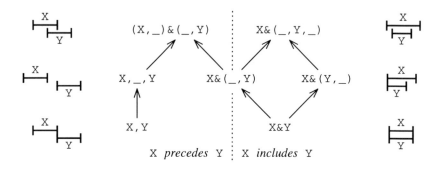

Figure 23. Partial Order of Superposition

by the second case, where Y can begin any time after X ends; this in turn is subsumed by the third case, which only requires that Y not begin before X does, nor end before X does. We have generalized this to a partial order, illustrated in Figure 23, that is arguably complete with respect to possible relations between spans of features [Searls, 1989b].

If, in the definition (101), X and Y were not string variables but were instantiated to the start symbols of two distinct grammars (which is allowed by the definition) then clearly $X\&Y$ would produce the *intersection* of the languages defined by those grammars [Pereira and Shieber, 1987]. The consequences of this will be explored in the next section.

7 Functional Linguistics of Biological Sequences

To this point we have dealt formally only with the *structural* nature of nucleic acids, which is amenable to linguistic formulation because of its relative simplicity; we will find that a *functional* or informational view of the language of biological sequences is less clear cut. This in no way weakens the results presented to this point. The closure properties derived for operations on nucleic acids, for example, apply to *any* language encoded in DNA or in any other string for which those operations are defined. Rather, the greater richness of the language of genes and proteins indicates all the more the need for a well-founded descriptive paradigm. Moreover, it will be seen that the most interesting aspects of biological languages may reside at the point where structural and functional components interact.

A functional view will also allow us to expand our horizons beyond the relatively local phenomena of secondary structure, to large regions of the genome or even entire genomes (represented formally, perhaps, as strings derived by concatenation of chromosomes). This will allow us in turn to reason linguistically about processes of evolution, at least at a conceptual level.

It may be supposed that this distinction between structural and functional linguistics corresponds to the conventional one drawn between syntax and semantics. There is much to recommend this, insofar as gene products (i.e. proteins) and their biological activities may be thought of as the *meaning* of the information in genes, and perhaps entire organisms as the meaning of genomes. On the other hand, the gene grammars presented earlier clearly demonstrate a syntactic nature, and as such grammars are further elaborated with function-specific "motifs" it may be difficult to make a sharp delineation between syntax and semantics. Ultimately, the semantics of DNA may be based on evolutionary selection; a certain view of syntax may allow sequences that do not support life (or not very well), just as syntactically-valid English sentences may nevertheless be nonsensical. The discussion that follows will not attempt to resolve where such a line should be drawn, though the potential utility of the distinction should perhaps be borne in mind.

7.1 The Role of Language Theory

In examining the functional aspects of the language of biological sequences, it becomes important to set out more precisely the goals of a language-theoretic approach. There are at least four broad roles for the tools and techniques of linguistics in this domain: *specification, recognition, theory formation,* and *abstraction.* By specification we mean the use of formalisms such as grammars to indicate in a mathematically and computationally precise way the nature and relative locations of features in a sequence. Such a specification may be partial, only serving to constrain the possibilities with features that are important to one aspect of the system. For example, published diagrams of genes typically only point out landmarks such as signal sequences, direct and inverted repeats, coding regions, and perhaps important restriction sites, all of which together clearly do not completely define any gene. However, a formal basis for such descriptions could serve to establish a *lingua franca* for interchange of information, and a similar approach may even extend to description of sequence analysis algorithms, as will be seen in a later section.

Moreover, such high-level descriptions can merge into the second role for linguistics, that of recognition. This simply refers to the use of grammars as input to parsers which are then used for pattern-matching search—that is, syntactic pattern recognition—of what may be otherwise uncharacterized genomic sequence data. We have seen that, in practice, these uses of linguistic tools tend to depart from the purely formal, for reasons of efficiency, yet a continued cognizance of the language-theoretic foundations can be important. As an example, the discovery of pseudoknots in RNA has spurred the development of new secondary structure prediction algorithms to improve on programs that, possibly without the developers explicitly realizing it, were limited to dealing with context-free structures [Abrahams et al., 1990].

The third role of linguistics is for the elaboration of *domain theories* that in some sense model biological structures and processes. In this case, other grammatical objects in addition to terminal strings (e.g. nonterminals, productions, and even parse trees) would have specific biological semantics attributed to them, and would be developed as postulates that are testable by parsing actual positive and negative exemplars. A number of possibilities along these lines will be discussed in section 2.9 of this article. Machine learning techniques could be expected to be most useful with regards to this role, to the extent that they could be made to assist in theory formation and modification.

The fourth role of linguistics, that of abstraction, can be seen as the most conceptual insofar as its goal would be an understanding of the language of biological sequences viewed mathematically, purely as sets of strings that are at some level meaningful in a biological system. One way to define such a language would be to imagine the set of all genomes that exist in viable organisms; however, this is severely limiting insofar as there are probably many such strings that have never existed, yet would support life. This distinction, between the set of strings that exist and the set that *can* exist, parallels one drawn in natural language, between *performance* and *competence* [Chomsky, 1965]; performance refers to actual instances of the use of language, while competence refers to the intrinsic capabilities of users to generate and recognize a language. An orientation toward the latter, in any domain, can be expected to lead to more universal, intensional descriptions than an approach based simply on inventories of extant strings. Of course, such incomplete sets of instances may be important sources of information in developing linguistic descriptions, e.g. consensus sequences for regulatory regions. In many cases, though, we may derive notions of competence by observing the biological machinery that manages the strings, e.g. transcription, translation, etc. As long as our knowledge of these phenomena remains incomplete, however, these languages must remain abstractions, particularly at the level of genomes. Still, we will see that they may constitute tools for abstract reasoning and thought experiments, and the sensation that they are unfathomable must not discourage the practical application of linguistic techniques, and the ideas gleaned from this type of analysis, in the other roles described above.

7.2 The Language of the Gene

In some situations genes are superimposed so as to create ambiguity, e.g. in the cases of multiple start sites for transcription, alternative splicing, and even "nested" genes. Thus, over the same stretch of DNA there would be multiple leftmost derivations for any grammar specifying a gene, with each derivation corresponding to a gene product. Such ambiguity suggests that the corresponding language is nondeterministic, and thus not regular. However, it must be emphasized that this is not in itself a formal proof that the language of DNA is not regular, since we have prejudiced our grammar by requiring that it capture the notion of "gene" as a nonterminal, indeed one that corresponds to a single gene product. As was the case for the formal language of (19), there may be other, perhaps less intuitive grammars that are unambiguous, specifying the same language as the ambiguous gene-oriented grammar. For example, much of the observed variation is post-transcriptional in nature, so that it may be that the ambiguity is not actually inherent at the DNA level, but resides in other cellular processes, beyond the gene itself. Thus, perhaps a transcript-oriented grammar might be unambiguous. However, we know that transcription itself can vary over time within the same region, as in the case of overlapping "early" versus "late" transcripts in certain viruses; even at the level of coding regions there is overlap, including instances of multiple reading frames. Thus, there seems to be good empirical evidence that any grammar related to genes, or purporting to model underlying biological processes at the gene level, would not be regular.

We arrive at this notion of ambiguity of gene products by viewing derivation as analogous to gene expression. In terms of information encoded, however, we must ask if such superposition is *required* of the language, rather than simply allowed. The importance of this is that it would necessitate the *intersection* of languages, under which some important language families are not closed. Returning briefly to a structural theme, consider attenuators (Figure 12), which we gave as examples of strings that are ambiguous as regards the language of secondary structure since they allow alternative folding. However, from a functional perspective, the genes that use attenuators require this secondary structure for the regulatory mechanism to work, so that the language must in fact intersect the two cases. Since the mechanism depends on orthodox secondary structure, it is CFLs, as in (54), that are being intersected, but the resulting language is greater than context-free because it necessarily contains direct repeats. While it happens to be an IL, it is a fact that any recursively enumerable language can be expressed as a homomorphism of the intersection of two context-free languages, so that there are potentially even more serious linguistic consequences to superposition of non-regular elements.

The process of gene expression by its nature suggests that genes are superpositional in another sense, reflecting the successive steps of transcription, processing, and translation, all encoded within the same region. To the extent that we wish any descriptive grammars to model these underlying processes, which occur at different times, in different places in the cell, and using different mechanisms, it would seem that such processes should be represented by separate, well-factored grammars. The projection of all the corresponding functional and control elements for these processes onto the same region of DNA should then be captured in a requirement that the respective grammars all parse that DNA successfully. Note that this would also make it much easier to model situations such as the transcriptional variants that produce untranslatable messages, as described for the globin gene grammars above; all that would be required would be to alter the RNA processing grammar (that recognizes splice junctions) and drop the translation grammar altogether.

If we accept that separate cellular processes should be modelled by distinct grammars, and that the underlying language represents the superposition of the resulting distinct languages, then again the language may tend upwards on the Chomsky hierarchy by virtue of intersection. If it is CFLs that are being intersected, it may also be the case that we can never know the final status of the language, since it is undecidable whether the intersection of CFLs is a CFL or not. For that matter, even if we could arrive at a context-free grammar that completely described all aspects of a gene, we might not be able to show that it was non-regular, since in general it is undecidable if nondeterministic CFLs (or above) are equivalent to some RL [Hopcroft and Ullman, 1979].

7.3 The Language of the Genome

The notion of derivations corresponding to gene products would appear to be a useful one, since it formally establishes the analogies between parsing and gene expression, and between parse trees and gene structure, which are inherent in the first sample gene grammars given above. It also allows us to adapt the discussion to wider questions of the differential control of gene expression in different tissues and developmental stages. For example, if we equate successful parsing with gene expression, we must concede that a substring that is a gene at one time may not be a gene at another. This is troublesome, unless we view genes in the context of the genome as a whole. If the genome is inherently ambiguous, then multiple global derivations could correspond to particular cell types at particular times and under particular conditions. Any given derivation may or may not call for the gene subderivation in question. From this viewpoint, it might be better to name the corresponding nonterminal *expressed-gene* rather than simply *gene*.

Does this mean, though, that in any *given* fixed global state of differentiation, etc., genes and gene expression may yet be deterministic? For, at a local level the apparent ambiguity of overlapping genes, or of expressed vs. unexpressed genes, does not mean that such an ambiguity necessarily exists at any given time in the cell; there may be external, regulatory factors that "tip off" some cellular recognizer and thus specify one or the other of the available parses. In this model there could be distant elements specifying such regulatory factors in an overall genomic language, acting against ambiguity that may otherwise be present within isolated segments. Indeed, grammar-based approaches have been proposed for simulating gene regulatory systems [Searls, 1988], and for modelling their genomic arrangement using transformational grammars (see section 2.9) [Collado-Vides, 1989b]. However, such mechanisms by and large exert their effects via exogenous elements (such as DNA-binding proteins) whose biochemical activity would seem to be necessarily "ambiguous," if only at threshold levels. It is difficult to imagine a language recognizer sophisticated enough to precisely simulate regulation that ultimately depends on the physical chemistry of molecules moving through a cell. Thus, whatever the cell might do to chart its fate deterministically, would seem to be inaccessible to any linguistic *description* of the genome out of context.

Perhaps the most telling evidence for this view is the totipotency of germline DNA, and the pluripotency of many somatic cells. That is, not only must the genome be ambiguous because it has the capacity to specify a wide variety of cell types at different times and places in development, but any counterargument based on a notion of deterministically programmed differentiation fails in the face of the many examples of dedifferentiation and developmental plasticity in biology—as clear a case for nondeterminism as could be wished. Therefore, we are left with a strong sense that the language of genes and even of the genome as a whole, must be at least context-free.

Recently an interesting proof has been offered for gene regulatory systems being greater than context-free, based on the fact that there need be no particular spatial relationship on the genome between genes coding for soluble regulatory elements and the genes those elements regulate [Collado-Vides, 1991b]. This being the case, an array of such regulatory genes and their target genes, which clearly form dependencies, are presumably free to arrange themselves so as to cross those dependencies, so that the language describing such arrangements could not be a CFL. (This is formally argued using a method of proof involving the *pumping lemma* for CFLs, to be described in section 2.8.1.)

7.4 The Language of Proteins

Proteins also have three-dimensional structure, whose nature suggests that the functional language of proteins may in fact be structural in the same sense as nucleic acids, with similar linguistic consequences. Figure 24 depicts a hypothetical folded protein molecule, illustrating in a highly schematic way the conformational relationships among major secondary structure features like α-helices (the cylinder at the bottom), β-strands (the arrows in the center), and β-turns (the "kink" iconified at the upper right).

Pattern-directed inference systems like Ariadne [Lathrop, Webster and Smith, 1987] have been used to detect amino acid sequences that are likely to produce such structures, combining statistical evidence for the features themselves with a hierarchical model of their higher-level ordering, captured in what amounts to a regular expression. Such an approach must necessarily deal with patterns seen on the unfolded string of amino acids, but clearly

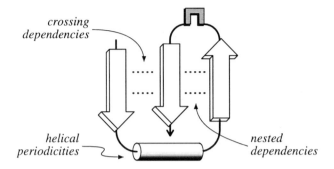

Figure 24. Protein Structure

these physical features also interact with each other in their three-dimensional conformation, not only through hydrogen bonding but also where charged moieties are brought into juxtaposition, or space-filling interactions occur, etc. These may be expected to display correlated changes over the course of evolution—i.e., dependencies.

Such interactions are suggested by the dotted lines between β-strands in Figure 24; note, however, that if those dotted lines are extended as the molecule is unfolded into a linear representation, the interactions on the right exhibit nested dependencies, and those on the left crossing dependencies, as in Figure 4. As we have seen, the former are characteristic of CFLs, and the latter of CSLs. Other such dependencies may be found, for instance, in α-helices which have one face in a hydrophobic milieu, and the other in a hydrophilic one; this will result in a series of periodic crossing dependencies.

The nested and crossing dependencies we have illustrated in inverted and direct repeats in nucleic acids are much more straightforward, corresponding to complementarity and equality of individual bases, respectively. Nevertheless, the dependencies in proteins, though more complex and varied (e.g. charge, bulk, hydrophilicity, catalytic activity within active sites, etc.) are likely to be tremendously important in terms of structure and function. Thus, it would appear that more sophisticated linguistically-based approaches to protein structure would be well-advised.

How might such non-regular functional languages interact with the non-regular secondary structures that occur in nucleic acids? They may, of course, be completely segregated, with the former confined to coding regions and the latter to control regions, introns, and structural species like tRNA and rRNA which have no polypeptide products. It is interesting to speculate, however, that nature with its usual parsimony may have elected to overlap phenomena on the DNA, for instance by favoring processed mRNA species that form secondary structure, for purposes of stability, transport, etc. We know that the resulting language intersection may act to increase the linguistic complexity of the system, particularly since both contributing languages may have nested dependencies, which in the case of simple inverted repeats do lead to a promotion from CFLs to ILs. In the next section, however, we will explore the intriguing possibility that functional CFLs may not even require context-free grammars, beyond what already exists in nucleic acid secondary structure, for their expression.

7.5 Structurally-Derived Functional Languages

The grammar of (48), which describes ideal orthodox secondary structure in nucleic acids, defines one *particular* CFL. It is interesting to note, though, that the capability to form secondary structure, as embodied in this grammar, can be "harnessed" to express other CFLs. We have seen this in several proofs, which have used intersection with RLs together with homomorphisms to arrive at distinct CFLs, such as (45) which produces (7). As another example, consider languages consisting of true (as opposed to biological) palindromes, (11). Using the language L_O of orthodox secondary structure determined by the grammar (48), and a homomorphism based on $\phi(g)=\phi(c)=0$, and $\phi(a)=\phi(t)=1$, we can see that

$$L_{P1} = \left\{ ww^R \mid w \in \{0,1\}^* \right\} = \phi\left(L_O \cap (\text{g+a})^*(\text{c+t})^*\right) \qquad (105)$$

Again, we have generated a new CFL from the generic language of secondary structure, and it would appear that this might be a fairly general capacity. However, for this example we have been forced to use all four bases—purines for the front of the palindrome, and pyrimidines for the back—raising the question of whether the utility of this tactic will be limited by the size of the DNA alphabet. For instance, it might appear that we would be unable to use L_O to express the language of true palindromes over an alphabet of size four:

$$L_{P2} = \left\{ ww^R \mid w \in \{0,1,2,3\}^* \right\} \qquad (106)$$

As it happens, though, we can *encode* this larger alphabet into dinucleotides via a homomorphism ψ, defined as follows:

$$\begin{array}{llll} \psi(0)=\text{gg} & \psi(1)=\text{ga} & \psi(2)=\text{ag} & \psi(3)=\text{aa} \\ \psi(\hat{0})=\text{cc} & \psi(\hat{1})=\text{tc} & \psi(\hat{2})=\text{ct} & \psi(\hat{3})=\text{tt} \end{array} \qquad (107)$$

As before, we will use purines for the front of the palindrome and pyrimidines for the back, but this time we use a dinucleotide to encode each digit in the final language. We must distinguish front and back digits for the moment, using the hat notation, in order for ψ to be a function, but we can strip off the hats later with another homomorphism:

$$\phi(x) = \phi(\hat{x}) = x \quad \text{for } x \in \{0,1,2,3\} \qquad (108)$$

In order to make use of the encoding, we must in fact apply ψ as an *inverse* homomorphism (under which CFLs are also closed). With these exertions, we see that it is indeed possible to specify the desired language:

$$L_{P2} = \phi\psi^{-1}\left(L_0 \cap ((g^+a)(g^+a))^*((c^+t)(c^+t))^*\right) \tag{109}$$

In fact, with appropriate encodings we should be able to specify any desired final alphabet, and with more sophisticated regular expressions we could take advantage of the ability of L_0 to specify iterated or nested structures as well. The remarkable thing about these specifications is that a variety of CFLs are being expressed using the "general purpose" stack mechanism of secondary structure together with only an RL in the primary sequence and some "interpretation" $\phi\psi^{-1}$.

If the notion of the interpretation as a composition of a homomorphism with an inverse homomorphism seems odd, note that nature already uses encodings of this type, in the form of amino acid codons:

$$\psi(\text{ser}_1)=\text{ucg} \qquad \psi(\text{ser}_2)=\text{uca} \qquad \psi(\text{ser}_3)=\text{ucc} \qquad \psi(\text{ser}_4)=\text{ucu}$$

$$\psi(\text{phe}_1)=\text{uuc} \qquad \psi(\text{phe}_2)=\text{uuu} \qquad \psi(\text{met}_1)=\text{aug} \qquad \text{etc.} \dots \tag{110}$$

$$\phi(x_i)=x \quad \text{for } x\in \{\text{ser},\text{phe},\text{met}, \cdots \}$$

where ψ now ranges over triplets from the slightly different alphabet of RNA, $\Sigma_{RNA}=\{\text{g,c,a,u}\}$. In this case, the interpretation $\phi\psi^{-1}(w)$ for $w\in \Sigma_{RNA}^{3n}$) will yield the corresponding polypeptide of length n (ignoring questions of alternative reading frame and stop codons). Here ψ establishes the encoding, and ϕ captures the degeneracy of the triplet code. It is easy to imagine other homomorphic interpretations of a similar nature being embodied, for instance, in DNA binding proteins involved in gene regulation (which in fact are often associated with regions of dyad symmetry).

This leads us to the question of whether *any* CFL, e.g. arbitrary functional languages, could be expressed by an RL superimposed on sequence with secondary structure, together with some interpretation to act as an "adaptor" to the new domain. An important characterization theorem [Chomsky and Schutzenberger, 1963] states that any CFL can in fact be specified as a homomorphism of the intersection of some RL with a language belonging to a family known as the *semi-Dyck* languages. A semi-Dyck language D_r consists of all well-balanced, properly nested strings of r types of parentheses; for example, for D_3 consisting of ordinary parentheses, square brackets, and curly braces, we would have

$$[\{\}([])]\{[]\} \in D_3$$
$$(\}\{)][\notin D_3 \tag{111}$$
$$\{[(\})] \notin D_3$$

The grammar describing semi-Dyck languages is tantalizingly close to that of (48) for L_0, since open parentheses must be matched by closed ones in a manner quite similar to base-pairing in secondary structure. Moreover, the minimum alphabet required for a semi-Dyck language to express any CFL, in order to be able to encode larger alphabets via inverse homomorphisms [Harrison, 1978], is one with two types of parentheses for a total of four elements—exactly what nucleic acids provide. However, nucleic acid secondary structure in fact represents a full or two-sided Dyck language, i.e. one for which corresponding parentheses facing *opposite* directions, as in (111b), can also pair. In addition, we know that non-orthodox secondary structure is allowed, such as pseudoknots, which are analogous to (111c). Thus, we must leave open the question as to what the exact expressive power of this paradigm may be, not to mention the question of whether any use is made of it *in vivo*.

8 Evolutionary Linguistics

Evolution is a process that provides many interesting complications in the linguistic analysis of biological systems, as suggested by the closure results observed for the evolutionary operators of (76). In this section we will investigate some of those complications, show how grammars may be applied to describe not only evolution itself but also algorithmic tools used to compare strings that have undergone evolutionary change, and finally, discuss the prospects of extending phylogenetic analysis from strings to languages.

8.1 Repetition and Infinite Languages

We have seen from the closure results given previously that typical evolutionary rearrangements may in the right circumstances lead to a "jump" up the Chomsky hierarchy. For example, duplications create copy languages, which are not CFLs. However, we must take care to note that, simply because a language contains strings with duplications, does not mean that it is greater than context-free—once again, unbounded duplications must be *required* (or, in an evolutionary sense, actively maintained) for this to be so.

In fact, it can be shown that, even in an RL, sufficiently long strings *must* contain substrings that are allowed to occur there as tandem repeats and still leave the resulting string within the given RL. To wit, for the FSA recognizing an RL to recognize any string longer than the number of nodes or states in that FSA, some of those nodes will of necessity be visited more than once, so that there must be a *cycle* in the directed graph of the FSA. This being the case, it must also be possible to traverse that cycle *any* number of times, and thus the original string can have any number of tandem repeats at that position, and still be guaranteed to be in the RL specified by that FSA. This reasoning, a variation on the "pigeonhole principle," is known as the *pumping lemma* for RLs. There is a similar result for the CFLs, commonly used to prove non-context-freeness, which essentially says that for sufficient-ly long strings derived from a context-free grammar some nonterminal must recur in the same subderivation, and this subderivation can thus be "pumped" any number of times.

This in itself need not have far-reaching consequences, since the repeat may only be of length one—in fact, simple gaps in the DCGs we have given satisfy the requirement. However, it does raise an issue related to the arbi-trary extent of the repeats. If an RL contains only strings shorter than the number of nodes in its FSA, it need not have a cycle, nor a tandem repeat. This would necessarily be a finite language, and in fact *any* finite language is an RL; this can be seen from the fact that a finite set of strings can be specified by a finite, regular grammar by simply listing every terminal string in the language as a disjunct arising from the start symbol.

Thus, if the language of DNA is indeed not regular, it must be infinite. This is an assumption that has been implicit in the grammars we have written to this point, which perhaps should be examined. It could be argued that the set of all DNA molecules (or genes, or genomes, etc.) that have ever existed is finite, so that the abstraction of the language of DNA is regular. However, recall that our preferred notion of language as abstraction deals with the *ca-pacity* of such languages to encompass all syntactically correct variations. DNA must be potentially non-regular, certainly to the extent one believes that it can specify an infinite variety of life—i.e. that there can be no com-plete list of possible genomes, such that no additional genome is imaginable that is different by even a single nucleotide from one already in the list. The fact of evolution adds particular force to this argument, when we realize that it is possible for the language to evolve entirely new capacities; indeed, it has apparently done this over time, e.g. at the point that eukaryotes arose.

It might also be argued that a biological language must constrain the lengths of strings, since there are practical problems with arbitrarily large genomes. For example, the bacteriophage lambda protein capsid places a limit on the size of the genome it must encapsulate; not much more than 50,000 nucleotides can physically fit inside. (In fact, a form of pumping lemma applies to this phage: since the total protein in the capsid exceeds the coding capacity of the genome, it follows that capsid proteins must be "repetitive", i.e. many identical proteins are employed in a crystalline array to achieve a large enough structure to contain the genome [Watson et al., 1987].) Thus, there would seem to be a finite number of possible phage lambda genomes. However, one can imagine mutations that alter the capsid proteins to allow an additional nucleotide insertion or two, and it becomes difficult to say where the limits are, in a system which contains the potential for respecifying the rules of its own game. Again, if we widen this to in-clude every species that could theoretically exist, a finite language is even harder to conceive, though there may be no formal nonexistence proof. In broader terms, even the alphabet is conceivably subject to change, as indeed may have occurred in prebiotic evolution.

Such discussions may only be of theoretical interest, since if any succinct specification is indeed possible for the potential combinatoric variation of even the relatively minuscule phage lambda genome, it may well require a powerful grammar that is "artificially" regularized with constraints, but which in outward form and every other respect is non-regular. The invocation of semantic constraint or selection might well serve this purpose. Retreating somewhat from this broadest possible abstraction, though, we can examine the case for infinite individual features, such as inverted repeats. There are probably only finitely many Type II restriction enzyme recognition sites, for example, since these are mostly inverted repeats either four or six nucleotides in length, which is about the limit of what these proteins can span on the DNA (ignoring for the moment the possibility of "changing the rules"). Are other inverted repeats of interest also limited in similar ways, e.g. is there a longest practicable stem structure in an RNA molecule? Even if a consensus for such an absolute maximum could be arrived at, it would seem that this misses the point that the self-embedding rule permitting unlimited recursion expresses the mechanical *capacity* of nucleic acids to form these structures in arbitrary lengths, and to properly capture the nested dependencies they entail.

We began this section by saying that the fact that strings in a language contain duplications does not imply that that language is not a CFL or RL. On the other hand, we can infer from the pumping lemmas that any CFL or infinite RL must allow strings with arbitrary numbers of duplications. It is only if direct repeats of arbitrary extent are for some reason required by the genome that it must be greater than context-free on this account. One sense in which duplications may be said to be required is an evolutionary one, since a primary mechanism of adaptation and change is for a gene to be duplicated and then for the copies to diverge. In fact, we can view the strings that are "pumped" in the pumping lemma as genes themselves, specified at a general enough level to allow divergence after they are duplicated. (They need not be completely general, though—a specific globin gene, for instance, can be thought of as having been pumped in this manner to create the globin gene regions.) For that matter, a diploid genome itself may be said to be a copy language, with the duplication required for the generation of diversity by recombination between homologous chromosomes.

The argument that duplications are required since they reflect a mechanism of evolution is somewhat indirect, if not circular; we could make a stronger case that the functional language of DNA is greater than context-free if functional duplications were required by the physiology of the cell. One example might be immunoglobulin variable region gene copies; though they are not exact duplicates, they serve the same function and their arrangement is required to generate diversity economically. Gene *amplification* is another mechanism whereby gene copy numbers (in this case, exact copies) increase or decrease according to physiological demand. Once again, we see that the *generation* of specific such duplications can occur by pumping RLs or CFLs, but any *requirement* that duplications of arbitrary composition be a feature of a general functional language in order for organisms to survive would seem to raise the abstracted language beyond context-free.

8.2 Mutation and Rearrangement

A simple point mutation can be modelled grammatically by a rule that produces a side effect on the input string, e.g. through the use of terminal replacement in DCGs:

$$\texttt{point\_mutation([From],[To]), [To] --> [From].} \qquad (112)$$

This rule consumes no net input, but effectively just overwrites the base *From* with *To*. Such rules can be used in actual derivations by leaving uninstantiated the remainder portion of the difference list or span, e.g.

$$\texttt{(\_, point\_mutation(X,Y), \_) ==> Input/Output.} \qquad (113)$$

where *Input* but not *Output* is initially bound, will produce every version of *Input* in which X's have been mutated to Y's. We can write other grammars to delete and insert bases:

```
deletion(X) --> [X].
insertion(X), [X] --> [].                              (114)
```

We can also generalize these rules for single base mutations to use string variables instead for "block" mutations, e.g.

$$\texttt{substitution(From,To), To --> From.} \qquad (115)$$

With this expanded repertoire, we can succinctly represent a range of genomic rearrangements that occur on an evolutionary scale, corresponding to the formal definitions of (76):

```
duplication, X, X --> X.
inversion, ~X --> X.
transposition, Y, X --> X, Y.                          (116)
deletion --> X.
```

This then allows us to write the most "top-level" rule of all, that for evolution itself:

```
evolution --> [] | event, evolution.
event, X --> X,                                        (117)
(inversion | deletion | transposition | duplication).
```

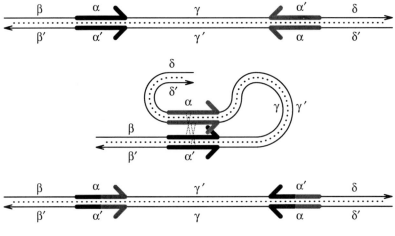

Figure 25. Inversion

This simply states that *evolution* consists of an *event* followed by more evolution. The rule for *event* is just a disjunctive list of possible rearrangements, and the variable X allows for arbitrary excursions down the molecule to the site where the event is to occur. We have employed a version of this grammar, which uses a random number generator for event and site selection, to simulate such evolution at the level of blocks of sequence.

More sophisticated rearrangements can also be described. For instance, an arbitrary number of duplications and reduplications can be accomplished with

```
duplication, X, X --> X | duplication, X.          (118)
```

which consumes a string and replaces two copies, but can also recursively call itself first. Combined with other forms of mutation, such a rule could, for instance, model saltatory replication involving duplications of duplications, etc., postulated to occur in mouse satellite DNA evolution [Lewin, 1987].

Some inversions are thought to occur as a result of homologous recombination between inverted repeats, as illustrated in Figure 25; examples include the tail protein of phage *Mu*, and the flagellar antigen of *Salmonella* [Watson et al., 1987]. This situation can be described using what amounts to a literally context-sensitive rule (though it is in fact unrestricted in format):

```
inversion, R, ~I, ~R --> R, I, ~R.          (119)
```

Similarly, regions between direct repeats, such as transposable elements, may be excised as circular elements, as shown in Figure 26. Excision can be

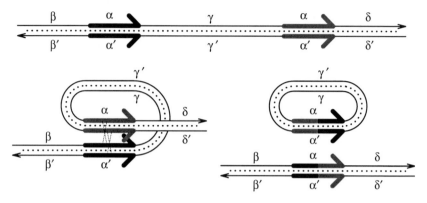

Figure 26. Excision and Integration

specified using string variable replacement, returning the excised circular fragment as a parameter, O:

$$excision(O), \ S \ \text{-->} \ S, \ X, \ S, \quad (120)$$
$$\{(S,X)\text{==>}O/O\}.$$

We concatenate S and X using recursive derivation *generatively*, i.e. running the parse backwards. What is more, the structure that is generated, O/O, is a Prolog list that has itself as its own remainder, that is, a circular list. While these are awkward to handle in practice, they allow us to write a rule for the reverse reaction, that of a site-specific *integration* of a circular molecule at some substring S which it has in common with a linear molecule:

$$integration(O), \ S, \ X, \ S \ \text{-->} \ S, \quad (121)$$
$$\{(\_,S,X,S,\_)\text{==>}O/O\}.$$

These and other grammars describing genome-level rearrangements are described in greater detail in [Searls, 1989a]. Our experience indicates that seemingly arbitrary such rearrangements can be quite concisely specified using SVGs. Though in a pure logic implementation they are not practical for large scale parsing, the grammar framework should be a good one in which to house more efficient lower-level algorithms to make this practicable, in a manner that will be described below.

Many of the rules in this section are unrestricted in format, though the string variables complicate the analysis somewhat. However, we can see that in one sense any grammar describing evolutionary change must in fact be greater than context-sensitive, by examining the phenomenon of recursive duplication as suggested by the grammar of (118). The ability to create any number of duplications of arbitrary substrings on the input indicates that no linear-bounded automaton could recognize such a language, since these automata are limited to space which is linear in the size of the input, while the grammars can "grow" a given input string to an arbitrary extent. This does not mean that the strings of a language which is the *product* of an evolutionary grammar are necessarily greater than context-sensitive, since we have seen that we can recognize any number of direct repeats with an SVG that falls within the ILs.

8.3 Comparison of Strings

The use of grammars for sophisticated pattern-matching search was proposed above, where it was also demonstrated that they are likely to be better-suited to the domain, at least in terms of expressive power, than current regular-expression based systems. Another form of search that is even more prevalent in molecular biology, however, is based on the detection of similarities between strings, rather than between a pattern and a string.

In the example grammars given above, it was seen that a simple cost function could be used to allow some degree of mismatching in the course of a parse. Generalizing this to allow not only base substitutions but insertions and deletions (collectively, *indels*) we can conceive of a derivation from string to string, e.g.

$$\text{``gaataattcggctta''\$Cost ==> ``gacttattcgttagaa''} \qquad (122)$$

where the "cost" would be, for instance, the *string edit distance* between the strings, or the total number of substitutions and indels required in the derivation; note how this linguistic formulation is different than the input/output model of mutation described above. We can implement this as a DCG:

```
[]$0 --> [].
[H|T]$Cost --> [H], T$Cost.      % bases match; zero cost
[H|T]$Cost --> [X], {X\==H}, T$Sub, {Cost is Sub+1}.
[_|T]$Cost --> T$Ins, {Cost is Ins+1}.              (123)
String$Cost --> [_], String$Del, {Cost is Del+1}.
```

However, there will be a very large number of such parses, of which we are only interested in the minimum cost parse. The corresponding minimal parse tree will indicate a probable *alignment* between the initial and terminal string, which may be significant should they be evolutionarily related. We can use the Prolog "bagof" operation to collect all parses and determine the minimum:

```
best(From$Cost ==> To)  :-
     bagof(Cost,(From$Cost ==> To),Bag),            (124)
     minimum(Bag,Cost).
```

```
Str1$Cost --> input(Str0),       % consult chart first
    {chart(Str0,Str1,Cost-Move)}, !,
    path(Move,Str1).
_$0 --> [].                      % end of input string
[]$0 --> _.                      % end of test string
[X|Y]$Cost --> input([H|T]),     % recursively find best path
    { Y$Sub0 ==> T, (X==Y -> Sub=Sub0; Sub is Sub0+1),
      [X|Y]$Ins0 ==> T, Ins is Ins0+1,
      Y$Del0 ==> [H|T], Del is Del0+1,
      minimum([Sub-sub,Ins-ins,Del-del],Cost-Move),
      assert(chart([H|T],[X|Y],Cost-Move)), ! },
    path(Move,[X|Y]).


input(S,S,S).    % extracts input list from difference lists


path(sub,[_|R]) --> [_], R$_.    % performs specified types
path(ins,X) --> [_], X$_.        % of moves on input string
path(del,[_|R]) --> R$_.         % relative to initial string
```

Figure 27. A Dynamic Programming Alignment Grammar

but this is of exponential complexity, due to the large amount of wasteful backtracking and reparsing entailed. We have investigated the characteristics of CKY-based algorithms for finding the minimum-cost parse, and find that this can be accomplished in $O(n^3)$ time, with the performance improving the better the fit of the original strings [Searls, unpublished results]. Others have described "error-correcting" parsers based on Earley's algorithm that will find minimum cost parses for arbitrary grammars (not just the string derivations above), also in $O(n^3)$ time [Aho and Peterson, 1972].

These results compare unfavorably with dynamic programming algorithms for minimum-distance alignment that are currently used in molecular biology, which execute in $O(n^2)$ time, and can be further improved by techniques involving preprocessing, hashing, suffix trees, etc. However, the parsing algorithms offer the opportunity for generalization to pattern-matching search at a higher level of abstraction than terminal strings, for instance permitting differential weighting of features, mutations involving entire features, and so on. Moreover, we have also been able to implement several traditional "algorithmic" approaches in grammar form, such as the dynamic programming alignment algorithm given in Figure 27.

This implementation of the simplest form of distance-optimal alignment algorithm [Sellers, 1974] uses the Prolog database to record current best scores and "moves" at each position of a comparison matrix between two strings, and prevents reparsing the same path multiple times. This grammar is clearly not optimal, and in fact it is not likely that any list-structured language could compete with procedural languages, but the ease and flexibility of the approach suggest the utility of grammars for rapid prototyping and modification of such algorithms. We have done this with a number of algorithms not ordinarily thought of as amenable to parsing, such as Fast Fourier Transforms [Searls, 1989b]. When embedded in higher-level grammars, the algorithms can then be tuned at leisure and eventually replaced with procedural code or hardware, while retaining the linguistic framework where hierarchical abstraction is of greatest benefit. As noted, we are exploring such an approach that would use signal processing hardware to implement primitive operations on string variables very efficiently [Cheever et al., 1991].

8.4 Phylogeny of Languages

Once we have embraced the notion of languages described abstractly rather than as collections of instances, we can perhaps begin to extend to the former more of the analytical tools already applied to the latter. One such tool would be phylogenetic trees, which are currently developed in general for single genes treated as strings. As illustrated at the left in Figure 28, representative strings from different species may be compared to find all the pairwise evolutionary distances, and then a tree created which postulates ancestral sequences and connections among them in such a way as to, for example, minimize the total change required. Exactly how such trees should be constructed, and distances between strings measured, is controversial and an area of active research, but it would seem that any effective notion of distance between two objects ought to conform to the basic mathematical axioms of a *metric space*; given some function δ which measures the distance between a and b, this would require that:

$$\delta(a,b) = \delta(b,a) \qquad \qquad symmetry$$

$$\delta(a,b) = 0 \;\; iff \;\; a=b \qquad \qquad identity \qquad (125)$$

$$\delta(a,b) \leq \delta(a,c) + \delta(c,b) \qquad triangle\ inequality$$

In fact, many (but not all) common methods of measuring string edit distances based on simple mutational models do adhere to these axioms.

Consider the possibility of a phylogenetic tree of languages which, instead of measuring degree of mutational change over individual strings, somehow measured distances between abstracted descriptions, e.g. grammars. Thus, it might be possible to focus the concept of evolutionary distance at a higher level, for instance describing major rearrangements as in the evolutionary grammars above, but perhaps also dealing with structural and functional aspects of the differences between organisms and groups of organisms. This

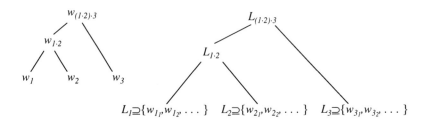

Figure 28. Phylogenetic Trees of Strings (left) and Languages (right)

idea is illustrated at the right in Figure 28, where the leaves of the tree represent sets of strings rather than individual strings. While one could in theory simply collect all the genomes from each of a number of individuals in a species and call this the language, we can by now see the virtues of concise, possibly grammar-based descriptions that freely allow variation within a species and constrain only what is critical to the "definition" of that species. Putting aside for the moment the known difficulties of such grammatical inference, we consider some of the formal consequences of such an idea.

We see first that, while the languages we are creating for each species will have many characteristics in common, they should nevertheless be pairwise disjoint; any language that claims to describe horses should contain no instance of a human being, and vice versa. Moreover, the non-leaf languages describing postulated ancestors should also in general be disjoint from present-day species. That is, we must avoid the mistake of inferring ancestors that simply *subsume* all their descendants, or else we will not have captured descriptions of change. Note, however, that we may choose to compare languages other than those of species. By generalizing languages to higher taxonomic levels, e.g. for eukaryotes versus prokaryotes, we would be distinguishing much more fundamental cellular machinery than we would by generalizing only to the level of humans versus chimpanzees, or even vertebrates versus invertebrates.

Finally, we would need a distance metric δ acting over languages, or grammars specifying those languages. With this, however, we can see some potential difficulties should the languages in question be non-regular. For we know that, given arbitrary CFLs or CSLs L_1 and L_2, it is in general undecidable whether $L_1 = L_2$. How, then, can we establish a δ which we are assured does not violate the identity axiom of (123b) whenever $\delta(L_1, L_2) = 0$? Thus, languages may not be so easy to compare. In fact, it is also undecidable whether L_1 and L_2 are pairwise disjoint, so we may not even be able to tell if our languages or their ancestors are truly distinct.

Thus, while the ideal of comparing abstract descriptions of genes or genomes holds great appeal, there are serious practical and theoretical problems to be overcome. Nevertheless, there are many avenues to explore, such as restricting the comparison to regular aspects of these languages, perhaps by confining the area of interest to specific phenomena. This approach has been used by [Overton and Pastor, 1991; Pastor, Koile and Overton, 1991], who restrict their attention to instantiated parse trees describing major features of genes and their regulatory regions in predicting the locations of those features in novel genes. Another approach is to focus on simple lexical and prelexical elements, following the methodology of the field of classical linguistics where prototypic languages are inferred from changes in basic vocabulary sets. Similar techniques have been used for biological sequences, for instance, by [Brendel et al., 1986; Pietrokovski et al., 1990]. As for the methodology of inducing grammars, a recent proposal would use logic grammar "domain descriptions" of DNA regulatory regions as a starting point for connectionist learning programs, which would in effect "tune" the general grammar by modifying and refining it [Noordewier and Shavlik, personal communication]. Others have used model-based learning to derive grammar-like descriptions of signal peptides [Gascuel and Danchin, 1988], and grammatical inference techniques to study *E. coli* promoter sequences [Park and Huntsberger, 1990] and 5'-splice sites in eukaryotic mRNAs [Kudo et al., 1987].

9 Conclusion

"Precisely constructed models for linguistic structure can play an important role, both negative and positive, in the process of discovery itself. By pushing a precise but inadequate formulation to an unacceptable conclusion, we can often expose the exact nature of this inadequacy and, consequently, gain a deeper understanding of the linguistic data. More positively, a formalized theory may automatically provide solutions for many problems other than those for which it was explicitly designed." [Chomsky, 1957]

Treating genes and potentially entire genomes as languages holds great appeal in part because it raises the possibility of producing concise generalizations about the information contained in biological sequences and how it is "packaged". One hopes that grammars used for this purpose would comprise a model of some underlying physical objects and processes, and that grammars may in fact serve as an appropriate tool for theory formation and testing, in the linguistic tradition. This article has suggested a number of ways in which this might occur, many of which are summarized below:

Parse trees may reflect secondary structure. It is considered a virtue of natural language grammars for their parse trees to capture schematically some inherent structure of a sentence (see, for example [Gazdar, 1985]). The reader is invited to draw parse trees from some of the orthodox secondary structure grammars of section 2.4, and observe how remarkably their outlines conform to the actual physical structures described. As we have noted, this extends also to alternative secondary structures, modelled by ambiguous grammars.

Grammar nonterminals might model biochemical entities. For example, nonterminals representing DNA-binding proteins could "rewrite" as the appropriate consensus binding sites, which would be especially useful in cases where proteins or protein complexes bind several sites and bring them into physical proximity as a result. Such complexes, and indeed other "layered" protein-protein interactions as well (e.g. the complement cascade in immunology [Watson et al., 1987]), could also be modelled hierarchically by grammars.

Grammar rules could describe intra-molecular interactions. The nonterminals in secondary structure grammars can be viewed as representing the hydrogen bonding between complementary bases. Generalizing this, other forms of chemical interaction or dependencies between distant sites in a macromolecule could be modelled, as suggested above for protein structure. Just as parse trees can depict secondary structure, more complex structures might be specified quite literally using grammar formalisms from the field of syntactic pattern recognition in which terminals are actually two- or three-dimensional subgraphs connected by derivation [Fu, 1982].

Greater-than-context-free grammars can model mutation and evolution. As was seen in section 2.8.2, rules producing side-effects on the input string can capture these processes, and the ability of such grammars to take account of lexical elements (i.e. "contexts") that could control such processes is particularly attractive. *Transformational grammar,* subsequently developed by Chomsky to account for, among other things, "movement" phenomena in natural language, might also be useful in describing the allowable variations on the *deep structure,* or canonical syntax, of a gene (together, perhaps, with its regulatory elements [Collado-Vides, 1989a,b]).

Grammar derivation could model gene expression. The notion of successful derivation from a gene grammar being analogous to the expression of that gene in the cell was discussed at length in section 2.7. In this model, nonterminals thus represent gene products and their component parts, or, in the context of gene regulation, the aggregate of lexical and "environmental" elements required to accomplish expression at a given time and place.

Parsing might mimic certain biochemical processes. Such environmental elements of gene expression are of course problematic, but we have suggested elsewhere how parsing might yet be a suitable simulation tool for these control systems [Searls, 1988]. It is interesting to note how recursive rules in a left-to right parser resemble the physical action of certain *processive* enzymes that travel along nucleic acid molecules, even in some cases performing a kind of "backtracking" error correction. The suitability of even more basic language-theoretic operations for depicting biological processes like replication and recombination was noted in section 2.5.

Besides the potential role of linguistic tools in modelling of biological systems, we have also discussed at length the use of grammars for specification (both of sequence elements and of algorithms), pattern-matching search, and as abstractions that could lead to insights about the organization of genetic information and its tractability to computational approaches. It seems clear that the detection and analysis of genes and other features of the genome could benefit from parser technology and a general awareness of the linguistic properties of the domain. The notion of a comprehensive grammar describing the genome or even individual genes in their full generality is clearly quixotic, but the effort to approach this ideal may yet afford a better understanding of what is surely a fundamentally linguistic domain.

Acknowledgements

The author wishes to thank Drs. Lynette Hirschman and Chris Overton for careful reading of early drafts and, along with Drs. Erik Cheever, Rebecca Passonneau, and Carl Weir, for many helpful discussions. The author is also grateful to Dr. Ross Overbeek and his student Ron Taylor, and to Drs. Mick Noordewier and Jude Shavlik, for acquainting him with their work in progress. Invaluable comments and suggestions were provided by Jim Tisdall in the area of formal language theory. A special debt is owed to Dr. Allen Sears for his enthusiastic patronage of these efforts. This work was supported in part by the Department of Energy, Office of Energy Research, under genome grant number DE-FG02-90ER60998.

Note

[*] Abbreviations used: BNF: Backus-Naur form; CFL: context-free language; CSL: context-sensitive language; CKY: Cocke-Kasami-Younger (parsing algorithm); DCG: definite clause grammar; FSA: finite state au-

tomaton; GSM: generalized sequential machine; IL: indexed language; L-system: Lindenmayer system; PDA: pushdown automaton; RL: regular language; SVG: string variable grammar.

Bibliography

J. P. Abrahams, M. van den Berg, E. van Batenburg, and C. Pleij. Prediction of RNA Secondary Structure, Including Pseudoknotting, by Computer Simulation. *Nucleic Acids Res.* 18:3035-3044, 1990.

A. V. Aho and T. G. Peterson. A Minimum Distance Error-correcting Parser for Context-free Languages. *SIAM J. Comput.* 1(4):305-312, 1972.

J. F. Allen. Maintaining Knowledge about Temporal Intervals. *Comm. of the ACM* 26:832-843, 1983.

J. F. Allen. *Natural Language Understanding.* Benjamin/Cummings, Menlo Park, 1987.

V. Brendel and H. G. Busse. Genome Structure Described by Formal Languages. *Nucleic Acids Res.* 12:2561-2568, 1984.

V. Brendel, J. S. Beckmann, and E. N. Trifinov. Linguistics of Nucleotide Sequences: Morphology and Comparison of Vocabularies. *J. Biomol. Struct. Dynamics* 4:11-21, 1986.

J. Bresnan, R. Kaplan, S. Peters, and A. Zaenen. Cross-serial Dependencies in Dutch. *Linguistic Inquiry* 13:613-636, 1982.

E. A. Cheever, G. C. Overton, and D. B. Searls. Fast Fourier Transform-based Correlation of DNA Sequences Using Complex Plane Encoding. *Comput. Applic. Biosci.* 7(2)143-159, 1991.

N. Chomsky. *The Logical Structure of Linguistic Theory.* The University of Chicago Press, Chicago (1975), 1955.

N. Chomsky. *Syntactic Structures.* Mouton, The Hague, 1957.

N. Chomsky. On Certain Formal Properties of Grammars. *Informat. Control* 2:137-167, 1959.

N. Chomsky. Formal Properties of Grammars. In D. Luce, R. Bush, and E. Galanter, editors, *Handbook of Mathematical Psychology II.* John Wiley & Sons, New York, 1963.

N. Chomsky and M. P. Schutzenberger. The Algebraic Theory of Context-free Languages. In P. Braffort and D. Hirschberg, editors, *Computer Program–ming and Formal Systems,* pp. 118–161. North-Holland, Amsterdam, 1963.

N. Chomsky. *Aspects of the Theory of Syntax.* MIT Press, Cambridge, 1965.

J. Collado-Vides. A Transformational-grammar Approach to the Study of the Regulation of Gene Expression. *J. Theor. Biol.* 136:403-425, 1989a.

J. Collado-Vides. Towards a Grammatical Paradigm for the Study of the Regulation of Gene Expression. In B. Goodwin and P. Saunders, editors, *Theoretical Biology: Epigenetic and Evolutionary Order,* pages 211-224. Edinburgh University Press, 1989b.

J. Collado-Vides. A Syntactic Representation of Units of Genetic Information. *J. Theor. Biol.* 148:401-429, 1991a.

J. Collado-Vides. The Search for a Grammatical Theory of Gene Regulation Is Formally Justified by Showing the Inadequacy of Context-free Frammars. *Comput. Applic. Biosci.* 7(3):321-326, 1991b.

W. Ebeling and M. A. Jimenez-Montano. On Grammars, Complexity, and Information Measures of Biological Macromolecules. *Math. Biosci.* 52:53-71, 1980.

K. S. Fu. *Syntactic Pattern Recognition and Applications.* Prentice-Hall, Englewood Cliffs, 1982.

O. Gascuel and A. Danchin. Data Analysis Using a Learning Program, a Case Study: An Application of PLAGE to a Biological Sequence Analysis. In *Proceedings of the 8th European Conference on Artificial Intelligence*, pages 390-395, 1988.

D. Gautheret, F. Major, and R. Cedergren. Pattern Searching/Alignment with RNA Primary and Secondary Structures: An Effective Descriptor for tRNA. *Comput. Applic. Biosci.* 6(4):325-331, 1990.

G. Gazdar. Applicability of Indexed Grammars to Natural Languages. CSLI-85-34, Center for the Study of Language and Information, Stanford, 1985.

M. A. Harrison. *Introduction to Formal Language Theory.* Addison-Wesley, Reading, 1978.

T. Head. Formal Language Theory and DNA: An Analysis of the Generative Capacity of Specific Recombinant Behaviors. *Bull. math. Biol.* 49(6):737-759, 1987.

J. E. Hopcroft and J. D. Ullman. *Introduction to Automata Theory, Languages, and Computation.* Addison-Wesley, Reading, 1979.

M. A. Jimenez-Montano. On the Syntactic Structure of Protein Sequences and the Concept of Grammar Complexity. *Bull. math. Biol.* 46(4):641-659, 1984.

M. M. Konarska and P. A. Sharp. Structure of RNAs Replicated by the DNA-dependent T7 RNA polymerase. *Cell* 63:609-618, 1990.

M. Kudo, Y. Iida, and M. Shimbo. Syntactic Pattern Analysis of 5'-splice Site Sequences of mRNA Precursors in Higher Eukaryotic Genes. *Comput. Applic. Biosci.* 3(4):319-324, 1987.

R. H. Lathrop, T. A. Webster, and T. F. Smith. Ariadne: Pattern-directed Inference and Hierarchical Abstraction in Protein Structure Recognition. *Comm. of the ACM* 30:909-921, 1987.

B. Lewin. *Genes.* John Wiley & Sons, Inc., New York, third edition, 1987.

A. Lindenmayer. Mathematical Models for Cellular Interaction in Develop–ment. *J. Theor. Biol.* 18:280-315, 1968.

G. C. Overton and J. A. Pastor. A Platform for Applying Multiple Machine-learning Strategies to the Task of Understanding Gene Structure. In *Proceedings of the 7th Conference on Artificial Intelligence Applications*, pages 450-457. IEEE, 1991.

K. Park and T. L. Huntsberger. Inference of Context-free Grammars for Syntactic Analysis of DNA Sequences. In *AAAI Spring Symposium Series*, Stanford, 1990. American Association for Artificial Intelligence.

J. A. Pastor, K. Koile, and G. C. Overton. Using Analogy to Predict Functional Regions on Genes. In *Proceedings of the 24th Hawaii International Conference on System Science*, pages 615-625, 1991.

S. Pietrokovski, J. Hirshon, and E. N. Trifonov. Linguistic Measure of Taxonomic and Functional Relatedness of Nucleotide Sequences. *J. Biomol. Struct. and Dyn.* 7(6):1251-1268, 1990.

F. C. N. Pereira and S. M. Shieber. *Prolog and Natural-Language Analysis.* Center for the Study of Language and Information, Stanford, 1987.

F. C. N. Pereira and D. H. D. Warren. Definite Clause Grammars for Language Analysis. *Artif. Intell.* 13:231-278, 1980.

P. A. Pevzner, M. Y. Borodovsky, and A. A. Mironov. Linguistics of Nucleotide Sequences: I. The Significance of Deviation from Mean Statistical Characteristics and Prediction of the Frequency of Occurence of Words. *J. Biomol. Struct. and Dyn.*, 6:1013-1026, 1989a.

P. A. Pevzner, M. Y. Borodovsky, and A. A. Mironov. Linguistics of Nucleotide Sequences: II. Stationary Words in Genetic Texts and Zonal Structure of DNA. *J. Biomol. Struct. and Dyn.*, 6:1027-1038, 1989b.

C. W. A. Pleij. Pseudoknots: A New Motif in the RNA Game. *Trends in the Biosci.* 15:143-147, 1990.

P. M. Postal and D. T. Langendoen. English and the Class of Context-free Languages. *Computational Linguistics* 10:177-181, 187-188, 1984.

P. Prusinkiewicz and J. Hanan. *Lindenmayer Systems, Fractals, and Plants*, volume 79 of *Lecture Notes in Biomathematics*. Springer-Verlag, New York, 1989.

S. M. Schieber. Evidence Against the Context-freeness of Natural Language. *Linguistics and Philosophy* 8:333-343, 1985.

J. L. Schroeder and F. R. Blattner. Formal Description of a DNA Oriented Computer Language. *Nucleic Acids Res.* 10:69, 1982.

D. B. Searls. Representing Genetic Information with Formal Grammars. In *Proceedings of the 7th National Conference on Artificial Intelligence*, pages 386-391. American Association for Artificial Intelligence, 1988.

D. B. Searls. Investigating the Linguistics of DNA with Definite Clause Grammars. In E. Lusk and R. Overbeek, editors, *Logic Programming: Proceedings of the North American Conference on Logic Programming*, volume 1, pages 189-208. Association for Logic Programming, 1989a.

D. B. Searls. Signal Processing with Logic Grammars. *Intelligent Systems Rev.* 1(4):67-88, 1989b.

D. B. Searls and S. Liebowitz. Logic Grammars as a Vehicle for Syntactic Pattern Recognition. In *Proceedings of the Workshop on Syntactic and Structural Pattern Recognition*, pages 402-422. International Association for Pattern Recognition, 1990.

D. B. Searls and M. O. Noordewier. Pattern-matching Search of DNA Sequences Using Logic Grammars. In *Proceedings of the 7th Conference on Artificial Intelligence Applications*, pages 3-9. IEEE, 1991.

P. H. Sellers. On the Theory and Computation of Evolutionary Distances. *SIAM J. Appl. Math.* 26:787-793, 1974.

B. Shanon. The Genetic Code and Human Language. *Synthese* 39:401-415, 1978.

T. A. Sudkamp. *Languages and Machines*. Addison-Wesley, Reading, 1988.

J. D. Watson, N. H. Hopkins, J. W. Roberts, J. A. Steitz, and A. M. Weiner. *Molecular Biology of the Gene*. Benjamin/Cummings, Menlo Park, 1987.

3

Neural Networks, Adaptive Optimization, and RNA Secondary Structure Prediction

Evan W. Steeg

1 Introduction

The RNA secondary structure prediction problem ($2°RNA$) is a critical one in molecular biology. Secondary structure can be determined directly by x-ray diffraction, but this is difficult, slow, and expensive. Moreover, it is currently impossible to crystallize most RNAs. Mathematical models for prediction have therefore been developed and these have led to serial (and some parallel) computer algorithms, but these too are expensive in terms of computation time. The general solution has asymptotic running time exponential in N (i.e., proportional to 2^N), where N is the length of the RNA sequence. Serial approximation algorithms which employ heuristics and make strong assumptions are significantly faster, on the order of N^3 or N^4, but their predictive success rates are low — often less than 40 percent — and even these algorithms can run for days when processing very long (thousands of bases) RNA sequences. Neural network algorithms that perform a multiple constraint satisfaction search using a massively parallel network of simple processors may provide accurate and very fast solutions.

This paper describes research into neural network algorithms for the prediction of RNA secondary structure from knowledge of the primary structure. Some background on both the computer science and molecular biology aspects of the problem is provided, new methods are proposed, and the results of some simple, preliminary experiments are described [Steeg, 1989].

There are several goals motivating research into this area:

1. A fast and accurate algorithm for predicting RNA secondary structure is sought. It is hoped that an approach that formalizes the problem explicitly as an optimization problem and that incorporates a fine-grained parallelism and the machine learning ability of neural networks will lead to a good algorithm.

2. It is an interesting test of the ability of a neural net (and in particular the MFT neural net) to learn some of the key parameters of a natural structure-to-structure mapping, in this case RNA primary structure to secondary structure. Fast learning and good generalization are among the important goals in the learning experiments.

3. Finally, the work described may be thought of as an early testing ground for neural network and other parallel distributed processing (PDP) methods in molecular structure prediction — the $2°RNA$ problem is related to the more difficult problems of the prediction of protein secondary and tertiary structure.

1.2 Organization of the Chapter

In Section 2, the RNA secondary structure prediction problem is introduced, and the necessary mathematical definitions and physical and chemical terms are explained.

Section 3 defines the problem more formally in terms of a general class of search problems. The most commonly used search algorithms are discussed, and then a few of the most successful or important serial RNA secondary structure prediction algorithms are described in this context. This provides a brief historical summary of previous work within a unified formal framework.

Our methods are described in Section 4. We discuss neural networks and the particular class of Hopfield nets, Boltzmann Machines, and Mean Field Theory (MFT) networks used in our research. We then define the mapping of the $2°RNA$ problem onto the network, and explain the biochemical and physical assumptions implicit in our approach in terms of a simple graph theory problem. Finally, reference is made to some previous work in *protein* structure prediction with neural networks in order to illustrate the issue of representation of constraints.

Section 5 describes the results of the experiments. There is an analysis of the basic models employed in terms of speed of convergence, speed of learn-

ing, generalization abilities, accuracy of structure prediction, stability of solutions, and hardware/memory complexity.

Conclusions about the theory and experiments are offered in Section 6,
along with some proposals for future work.

2 Secondary Structure of RNA: Its Importance and Methods of Determination

A molecule of RNA consists of a long chain of subunits, called ribonu-
cleotides. Each ribonucleotide contains one of four possible bases: adenine,
guanine, cytosine, or uracil (abbreviated as A,G,C,U respectively). It is this
sequence of bases, known as the *primary structure* of the RNA, that distinguishes one RNA from another.

Under normal physiological conditions, a ribonucleotide chain can bend
back upon itself, and the bases can hydrogen-bond with one another, such
that the molecule forms a coiled and looped structure. The pattern of hydrogen bonding is generally called the *secondary structure*, while the conformation of the molecule in 3-dimensional space is called the *tertiary structure.*
The base-to-base interactions that form the RNA secondary structure are primarily of two kinds — hydrogen bonding between G and C and hydrogen
bonding between A and U, as was first described by Watson and Crick in
[1953]. (See Figure 1.) In fact, there is evidence of non-Watson-Crick base-
pairing in such nucleic acids as the tRNAs, but these are considered to derive
from the tertiary structure produced by large regions of secondary structure
containing Watson-Crick basepairing. For the sake of simplicity, such base-
pairing is mostly ignored in this paper.

Genetic information, the set of instructions that directs cell maintenance,
growth, differentiation, and proliferation, is encoded in DNA molecules.
RNA serves two biological purposes: It is the means by which information
flows from DNA into the production of proteins, the catalysts and building
blocks of cells; it also acts as a structural component of ribosomes and other
complexes. It is the secondary structure, and the resulting tertiary structure,
that determine how the RNA will interact and react with other cell components.

Work on the determination of RNA secondary structure has been carried
out for decades by a number of research groups. The classical approach is direct observation of a molecule's secondary structure using X-ray crystallography. More indirect methods involve specific cleavage of the RNA by enzymes called ribonucleases. Much research has gone into the promising
approach of computational *prediction* of secondary structure from knowledge of primary structure. The general method has been to search for
configurations of maximum base-pairing or of minimum free energy.

There are two basic problems encountered in the prediction approach.

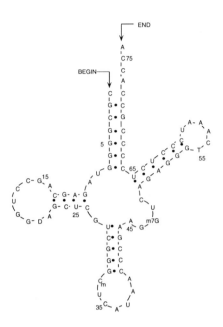

Figure 1. The figure is a 2-d representation of a tRNA molecule. The dots between bases (letters) represent basepairing. The numbers represent the numbering of bases in the sequence. (After [Sankoff et al. 1983]).

First is the need for accurate measures of the free energies of the various possible substructural components — of individual basepairs as well as stems, loops, and bulges. Second, the space of possible secondary structures for a given sequence is extremely large; a systematic search through all possible configurations for a minimum-energy structure can be prohibitively slow even on fast computers.

2.1 Structure and Free Energy—A Mathematical Model

We represent[1] an RNA molecule as a sequence S of symbols : $s_1 \, s_2 \ldots s_n$, where s_i is one of G,C,A, or U. A subsequence of S may be called a "sequence" where no confusion will occur. A sequence or subsequence may also be called a "string".

Given a sequence S, we represent the secondary structure of S by the upper right triangular submatrix of an *n*-by-*n* matrix **A**. A_{ij} is 1 if *paired(i, j)*, i.e., (for $i < j$), if the bases at positions i and j in the sequence are paired, and is 0 otherwise. (See Figure 3.) The secondary structure may then also be represented by a list **P** of pairs, where (i, j) is in **P** if and only if *paired(i, j)*. A pairing itself will sometimes be referred to as $i \bullet j$.

The subsequence from s_i to s_j is written $[\mathbf{i}, \mathbf{j}]$. A subsequence is *proper* with respect to a secondary structure P if, for every paired element in the subsequence, its partner is also in the subsequence. If $i \bullet j$ is a pair and $i < r < j$ then we say $i \bullet j$ *surrounds* r. Likewise $i \bullet j$ *surrounds* $r \bullet s$ if it surrounds both r and s. (The rule against knots dictates that given $r \bullet s$, if $i \bullet j$ surrounds either r or s, then it surrounds both.) Subsequence $[\mathbf{i}, \mathbf{j}]$ is closed with respect to a structure P if (i, j) in P. A pair $p \bullet q$ or an element r in proper string $[\mathbf{i}, \mathbf{j}]$ is *accessible* in $[\mathbf{i}, \mathbf{j}]$ if it is not surrounded by any pair in $[\mathbf{i}, \mathbf{j}]$ except possibly $i \bullet j$. It is accessible from $i \bullet j$ if i and j are paired. A *cycle* c is a set consisting of a *closing pair* $i \bullet j$ and all pairs $p \bullet q$ and unpaired elements r accessible to it.

We can distinguish two kinds of constraints on the forming of an RNA secondary structure: *hard* and *soft* constraints (*constraints* and *costs* are the terms often used in optimization work). Hard constraints dictate that certain kinds of pairings cannot occur at all; soft constraints are those imposed by thermodynamics upon the classes of possible structures. Hard constraints determine which structures are "legal"; soft constraints determine which structures are *optimal.*. The hard constraints are:

1. (Watson-Crick pairing): If **P** contains (i, j) then s_i and s_j are either G and C, or C and G, or A and U, or U and A. (This may be easily extended to include the relatively rare GU pairings.)

2. There is no overlap of pairs. If **P** contains (i, j), then it cannot contain (i, k) if $k \neq j$ or (k, j) if $k \neq i$.

3. For all i, (i, i) cannot be in **P**.

4. Knots are not allowed: If $h < i < j < k$, then **P** cannot contain both (h, j) and (i, k).

5. No sharp loops are allowed: If **P** contains (i, j), then i and j are at least 4 bases apart.

The soft constraint on possible secondary structures **P** for **S** is simple: **S** will assume the secondary structure **P** that has *minimum free energy*.

A secondary structure **P** for **S** can be described in a natural and unique way as composed of substructures of four kinds: loops, bulges, stacked pairs (a stack of pairs is called a *stem*), and external single-stranded regions. The *cycles* of **P** are its loops, bulges, and stacked pairs. It is useful here to provide some definitions of cycles.

1. If **P** contains $i \bullet j$, $(i + 1) \bullet (j - 1)$, ... $(i + h) \bullet (j - h)$, each of these pairs (except the last) is said to *stack* on the following pair. Two or more such consecutive pairs is called a *stacked pairs* cycle.

2. If **P** contains $i \bullet j$ but none of the surrounded elements $i + 1$ ... $j - 1$ are

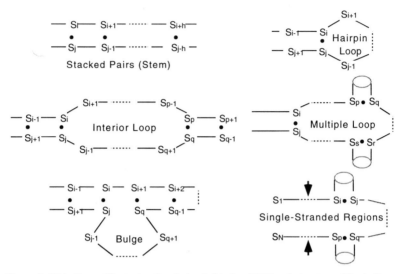

Figure 2. This figure illustrates the six basic kinds of RNA substructure. The indices S_i etc., represent base numbering, and the dots represent basepairing. (After [Sankoff et al. 1983]).

paired, then the cycle is a *hairpin loop*. (Many molecular biologists use "hairpin" to refer to a stem with a loop of size 0 or 1 at the end, i.e., a stem with virtually no loop. These structures are not allowed within our model, and it is not certain that such structures occur *in vivo* [Altona *et al.*, 1988].)

3. If $i + 1 < p < q < j -1$ and **P** contains $i \cdot j$ and $p \cdot q$, but the elements between i and p are unpaired and the elements between q and j are unpaired, then the two unpaired regions constitute an *interior loop*.

4. If **P** contains $i \cdot j$ and $i \cdot j$ surrounds two or more pairs $p \cdot q, r \cdot s,...$ which do not surround each other, then a *multiple loop* is formed.

5. If **P** contains $i \cdot j$ and $(i + 1) \cdot q$, and there are some unpaired elements between q and j, (or, symmetrically, if **P** contains $i \cdot j$ and $p \cdot (j - 1)$ and there are unpaired elements between i and p), then these unpaired elements form a *bulge*.

6. Let r be a sequence of elements in the sequence. If r is unpaired and there is no pair in **P** surrounding r, then we say r is in a *single-stranded region*.

In addition to these widely-accepted definitions of common substructure types, there is the interesting phenomenon of *pseudo-knots* [Waterman and Smith, 1978; Pleij, 1989]. Our current model makes no provision for the prediction of such anomalous structures.

The classical (Tinoco-Uhlenbeck) approach to specifying the free energy $E(P)$ of a secondary structure rests on the hypothesis that the free energy is a sum of the free energy values of P's cycles.

$$E(P) = \Sigma_i\, E(c_i)$$

Even if we accept as a working assumption the equation given above, we are left with the task of specifying free energy values for the primitive substructures. For this we must turn to empirical biochemistry.

2.2 The Tinoco-Uhlenbeck Theory

Much progress has been made on the problem of assigning free energy values to substructures. Although considerable theoretical work has been done, the most useful free energy data have been extrapolated from experiments on particular kinds of RNA. Much of the most important work has been carried out by Tinoco and Uhlenbeck [Tinoco, Uhlenbeck and Levine, 1971; Tinoco *et al.*, 1973].

A reasonable first attempt at solving the *2°RNA* problem would probably incorporate a detailed physical model of molecular structure. A mathematician might define a ball and stick model (balls for nucleotides, sticks for bonds) of an RNA molecule of length N, with $2N - 4$ variable angles and $(N - 1)(N - 2)/2$ potential energy functions for all pairwise hydrogen bond interactions. But the number of possible conformations is then an exponential function of the degrees of freedom. Such a model would prove computationally intractable for even the smallest RNA molecules.

Fortunately, Tinoco and others have simplified the problem, arguing that only the existence or nonexistence of particular hydrogen bonds matters; they have also provided empirical evidence that this simpler model has predictive power. Methods for relating free energy values to the size, shape, and base composition of secondary substructures, sometimes known as the "Tinoco Rules", can be viewed as a means of abstracting away from much of the complex thermodynamics of hydrogen bonding, Van der Waals forces, rotation of covalent bonds, and steric hindrance.

The Tinoco free energy data may be found in [Tinoco, Uhlenbeck and Levine, 1971; Tinoco *et al.*, 1973]. Summarized below are the most important general ideas. It is important to qualify these ideas by noting that the $E(c)$ free energy estimates for cycles are only estimates. The values cannot be determined with great accuracy, but they serve as useful, if sometimes crude, approximations of physical reality.

The most stable secondary structures, those having the lowest free energy, are long chains of stacked pairs. That is, a stem is the only kind of cycle which contributes negative free energy to the structure. The particular free energy value for a given stacked pair depends upon the two bases that are bonding, as well as a *local context*, i.e., the base composition of the closest stacked pairs to its upper right and/or lower left in the matrix. Loops and bulges raise the free energy roughly in proportion to their size, that is, the number of elements that are left unpaired between the two elements that are paired. Beyond a certain size, loop and bulge energies seem to grow proportionally to the *log* of the unpaired length. Thus, a certain minimum number of stacked pairs is required to support a loop or bulge interior to the stacked pairs.

2.2.1 On The Minimal Free Energy Assumption. Molecular biologists commonly accept as an axiom that a full-length RNA molecule exists in its lowest energy thermodynamic state. After transcription, the molecule "breathes" in solution; that is, weak, non-covalent molecular interactions (Van der Waals forces, hydrogen bonds, etc.) form, break, and reform. Finally, the molecule settles into its lowest energy state — the secondary structure which the neural net algorithms described herein attempt to predict.

There are certain exceptions and caveats to the above axiom. The sequential generation, during transcription, of an RNA molecule can trap it in a local optimum. An example of this is attenuation, a regulatory mechanism for some bacterial operons (summarized in [Stryer, 1981]). In other cases, an RNA molecule will be forced into a particular configuration by its interaction with other molecules, usually proteins. However, the minimum free energy configuration provides a baseline with which the in vivo molecule can be compared. Moreover, the techniques described herein are able to accommodate such phenomena; particular substructures can be "clamped" while the rest of the representation of a molecule is folded using the free energy constraints. With these qualifications in mind, let us proceed with the description of the theory and techniques used by others and in this project, while following the classical simplifying assumption that minimal free energy is the determinant of secondary structure.

2.3 Serial Algorithms

The development of serial algorithms for the *2°RNA* problem starts with the following equation. Let **P** be a secondary structure and suppose that [**i, j**] is proper. Consider the secondary structure P_{ij} on [**i, j**] induced by **P**. P_{ij} consists of all pairs from **P** whose elements belong to [**i, j**]. Suppose P'_{ij} is any other secondary structure on [**i, j**]. If we substitute P'_{ij} for P_{ij} in **P**, then the result is a valid secondary structure. That is,

$$P^* = (P - P_{ij}) \cup P'_{ij}$$

is a valid secondary structure. Then, from the above equation it follows that

$$E(P^*) = E(P) - E(P_{ij}) + E(P'_{ij})$$

Therefore, if **P** is optimal on [**1, N**] then P_{ij} is optimal on [**i, j**].

These facts serve as the mathematical basis for the serial algorithms for RNA structure prediction, and they define a basic recursive scheme which most of the algorithms follow [Sankoff *et al.*, 1983]. The reason that the algorithm in general is exponential is that every subsequence is broken into all of its possible cycles and single-stranded regions, and each of these defines a subsequence that must be analyzed and broken into its cycles, and so on. The intolerable running times can be avoided by using dynamic programming in order to compute the energy of each cycle only once, and by relying on strong assumptions about the free energy function. (Mainly, the assumption is that one need not calculate the energies of all subcycles in order to obtain the free energy of a cycle; thus, the expensive recursion is avoided.) The details of these algorithms differ and will be explored in more depth below.

The other class of algorithms in use sacrifices claims of optimality in order to obtain small polynomial running times. In these algorithms, the basic idea is to collect a set of pairs of complementary subsequences (subsequences which could form chains of stacked pairs). This is a simple $O(N^2)$ operation. Then some heuristic is employed to combine these into possible secondary structures and more heuristics are applied in order to choose "good" secondary structures.

3   Search Algorithms

3.1 *2°RNA* as a Search Problem.

The development of the simplified Tinoco model of free energy in RNA secondary structure has allowed researchers to work with a high-level descriptive model that is independent of the low-level physics. In effect, the focus upon mere existence or non-existence of hydrogen-bonded basepairing reduces the problem to a discrete space that can be put into one-to-one correspondence with a planar graph. Global energy minimization is implemented as a discrete optimization problem. A discrete optimization problem can be formulated as a *search* problem — a search through the space of possible structures for the optimal structure.

Given the definitions of basepairing and secondary structures in RNA, it is easy to see that an RNA sequence may have unimaginably many secondary structures. Even if restricted to the chemically possible structures, as defined by the hard constraints given in Section Two, the number of secondary structures for a given RNA can be unmanageably high. To attempt to find an *optimal* secondary structure, then, is to perform a search for the one (or few) "very good structures" among the multitude of "pretty good" and "bad" ones. The problem then is to find ways to restrict the search space and/or to speed up the search through parallelism or by using finely tuned physical parameters to recognize quickly the thermodynamically best structures.

Looking at the *2°RNA* as a search problem will enable us to make clear and insightful comparisons of the many solution methods proposed. In this section, the RNA secondary structure problem is formally defined in terms standard to search problems in computer science.

3.1.1 Defining the Search Space. Let N, a natural number, be given.Let Σ (as in "s" for "sequence") be the set of RNA sequences of length N, that is,

$$\Sigma = \{G, C, A, U\}^N.$$

Let Π (as in "p" for "pairs") be the set of secondary structures for sequences of length N, that is,

$$\Pi = \{0, 1\}^{N^2}$$

Then if T (as in "Tinoco") is a function that assigns free energy values to secondary structures, our search space for the problem is, formally,

> Given some T,
> $\{(S, P), T(P)\}$ where $S \in \Sigma$, $P \in \Pi$ and $T: \Sigma \rightarrow \Re$

(Where a particular sequence S is considered, and no confusion should result, we will omit the S argument and use $T(P)$.)

The problem then is:

> Given a sequence $S \in \Sigma$, construct a secondary structure $P \in \Pi$ such that $T(P) \leq T(P')$ for all $P' \in \Pi$

3.2 Classes of Search Algorithm

We discuss here some standard classes of search algorithms, because their analysis sheds some light on the previous approaches to RNA structure prediction as well as on our new methods.

3.2.1 Optimal Algorithms and Exhaustive Search. In terms of the search space formulation given earlier, what does an exhaustive search algorithm do? Clearly, it considers *every point* **P** in the space of valid secondary structures for sequence **S**. For each such point, it calculates the free energy $T(P)$. It then chooses the **P** with the lowest T value, and outputs **P**.

A simple recurrence relation defining the exhaustive search may be derived by considering the assumptions and definitions from Section 2:

The assumption about the additivity of free energy among cycles:

$$E(P) = \Sigma_i E(c_i)$$

Substitutivity of structures:

> If **P** is optimal on [**1, N**] then P_{ij} is optimal on [**i, j**], if [**i, j**] is proper.

Taking these and performing some algebra, one may derive the following rule. The free energy value for the optimal secondary structure on [**i, j**] is given by

$$T(i, j) = min\left\{0, \ C(i, j), \ \min_{i \leq h < j}\left[T(i, h) + T(h+i, j)\right]\right\}$$

where $C(i, j) = \min_{k \geq 1} \min_{\mathbf{c}}[E(S) + \Sigma_{(a_h, b_h)} C(a_h, b_h)]$, $\mathbf{c}$ representing k–cycles from i to j, is the optimal energy for $[\mathbf{i}, \mathbf{j}]$ if we close it (i.e., if i and j are paired). If $[\mathbf{i}, \mathbf{j}]$ is not *closable*, that is, if (i, j) is not a Watson-Crick pair or if $j - i < 4$, then $C(i, j)$ is taken to be infinity.

This analysis is due to Sankoff *et al.*, and further details may be found in [Sankoff *et al.*, 1983]).

A search algorithm simplistically defined in terms of such a recurrence relation is inherently inefficient. The algorithm recursively recomputes the same answer — the T value — for each subsequence many times. *Dynamic programming* methods work by filling in a table of subproblem values for subsequent repeated lookup, and offer dramatic time savings for problems which are composed of only a polynomial number of subproblems. However, the complexity concerns for the $2°RNA$ problem do not derive solely from the choice of full recursion versus dynamic programming. The complexity in the general algorithm stems from the number of possible cycles that have to be considered for each substring if multiple loops of arbitrarily high order are allowed. That is, the number of subproblems is exponential in the size of N. This fundamental complexity is not decreased if the algorithm looks up the energy for each possible cycle in a table instead of visiting each cycle substring recursively.

3.2.2 Approximation and Heuristic Algorithms. An exhaustive search for the best secondary structure is not feasible. Some restrictive assumptions have to be made, and some potential structures ruled out of consideration. Exactly which assumptions to make, and which classes of structures to ignore is a deep and difficult problem. Some heuristic choices have to be made, and in the end one has to settle for an approximation algorithm, an algorithm which is believed to "often" provide a "good" solution, if not always the optimal one.

3.2.3 Restrictions on the Search Space. In [Sankoff *et al.*, 1983], the basic exhaustive search algorithm is shown to have time complexity of $O(r^2 (rN)^{2crN})$, where r is the proportion of unpaired bases in the sequence (often taken to be around 3/4), and c is a number providing a proportional limit on the order k of a loop within some $[\mathbf{i}, \mathbf{j}]$ (for example, it is found that usually $k \leq (j - i)/7$, so $c = 1/7$). The simplest way to modify the exhaustive search algorithm described above in order to make it efficient is to restrict the number and kind of secondary structures to be considered, and the complexity of energy functions, while employing the same basic algorithmic structure.

Two obvious and useful restrictions to make are

1. to ignore multiple loops with order $k > k_0$ for some small k_0, and/or

2. to weaken the requirement that the algorithm work for arbitrary functions $T(s)$ for any cycle s.

Before reviewing previous work on $2°RNA$ algorithms, it is instructive to consider a few more general search methods.

3.2.4 Local Search. A large and interesting class of algorithms is the class of local search algorithms. A local search algorithm has this basic form: Assume we have a measure $g(x)$ of the "goodness" of a solution x. (Goodness may be defined analytically or in terms of heuristic and subjective criteria.)

1. Start with a random solution (or some easily-obtained solution).

2. Apply to the current solution some transformation L_i from a given set of transformations. The resulting solution becomes the new current solution.

3. Repeat until no transformation in the set improves the current solution.

The resulting solution may or may not be globally optimal. Of course, if the set of transformations includes every transformation that can take one solution into another, then we have essentially the exhaustive search method — and its high computational expense. The point of local search algorithms is to use a set of transformations that can be considered (hence the set should be small) and applied (so they must be efficient) in a small amount of time and space. If the set is small and the transformations easy, then the solutions that can be transformed one to another are considered "near", and hence the transformations are "local". The result of a local search is a *locally optimal* solution, also called simply a *local optimum*. The best solution overall is the (or a) *global optimum*. One can hope, if the transformation set is a good one, that the local optima found are at least very close to the global optimum (optima).

A Hopfield network, as discussed below, is a highly parallel neural net method of local search. The Boltzmann Machine and MFT networks represent (stochastic and deterministic, respectively) ways to change this into a more *global* search method.

3.2.5 Greedy Algorithms. The local search algorithms build whole solutions and then transform them repeatedly. A large number of heuristic algorithms build solutions incrementally. The greedy algorithms are in this class.

In a greedy algorithm, at any stage in the building of a solution it is the locally optimal step that is chosen. For example, a greedy Traveling Salesman algorithm would, having computed a path from C_1 through C_k, choose for the next section the city which is closest to C_k, though that choice might result in a suboptimal final path. A simplistic greedy algorithm for $2°RNA$ might calculate a structure for an ever larger segment of the RNA sequence. At step k it would have a secondary structure for $[1, k - 1]$ and would grow the solution by finding the best way to force the kth base onto the current structure. In general, this would generate a rather poor solution; however, Martinez [1984] has a biological justification for a particular greedy approach, and his method achieves good results on some RNA sequences.

3.2.6 Monte Carlo Methods, Simulated Annealing. "Simulated anneal-ing" is a method, adapted from statistical mechanics and inspired by anneal-ing procedures in metallurgical processing, of employing stochastic functions in search procedures. Derived from theoretical work in [Metropolis et al., 1953] and popularized in [Kirkpatrick, Gelatt and Vecchi, 1983] as an opti-mization technique, simulated annealing is one example of a "Monte Carlo" method of probabilistic numerical simulation.

The simulated annealing procedure is a way of doing a local search with-out becoming stuck in "bad" local minima. The method is simple:

1. Define a set of local transformations L_i (as in any local search) on the so-lution space.
2. Define a stochastic function Φ from solutions (states) and *temperature* val-ues $(T \geq 0)$ to transformations, such that

- The probability $\pi_i(x, T)$ of picking transformation L_{i}, for some constant temperature T, when the current solution is x, varies directly with its "goodness" as a move, i.e.

  If $g(L_i(x)) > g(L_j(x))$ then $\pi_i(x, T) > \pi_j(x, T)$.

- The degree to which the probability of a move depends on its goodness is higher as T is lowered. In other words, T is a measure of the *randomness* in the move-generation process. Φ is the move-generation function, which employs the probabilities π_i.

3. Choose a *temperature T, T > 0*.
4. Repeat while $T > 0$:

    (a) Choose a transformation and transform the current solution **x** by
    x:= $\Phi(\mathbf{x}, T)(\mathbf{x})$

    (b) If acceptable(x) then quit.

    (c) Decrement T

As Kirkpatrick, Gelatt and Vecchi [1983] have pointed out, the simulated annealing technique is a type of adaptive divide-and-conquer, with the basic features of a solution appearing at high temperatures, leaving the specific de-tails to be determined at lower temperatures. There is a very natural way to map simulated annealing onto neural nets, and this, the Boltzmann Machine, is discussed in Section 4.4

3.3 Previous Work on 2°RNA

Historically, the systematic investigation into prediction of nucleic acid secondary structure has been marked by three major phases, each represented by a particular approach that dominated: 1) heuristic search over the sec-ondary structure matrix or a large space of possible stacking regions, 2) dy-namic programming approaches to building an optimal structure in a few passes, and 3) incorporation of auxiliary information and kinetic or evolutionary assumptions into folding rules.

Pipas and McMahon [1975] designed an algorithm that performs a search in three passes. The first pass constructs a list of all possible stems of a certain size. The second pass scans this list for stacking regions that are *compatible* (meaning they form no knots and share no bases in common). In the final pass the algorithm performs an exhaustive search for the set of compatible stacking regions with the lowest free energy (using the Tinoco rules [Tinoco, Uhlenbeck and Levine, 1971]).

In terms of search spaces, this algorithm can be viewed as using two passes to construct a subset of Π — the subset consisting of those structures containing stacking regions of at least a certain size. The third pass then searches Π exhaustively for the P which minimizes $T(P)$ for some given T.

The Studnicka algorithm [Studnicka *et al.*, 1978], like Pipas and McMahon's, begins by constructing a list of all the possible stacking regions. In the second stage, the algorithm enforces compatibility constraints between sets of regions. Instead of ignoring conflicting regions, as the Pipas-McMahon algorithm does, the Studnicka algorithm pares down the regions until compatibility is achieved for the now-smaller regions. The next pass combines the regions into large structures of order $k \leq 2$ (i.e., multiple loops not allowed). A final stage permits the user to combine these large structures into secondary structures of arbitrary complexity.

Such an algorithm can examine structures of high order k (the number of loops in a multiple loop) without the exponential time complexity seen in the general recursive algorithm. This is because the set of high-order structures that the algorithm can construct is severely restricted by the initial constraint of building structures with a set of existing stacking structures. For example, if building a structure from stems A, on $[\mathbf{i}, \mathbf{j}]$, and B, on $[\mathbf{p}, \mathbf{q}]$, one already rules out all combinations of structures over subsequences $[\mathbf{r}, \mathbf{s}]$ where $i < r < j$, or $i < s < j$, or $p < r < q$, or $p < s < q$. An exponential explosion of possible structures is excised from the search space *a priori*.

Nussinov's group [Nussinov *et al.*, 1978; Nussinov and Jacobson, 1980] was among the first to apply dynamic programming to the $2°RNA$ problem. The Nussinov algorithms build an optimal secondary structure (subject to certain restrictive assumptions) in one pass. The algorithms are similar in structure to a basic dynamic programming version of the general recursive search algorithm [Sankoff *et al.*, 1983], except that Nussinov made simplifying assumptions about structure and energy. The first version [Nussinov *et al.*, 1978] ignores the destabilizing effects of loops, and simply attempts to maximize basepairing. The second version imposes a simple linear penalty on loop size.

All of the above display either unrealistic assumptions about the free energy of substructures, and/or have high time complexity ($O(N^5)$ for Studnicka) or space complexity.

3.3.1 Recent Advances with Dynamic Programming. With the interesting exceptions of the Martinez work and Major, *et al* [1991], the current "state of the art" in serial *2°RNA* algorithms is a set of recent dynamic programming approaches.

Sankoff, Kruskal, Mainville, and Cedergren [Sankoff *et al.*, 1983] have described algorithms that restrict the order of multiple loops to $k \leq 2$. In the case of arbitrary energy functions for loops, they report running times of $O(N^4)$. When the energy function for loops is restricted to the linear case, the result is an $O(N^3)$ algorithm. Zuker [Zuker and Stiegler, 1981], and Waterman and Smith [1978] have proposed similar algorithms within this range of time complexity.

In a theoretical computer science paper [1988], Eppstein, Galil, and Giancarlo describe an algorithm with running time $O(N^2 log^2 N)$ for the $k \leq 2$ case where the energy function for loops is assumed to be convex function of the number of exposed bases (bases accessible from the loop's closing pair). (See [Eppstein, Galil and Giancarlo, 1988] for the definitions of convex and concave.)

Several of the dynamic programming algorithms can be parallelized quite effectively, typically by using a wavefront method to trade $O(N)$ processors for an $O(N)$ factor in running time.

3.3.2 Martinez. Martinez [1984; 1988] takes a very different approach to minimizing free energy of molecules. Instead of building a structure using purely combinatorial methods, his *kinetics*-based method simulates the folding as it might actually occur in the molecule.

The Martinez folding rule, which defines the order in which parts of the final secondary structure are built in his algorithm, is simple:

Of all the remaining unformed stems which are compatible with those constituting the current structure, choose the one with the largest equilibrium constant (of association). This structure is the one whose formation is the most thermodynamically favored chemical reaction.

In search method terms, Martinez's method is a form of greedy algorithm. In particular, it has the property that it removes $(j-i)^3$ points from the search space of possible remaining structures at each step, where i, j are the beginning and end indices of the subsequence which supports the chosen stem. The time complexity of this algorithm is only $O(N^2)$.

The Martinez method is very promising. It has been shown to work on some medium-length (200-500 bases) sequences. The method is based on a fairly speculative but interesting evolutionary assumption, and is expected to be most successful in predicting the structures of RNAs whose secondary structure is essential to function (e.g., tRNAs and rRNAs).

3.4 The MFT Network Search for Optimal RNA Structures

In terms of the search model discussed above, our neural network method may be described as a highly parallel distributed search, wherein each possible RNA secondary structure representation is distributed over many "processing units" (one unit for each possible base-pairing) and wherein several potential secondary structures for the input sequence are represented simultaneously. *Conflict* (w.r.t. constraint violation) between possible substructures is implemented by inhibitory connections between units in the respective substructures, and *support* (stem compatibility) is implemented by excitatory constraints.

Points in the $2°RNA$ search space are considered many at a time, as they *compete* during the MFT network relaxation process. The MFT relaxation algorithm is intended to avoid bad locally-optimal points in the space in favor of more globally-optimal solutions. The MFT learning algorithm is intended to make this search easier by refining the parameters of this competition over many trials with a training set of sequence and structure data. Connection weights constrain the dynamics of network relaxation, and can be seen as an implicit representation of *knowledge*, both analytic and heuristic, that aids the search process by pushing the network state transition process in particular directions and towards particular solutions in the solution space (π, $\{T(P)\}$).

4 Methods

This section describes our methods, and in particular it defines the neural network model of RNA secondary structure used in the experiments. The model is an example and an extension of the Mean Field Theory (MFT) machine originally proposed by Hopfield and Tank [1985] and later described and used by Peterson and Anderson [1987], among others. The MFT machine is a deterministic approximation of a Boltzmann Machine, which is a stochastic variant of a Hopfield net. The representation used is one wherein an RNA secondary structure matrix is mapped directly onto a Hopfield net, with every unit representing a basepairing.

In the first subsection, neural networks are introduced and some reasons behind the choice of neural networks, and specifically one-layer nets, are offered. Next, the MFT network and its intellectual roots (Boltzmann Machine and Hopfield network) are introduced. Then we define our mapping of the $2°RNA$ problem onto a Hopfield net architecture. Finally, some issues in the modelling of molecular structure are discussed with reference to our work as well as other work on neural networks and molecular structure prediction.

4.1 Neural Networks

Artificial neural networks are models of highly parallel and adaptive computation, based very loosely on current theories of brain structure and activity. There are many different neural net architectures and algorithms, but the basic algorithm which all artificial neural nets share is the same. Assume a collection of simple processors ("units") and a high degree of connectivity, each connection having a *weight* associated with it. Each unit computes a weighted sum of its inputs (then may plug this sum into some nonlinear function), assumes a new level of activation, and sends an output signal to the units to which it is connected. In many of the models, the network settles into a stable global state under the influence of external input that represents an interpretation of the input or a function computed on the input. This settling process, called relaxation, performs a parallel search.

4.1.1 Neural Network Applications. Besides being the focus of *connectionist* research into models of brain function and cognition, neural networks have been applied with some success to optimization problems and function approximation. Optimization problems attacked with neural nets include the Traveling Salesman problem (TSP) and graph partitioning [Peterson and Soderberg, 1989], and process scheduling [Hellstrom and Kanal, 1990].

The *2°RNA* problem possesses several important features of the kind of problem at which neural network methods excel:

- Complexity: The problem has a large space of variables (search space).

- Redundancy: The set of reasonable, though not necessarily optimal, solutions is large, and many roughly equivalent solutions have variable values in common.

- Parallelism: Neural nets, of course, bring a parallel approach to any problem. Some problems seem inherently parallel (e.g., low-level vision), and the simultaneous consideration of and competition between possible solutions might well be the correct paradigm for the molecular folding prediction problems.

- Noise-tolerance: The problem may require the processing of very noisy or incomplete input data, and one would still like a reasonable answer.

In addition to these general neural net advantages, there are reasons for favoring the particular architectures chosen in this project. The stochastic nature of the simulated annealing procedure of the Boltzmann Machine might model well the thermodynamics of free energy minimization of an RNA molecule. The relationships among statistical mechanical models of spin glasses, neural networks, and biological macromolecules is an active research area [Stein, 1985; Anderson, 1988].

4.2 Architectures

A particular neural network architecture may be defined by specifying the following (list taken from [McClelland, Rumelhart and the PDP research group, 1986]):

- A set of processing units
- A set of activation states for the units
- An output function for each unit
- A pattern of connectivity among units
- A propagation rule for propagating patterns of activity through the network
- An activation rule for combining a unit's inputs with its activation level to produce a new activation level
- A learning rule whereby patterns of connectivity are modified by experience

In most neural net models of computation, the processing of an input vector, i.e., the solving of a particular instance of a problem, occurs through the network relaxation process. This is the process wherein the units in the network change their individual states in accordance with an update rule in order to maximize some global measure of "harmony" or minimize "energy" or constraint-violation.

4.3 Learning in Neural Networks

In most neural net models of computation, the processing of an input vector, i.e., the solving of a particular instance of a problem, occurs through the network relaxation process. The information needed for a neural net to solve a problem is largely stored in the connection weights between units. The process whereby the weights are modified in order to improve network performance is called, appropriately enough, *learning* or *training*.

There are several kinds of network learning procedures, but most fall into one of two broad classes: the *supervised* and the *unsupervised* learning procedures. The research described in this report concerns only supervised learning procedures.

In supervised learning, the connection weights between units are modified in order to reduce some measure of error — the error being a weighted difference between what the network outputs in response to a particular input and what one desires the network to produce in response to that input. Just as the relaxation process may be seen as a search through the space of possible network activation states for the state(s) with the lowest energy (lowest error, highest harmony, etc.), the learning process is the search through the weight space of the network for the set of connection weights that minimizes error in processing the training inputs. However, one desires that the learning procedure demonstrate some degree of *generalization*. That is, the weight modifications should enhance performance on whole classes of possible inputs represented by the trial patterns – not just on the trial patterns themselves.

The focus of this report is on *2°RNA*, which is essentially a large optimization problem; but we require the networks also to learn a function, a mapping between RNA sequences and secondary structures, by successively refining estimates of a few network variables in order to reduce predictive error.

4.4 Hopfield Nets, Boltzmann Machines, and MFT Networks

Hopfield [1982] formalized the idea of a massively parallel and highly interconnected network performing a constraint satisfaction search. He introduced a cost function, termed *energy*, which is a measure of system-wide constraint violation. He then showed that the connection weights in a network encode locally minimum energy states, and that, using a suitable activation updating rule, these minimum energy states are exactly the stable states of the network. In particular, a unit u_k's contribution to the network's energy can be computed locally:

$$\Delta E_k = E_{(a_k=0)} - E_{(a_k=1)} = \left(\Sigma_i \, a_i \, w_{ki} \right).$$

where a_i is the activation level of the *ith* unit, and w_{ij} is the connection weight between the *ith* and *jth* units. The unit turns/remains on/off depending on which state lowers the network's energy.

Since the absolute value of the energy is bounded by the weights, the search is guaranteed to converge, if asynchronous node updating is used. However, like other gradient search methods, the procedure may only find a locally optimal solution. (This was not especially problematic in Hopfield's early work, because the networks were intended as a model for content-addressable memory. The "memorized" states were exactly the locally minimum states, and all the network was required to do was to *complete* one of the stored states, i.e., to fall into a local minimum.)

In order to design Hopfield-like nets that can escape local minima, researchers have adopted the *simulated annealing* technique, and thereby developed the Boltzmann Machine (BM) [Ackley, *et al* 1985] . In a BM, the following stochastic updating rule (or a variant thereof) is used:

> Each unit sets its activation state to 1, regardless of previous state, with probability
> $$P_k = 1/(1 + e^{-\Delta E_k/T})$$

where T, called *temperature*, is a measure of randomness in the system. At higher temperatures, high randomness permits state changes to be relatively independent of the energy, thus allowing the system to escape from local minima. At lower temperatures, configurations with low energy are more heavily favored. Thus, by using an annealing schedule whereby the temperature is gradually lowered or alternately raised and lowered, it is possible to avoid certain local minima and to find more globally optimal solutions. Actual performance in practice depends greatly on the topology of the energy surface for the particular problem and encoding.

An alternative method for avoiding local minima and generally speeding up the search for some problems is to use *continuous activation* models. In [1985] Hopfield and Tank introduced a model in which activation levels (and hence outputs) take values from a fixed interval (in this case [0,1]) instead of the set {0, 1}. Such networks are based on a *Mean Field Theory* approximation to Boltzmann Machines and are thus called *MFT machines* or *MFT networks*. The MFT algorithm replaces the stochastic state transitions of the BM with a set of deterministic equations. The solutions to these equations, for each given temperature, represent *average* values of the corresponding quantities (correlations or co-occurrences between states of all units) computed from extensive and time-consuming sampling in the BM. The continuous output has the effect of smoothing the energy surface. In the binary model, the search procedure can be viewed as moving along the edges of an M-dimensional hypercube (where M is the number of units); whereas, in the continuous model, the search can move smoothly *within* the hypercube. In terms of an energy surface, a Boltzmann Machine performs stochastic hillclimbing (or hill-descending); MFT recasts it into deterministic motion through a smoother landscape. "Rather than scaling hills, one takes them away" [Peterson and Anderson, 1987]. Like the binary model, the continuous model is not guaranteed to find globally optimal configurations. Nevertheless, simulations of such a net which encoded the Travelling Salesman Problem did produce reasonably good solutions in a short period of time. In contrast, solutions found using the binary model proved to be only slightly better than random [Hopfield and Tank, 1985]. Peterson and Anderson [1987] have extended this approach and have tested the algorithm on several important optimization and learning problems, with favorable results.

The details of the derivation of the MFT model from the Boltzmann Machine model may be found in [Peterson and Anderson, 1987]. It turns out that the update rule for each of the continuously-valued units in a network is

$$V_i = tanh\left(\sum_j \frac{w_{ji}V_j}{T}\right)$$

and the iterative algorithm becomes

$$V_i^{new} = tanh\left(\sum_j \frac{w_{ji}V_j^{old}}{T}\right)$$

The above equations define the MFT relaxation scheme. The learning algorithm is equally straightforward. V_i is really an estimate of $<a_i>$, the time average taken for the state of unit u_i. What is needed for learning is the equivalent, V_{ij}, of the correlations $<a_ia_j>$ between connected units sampled in the Boltzmann Machine learning algorithm:

$$V_{ij} = \frac{1}{2}\left(tanh \left(\sum_{k} \frac{w_{jk}V_{ik}}{T} \right) + tanh \left(\sum_{k} \frac{w_{ik}V_{jk}}{T} \right) \right)$$

which reduces under certain conditions to

$$V_{ij} = V_i V_j$$

Let V_{ij}^{+} be the V_{ij} value for units u_i and u_j in a relaxation run wherein the input units are activated by an input vector v_{in} and the output units are "clamped" (forcibly set and maintained) to represent vector v_{out}; and let V_{ij}^{-} be the V_{ij} value when the machine runs with no clamping of the output units in response to the input v_{in}. Then the weight update (learning) rule is the following.

If $V_{ij}^{+} > V_{ij}^{-}$ then increment w_{ij}.

If $V_{ij}^{+} < V_{ij}^{-}$ then decrement w_{ij}.

The increment must be proportional to $V_{ij}^{+} - V_{ij}^{-}$ and the V_{ij} quantities are usually averaged across cases (learning samples).

4.5 Defining an MFT Machine Model of 2°RNA

4.5.1 The Underlying Architecture: A Hopfield Net The Hopfield net was chosen primarily because there is a very natural mapping of the 2°RNA problem onto this architecture. Basically, the network is a direct representation of an RNA secondary structure matrix. Each matrix position is represented by a single unit. An activation value of 1 means that the corresponding matrix element has a 1, and hence an hypothesis that the corresponding two bases in the RNA sequence are paired; a 0 in the same unit represents an hypothesis that the bases are not paired. A value between 0 and 1, if analog values are used, stands for a relative probability of the two bases being paired.

Symmetric connections are chosen because there must be signals (inhibitory or excitatory) between units and there are no privileged units — all the matrix positions are, *a priori*, equally valid, although particular combinations of them are invalid.

4.5.2 Representing the Problem: Deriving the Energy Function. Recall the Hopfield result [1982] that the equations of motion for a symmetrically connected network lead to convergence to a stable state. A stable state is one in which the outputs of all units remain constant. Under certain conditions (asynchronous node update according to the local updating rule), the network's stable states are the local minima of the quantity

$$E = -\frac{1}{2}\sum_{i=1}^{M}\sum_{j=1}^{M}w_{ij}a_i a_j - \sum_{i=1}^{M}a_i I_i$$

where E is a measure of *energy*. (This term is not to be confused with the free energy of an RNA molecule; we will attempt to make it clear which use is intended in each situation.) M is the number of units, a_i is the activation level of the ith unit, and w_{ij} is the connection weight between units i and j. I_i is a level of external input to the system, a *bias* for each unit.

In mapping the $2°RNA$ problem onto a Hopfield net, the network must be described by an energy function in which the lowest state corresponds to a legal and optimal RNA secondary structure. Low energy in the network must correspond to low free energy in the simulated RNA molecule.

Assume that the network has $M = N(N-1)/2$ units (where N is the length of the RNA molecule), so that, intuitively, the network represents the upper right triangular submatrix of the RNA secondary structure matrix. (See Figure 3.) Assume that each unit receives input telling it the composition of the two bases whose possible pairing it represents (e.g., it receives a constant

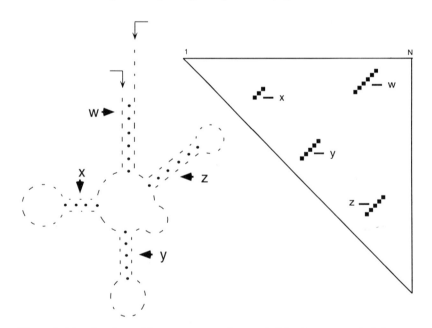

Figure 3. Mapping the problem onto a neural network: The diagram on the left represents a tRNA secondary structure. On the right is its representation on a secondary structure matrix, where each cell corresponds to a possible base pairing. The large diagonal in the upper right of the matrix represents the main stem; the other diagonals represent the smaller, subordinate stems.

signal of 00 01 for (G,C), etc.).

First, we want a term in the energy definition which tells us that the opti-

$$E = \alpha/2 \sum_R \sum_i \sum_{j \neq i} a_{R_i} a_{R_j} + \beta/2 \sum_i \sum_R \sum_{C \neq R} a_{R_i} a_{C_i} +$$

$$\gamma/2 \sum_R^N \sum_C^N \sum_{z=0}^{C-N} \sum_{y=0}^{N-y} a_{RC} a_{R+z, C+y}$$

mal states are ones which enforce the hard constraints on RNA secondary structure. There should be only one unit active in any row, only one active in any column, and there should be no knotting. Consider the local minima of the following quantity:

(all summations are from 1 to N except where indicated), where R ranges over rows of the network, C over columns, and i and j count up to the length of the respective row or column.

Note that the first term is 0 iff each row R contains only one or fewer active units; the second term is 0 iff each column C contains only one or fewer active units; and the third term is 0 iff there are no knots. Therefore if a network incorporates this energy function, the stable states of the network favor representations of legal RNA secondary structures.

There remains the task of representing constraints on optimal secondary structures. Basically, what is wanted is this: Favor the formation of stacked pairs, with the precise negative energy contribution given by the Tinoco local context value for two adjacent stacked pairs. Impose a penalty for large loops and bulges, the penalty growing with the size. (In the experiments performed, the local context values were not represented, and their omission did not prevent good performance on the small tRNA sequences. However, it is expected that accurate predictions for longer molecules will require local context values.)

Add to the equation for E, the global network energy, the following terms:

$$\mu/2 \sum_R^N \sum_C^N \sum_{z=0}^{C-R} \sum_{y=0}^{N-y} f_d(R, C, R = z, C - y) a_{RC} a_{R+z, C-y}$$

and

$$\sum_R^N \sum_C^N f_b(R, C)$$

where $f_d(i, j, k, l)$ is some function of the distance between two units (i, j) and (k, l), and $f_b(i, j)$ is a function of the indices of a unit which returns some value representing the tendency of a basepair to form. (For example, a high value is returned for indices representing a $G \cdot C$ pair, and low or zero value returned for a $C \cdot U$ pair.)

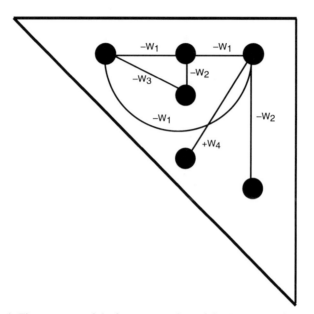

Figure 4. The structure of the basic network used for RNA secondary structure pre-diction. W_1 is the inhibitory signal between elements of a row; W_2 is the inhibitory signal between elements of a column; W_3 is the inhibitory signal that prevents knot-ting; W_4 is the excitatory signal between elements of possible secondary structures.

Setting the Connection Weights and Node Weights. Through the ener-gy function definitions above and the earlier definition of energy minima for Hopfield nets, a set of connection weights is implicitly defined. The first three terms define inhibitory connections, with weights α, β, γ respectively, between elements in the same rows or columns or elements whose conjunc-tions form knots. The fourth term defines excitatory connections, with weight μ, between elements diagonal (in the "good" direction, i.e., not the knot di-rection) to each other. The fifth term defines the node weights, the bias for each unit. The bias of a unit influences the tendency of a unit to be active, ir-respective of the influence of other units acting on it via connection weights. The bias is used in this model to represent the basic probability of a particu-lar basepairing, independent of constraints imposed by other possible pair-ings. (Figure 4 illustrates the connection structure of the basic network.)

It is important to understand the limitations of this representation and how this relates to heuristic knowledge and to machine learning. The global pa-rameters $\alpha, \beta, \gamma, \mu$ (and through these, the connection weights w_{ij}), f_d, and f_b must embody a combination of information about both the problem and pa-rameters particular to the computational architecture. Analysis of the prob-lem and of Hopfield networks has led to this mapping of problem to architecture, but it is not currently possible to derive analytically, from biochemical knowledge, precise optimal values for the global parameters. It is therefore necessary to make educated guesses at initial values (i.e., employ heuristic knowledge) and to adapt the weights over several learning trials in order to improve the representation and improve performance. It may be that adaptive networks also learn so well that they, in addition to improving their ability to represent existing biochemical knowledge, actually derive unknown or refine known physical parameters of the RNA folding process.

Input, Output, and Hidden Units. The structure of the network as defined for this project differs somewhat from most other Hopfield or Boltz-mann applications. There are no separate input or output units, and no hidden units. The input sequence (binary representations of the bases G, C, A, U, and perhaps modified bases) is read into the rows and columns so that each unit receives input representing the identities of the two bases whose possible pair the unit represents — one represented by the row index and one by the column index. The bias term I_k for each unit u_k is then set accordingly. The connection weights are already determined and remain fixed during the processing of the particular sequence.

The output of the network is the set of activation levels of all the units, measured in analog (as numbers between 0 and 1) or binary, and preferably represented in a format like the RNA secondary structure matrix.

There are no hidden units in the models used thus far, although there are models under consideration which may use hidden units to represent the more complex higher-order relationships between distant substructures that will probably be needed for accurate prediction of very long RNA sequences.

4.6 Learning the Connection Weights and Learning RNA Structure

In this project, an effort was made to take as much advantage as possible of regularities in the problem (in the search space) in order to define an architecture wherein fast and useful learning is possible. If most work on predicting protein secondary structure [Qian and Sejnowski, 1988] seems to assume that all the important information in the sequence-to-structure mapping is *local*, the work described here assumes only that such information is either *local or uniform* across the net.

In particular, we hypothesize that there are a few (fewer than ten) important parameters, potentially obtainable through learning from examples, that determine the global sequence-to-structure mapping for RNA. Our current model employs α, β, γ, μ. These few quantities, once learned, can then be combined and replicated in some recursively specifiable way across the net in order to construct connection weights. The problem, then, is to define these few parameters as variables defining a learning space, and to devise a simple way to construct connection weights from these variables. Then the learning procedure would, instead of incrementing or decrementing each individual weight w_{ij} on each pass through the net, only update the corresponding global learning variable. After learning, the weights would then be constructed from the variables and used in the relaxation search. This is in fact what was done in this project, and the details are given below.

Such a learning scheme is beneficial in three ways. First, it probably provides for more accurate and robust learning, as it tends to ensure that key global parameters — and not just positional correspondences found in the learning samples — are what is learned. Second, the very small variable space (less than 10 instead of $O(N^4)$ or $O(N^2)$) that is optimized during learning makes for huge decreases in learning time. Third, and perhaps most interesting, it probably allows for some degree of scale-invariant learning. That is, it should be possible to achieve useful learning and structure prediction on a set of RNA sequences of different sizes, since the indices of particular units and connections do not have to match up exactly. Such scale-invariance over a very small range of sequence lengths is demonstrated in the experiments described below. In sum, the parameterization is a regularization scheme.

4.6.1 The Learning Variables and Learning Procedure. Following the derivation of the energy function given above in the introduction to the Hopfield net representation of $2°RNA$, one sees the obvious candidates for global learning variables. Corresponding to the α, β, γ, and μ are RowInhibition, ColumnInhibition, KnotInhibition, DiagonalExcitation.

The MFT learning algorithm, modified for our global learning method, becomes (for a network of M units):

for each training iteration k ·
  for each learning example sequence s
    $Phase^+(s)$
    $Phase^-(s)$
    for $i = 1$ to M
      for $j = i + 1$ to M
        $\delta := \eta((V_i V_j)^+ - (V_i V_j)^-)$
        if (u_i; u_j are in the same row) then
          RowInhibition := RowInhibition $- \delta$
        else if (u_i, u_j are in the same column) then
          ColumnInhibition := ColumnInhibition $- \delta$
        else if (u_i, u_j form a knot) then
          KnotInhibition := KnotInhibition $- \delta$
        otherwise
          DiagonalExcitation = DiagonalExcitation $- \delta$
  endfor; endfor; endfor; endfor

η is the *learning rate parameter*. $Phase^+(s)$ normally means to run the network relaxation process on input s with the output clamped (this provides the

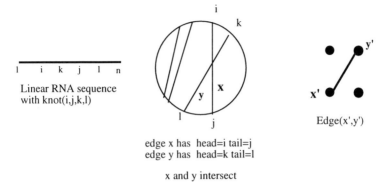

Figure 5. Graph theoretical interpretation of RNA secondary structure. On the left is a linear representation of the RNA sequence 1-n with a knot involving i,j,k and l. In the center is a circle graph (Referred to as G in the text) derived from the linear sequence. On the right is an edge adjacency graph (G' in the text) derived from the circle graph.

teaching input, the supervision in supervised learning). *Phase⁻(s)* means run the network relaxation on input sequence *s* with the output unclamped. Similarly, the +,− superscripts refer to the correlations gathered in the clamped and unclamped phases of learning. (In our described experiments the networks contain no hidden units, and therefore no distinct *Phase⁺(s)* relaxation is needed. Instead, the $(V_iV_j)^+$ numbers are simply and quickly calculated from a vector representing the desired network outputs

4.6.2 Constructing the Weights from the Learning Variables. The mapping from learning variables to connection weights is quite straightforward, and follows from the definition of the system energy function *E* given in an earlier section.

The inhibitory weights used are exactly the corresponding global learning variables, e.g., (w_{ij}:= *KnotInhibition*) if the bases represented by units u_i, u_j form a knot. For the other, excitatory connections, the DiagonalExcitation is multiplied by the value returned by a distance function applied to *i* and *j*. The unit bias terms I_i are not affected by the learning procedure. They are determined by basepair identity as described earlier, along with a factor representing the distance $(i - j)$, used to account for loop penalties.

4.7 Graph-Theoretic Analysis of the Methods

It is possible to explain the mapping of the *2°RNA* problem onto neural networks in terms of the mathematical theory of circle graphs and edge-adjacency graphs, and thereby to relate the problem to a set of well-known combinatorics problems.

Consider an RNA sequence **S**: $s_1s_2 \ldots s_n$, where s_i is one of G, C, A, or U. A secondary structure **P** for **S** may be represented by a circle graph **G**, wherein the n nodes are points around a circle and the edges (i, j) correspond to basepairs (i, j). (See Figure 5.) Edges that cross correspond to knots. All of the substructure types and constraints on structures defined in Section 2 may be described in terms of the circle graph. (Details may be found in [Nussinov and Jacobson, 1980; Takefuji et al., 1990].)

Consider next a graph **G'** with the number of nodes equal to the number of edges in **G**, and an edge (x', y') in **G'** for each pair of edges $x = (i, j)$, $y = (k, l)$ in **G** that intersect. **G'** is the edge-adjacency graph for **G**. (See Figure 5.)

It is clear from the above that the 2°RNA problem is closely related to the problem of finding the maximal independent set (the largest set of nodes such that none of them are connected to another node in the set) of the edge adjacency graph **G'** of a circle graph **G** for an RNA sequence S. Takefuji and coworkers [Takefuji et al., 1990] designed a neural network that finds locally optimal solutions of the general graph MIS problem, and pointed out the connection to predicting RNA structure.

While the similarity to the graph theoretic problem provides useful insights into the essential complexity of the 2°RNA problem, it is important to recognize the limits of this similarity. To solve the graph MIS problem, even exactly (an NP-complete task), corresponds to finding the largest set of possible basepairs such that none of them form knots. Clearly, this is not necessarily the optimal RNA secondary structure. Some attempt must be made to represent different stacking energies, the contribution of one stem to another in a multiple loop, and other real biochemical and physical constraints. Such attempts were made in our work, and machine learning was made central to our model in order to further refine the representation, but there is room for future work in exploring, possibly through graph theory, better problem representations for parallel networks.

4.8 Evaluating Models and Mappings

Having defined the particular kind of one-layer neural network model used, and the mapping of the 2°RNA problem onto the network model, it is instructive to review the nature of the constraints and the information flow within problem representations and some of the issues in representing in particular the RNA molecule and the molecular folding process.

4.8.1 Global and Local, First-Order and Higher-Order. When analyzing the constraints inherent in a problem, and before choosing a representation, one may consider three dimensions along which the adequacy of a representation (and hence a solution) will be judged. These three dimensions are *locality*, *order*, and *completeness of* information.

A representation for molecular structure prediction may capture simultaneously information on all parts of the molecule, or it may only represent a piece at a time. We say that a representation is *local* if it contains information from only a section of k elements (bases, or amino acids) at any time. It is *global* if $k = length(molecule)$. A representation is:

1. *first-order* if it captures interactions between primitive elements. In the $2°RNA$ problem, this means it captures base-pairing.

2. *second-order* if it captures interactions between interactions between elements. For example, the representation of stems, as resulting from interactions between basepairs, is second order.

3. *third-order* if it captures interactions between second-order objects. The representation of thermodynamic competition between possible RNA substructures is third-order.

4. *nth-order*, generally, if it captures interactions between (n-1)st-order objects and events.

Completeness refers to how much of the information, in a given local "window" and of a particular order, is captured.

Obviously, one ought to strive for a global, complete, and higher-order representation of a problem. Also obvious is that there is a trade-off involved: The more global and complete a representation is, and the higher its order, the higher is the computational complexity.

The serial algorithms for RNA secondary structure prediction are slow precisely because they compute with higher-order information in finding optimal substructures, and they do this serially over the entire molecule. A sequential computer generally can act globally only by covering a section at a time and iterating over the whole sequence, and this leads to long running times. Generally, the (non-neural) parallel algorithms do not differ drastically in their logical structure from the serial programs. Rather, they perform essentially the same steps but do it over $O(N)$ processors and thus achieve an $O(N)$ time savings.

The other work with neural nets on molecular structure, including Qian and Sejnowski's protein secondary structure prediction project [1988] (and see also [Bohr *et al.*, 1988]) is based on local approaches. Sejnowski used feed-forward nets which captured only local ($k = 13$) information. The fairly low accuracy of local methods (of which neural net methods are the best) and the surprising fact that, as Qian and Sejnowski discovered, higher-order representations did not seem to raise the predictive accuracy, indicate that more global information must be captured, perhaps using global constraint-satisfaction [Friedrichs and Wolynes 1989] or pattern recognition [Greller *et al* 1991]. Research groups also use local representations and neural networks to predict local aspects of protein *tertiary* structure [see Bohr *et al.*, 1990 and Holbrook, Muskal and Kim, this volume]. In RNA secondary structure, global interactions are probably more common than in protein secondary structure, and absolutely must be captured in the representation used by any computational method.

The neural net models used herein are intended to be global and higher-order. The representation is explicitly higher-order, as the primitives (the processing units) stand for possible basepairs. Connection weights between the (2nd-order) units represent constraints on substructure types and competition between possible structures, which is third-order information. This premise implies a particular hardware complexity: $O(N^2)$ units and $O(N^3)$ or $O(N^4)$ connections, depending on how much of, and how globally, the third-order relationships are to be captured. (All of the 2nd-order information is represented, for the whole molecule, thus requiring $N(N-1)/2$ units.)

This hardware complexity is very expensive — prohibitively so, for very large RNA molecules. Thus one of the long-term goals of this project is to find ways, using separate processing stages, approximation methods, and forms of "time-sharing" on parallel hardware, to reduce this hardware cost significantly.

On the other hand, this neural net approach offers a large potential advantage in terms of complexity. It is believed that the costs of computation on this problem are "paid all at once", in the amount of parallel hardware, when using these methods. There are *no additional incremental orders of complexity added* when more general structures are handled. Relaxing an assumption about the energy contribution of loops, or about the complexity of multiple loops that are allowed, for example, can raise the runtime complexity of a serial algorithm from $O(N^3)$ to $O(N^6)$ or worse; handling the general case — all secondary structures are possible — mandates an exponential algorithm. However, to handle the general case with the simple model presented in this report requires only an $O(N^2)$-processor, fully-connected Hopfield net.

5 Experiments and Results

5.1 General Assumptions and Methodology

In the main set of experiments the basic problem representation outlined in Section Five, with $O(N^2)$ units, was used. The RNA sequences were limited to a standard length of 30 bases. In particular, the first thirty bases of each of 41 tRNAs were used (35 training, 5 test, and 1 for playing around with). These truncated sequences do not represent autonomous naturally-occurring molecules. However, in order to make the experiments more manageable, this limitation was considered necessary.

Because the 30-base sequences do not occur naturally except as components, there are no published secondary structures for them. Therefore, the secondary structures used in the training set of the supervised learning experiment were those determined by Zuker's serial program for RNA secondary structure prediction, described in [Zuker and Stiegler, 1981]. The Zuker program is widely used and we assume it can be trusted to find the best structures for such very small sequences.

As mentioned in an earlier section, in these experiments we did not represent the local context effects on stacking energies. This omission was made for the sake of simplicity, and it did not prevent the nets from achieving good results on small RNAs (length 30, and, in a few preliminary experiments with our multiresolution model, lengths from 100 to 130). However, success on much longer sequences probably requires the local context information, or indeed a very different problem-to-network mapping.

5.1.1 Update Algorithm and Annealing Schedule. The network relaxation algorithm used in all experiments was the MFT algorithm described in Sections Four and Five. A sweep through the network consisted of $N(N - 1)/2$ node updates; the choice of which node to update was made randomly each time. The updating was also asynchronous. The network was run for a given number of sweeps, unless stability (thermodynamic equilibrium) was achieved before reaching that number; a check for stability was made after each sweep.

In every experiment, the annealing schedule followed the same basic form: $T_{init} = 100$, $T_{final} = 1$, and $\Delta T = (T_{init} + 1)/n_{sweeps}$ for each sweep.

5.1.2 Dissimilarity and Predictive Accuracy. We define D, the structural dissimilarity between two RNA secondary structures (true or predicted) to be the proportion of possible basepairings on which they disagree:

$$\sum_{i=1}^{N-1} \sum_{j=i+1}^{N} \frac{2[round(a_{ij}) - b_{ij}]^2}{N(N-1)}$$

where a_{ij} and b_{ij} are the units in row i and column j in the secondary structure matrix representation of the network and of the known secondary structure, respectively. The *round()* function rounds a number $n \in [0, 1]$ to 0 or 1.

Predictive accuracy of a method for a given RNA sequence is therefore measured as the number of correct positional matches between the secondary structure matrix (prediction) and the actual known secondary structure, as a percentage of the total number of cells in the matrix. That is, it is $100/D$.

There are many ways to look at the problem of dissimilarity among sequences and structures. It is true that tRNAs are known to share a particular overall shape — often called the "clover leaf" pattern — that is, a main stem and loop with three smaller subordinate stem/loop structures. However, it is very important to note that the forty tRNAs used in these experiments differ significantly both in terms of base composition and the particular places in the sequences where the stems occur. They also vary somewhat in length — from 107 to 131 bases.

The initial subsequences used in the first experiments display even more diversity than the full-length tRNAs. Their thermodynamically optimal sec-

Accuracy
(% correct)

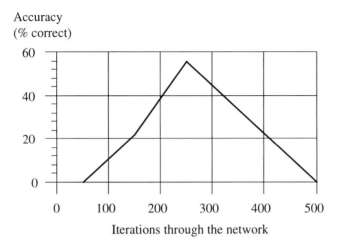

Iterations through the network

Figure 6. Predictive accuracy as a function of relaxation time, for the network with pre-set weights, with no learning

ondary structures, as determined by the Zuker program, do not all share the same overall structure. Some have one stem, others have two or three. The positions of the stems and loops also differ greatly. These general judgments concerning dissimilarity are valuable, but quantitative measures are also needed. The measurement of sequence homology is of course a standard tool in molecular biology. However, it is not especially relevant in these experiments, as sequences with a high degree of homology can produce very different secondary structures, and sequences with very similar structures can have a low degree of homology. Therefore, the positional matching measure of structure similarity described above, though not an ideal measure, is preferable in this case. The average structural dissimilarity among the training and test structures for the length-30 subsequences experiments was calculated to be 83 percent.

5.2 Pre-set Connection Weights, No Learning

The first experiment tested the predictive ability and examined the dynamics of a network with pre-set connection weights processing a particular 30-base sequence (initial subsequence of a tRNA from *Clostridium pasteurianum*).

The weights were set by hand, based on rough calculations of Hopfield-energy values for some desired network states corresponding to "legal" (though not actual) RNA secondary structures and the results of 20 trial-and-error runs of the simulator. The sequence was read into the network, the bias terms I_i initialized, and the network allowed to run the MFT algorithm for 500 sweeps through the net. Figure 6 is a plot of the number of sweeps against predictive accuracy for the simulation described.

Test Accuracy
(% correct)

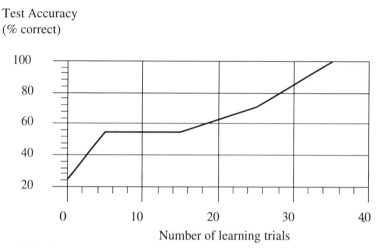

Number of learning trials

Figure 7. Predictive accuracy as a function of number of learning passes, 500 iterations on learning trials, 200 iterations on test.

Clearly, the preset network made some progress from a random state towards reasonable guesses at secondary structure. However, the predictive accuracy remained low (less than 60%), and the best solution obtained was not stable: after 250 iterations the network moved toward less optimal structures. The next section shows the degree to which learning improved the accuracy and stability of structure prediction.

5.3 Learning the Connection Weights

The second experiment was intended to test the capability of the basic MFT network to learn to predict RNA secondary structure, and to use the learned information to produce faster, more accurate, and more stable predictions than the network whose weights were preset.

5.3.1 The Learning Algorithms. The MFT learning algorithm described in Sections 4 and 5, modified to fit the small learning space approach, was used in the learning experiments. A set of 35 sequence/structure samples was used for supervised learning. Each sample was run through the "plus" and "minus" (clamped and unclamped) phases once. Thus there were only 35 learning passes in each experiment. The global learning variables, from which the connection weights were derived, were updated after each pass. A pass using the *test sequence*, the 30-base segment from the *C. pasteurianum* tRNA, was tried at various intervals throughout the learning experiment to test the abilities of the changing network. Note that a) the test sequence was not among the training sequences, and b) the learning variables and weights were not changed after a pass using the test sequence.

In the learning experiments, the network's initial weights were set to a

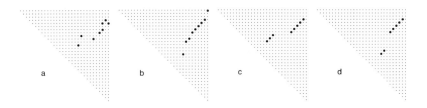

Figure 8. Network after 0; 5; 15 and 25; and 35 Learning Passes. (a) represents the net after 0 learning sweeps, (b) is 5 sweeps, (c) shows the net after both 15 and 25 sweeps, and (d) shows the output at the end, after 35 sweeps.

configuration that achieved better than random performance (15%) on a sequence that was neither a test nor a training sequence.

5.3.2 Results. Two experiments were performed, on five different test sequences: initial subsequences from tRNAs from *C. pasteurianum, Bacillus megaterium, Streptococcus faecalis, Mycoplasma capricolum,* and *Mycoplasma mycoides capri.* The experiments used the same initial weight configuration, the same learning rate, and the same annealing schedule. The results were very similar, so we describe the results for the same *C. pasteurianum* tRNA fragment used earlier.

In each experiment 200 sweeps were made through each annealing (minus phase) of the training sample. Only 100 sweeps were made through the network during the relaxation on the test sequence. The next diagram (Figure 7) is a plot of the accuracy of performance of the network after 0; 5; 15; 25; and 35 learning passes. Figure 8 displays network activation (output) diagrams for these snapshot points. Figure 8d is the correct structure (as predicted by the Zuker program). It is clear that the network did improve its performance drastically over the learning period. Also, its performance became quite good: It achieved perfect predictive accuracy after 35 learning passes. It is interesting also to note the steep improvement during the first 5 passes.

In a recent paper, Takefuji *et al.* [1990] report similar results with their non-learning neural net method for solving near-MIS of circle graphs. Their method found good structures (in 2 cases, structures more stable than those predicted by serial methods) for three RNA sequences of lengths 38; 59; and 359 bases.

6. Conclusions and Future Work

6.1 Conclusions

This report presents a new class of methods for predicting RNA secondary structures from sequences. The methods use artificial neural networks based on the Boltzmann Machine model and the Mean Field Theory deterministic approximations to the Boltzmann Machine.

The methodology described in this paper is:

- Formulate the 2°*RNA* problem as problem of optimization and search.

- Map the search problem onto a Hopfield network (typically a method of highly parallel local search). This mapping can be understood in terms of some simple combinatorics and graph theory.

- Avoid the problem of Hopfield local minima by using the MFT network training and relaxation algorithms, which implement a deterministic and "analog" (continuous) version of the stochastic Boltzmann Machine.

- Use the MFT learning algorithm and a highly-structured connection weight-sharing scheme to adjust a small set of parameters in the network's representation of the sequence-to-structure mapping, in order to improve performance over time.

After an introduction to the problem and a review and analysis of search techniques and neural network algorithms, the results of some preliminary experiments were reported.

Experiments were performed on a set of 35 tRNA sequences and fragments thereof, using neural network simulators implemented on serial computers. Conclusions drawn from the experiments include:

- At least on small RNA sequences, a properly-configured MFT neural network can learn a few global parameters from which connection weights can be derived that enable the accurate prediction of secondary structures. Related work on neural network methods without learning [Takefuji *et al.*, 1990] demonstrates that these methods may also work on moderate-sized RNAs.

- The learning can be very efficient. 35 learning examples, each passed through the network once, sufficed in the experiments. On each learning pass, fewer than 400 iterations through the network always sufficed. This fast and powerful learning is made possible by a method that constructs a very small learning space (4 or 5 variables) for an RNA secondary structure network. This method also enables a degree of scale-invariant learning.

- With the learned weights, the networks were able to converge quickly to exactly accurate solutions on the test sequences. 200 or fewer iterations were required.

- A degree of generalization is possible. The test sequences were not part of any of the learning sample sets, and in fact differed significantly from many of the learning samples.

6.2 Future Work

6.2.1 Interpreting the Network Dynamics; Representing Molecular Dynamics. The dynamics of MFT networks configured for the *2°RNA* problem are interesting enough to warrant further study. In particular, one would like to discover whether the dynamics of a relaxation search implement a particular, realistic *folding pathway* for an RNA molecule. The networks *seem* to mirror Martinez's kinetically-driven sequential cooperativity search: large stems form first and constrain the set of possible small stems; and at each stage the most thermodynamically favored stems appear. It would be interesting to investigate whether such behavior is inherent in the MFT approach, or whether it is an artifact of particular sequences or particular parameter settings.

In general, the currently prevailing models for molecular structure prediction with neural networks share an essentially *static* approach to the problem. In other words, a mapping is sought between sequence and final secondary or tertiary structure, making no use of intermediate stages of folding. Future research should explore ways to integrate kinetic effects and dynamical processes.

6.2.2 Interpreting Continuous Activation Levels., Throughout this project, we chose to round the activation states of the units to 0 or 1 when reading them as output. The MFT relaxation algorithm also tends to drive the activation values very close to their extrema. Thus all discussion was in terms of elements being paired or unpaired. However, it has been pointed out that in many cases network activation levels, read as real numbers, can be interpreted in terms of probabilities. Perhaps the network models could be used, like several other RNA structure prediction programs, to predict ensembles of near-optimal structures.

6.2.3 Bringing More Knowledge to Bear on the Problem. The simple representations of ribnucleotides (or amino acids) used typically in computer programs are very limited. A ribonucleotide is in reality more than a symbol; it is a molecule, with physical structure and several important physical and chemical properties that can be measured. Good simulation/prediction programs should probably represent these structural units as vectors, linear combinations of basis vectors representing physical and chemical characteristics, like molecular weight, steric configuration, charge, magnetic dipole, and hydrophobicity [Nakai, *et al* 1988; Hunter, 1992].

Phylogeny is another source of information. How can knowledge of the structure and sequence of one molecule be used to predict the structure of another molecule whose sequence is homologous or whose function is the same? Major *et al* [1991] describe a system for RNA secondary and tertiary structure prediction that combines geometric, energetic, phylogenetic and functional information within a symbolic constraint satisfaction framework.

Their results are impressive and lead one to wonder whether the addition of statistical induction (machine learning) methods might refine their existing knowledge base and produce even better results.

6.2.4 Tests on Longer RNA Sequences. Obviously, the methods described herein should be tested on larger RNAs, despite the space complexity problems afflicting the current versions of the basic algorithm (see below). The adaptive optimization approach seems to perform very well on small pieces of RNA when we have a reasonably large set of representative training data. However, a very similar but non-adaptive method [Takefuji, *et al,* 1990] has also apparently been made to work well on some small RNAs. I do not believe that neural networks with weights set "by hand", or graph-planarization algorithms that ignore thermodynamic subtleties, will scale up well to larger structure prediction problems. Larger scale experiments with adaptive algorithms will help us to determine whether a sufficient number of RNA sequences and solved structures are available to allow machine learning methods to refine and augment the very incomplete communal knowledge --- theoretical and empirical --- on the thermodynamics, kinetics, and molecular evolutionary history of RNA folding.

6.2.5 Coarse-Grained and Multiresolution Search. The representation described in Section 4 is useful because it is based on an obvious mapping of the RNA secondary structure matrix onto a neural net model, and is therefore easily understood. However, it is not very efficient in its use of hardware (simulated hardware, in the near term). The representation employs $O(N^2)$ processing units. (In fact, it employs exactly $N(N-1)/2$ units.) We have begun to develop ways to approximate such large nets with much smaller ones, by making assumptions about the covariance of members of clusters of units and then using single units to represent clusters of units. In the RNA secondary structure prediction problem, the clusters of interest are those diagonal clusters of units (corresponding to diagonals in the $2°RNA$ matrix) representing *potential stems* in the secondary structure.

The key to making such coarse-grained or multiresolution methods work, indeed the key to making any neural network method successful in molecular structure prediction, is to find a sensible mapping of the problem onto the network. Neural networks offer challenges in representing the static and dynamic structures of RNA (or protein), but success brings the benefits of massive parallelism and the simple, computable, and differentiable error measures needed for gradient descent and adaptive improvement in structure prediction. Solving the representational problems will lead to an entirely new class of fast, parallel, adaptive methods for predicting and simulating physical systems.

Notes

1. Much of the notation and many of the definitions in this section are adopted from [Sankoff et al., 1983]. We found their exposition on secondary

structure types and constraints to be the clearest by far, and we hope that their notational conventions become a standard in the field. Their text is copyright©, 1983, American Telephone and Telegraph Company, and used by permission.

Acknowledgements

The author would like to thank Dr. Geoffrey Hinton for helpful and insightful suggestions and critiques, and Dr. Rick Collins for his careful review of the original thesis. Thanks are also due to Dr. Carol Miernicki Steeg and Sarah Lesher for proofreading and helpful discussions and to Desirée Sy for editing and formatting help. The author appreciates the help of Raj Verma, Sudarsan Tandri, and Tim Horton with graphics and diagrams and Carol Plathan and Marina Haloulos with Macintosh tasks. Conversations with Dr. Larry Greller, Dr. F. Ray Salemme, and the UofT Connectionist Research Group have been very helpful in clarifying some ideas first described in the 1989 M. Sc. thesis.

Finally, the author gratefully acknowledges the support of the Natural Sciences and Engineering Research Council of Canada, the University of Toronto and its Connaught Fellowship Fund, and the E.I. Du Pont de Nemours & Co. in Delaware.

References

Ackley, D. H., Hinton, G. E., and Sejnowski, T. J. (1985) A Learning Algorithm for Boltzmann Machines. Cognitive Science, 9:147-169.

Altona, C., van Beuzekom, A. A., Orbons, L. P. M., and Pieters, M. L. (1988).Minihairpin Loops in DNA: Experimental and Theoretical Studies. In *Biological and Artificial Intelligence Systems*, pages 93-124. ESCOM Science Publishers B.V., Kingston, New York.

Anderson, P. W. (1988). Spin Glass Hamiltonians: A Bridge Between Biology, Statistical Mechanics and Computer Science. In Pines, D., editor, *Emerging Syntheses in Science*. Addison-Wesley, Santa Fe, NM.

Bohr, H., Bohr, J., Brunak, S., Cotterill, R. M., Lautrup, B., Norskov, L., Olsen, O. H., and Petersen, S. B. (1988). Protein Secondary Structure and Homology by Neural Networks: The Alpha-helices in Rhodopsin. *FEBS Letters*, 241:223-228.

Bohr, H., Bohr, J., Brunak, S., Cotterill, R. M. J., Fredhom, H., Lautrup, B., and Petersen, S. B. (1990). A Novel Approach to Prediction of the 3-Dimensional Structures of Protein Backbones by Neural Networks. *FEBS Letters*, 261:43-46.

Eppstein, D., Galil, Z., and Giancarlo, R. (1988). Speeding up Dynamic Programming. In *Proceedings: Foundations of Computer Science. IEEE*.

Friedrichs, M. S. and Wolynes, P. G. (1989). Toward Protein Tertiary Structure Recognition by Associative Memory Hamiltonians. *Science*, 246:371-373.

Greller, L. D., Steeg, E. W., and Salemme, F. R. (1991). Neural Networks for the Detection and Prediction of 3D Structural Motifs in Proteins. In *Proceedings of the Eighth International Conference on Mathematical and Computer Modelling*, College Park, Maryland.

Hellstrom, B. J. and Kanal, L. N. (1990). Asymmetric Mean-field Neural Networks for Multiprocessor Scheduling. Computer Science UMIACS-TR-90-99, University of Maryland, College Park, Maryland.

Holley, L. H. and Karplus, M. (1989). Protein Secondary Structure Prediction with a Neural Network. *Proceedings of the National Academy of Sciences U.S.A.*, 86:152- 156.

Hopfield, J. and Tank, D. (1985). Neural Computation of Decisions in Optimization Problems. *Biological Cybernetics*, 52:141-152.

Hopfield, J. J. (1982). Neural Networks and Physical Systems with Emergent Collective Computational Abilities. *Proceedings of the National Academy of Sciences U.S.A.*, 79:2554-2558.

Hunter, L. 1992 . Representing Amino Acids with Bitstrings. Submitted to *Computer Applications in the Biosciences*; code available by electronic mail from hunter@nlm.nih.gov.

Kirkpatrick, S., Gelatt, C. D., and Vecchi, M. P. (1983). Optimization by Simulated Annealing. *Science*, 220:671-680.

Major, F., Turcotte, M., Gautheret, D., Lapalme, G., Fillion, E., and Cedergren, R. (1991) The Combination of Symbolic and Numerical Computation for Three-dimensional Modeling of RNA. *Science*, 253:1255-1260.

Martinez, H. M. (1984). An RNA Folding Rule. *Nucleic Acids Research*, 12:323-334.

Martinez, H. M. (1988). An RNA Secondary Structure Workbench. *Nucleic Acids Research*, 16(5):1789-1798.

McClelland, J. L., Rumelhart, D. E., and the PDP Research Group (1986). *Parallel Distributed Processing: Explorations in the Microstructure of Cognition. Volume II.* Bradford Books, Cambridge, MA.

Metropolis, N., Rosenbluth, A. W., Rosenbluth, M. N., Teller, A. H., and Teller, E. (1953). Equations of State Calculations by Fast Computing Machines. *Journal of Chemical Physics*, 6:1087-1091.

Nakai, K., Kidera, A., and Kanehisa, M. (1988) Cluster Analysis of Amino Acid Indices for Prediction of Protein Structure and Function. *Protein Engineering*, 2(2):93-100.

Nussinov, R. and Jacobson, A. (1980). Fast Slgorithm for Predicting the Secondary Structure of Single-stranded RNA. *Proceedings National Academy of Sciences, U.S.A.*, 77:6309-6313.

Nussinov, R., Piecznic, G., Grigg, J. R., and Kleitman, D. J. (1978). Algorithms for loop matchings. *SIAM Journal of Applied Mathematics*, 35(1):68-82.

Peterson, C. and Anderson, J. (1987). A Mean Field Theory Learning Algorithm for Neural Networks. MCC Technical Report EI-259-87, Microelectronics and Computer Technology Corporation, Austin, TX.

Peterson, C. and Soderberg, B. (1989). A New Method for Mapping Optimization Problems onto Neural Networks. *International Journal of Neural Systems*, 1.

Pipas, J. M. and McMahon, J. E. (1975). Methods for Predicting RNA Secondary Structures. In *Proceedings of the National Academy of Sciences, U.S.A.*, volume 72, pages 2017-2021.

Pleij, C. W. A. (1990) Pseudoknots: a New Motif in the RNA Game. *Trends in Biochemical Sciences*, 15:143-147.

Qian, N. and Sejnowski, T. J. (1988). Predicting the Secondary Structure of Globular Proteins Using Neural Network Models. *Journal of Molecular Biology*, 202:865-884.

Sankoff, D., Kruskal, J. B., Mainville, S., and Cedergren, R. J. (1983). Fast Algorithms to Determine RNA Secondary Structures Containing Multiple Loops. In Sankoff, D. and Kruskal,

J. B., editors, *Time Warps, String Edits, and Macromolecules: The Theory and Practice of Sequence Comparison.* Addison-Wesley, Reading, MA.

Steeg, E. W. (1989). Neural Network Algorithms for RNA Secondary Structure Prediction. Master's thesis, University of Toronto Computer Science Dept.

Steeg, E. W. (1990). Neural Network Algorithms for RNA Secondary Structure Prediction. Technical Report CRG-TR-90-4, University of Toronto Computer Science Dept., Toronto, Canada.

Steeg, E. and Takefuji, I. (1991) Comments on Parallel Algorithms for Finding a Near Maximal Independent Set of a Circle Graph; and Author's Reply. *IEEE Transactions Neural Networks*, 2(2):328-329.

Stein, D. L. (1985). A Model of Protein Conformational Substates. *Proceedings of the National Academy of Sciences, U.S.A.*, 82:3670-3672.

Stryer, L. (1981). *Biochemistry, 2nd Edition.* W. H. Freeman and Company, San Francisco.

Studnicka, G. M., Rahn, G. M., Cummings, I. W., and Salser, W. A. (1978). Computer Methods for Predicting the Secondary Structure of Single-stranded RNA. *Nucleic Acids Research*, 5(9):3365-3387.

Takefuji, I., Chen, L.-L., Lee, K.-C., and Huffman, J. (1990). Parallel Algorithms for Finding a Near-maximum Independent Set of a Circle Graph. *IEEE Transactions on Neural Networks*, 1(3):263-267.

Tinoco, I., Borer, P. N., Dengler, B., Levine, M. D., Uhlenbeck, O. C., Crothers, D. M., and Gralla, J. (1973). Improved Estimation of Secondary Structure in Ribonucleic Acids. *Nature New Biology*, 246:40-41.

Tinoco, I., Uhlenbeck, O. C., and Levine, M. D. (1971). Estimation of Secondary Structure in Ribonucleic Acids. *Nature (London)*, 230:362.

Waterman, M. S. (1978). *Advances in Mathematics: Supplementary Studies Vol. I, Studies in Foundations and Combinatorics.* Academic Press, New York.

Waterman, M. S. and Smith, T. F. (1978). RNA Secondary Structure: A Complete Mathematical Analysis. *Mathematical Biosciences*, 42:257-266.

Watson, J. D. and Crick, F. H. C. (1953). Molecular Structure of Nucleic Acids. A Structure for Deoxyribose Nucleic Acid. *Nature (London)*, 171:737-738.

Wilcox, G. L. and Poliac, M. O. (1989). Generalization of Protein Structure from Sequence Using a Large Scale Backpropagation Network. UMSI 89/22, University of Minnesota Supercomputer Institute, 1200 Washington Avenue South, Minneapolis, MN 55415.

Wolpert, D. H. (1990) Constructing a Generalizer Superior to NETtalk via a Mathematical Theory of Generalization. *Neural Networks*, 3(4):445-452.

Zuker, M. and Stiegler, P. (1981). Optimal Computer Folding of Large RNA Sequences Using Thermodynamics and Auxiliary Information. *Nucleic Acids Research*, 9:133-148.

4

Predicting Protein Structural Features With Artificial Neural Networks

Stephen R. Holbrook, Steven M. Muskal

and Sung-Hou Kim

1 Introduction

The prediction of protein structure from amino acid sequence has become the Holy Grail of computational molecular biology. Since Anfinsen [1973] first noted that the information necessary for protein folding resides completely within the primary structure, molecular biologists have been fascinated with the possibility of obtaining a complete three-dimensional picture of a protein by simply applying the proper algorithm to a known amino acid sequence. The development of rapid methods of DNA sequencing coupled with the straightforward translation of the genetic code into protein sequences has amplified the urgent need for automated methods of interpreting these one-dimensional, linear sequences in terms of three-dimensional structure and function.

Although improvements in computational capabilities, the development of area detectors, and the widespread use of synchrotron radiation have reduced the amount of time necessary to determine a protein structure by X-ray crystallography, a crystal structure determination may still require one or more man-years. Furthermore, unless it is possible to grow large, well-ordered crystals of the protein of interest, X-ray structure determination is not even an option. The development of methods of structure determination by high resolution 2-D NMR has alleviated this situation somewhat, but this technique is also costly, time-consuming, requires large amounts of protein of high solubility and is severely limited by protein size. Clearly, current experimental methods of structure determination will not be able to cope with the present and future need for protein structure determination.

Efforts toward protein structure prediction have come from two general directions and their hybrids. The first, a molecular mechanics approach, assumes that a correctly folded protein occupies a minimum energy conformation, most likely a conformation near the global minimum of free energy. Predictions are based on a forcefield of energy parameters derived from a variety of sources including *ab initio* and semi-empirical calculations and experimental observations of amino acids and other small molecules [Weiner, *et al* 1984]. Potential energy is obtained by summing the terms due to bonded (distance, angle, torsion) and non-bonded (contact, electrostatic, hydrogen bond) components calculated from these forcefield parameters [Weiner & Kollman, 1981]. This potential energy can be minimized as a function of atomic coordinates in order to reach the nearest local minimum. This method is very sensitive to the protein conformation at the beginning of the simulation. One way to address this problem is use molecular dynamics to simulate the way the molecule would move away from that (usually arbitrary) initial state. Newton's equations of motion are used to describe the acceleration of atoms in a protein with respect to time; the movement in this simulation will be toward low energy conformations. The potential energy of the molecule can also be minimized at any point in a dynamics simulation. This method searches a larger proportion of the space of possible confirmations.

Nevertheless, only through an exhaustive conformation search can one be insured to locate the lowest energy structure. Even restricting the representation of a confirmation of a protein as much as possible, to only a single point of interest per amino acid and two angles connecting the residues, the combinatorial aspect of an exhaustive search lead to difficult computational problems [Wetlaufer, 1973]. Under the further simplification of restricting each atom in the protein chain to a discrete location on a lattice [Covell & Jernigan, 1990] and searching the conformation space with very simple energy equations, the exhaustive search method is feasible for only small proteins. Alternatively, conformational space may be sampled randomly and sparsely by monte carlo methods with the hope that a solution close enough to the global energy minimum will be found so that other methods will be able to converge to the correct conformation. Given an approximately correct model from either monte carlo searches or other theoretical or experimental approaches, the technique of molecular dynamics has become the method of choice for refinement, or improvement, of the model. This approach allows the moving molecule to overcome some of the traps of local energy minima in its search for a global minimum.

In general, the energetics approach of molecular mechanics is fraught with problems of inaccurate forcefield parameters, unrealistic treatment of solvent, and landscapes of multiple minima. It appears that this direction will be most valuable in combination with other methods which can provide an approximate starting model.

The second major focus of research toward predicting protein structures from sequence alone is a purely empirical one, based on the databases of known protein structures and sequences. This approach hopes to find common features in these databases which can be generalized to provide structural models of other proteins. For example, the different frequencies at which various amino acid types occur in secondary structural elements; helices, strands, turns and coils, has led to methods [Chou & Fasman, 1974a; Chou & Fasman, 1974b; Garnier, Osguthorpe & Robson, 1978; Lim, 1974a; Lim, 1974b] for predicting the location of these elements in proteins. Even more powerful and now widely used is the prediction of tertiary structure by sequence homology or pattern matching to previously determined protein structures [Blundell, Sibanda & Pearl, 1983; Greer, 1981; Warme, et al, 1974] or structural elements, such as zinc binding fingers, helix-turn-helix DNA binding motifs and the calcium binding EF hand. A portion of a target protein that has a sequence similar to a protein or motif with known structure is assumed to have the same structure. Unfortunately, for many proteins there is not sufficient homology to any protein sequence or sub-sequence of known structure to allow application of this technique. Even proteins thought to have similar structures on functional grounds may show such little sequence similarity that it is very difficult to determine a proper sequence alignment from which to propose a molecular model.

Thus, an empirical approach, which derives general rules for protein structure from the existing databases and then applies them to sequences of unknown structure currently appears to be the most practical starting point for protein structure prediction. Various methods have been used for extracting these rules from structural databases, ranging from visual inspection of the structures [Richardson, 1981], to statistical and multivariate analyses [Chou & Fasman, 1974; Krigbaum & Knutton, 1973]. Recently, artificial neural networks have been applied to this problem with great success [Crick, 1989]. These networks are capable of effecting any mapping between protein sequence and structure, of classifying types of structures, and identifying similar structural features from a database. Neural network models have the advantage of making complex decisions based on the unbiased selection of the most important factors from a large number of competing variables. This is particularly important in the area of protein structure determination, where the principles governing protein folding are complex and not yet fully under-

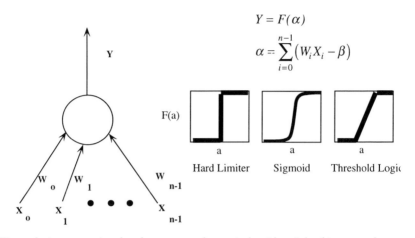

Figure 1. A computational node represented as a circle with weighted inputs and out-put shown as arrows. The formula for summation of weighted input and bias (b) is given, as well as three common functional forms of nonlinearity which may be used by the node to determine output

stood. The researcher is then able to explore various hypotheses in the most general terms, using the neural network as a tool to prioritize the relevant information.

The remainder of this review will discuss neural networks in general including architecture and strategies appropriate to protein structure analysis, the available databases, specific applications to secondary and tertiary structure prediction, surface exposure prediction, and disulfide bonding prediction. Finally, we will discuss the future approaches, goals and prospects of artificial neural networks in the prediction of protein structure.

2. Artificial Neural Networks

Artificial neural networks appear well suited for the empirical approach to protein structure prediction. Similar to the process of protein folding, which is effectively finding the most stable structure given all the competing interactions within a polymer of amino acids, neural networks explore input information in parallel. . Inside the neural network, many competing hypotheses are compared by networks of simple, non-linear computation units. While many types of computational units exist, the most common sums its inputs and passes the result through some kind of nonlinearity. Figure 1 illustrates a typical computational node and three common types of nonlinearity; hard limiters, sigmoidal, and threshold logic elements. Nearly every neural network model is composed of these types of computational units. The main

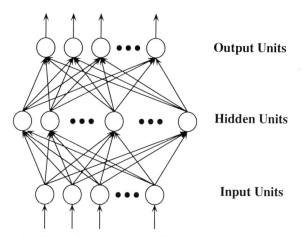

Figure 2. A three layer feedforward neural network. The circles represent the computational nodes which integrate input from the preceding layer and transmit a signal to the next layer. Arrows represent weighted links (connections) between these nodes which modulate incoming signals. The three layer network presented is the most common, but additional layers are possible.

differences exist in topology (node connectivity), methods of training, and application. This article will focus primarily on one type of network, the feedforward network trained with backpropagation for rule extraction purposes. Networks are termed feedforward because information is provided as input and propagated in a forward manner, with each computational unit integrating its inputs and "firing" according to its non-linearity. The following sections will describe in more detail the characteristics of feedforward networks, the preferred method of training with backpropagation, and useful techniques for network optimization.

2.1 Feedforward Networks

A typical feed-forward network is depicted in Figure 2. These networks are often composed of two to three layers of nodes; input and output or input, hidden, and output. Each network has connections between every node in one layer and every other node in the layer above. Two layer networks, or perceptrons, are only capable of processing first order information and consequently obtain results comparable to those of multiple linear regression. Hidden node networks, however, can extract from input information the higher order features that are ignored by linear models.

Feedforward networks are taught to map a set of input patterns to a corresponding set of output patterns. In general, a network containing a large enough number of hidden nodes can always map an input pattern to its corresponding output pattern [Rumelhart & McClelland, 1986]. Once such networks learn this mapping for a set of training patterns, they are tested on examples that are in some way different from those used in training. While most feedforward networks are designed to maximize generalization from training examples to testing examples, some networks are intentionally forced to memorize their training examples. Such networks are then tested with either an incomplete or subtly different pattern. The output of the network will be the memory that best matches the input..

2.2 Training Procedure

The process of training a feedforward network involves presenting the network with an input pattern, propagating the pattern through the architecture, comparing the network output to the desired output, and altering the weights in the direction so as to minimize the difference between the actual output and the desired output. Initially however, the network weights are random and the network is considered to be ignorant. While many algorithms exist for training, clearly the most frequently used technique is the method of backpropagation [Rumelhart, Hinton & Williams, 1986]. Backpropagation involves two passes through the network, a forward pass and a backward pass. The forward pass generates the network's output activities and is generally the least computation intensive. The more time consuming backward pass involves propagating the error initially found in the output nodes back through the network to assign errors to each node that contributed to the initial error. Once all the errors are assigned, the weights are changed so as to minimize these errors. The direction of the weight change is:

$$\Delta W_{ij} = \upsilon \cdot \delta_j \cdot O_i \tag{1}$$

where W_{ij} is the weight from node i to node j, v is a learning rate, δ_j is an error term for node j, O_i is either the output of node i or an input value if node i is an input node. If the node j is an output node, then

$$\delta_j = F'_j(net_j) \cdot (T_j - O_j) \tag{2}$$

with

$$net_j = \sum_i (W_{ij} \cdot O_i) \tag{3}$$

where $F_j'(net_j)$ is the derivative of the nonlinear activation function which maps a unit's total input to an output value, T_j is the target output of the output node and O_j is the actual output. If node j is an internal hidden node, then

$$\delta_j = F'_j(net_j) \cdot \sum_{k>j} (\delta_k \cdot W_{jk}) \tag{4}$$

The weight change as described in Equation 1 can be applied after each example, after a series of examples, or after the entire training set has been presented. Often momentum terms are added and weight changes are smoothed to effect faster convergence times. Regardless of the training recipe however, the main goal of the network is to minimize the total error E of each output node j over all training examples p:

$$E = \sum_p \sum_j \left(T_j - O_j\right)^2 \tag{5}$$

2.3 Network Optimization

Because the rules in most input-output mappings are complex and often unknown, a series of architecture optimizing simulations are required when testing each hypothesis. Examples of such optimizing experiments include varying input representation, numbers of hidden nodes, numbers of training examples, etc. In each case, some measure of network performance is evaluated and tabulated for each network architecture or training condition. The best performing network is chosen as that which performs the best on both the training and testing sets.

With networks containing hidden nodes, training algorithms face the problem of multiple-minima when minimizing the output error across all training patterns. If the error space is rugged, as is often the case in hidden node networks, the multiple-minima problem can be a serious one. To combat this problem, researchers often permute their training and testing sets and train a number of times on each set, while reporting the best performing network for each simulation. The variance between training and testing sets as well as between training sessions helps to describe the complexity of the weight space as well as the input-output mapping.

Generally smooth trends in performance levels immediately point to optimal network architectures. One nuisance to those who are designing networks to generalize from training examples to testing examples, however, is the concept of memorization or overfitting: the network learns the training examples, rather than the general mapping from inputs to outputs that the training set exemplifies. Memorization reduces the accuracy of network generalization to untrained examples. Sure signs of undesired memorization become apparent when the network performs much better on its training set than on its testing set; and typically, this results when the network contains far more weights than training examples. When undesired memorization results, the researcher is forced to increase the numbers of training examples, reduce node connectivity, or in more drastic situations, reduce the number of input, hidden, and/or output nodes. Increasing the number of training examples is by far the best remedy to the effects of memorization. But more often than not, especially in the area of protein structure prediction, one is constrained with a relatively small database. If it is not possible to increase the database of training examples, the next best choice is to reduce the network connectivity. This, however, poses the problem of deciding on which connections to remove. Here, some have tried removing those connections that are used the least or that vary the most in the training process. This process of network pruning, however, often slows the already lengthy training process and should be done with caution. Finally, reducing the number of network nodes is the least desirable of all approaches since it often results in hiding key information from the network, especially if the number of input nodes is reduced. Similarly, reducing the number of hidden nodes often results in unacceptable input-output mappings; while reducing the number of output nodes, often results in mappings that are no longer useful. Clearly, undesired memorization is one of the greatest drawbacks with neural network computing. Until methods for alleviating the problem are developed, researchers are forced to be clever in their design of representations and network architecture.

Feedforward neural networks are powerful tools. Aside from possessing the ability to learn from example, this type of network has the added advantage of being extremely robust, or fault tolerant. Even more appealing is that the process of training is the same regardless of the problem, thus few if any assumptions concerning the shapes of underlying statistical distributions are required. And most attractive is not only the ease of programming neural network software, but also the ease with which one may apply the software to a large variety of very different problems. These advantages and others have provided motivation for great advances in the arena of protein structure prediction, as the following sections suggest.

2.4 Protein Structure and Sequence Databases

Application of an empirical approach to protein structure prediction is entirely dependent on the experimental databases which are available for analysis, generalization and extrapolation. Since all of the studies discussed below are dependent on these databases, a brief discussion of their contents is appropriate.

The Brookhaven Protein Data Bank [Bernstein et al, 1977], or PDB, currently (April, 1990) contains atomic coordinate information for 535 entries. These entries are primarily determined by X-ray crystallography, but some more recent entries are from two-dimensional NMR and molecular modeling studies. Of the 535 entries, 37 are nucleic acids, 10 are polysaccharides and 27 are model structures. Of the remaining entries many of the proteins are essentially duplicated, with either minor amino acid changes due to biological source or specific mutation or with different ligands bound. Taking these factors into account, one can estimate that the Protein Data Bank, currently contains 180 unique protein coordinates sets. Besides the x, y, z coordinates of the non-hydrogen atoms of the proteins and bound co-factors, the following information is included in the Protein Data Bank entries: protein name, a list of relevant literature references, the resolution to which the structure was determined, the amino acid sequence, atomic connectivity, the researcher's judgement of secondary structure and disulfide bonding pattern, and also may contain atomic temperature factors (measure of mobility), coordinates of bound water molecules and other ligands, a discussion of the refinement scheme and its results (estimate of error), and other miscellaneous comments the depositors may wish to make.

In addition to the information directly available from the PDB several computer programs are available both through Brookhaven and from external sources for calculation of additional structural parameters from the entries. These programs calculate such values as the main chain conformational angles phi and psi, the side chain torsion angles, the surface area accessible to a water molecule, distances between all residue pairs in the form of a matrix and may also make automatic assignments of disulfide bonds, secondary structure and even super-secondary structure folding patterns. The most widely used of these programs and the one employed for most of the neural network studies is the DSSP program of Kabsch and Sander [Kabsch & Sander, 1983].

Because of the difficulty of the experimental methods of protein structure determination, the number of known three-dimensional protein structures is much less than the number of protein sequences which have been determined. It is vital, then, to merge this information together with the structural information of the PDB in attempts to predict protein structure. The Protein Identification Resource [George, et al, 1986] or PIR, as of December 31, 1989 contained 7822 protein sequences consisting of 2,034,937 residues. The amino acid sequences of these proteins were determined either by chemical sequencing methods or inferred from the nucleic acid sequences which code for them. The PIR database contains, in addition to amino acid sequence, information concerning the protein name, source, literature references, functional classification and some biochemical information.

An even larger database of sequences is found in the GENBANK collection of nucleic acid sequences. Many of these sequences code for proteins whose sequences may be obtained by a simple translation program. The nucleic acid sequences which code for proteins may eventually become the source for additional entries in the PIR, but because of the rapid growth of both the GENBANK and PIR databases there currently is a large backlog of sequences to be added to these data banks.

A variety of computer programs also are available for analysis of the protein sequence database, the PIR. These programs include those which calculate amino acid composition, search for sequence similarity or homology, conserved functional sequences, plot hydrophobicity and predict secondary structure.

Secondary Structure

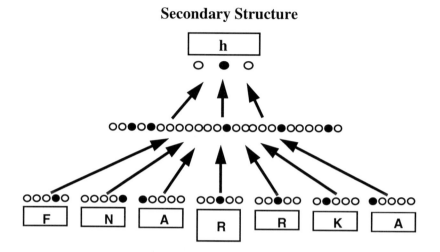

Figure 3. A feedforward neural network of the type used by Qian and Sejnowski [1988] for the prediction of secondary structure from a window of input amino acid sequence. Active nodes are shaded and the connections between each node and all other nodes above it are illustrated schematically by arrows. Only 5 input nodes are shown for each amino acid although 21 were used.

3 Secondary Structure Prediction with Neural Networks

At present, the largest application of feedforward neural networks in the world of protein structure prediction has been the prediction of protein secondary structure. As secondary structures (α-helices, β-strands, β-turns, etc) are by definition the regions of protein structure that have ordered, locally symmetric backbone structures, many have sought to predict secondary structure from the sequence of contributing amino acids [Chou & Fasman, 1974a; Chou & Fasman, 1974b; Garnier, Osguthorpe & Robson, 1978; Lim, 1974a; Lim, 1974b[. Recently though, Qian and Sejnowski (1988], Holley and Karplus [1989], Bohr *et al.* [1988], and McGregor *et al.* [1989] have applied neural network models to extract secondary structural information from local amino acid sequences and have achieved improved secondary structure prediction levels over that derived by statistical analysis [Chou & Fasman, 1974a; Chou & Fasman, 1974b].

3.1 α-Helix, β-Strand, and Coil Predictions

The general hypothesis taken when attempting to predict secondary structure is that an amino acid intrinsically has certain conformational preferences and these preferences may to some extent be modulated by the locally surrounding amino acids. Using this information, network architectures of the

Window Size	$Q_3(\%)$	C_α	C_β	C_{coil}
1	53.90	0.11	0.14	0.17
3	57.70	0.22	0.20	0.30
5	60.50	0.28	0.26	0.37
7	61.90	0.32	0.28	0.39
9	62.30	0.33	0.28	0.38
11	62.10	0.36	0.29	0.38
13	**62.70**	**0.35**	**0.29**	**0.38**
15	62.20	0.35	0.31	0.38
17	61.50	0.33	0.27	0.37
21	61.60	0.33	0.27	0.32

Table 1. Dependence of testing accuracy on window size (adapted from Qian & Sejnowski, 1988). Q_3 is average percent correct over three predicted quantities (α, β, coil). C is correlation coefficient for each prediction type, as defined by Mathews [1975].

type in shown in Figure 3 have been designed to predict an amino acid's secondary structure given the sequence context with which it is placed.

Qian and Sejnowski [1988] and others [Holley & Karplus 1989; Bohr *et al.* 1988] have shown that a locally surrounding window of amino acids does improve prediction levels as shown in Table 1. This table indicates that when the size of the window was small, the performance on the testing set was reduced, suggesting that information outside the window is important for predicting secondary structure. When the size of the window was increased beyond 6 residues on each side of a central residue, however, the performance deteriorated. Therefore, when using only local sequence information, residues beyond 6 residues in each direction contribute more noise than information in deciding a central amino acid's secondary structure.

Further attempts at improving prediction levels by adding a variable num-

Hidden Units	$Q_3(\%)$
0	62.50
5	61.60
10	61.50
15	62.60
20	62.30
30	62.50
40	62.70
60	61.40

Table 2. Testing of secondary structure prediction versus number of hidden nodes. (adapted from Qian & Sejnowski, 1988)

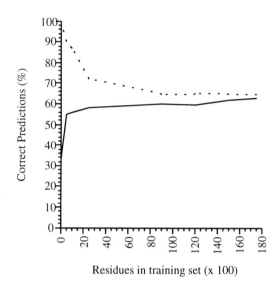

Figure 4. Relationship between prediction accuracy on the Training and Testing sets and number of residues in the Training set. Adopted from Qian and Sejnowski [1988]i

ber of hidden nodes as seen in Table 2 were only slightly successful. In fact, the best performing network containing 40 hidden nodes offers only a small improvement over the network containing 0 hidden nodes. This result suggests that the mapping between flanking amino acid sequence and an amino acid's secondary structure is of first order, requiring little if any higher order information (information due to interactions between 2 or more residues in the input sequence).

Further studies showed the maximum performance of the network as a function of the training set size as seen in Figure 4. The maximum performance on the training set decreases with the number of amino acids in the training set because more information is being encoded in a fixed set of weights. The testing set success rate, however, increases with size because the larger training set increases the network's generalization ability. Figure 4 nicely depicts the concept of memorization. When the training set is small, the network can memorize the details and suffers on the testing set. When the training set is large, memorization is not possible and generalization is forced. Furthermore, Figure 4 suggests that any additional increase in the size of the training set is unlikely to increase the network's testing performance, implying that more information for predicting secondary structure is required than that contained in a window of 13 consecutive amino acids. This missing information is undoubtedly in the tertiary contacts between residues in the proteins. The three-dimensional fold of the protein chain en-

Method	$Q_3(\%)$	C_α	C_β	C_{coil}
Chou-Fasman	50.00	0.25	0.19	0.24
Garnier	53.00	0.31	0.24	0.24
Lim	50.00	0.35	0.21	0.20
Qian & Sejnowski - 1	62.70	0.35	0.29	0.38
Qian & Sejnowski - 2	64.30	0.41	0.31	0.41
Holley & Karplus	63.20	0.41	0.32	0.36

Table 3. Accuracy comparison of methods of secondary structure prediction. Qian & Sejnowski - 1 is their perceptron network, Qian & Sejnowski - 2 includes a smoothing network using predictions from the first network as input. See text.

velopes most of the amino acids in a unique environment, thus modifying their inherent tendencies toward a particular secondary structure. A prediction limit is therefore approached when only local sequence information is available.

The performance of Qian and Sejnowski's network compared to those prediction methods of Garnier *et. al.* [1978], Chou & Fasman [1974b], Lim [1974], and Holley & Karplus [1989] is shown in Table 3. Clearly, the neural networks out-perform those methods of the past. Approximately 1% of the 11% improvement in Table 3 between Garnier's method and the neural network method is attributed to the difference between the network's training set and the set of proteins used to compile Garnier's statistics.

One benefit of using networks containing no hidden nodes is the ease with which the network weights can be interpreted. While Sanger [Sanger, D., Personal Communication] has developed a method of weight analysis for hidden node networks called contribution analysis, the technique is still in its infancy. Until more researchers turn to this or other methods of hidden node network weight analysis, graphical representations of the weights from input to output nodes will have to suffice.

Figure 5 details the relative contribution to the decision of a secondary structure made Qian and Sejnowski's network for each amino acid at each window position. Here, correlations between each amino acid's sequence specific secondary structure preference and its physical properties can be readily extracted.

In a parallel study to that of Qian and Sejnowski, Holley and Karplus [1989] have designed a similar network for prediction of secondary structure. Their optimal network contains an input layer of 8 amino acids on either side of the residue of interest (window size equals 17), a hidden layer of two nodes and an output layer of two nodes. The two node output layer describes three states: helix, strand and coil by taking on values of 1/0, 0/1 and 0/0 respectively. Since the actual values of these nodes lie between 0 and 1, a cutoff value or threshold was determined which optimized the network predic-

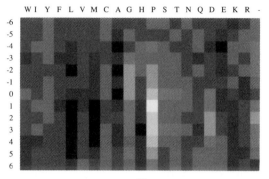

(A)

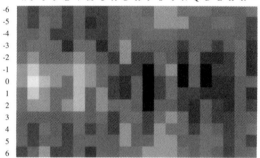

(B)

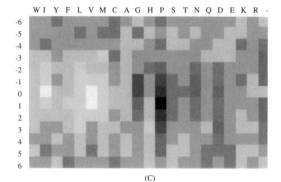

(C)

Figure 5. The relative values of the connection weights obtained by Qian and Se-
jnowski [1989] in their perceptron network for prediction of helix (a), strand (b) and
coil (c) from amino acid sequence. For each window position and amino acid type
the weight of its link to the next layer is represented as a shade of gray. Darker
shades indicate higher weights. The amino acid residues in this and following simi-
lar figures are in order of decreasing hydrophobicity according to Eisenberg [1984]

tion. The maximum overall prediction accuracy on the training set was 63.2% (Table 3) over three states with C_α 0.41, C_β 0.32 and C_{coil} 0.36 which are very similar to the results discussed previously. They also noted an increase in prediction accuracy for residues near the amino-terminus and for highly buried versus partially exposed β-strands. Finally, residues with higher output activities were found to be more accurately predicted, i.e. the strongest 31% of predictions were 79% correct. The Holley and Karplus perceptron network has recently been implemented on an IBM-compatible microcomputer and shown to reproduce their results [Pascarella & Bossa, 1989].

Attempting to extend these studies, Bohr et al. [1988] designed three separate networks to predict simply if a residue was in a helix or not, strand or not, and coil or not given a window of 25 residues on each side of a central amino acid. Clearly, by the size of this network, memorization was inevitable. But they, as will be mentioned in their approach to tertiary structure prediction, seem to desire memorization. In fact, their approach seems to have led to a new measure of homology.

Again using a window of 25 residues on each side of a central amino acid, but extending the output to α-helix, β-strand, and coil, Bohr et al. trained a network similar to Qian and Sejnowski's on one member of a homologous pair of proteins. The percent performance on the other protein, then, indicated the degree of homology. In this way, Bohr et al. used to their advantage the concept of network memorization to determine the degree of similarity between protein sequences, without requiring any sequence alignment.

In a practical application of neural networks for the prediction of protein secondary structure, a prediction of helix and strand location was made for the human immunodeficiency virus (HIV) proteins p17, gp120 and gp41 from their amino acid sequences [Andreassen, et al, 1990]. The input layer used an amino acid sequence window of 51 residues (1020 binary units) and a hidden layer of 20 units. Separate networks were trained for α-helices and β-strands and used in their prediction.

3.2 β-turn Predictions

In order for proteins to be compact, folded structures that pack their secondary structures into remarkably small volumes [Richardson, 1981; Rose, 1978], they must have a number of chain reversals. β-Turns are a specific class of chain reversals localized over a four-residue sequence[Richardson, 1981; Venkatachalam, 1968] and are defined by having a distance between $C\alpha(i)$ and $C\alpha(i+3)$ of < 7A. Seven classes (I,I',II,II',VIa,VIb,VIII) and a miscellaneous category (IV) have been defined [Richardson, 1981; Venkatachalam, 1968; Lewis, Momany & Sheraga, 1973] and differ by hydrogen bond interactions between involved residues. The most common classes of turns being I and II (41 and 26% of all turns), for example, have a specific

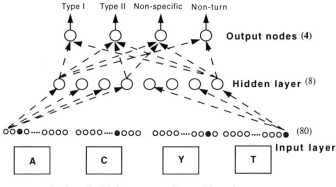

Figure 6. The network architecture used by McGregor, et al. for identification of β-turns. The input layer is a sequence of 4 amino acids comprising aβ-turn or non-turn presented to the network as 20 nodes per amino acid. The output layer has one node per turn (or non-turn) type. Shaded circles indicate activated nodes and dashed arrows schematically represent the weighted links between all node.

hydrogen bond interaction between the C=O of residue i and the N-H of residue i+3.

Similar to the prediction of α-helices and β-strands, network predictions for β-turns begin with the hypothesis that the information necessary to force the sequence of amino acids into a β-turn exists locally in a small window of residues. The network architecture designed to further this notion is depicted in Figure 6. Once again, the input to the network encodes a string of amino acids. The output classifies the sequence as one of four types, Type I, Type II, Non-Specific, or Non-turn.

Because the window size is fixed at four by the definition of β-turns, the only network optimizing simulations required were those that determine optimal numbers of hidden nodes. McGregor *et al.* [1989] have reported, as shown in Table 4 a network performance with 0 (perceptron) and 8 hidden nodes. Statistics were calculated for six different testing sets and the mean value is indicated. Table 4 also compares the performance of these networks to the method of Chou and Fasman [1974b]. The low values for the overall prediction accuracy reflect the stringent requirement that all four residues in the β-turn must be correctly predicted. On an individual residue basis, 71% of the predictions are correct compared to a chance level of 58%.

A commonly occurring issue addressed in this paper is how to adjust the relative ratio of the four different turn types (different outputs) in the training set. Since the numbers of types of turns and non-turns differ considerably, it was important to decide how frequently to sample each input type. Sampling

Prediction Method	% correct	$C_{\beta\text{-turn}}$
Perceptron	24.1	0.177
Hidden Layer Network	26.0	0.202
Chou-Fasman	20.6	0.167

Table 4. Statistics for β-turn prediction

of each type with equal frequency led to a large overdetermination of turns, however if the sequences were sampled according to the frequency at which they actually occur then all the predictions were for non-turns. The authors finally used a trial and error approach, obtaining the best results by sampling type I, II, non-specific turns and non-turns in the ratio 6:3:8:34, approximately the correct ratio except that the non-turns were reduced by a factor of six. This biased distribution of examples may partially account for the low prediction performance obtained with this network.

3.3 Secondary Structure Composition Predictions

Given the above mentioned work, it appears that the information encoded in small windows of local sequence is sufficient to correctly predict approximately two-thirds of a protein's secondary structure [Qian & Sejnowski, 1988; Holley & Karplus, 1989; McGregor, et al, 1989]. Because of this less than satisfactory rate of prediction, many have sought to improve the accuracy of secondary structure predictions by adjusting predictions based on a consensus of many predictive methods [Nishikawa & Ooi, 1986], the secondary structure of seemingly similar proteins [Nishikawa & Ooi, 1986; Levin & Garnier, 1988; Zvelebil, *et al*, 1987], and an *a priori* knowledge of secondary structure composition [Garnier, *et al,* 1978]. In attempts to predict the latter, others have noted that there exists a correlation between secondary structure composition and amino acid composition [Crick, 1989; Nishikawa & Ooi, 1982; Nishikawa, *et al*, 1983].

Neural networks have recently been applied by Muskal and Kim [1992] to the problem of mapping amino acid composition to secondary structure composition. They trained a network to map a string of real numbers representing amino acid composition, molecular weight and presence or absence of a heme cofactor onto two real valued output nodes corresponding to percent α-helix and percent β-strand. A second, or tandem, network was used to detect memorization and maximize generalization.

Networks with and without hidden nodes were able to accurately map amino acid composition to secondary structure composition. The correlations between predicted and real secondary structure compositions for the networks containing no hidden nodes are quite similar to those obtained by techniques of multiple linear regression [Krigbaum & Knutton, 1973; Horne, 1988] and by standard statistical clustering methods [Nishikawa & Ooi,

1982; Nishikawa, et al, 1983], while those obtained with hidden node networks are considerably greater.

The improved performance with networks containing hidden nodes is likely a result of the information contained in combinations of the quantities of each amino acid type, i.e. x amount of Ala with y amount of His. Perhaps secondary structure content is dependent both on composition individual amino acids and on combinations of these compositions. Therefore, in the interest of *de novo* and secondary structure design, serious consideration of potential protagonist and/or antagonist amino acid composition combinations may lead to improved success rates.

The hidden node network's high accuracy, however, (within ±5.0% and ±5.6% for helix and strand composition respectively) is the best predictive performance for secondary structure composition to date and can be attributed to the non-linear mapping of multi-layer neural networks. It should be noted that the error in these predictions is comparable to the errors associated with the experimental technique of circular dichroism (Johnson, 1990).

Utilizing the network weights made available from Qian and Sejnowski [1988] and counting secondary structure predictions, total average errors for helix, strand, and coil composition were approximately ±9.1%, ±12.6%, and ±12.9% respectively. By correcting for predicted secondary composition, Qian and Sejnowski's predictions can be altered to improve the prediction rate from 64% to 67%. Clearly, though secondary structure composition predictions are useful and can offer some improvement to secondary structure prediction, secondary structure predictions do appear to have reached a plateau. This leveling of secondary structure predictions has inspired more effort in the direction of predicting tertiary interactions, as the next sections will suggest.

4 Prediction of Amino Acid Residues on the Protein Surface

The residues on a protein surface play a key role in interaction with other molecules, determine many physical properties, and constrain the structure of the folded protein. Surface exposure of an amino acid residue can be quantified as the area accessible to a water molecule in the folded protein [Lee & Richards, 1971]. The calculation of solvent accessibility, however, has generally required explicit knowledge of the experimentally determined three-dimensional structure of the protein of interest.

Recently, Holbrook, *et al* [1990] have applied neural network methods to extract information about surface accessibility of protein residues from a database of high-resolution protein structures. Neural networks of the type seen in Figure 7 were trained to predict the accessibility of a central residue in context of its flanking sequence.

In order to predict surface exposure of protein residues, it is first neces-

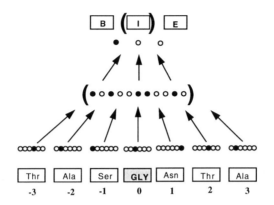

Figure 7. Neural network architecture used for the prediction of solvent accessibility of amino acid residues in proteins. Each amino acid in the window was represented by activating one of 21 binary input nodes. The output consisted of either one, two, or three nodes, corresponding to either a continuous, binary (buried/exposed) or ternary (buried/intermediate/exposed) definition of accessibility

sary to define categories for the buried and exposed residues. Recent definitions [Rose, *et al*, 1985] use the fractional exposure of residues in folded proteins compared with a standard, fully exposed state such as found in extended tripeptides. In the network analysis, two definitions of surface accessible residues were used: 1) a binary model in which buried residues are defined as those with less than 20% of the standard state exposure and accessible residues as those greater than 20% fully exposed and 2) a ternary model in which a residue is either fully buried (0-5% exposure), intermediate (5-40%) exposure, or fully accessible (greater than 40% exposure). A continuous model, which required prediction of the actual fractional exposure was also explored.

The neural networks used in this study contained either zero (perceptron) or one hidden layers and weights set by backpropagation (see Figure 7). The protein sequences were presented to the neural networks as *windows,* or subsequences, of 1-13 residues centered around and usually including the amino acid of interest, which slide along the entire sequence. For experiments involving only the flanking residues, the central residue was omitted from the window.

4.1 Binary Model

Window size was varied between 1 (no neighbors) and 13 (6 amino acids on either side of the central) residues for both training and testing networks containing two outputs. Table 5 shows the results of these experiments. The correct overall prediction for the training set is seen to reach a maximum of about 74% at window size 11 (-5:5) with a correlation coefficient of 0.48. The highest percentage of correct prediction, 72%, and correlation coefficient, 0.44, for the testing set was obtained with a window size of 9 (-4:4) residues. This is only a 2% increase over the 70% obtained with networks trained on patterns of only single amino acids (window size 1). To investigate the significance of this difference and the influence of flanking residues on exposure or burial of the central residue a network using examples consisting of *only* the flanking residues and excluding the central residue was trained and tested on the same databases. This network was able to predict exposure of the central residue in 55.3% of the cases with a correlation coefficient of 0.10 indicating that the sequence of the flanking residues has a small, but significant effect on exposure of the central residue.

Analysis of the predictive capacity of the trained network as a function of location of the residue being predicted in the protein sequence indicated that the residues at the extreme N-terminus can be predicted with much greater accuracy than the protein as a whole. The 10 amino terminal residues of the proteins in the testing set can be correctly predicted in 84% of the cases (correlation coefficient 0.50). A similar, but smaller effect is seen for the residues at the carboxy-termini where 75% of the predictions are correct (correlation coefficient 0.47). The high predictability of the N-terminal residues may reflect the fact that this is the first region of the protein synthesized and as such exists transiently in a different environment from the remainder of the protein. It should also be noted that both the N-terminal and C-terminal portions of the chain are more hydrophilic than the bulk of the protein.

An advantage of neural network analysis is that a prediction of surface exposure is based on quantitative activity values at each of the output nodes. Therefore a confidence level may be assigned to each prediction based on the strength of the output activities. While the accuracy of prediction increases with the minimum activity accepted, a corresponding decrease is seen in the percent of the total residues whose accessibility is predicted. For example, using the binary model of accessibility, while 100% of tested residues are predicted with an accuracy of 72%, over half of the residues with the strongest activities are predicted with greater than 80% accuracy.

4.2 Ternary Model

The use of a three state exposure model offers several advantages over the two state model. First, the definition of buried and exposed residues is clarified since intermediate cases are classified as a third category. Second, it is possible to reproduce the observed distribution more closely by allowing more classes. Finally, if it is not necessary to distinguish between fully and partially exposed residues, it is possible to predict exposure with very high accuracy. In experiments involving three-state prediction (buried, partially exposed, and fully exposed), window size was from 1 to 9 residues, at which

Window Size	%Correct Train Binary	%Correct Test Binary	%Correct Train Ternary	%Correct Test Ternary
1	69.1	70.0	49.1	50.2
3	70.1	69.5	52.4	51.1
5	71.0	70.8	54.1	50.1
7	71.9	71.8	**55.9**	**52.0**
9	**72.5**	**72.0**	57.5	49.8
11	73.9	71.8	-	-
13	73.4	70.7	-	-

Table 5. Solvent exposure predictions

point prediction of the testing set began to decrease. Table 5 gives the results of these experiments for both the training and testing datasets. For both datasets, the fully buried and exposed residues are predicted with greater accuracy than the partially exposed residues As in the experiments with a binary representation, the exposed residues in the testing set are consistently predicted approximately 10% more accurately than the buried. The overall peak in prediction with the ternary model occurs for the testing set at window size 7 (-3:3) after which a decline occurs. Experiments with networks containing a hidden layer of computational nodes between the input and output layers resulted in an improvement in prediction for window size 7 and three output states. The maximal improvement was observed when using 10 hidden nodes, which predicted the testing set with 54.2% overall accuracy, compared to the best prediction of 52.0% with a perceptron network.

Using this three state network with hidden nodes, a residue which is predicted to be fully exposed was actually found to be fully or partially exposed over 89% of the time, while a residue predicted to be buried was found fully or partially buried in 95% of the cases. The difference in prediction percentage for buried and exposed is in large part due to overprediction of the fully exposed state and underprediction of the fully buried state by the network. If only fully exposed or fully buried residues are considered (cases observed or predicted to be partially exposed are ignored) the states are predicted correctly for 87% of the residues. The hydrophobic residues were predicted with very high accuracy (86-100%) as are the hydrophilic residues (75-100%). The ambiphilic residues glycine and threonine were, as expected, predicted with less accuracy (68% and 60% respectively), but the ambiphilic residues methionine, alanine and histidine are predicted with 90-100% accuracy. Even the hydrophobic residue valine is correctly predicted to be exposed in one case and the hydrophilic residue proline is predicted correctly to be buried in one case.

4.3 Continuous Model

In order to assess the potential for prediction of the percent of fractional exposure without regard to arbitrary definitions of burial and exposure, a direct mapping can be effected from amino acid sequence represented in a binary form as described above (21 nodes per residue) to fractional exposure (S. Holbrook, unpublished results). This mapping utilized real numbers (the actual or predicted fraction exposures of the central residue) as the output nodes which are fit in the training process. Using a window size of 9 amino acid residues, the training set converged at a correlation coefficient of 0.561 with an average deviation between observed and calculated exposure of 17%. This trained network was able to reproduce the exposures of the residues in the testing set with a correlation coefficient of 0.508 and average deviation of 18%.

4.4 Analysis of Network Weights

Examination of the network weights allowed the physical interpretation of the major factors influencing residue exposure. From the plot of network weights in the binary model shown in Figure 8, it is apparent that the primary factor governing exposure of the strongly hydrophobic and hydrophilic residues is the identity of the central amino acid itself, however for neutral or ambiphilic residues such as proline and glycine the flanking sequence is more influential. Nevertheless, the weights show that hydrophobic residues 2 or 3 amino acids before or after the central amino acid favor its burial. This is likely due to the preponderance of buried residues in β-strand and to a lesser degree α-helical structures and the periodicity of these structures. Since exposed residues are favored over buried in turn and coil regions, exposure of the central residue is favorably influenced by neighboring residues such as proline and glycine which preferentially are found in these regions. As turns and coils are not periodic structures, less positional specificity is observed for the exposed residues than for buried residues which prefer regular secondary structure.

The weights to the output nodes of the three state model show a greater contribution of neighboring residues to the exposure of the central residue, especially for the intermediate (partially exposed) node, which is not strongly determined by the central residue alone (not shown). The weights (not shown) suggest that larger residues (i.e. W, H, Y and R) tend towards intermediate exposure (correlation coefficient 0.35) regardless of their hydrophobicity. Generally, high weights for neighboring hydrophobic residues tend to favor burial of the central residue and high weights for neighboring hydrophilic residues favor exposure of the central residue.

In summary, neural network models for surface exposure of protein residues make highly accurate predictions of accessibility based solely on the

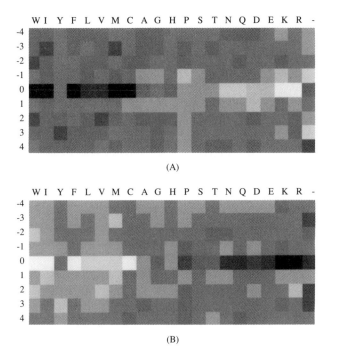

WI Y F L V M C A G H P S T N Q D E K R -

(A)

WI Y F L V M C A G H P S T N Q D E K R -

(B)

Figure 8. Network weights for binary model of surface exposure.. (a) is the weight matrix for the buried residue predictions, and (b) is the matrix for the exposed residue predictions.

identity of the amino acid of interest and its flanking sequence. This capability is a valuable tool to molecular biologists and protein engineers as well as to those concerned with the prediction of protein structure from sequence data alone.

5 Prediction of Cysteine's Disulfide Bonding State

The bonding states of cysteine play important functional and structural roles in globular proteins. Functionally, cysteines fix the heme groups in cytochromes, bind metals in ferredoxins and metallothioneins, and act as nucleophiles in thiol proteases. Structurally, cysteines form disulfide bonds that provide stability to proteins such as snake venoms, peptide hormones, immunoglobulins, and lysozymes.

Because free thiols are unstable relative to S-S bridges in the presence of oxygen, cysteines are typically oxidized into disulfide bonds in proteins leaving the cell; and conversely, because S-S bridges are unstable relative to free

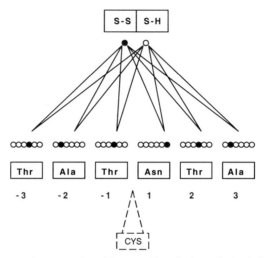

Figure 9. The cysteine network architecture. For clarity, only 6 window positions (3 amino acids to the N-terminal and 3 amino acids to the C-terminal side of the omitted centered cysteine) and 6 nodes per window position are illustrated. The net is a perceptron with two output nodes, one for disulphide bonded cysteines (S-S) and one for hydrogen bonded (S-H).

thiols in reducing environments, cysteines are typically reduced in proteins that remain inside the cell. Predictions of the disulfide bonding state of cysteines based only on this criterion, however, result in failures for extracellular proteins containing free thiols such as actinidin, immunoglobulin, papain, and some virus coat proteins and for cystine containing intracellular proteins such as trypsin inhibitor, thioredoxin, and superoxide dismutase. Furthermore, to base positive disulfide bond predictions on high cysteine content and even parity result in failures for ferredoxins, metallothioneins, and some cytochromes. Clearly, predictions based on these simple rules fail to capture the unique micro-environments a protein structure imposes on its cysteines to define their disulfide bonding states.

Recently, Muskal *et al.* [1990] used a network of the architecture seen in Figure 9 to predict a cysteine's disulfide bonding state, with the presumption that it is the local sequence that influences a cysteine's preference for forming a disulfide bond. The networks were of the feedforward type containing no hidden nodes (perceptrons). Because every sequence presented to the networks contained a centered cysteine, the input layer encoded a window of amino acid sequence surrounding but not including, the central cysteine, as shown in Figure 9

Network performance depended on the size of the window around a centered cysteine. For testing, 30 examples were randomly selected (15 exam-

Window	%Train	$C_{ss\text{-bond}}$	%Test	$C_{ss\text{-bond}}$
-1:1	65.7	.30	60.0	.22
-2:2	72.8	.45	66.7	.34
-3:3	79.1	.57	73.3	.51
-4:4	83.9	.67	73.3	.48
-5:5	85.7	.71	**80.0**	**.61**
-6:6	88.2	.76	80.0	.60
-7:7	91.4	.82	80.0	.61

Table 6: Dependence of training and testing success of the cysteine net on window size. Window of –x:x has x amino acids on either side of the cysteine. C's are Mathews [1975] correlation coefficients.

Run	%Correct Train		%Correct Test	
	S-S	S-H	S-S	S-H
1	89.7	83.3	80.0	80.0
2	89.4	82.3	80.0	80.0
3	89.7	83.3	90.0	70.0
4	90.2	83.0	70.0	90.0
5	90.5	83.0	70.0	100.0
6	90.5	84.3	90.0	70.0
7	90.0	82.7	90.0	70.0
Average	90.0	83.1	81.4	80.0

Table 7. Cross validation runs for cysteine network with window –5:5.

ples of sequences surrounding disulfide bonded cysteines; 15 examples of sequences surrounding non-disulfide bonded cysteines) from the pool of 689 examples, leaving the remaining 659 examples for a training set. The influence of flanking sequence on a centered cysteine was determined by increasing window of sequence surrounding the cysteine and tabulating the network's predictive performance. As seen in Table 6, the network's performance on both the training and testing sets increases with increasing window size. It should be noted that after window -7:7 (14 flanking amino acids, 21 nodes per amino acid, 2 output nodes, and 2 output node biases corresponds to 14 * 21 * 2 + 2 = 590 weights), the number of weights begins to exceed the number of training examples. As a result memorization becomes apparent after a window of -6:6, suggesting that the windows -5:5 or -6:6 are optimal for predictive purposes. Furthermore, Table 6 shows that trained networks made accurate predictions on examples never seen before thus supporting the hypothesis that a cysteine's propensity and/or aversion for disulfide bond formation depends to a great extent on its neighbors in sequence.

Network performance for each set was evaluated by testing on a random

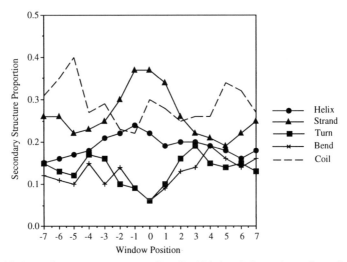

Figure 10. Secondary structure surrounding disulfide bonded cysteines. Secondary structure proportion is calculated by summing number of individual secondary structure types and dividing by the total number of secondary structure occurring in that window position. Secondary structure assignments were made by the method of Kabsch and Sander [1983].

subset of 20 examples (10 examples of sequences surrounding disulfide bonded cysteines; 10 examples of sequences surrounding non-disulfide bonded cysteines) taken from the pool of 689 examples after training on the remaining 669 examples. Each experiment was conducted independently on networks with a window -5:5 (5 amino acids to the left and 5 to the right of a central cysteine).

After window size experiments were completed, 7 independent training and testing experiments were conducted so as to determine an average performance that was not dependent on any particular training and testing set. Table 7 indicates that a network can be trained to predict disulfide bonded scenarios 81.4% correctly and non-disulfide bonded scenarios 80.0% correctly. Trained networks made accurate predictions on sequences from both extracellular and intracellular proteins. In fact, for the extracellular proteins actinidin, immunoglobulin, and papain, the odd cysteines not involved in disulfide bonds were correctly predicted as such. Likewise, for the intracellular cystine-containing proteins such as trypsin inhibitor and superoxide dismutase, every cysteine's state was correctly predicted.

Figure 10 shows the secondary structure proportion as a function of window position for disulfide bonded cysteines. Here the sequences surrounding and including half-cysteines seem to prefer the extended conformation of β–sheets over that of turns and bends. The secondary structural preferences of

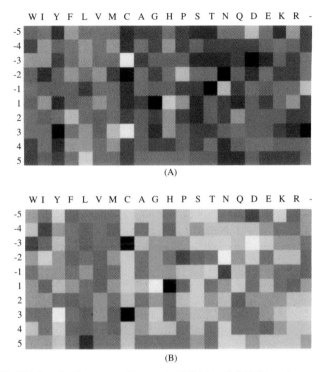

Figure 11. Weights for the connections to the S-S (a) and S-H (b) nodes averaged over the 7 network experiments in Table 8. Dark shades indicate high and light shades indicate low S-S (S-H) propensity.

half-cysteines perhaps enable the high prediction rate of a cysteine's disulfide bonding state. Note that in Figure 10, beyond ±5 residues from the central half-cystine (coinciding with the selected network window size) the preferences for any secondary structure are greatly reduced.

Figure 11 is a graphical depiction of the weights averaged from the seven network experiments. Note that cysteines at positions ±3 are not very conducive towards disulfide bond formation. This can be explained by the frequent occurrence of CYS-x-x-CYS in heme and metal binding proteins. However, cysteines at position ±1 increase the propensity considerably. This can be explained by the frequent occurrence of CYS-CYS in extracellular proteins, where the cysteines can form a basis for linking three chain segments in close proximity. Figure 11 also shows a positive influence of closely centered β-sheet forming residues such as ILE, TYR, and THR on disulfide bond formation.

The contribution an individual amino acid may have towards disulfide bond formation, irrespective of window position, can be seen in Figure 12.

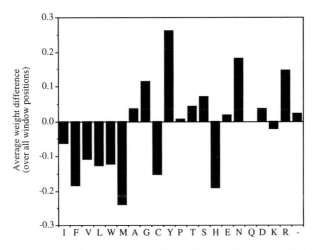

Figure 12. Amino acid contribution to disulphide bond formation. Weights from the 7 network experiments in Table 8 were averaged for each amino acid over all window positions. Bars represent the weights to the S-H node subtracted from the weights to the S-S node. Bars above the midline indicate a propensity to form S-S bonds, and those below tend to form S-H bonds.

One clear pattern is that the residues contributing *towards* S-S bond formation are polar and/or charged while those *against* formation are primarily hydrophobic. The effects of a locally hydrophobic environment could help to bury a cysteine to make it less accessible to other cysteines, thus reducing the chances of disulfide bond formation. Conversely, the effects of a locally hydrophilic environment could help to maintain cysteines in solution thus making them more accessible to one another and to increases the chances of disulfide bond formation.

The most striking features in Figure 12 exist between similar amino acids. TYR, for example, is highly conducive towards disulfide bond formation, yet PHE and TRP disfavor formation quite strongly. Electrostatic interaction between the edge of aromatic rings and sulfur atoms is found to be more frequent between aromatics and half cysteines than with aromatics and free cysteines. Figure 13 also suggests that TYR will favor disulfide bond formation over the other aromatics simply because PHE and TRP lack hydrophilic character. Likewise, ARG suggests S-S formation more strongly than LYS. Again, hydrophilic arguments find ARG more polar and thus more favorable for S-S formation. Less obvious, however, is the strong S-S propensity of ASN relative to GLN. Perhaps it is ASN's smaller size that better enables the close approach of a potential half-cystine. Consistent with this, the S-S propensity of GLY, ASP and SER exceed that of their slightly larger counter-

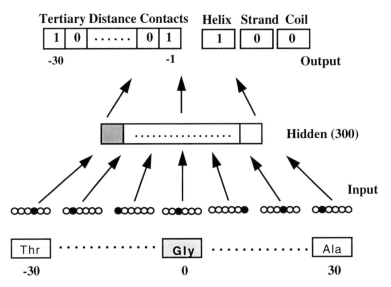

Figure 13. Network for prediction of protein tertiary structure. Input window is 30 residues to either side of the residue of interest, each represented by 20 nodes (one of which is activated). The output level consists of two parts; a window of 30 residues corresponding to those to the left of the central in the input which contains a 0 or 1 reflecting whether the residue is within 8Å of the central position. The other 3 output nodes specify the secondary structural type of the central residue.

parts ALA, GLU and THR. These differences in S-S propensity between otherwise very similar amino acids may make feasible the stabilization and/or destabilization of disulfide bonds through the site-directed mutagenesis of sequences surrounding half-cysteines.

The results of this network analysis suggest that tertiary structure features, such as disulfide bond formation, may be found in local sequence information. More experiments will need to be conducted to further exploit the information content in local amino acid sequence. Perhaps this will suggest a new twist to protein structure prediction.

6 Tertiary Structure Prediction with Neural Networks

Bohr, *et al*, [1990] recently reported the use of a feedfoward neural network trained by backpropagation on a class of functionally homologous proteins to predict the tertiary folding pattern of another member of the same functional class from sequence alone. The basis of this approach is that the commonly used binary distance matrix representation of tertiary protein structure, will be similar for members of a homologous protein family. In this representation the protein sequence is plotted along both the vertical and horizontal axes and points are placed on the graph to indicate where two C_α positions are within a specified distance in the three-dimensional structure. The network using tertiary structure information given as binary distance constraints between C_α atoms as well as a three-state model of secondary structure in the output layer and a sliding window of amino acid sequence as the input layer of a three-layer network is shown in Figure 13.

The input layer encompassed a window of -30 to +30 residues around the residue of interest (central residue) and the output a window of the 30 residues preceding the central residue. For input, each amino acid position was defined by 20 nodes each with a value of zero except for the one corresponding to the actual amino acid which had a value of one. The output layer consisted of 33 nodes, 30 representing the residues preceding the central residue and having values of zero or one depending on whether the distance to the central residue was less than or greater than 8 Å (in some cases 12 Å was used) respectively, and three nodes indicating secondary structure of helix, sheet, or coil.

This network is characterized by a very large number of computational nodes and variable weights. For input 1220 units (20x61) were used, in the hidden layer 300-400 units, and in the output 33 units. The total number of weighted links is therefore 375,900 or 501,200 for the two types of networks used. Clearly, a network containing this many weights has the capacity to memorize the small training set of 13 protease structures. The learning of the training set to a level of 99.9% on the binary distance constraints and 100% on the secondary structure assignment, indicates that the network memorizes the training set effectively, but is unlikely to incorporate generalizations. Thus, although the architecture is quite different, the application of this feedforward network is analogous to an associative memory network.

This network is quite similar to the associative memory Hamiltonian approach which has been applied for tertiary structure prediction [Friedrichs & Wolynes, 1989], thus raising the possibility that an associative memory type neural network may be useful for the storage and retrieval of protein three-dimensional folding patterns. However, it is doubtful whether this approach can predict tertiary structure of proteins which are not homologous to proteins on which the network was trained

7 Long Range Goals

While the ultimate goal of protein structural prediction is obviously to produce a complete set of three-dimensional atomic coordinates solely from the amino acid sequence, the best approach to this goal and the most important intermediate goals are still not defined. First, it should be realized that there is no such thing as a unique set of three-dimensional coordinates of a

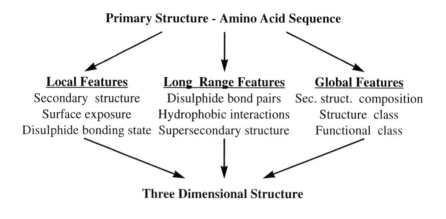

Figure 14. A possible strategy for protein structure prediction.

protein: i.e. all proteins are mobile to a greater or lesser degree and most can assume different conformations depending on environment, ligands or substrates, or complex formation. This structural variability has been observed both by NMR methods in solution and X-ray studies in crystals. The database for most theoretical studies, however, concentrates on an equilibrium or most stable conformation usually as observed in a crystal structure. Our goal, currently, must be narrowed to determining this "sample conformation" which likely corresponds to one of the minimum energy states. Now the question arises as to whether it is possible to determine this "protein structure" or at least an approximation of it from information contained in the structural and sequence databanks. It now appears that in some cases this is possible and in others the data is insufficient. For example, highly homologous proteins likely share very similar structures, while on the other hand large classes of proteins exist for which little or no structural information is available such as membrane proteins and specialized structural proteins.

Thus, a more practical if less idealistic approach, will be to concentrate efforts on the prediction of well understood structural features such as secondary structure, surface exposure, disulfide bond formation, etc. while keeping sight of the final goal of predicting a complete tertiary structure. This stairstep approach will not only provide valuable tools for molecular biologists, biochemists and protein engineers, but will also provide insight into protein structure by forcing an overall critical view of the set of known protein structures. Figure 14 illustrates the overall scheme in this approach to protein structure prediction.

8 Conclusions

The studies discussed above clearly demonstrate the power of the artificial neural network in extracting information from the protein structure database and extrapolating to make predictions of protein structural features from sequence alone. It should also be clear that so far almost all studies have utilized simple backpropagation networks. While these types of networks will continue to be widely used, it may be that the next round of advances in protein structure will involve other types of networks such as associative memory, Kohonen, or Hebbian (see, e.g., Steeg's chapter in this volume). Already, the promise of an associative memory approach has been observed. Neural networks comprise a powerful set of tools which have reached the stage where biochemists and structural biologists, and not just computer scientists, can now attack the problems of their choice. The results of these studies will depend on their ingenuity in problem formulation, network design and the informational storage of the databases. We can look forward to a rapid growth in the number of biologists using these methods.

References

Andreassen, H., Bohr, H., Bohr, J., Brunak, S., Bugge, T., Cotterill, R. M. J., Jacobsen, C., Kusk, P., Lautrup, B., Petersen, S. B., Saermark, T., & Ulrich, K. (1990). Analysis of the Secondary Structure of the Human Immunodeficiency Virus (HIV) proteins p17, gp120, and gp41 by Computer Modeling Based on Neural Network Methods. *J. Acquired Immune Deficiency Syndromes, 3*, 615-622.

Anfinsen, C. G. (1973). Principles that Hovern the Golding of Protein Vhains. *Science, 181*, 223.

Bernstein, F. C., Koetzle, T. F., Williams, G. J. B., Meyer, E. F. J., Brice, M. D., Rodgers, J. R., Kennard, O., Shimanouchi, T., & Tasumi, M. (1977). The Protein DataBank: A Computer-based Archival File for Macromolecular Structures. *J. Mol. Biol., 112*, 535-42.

Blundell, T., Sibanda, B. L., & Pearl, L. (1983). Three-dimensional Structure, Specificity and Catalytic Mechanism of Renin. *Nature, 304*, 273-275.

Bohr, H., Bohr, J., Brunak, S., Cotterill, R. M., Lautrup, B., Norskov, L., Olsen, O. H., & Petersen, S. B. (1988). Protein Secondary Structure and Homology by Neural Networks. The Alpha-helices in Rhodopsin. *Febs Lett, 241*(1-2), 223-8.

Bohr, H., Bohr, J., Brunak, S., Cotterill, R. M. J., Fredholm, H., Lautrup, B., & Petersen, S. B. (1990). A Novel Approach to Prediction of the 3-dimensional Structures of Protein Backbones by Neural Networks. *Febs. Lett., 261*, 43-46.

Chou, P. Y., & Fasman, G. D. (1974a). Conformational Parameters for Amino Acids in Helical, Sheet and Random Coil Regions From Proteins. *Biochem., 13*, 211.

Chou, P. Y., & Fasman, G. D. (1974b). Prediction of Protein Conformation. *Biochem., 13*, 222.

Covell, D. G., & Jernigan, R. L. (1990). Conformations of Folded Proteins in Restricted Spaces. *Biochem., 29*, 3287-3294.

Crick, F. (1989). The Recent Excitement About Neural Networks. *Nature, 337*, 129-132.

Eisenberg, D. (1984). Three-dimensional Structure of Membrane and Surface Proteins. *Ann. Rev. Biochem., 53*, 595-623.

Friedrichs, M. S., & Wolynes, P. G. (1989). Toward Protein Tertiary Structure Recognition By Means of Associative Memory Hamiltonians. *Science, 246*, 371-373.

Garnier, J., Osguthorpe, D. J., & Robson, B. (1978). Analysis of the Accuracy and Implications of Simple Methods for Predicting the Secondary Structure of Globular Proteins. *J. Mol. Biol., 120*, 97.

George, D. G., Barker, W. C., & Hunt, L. T. (1986). The Protein Identification Resource (PIR). *Nucl. Acids Res., 14*, 11-15.

Greer, J. (1981). Comparative Model-building of the Mammalian Aerine Proteases. *J. Mol. Biol., 153*, 1027-1042.

Holbrook, S. R., Muskal, S. M., & Kim, S. H. (1990). Predicting Surface Exposure of Amino Acids from Protein Sequence. *Protein Eng, 3*(8), 659-65.

Holley, L. H., & Karplus, M. (1989). Protein Secondary Structure Prediction with a Neural Network. *Proc Natl Acad Sci U S A, 86*(1), 152-6.

Horne, D. S. (1988). Prediction of Protein Helix Content from an Autocorrelation Analysis of Sequence Hydrophobicities. *Biopolymers, 27*(3), 451-477.

Johnson, W. C., Jr. (1990). Protein Secondary Structure and Circular Dichromism: A Practical Guide. *Proteins, 7*, 205-214.

Kabsch, W., & Sander, C. (1983). Dictionary of Protein Secondary Structure: Pattern Recognition of Hydrogen-Bonded and Geometrical Features. *Biopolymers, 22*, 2577-2637.

Krigbaum, W. R., & Knutton, S. P. (1973). Prediction of the Amount of Secondary Structure in a Globular Protein from Its Aminoacid Composition. *Proc. Nat. Acad. Sci. USA, 70*(10), 2809-2813.

Lee, B. K., & Richards, F. M. (1971). The Interpretation of Protein Structures: Estimation of Static Accessibility. *J. Mol. Biol., 55*, 379-400.

Levin, J. M., & Garnier, J. (1988). Improvements in a Secondary Structure Prediction Method Based on a Search for Local Sequence Homologies and Its Use as a Model Building Tool. *Biochim. Biophys. Acta, 955*(3), 283-295.

Lewis, P. N., Momany, F. A., & Sheraga, H. A. (1973). Chain Reversal in Proteins. *Biochim. Biophys. Acta, 303*, 211-229.

Lim, V. I. (1974a). Algorithms for Predictions of Alpha-Helical and Beta-Structural Regions in Globular Proteins. *J. Mol. Biol., 88*, 873.

Lim, V. I. (1974b). Structural Principles of the Globular Organization of Protein Chains. A Stereochemical Theory of Globular Protein Secondary Structure. *J. Mol. Biol., 88*, 857.

Mathews, B. W. (1975). Comparison of the Predicted and Observed Secondary Structure of T4 Phage Lysozyme. *Biochim. Biophys. Acta, 405*, 442-451.

McGregor, M. J., Flores, T. P., & Sternberg, M. J. (1989). Prediction of Beta-turns in Proteins Using Neural Networks. *Protein Eng, 2*(7), 521-6.

Muskal, S. M., Holbrook, S. R., & Kim, S. H. (1990). Prediction of the Disulfide-bonding State of Cysteine in Proteins. *Protein Eng, 3*(8), 667-72.

Muskal, S. M., & Kim, S.-H. (1992). Predicting Protein Secondary Structure Content: A Tandem Neural Network Approach. *J Mol Biol, in press.*,

Nishikawa, K., Kubota, Y., & Ooi, T. (1983). Classification of Proteins into Groups Based on Amino Acid Composition and Other Characters. I. Angular Distribution. *J. Biochem., 94*, 981-995.

Nishikawa, K., & Ooi, T. (1982). Correlation of the Amino Acid Composition of a Protein to Its Structural and Biological Characteristics. *J. Biochem., 91*, 1821-1824.

Nishikawa, K., & Ooi, T. (1986). Amino Acid Sequence Homology Applied to the Prediction of Protein Secondary Structures, and Joint Prediction with Rxisting Methods. *Biochim. Biophys. Acta, 871*, 45-54.

Pascarella, S., & Bossa, F. (1989). PRONET: A Microcomputer Program for Predicting the Secondary Structure of Proteins with a Neural Network. *CABIOS, 5*, 319-320.

Qian, N., & Sejnowski, T. J. (1988). Predicting the Secondary Structure of Globular Proteins Using Neural Network Models. *J Mol Biol, 202*(4), 865-84.

Richardson, J. S. (1981). The Anatomy and Taxonomy of Protein Structure. *Adv. in Prot. Chem., 34*, 167-339.

Rose, G. D. (1978). Prediction of Xhain Rurns in Globular Proteins on a Hydrophobic Basis. *Nature* (London), *272*, 586.

Rose, G. D., Geselowitz, A. R., Lesser, G. J., Lee, R. H., & Zehfus, M. H. (1985). Hydrophobicity of Amino Acid Residues in Globular Proteins. *Science, 229*, 834-838.

Rumelhart, D. E., Hinton, G. E., & Williams, R. J. (1986). Learning Representations by Back-propagating Errors. *Nature,* 323, 533-536.

Rumelhart, D. E., McClelland, J. L., & group, t. P. r. (1986). *Parallel Distributed Processing: Explorations in the Microstructure of Cognition* . Cambridge, MA: MIT Press.

Venkatachalam, C. M. (1968). Stereochemical Criteria for Polypeptides and Proteins. V. Conformation of a Aystem of Three Linked Peptide Units. *Biopolymers, 6*, 1425-1436.

Warme, P. K., Momany, F. A., Rumball, S. V., Tuttle, R. W., & Scheraga, H. A. (1974). Computation of Structures of Homologous Proteins. Alpha-lactalbumin from Lysozyme. *Biochem., 13*, 768-782.

Weiner, P. K., & Kollman, P. A. (1981). AMBER: Assisted Model Building with Energy Refinement. A General Program for Modeling Molecules and their Interactions. *J. Comp. Chem., 2*, 287-303.

Weiner, S. J., Kollman, P. A., Case, D. A., Singh, U. C., Ghio, C., Alagona, G., Profeta, S., Jr., & Weiner, P. (1984). A New Force Field for Molecular Mechanical Simulation of Nucleic Acids and Proteins. *J. Am. Chem. Soc., 106*, 765-784.

Wetlaufer, D. B. (1973). Nucleation, Rapid Folding and Globular Intrachain Regions in Proteins. *Proc. Natl. Acad. Sci. USA, 70*, 697.

Zvelebil, M. J., Barton, G. J., Taylor, W. R., & Sternberg, M. J. (1987). Prediction of Protein Secondary Structure and Active Sites Using the Alignment of Homologous Sequences. *J. Mol. Bio., 195*(4), 957-61.

5

Developing Hierarchical Representations for Protein Structures: An Incremental Approach

Xiru Zhang & David Waltz

1 Introduction

The protein folding problem has been attacked from many directions. One set of approaches tries to find out correlations between short subsequences of proteins and the structures they form, using empirical information from crystallographic databases. AI research has repeatedly demonstrated the importance of representation in making these kinds of inferences. In this chapter, we describe an attempt to find a good representation for protein substructure. Our goal is to represent protein structures in such a way that they can, on the hand, reflect the enormous complexity and variety of different protein structures, and yet on the other hand facilitate the identification of similar substructures across different proteins. Our method for identifying a good representation for protein structure is embodied in a program called GENEREP[1], which automatically generates hierarchical structural representations for a protein of known structure.

Our approach proceeded in three stages. First, we selected a set of objectively definable primitives that captured all local information in as compact a form as possible. This step was accomplished by an unusual variation on principal component analysis. Using these primitives to represent proteins of known structure, we then looked for commonly co-occurring collections of primitives, which we used to define substructure families by an analog of k-means classification. Finally, we looked at how these families of structures are combined in sequence along a protein chain by heuristically inferring finite state automata that use the structure families to recognize proteins of known structure.

We hope this paper can serve both the AI and molecular biology communities. We believe the techniques described here are generally useful in designing representations for complex, ordered data in general, such as speech processing or economic predictions. We also present the derived representation as a useful tool for analysis of protein structures in biological domains. Our representation captures much of the important information about a protein conformation in a very compact form, which is more amenable to analysis than many of the alternatives.

2 Why Worry About Representation of Protein Structures?

2.1 The Issue of Representation in AI

The importance of representation in problem solving has long been emphasized in AI; see, for example, [Brachman & Levesque, 1985]. Researchers in the recent resurgence of connectionism have also started to realize its importance [e.g. Tesauro & Sejnowski, 1989]. A general lesson from AI is that good representations should make the right things explicit and expose natural constraints. In most of the traditional AI work, representations were designed by users and hand-coded; see [Charniak & McDermott, 1985] and [Winston, 1984] for summary of such work. Recently, with the development of connectionism, it has been shown that interesting representations can also be computed "on the fly" from the input data. For example, [Hinton, 1988] developed internal representations for family relationships by training an auto-association networks with a set of examples; [Ellman, 1989] trained a recurrent network on a corpus of sentences, and the network was able to abstract noun/verb agreement. Researchers in computer vision have also been concerned with computing concise representations of large amounts of visual input data [Sanger, 1989; Saund, 1988]. Here, we attempt to bring some of this experience to bear in developing representations of protein structure.

2.2 Existing Representations of Protein Structures

A common format of known protein structure data (such as in

Brookhaven Protein Databank) gives lists of 3D coordinates for the atoms of all of the amino acids in a protein. This is not a good representation for the purpose of structure prediction because it is difficult to identify similar sub-structures across different proteins and, consequently, difficult to carry out generalization and abstraction.

Another way to represent the three-dimensional structures is to use a "distance matrix." For a protein sequence of N residues, the corresponding distance matrix contains NxN entries, each representing the distance between the C_α atoms of a pair of residues. Similar to the 3D-coordinate representation, a distance matrix carries almost all the information about the protein structure (except the handedness of a helix), but still it is not obvious how to build an abstraction hierarchy on top of it.

Another common way to represent the protein structure is to assign each residue in the protein to one of several secondary structure classes. Secondary structure is a relatively coarse characterization of protein conformation, indicating basically whether the amino acid residues are packed closely (α helix) or stretched into an extended strand (β sheet). Parts of proteins that don't match either category are generally labeled random coil.

Research so far on protein structure prediction has mainly focused on predicting secondary structures, e.g. [Qian & Sejnowski, 1988; Levin, Robson & Garnier, 1986; Chou & Fasman, 1974; Rooman & Wodak, 1988]. However, given the 3D coordinates of all the residues in a protein, researchers differ on how to assign secondary structures. There is broad agreement on what a typical α helix or β sheet is, but a real protein structure is complicated, and non-typical cases are common.[2] Coil is not really one class of local structures, but rather it includes many very different structures. Also, though it is known that groups of α helices and/or β sheets often form higher level structures (often called super-secondary structures) [Richardson, 1981]—and some researchers have even tried to predict particular super-secondary structures, such as $\beta\alpha\beta$ [Taylor & Thornton, 1984]—there has not been a rigorous, generally agreed way to identify different super-secondary structures in the known proteins.

The Ramachandran plot [Schulz & Schirmer, 1979], plots ϕ vs. ψ angles for all the residues in the set of protein structures used in this work. The definition of these angles is shown in Figure 1, and a Ramachandran plot is shown in Figure 2. We can see that the angles are not evenly distributed. There are two dense regions; these correspond to α helices and β sheets, respectively. We can also see clearly that this categorization does not capture the richness and variety in protein structure.

Thus, a good representation for protein structures is in demand for the purpose of structure prediction. It should produce a coherent description of protein structures at the residue level, secondary structure level and super-secondary structure level.

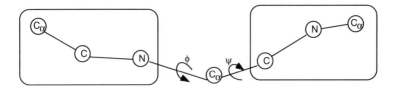

Figure 1. The definition of phi (φ) and psi (ψ) angles in a peptide chain. Most of the bond angles and bond lengths in an amino acid are quite rigidly fixed, as is the peptide bond that holds the amino acids together. There are two principal degrees of freedom in the backbone of a peptide chain: These angles are defined around α carbons by the indicated planes.

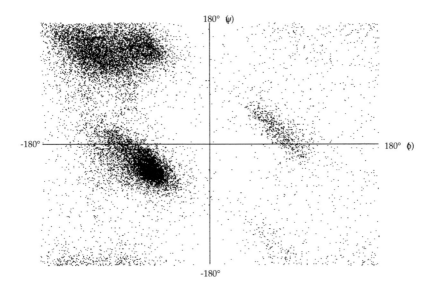

Figure 2. A Ramachandran plot of the φ versus ψ angles found in our dataset. Notice that although there are two main groups, there is significant variance within the groups, and many points outside of them.

3 Method

Our goal is: given the 3-D coordinates of all the residues in a protein, generate a representation that can both reflect the enormously complexity of protein structures and facilitate the identification of similar substructures across different proteins. This is exactly the kind of representation problem AI has been concerned with. Ideally, it should be possible to describe a protein structure at several levels of abstraction, so we desire a hierarchical representation.

We have taken an incremental, bottom-up approach in developing representations for protein structures. The first step is to find a set of lowest level primitives with which we will build higher level structures. These primitives must capture as much relevant information about the structure as possible, and do so in a maximally compact way. In order to define the base level, we apply a neural network-based techniques related to principal component analysis to a dataset that contains the structural state of each residue in a large number of proteins.

The second step is to group continuous stretches of structural states to form local structures, roughly corresponding to what have been called secondary structures. We take the primitives we developed in step one, and use them to find groups of similar residues, using a method related to k-means classification; this provides a level of description roughly commensurate with secondary structure. Finally, we assemble our groups of related local structures to form higher level structures, which corresponds to super-secondary structures.

The advantages of this approach are (a) given a protein's residue coordinates, it can generate representations at all three levels discussed above automatically—higher level representations are built upon lower level ones; (b) these representations are grounded on a few objective, observable structural parameters whose accuracy depends only on the accuracy of the crystal data, rather than some subjective judgment; (c) it is straightforward to compute a distance (similarity/difference) between any two structures in this representation; thus when categories are formed, it is possible to compute how different one category is from another, or how far a particular instance is from the mean for each category.

All of the inference was done on a subset of protein structures taken from the Brookhaven Protein Databank. The subset consisted of 105 non-homologous protein structures; we call our subset the Protein Structure DataBase (PSDB) in the following discussion.

3.1 Defining Primitives

3.1.1 Source data. Abstraction and generalization must be solidly grounded. In this work, each residue in a protein in PSDB is associated with a number of structural parameters. The three parameters used here are the dihedral angles (ϕ, ψ) and water accessibility (ω)[3]. Dihedral angles represent a residue's spatial orientation relative to its two immediate neighbors in the protein sequence, and the water accessibility reflects whether the residue is on the surface of or inside the protein. ω is included here because it is generally believed that hydrophobic interaction plays an important role in protein folding. Also, whether a residue is on the surface of or inside a protein is an important source of structural information.[4] The residue state vector for residue i is defined as a 9-tuple:

$$SV_i = <\omega_{i-1}, \Phi_{i-1}, \Psi_{i-1}, \omega_i, \Phi_i, \Psi_i, \omega_{i+1}, \Phi_{i+1}, \Psi_{i+1}>$$

That is, each SV_i depends on residue i's ϕ, ψ and ω parameters and on those of its two nearest neighbors in the sequence. In this work, ω takes a binary value: either 0 (inside) or 1 (on surface). ϕ and ψ are are rounded to the nearest multiple of 20 degrees. Any pair of residues that have at least 3 identical angles and no angles that differ by more than 20 degrees are forced to have identical state vectors. Residue state vectors include all aspects of protein structure of concern here; it is on this basis that the abstraction hierarchy is built.

All the state vectors for all of the residues in the entire PSDB were computed, and 7159 distinct residue state vectors were found. This is a highly nonrandom distribution; in theory, there are about $3.8*10^7$ possible residue state vectors. In addition, the histogram of occurrence of vectors is highly skewed. The mean number of times a state vector occurs in the database is 3; the most frequent one occurs 2027 times.

3.1.2 Computing Canonical Representations by an Auto-association Network. Computing the state vector for each amino acid residue in a protein structure provides a great deal of information about the structure, but in a less than ideal form. The elements of the state vectors are highly dependent upon each other, and it is unclear how to measure the distance between a pair of vectors. The different dimensions of the vector have different value ranges and value distributions; it is not clear how to weight their relative importance. A canonical representation is needed to make useful information explicit and strip away obscuring clutter. Our approach was to use an auto-associative back-propagation network [McClelland & Rummelhart, 1986] to automatically identify the intrinsic features implied in the state vectors.

It has been shown that, when properly designed, the hidden unit values of an auto-association back-propagation network will identify the intrinsic features of its inputs [Bourlard & Kamp, 1988; Saund, 1986]. A network trained to reproduce values at its input units (within a given accuracy) using a smaller number of hidden units has found a more compact encoding of the information in the input unit values. This process is related to principal component analysis (see section 5). In addition, something else is available for free: if the hidden unit values for each residue state vector are used as its new representation, the lower half of the trained network (input→hidden layers) can be used as an encoder, and the upper half (hidden→output layers) can be used as a decoder.

At this point, we needed a mapping of the state vectors to binary vectors as required by the autoassociative network encoding process. Since the accuracy of ϕ and ψ angles is around 20° in PSDB, and these angles range over [-180°, 180°], 18 units are used to encode one angle. The unit activity then is smeared by a Gaussian function to the unit's neighbors, thus similar angle values will have encodings near each other in Hamming space. This encoding of real values is similar to that in [Saund, 1986]. Four units are used to encode each ω value. This is required so that the backpropagation error signal for ω will not be overwhelmed by that from the angles. The network and encoding are shown in Figure 3.

After the network is trained on all of the state vectors, it can be used as an encoder and decoder, to translate from state vectors to the newly defined primitives. Each residue state vector can be mapped to a 20-element vector on [0,1] obtained from the 20 hidden units of the backpropagation network. These are called residue feature vectors. But treating the production of these vectors solely as a blackbox encoding is somewhat unsatisfying; what do the values of the hidden units mean?

Each hidden unit captures certain features of the input vectors. One example is a hidden unit which is sensitive primarily to the first, fourth and seventh position of the input vectors, that is, to the ω values. For example, when the input vectors have the form $<0,?,?,0,?,?,0,?,?>$[5], the output of the 6th hidden unit is always close to 0. Another, more complex example demonstrates a distributed representation: when one hidden node is low ($V_0 \leq 0.3$) and another hidden node is high ($V_2 \geq 0.8$) the input vectors are always of the form $<?,?,?,?,?,?,?,-120,160>$, indicating the beginning of a β sheet.

The hidden unit value distributions were plotted for all 7159 distinct residue state vectors. The values of each of the hidden nodes over the range of training examples took on one of three distinctive distributions: bimodal, multimodal and normally distributed. Figure 4 shows one example from each kind.

We now have a method for translating objective information about the amino acid residues in a protein structure into a set of independent, compatible features. The next step is to assemble these examples of protein structure into general classes, based on the feature vectors we have just defined. These features provide the basis for an objective, general classification.

3.2 Finding Common Structures Using the Primitives

We claim that the hidden unit values represent intrinsic features of the network inputs. The residue feature vector representation not only provides a good representation for clustering, but also a way to measure the "distance" between different clusters (how similar two classes are) and the "distance" between a particular instance and the center of the cluster it belongs to (how typical it is to the class). This distance measure allows us to apply a standard clustering algorithm to find groups of similar structures from the examples that we have.

3.2.1 The Clustering Algorithm. The clustering on the 7159 20-element residue feature vectors was carried by a clustering procedure implemented on the Connection Machine CM-2 which is similar to K-means clustering.[6] Briefly, it does the following:

1. Get arguments: n — the number of clusters required; m — the number of iterations desired;

2. Randomly select n vectors from the 7159 residue feature vectors as "seeds" of the n clusters;

3. For each of the rest of the feature vectors, find the closest seed and put

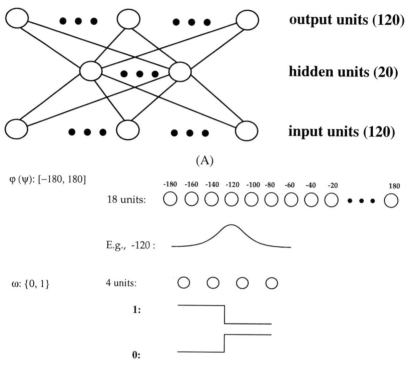

(A)

(B)

Figure 3. The design of an auto-association backpropagation network for transform-ing the residue state vectors to a canonical form. (A) The net contains 120 input units, 20 hidden units, and 120 output units. After training, the hidden unit values are taken as the canonical form. (B) The parameters φ and ψ are encoded as the activities of the input/output units in the backpropagation network by quantizing the angle to the nearest multiple of 20° and smearing the value over several neighbors. ω, which is binary, is encoded with four bits.

the vector into that cluster;

4. Compute the deviation in each cluster, then compute the average deviation of all clusters;

5. Repeat m times from Step 2 to Step 4 above, and select as the result the
   clustering that has the smallest average deviation.

3.2.2 Clustering Results. Therefore, a classification of residue state vectors based on the feature vectors should put similar structural states into the
same class. Using a method related to K-means clustering, the residue feature vectors were classified into clusters with small average deviations. We
looked for something around 20 classes at the beginning, and we found that
using 23 clusters produced the grouping with the smallest overall deviations.

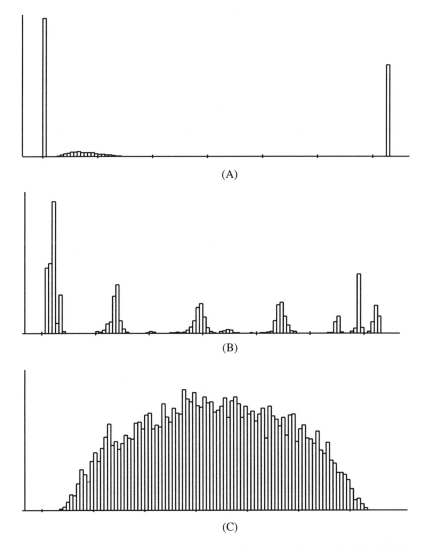

Figure 4. Three kinds of distributions of the hidden unit values. (a) V_6 (The 6th hidden unit). This kind of hidden units divides all the inputs into two classes. There are six hidden units with this kind of distribution. (b) V_1. This kind of units classifies all the inputs into a few categories. There are six such units. (c) V_0. Eight units have this kind of normal distribution.

Figure 5 shows an example of a cluster. 50 residue state vectors from this cluster are plotted by ϕ/ψ angle. It is clear that they share strong family resemblance. The 23 residue structural classes found by the clustering procedure are denoted by $C_1, C_2, ..., C_{23}$.

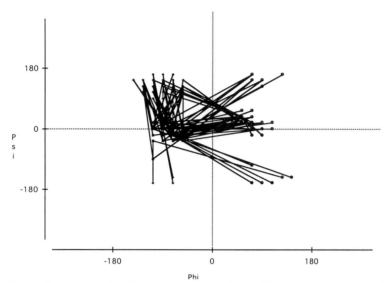

Figure 5. A cluster of residue state vectors made by a K-mean clustering procedure. Three consecutive <ϕ, ψ> pairs are three points on the $\phi - \psi$ plane joined by two straight lines, each line starts with a ∘, goes through an x and ends with a +. ω's are not displayed here.

3.3 Correlation Between Residue State Classes And Amino Acids

It was found that there are strong amino acid preferences for each of the 23 classes computed above. That is, some amino acids appear very frequently (or rarely) in particular classes. Figure 6 shows the results of a χ^2 correlation test between the 20 amino acids and the 23 classes in PSDB.

3.4. Identification of Common Substructures

In PSDB, strong correlations exist among structural classes C_1, C_2, ... C_{23} themselves, also. That is, in a protein, when C_i occurs at one place, some C_j tends to occur at another place. A number of class patterns were identified based on this kind of correlation.

3.4.1 Labeling the Residues with Structural Classes. Given 3D protein structure, we can compute a 20-element feature vector for each residue by the trained lower half of the auto-association network in Figure 8. Then from the feature vector, we can determine which of the 23 structural classes the residue belongs to. Thus all the residues in the sequence can be labeled for structural class membership. That is, the structure of the protein can be represented as (assuming there are n residues):

$$C^2 C^3 C^4 C^5 C^6 C^7 \ldots C^{n-1}$$

where $C^i \in \{C_1, C_2, \ldots C_{23}\}$, i = 2, 3, ... (n-1). The first and the last residues each have only one neighbor residue, and thus their structural class-

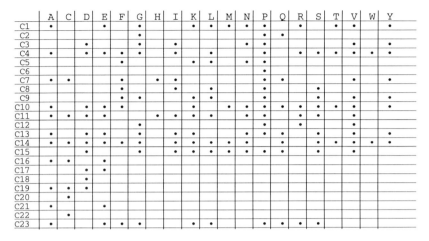

Figure 6. The contingency table for χ^2 tests on the correlations between amino acids and classes. Each column corresponds to an amino acid, and each row corresponds to a class. A mark means the corresponding amino acid and class are correlated with a confidence level >95%

es cannot be computed.

3.4.2 Repetitive Patterns. It is known that there are some repetitive local structures in proteins, mainly α helices and β sheets. Pattern matching techniques using fixed pattern size do not work here because α helices and β sheets occur with different lengths. Finite state automata (FSA's) can easily recognize sequences of symbols of variable length. A set of heuristics was used to inductively generate FSA's from instances in PSDB, and these automata were then used to identify all the similar structures. The heuristics used were:

(1) $C_i \, C_i \, ... \, C_i \, (N, M) \rightarrow C_i^+$

(2) $C_i \, ... \, C_i \, C_j \, ... C_j \, C_i \, C_i ... \, C_j ... \, (N, M) \rightarrow (Ci^*Cj^*)^+$

Heuristic (1) says that if in a protein sequence, a structural class C_i occurs continuously along the sequence for at least N residues, and this occurs in M different protein sequences, then generate regular expression C_i^+ as a general representation for such continuous, repetitive local structures.[7] Heuristic (2) is similar to (1), except that it deals with two interleaving structural classes C_i and C_j.

Four regular expressions (representing the FSA's) were generated from protein sequences labeled with 23 classes $\{C_1, C_2, ... C_{23}\}$:

(1) $RE_1 = C_{21}^+$

(2) $RE_2 = C_{14}^+$

(3) $RE_3 = (C_1{}^*C_{21}{}^*)^+$

(4) $RE_4 = (C_{17}{}^*C_{23}{}^*)^+$

The average residue state vector values for these classes are:

	ω_1	ϕ_1	ψ_1	ω_2	ϕ_2	ψ_2	ω_3	ϕ_3	ψ_3
C_{21}:	<0.3	-54	-32	0.3	-67	-34	0.0	-75	-36>
C_1:	<0.3	-61	-26	0.4	-46	-37	1.0	-65	-26>
C_{14}:	<0.2	-92	104	0.0	-104	110	0.0	-88	93>
C_{17}:	<0.4	-93	107	0.3	-81	108	1.0	-88	116>
C_{23}:	<0.3	-73	70	1.0	-89	113	0.0	-82	96>

These repetitive patterns correspond to α helices (RE_1 and RE_3) and β sheets (RE_2 and RE_4). The main difference between RE_1 and RE_3, and between RE_2 and RE_4 is whether the local structure is on the surface of or inside proteins.

3.4.3 Non-repetitive Structural Class Patterns. After the repetitive local structures were identified, structural classes that occur often at the beginning or the end of RE_1, RE_2, RE_3 and RE_4, and non-repetitive class patterns that happen frequently in PSDB were found. Some interesting phenomena were observed. For example, class pattern $C_{10}C_7$ occurs often at the beginning of RE_3 (61 times in PSDB), but never occurs at the end of RE_3 while class pattern C_3C_4 occurs 79 times at the end of RE_3, but never at the beginning. This suggests that classes in these two sets are not just variations of the classes inside RE_3, but rather they have specific preference for places they occur. Also about 100 non-repetitive class patterns (with length ≥ 4) were found that occur 20 times or more in PSDB.

Table 3 shows how many α helices and β sheets (identified by RE_1, RE_2, RE_3, RE_4) have common sequences proceeding them (heads) or sequences that follow them (tails) in PSDB. More than 75% of the helices and sheets have both head and tail ((413-89-11)/413 = 75.9%, (695-137-21)/695 = 77.3%). Only 3% of the helices and sheets have neither head and tail (11/413 = 2.7%, 21/695 = 3%). Thus, the occurrences of the heads and the tails suggests strongly the existence of the corresponding secondary structures.

Finally, groups of RE_i's are found that are close to each other in space and less than 15 residues apart along the sequence. For example, $RE_2...RE_3...RE_2$ (two sheets with a helix in between) occurs 18 times in PSDB. This is an example of what has been called super-secondary structure.

4 Summary and Discussion

4.1 Protein Structures

The success of protein structure prediction research depends on whether "rules" can be found that govern the correspondence between amino acid se-

Head and Tail of Helices and Sheets

RE's	Total	Lack One	Lack Two	Lack Head	Lack Tail
RE_1 & RE_3	413	89	11	54	57
RE_2 & RE_4	695	137	21	86	93

Table 3. The number of occurrences of the ``heads'' and the ``tails'' of the secondary structures identified by RE_1, RE_2, RE_3, RE_4.

quences and structures they form. We argue that representation plays an important role here—good representation exposes natural constraints.

In this paper, starting with a few primitive structural features about residues and some generalization techniques, we have developed representations for protein structures at several levels. As shown elsewhere [Zhang, 1990], we obtained a much higher secondary structure prediction accuracy with this representation than other representations; these representations greatly facilitate the prediction of protein structures. The correlations among structures at different levels revealed by these representations impose constraints about which amino acids will form what structures and where (in relation to other structures). This suggests that instead of predicting the state of each residue as an isolated individual (which is the case in most secondary structure prediction work today), the structural states of all the residues in a protein should be treated as a mutually related whole. The structure hierarchy described in this chapter is one way that these relations can be found and represented.

The representation here also has its limitations. Right now it only covers certain super-secondary structures—those that are close to one another in space and not very far away from each other along the sequence. It cannot account for all the global interactions.

4.2 General

In this paper, several computational tools have been successfully applied to the problem:

Feature Extraction. This was done by an auto-association network and proved to be a very useful tool for the purpose. Auto-association networks have been shown to be similar to principal component analysis [Bourlard, et al., 1988]. However, with non-linear input/output units, their dynamics are not yet fully understood. A principal component analysis method was applied to the same problem but did not produce as good a result in terms of forming meaningful clusters of protein local structures. One explanation for this is that the original dimensions need to be properly weighted in the principal component analysis to be successful.

Primitive Identification In this chapter, clustering of the original data based on their canonical features gave rise to meaningful categories. This gives an interesting example about the relationship between symbolic and non-symbolic reasoning: the original data — ϕ, ψ angles and ω's — are clearly non-symbolic, and yet the labels for the final structural classes are symbolic. These symbols (which correspond to the structural classes) emerged from the computation on non-symbolic data. They facilitate reasoning by identifying similar things and omitting details (abstraction!). They differ from the symbols in classic AI in that they are "backed up" by non-symbolic (numeric) information, so they can be compared, combined or broken into smaller pieces.

Correlation Among Primitives. Finite state automata and pattern matching techniques have been used to determine correlations among representation primitives. The sequential nature of the input data was explored to make such techniques applicable.

The above techniques could be applied to other representations of protein structures such as the distance matrix, or to problems in other domains (maybe in slightly different form), such as speech recognition and text processing. It is hoped that the lessons learned in this work will shed light on research in these domains as well.

Acknowledgment

We would like to thank Jill L. Mesirov and Robert Jones of Thinking Machines Corporation for many comments and suggestions on this work, and Chris Sander for providing the DSSP program and for helpful discussions. This work was supported in part by the Defense Advanced Research Projects Agency, administered by the U.S. Air Force Office of Scientific Research under contract number F49620-88-C-0058, while the first author was a graduate student at Brandeis University, and in part by Thinking Machines Corp. Cambridge, MA, both author's current affiliation.

Notes

1. It stands for "GENErate REPresentations."

2. When comparing the assignment of secondary structures by crystallographers and the one by Kabsch and Sander [Kabsch, 1983] (which is commonly used by structure predictors) for some protein sequences in Brookhaven Protein Databank, we found that they classify as many as 20% of the residues differently.

3. These parameters were computed from PSBD atomic coordinates by Kabsch and Sander's program DSSP.[Kabsch, 1983]

4. w is based on the number of water molecules bound to each residue. The w value computed by DSSP is normalized to be in [0, 1].

5. Where ? means any value.

6. Anand Bodapati at Thinking Machines Corp. kindly provided the initial

code. We modified it to suit our need.

7. The regular expression also specifies a FSA that can recognize all the sequences that can be represented by this expression.

References

Bourlard, H. & Kamp, Y. (1988). Auto-Association by Multilayer Perceptrons and Singular Value Decomposition. *Biological Cybernetics,* 59: 291-294.

Brachman, R. & Levesque, H. (1985). *Readings in Knowledge Representation.* Morgan Kaufmann,

Charniak, E. & McDermott, D. (1985). *Introduction to Artificial Intelligence .* Reading, MA: Addision-Wesley.

Chou, P. & Fasman, G. (1974). Prediction of Protein Conformation. *Biochemistry, 13*(2),

Ellman, J. (1989). *Representation and Structure in Connectionist Models* (CRL TR 8903). Center for Research in Language, UCSD.

Hinton, G. (1988). Representing Part-Whole Hierarchies in Connectionist Networks. In *Proceedings of the Tenth Annual Conference of the Cognitive Science Society* (pp. 48-54).

Kabsch, W. & Sander, C. (1983). Dictionary of protein secondary structure: pattern recognition of hydrogen-bonded and geometrical features. *Biopolymers, 22*(12), 2577-2637.

Levin, J. M., Robson, B. & Garnier, J. (1986). An algorithm for secondary structure determination in proteins based on sequence similarity. *205*(2), 303-308.

McClelland, J. & Rummelhart, D. (1986). *Parallel Distributed Processing.* Cambridge, MA: MIT Press,

Qian, N. & Sejnowski, T. (1988). Predicting the Secondary Structure of Globular Proteins Using Neural Network Models. *Journal of Molecular Biology, 202,* 865-884.

Richardson, J. (1981). The Anatomy and Taxonomy of Protein Structure. *Advances in Protein Chemistry, 34,* 167-339.

Rooman, M. & Wodak, S. (1988). Identification of Predictive Sequence Motifs Limited by Protein Structure Data Base Size. *Nature, 335*(1), 45-49.

Sanger, T. (1989). *Optimal Unsupervised Learning in Feedforward Neural Networks* (1086). MIT Artificial Intelligence Laboratory.

Saund, E. (1986). Abstraction and Representation of Continuous Variables in Connectionist Networks. In *Proceedings of Fifth National Conference On Artificial Intelligence* (pp. 638 - 644). Morgan Kaufmann.

Saund, E. (1988). *The Role of Knowledge in Visual Shape Representation* (1092). MIT Artificial Intelligence Laboratory.

Schulz, G. E. & Schirmer, R. H. (1979). *Principles of Protein Structure .* New York: Springer-Verlag.

Taylor, W. & Thornton, J. (1984). Recognition of Super-secondary Structure in Proteins. *Journal of Molecular Biology, 173,*

Tesauro, G. & Sejnowski, T. J. (1989). A Parallel Network that Learns to Play Backgammon. *Artificial Intelligence, 39,* 357-390.

Winston, P. (1984). *Artificial Intelligence* (2nd ed.). Reading, MA: Addison-Wesley.

Zhang, X. (1990). *Exploration on Protein Structures: Representation and Prediction.* Ph.D., Brandeis University,

6

Integrating AI with Sequence Analysis

Richard Lathrop, Teresa Webster, Randall Smith,
Patrick Winston & Temple Smith

1 Introduction

This chapter will discuss one example of how AI techniques are being integrated with, and extending, existing molecular biology sequence analysis methods. AI ideas of complex representations, pattern recognition, search, and machine learning have been applied to the task of inferring and recognizing structural patterns associated with molecular function. We wish to construct such patterns, and to recognize them in unknown molecules, based on information inferred solely from protein primary (amino acid) sequences. Besides its intrinsic interest as a difficult machine learning task of induction from complex and noisy data, this is of interest in the empirical domain for:

• suggesting targets for genetic manipulation in known molecules;

• suggesting functional identification and confirmatory tests in unknown or newly discovered molecules; and

• increasing general scientific knowledge by suggesting essential structural elements encoding molecular function.

The work described in this chapter is part of a larger ongoing effort to associate symbolic structural patterns with functionally defined classes of proteins. The basic question that we seek to address is: How can we recognize and relate protein function and structure? In the cases of interest to us, one typically has a defining set of sequences (instances) exhibiting the structure or function of interest, plus some biological or chemical experimental data which is believed to be relevant. The task is to inductively construct the pattern(s) which detect regularities implicit in the set of defining sequences, and which discriminate them from all other sequences. In machine learning terms, this is a task of concept acquisition from positive and negative examples. Positive examples are sequences which exhibit the structure or function under study, and negative examples are sequences which do not.

A pattern-based model is an excellent starting point for a feedback loop between experimental testing of the model and model refinement. For example, the pattern-based modeling of the classical mononucleotide binding fold (MBF) in tRNA synthetases [Webster et al. 1987] and the simian virus 40 (SV40) and polyomavirus large tumor (large-T) antigens [Bradley et al. 1987] led to site-directed mutagenesis in SV40 at the site suggested by the pattern match. The experimental manipulation [Bradley et al. 1987] verified the MBF location there. Continued theoretical study [Figge et al. 1988] led to a common pattern in the SV40 large-T, E1A, and myc oncoproteins (cancer-related proteins), all of which co-transform cells (induce cancer-like growth) with ras. Experimental work [Grasser et al. 1988, DeCaprio et al. 1988, 1989] found that phosphorylation of the region matched by the pattern in SV40 large-T was associated with binding the retinoblastoma (Rb) protein (a protein that apparently suppresses cancer-like cell division, unless it is bound and inactivated). The region matched by the same pattern in E1A [Figge et al. 1988] was experimentally substituted for the region matched in SV40 large-T, and the resulting domain exchange was found experimentally to bind Rb [Moran 1988]. Experimental work confirmed that E1A also binds Rb [Whyte et al. 1988, Lillie and Green 1989]. A generalization of the pattern matched two additional proteins, E7 and CDC25, suggesting their Rb binding [Figge and Smith 1988]. Subsequent experimental work [Storey et al. 1988, Goldsborough et al. 1989] demonstrated that the degree of pattern match (its differential similarity score) in papillomavirus (the virus responsible for warts) E7 was linked to the degree of biological activity. As predicted, further experimental work [Munger et al. 1989, Dyson et al. 1989, 1990] verified that E7 binds Rb. Theoretical attempts to further generalize the pattern led to the discovery of a new pattern [Zhu et al. 1990] for transcriptional activators (a large class of proteins that bind to DNA and activate genetic transcription). In experimental work continuing the Rb binding studies, Breese *et al.* [1991] constructed a number of small (14 residue) peptides containing the sequence regions matched by the pattern, demonstrated that they bound Rb, and verified the secondary structure part of the pattern with circular dichroism measurements. Further theoretical work led to the proposal of a full three-dimensional model [Figge *et al.*, submitted] of the binding site in proteins that bind Rb. This prediction now awaits experimental test.

The basis for the theoretical approach is that common functions often correlate with common protein structures, domain folding types, supersecondary structures and/or a few invariant or equivalent amino acids. This is true even for proteins with very different primary sequences. Biologically, a mutation that distorts a functionally important structure tends to produce an unviable organism and so tends not to propagate. Other mutations often have little effect and so are passed to offspring. Consequently, functionally important structure tends to be conserved, and functionally irrelevant structure tends to drift. If the functionally related sequences exhibit sufficient evolutionary diversity, a conserved functional "signal" may be distinguishable above the "noise" of mutational drift.

Unfortunately, although similar protein sequences generally indicate similar folded conformations and functions, the converse does not hold [Creighton 1983]. There are proteins, e.g., the nucleotide binding proteins [Rossman *et al.* 1974; Birktoft and Banaszak 1984], in which the secondary and tertiary structure encoding a common function is conserved while primary sequence similarity is almost non-existent. Methods which detect similarities solely at the primary sequence level have difficulty addressing functional associations in such sequences. A number of features, often only implicit in the protein's primary sequence of amino acids, are important in determining structure and function.

We attempt to identify patterns which are characteristic of a structural motif assumed to carry out some particular function. Our approach involves searching for a pattern which is shared by a defining set of functionally related proteins (positive instances of the function), and which does not appear in other proteins (negative instances, comprising the control set). The features we employ can be predicted or inferred (even if only statistically) from the primary structure. An initial "complex pattern" of a structural motif potentially involved in carrying out the common function is iteratively refined in order to maximize its discrimination between the positive and negative instances. The resulting pattern is a preliminary model for the relationship between a protein's structure and function, grounded in its amino acid sequence, which includes an identification of a functional site(s) as well as structural elements characteristic of that function. In the machine learning literature, this is sometimes referred to as the "concept" associated with the positive set. Regions of protein sequences matched by the pattern may suggest potential sites for experimental work. Because the inference is grounded in the primary sequence, the model is also suitable for hypothesizing the function in unknown proteins for which the primary sequence may be the only information available.

We have decomposed our pattern-based approach into a series of subproblems, each addressing a small part of the puzzle:

(1) ARIADNE [Lathrop *et al.* 1987] approaches our basic question by searching an annotated protein sequence for a complex pattern describing a structural motif assumed to be correlated with function. It employs hierarchical object-oriented representations of both pattern and protein, graph-based sequence and annotation representations, procedural attachment of user-defined match functions, and a complex user-extensible structural pattern language that supports pattern element weights, gaps, annotations and weights attached to the annotations, and so forth.

(2) The ability to match an unknown protein sequence against a complex pattern introduces the question of: Where does the complex pattern come from? ARIEL [Lathrop 1990, Lathrop *et al.* 1990, 1992] functions as an "Induction Assistant" for the biologist engaged in constructing such patterns. It applies massively parallel symbolic induction to the task of refining an initial seed pattern to increase the discrimination between positive and negative instances. Machine learning heuristics for the main pattern language components have been implemented on a massively parallel computer. These manipulate class membership terms, interval relationships, pattern element weights, and an overall match threshold. The time complexity of these machine learning heuristics techniques is essentially constant, and their space complexity essentially linear, in the number of instances in the training set.

(3) But now the further question arises: Where does the seed pattern come from in the first place? PIMA [Smith and Smith 1990, 1992] inductively constructs primary sequence patterns common to a functionally-related family of proteins, using a modified dynamic programming alignment method. These patterns can be more diagnostic for functional family membership than using any member of the family as a probe sequence.

The chapter begins with a background section, following which we examine each of these three areas in detail. No discussion of pattern-based sequence analysis is complete without some mention of statistical reliability, and we close the chapter with a brief discussion of this important topic.

2 Background

One of the fundamental problems in molecular biology is that of relating a protein's structure and function to its amino acid sequence. Kolata [1986] terms this difficult problem "cracking the second half of the genetic code".

Among the problems involved are: relating the protein primary sequence to higher structural levels of protein organization (including secondary, super-secondary, domain, tertiary and occasionally multi-protein quaternary structural levels); identifying the structural elements which are the determinates of a protein function (structural elements here refers broadly to all levels of protein structure); describing the organizational constraints (or patterns) that hold between such elements; and inferring the function and structure in new or unknown proteins.

Before 1959 it was generally assumed that every unique protein sequence would produce a three-dimensional structure radically different from every other protein structure. The subsequent accumulation of X-ray determined protein structures has shown that proteins tend to have a limited number of three-dimensional arrangements. Also, proteins with similar functions often have similar structure. It is this regularity of protein structure that makes it possible to investigate the relationships between sequence, encoded structure, and biological function.

The problem is, of course, difficult and complex. Approaches fall into four broad categories, two experimental and two analytical:

(1) Analysis of physical data generated from proteins, such as X-ray and nuclear magnetic resonance (NMR) data. The most rigorous way to connect primary sequence to function is through X-ray analysis of co-crystal structures, which provide a three-dimensional picture of the protein molecule bound to its substrate. Unfortunately the availability of such data is quite limited. For most proteins, crystals suitable for X-ray analysis prove difficult to obtain, and the experimental and analytical process may require years to determine a single structure (where possible at all). NMR is currently possible only for small proteins, due to resolution limitations inherent in the experimental techniques.

(2) Genetic and crosslinking experimental studies which highlight potentially important functional regions. Functional change associated with amino acid substitutions, deletions and insertions can correlate amino acid positions or regions with functional determinates. The crosslinking of substrates to nearby amino acids supports their association with binding sites. These are often the result of sophisticated laboratory techniques, and the data is usually difficult and laborious to obtain.

(3) Prediction of protein three-dimensional structure and/or function directly from the primary sequence. There are three major approaches. The first (3a) is to attempt to predict three-dimensional backbone conformation by attempting to fold the protein sequence directly from first principles. These methods generally employ empirical potential energy functions. They are very computationally intensive and currently rather unsuccessful, although an active area of research with hope for the future. The second approach (3b) is to predict structure based on similarity to a known three-di-

mensional structure. This approach is related to the first in using empirical potential energy functions, but uses them to refine an initial fit obtained from a known structure rather than to fold the chain *ab initio*. Success depends on the degree of similarity between the known and modeled structures. If the similarity is sufficiently great this method can give very good results, but many sequences fail to exhibit appreciable primary similarity to any known structure. The third (3c) comprises a wide variety of secondary and tertiary structure prediction schemes that attempt to use empirical or statistical rules of one form or another.

(4) Comparative analysis of primary sequences (or of physical values inferred from the primary sequences). There are two related approaches. The first (4a) is to compare primary sequences directly to each other. If significant similarity occurs between a protein of interest (the query) and a protein of known structure or function, one can reason by analogy that they share similar structure and function. If the similarity is great enough this inference is almost always correct. The second (4b) is to compare primary sequences to a structural or functional pattern. If a match to a known pattern occurs one can infer that the protein of interest shares the structure or function associated with the pattern. While a pattern-based approach has often been shown to be a more sensitive detector than direct primary sequence similarity to any single query sequence, the validity of the inference depends on the sensitivity and specificity of the pattern.

Others might reasonably classify some approaches differently, as many overlap or share characteristics. Some of the references below touch several of these areas and have been arbitrarily categorized. In any case our intent is not a rigorous ontological division of the field, but only a pedagogical aid to structure the presentation.

Approach (1) and (2) above rely on experimental methods that are outside the scope of this chapter, even though computational methods are often crucial in the interpretation of the experimental data. For example, the interpretation of X-ray crystal diffraction data to yield the three-dimensional placement of atoms is extremely computationally intensive. Hayes-Roth *et al.* [1986] have applied AI constraint-based techniques to the problem of inferring protein structure from NMR experimental data; Glasgow, *et al.* and Edwards, *et al.* in this volume also describe AI systems that address these approaches.

Approaches (3) and (4) rely almost completely on the development and implementation of analytical and computational methods. Most of the methods that have been developed for approach (3) apply to attempts to model the three-dimensional placement of atoms in the protein, either numerically or by assigning a qualitative structural class to the sequence or subsequences. While quantum mechanics provides a solution in principle to this problem, it is impractical for molecules such as proteins which may contain many thousands of atoms. Consequently a variety of clever innovations have been used instead. Most of these are beyond the scope of this chapter and its focus on sequence analysis, although some of the methods employed for (3c) use pattern-based or machine learning techniques. Approach (3c) is described elsewhere in the present volume, e.g. in the chapters of Holbrook *et al.*, and Hunter. Zhang *et al.* [1992] applied parallel processing machine learning methods to find regularities in three-dimensional protein structure. A few examples of related techniques include Bohr *et al.* [1990], Bowie *et al.* [1991], Clark *et al.* [1990], Cohen *et al.* [1989], Fasman [1989], Holbrook *et al.* [1990], Holley and Karplus [1989], King and Sternberg [1990], Maclin and Shavlik [1992], Major *et al.* [1991], McGregor *et al.* [1989], Muskal *et al.* [1990], Noordewier *et al.* [1990], Ponder and Richards [1987], Qian and Sejnowski [1988], Rawlings *et al.* [1985], Thornton *et al.* [1991], and Towell *et al.* [1990].

Comparative sequence analysis, approach (4), will be the focus of the remainder of the chapter. These methods proceed by comparing a sequence either to another sequence or to a pattern. Although this chapter is primarily directed towards protein sequences, many of the computational techniques are equally applicable to both protein sequences (strings from an alphabet of twenty letters) and DNA sequences (strings from an alphabet of four letters).

2.1 Comparing Primary Sequences to Each Other

By far the most common approach to relating a protein's amino acid sequence to its structure and function is by comparing its sequence to one or more known protein sequences [Wilbur and Lipman 1983; Pearson and Lipman 1988; Altschul *et al.* 1990]. Many important advances have been made by these methods, for example, when the sequence of an oncogene (cancer related gene) was found to be similar to sequences of human growth hormones [Doolittle *et al.*, 1983]. The highly similar sequences clearly related cancerous growth to defective normal cell growth.

The basic idea of most sequence comparison algorithms is to obtain a measure of the similarity (or distance) between two sequences. This usually reflects the minimum number of changes ("edit distance") required to convert one sequence into the other [Sellers 1974, Smith and Waterman 1981a,b]. For biological sequences, there are basically three types of mutation events commonly counted: point mutations, deletions, and insertions. These are "nature's typos:" NATORE, NTURE, and NATEURE. An alignment of such sequences is defined as an ordered sequence of n-tuples, each n-tuple containing one element, or null, from each sequence. For example:

```
N A T - U R E
N A T - O R E
N - T - U R E
N A T E U R E
```

is one alignment of these sequences. Alignments are usually constructed so as to maximize the measure of similarity (or minimize distance) between the sequences. For a few examples of related techniques, see Bacon and Anderson [1986], Barton [1990], Barton and Sternberg [1987a,b], Brutlag *et al.* [1990], Corpet [1988], Felsenstein [1988], Feng and Doolittle [1987], Fischel-Ghodsian *et al.* [1990], Hein [1990], Henneke [1989], Hunter *et al.* [1992], Sankoff and Kruskal [1983], Schuler *et al.* [1991] Taylor [1988a], Vingron and Argos [1989], Waterman [1984, 1986]. Parallel processing versions have been implemented by Collins *et al.* [1988] and Lander *et al.* [1988].

2.2 Comparing Primary Sequences to Patterns

Inspecting the four aligned sequences above, one might notice that their observed variability could be concisely represented by "NgTgvRE", if we assume that "g" (gap) matches zero or one characters of any type, "v" matches any one vowel, and each upper-case letter matches exactly itself. While direct sequence comparison often yields important information, in some cases it may be more desirable to derive a pattern representing the structure or function under study and then compare sequences to that pattern. This is because a pattern is often a more sensitive detector of the regularity under study than any single sequence, due to the "noise" in the rest of the sequence. Further, elements of the pattern often highlight biologically important aspects of the protein.

What is required to compare a pattern to a protein? We must: (1) represent the protein and the pattern to the computer; (2) have an algorithm which performs the comparison; and (3) somehow obtain a pattern to compare. These are all closely related, of course, but we shall adopt this division as an organizing theme.

For pattern matching purposes, the simplest protein representation is a linear sequence denoting its amino acids. This basic amino acid sequence is sometimes annotated with additional information, representing additional features (known or inferred) of the sequence. The degree of annotation possible is a function of the level of our knowledge.

At a minimum; most useful patterns must be able to represent protein positions in which any of several alternate amino acids are acceptable (amino acid physico-chemical classes), as well as regions in which a variable number of amino acids may occur (variable-length gaps). Beyond this, the ability to tolerate a certain amount of mismatch to a pattern lends robustness in the face of mutational diversity. Weights or frequencies are often used to specify greater tolerance in some positions than in others. There is a great deal of effort in the field aimed at extending the power, flexibility, and expressive power of patterns beyond these simple desiderata. Protein sequences fold up to form complex dynamic mechanisms, in which mutations, interactions and dependencies abound. Representations which capture in a manageable way the complexity inherent in Nature may expose some of her regularities more clearly.

The simplest pattern match algorithm possible is an exact match to a literal string. This fails to handle most of the naturally occurring variability in biological sequences. The necessary robustness for inexact matches can often be supplied by the pattern match algorithm instead of the pattern itself. For example, regular expression-based patterns (which specify an exact match in the usual finite state machine construction) can be made more robust by a match algorithm which allows some mis-matches before discarding a potential match.

In some cases the pattern to compare may come directly from biochemical investigation, known three-dimensional structures, analysis of genetic or mutational data, knowledge of similar sequences or patterns, and other sources. Such information is not often available in sufficient quantity and quality to form the sole basis for pattern construction, although it may be adequate to provide initial guesses or seed patterns. Consequently, inductive construction of the pattern is often necessary. The simplest pattern discovery method is to align the sequences maximizing the number of matching amino acids, then construct a consensus sequence from the conserved regions by assigning each consecutive pattern position to consecutive aligned sequence positions. The pattern above, "NgTgvRE", was constructed in this way. This simple method may fail to find patterns in defining sets having widely diverse primary sequences, and consequently more sophisticated approaches are often desirable. Pattern induction techniques fall broadly into two classes, depending on whether a sequence alignment is performed to bring sequence positions into explicit correspondence with each other before pattern discovery is attempted, or not. There is an intermediate set of techniques for which sequence alignment and pattern discovery proceed in alternating cycles. A number of the approaches are "semi-automatic" in actual domain practice, the domain expert applying domain knowledge by direct manual intervention where deemed appropriate or desirable. Any existing experimental data may be used, either as a source of additional clues in the pattern construction process, or to substantiate the pattern once discovered (for example, by verifying that the pattern elements and the positions of matches within the sequences reflect experimentally known associations between sequence position and function).

Hierarchical pattern-matching was pioneered by Abarbanel [1985] and Cohen et al. [1983, 1986], and these researchers originated the term "complex pattern". Cohen et al. [1991a,b] added a meta-level of control knowledge. Taylor and Thornton [1983] originated the use of secondary structure predictions and hydropathy (hydrophobicity) in super-secondary structure patterns. An explicit machine learning approach to pattern discovery in protein sequences was developed by Gascuel and Danchin [1986]. Automatic evaluation of functional patterns was described by Guigo et al. [1991].

Hodgman [1986] describes a pattern library. The chapter by Searls in the present volume discusses complex grammars for biosequences. A few related examples include Abarbanel *et al.* [1984] Barton [1990], Barton and Sternberg [1990], Blundell *et al.* [1987], Bork and Grunwald [1990], Boswell [1988], Cockwell and Giles [1989], Gribskov *et al.* [1987, 1988], Hertz *et al.* [1990], Lawrence and Reilly [1990], Myers and Miller [1989], Owens *et al.* [1988], Patthy [1987, 1988], Sibbald and Argos [1990a], Smith *et al.* [1990], Smith and Smith [1989], Staden [1989], Stormo [1990], Stormo and Hartzell [1989], Taylor [1986, 1988b], Thornton and Gardner [1989], Waterman and Jones [1990], and Webster *et al.* [1989].

Comparative sequence analysis has been an active and fruitful area for the application of computation to biological problems, and a number of very clever techniques have been devised. The discussion and references above provide only an initial window. Next we turn our attention to examining our approach to integrating AI techniques with existing domain methods for sequence analysis. The approach uses three systems: ARIADNE, which matches a complex pattern to an annotated protein sequence; ARIEL, which inductively constructs these complex patterns by refining one or more "seed" patterns; and PIMA, which constructs seed patterns given a family of proteins.

3 ARIADNE[1]

ARIADNE was developed to explore representation and match algorithm issues. Our motivation was to allow a more complex representation of protein sequences, in order make richer information sources explicitly available; and correspondingly, to provide a more complex pattern language in which to express similarities among proteins at a higher level than primary sequence. Because the "best" indicators of protein structure are surely not yet known, both protein and pattern representations had to be easily extensible. In turn, the matching algorithm had to be flexible enough to support unknown future extensions to the representations; extensible itself in order to easily support novel match behavior; and also efficient enough to quickly match complex patterns to large sets of protein sequences. The resulting system facilitates direct expression and manipulation of higher-order structures. It identifies the optimal match between a given complex pattern and protein sequences annotated with various inferred features, by abstracting intermediate levels of structural organization. Inference is grounded solely in knowledge derivable from the primary sequence.

A biologist first hypothesizes a possible protein structure, based on biochemical knowledge (for example, Figure 1a). This is used to form a pattern describing the hypothesized common features, as a sequence of primary sequence elements and their annotations (for example, Figure 1b). It is often convenient to be able to describe the pattern in terms of hierarchical group-

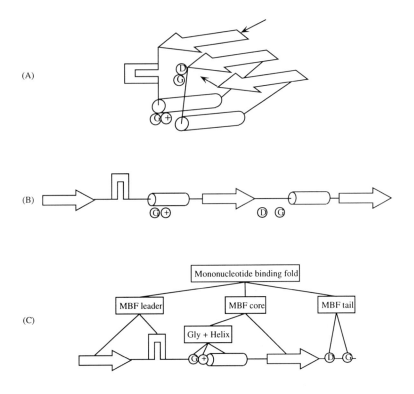

Figure 1 (a) Schematic of the Mononucleotide Binding Fold-like Structure. Beta-sheet strands are represented by arrows, alpha-helices by cylinders, and beta-turns by angular bends. (b) The Mononucleotide Binding Fold Unfolded into a Linear Sequence. The first beta-strand/beta-turn/alpha-helix/beta-strand sequence will form the basis of the structural descriptor below. Key amino acids have been labeled.. (c) The Unfolded Mononucleotide Binding Fold as Hierarchical Groupings. It is often convenient to be able to describe a structure in terms of intermediate levels. This figure appeared as figure 3 of Lathrop et al. (1987).

ings of sub-patterns (for example, Figure 1c). ARIADNE receives as input these pattern(s), and also one or more annotated protein primary sequences.

ARIADNE's biological structure knowledge is encoded in a number of pattern/action inference rules: an antecedent (pattern) that describes a relationship between structural elements, and a consequent (action) that executes in a context with variables bound to reflect the current state of the match (the consequent usually, but not always, hypothesizes the presence of a higher-order structure). Patterns are represented as a hierarchy of sub-patterns, each level an inference based on sub-patterns at lower levels. The target protein is searched for regions which are plausibly similar to the rule antecedent. A dif-

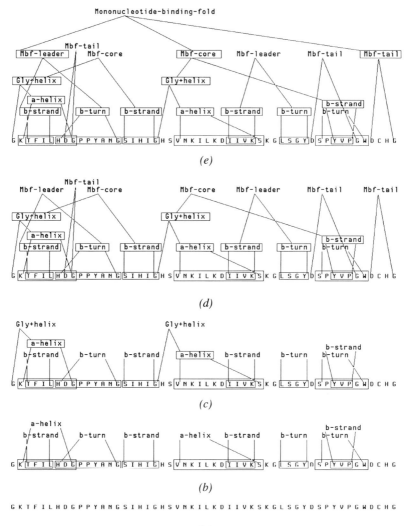

Figure 2 (a) E. coli *Isoleucyl-tRNA synthetase (residues 48-99 of 939 residues). Primary sequence input to ARIADNE. (b)* E. coli *Isoleucyl-tRNA synthetase (residues 48-99 of 939 residues). Secondary structure predictions (Chou and Fasman, 1978; Ralph et al. 1987) input to ARIADNE. (c)* E. coli *Isoleucyl-tRNA synthetase (residues 48-99 of 939 residues). Intermediate predictions constructed by ARIADNE. (d)* E. coli *Isoleucyl-tRNA synthetase (residues 48-99 of 939 residues). Intermediate predictions constructed by ARIADNE. (e)* E. coli *Isoleucyl-tRNA synthetase (residues 48-99 of 939 residues). Final prediction constructed by ARIADNE. No other occurrences of Mononucleotide-Binding-Fold are predicted in this sequence. This figure appeared as figure 4 of Lathrop et al. (1987).*

Enzyme	Source	beta-A — turn — G[H,N,Q] alpha-B — beta-B	Descriptor 1 1&2
Met	E. coli	5 KRILVTCALPYANGSIH LGHMLEHIQADVWVRYQRMRGH EVHFICADDAHG	+ +
	S. cerevisiae	197 NILITSALPYVN YVPHLGNIIGSVLSADIFARYCKGHNYNA	+ −
Tyr	E. coli	31 PIALYCGFDPTADSLHLGHLVPLLCLKRFQQAGHKPVALVGGAT	+ +
	B. stearothermophilus	RVTLYCGFDPTADSLHIGHLATILTMRRFQQAGHKPIALVGGAT	+ +
Ile	E. coli	30 IFILHDGPPYANGSIHIGHSVNKILKDIIVKSKGLSGYDSPYVPGWDCHG	+ +
	S. cerevisiae	50 EFTFFDGPPFATGTPHYGHILASTIKDIVPRYATHTGHHVERRFGWDIHG	+ +
Gln	E. coli	26 ITVHTRFPPEPNGYLHIGHAKSIGLNFGIANDYKGNCHLRFDD	− −
	S. cerevisiae	251 KVRTRFPPEPNGYLHIGHSKAIMVNFGYAKVYHNQTCYLRFDD	− −
Trp	B. stearothermophilus	1 MKTIFSGIQPSGVITIGNYIGALRQFVELQHQYNCYFCIQHAITVWQDPH	+ +
	E. coli	4 RIVFSGRQPSGELTIGNYMGALRQWVKMQQDYHCIYCIVDQH	+ +
	S. cerevisiae	35 ATVFSHIDPTGCFHLGHYLGAYRVWYTMCCELKQGQELIFBV	− −
Ala	E. coli	152 RIIRINDMKGAPYASGNFWRMGGIGPCDPCTEIFYDHG	+ +
	E. coli	488 FVVVLCQTPFYAESGGQVGDKGELKGANFSFAVEDIQK	+ +
Gly	E. coli beta-subunit	300 NFIFVANIESKDPQQIISGNEKVVRPRLADAEFFFNTDR	+ +
Asp	S. cerevisiae	78 LPLIQSRDSDRIGQKRVKFVDLDEAKDSDKEVLFRARVHNTRQQQATLAFLILRQG	+ +
Glu	E. coli	1 MKIKTRFAPSPTGYLHVGGARTALYSWLFARRHGGEFVLR	− −

Figure 3. Proposed alignment of aminoacyl-tRNA synthetase sequences with the first beta-alpha-beta fold of a mononucleotide bindinglike structure. The regions predicted to fold into beta-A, the turn, alpha-B, and beta-B are enclosed in the first, second, third and fourth solid box, respectively, of each sequence. Sequences which match the composite descriptor and/or descriptor 1 are indicated with a "+" to the right of the figure. Secondary structure assignments for the B. stearothermophilus Tyr-tRNA synthetase and E. coli Met-tRNA synthetase X-ray structures are indicated with an underline. Dashed boxes indicate weakly predicted secondary structure elements. This figure is adapted from figure 5 of Webster et al. (1987), which includes references for the sequences.

ferential similarity score between the pattern and the target protein elements is computed, and the rule fires where this equals or exceeds some user-specified threshold. When the rule fires, its consequent typically creates a new entry in the overlay of inferred structures. The new entry can enable the firing of subsequent rules. For example, Figure 2a-e shows the hierarchical pattern matching of the mononucleotide binding fold pattern (Figure 1) to an annotated protein sequence.

The output describes, for each input protein, which (sub)pattern(s) matched; what their support in the annotated protein sequence was; and the computed similarity score between the (sub)pattern(s) and the protein elements in the support. From the patterns and their match support, it is possible to construct a local alignment of the matched members of the family, by aligning elements which support the same pattern. For example, Figure 1a-c shows a pattern for a mononucleotide binding foldlike structure, and Figure 3 shows the local alignment induced by the matches of the pattern to the positive sequences. If the the input sequences are divided into the positive (defining) and the negative (control) sets, it is also possible to obtain the sensitivity/specificity spectrum of the pattern as the threshold similarity score varies. These take the form of 2x2 contingency tables (see the section on Significance, Validity, and Pattern Quality, below) for each possible setting of the threshold score, as well as a graph summarizing the spectrum of sensitivity and specificity attainable as the threshold varies.

3.1 ARIADNE Protein Representation

We enriched the protein sequences by explicitly annotating the sequences with information which normally is only implicit in the sequence. For example, secondary structure predictions [Chou and Fasman, 1978; Garnier *et al.* 1978], hydropathy and amphipathy weighted average profiles [Eisenberg *et al.* 1982, 1984], and various charge templates and clusters [Karlin *et al.* 1989, Zhu *et al.* 1990], all contain clues to higher levels of organization. All are implicit in, but can be inferred from, the amino acid sequence. By explicitly annotating the protein sequence with these implicit information sources (often computed externally by existing domain programs), we can make the additional structural clues they contain directly available to the pattern match process. For example, Figure 2b shows a protein sequence annotated with secondary structure predictions [Ralph *et al.* 1987]. Any information source which usefully distinguishes certain subsequences of the protein may be employed.

Although the amino acid sequences are inherently strings in a twenty-letter alphabet, we represent the instance as an object-oriented directed graph. Nodes and arcs are the typed and weighted data objects. Typed nodes in our graph represent the twenty amino acid types found in protein sequences. They participate in a user-extensible class generalization hierarchy depending on amino acid physico-chemical properties (volume, charge, hydropathy, and so forth). Directed arcs annotate the sequence with extended higher-level features. The arc type reflects the feature type, and the arc connects the node that begins the feature to the node that ends it. Arcs represent the annotations to the protein sequence supplied in the input data, as well as the higher-level structural organization inferred as a result of pattern matching. For example, nodes represent the protein sequence shown in Figure 2a, while arcs represent both the input secondary structure predictions shown in Figure 2b and the subsequent pattern matches shown in Figure 2c-e.

This approach allows a uniform treatment of information derived from both external and internal sources. Both are treated as annotations to the protein sequence, which make explicit some information previously implicit in the sequence but inferrable from it. This is similar in some respects to a "blackboard" architecture [Erman and Lesser 1975]. The hierarchical organization of protein structure in the domain is readily mirrored, and hierarchical patterns are easily supported. Because each extended feature represents its own beginning and end, overlapping features of the same type are distinct. This facilitates representation of the annotated structural correlates and inferred structures. The major alternative approach (in a purely string-based sequence representation) is to mark the individual string characters with tokens indicating which feature types they occur within; but then overlapping features of the same type lose their boundaries and hence their individual identities, inseparably blurring together.

3.2 ARIADNE Pattern Language.

ARIADNE's pattern language is divided into primitive and composite pattern elements. Primitive patterns usually appear only as components in composite patterns. Their match behavior is completely determined by three attached procedures that directly inspect and manipulate the target protein data structures:

1. GENERATE-EXPANSIONS returns a list of possible pairings of the pattern element to target protein elements.

2. SIMILARITY-SCORE returns the similarity score that the pattern element actually attains on any given pairing to target protein elements.

3. MAX-POSSIBLE-SCORE returns (an upper bound on) the maximum similarity score the pattern element could ever achieve.

A number of useful primitive pattern elements are provided by default. These include the twenty primitive amino acids; their various physico-chemical classes (e.g., positively charged, hydrophobic, H-bond donors, etc.); several spacer (gap), overlap, positioning, and containment operators; features in various numeric transforms of the amino acid sequence (e.g., amphipathy peaks are often associated with surface helices); primitives for recognizing sequence annotations (including user-defined annotations); and so forth.

However, ARIADNE is predicated on the assumption that we do not yet know the best structural features with which to analyze all proteins. The intent is to provide a development framework wherein pattern primitives with complex behavior can easily be created in response to new needs, as domain knowledge expands through exploration and experimentation. ARIADNE therefore provides a framework of procedural attachment for the user to define new primitive pattern elements, with new match behavior. This is done by allowing the user (or more likely, a programmer working with the user) to write new procedures for the three determinates of primitive match behavior above. Also, any annotation type used to annotate the input protein sequence automatically induces a corresponding primitive element that recognizes occurrences of the annotation. Thus the pattern language is extensi-

ble either by defining new annotations, or by directly coding the match behavior of new primitives.

A composite pattern is defined by giving a list of the lower-level subpat-
terns and relationships required as support. Its match behavior is completely
determined by the match behavior of its components. Hierarchical pattern
construction and matching is supported because recognition of a hierarchical
organization from low-level detail proceeds most naturally by hierarchical
construction of the intervening patterns. This is implemented internally by
annotating the protein to reflect the newly inferred structure, in exactly the
same way as we annotated the protein on input to reflect structure inferred by
domain programs. Each instance of a composite pattern, when recognized in
a low-level description, becomes available as a feature element for higher-
order composite patterns. In this way a pyramid of inferences may connect
the low-level features to the more abstract.

3.3 ARIADNE Pattern Matching Algorithm.

The power of pattern-directed inference (e.g., rule-based expert systems)
is well known, as is its applicability to molecular biology [Friedland and
Iwaskai 1985]. One of the first such systems ever constructed, DENDRAL
[Lindsay et al. 1980], also performed the task of chemical structure recognition. However, we allow flexible rule invocation based on a controllable degree of partial pattern similarity. This is implemented by an A* search [Win-
ston 1984] through the space of target protein subsequences.

The search for a differential similarity to a composite pattern consists of
attempting to pair each component subpattern to an admissible subset of target objects. A partial pairing, constructed at some intermediate stage, might
pair only some of the pattern components. For a given composite pattern,
ARIADNE's search space is the set of all possible partial pairings. The single start state in this search space is the empty partial pairing, and goal states
are complete pairings of all pattern components. An operator which carries
one partial pairing into its successors, is to expand the next unpaired pattern
component by hypothesizing pairings to every admissible set of target objects. By applying this operator first to the start state and then iteratively to
resulting partial pairings, all complete pairings may be found. Typically, a
single new target object is created for each pair showing a positive similarity
(Figure 2c-e). For example, in Figure 2c the pattern "Gly+helix" is shown
matching its components "G" and "a-helix". Each time a complete pairing is
found, a new "Gly+helix" object is created.

Viewed from top-to-bottom, the added target objects impose a hierarchical
organization. Viewed from left-to-right they impose a lattice structure because of the partial ordering, "followed-by", inherited from the underlying
linear chain. Pattern recognition consists of exploring alternate pathways
through the lattice structure. For example, in Figure 2b the target object rep-

resenting the first lysine (the first "K" in "G K T F ...") may be followed either by a threonine object ("T") or by an object representing a beta-strand prediction. The beta-strand object, in turn, may be followed either by a histidine object ("H") or by a beta-turn object. This permits structural elements (at any level) to be manipulated and searched as a unit, independent of their actual length or composition.

Complete pairings are ordered by a similarity score and only the higher-scoring ones are of interest, so an efficient search strategy is desirable. The well known A* search [Winston 1984] efficiently accommodates differentially inexact similarities to a pattern and tends to focus search effort on the most promising candidates. A* is a best-first branch-and-bound search with dynamic elimination of redundant pairings and an optimistic estimate of the contribution of the remaining unpaired pattern components. (The elimination of redundant pairings may optionally be suppressed.) Optimality and convergence are both guaranteed.

The key to A* search is in the selection of which partial pairing to expand. Each partial pairing has a "best possible score", which is the highest score that the most favorable possible pairing of yet-unpaired pattern components could ever yield. At each step the partial pairing with the highest BEST-POSSIBLE-SCORE is selected. If its BEST-POSSIBLE-SCORE is below the threshold the search can fail immediately, as no partial pairing could possibly exceed the threshold. Similarly, if it is a complete pairing then no other partial pairing can ever complete to a higher score. Otherwise, its next unpaired pattern is expanded and the algorithm iterates. It is possible to enumerate all complete pairings in decreasing order of similarity score, pausing and continuing the search at will.

3.4 Discussion of ARIADNE

The principle sources of power in ARIADNE are:

- The ability to utilize multiple, unreliable, inconsistent knowledge sources. Since no prediction scheme produces accurate predictions, any inference procedure which vitally depended on the consistency of its database (e.g., some forms of theorem-proving) would be ineffective.

- The use of a pattern-similarity measure to guide flexible invocation of inference rules. This conveys a degree of robustness in the face of pattern fluctuations such as mutations.

- Implementation of the rule-invocation similarity measure as an A* search. This provides an efficient enumeration of match candidates, in order of decreasing similarity.

- A flexible framework for pattern language development and extension. This is important because all the appropriate pattern elements are surely not yet known.

- Explicit identification and representation of the intermediate hierarchy, which helps in several ways:

  - Many of the higher-order (super-secondary) structures of interest are most effectively expressed in terms of lower and intermediate levels of hierarchy (secondary structure groupings), and not directly at the lowest level of description.

  - Handling patterns in small pieces encourages selective pattern refinement.

  - Expressing patterns consisting of key residues embedded in secondary structures involves the interaction of different hierarchical levels.

  - Breaking a large pattern into pieces increases search efficiency by reducing the potentially exponential time dependency on pattern size.

The approach presented here is limited to detecting similarities in sequence patterns of known and/or predicted structural elements. To the extent that hypotheses of interest can be expressed in the form of a structural pattern, ARIADNE provides a powerful and efficient vehicle for finding supporting regions in the target proteins. However, no use is currently made of primary sequence similarities (or homologies), which would provide additional evidence for favoring some matches over others (particularly similarity of sequence elements in between paired pattern elements across the defining set). No direct use is made of three-dimensional spatial constraints. The secondary structure predictions remain inherently inaccurate, even though trade-offs can be made between reliability and coverage. Some three-dimensional structural motifs are composed from elements widely dispersed in the primary sequence but folded to be contiguous in space, and these are unlikely to be seen by any method which draws its power from exploiting constraints which are local in the sequence. No attempt has been made to encode or exploit "expert rule-of-thumb" knowledge of general biochemical heuristics.

Construction of abstract structural hypotheses implies that low-level features meet the additional constraints imposed by higher-order patterns and relationships. These constraints take two forms: requiring a specified relationship with an element unambiguously present in the primary input (e.g., key amino acids); and requiring a specified relationship with other predicted or inferred features. Importantly, in a hierarchical pattern recognizer the structure imposed by higher-order patterns implies strong constraints on the admissibility and interpretation of low-level features, because those not fitting into a higher-level pattern will be dropped. A pattern acts to prune the (uncertain, heuristic, empirical) low-level features by selective attention, based on the strong constraint of fitting into higher-order organization (see

Figure 2a-e). Low-level features will be interpreted in terms of the expectations encoded in the patterns being searched for.

This has both good and bad aspects. When an intelligent agent (e.g., a biologist) hypothesizes and searches for the existence of a particular pattern based on supporting biochemical or circumstantial evidence, selective feature attention extends that evidential support down to low-level feature selection, and features supporting the pattern will be propagated upward. When a large number of patterns are sought randomly in a large number of targets (as in a database search), then each pattern will impose its own selective bias and additional confirming experimental evidence should be sought. In either case, an important estimate of the false positive (resp. false negative) rate may be had by testing a control set known not to (resp. known to) actually satisfy the pattern.

4 ARIEL[2]

Although ARIADNE provides a powerful and flexible means to match a complex pattern against a group of protein sequences, it raises the question, "Where do the patterns come from?" One methodology for pattern construction by a domain expert was described in [Webster *et al.* 1988]. An initial pattern is refined in an iterative loop consisting of:

a. matching the pattern against the positive and negative instances;

b. evaluating the performance (sensitivity and specificity) of the pattern; and

c. modifying the pattern and repeating.

Even in cases where a clear idea of actual structure provides an initial seed pattern, transforming that into the final pattern that best separates the positive and negative sequences involves a potentially large search through pattern space. ARIEL [Lathrop 1990, Lathrop *et al.* 1990, 1992] functions as an "Induction Assistant" to the domain expert engaged in such a process. It automates and parallelizes parts (a), (b), and the low-level aspects of part (c), of the methodology above, while the domain expert provides high-level control and direction (see Figures 4 and 5). Symbolic induction heuristics ("operators") are provided for the major syntactic components of the pattern language. Various amino acid classes may be explored at primary sequence positions; inter-element intervals (gaps) may be varied; weights associated with the several pattern elements may be increased or decreased; the overall match threshold may be changed; and pattern elements may be added or deleted.

ARIEL runs on a CM-2 Connection Machine, and implements efficient massively parallel machine learning algorithms for several symbolic induction heuristics (of the sort familiar to the symbolic machine learning commu-

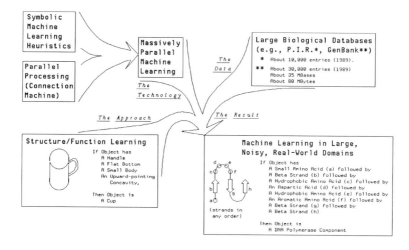

Figure 4 . Overview of ARIEL. Structure/function relationships, massively parallel processing, symbolic machine learning, and on-line biological databases converge in learning structure/function patterns as discussed in this chapter. This figure appeared as figure 1 of Lathrop et al. (1990).

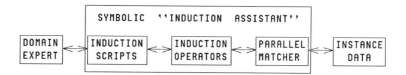

Figure 5. Logical system architecture. he domain expert invokes induction scripts on a ``parent" pattern (terms are explained in the text). Induction scripts consist of a sequence of induction operators, separated by filters. Induction operators construct a set of syntactically variant patterns (``children") from the parent. A subset of the children (the ``induction basis set") is matched against the instance data using the parallel matcher. The results are returned to the induction operator, which composes them to compute the performance of the remaining children. All the evaluated children are returned to the script, which uses filters to prune unpromising possibilities. The surviving results of the script are returned to the domain expert. Scripts and filters execute in the serial front-end host, while induction operators and matching execute mostly in the parallel hardware. This figure appeared as figure 2 of Lathrop et al. (1990).

MATCHING AND INDUCTION IN PARALLEL HARDWARE

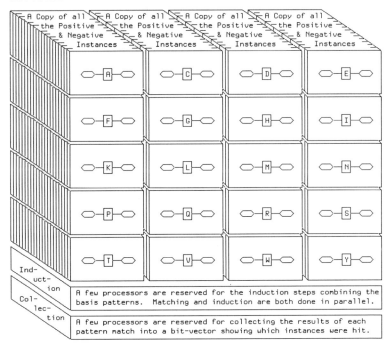

Figure 6. Schematic organization of parallel hardware usage. An induction operator can be decomposed into a ``basis set'' of multiple patterns (shown as boxed letters representing different pattern terms, flanked by lozenges representing preceding and following pattern components). These may be applied to multiple copies of the full positive and negative instance sets in parallel (each copy of the sets is shown fronted by the pattern matched against it, with vertical ``slices'' representing the individual instances). All patterns may be matched against all instances in parallel. The results may be recombined, also in parallel, within the few induction processors. This figure appeared as figure 3 of Lathrop et al. (1990).

nity as Climb-Tree, Drop-Link, Expand-Range, and so forth; for example, see Winston [1984]). We have parallelized both the match and the induction steps (see Figure 6). First an efficient, noise-tolerant, similarity-based parallel matching algorithm was developed. (See Figure 7.) The parallel matcher was used as infrastructure to construct efficient parallel implementations of several symbolic machine learning induction operators. (See Figure 8 for an example of an induction operator.) Finally, the induction operators were sandwiched together, separated by filters (both syntactic and empirical), to compose a crude form of induction scripts. These are invoked by the domain expert. (See Figure 9 for an example of an induction script.) Scripts and

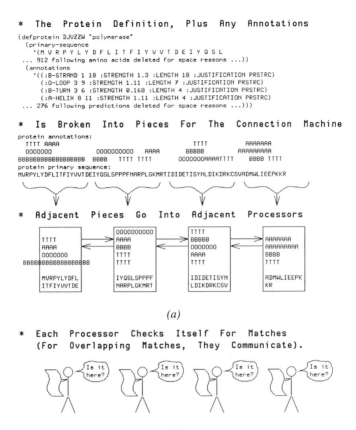

```
*  The  Protein  Definition,  Plus  Any  Annotations
(defprotein DJVZZW "polymerase"
  (primary-sequence
   '(M U R P Y L Y D F L I T F I Y V V T D E I Y Q S L
   ... 912 following amino acids deleted for space reasons ...))
  (annotations
   '(((:B-STRAND 1 18 :STRENGTH 1.3 :LENGTH 18 :JUSTIFICATION PRSTRC)
     (:O-LOOP 3 9 :STRENGTH 1.11 :LENGTH 7 :JUSTIFICATION PRSTRC)
     (:B-TURN 3 6 :STRENGTH 0.168 :LENGTH 4 :JUSTIFICATION PRSTRC)
     (:A-HELIX 8 11 :STRENGTH 1.11 :LENGTH 4 :JUSTIFICATION PRSTRC)
   ... 276 following predictions deleted for space reasons ...)))
```

```
*  Is  Broken  Into  Pieces  For  The  Connection  Machine
protein annotations:
TTTT AAAA                                TTTT       AAAAAAA
0000000            0000000000   AAAA      BBBBB      AAAAAAAAA
BBBBBBBBBBBBBBBBB   BBBB    TTTT TTTT   0000000AAAATTTT   BBBB  TTTT
protein primary sequence:
MVRPYLYDFLITFIYVVTDEIYQSLSPPPFNARPLGKMRTIDIDETISYNLDIKDRKCSVADMWLIEEPKKR
```

```
*  Adjacent  Pieces  Go  Into  Adjacent  Processors
```

(a)

```
*  Each  Processor  Checks  Itself  For  Matches
   (For  Overlapping  Matches,  They  Communicate).
```

(b)

Figure 7. Embedding and matching instances in the machine. Instances occur in very different lengths, but a constant-sized segment is placed in each processor. During the match phase, each processor checks only the constant-sized segment it contains. A communication protocol handles matches which extend over several processors. This figure appeared as figure 1.6 of Lathrop (1990).

filters execute in the serial front-end host, while induction operators and matching execute mostly in the parallel hardware.

Initial input to ARIEL consists of one or more seed patterns, and also two sets of protein primary sequences (one positive, one negative) annotated as described above. The proteins are loaded into static data structures in the parallel hardware at start-up. Thereafter the domain expert and ARIEL iterate through the pattern construction loop (a, b, c) described above. At each iteration, the domain expert invokes an induction script on a "parent" pattern. A single script may chain together several induction operators and filters. In-

* Given Pattern, Pick A Term Corresponding to A Leaf Or Class

* Copy Pattern Once For Each Leaf, Substituting In Each Leaf

* Load Each Pattern Copy Into A Full Instance Set In The CM

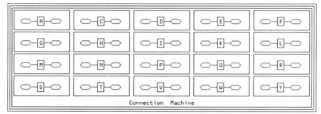

Connection Machine

* Match Every Pattern To Every Protein In Parallel (Unit Time)

(a)

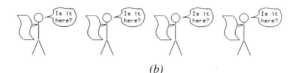

(b)

* Each Pattern Generates Its Characteristic Bit-Vector Of Matches

○─[A]─○   0001000100001000000001000100100001000000000000010000000000100001001010000000000...

○─[G]─○   1000100000000000000001001001000001000000001001011000000001110010000001000000000001000...

○─[S]─○   0001000000010010010000100100010001000101010010000000100000100100100010001001001000001...

↓ Logical OR ↓ Logical OR ↓ Logical OR ↓ Logical OR ↓ Logical OR ↓

○─[SMALL]─○ 1001100100011010010011110110110011100101101111001001001111011100101111010001001001...

* The Matches Generated by Substituting Any Class At That Term
  Are Exactly The Logical 'OR' Of Its Constituents' Matches.

The matches to the pattern if SMALL were   SMALL   Because the amino acid class
to be substituted in that position are   ╱│╲   SMALL is exactly the union of
exactly the union of the matches to the   A G S   its constituents, A, G, and S.
patterns with A, G, and S substituted there.

* Logical 'OR's For All Classes Are Computed In Parallel

Consequently, we return the result of substituting every possible class of amino acids at that position,
then matching each of the resulting patterns against every protein in the functional and control sets,
all in little more than the time for one processor to match its own protein fragment to one pattern.

(c)

Figure 8. Induction operator example of CLASS-INDUCTION. This explores optimizations attainable by replacing a specified term in the parent pattern (the term HYDROPHOBE as illustrated here) by every other term from the generalization hierarchy (its replacement by SMALL is shown here for concreteness, but its replacement by every other term in the generalization hierarchy is also computed in parallel). This figure appeared as figure 4 of Lathrop et al. (1990).

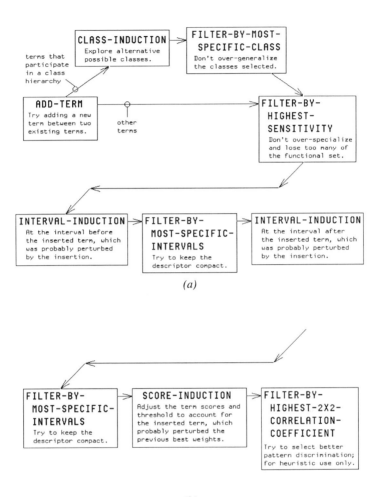

Figure 9.   Induction script example of ADD-TERM-AND-REFINE. A script consists of a series of induction operators, separated by filters to prune unpromising candidates. These chain together common sequences of induction operators. Each induction operator generates and evaluates a large number of candidate patterns. Each filter step removes patterns based on some criteria. In the script shown here, the operator ADD-TERM is first applied to the parent pattern. If the term participates in a class generalization hierarchy, CLASS-INDUCTION is then applied to explore appropriate class terms. INTERVAL-INDUCTION is next applied, to adjust the intervals before and after the added term. Finally, SCORE-INDUCTION adjusts the term scores and threshold. This figure appeared as figure 5 of Lathrop et al. (1990).

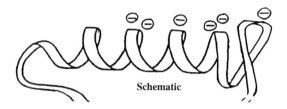

Schematic

Elements					
Local Hydrophobic {-1, 7} profile minimum	alpha-helix with acid-faced segment	{-1, 8} Local Hydrophobic profile maximum	[V L I] {4, 8}	ß-turn {-5,0}	D

Weights						
If absent	-0.5	-	-	-0.5	-	-1.5
If present	+0.5	function of net template charge	0.0	+0.5	0.0	+1.5
Space skipped if absent	+1	+16	+1	+1	+4	+1

Figure 10. The pattern found to be most diagnostic of a class of transcriptional acti-
vators containing the steroid hormone receptors. The schematic diagram was drawn
by a domain expert. The remainder of the figure describes the pattern found by
ARIEL. The pattern elements must be found in sequence. Elements in curly braces
{n, m} are allowed spaces between elements, where n is the minimum distance and m
is the maximum. Note that a negative value for n allows the beginning of the follow-
ing element to overlap the end of the preceding element. The weights given corre-
spond to the pattern elements that they are below. All weights are relative to a pattern
match threshold of +3.5 (see text). The spacer elements do not have weights; if the
match is within the allowed space limits, the weight is zero, and if not, the weight is
negative infinity.

duction operators construct a set of syntactically variant patterns ("children")
from the parent pattern. Only a subset of the children (the "induction basis
set") is actually matched against the instance data, and from these the performance of the remaining children is computed. Filters prune unpromising possibilities. Finally, surviving children are returned to the domain expert, and
the loop iterates. At the end of the session, output consists of a number of
patterns evaluated for their sensitivity and specificity against the data set (see
the section on Significance, Validity, and Pattern Quality, below), as well as
the spectrum of sensitivity and specificity explored across pattern space.

Figure 10 shows a schematic representation (drawn by the domain expert)
of the pattern found to be most diagnostic of a class of transcriptional activa-

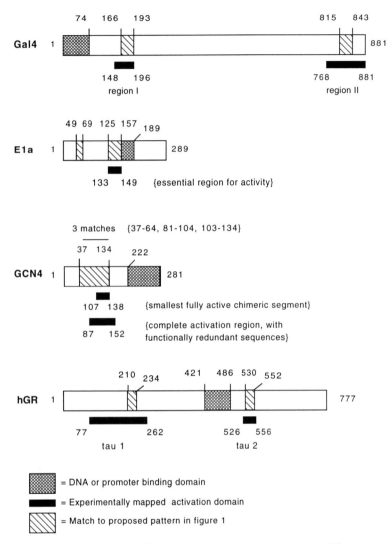

Figure 11 . Schematic of Four Transactivating Proteins. A schematic of four transactivating proteins showing the relative positions of the pattern matches, DNA binding domains, and experimentally mapped regions essential to that activity (hGR (Hollenberg and Evans 1988); E1a (Lillie and Green 1989); Gal4 (Ma and Ptashne 1987); and GCN4, (Hope et al. 1988)) These regions were used in the pattern construction, and so cannot be considered experimental verification of the pattern. Nonetheless, the close correspondence between pattern matches and functionally essential regions illustrates the potential utility of the pattern match for guiding future experimental work in unknown transactivating proteins. This figure appeared as figure 2 of Zhu et al. (1990).

tors containing the steroid hormone receptors, as well as the corresponding pattern as refined by ARIEL. Figure 11 shows in schematic four transcriptional activating proteins with the relative positions of the pattern matches and the experimentally mapped activation domains known to be essential to the function. These regions were used in the pattern construction, and so cannot be considered experimental verification of the pattern. Nonetheless, the close correspondence between pattern matches and functionally essential regions illustrates the potential utility of the pattern match for guiding future experimental work in unknown transactivating proteins.

4.1 ARIEL Protein and Pattern Representations.

ARIEL accepts as input the same annotated protein sequences as ARIADNE. Internally, ARIEL employs a graph-based pattern representation similar to ARIADNE, but it is not fully object-oriented due to data storage considerations arising from the massively parallel Connection Machine implementation. The major differences are that (1) the protein data structure is static, and so neither patterns nor target objects can be hierarchically constructed because annotations cannot be dynamically added; and (2) the annotations are implemented as typed weighted pointers, rather than as full-fledged objects in an object-oriented style, and so lack the notion of "containing" the amino acids which compose them.

ARIEL currently implements a restricted subset of the pattern language generality provided by ARIADNE. Only the most commonly used language terms (pattern elements) from ARIADNE are currently included. The set of ARIEL language primitives was fixed by choosing the ARIADNE language constructs that had been found to be most useful in the domain task. ARIADNE was designed to be a research vehicle into useful language constructs for the domain; consequently its pattern primitives are expressed in arbitrary LISP code making the language nearly arbitrarily user-extensible. ARIEL was designed to be a research vehicle into parallel symbolic induction; consequently it has a fixed set of pattern primitives whose semantics are directly encoded in the primitive hardware. ARIEL's pattern language permits description of nodes and their generalization classes, arcs, weights, threshold, and interval relationships. A pattern consists of a series of TERMS separated by INTERVALS. A THRESHOLD governs the overall match quality required to qualify as a successful match.

Each term specifies either a node class or an arc type. The semantics of a term specifying a node class are to match to a node belonging to that class. The semantics of a term specifying an arc type are to match to and traverse an arc of that type. Terms carry an associated SCORE-IF-ABSENT and SCORE-IF-PRESENT that govern how the pattern term matched against instance features contributes to the overall match score. These may indicate either a numeric score, minus infinity, or the weight attached to the instance feature. Arc type terms indicate a default length, usually set to the average length of arcs of that type. Intervals separate adjacent pattern terms. The interval between two terms governs where to look for the next term after having found the previous one. An interval consists of a fixed part (representing a mandatory offset from the preceding term) and a variable part (indicating a window length within which to look for the next term), and thus is equivalent to a variable-length gap in specifying a minimum and maximum number of amino acids to skip.

4.2 Pattern Matching in Parallel Hardware.

The induction mechanisms are built upon, and call as a subroutine, a parallel matching algorithm. Virtually all processors in the parallel hardware (over 98%) are of type MATCH, and receive a pattern to test and an instance segment to match against it. A few processors are of type COLLECTION, and collect the global results of the match. A few processors are of type INDUCTION, and are used to combine the results of the induction operators (see Figure 6).

Both the pattern, and the instance data against which it is matched, are stored in the private data of a processor (see Figures 6 and 7). Once loaded, the instance data is permanently resident in the processor. New patterns are broadcast to the processors at the beginning of each match cycle. Bit-vectors are transmitted back to the host when the cycle ends. Thus the communication channel between front-end host and parallel hardware is of low bandwidth.

Large proteins are broken into several segments and stored in several adjacent processors. A communication protocol handles cases in which a successful match spans more than one processor. Each instance is assigned a unique bit position in a bit vector, which is stored with the instance in the processor. When each match cycle is complete, each processor compares the highest score achieved by any match terminating in its segment to the threshold from the pattern. If the threshold is met or exceeded, that processor sends (with logical inclusive OR) the instance bit representing its protein to the collection processor for that pattern. There is one collection processor dedicated to each pattern concurrently matched. Bits sent by processors meeting or exceeding the threshold set the corresponding bit in the collection processor, and thereby specify that the corresponding instance matched that pattern. Each collection processor winds up with a global bit-vector corresponding exactly to the successfully matched instances of its associated pattern.

Because we usually use no more than one or two hundred instances in the positive and negative sets, but have thousands of processors, it is possible to hold many duplicate copies of the full sets of positive and negative instances in the parallel hardware. Each full copy of the positive and negative instances is called a full instance set, and the processors holding them a full processor set. Matching one pattern against one instance is independent of matching another pattern against a different instance, and so can be done in parallel (see Figures 6, 7 and 8). We put different patterns in each full processor set, but each processor in the same full set receives the same pattern. By matching against all of these concurrently, we obtain the result of matching many different patterns exhaustively against all the positive and negative instances, in essentially the real time taken to match one pattern against one segment of one instance.

For the domain studied here, this yields the following attractive match properties:

- Nearly Constant Time in Number of Instances; because the match against each instance is independent and concurrent. The only time dependency on number of instances occurs in transmitting the bit-vectors, an operation that consumes a tiny fraction of the time of the match.

- Nearly Linear Space in Total Instance Pool Size; because we need but one processor per segment. The space dependency on number of instances involves storing the instance data together with the instance-ID.

- Nearly Constant Time in Instance Size; because an instance is segmented and split over several processors. Any one processor looks only at a constant-length segment regardless of the total length of the instance. Communication costs for following arcs from one processor to another are nearly constant in instance size because the domain has high locality (i.e., arcs are mostly short).

- Most Communication Local for Domains With High Locality; because if the domain is sufficiently local, most communication except the global bit-vector OR used to compute the characteristic set can use local communication with adjacent processors.

- Nearly All Non-Local Communication Evenly Distributed in Both Source and Destination (No Bottlenecks or Collisions); because except for the global bit-vector OR, all non-local communication has unique source and unique destination.

- Space Constant Adjustable to Available Hardware, for Nearly 100% Processor Utilization; because we can vary the length of the segment we put in each processor. Decreasing the length uses more processors, increasing it uses fewer. We can vary it to fill the machine.

- Works on real-world problems using realistic hardware; for example the transcriptional activator pattern from Zhu *et al.* [1990] was run on an 8K CM-2 Connection Machine.

These bounds fail to be exactly constant or linear because each match processor must also store and transmit its own instance-ID (specifying the bit position corresponding to its instance). A binary encoding of the instance-ID must consume at least log N bits, forcing the formal time complexity to O(log N) and the formal space complexity to O(N log N). However, bounding the size of the binary instance-ID by as few as 64 bits (tiny compared to the many tens of thousands of bits consumed by the typical instance itself, and less than 1/10 of 1 percent of each CM-2 processor's 64K bits of private memory) would suffice for well over ten sextillion instances, certainly far beyond the foreseeable future of parallel hardware. The time consumed in processing the instance-ID is currently trivial compared to seconds or even minutes for the match process itself, and the space consumed so small relative to other uses that the implementation actually encodes the instance-ID as a single bit set in a large bit-field for simplicity. Once the match and induction steps are complete, transmitting the bit-vector back to the front-end host incurs a small communication cost of one bit per instance per pattern.

4.3 ARIEL Pattern Induction Mechanisms.

Induction operators have been provided for the main pattern language components: class membership terms, interval relationships, weights and a threshold, and pattern elements. Each operator seeks to explore a single characteristic class of perturbations to the original pattern, related to a specific pattern language component. An induction operator transforms one initial pattern (parent) into a set of related patterns (children), and evaluates their performance on the positive and negative instances.

One of the main points of this research is to demonstrate parallel induction algorithms rendering it unnecessary to actually match each and every child pattern against the instances in order to evaluate its match performance. Matching each child pattern would be an undesirable waste of our computing resources, because the match step consumes most of the time and space of the system. Instead, we find a subset of pattern space (an "induction basis set") from which, once the performance of that subset is known, we can readily infer the exact performance of the other child patterns implied by the induction operator. Thus we match only a few child patterns against the instance data, and use those results to compute what the match performance of other children would be.

For example, CLASS-INDUCTION operates on a language term that participates in a class generalization network (often termed an A-Kind-Of, or AKO, hierarchy). In the domain, this corresponds to the physico-chemical classes of amino acids. The effect of applying CLASS-INDUCTION to a term in a pattern is to explore all new pattern variants which may be constructed by changing its class to any other class in the generalization hierarchy. As shown in Figure 8, for this operator the "induction basis set" can be just the leaves (or some suitable subset of the class hierarchy). In CLASS-

INDUCTION these are the children which substitute individual amino acids (leaves of the generalization hierarchy) at the position of interest. In the example of Figure 8, the class SMALL is composed of the leaves A, G, and S. The instances matched by a child substituting SMALL at a given term are exactly the union of the instances matched by the three children substituting A, G, or S. In general, each class is just the union of its leaves, so the instances matched by a child substituting any given class at the term are exactly the union of the instances matched by children substituting one of the leaves making up the class. Match performance on instance data is encoded in a bit-vector indicating which instances matched a pattern (by whether the bit corresponding to a given instance is on or off). Pattern results for the leaves can be merged by ORing together their bit-vectors of hit instances according to the union comprising the class. Figure 8 shows how the match bit-vector of the child substituting SMALL is computed by ORing the bit-vectors obtained from A, G, and S. The SMALL child is never actually matched to the instances.

The time required to explore all the children is nearly independent of either the number of instances or the number of class terms in the generalization hierarchy because both the match and the induction steps occur in parallel hardware. Provided sufficient parallel hardware is available, in little more than the time taken to match one pattern within one processor, we have effectively evaluated every pattern which can be formed from the parent by substituting any generalization class for the specified term, against every instance in the positive and negative sets. (Throughout this section, the discussion is phrased as if sufficient hardware were available. The hardware requirements are linear in the instance data size, and we have been able to solve real problems using an 8K Connection Machine. Thus, this is not an unreasonable simplification. The actual implementation adjusts to accommodate the hardware available, automatically iterating when an instance basis set will not entirely fit in the available processors.)

The other induction operators function similarly. The key is the decomposition of the syntactic operation on a pattern in such a way that we actually match against the instance data only a subset of the children (the "induction basis set"), but can then compute the results for all the other children without actually matching against them.

One important induction operator explores variations in a range of values, such as the interval separating two adjacent terms. The children are patterns that vary from the parent by having a different interval (a mandatory offset plus an active window within which the following term may appear, specifying a variable-length gap) separating the two terms. The corresponding induction basis set would be the intervals having offsets of different lengths and an active window of width one. From the appropriate union of these primitive ("basis") intervals we can construct every other interval in the set of child patterns, i.e., intervals with an arbitrary offset and window. Consequently, from the OR of the bit-vectors associated with these "basis" patterns we can compute the bit-vectors to asssociate with every other child pattern. Thus we evaluate every pattern which can be formed by substituting a different interval between the two adjacent terms, again in little more than the time taken to match one pattern within one processor.

Another induction operator explores variations in the overall match threshold. Although there are potentially an infinite number of children, we are really interested only in the critical set of threshold values at which some instance switches between being matched and not matched. Rather than explicitly constructing each possible child, this induction operator finds these critical values using the global maximum instruction implemented by the parallel hardware. First the parent pattern is matched as described in the previous section. The maximum score achieved in any processor is retrieved and treated as the threshold. As above, the bit-vector OR of instances matching at this threshold is retrieved, and the corresponding child is constructed. Successively each distinct next lower score is retrieved and treated as the threshold, and the corresponding bit-vector and child constructed. In this way we rapidly evaluate the match performance of all children, while performing the match step only once.

Computing the induction operator for term weights is more subtle. It explores simultaneous changes to the threshold and the SCORE-IF-ABSENT and SCORE-IF-PRESENT parameters of any single term. (In practice we compute this operator for all terms in parallel, but the exposition is simpler when only a single term is considered.) For a given term, the basis set consists of two child patterns: one with SCORE-IF-ABSENT zero and SCORE-IF-PRESENT minus-infinity, the other with the values reversed. These two patterns are matched against the instance data, and their match performances for each different setting of the match threshold evaluated as just described. The instances matched by either one of these patterns at any setting of the threshold is identical to those that same pattern would match if its zeroed score were set to the negative of the match threshold and the threshold were set to zero. Also, the match support for this term in the two patterns is necessarily disjoint. Consequently, we can compute a child term that matches the union of the instance matches of both patterns at any of the match thresholds individually, by setting the child's SCORE-IF-ABSENT to the negative of the threshold chosen for the first pattern, its SCORE-IF-PRESENT to the negative of the threshold chosen for the second pattern, and its threshold to zero. Thus we evaluate every pattern which can be formed by substituting a different SCORE-IF-ABSENT and SCORE-IF-PRESENT at a single given term and simultaneously changing the match threshold to any value, again in little more than the time taken to match one pattern within one processor.

The set of induction operators as a whole is suitable for use in a heuristic search through pattern space. Their major strength is that a whole class of characteristic perturbations may be explored rapidly. This greatly speeds the search for a pattern which satisfactorily discriminates positive from negative instances; eliminates the whole lowest level of search planning complexity that previously attended to exploring each class of perturbations efficiently; and allows a more systematic search through pattern space. Their major weakness is that, because they explore only one major characteristic at a time, they are poor at detecting interaction effects. This is only partially compensated for by the use of induction scripts, which automatically chain together some of the more common interactions.

Induction scripts are constructed by sequencing induction operators together in a pipeline, separated by filters to prune unpromising candidates. For example, the script for adding a new term (see Figure 9) involves first exploring the class generalization hierarchy (to find plausible terms to add), then exploring different intervals before and after the new term (because the insertion will disturb the previous spacing), and finally exploring different weights for the new term, and a new match threshold. Overall, the induction scripts implement a variant of symbolic hill-climbing beam search through symbolic pattern space. The search is analogous to hill-climbing because each induction operator modifies only one aspect of a pattern at a time, just as hill-climbing search steps in one direction at a time, and because we seek to go "uphill" as determined by increasing sensitivity and specificity (this is not a single "direction"). It is analogous to beam search because filters retain a number of promising candidates at each stage.

4.4 Discussion of ARIEL

The resulting induction scripts are a fairly crude search heuristic. The pruning of intermediate patterns may be too aggressive at some step and so discard a possible variant. The scripts are also limited in that they contain no conditionalization, no parameterization, and no variables. There is currently no automated effort to systematically explore all alternative avenues from step to step within an induction script, nor from script to script. The scripts and operators use a "generate and test" strategy for finding candidate patterns, and so are less direct than methods which construct candidate patterns by inspecting and manipulating the instances (as does PIMA, discussed in the next section).

In spite of their current limitations, in practice the scripts prove to be reasonably effective at exploring different possibilities and focusing computational effort into useful areas. The scripts raise the general level of abstraction at which the domain expert plans the search through pattern space. By removing the necessity to expend planning effort on low-level induction steps the domain expert is freed to formulate higher-level plans at a higher level of abstraction, covering more possibilities with each planning step. Fu-

Amino Acid Classes   Match score

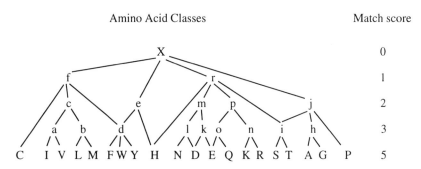

Figure 12. The amino acid class hierarchy used to construct AACC patterns during multi-alignment. Uppercase characters, one-letter amino acid codes; lowercase characters, designated amino acid classes; X, wild-card character representing one amino acid of any type. The match score between any two aligned elements equals the score assigned to the minimally inclusive class in the hierarchy that includes both elements. [From Smith and Smith, 1992].

ture improvements to ARIEL would add a planning component on top of (and interacting with) the induction scripts, rather than attempting to expand the scope and coverage of the script-based search approach itself (see Hunter's chapter in this volume on the relationship of planning to learning).

5 Covering Pattern Construction (PIMA) and Search (PLSEARCH) Tools

As ARIEL provides an automated method to construct complex patterns from seed patterns, we now ask: "Where does the seed pattern come from in the first place?" A completely automated method for seed pattern construction is provided by PIMA (our Pattern-Induced Multiple Alignment program), which uses a modified dynamic programming algorithm to inductively construct primary sequence patterns common to a family of functionally-related proteins [Smith and Smith, 1990, 1992].

PIMA employs a pre-defined set of amino acid classes (based on a physico-chemical generalization hierarchy, Figure 12) to construct a primary sequence pattern from a dynamic programming generated alignment. Given an alignment between two sequences generated using the Smith and Waterman [1981b] local optimal alignment algorithm, an "Amino Acid Class Covering" (AACC) pattern can be constructed from the alignment by identifying the smallest amino acid class which includes (covers) each pair of aligned amino acids. If two identical amino acids are aligned at a position, then the symbol

A. Trypsinogen/Venom serine proteases

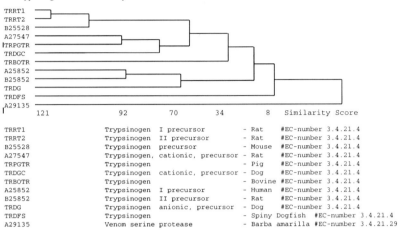

```
TRRT1
TRRT2
B25528
A27547
ITRPGTR
TRDGC
TRBOTR
A25852
B25852
TRDG
TRDFS
A29135

        121          92        70      34         8    Similarity Score
```

```
TRRT1     Trypsinogen  I precursor          - Rat    #EC-number 3.4.21.4
TRRT2     Trypsinogen  II precursor         - Rat    #EC-number 3.4.21.4
B25528    Trypsinogen  precursor            - Mouse  #EC-number 3.4.21.4
A27547    Trypsinogen, cationic, precursor  - Rat    #EC-number 3.4.21.4
TRPGTR    Trypsinogen                       - Pig    #EC-number 3.4.21.4
TRDGC     Trypsinogen  cationic, precursor  - Dog    #EC-number 3.4.21.4
TRBOTR    Trypsinogen                       - Bovine #EC-number 3.4.21.4
A25852    Trypsinogen  I precursor          - Human  #EC-number 3.4.21.4
B25852    Trypsinogen  II precursor         - Rat    #EC-number 3.4.21.4
TRDG      Trypsinogen  anionic, precursor   - Dog    #EC-number 3.4.21.4
TRDFS     Trypsinogen                       - Spiny Dogfish #EC-number 3.4.21.4
A29135    Venom serine protease             - Barba amarilla #EC-number 3.4.21.29
```

B. Covering pattern constructed from the above cluster.

```
1                 20 21                  40 41                  60 61                  80
lllhXaaGGXXCXX1XXPbX XXcXXXXigFCGXkLIXXXW VakApHCX1XXclaiLG1XX XXXX1XXEXcXXXXXXcXXP 80
lX1XXXcllgDIcLIiLXlX XXX1X1aXXaXLP1XXXXXG lXXXaXGWGXXX1gXXXXX1 XX1CX1XXacX1XXC1XXYX 16(
GgaXX1XcCXGcc1GGXDkC XGDSGGPaaX1GXcQGaaSW 200 GXXgCAXXXXPpcXXiVclb aXWIl1XaA /22!
```

C. Pattern constructed from 4 protein tyrosine kinase sequences

```
1                 20 21                  40 41                  60 61                  80
lXaXXaXXXaXXcXXXX1XX XXXXX1XgggX1X111lX1 ghlAgX1cXXcXgggXXXX1 laXXXXXXXXXXXXXX1XXX 80
XXXggXXXXXcXXXXNXXaX XgggggggXXXXX1XX1XXX 1XXXXXXXX1iXXaXXXGXX XX1XiX1XXXXXXXgg1X1 16(
XXaXXcXXXXXXXXXX1lc XXXX1XXXXXXXc1XgglX X1XX1XXgggggggg1XX1gg 1XXXXXXXTXXXXX1XXXX 24(
X1XXXXXXXXXXXXXXaXX XXXXXXXXXXcaXXXXcXX XXXXXXXXXXXXXXXXXgggg XXXXXcXbX1XXXXgg1XXX 32(
XXXXXSXXXXaXX1XXXgg ggggggggglcXR1laXLXX1 LG1GXFGXVcXp1XXXaXXX XXXXXVAVKXa11gAlX1XX 40(
XXcX1EXlac1XcXgXXlaa lccGXck1XXPXccaXEcXX XG1LXXbLilgggggggggg gggggggggggggggggggg 48(
gggXXXXXXXXXXGXgggggg ggggggggggggggggggg ggggggggggggggggggg gggggggggXXXXcX1caX 56(
cXX1aXXGMXbLXXX1cVHR  DLAXRNccaX1XXXcKIXDF GcXRDacll1XYXXXX1XXa PaiWMXXESaXXXXbTTXSD 64(
cWSFGaaLWEIXkcpX1PbX XaXX11Xcg1XaXlGXXcX1 PXXXXX1cXXaMXXCWlX1X 1XgggXXXX1XcXXXXggi 72(
XXXXXcXXXXX1XXXXXX1X XXggggGXXXX1XXXcP                                      /75'
```

Figure 13. (A) A binary dendrogram constructed by clustering the pair-wise scores for a set of serine protease-related sequences using a maximal linkage rule. (B) The AACC pattern generated from this cluster. Upper case characters: IUPAC one-letter amino acid codes; lower case characters: amino acid classes: a=[ILV], b=[FWY], c=[ILVFWYCM], h=[DE], i=[HKR], j=[NQ], k=[ST], l=[DEHKRNQSTBZ], p=[AG], X=wild-card (1 amino acid of any type), g= gap character (0 or 1 amino acid of any type). The 8 cysteine residues forming the 4 disulfide bonds that are common to this set of proteases are all present in the pattern and are shown highlighted in bold/underlined type. The highlighted regions at positions 178-188 and 199-200 are at the substrate binding site; the former region contains the "GDSG" motif conserved in known serine proteases. Highlighted positions 46 and 91, along with position 184 constitute the active site charge relay system. (C) AACC pattern constructed from 4 protein serine/threonine kinase sequences: human insulin receptor (NBRF/PIR locus A05274) and feline trk (locus A25184), mouse PDGF receptor (locus A25742) and human ret (locus TVHURE). Six conserved regions previously identified within the catalytic domains of protein serine/threonine kinases are shown highlighted. [Adapted from Fig. 4 of Smith and Smith, 1990].

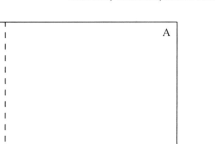

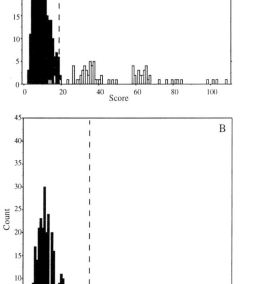

*Figure 14. Match score distributions comparing AACC pattern vs. sequence matches
(A) to sequence vs. sequence matches (B). (A) An AACC pattern was constructed
from 4 protein tyrosine kinase sequences (Fig. 14C) and matched to 2 control sets: a
positive control set composed of 81 protein kinase (PK) related sequences (white
bars) and a negative control set 313 non-PK-related sequences (black bars;
mean±s.d=10.88±4.60); where the two sets of matches overlap, the smaller bar at
each position is shown in the foreground; at those positions where the bars are the
same height, a single stippled bar is displayed. The dashed line indicates the 99th
percentile of the negative control scores. (B) Score distributions of a single PK sequence (human ret, locus TVHURE) matched against the same positive (white bars)
and negative (black bars; mean±s.d=13.59±6.59) control sets described above. As in
(A), the dashed line indicates the 99th percentile of the negative control set. [From
Smith and Smith, 1990]*

for that amino acid is placed at the corresponding position in the pattern. In the other case, two non-identical residues are aligned, and the smallest covering class (represented by a lower-case characters in Figure 12) is placed at that position. Positions in an alignment where an amino acid was is paired to the null element are converted into gap characters (`g') in patterns. The dynamic programming algorithm has been extended such that each gap character can function as 0 or 1 amino acid of any type during subsequent pattern alignment (described below). This is analogous to the way variable spacing can be specified in a regular expression pattern.

Given an unaligned set of protein sequences from a homologous family (such as all alpha globin sequences), a single primary sequence pattern, representing the conserved sequence elements common to all members of the family, can be constructed. The method involves using patterns constructed from pairwise alignments as input for subsequent rounds of alignment and pattern construction. First, all pairwise alignments between sequences in a set are performed. The resulting pairwise scores are then clustered using a maximal linkage rule [Sneath and Sokal, 1973] to generate a binary dendrogram (i.e., tree; Figure 13). The two most similar sequences in the clustered set are then aligned and a covering pattern constructed as described above. Patterns are similarly constructed for each node in the tree by sequentially moving down the tree, aligning at each step the patterns or sequences connected by the next most similar node, until a single "root" pattern is constructed for the entire set. The root pattern represents those conserved primary sequence elements common to all members of the set.

In a manner analogous to a regular expression pattern, covering patterns so constructed will match with equal score all of the sequences from which the pattern was derived. Indeed, these covering patterns can be directly translated into standard regular expression patterns. This pattern construction algorithm can be thought of as a method to construct a single regular expression pattern for a set of homologous sequences, and our modified dynamic programming algorithm is, in essence, a method to perform "regular expression matching with mismatching" (the latter problem has been approached differently by [Myers and Miller, 1989]).

Covering patterns can be more diagnostic for family membership than any of the individual sequences used to construct the pattern. This can be shown by comparing the diagnostic capability of a pattern with that of the sequences used to construct the pattern. An example of this is shown in Figure 14, where a pattern constructed from four sequences taken from the protein kinase (PK) family is matched against (1) a positive control set of 80 PK sequences, and (2) a negative control set of 313 different sequences not related to the PK family. For the PK pattern, only four PK sequences in the positive set had match scores less than the 99th percentile of the negative control set (Figure 14a). Using the same 99th percentile criterion for determining false negative (FN) matches, the four individual PK sequences generated 46, 29, 23, and 20 FN matches (the example with 20 FN matches is shown in Figure 14b).

There are two apparent reasons why covering patterns can be more diagnostic than the sequences used to construct them. First, in sequence vs. sequence alignments, mismatch and gap penalties generated at non-conserved positions can easily outweigh the match scores contributed at the limited number of conserved sites. This is especially true in families such as the PKs which encompass a diverse set of sequences with low overall sequence similarity. In the patterns, non-conserved positions are converted into "wild-card" (X) and gapped (g) characters that do not contribute to mis-matching. Second, chance similarities between non-conserved regions of any single positive instance sequence and non-related sequences can broaden the score distribution of the negative control set. Non-conserved site/regions are not represented in the patterns and thus such chance similarities are eliminated.

5.1 An Application of PIMA.

Using the covering pattern construction methodology described above, we have constructed a database of covering patterns for all sequence families in the SWISS-PROT Protein Sequence Database. Families of related protein sequences were identified by performing all possible pairwise comparisons between all sequences in the SWISS-PROT database (i.e., "running the database against itself") using BLAST, an ultra-fast k-tuple search program [Altschul et al., 1990]. The resulting set of pairwise scores was then clustered into families using a maximal-linkage clustering algorithm. The covering pattern construction program was then used to generate a single primary sequence pattern for each family. The current pattern library (release 4, based on SWISS-PROT release 13) contains 2026 patterns derived from all families of 2 or more members (encompassing 10664 of the 13837 sequences in the database). In collaboration with the Human Retrovirus and AIDS Sequence Database, we have also constructed a pattern library for all gene families of HIV (AIDS) -related viruses. Biologists with new sequences of unknown function can search these pattern databases with PLSEARCH (Pattern Library SEARCH), a pattern search tool that utilizes PIMA's pattern alignment algorithm. As described above, pattern searches can be more sensitive than conventional sequence vs. sequence database search programs since covering patterns can be more diagnostic for family membership than any of the individual sequences used to construct a pattern. We are also using these primary sequence patterns as "seed" inputs to construct complex hierarchical patterns using ARIEL's pattern induction system.

6 Significance, Validity, and Pattern Quality

"Validity, in a metric sense, is how well the test actually measures what its name indicates that it measures the degree to which the test reports what it purports to report."

—R. G. Lathrop [1969]

Questions of significance and validity are familiar fare to the statistics and machine learning communities. Here we briefly touch on these issues with respect to protein sequence patterns (see also [Felsenstein 1988; Karlin and Macken 1991; Karlin *et al.* 1991]). The issue is of more than theoretical concern to the domain practitioners: on more than one occassion, a pattern for some defining class has been published which, while indeed matching the defining (positive) set, subsequently was found to match almost every other sequence in the sequence databases as well! Such a pattern is of little value.

At a minimum, patterns must be tested against both a positive and a negative set of sequences. The result yields a 2x2 contingency table:

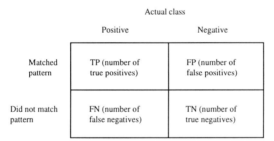

| | Actual class | |
	Positive	Negative
Matched pattern	TP (number of true positives)	FP (number of false positives)
Did not match pattern	FN (number of false negatives)	TN (number of true negatives)

While this provides a complete description of the pattern behavior on both positive and negative sequences, other derivative statistics are also useful:

$$Sensitivity = \frac{TP}{TP + FN}$$

$$Specificity = \frac{TN}{TN + FP}$$

$$Positive \; Predictive \; Value = \frac{TP}{TP + FP}$$

$$2x2 \; Correlation \; Coefficient = \frac{(TP \cdot TN - FP \cdot FN)}{\sqrt{(TP + FP) \cdot (FP + TN) \cdot (TN + FN) \cdot (FN + TP)}}$$

In particular, sensitivity and specificity should always be reported for any published pattern. A pattern which achieves 1.0 for both sensitivity and specificity exhibits perfect discrimination and is sometimes refered to as "diagnostic". Patterns may be quite useful even if their sensitivity and specificity are not both 1.0, but these values must be known for its full utility to be realized. For example, a pattern for alpha helices that achieved 1.0 sensitivity but only 0.75 specificity would be quite useful— it would guarantee to find every alpha helix, although it would over-predict somewhat. Similarly, a pattern for alpha helices that achieved only 0.75 sensitivity but 1.0 specificity also would be quite useful— it would not find every alpha helix, but it would guarantee complete confidence in the matches it did find. Nonetheless, matches to these two patterns would be interpreted very differently, and this is not possible unless their sensitivity and specificity are both known.

> "The word 'significantly' has a somewhat different meaning in statistics than it has in common usage. In everyday usage, a significant difference is one which is of practical import. A significant difference in statistical terms implies a difference that is unlikely to have occurred by chance alone."
>
> —R. G. Lathrop [1969]

The statistical significance of induced patterns is always of concern. This is especially so for those interested in applying AI methods. In our case, we have greatly enriched the expressive representational power of both the instance and the pattern languages relative to existing better-understood sequence-based languages current in the domain. Is it possible that their expressive power is now so rich that we could detect a discriminating "regularity" in any randomly drawn set, even when no such regularity existed, or existed solely due to chance? The nature of the domain hampers the usual methods for establishing significance, especially due to sequence similarity, sample bias, and the small size of typical defining sets. Additionally, any method in which the domain expert intervenes in any way cannot use the cross-validation (leave-one-out) verification methodology, because the domain expert cannot be "reset" between trials. Any method which refines patterns in an iterative loop cannot use methods such as a means test, analysis of variance, or chi square, all of which assume a single independent trial.

Nonetheless, the languages we use appear to more closely reflect the underlying domain ontology as understood by domain experts; the patterns inferred reflect plausible generalizations that are directly subject to experimental tests by domain experts; tests of the pattern against a control (negative) set not used in pattern construction can provide an unbiased estimate of the false positive rate; and pattern-based discrimination should always be related to the domain's existing scientific literature. In the end, any computational technique can do no more than supply a hypothesis. Verification occurs only in an experimental setting, where a prediction is compared to Nature. Clearly, more rigor is desirable, and statistical significance and validity is an area of inquiry where formal consideration by theoreticians and their methods would be welcome. The remainder of this section will briefly survey some of the domain-based issues that arise, making an attempt to discuss issues that are intrinsic to the general problem of inferring functional patterns in the domain rather than artifacts of our "Induction Assistant" approach.

Instances often share evolutionary history (known as "homology" in the domain), and hence fail to be independent of each other. These can be thought of as near-identical twins in an evolutionary sense. This is especially true of functionally related proteins, because related functions often spring from a common ancestral gene. Typically, the more recent the evolutionary divergence, the greater the degree of similarity (for example, functionally equivalent proteins from man and chimpanzee may differ by a few percent or less, while corresponding proteins from man and yeast may differ by more). This complicates the analysis of our positive (defining) set. The best current approach is to run a primary sequence similarity analysis beforehand. One may then count homologous families (clusters) as a single sequence for reporting purposes, or discard sequences until each family has but one remaining representative. Unfortunately, information is lost by these approaches, while dependencies undetectable by primary sequence similarity may still remain. Clustering methods proposed by Felsenstein [1985], Altschul et al. [1989], and Sibbald and Argos [1990b] promise to eventually provide a better approach. Here one can differentially weight each sequence relative to its similarity to other sequences, thereby attempting to retain the extra information present in their diversity while compensating for the partial lack of independence. However, the effect of cluster-based differential weights on any of the standard statistical tests of significance is unclear.

The available databases do not represent anything close to a uniform sampling of the space of all proteins. Rather, the sampling represents a highly skewed bias reflecting both the research interests of individual domain researchers (for example, hemoglobins and myoglobins are vastly over-represented in the protein sequence databases), and current technological limitations on what we can study (for example, membrane-bound proteins are vastly under-represented in the three-dimensional (folded shape) database because they are virtually impossible to crystallize). Thus it is currently impossible to construct a control set of negative instances whose distribution accurately reflects the space of all negative instances. One current approach is to construct a stratified negative set that attempts to sample the major protein groups systematically. Another common approach is to randomly sample the current databases, controlling for homology as discussed above.

Another problem, also familiar to the statistics and machine learning communities, arises from the small size of typical defining sets (in many cases, only a few dozen positive instances, or less, are known to science, especially if highly similar sequences are removed). This raises the possibility of overfitting the data, also known as memorizing the training set. While cross-validation or jack-knife techniques may offer assistance, holding out a test set may leave an impoverished training set. Additionally, the domain issue of similar sequences is especially bothersome for these methods, and domain opinion is divided. The problem arises when a sequence in the test set is highly similar to another sequence in the training set. One school of thought asserts that, because the test sequence is essentially duplicated in the training set, the situation is as if the test sequence had not been held out at all and one is effectively testing on the training data, invalidating the trial. The contrary school of thought holds that, because similar sequences occur so frequently in Nature, the next unknown sequence that arises may be highly similar to a known sequence and one is effectively modeling an intrinsic domain fact, yielding a better estimate of expected performance in practice. The former position is probably preferable because more conservative, but opinions differ.

We close by pointing out several other minor protein-based violations of common underlying statistical assumptions. First, the positive and negative sets often differ in measurable ways from each other in ways unrelated to the phenomenon under test (for example, the average positive instance length is often significantly longer or shorter than the average negative instance). Second, the underlying distributions are not normal. However, most statistical tests are relatively insensitive to minor deviations from normality. Third, while the negative set is usually stratified or otherwise corrected for the sample independence problem, the positive set typically employs all the positive instances known to science (while compensating for homology as discussed above). Thus, the selection criteria for inclusion in the sets differs. Fourth, if homology is controlled for in the control set differently than in the defining set, then the degree of internal independence varies between the two sets.

Notes

1. Ariadne was the Cretan princess who gave Theseus a ball of thread, by which he found his way out of the Labyrinth after slaying the Minotaur.

2. ARIEL is a combination of ARI-adne and parall-EL, and also a pleasing character from Shakespeare's *The Tempest*

References

Abarbanel, R. M. (1985) *Protein Structural* Proteins *Knowledge Engineering*. Ph.D. diss., Univ. of California, San Francisco.

Abarbanel, R. M., Wieneke, P. R., Mansfield, E., Jaffe, D. A., Brutlag, D. L. (1984) "Rapid Searches for Complex Patterns in Biological Molecules." *Nucleic Acids Res.* 12:263-280.

Altschul S. F., Carroll R. J., Lipman D. J. (1989) "Weights for Data Related by a Tree." *Journal of Molecular Biology* 207:647-653.

Altschul, S. F., Gish, W., Miller, W., Myers, E. W., Lipman, D. J. (1990) "Basic Local Alignment Search Tool." *Journal of Molecular Biology* 215(3):403-410.

Bacon, D. J., Anderson, W. F. (1986) "Multiple Sequence Alignment." *Journal of Molecular Biology* 191:153-161.

Barton, G. J. (1990) "Protein Multiple Sequence Alignment and Flexible Pattern Matching." in *Methods in Enzymology,* ed. R. F. Doolittle, 183:403-429. Academic Press.

Barton, G. J., Sternberg, M. J. E. (1987a) "Evaluation and Improvements in the Automatic Alignment of Protein Sequences." *Protein Engineering* 1:89-94.

Barton, G. J., Sternberg, M. J. E. (1987b) "A Strategy for the Rapid Multiple Alignment of Protein Sequences." *Journal of Molecular Biology* 198:327-337.

Barton, G. J., Sternberg, M. J. E. (1990) "Flexible Protein Sequence Patterns: A Sensitive Method to Detect Weak Structural Similarities." *Journal of Molecular Biology* 212:389-402.

Bashford, D., Chothia, C., Lesk, A. M. (1987) "Determinants of a Protein Field." *Journal of Molecular Biology* 196:199-216.

Birktoft, J.J., Banaszak, L.J. (1984) "Structure-function Relationships Among Nicotinamide-adenine Dinucleotide Dependent Oxidoreductases." In *Peptide and Protein Reviews* ed. Hearn, M. T. W., 4:1-47, Marcel Dekker, New York.

Blundell, T. L., Sibanda, B. L., Sternberg, M. J. E., Thornton, J. M. (1987) "Knowledge-based Prediction of Protein Structures and the Design of Novel Molecules." *Nature* 326:347-352.

Bode, W., Schwager, P. (1975) "The Refined Crystal Structure of Bovine Beta-trypsin at 1.8 A Resolution." *Journal of Molecular Biology* 98(4):693-717.

Bohr, H., Brunak, S., Cotterill, R., Fredholm, H., Lautrup, B., Petersen, S. (1990) "A Novel Approach to Prediction of the 3-dimensional Structures of Protein Backbones by Neural Networks." *FEBS Letters* 261:43.

Bork, P., Grunwald, C. (1990) "Recognition of Different Nucleotide-binding Sites in Primary Structures Using a Property-pattern Approach." *Eur. J. Biochem.* 191:347-358.

Boswell, D.R. (1988) "A Program for Template Matching of Protein Sequences." *CABIOS* 4(3):345-350.

Bowie, J.U., Luthy, R., Eisenberg, D. (1991) "A Method to Identify Protein Sequences that Fold into a Known Three-dimensional Structure." *Science* 253:164-170.

Bradley, M., Smith, T.F., Lathrop, R.H., Livingston, D., Webster., T.A. (1987) "Consensus Topography in the ATP Binding Site of the Simian Virus 40 and Polyomavirus Large Tumor Antigens." *Proc. of the Natl. Acad. of Sciences USA,* 84:4026-4030.

Breese, K., Friedrich, T., Andersen, T.T., Smith, T.F., Figge, J. (1991) "Structural Characterization of a 14-residue Peptide Ligand of the Retinoblastoma Protein: Comparison with a Non-Binding Analog." *Peptide Res.* 4(4):220-226.

Brutlag, D.L., Dautricourt, J.-P., Maulik, S., Relph, J. (1990) "Improved Sensitivity of Biological Sequence Databases." *CABIOS* 6(3):237-245.

Chou, P.Y., Fasman, G.D. (1978) "Empirical Predictions of Protein Conformation." *Ann. Rev. Biochem* 47:251-276.

Clark D.A., Barton G.J., Rawlings C.J. (1990) "A Knowledge-based Architecture for Protein Sequence Analysis and Structure Prediction." *J. Mol. Graph.* 8:94-107.

Cockwell, K.Y., Giles, I.G. (1989) "Software Tools for Motif and Pattern Scanning." *CABIOS* 5(3):227-232.

Cohen, B. I., Presnell, S.R., Cohen, F.E. (1991a) "Pattern-based Approaches to Protein Structure Prediction." *Methods of Enzymology* 202:252-268.

Cohen, B. I., Presnell, S. R., Morris, M., Langridge, R., Cohen, F.E. (1991b) "Pattern Recognition and Pprotein Structure Prediction." *Proc. 24th Hawaii Intl. Conf. on System Sciences,* pp. 574-584, IEEE Computer Soc. Press, Los Alamitos, CA, USA.

Cohen, F. E., Abarbanel, R. M., Kuntz, I. D., Fletterick, R. J. (1983) "Secondary Structure Assignment for Alpha/beta Proteins by a Combinatorial Approach." *Biochemistry* 22:4894-4904.

Cohen, F.E., Abarbanel, R.M., Kuntz, I.D., Fletterick, R.J. (1986) "Turn Prediction in Proteins Using a Complex Pattern Matching Approach." *Biochemistry* 25:266-275.

Cohen, F.E., Gregoret, L., Presnell, S.R., Kuntz, I.D. (1989) "Protein Structure Predictions: New Theoretical Approaches." *Prog. Clin. Biol. Res.* 289:75-85.

Collins, J.F., Coulson, A.F.W., Lyall, A. (1988) The Significance of Protein Sequence Similarities. *CABIOS* 4(1):67-71.

Corpet, F. (1988) "Multiple Sequence Alignment with Hierarchical Clustering." *Nucleic Acids Res.* 16(22):10881-10890.

Creighton, T.E. (1983) *Proteins: Structure and Molecular Properties.* W.H. Freeman and Company, New York.

DeCaprio, J.A., Ludlow, J.W., Figge, J., Shew, J.-Y., Huang, C.-M., Lee, W.-H., Marsilio, E., Paucha, E., Livingston, D.M. (1988) "SV40 Large Tumor Antigen Forms a Specific Complex with the Product of the Retinoblastoma Susceptibility Gene." *Cell* 54:275-283.

DeCaprio, J.A., Ludlow, J.W., Lynch, D., Furukawa, Y., Griffin, J., Piwnica-Worms, H., Huang, C.-M., Livingston, D.M. (1989) "The Product of the Retinoblastoma Susceptibility GEne has Properties of a Cell Cycle Regulatory Component." *Cell* 58:1085-1095.

Doolittle, R.F., Hunkapillar, M.W., Hood, L.E., Davare, S.G., Robbins, K.C., Aaronson, S.A., Antoniades, H.N. (1983) "Simian Sarcoma Virus Onc Gene, v-sis, Is Derived from the Gene (or Genes) Encoding a Platelet-derived Growth Factor." *Science* 221:275-277.

Dyson, N., Howley, P.M., Munger, K., Harlow, E. (1989) "The Human Papilloma Virus-16 E7 Oncoprotein Is Able to Bind to the Retinoblastoma Gene Product." *Science* 243:934-937.

Dyson, N., Bernards, R., Friend, S.H., Gooding, L.R., Hassell, J.A., Major, E.O., Pipas, J.M., Vandyke, T., Harlow, E. (1990) "Large T Antigens of Many Polyomaviruses Are Able to Form Complexes with the Retinoblastoma Protein." *J. Virology* 64:1353-1356.

Eisenberg, D., Weiss, R.M., Terwilliger, T.C. (1982) "The Helical Hydrophobic Moment: a Measure of the Amphilicity of a Helix." *Nature* 299:371-374.

Eisenberg, D., Weiss, R.M., Terewilliger, T.C. (1984) "The Hydrophobic Moment Detects Periodicity in Protein Hydrophobicity." *Proc. Natl. Acad. Sci. USA.* 81:140-144.

Emi, M., Nakamura, Y., Ogawa, M., Yamamoto, T., Nishide, T., Mori, T., Matsubara, K. (1986) "Cloning, Vharacterization and Nucleotide Dequences of Ywo cDNAs Rncoding Human Pancreatic Trypsinogens." *Gene* 41:305-310.

Erman, L.D., Lesser, V.R. (1975) "A Multi-level Organization for Problem Solving Using Many Diverse, Cooperating Sources of Knowledge." *Proc. Intl. Joint Conf. Artif. Intell.* (IJCAI-4), pp. 483-490.

Fasman, G.D. (1989) *Prediction of Protein Structure and the Principles of Protein Conformation,* Plenum Press, New York, pp. 193-316.

Felsenstein, J. (1985) "Phylogenies and the Comparative Method." *Amer. Naturalist* 125(1):1-15.

Felsenstein, J. (1988) "Phylogenies from Molecular Sequences: Inference and Reliability." *Annual Rev. Genetics* 22:521-65.

Feng, D.-F., Doolittle, R.F. (1987) "Progressive Sequence Alignment As a Prerequisite to Correct Phylogenetic Trees." *J. Mol. Evol.* 25:351-360.

Figge, J., Webster, T., Smith, T.F., Paucha, E. (1988) "Prediction of Similar Transforming Region in Simian Virus 40 Large T, Adenovirus E1A, and Cyc Oncoproteins." *J. Virology,* 62(5):1814-1818.

Figge, J., Smith, T.F. (1988) "Cell-Division Sequence Motif." *Nature* 334:109.

Fischel-Ghodsian, F., Mathiowitz, G., Smith, T.F. (1990) "Alignment of Protein Sequences Using Secondary Structure: a Modified Dynamic Programming Method." *Protein Engineering* 3(7):577-581.

Friedland, P., Iwaskai, Y. (1985) "The Concept and Implementation of Skeletal Plans." *J. Autom. Reasoning* 1(2):161-208.

Garnier, J., Osguthorpe, D.J., Robson, B. (1978) "Analysis of the Accuracy and Implications of Simple Methods for Predicting the Secondary Structure of Globular Proteins." *Journal of Molecular Biology* 120(1):97-120.

Gascuel, O., Danchin, A. (1986) "Protein Export in Prokaryotes and Eukaryotes: Indications of a Difference in the Mechanism of Exportation." *J. Mol. Evol.* 24:130-142.

Goldsborough, M.D., DiSilvestre, D., Temple, G.F., Lorincz, A.T. (1989) "Nucleotide sequence of human papillomavirus type 31: a cervical neoplasia-associated virus." Virology 171(1):306-11.

Grasser, F.A., Scheidtmann, K.H., Tuazon, P.T., Traugh, J.A., Walter, G. (1988) "In Vitro Phosphorylation of SV40 Large T Antigen." *Virology* 165(1):13-22.

Gribskov, M., McLachlan, A.D., Eisenberg, D. (1987) "Profile Analysis: Detection of Distantly Related Proteins." *Proc. Natl. Acad. Sci. USA* 84:4355-4358.

Gribskov, M., Homyak, M., Edenfield, J., Eisenberg, D. (1988) "Profile Scanning for Three-Dimensional Structural Patterns in Protein Sequences." *CABIOS* 4(1):61-66.

Guigo, R., Johansson, A., Smith, T.F. (1991) "Automatic Evaluation of Protein Sequence Functional Patterns." *CABIOS* 7(3):309-315.

Hanks, S.K., Quinn, A.M., Hunter, T. (1988) "The Protein Kinase Family: Conserved Features and Deduced Phylogeny of the Catalytic Domains." *Science* 241:42-52.

Hayes-Roth, B., Buchanan, B., Lichtarge, O., Hewette, M., Altman, R., Brinkley, J., Cornelius, C., Duncan, B., Jardetzky, O. (1986) "PROTEAN: Deriving Protein Structure from Constraints." *Proc. Fifth Natl. Conf. on Artificial Intelligence,* pp. 904-909, Morgan Kaufman, Los Altos, Calif.

Hein, J. (1990) "Unified Approach to Alignment and Phylogenies." in *Methods in Enzymology,* ed. R.F. Doolittle, 183:626-645. Academic Press.

Henneke, C.M. (1989) "A Multiple Sequence Alignment Algorithm for Homologous Proteins Using Secondary Structure Information and Optionally Keying Alignments to Functionally Important Sites." *CABIOS* 5:141-150.

Hertz, G.Z., Hartzell, G.W., Stormo, G.D. (1990) "Identification of Consensus Patterns in Unaligned DNA Sequences Known to be Functionally Related." *CABIOS* 6(2):81-92.

Hodgman, T.C. (1986) "The Elucidation of Protein Function from Its Amino Acid Sequence." *CABIOS* 2:181-187.

Holbrook, S., Muskal, S., Kim, S., (1990) "Predicting Surface Exposure of Amino Acids from Protein Sequence." *Protein Engineering* 3(8):659-665.

Hollenberg, S.M., Evans, R.M. (1988) "Multiple and Cooperative Trans-activation Domains of the Human Glucocorticoid Receptor." *Cell* 55:899-906.

Holley, L.H., Karplus, M. (1989) "Protein Structure Prediction with a Neural Network." *Proc. Natl. Acad. Sci. USA* 86:152-156.

Hope, I.A., Mahadevan, S., Struhl, K. (1988) "Structural and Functional Characterization of the Short Acidic Transcriptional Activation Region of Yeast GCN4 Protein." *Nature* 333:635-640.

Hunter, L., Harris, N., States, D. (1992) "Efficient Classification of Massive, Unsegmented Datastreams." *Proc. 10th International Machine Learning Workshop,* Morgan Kaufmann, Los Altos, CA, USA (forthcoming).

Itoh, N., Tanaka, N., Mihashi, S., Yamashina, I. (1987) "Molecular Cloning and Sequence Analysis of cDNA for Batroxobin, a Thrombin-like Snake Venom Enzyme." *J. Biol. Chem.* 262(7):3132-3135.

Karlin, S., Blaisdell B.E., Mocarski E.S., Brendel V. (1989) "A Method to Identify Distinctive Charge Configurations in Protein Sequences, with Applications to Human Herpesvirus Polypeptides." *Journal of Molecular Biology* 205:165-177.

Karlin, S., Bucher, P., Brendel, V., Altschul, S.F. (1991) "Statistical Methods and Insights for Protein and DNA Sequences." *Annu. Rev. Biophys. Biophys. Chem.* 20:175-203.

Karlin, S., Macken, C. (1991) "Some Statistical Problems in the Assessment of Inhomogeneities of DNA Sequence Data." *J. American Statistical Assoc.* 86:27-35.

King, R.D., Sternberg, M.J.E. (1990) "Machine Learning Approach for the Prediction of Protein Secondary Structure." *Journal of Molecular Biology* 216:441-457.

Kolata, G. (1986) "Trying to Crack the Second Half of the Genetic Code." *Science* 233:1037-1040.

Lander, E., Mesirov, J., Taylor, W. (1988) "Study of Protein Sequence Comparison Metrics on the Connection Machine CM-2." *Proc. Supercomputing-88.*

Lathrop, R.G. (1969) *Introduction to Psychological Research: Logic, Design, Analysis.* Harper and Row, New York.

Lathrop, R.H. (1990) Efficient Methods for Massively Parallel Symbolic Induction: Algorithms and Implementation. PhD. diss., Massachusetts Inst. of Technology, Cambridge, MA, USA.

Lathrop, R.H., Webster, T.A., Smith T.F. (1987) "ARIADNE: Pattern-directed Inference and Hierarchical Abstraction in Protein sSructure Recognition." *Communications of the ACM* 30(11):909-921.

Lathrop, R.H., Webster, T.A., Smith T.F., Winston, P.H. (1990) "ARIEL: A Massively Parallel Symbolic Learning Assistant for Protein Structure/Function." in *Artificial Intelligence at MIT: Expanding Frontiers,* ed. Winston, P.H., with Shellard, S., MIT Press, Cambridge, MA, USA.

Lathrop, R.H., Webster, T.A., Smith T.F., Winston, P.H. (1992) "Massively Parallel Symbolic Induction of Protein Structure/Function Relationships." in *Machine Learning, From Theory to Applications,* (ed.) Hanson, S., Remmele, W., Rivest, R.L., Springer-Verlag (forthcoming); reprinted from *Proc. 24th Hawaii Intl. Conf. on System Sciences* (1991), pp. 585-594, IEEE Computer Soc. Press, Los Alamitos, CA, USA.

Lawrence, C.E., Reilly, A.A. (1990) "An Expectation Maximization (EM) Algorithm for the Identification and Characterization of Common Sites in Unaligned Biopolymer Sequences." *Proteins* 7:41-51.

Leytus, S.P., Loeb, K.R., Hagen, F.S., Kurachi, K., Davie, E.W. (1988) "A Novel Trypsin-like Serine Protease (Hepsin) with a Putative Transmembrane Domain Expressed by Human Liver and Hepatoma cells." *Biochemistry* 27:1067-1074.

Lillie, J.W., Green, M.R. (1989) "Transcription activation by the adenovirus E1a protein." *Nature* 338:39-44.

Lindsay, R., Buchanan, B., Feigenbaum, E., Lederberg, J. (1980) *The DENDRAL Project* McGraw-Hill, New York.

Ma, J., Ptashne, M. (1987) "Deletion Analysis of GAL4 Defines Two Transcriptional Activating Segments." *Cell* 48:847-853.

Maclin, R., Shavlik, J.W., (1992) "Refining Algorithms with Knowledge-Based Neural Networks: Improving the Chou-Fasman Algorithm for Protein Folding" *Machine Learning* (forthcoming).

Major, F., Turcotte, M., Gautheret, D., Lapalme, G., Fillion, E., Cedergren, R. (1991) "The Combination of Symbolic and Numerical Computation for Three-dimensional Modeling of RNA." *Science* 253:1255-60.

McGregor, M., Flores, T., Sternberg, M. (1989) "Prediction of Beta-turns in Proteins Using Neural Networks." *Protein Engineering* 2(7):521-526.

Mikes, O., Holeysovsky, V., Tomasek, V., Sorm, F. (1966) "Covalent Structure of Bovine Trypsinogen. The Position of the Remaining Amides." *Biochem. Biophys. Res. Commun.* 24(3):346-352.

Moran, E. (1988) "A Region of SV40 Large T Antigen can Substitute for a Transforming Domain of the Adenovirus E1A Product." *Nature* 334:168-170.

Munger, K., Werness, B.A., Dyson, N., Phelps, W.C., Harlow, E., Howley, P.M. (1989) "Complex Formation of Human Papillomavirus E7 Proteins with the Retinoblastoma Tumor Suppressor Gene Product." *EMBO J.* 8:4099-4105.

Muskal, S., Holbrook, S., Kim, S. (1990) "Prediction of the Disulfide-bonding State of Cysteine in Proteins." *Protein Engineering* 3(8):667-672.

Myers, E.W., Miller, W. (1989) "Approximate Matching of Regular Expressions." *Bull. Math. Biol.* 51:5-37.

Noordewier, N.O., Towell, G.G., Shavlik, J.W. (1990) "Training Knowledge-based Neural Networks to Recognize Genes in DNA Sequences." *Proc. 1990 Neural Info. Processing Conf.*

Owens, J., Chatterjee, D., Nussinov, R., Konopka, A., Maizel, J.V.J. (1988) "A Fixed Point Alignment Technique for Detection of Recurrent and Common Sequence Motifs Associated with Biological Features." *CABIOS* 4:73-77.

Patthy, L. (1987) "Detecting Homology of Distantly Related Proteins with Consensus Sequences." *Journal of Molecular Biology* 198:567-577.

Patthy, L. (1988) "Detecting Distant Homologies of Mosaic Proteins." *Journal of Molecular Biology* 202:689-696.

Pearson, W.R., Lipman, D.J. (1988) "Improved Tools for Biological Sequence Comparison." *Proc. Natl. Acad. Sci. USA* 85:2444-2448.

Ponder, J.W., Richards, F.M. (1987) "Tertiary Templates for Proteins: Use of Packing Criteria in the Enumeration of Allowed Sequences for Different Structural Classes." *Journal of Molecular Biology* 193:775-791.

Qian, N., Sejnowski, T. (1988) "Predicting the Secondary Structure of Globular Proteins Using Neural Network Models." *Journal of Molecular Biology* 202:865-884.

Ralph, W.W., Webster, T.A. Smith, T.F. (1987) "A modified Chou and Fasman protein structure algorithm." CABIOS 3:211-216.

Rawlings, C.J., Taylor, W.R., Nyakairu, J., Fox, J., Sternberg, M.J.E. (1985) "Reasoning about protein topology using the logic programming language PROLOG." J. Mol. Graph. 3:151-157.

Rossman, M.G., Moras, D., Olsen, K.W. (1974) "Chemical and Biological Evolution of a Nucleotide-binding Protein." *Nature* 250:194-199.

Sankoff, D., Kruskal, J.B. (eds.) (1983) *Time Warps, String Edits, and Macromolecules: The Theory and Practice of Sequence Comparison.* Addison-Weslye, Reading, MA, USA.

Schuler, G.D., Altschul, S.F., Lipman, D.J. (1991) "A Workbench for Multiple Alignment Construction and Analysis." *Proteins* 9(3):180-90.

Sellers, P.H. (1974) "On the Theory and Computation of Evolutionary Distances." *Siam J. Appl. Math.* 26:787-793.

Sibbald, P.R., Argos, P. (1990a) "Scrutineer: a Computer Program that Flexibly Seeks and Describes Motifs and Profiles in Protein Sequence Databases." CABIOS 6(3):279-88.

Sibbald, P.R., Argos, P. (1990b) "Weighting Aligned Protein or Nucleic Acid Sequences to Correct for Unequal Representation." *Journal of Molecular Biology* 216(4):813-818.

Smith, H.O., Annau, T.M., Chandrasegaran, S. (1990) "Finding Sequence Motifs in Groups of Functionally related Proteins." *Proc. Natl. Acad. Sci. USA* 87:826-830.

Smith, R.F., Smith, T.F. (1989) "Identification of New Protein Kinase-related Genes in Three Herpes Viruses, Herpes Simplex Virus, Varicella-zoster Virus, and Epstein-Barr Virus." *J. Virology* 63:450-455.

Smith, R.F., Smith, T.F. (1990) "Automatic Generation of Primary Sequence Patterns from Sets of Related Protein Sequences." *Proc. Natl. Acad. Sci. USA* 87:118-122.

Smith, R.F., Smith, T.F. (1992) "Pattern-induced Multi-sequence Alignment (PIMA) Algorithm Employing Structure-dependent Gap Penalties for Use in Comparitive Protein Modelling." *Protein Eng.* 5:35-41.

Smith, T.F., Waterman, M.S. (1981a) "Comparison of Biosequences." *Adv. Appl. Math.* 2:482-489.

Smith, T.F., Waterman, M.S. (1981b) "Identification of Common Molecular Subsequences." *Journal of Molecular Biology* 147:195-197.

Sneath, P.H., Sokal, R.R. (1973) *Numerical Taxonomy* Freeman, San Francisco.

Staden, R. (1989) "Methods to define and locate patterns of motifs in sequences." CABIOS 5(2):89-96.

Storey, A., Pim, D., Murray, A., Osborn, K., Banks, L., Crawford, L. (1988) "Comparison of the In Vitro Transforming Activities of Human Papillomavirus types." *Embo. J.* 7(6):1815-1820.

Stormo, G.D. (1990) "Consensus Patterns in DNA" in *Methods in Enzymology,* ed. R.F. Doolittle, 183:211-221, Academic Press.

Stormo, G.D., Hartzell, G.W. (1989) "Identifying Protein-binding Sites from Unaligned DNA Fragments." *Proc. Natl. Acad. Sci. USA* 86(4):1183-1187.

Taylor, W.R. (1986) "Identification of Protein Sequence Homology by Consensus Template Alignment." *Journal of Molecular Biology* 188:233-258.

Taylor, W.R. (1988a) "A Flexible Method to Align Large Numbers of Biological Sequences." *J. Mol. Evol.* 28:161-169.

Taylor, W.R. (1988b) "Pattern Matching Methods in Protein Sequence Comparison and Structure Prediction." *Protein Eng.* 2:77-86.

Taylor, W.R., Thornton, J.M. (1983) "Prediction of Super-secondary Structure in Proteins." *Nature* 301:540-542.

Thornton, J.M., Flores, T.P., Jones, D.T., Swindells, M.B. (1991) "Protein Structure. Prediction of Progress at Last [News]" *Nature* 354:105-106.

Thornton, J.M., Gardner, S.P. (1989) "Protein Motifs and Data-base Searching." TIBS 14:300-304.

Towell, G.G., Shavlik, J.W., Noordewier, M.O. (1990) "Refinement of Approximate Domain Theories by Knowledge-Based Artificial Neural Networks" *Proc. Natl. Conf. on Artificial Intelligence (AAAI-90),* pp. 861-866.

Vingron, M., Argos, P. (1989) "A Fast and Sensitive Multiple Sequence Alignment Algorithm." *CABIOS* 5:115-121.

Waterman, M.S. (1984) "General Methods of Sequence Comparison." *Bull. Math. Biol.* 46:473-500.

Waterman, M.S. (1986) "Multiple Sequence Alignment by Consensus." *Nucleic Acids Res.* 14:9095-9102.

Waterman, M.S., Jones, R. (1990) "Consensus Methods for DNA and Protein Sequence Alignment." in *Methods in Enzymology,* ed. R.F. Doolittle, 183:221-237, Academic Press.

Webster, T.A., Lathrop, R.H., Smith, T.F. (1987) "Evidence for a Common Structural Domain in Aminoacyl-tRNA Synthetases Through Use of a New Pattern-directed Inference System." *Biochemistry* 26:6950-6957.

Webster, T.A., Lathrop, R.H., Smith, T.F. (1988) "Pattern Descriptors and the Unidentified Reading Frame 6 Human mtDNA Dinucleotide-Binding Site." *Proteins* 3(2):97-101.

Webster, T.A., Lathrop, R.H., Smith, T.F. (1989) "Potential Structural Motifs in Reverse Transcriptases" *Mol. Biol. Evol.,* 6(3):317-320.

Whyte, P., Ruley, H.E., Harlow, E. (1988) "Two Regions of the Adenovirus Early Region 1A Proteins Are Required for Transformation." *Nature* 334:124-129.

Wilbur, W.J., Lipman, D.J. (1983) "Rapid Similarity Searches of Nucleic Acid and Protein Data Banks." *Proc. Natl. Acad. Sci. USA* 80(3):726-730.

Winston, P.H. (1984) *Artificial Intelligence, 2nd ed.* Addison-Wesley, Reading, MA.

Zhang, X., Mesirov, J., Waltz, D., (1992) "A Hybrid System for Protein Secondary Structure Prediction" *Journal of Molecular Biology* (to appear).

Zhu, Q., Smith, T.F., Lathrop, R.H., Figge, J. (1990) "Acid Helix-Turn Activator Motif." *Proteins* 8:156-163.

Planning to Learn
About Protein Structure

Lawrence Hunter

1 Introduction

Discovery requires concerted effort. Human scientists actively seek out information that bears on questions they have decided to pursue. They design experiments, explore the implications of the knowledge they have, refine their questions and test alternative ideas. Although many discoveries are the result of unexpected observations, these surprises take place in the context of an explicit pursuit of knowledge.

Viewing scientific discovery as a kind of motivated action raises some basic issues common to goal-directed behavior generally: Where do desires (to know) come from? What are the actions that can be taken (to discover)? What are the resources those actions consume, and how are they allocated? How are decisions about selecting and combining actions made? The goal of this chapter is to describe a set of related systems for automated discovery in molecular biology, sketching a framework of a cognitive theory of discovery processes.

Automated process models of cognitive phenomena serve two functions. One is fundamentally scientific: such models provide a vocabulary for expressing theories of mental functioning and a framework for testing and comparing theories. The other role is a kind of engineering: these models are artifacts that, to the degree they are successful models, accomplish useful tasks, and which can extend human abilities. These functions are interrelated. The main scientific claim of most AI models of cognition is that a given model is *sufficient* to account for some complex cognitive phenomenon. Supporting a claim of sufficiency for a model of discovery involves writing a program that actually makes at least moderately significant discoveries.

Biologists hoping for useful tools from machine learning techniques can read this chapter as a description of some approaches to applying machine learning tools to biological problems, and as a promise for the eventual creation of an integrated framework for increased automaticity and coordination in the application of such tools. However, the main thrust of the chapter is to use the complexity and challenges inherent in the domain of molecular biology to argue for a new level of theorizing in machine learning, one that addresses issues such as the design of representations, the integration and coordination of multiple inference techniques, and the origin and transformation of specific desires for knowledge. I present arguments for the approach, and some examples, although this work does not offer significant empirical evaluation of the approach, nor a formal statement of its characteristics. This chapter is a preliminary exploration of a new set of problems for machine learning and discovery theories: expanding the scope of these theories to include the steps before and after data-driven inductive inference.

The chapter is divided into three sections: The first section outlines some theoretical concerns about existing approaches to automated discovery systems, and proposes a new kind of problem for machine learning research. The idea is to expand the purview of discovery systems to include the problems of data selection and representation, the automated selection and combination of inference methods, and the evaluation of alternative approaches. The second section describes in some detail an example of a partially automated scientific discovery process directed at the prediction of protein structure. This example includes the generation of appropriate representations and the integration of multiple inference methods. The process is analyzed to identify the kinds of decisions that scientists have to make before and after the inductive step itself, and to try to illuminate the context in which these decisions are made. In conclusion, the challenges inherent in developing testable theories that address these issues are considered.

2 Discovery in People and Machines

AI theories of scientific discovery have been around for more than a decade ([Lenat, 1979] was arguably the first such theory). Although the role of computation in science has grown enormously in the last ten years, AI theories of discovery have, as yet, played at best a minor part in this expansion. Scientific visualization, physical simulation systems and automated statistical analysis are now integral parts of scientific research, but as yet there isn't much AI.

There are a few examples of AI in molecular biology computing, particularly neural networks; for example, the cover of the 24 August 1990 issue of *Science* is a neural net prediction of the secondary structure of the HIV-1 Principal Neutralizing Determinant protein. However, to my knowledge, most of the applications of AI to scientific discovery have focused on *recapitulation,* or duplicating the historical record of a scientific insight [Shrager & Langley, 1990a]. Because the systems that have been so successful at recapitulation have yet to make any novel discoveries of their own, and because the computational methods embodied in these programs have not been adopted by the scientific community, there is reason to doubt at least the sufficiency of the theories underlying those systems to explain scientific thinking. Admittedly this is a high standard to apply, and there have been clear contributions of the previous work to understanding some of the subproblems of discovery. Nevertheless, demonstrations of the sufficiency of the proposed computational methods to accomplish useful scientific tasks are so far lacking.

What might be missing from the existing AI approaches to discovery? An indication can be found in the overview chapter from the leading collection on the topic, *Computational Models of Scientific Discovery and Theory Formation* [Shrager & Langley, 1990a]. In that overview, Shrager and Langley, two of the founders of the field, list the knowledge structures and processes addressed in their extensive survey of AI models of scientific discovery. The knowledge structures are: observations, taxonomies, laws, theories, background knowledge, models, explanations, predictions and anomalies (they also mention hypotheses, explorations, instruments and representations, but claim that the former set provides a sufficient basis for an account of scientific behavior). The processes found in AI models are: observation, taxonomy formation and revision, inductive law formation and revision, theory formation and revision, deductive law formation, explanation, prediction, experimental design, manipulation and evaluation (comparing a prediction with observations). They also note that assimilating a new theory into one's background knowledge, revising an entire theoretical framework, model formation and revision, and various activities related to the social and bodily embedded aspects of scientific activity are important, although not yet addressed by AI theories.

I found it striking that there is not a single reference to the interests or goals of the scientist in the entire survey. There is likewise no mention of a characterization of available inferential and data gathering abilities—no self-model of the scientist. As I will suggest in more detail below, discovery requires making decisions about how to pursue specific goals for knowledge, using a characterized collection of data-gathering and analytical tools under significant resource constraints. Explicit representations of desired knowledge, and models of the available methods for gathering and analyzing information are crucial components of this process. Some recent work in machine learning has raised this issue in other contexts, e.g., [Cox & Ram, 1992; des-Jardins, 1992; Hunter, 1989b; Hunter, 1990b; Ram & Hunter, 1992] and there is related psychological work, e.g., [Weinert, 1987] .

Existing AI theories of discovery are, almost universally, cast as methods for searching through a space of possible hypotheses for the point that somehow best fit the available data (e.g., [Langley, Simon, Bradshaw, & Zytkow, 1987; Shrager & Langley, 1990b] , although compare [Tweney, 1990]). The alternative presented here casts learning and discovery as planning processes, working from a knowledge goal to a selection of actions to take to achieve that goal, to the execution (and perhaps reaction or replanning) of those data gathering and inferential actions, ultimately resulting in the satisfaction of the goals for knowledge. Since planning is well known to be just another intractable search problem (in this case through the space of possible actions, rather than possible hypotheses), it is not immediately clear what the advantage of trading one intractable search space for another might be. The difference is in what these metaphors suggest about what the important research problems are in discovery. The hypothesis space view emphasizes the importance of evaluating theories in light of all the available data, and in revising theories given a new set of observations. The planning view emphasizes the importance of understanding how research questions are generated, how it is possible to characterize *a priori* or incrementally what information is likely to be relevant in addressing a question (and is therefore worth gathering or drawing inferences from) and how to select and combine inference methods to best address a particular question. Although the questions raised by the hypothesis space metaphor are clearly important, I believe that these other issues are also important, and currently underexplored.[1]

2.1 Selecting Data

It is perhaps obvious that scientists have particular interests in mind as they do their work. They do not simply examine all the information perceptually accessible to them and try to reach the best explanation of it. In fact, a large portion of scientific labor is devoted to acquiring information that is difficult to perceive, precisely because it is believed to be relevant to some question of interest. Making decisions about what data might be worth gathering is a fundamental component of the discovery process. Because there are limits on the kind and amount of information that can be gathered, and because there are limits on the amount of data that can be *considered* by any realistic inference process, the process of directing attention to potentially relevant data is a central one in scientific discovery.

Current machine learning (and automated discovery) approaches tend to use all the data that is available for inference. At first, this does not seem unreasonable; after all, why should a program ignore information that might be useful? For any particular learning or discovery task, it seems desirable to select as broad an array of potentially relevant phenomena as possible. It is within the ability of current methods to discover that an aspect of a training set is irrelevant, but hard to infer that something is missing, and even harder to infer what that missing element might be. However, this view makes an important tacit assumption, that it is possible to identify (and ignore) all the irrelevant aspects of the all information that may be available to a scientific discovery system.

As demonstrated in [Almuallim & Dietterich, 1991], no existing machine learning system learns well in the presence of many irrelevant features. Almuallim and Dietterich present a system that exhibits somewhat better performance at this task, but the limitation is still significant. When compared to the amount of information potentially available to a discovery program, the problem of selecting relevant information is quite clear. In the field of molecular biology alone, the number and complexity of the datasets currently available over the Internet is staggering. The amount of information available to a human scientist in his or her local library is larger by many orders of magnitude, and the amount of information potentially gatherable with modern laboratory instrumentation is even larger. The vastness of "all available data" demands that decisions about what aspects of the universe are worth considering must be made in order to solve any significant scientific problem. The question of how a program can decide what data might be relevant to a particular question is a central concern to both developing a cognitive theory of how scientists think and to engineering a discovery assistant that is capable of navigating the information resources of the Internet effectively.

The requirement that potentially relevant aspects of a problem be selected before learning can occur is currently addressed by current automated discovery research in two ways. Most obviously, researchers select a dataset to which their algorithm will be applied. Existing datasets are generally winnowed down to select samples with various desirable characteristics. Some data is ignored as irrelevant, and others are transformed so that the distributions of values are better matched to the characteristics of the learning system. Possible transformations include discretizing, scaling, and combining multiple fields. Second, researchers are making decisions about relevancy when they craft the representations that their programs use. It is often the case that even radically different machine learning methods (e.g., decision tree induction and neural networks) offer similar levels of performance on a given induction problem. The key issue in the successful application of many of these methods turns out to be the selection of a suitable representation. However, the process of designing representations is generally taken to be outside the computational theory proposed (and evaluated) by AI discovery research.

One of the goals of this chapter is to bring the question of deciding upon the structure and content of input representations to a machine learning system into the realm of the theory itself. This work differs from related efforts in constructive induction (e.g., [Rendell & Seshu, 1990]) in that it addresses the entire process, from selecting and segmenting data sources to representational transformations both before and during learning. The task, given a specification of desired knowledge, is to make well-founded decisions that address the following questions:

- *What kinds of data might be relevant to acquiring the desired knowledge?*

- *What sources of potentially useful data exist?*

- *Given the available sources of potentially useful data, how can a dataset that best matches the relevancy specification be retrieved?*

- *How should retrieved data be sampled or segregated? (e.g., for cross-validation)*

- *How should retrieved data be transformed? (e.g., to match a particular inference method)*

How can a discovery system make these decisions about what data might be worth considering and how to find and transform it to address a given problem? A decision-theoretic approach would suggest defining utility and cost functions. The utility of considering a set of data might be estimated based on a characterization of the desired outcome. This is a difficult problem. The PAGODA system [desJardins, 1992] uses a decision theoretic approach to select which of several sensory modalities is worth learning about next, based on an estimate of expected utility of learning. However, the assumptions that make this estimate computationally tractable are extremely stringent, requiring, among other things, that the utilities of learning about the various modalities do not interact, and that the effects of learning in each modality can be modeled accurately. The example described in section 3, below, applies a computationally simpler method to a making a decision that does not fit PAGODA's assumptions.

A model of the costs of acquiring and using data is also necessary. It is possible to make estimates of the cost of obtaining and using data, e.g., as [Horvitz, Cooper, & Heckerman, 1989] does in evaluating the tradeoff between gathering more data and taking action in certain medical contexts, or as [Holder, 1991] does in estimating the amount of inference necessary for maximum predictive accuracy of certain machine learning systems. Other data-related costs can be estimated by an analysis of how the performance of a particular inferential method depends on the characteristics of its input, or by the network costs, time, disk space or other factors involved in acquiring and using the data.

No matter how large the machine, or how massively parallel, programs are fundamentally unable to make all inferences from all the potentially usable information in a realistic setting. Sampling methods, incremental experimentation and other methods for exploring very large spaces are applicable to this problem, but the space of possible "features" of the universe mandates some kind of selective attention. A novel set of problems for machine learning and discovery research to explore involves the interrelated issues of how to represent the contents of sources of information, and how to estimate the costs and benefits of using a potential source of information.

2.2 Knowledge Goals

An estimate of the expected utility of a source of information depends on what how that information relates to the goals of the learner. Not all information is equally relevant to all questions. The specific goal(s) for knowledge being pursued by a discovery program are the basis on which judgments about the relevancy (and hence utility) of a given collection of data must ultimately be made. *Knowledge goals* must describe the content of desired knowledge (e.g., Marvin Minsky's home phone number, or a computable method for calculating protein secondary structure from sequence) rather than just its structure (e.g., biases that prefer the induction of short hypotheses). Relevancy is an inherently semantic concept; a relationship between meanings. Programs without an explicit, content-based representation of the knowledge they desire will not, in general, be able to make effective relevancy decisions to focus attention on potentially useful knowledge. To the degree that programs that do not reason about their own goals for knowledge are successful in acquiring desired knowledge, they will either have had their input data prescreened by the researcher or they will include a built-in, inflexible bias that encodes relevancy judgments, or both. These methods will work in some circumstances, and built-in relevancy biases that are effective in particular situations are important contributions to attacking the general problem, but these methods are not alone sufficient for a building a flexible and powerful discovery system.

Programs that represent and draw inferences from their own goals for knowledge have other advantages as well. In addition to being able to make decisions about what external stimuli to focus on, they are also able to use those goals to focus their internal memory and inferential capacities in such a way as to improve their performance. Programs with limitations on processing ability and memory capacity need to allocate inferential resources so as to facilitate the accomplishment of their goals; explicit representation of those goals makes this process more flexible. Such decisions are important for agents with bounded rationality, and have been useful in addressing difficult inferential problems [desJardins, 1992; Hunter, 1989a; Ram, 1989]

A second important aspect of the explicit representation of desires for knowledge is that it makes possible the automatic and dynamic choice of the inference method or methods that are most appropriate for each particular knowledge goal. A recent proof demonstrated that learning algorithms, very broadly defined, can evaluate only a small proportion of the hypotheses compatible with the experiences they have. That is, there is no general learning method, and "different classes of learning problems may call for different algorithms." [Dietterich, 1989] A general (i.e. human-like) learning system will therefore have to make choices about what method(s) to learn or discover in a particular context.

A mechanism for making choices about what to learn and how to learn it is a crucial component of an automated learning system. On what basis can such decisions be made? How well a particular learning method performs on a particular task depends crucially on the characteristics of the concept to be learned [Rendell & Cho, 1990] . Rendell's work shows that the true character of a concept effects how well a particular learning method works. In order to use the relationships between concept character and learning method that Rendell identified to direct the selection of a learning mechanism, the learning system must have some internal characterization of its target concept(s). A knowledge goal is such an internal characterization of a target concept; knowledge goals are the appropriate basis for making decisions about learning methods, data selection, and representation.

Knowledge goals may have another role to play in an integrated learning and discovery system. They may facilitate experience-based improvement of the learning process itself: learning how better to learn. In order for a discovery program to be able to evaluate its own performance, it must compare the actual result of inference with its original knowledge goals. This comparison may identify areas where additional inference would be beneficial. A record of the decisions made and an internal model of the learning and discovery process could be used to identify alternative approaches that could be explored, or to support systematic modifications to decision making within the learning and discovery processes themselves. This potential use of knowledge goals remains unexplored, but is supported by analogy to the use of goals and internal models in other kinds of learning (e.g., [Hunter, 1989a]).

2.3 Problem Transformation

In order to address a desire for knowledge, a discovery system must have both data that bears on the question and inferential abilities that apply to it.

However, there is an interaction between the available data and the requirements of the inferential method. The structure and representation of the data is often a determining factor in the successful application of an inferential technique. Many of the considerations in selecting the data to attend to described above also apply to the selection of which features of that data should be made explicit, and how.

Often this question is complicated by the need to reduce the complexity of the data. In order to learn a complex mapping, an inference system needs many examples. Formal results relate the ability of any learning system to learn a concept to the number of examples it has seen [Valient, 1984]. It is not possible to accurately induce complex concepts from small amounts of data. Most interesting scientific problems face this challenge. This problem can be addressed by simplifying the space of possible concepts considered or increasing the amount of data, or both.

The process of addressing a complex desire for knowledge by transforming it into a more tractable problem that can be addressed with available data is an important aspect of scientific creativity. Individual scientists appear to have quite different approaches to this problem, which may depend on training, experience, the desire to try (or demonstrate) some particular approach, and many other difficult to capture factors. Computational models of creative processes in understanding [Kass, 1990] may be relevant to this addressing this question.

In the specific examples described in the next section, a variety of transformations were applied data to reduce the size of a problem. Generalizations of these approaches are potentially applicable to reducing the complexity of many other induction problems. Six interrelated classes of transformations were applied:

- *Identify invariances* so portions of the space can be collapsed into equivalence classes. A simple example in structural domains is to collapse all translations or rotations of a structure into a single class.

- *Creating approximate equivalence classes*, for example, by clustering the data and ignoring distinctions within clusters.

- *Prune the space* e.g., by focusing on areas with a high density of examples or with more available information.

- *Decrease the resolution* of the distinctions made, for example by discretizing real values or increasing the grain size of a discrete measure.

- *Find correlated attributes* and develop proxy measures that reduce the correlated attributes to a single one

- *Find independent subspaces*, and solve them one at a time

There are many possible ways to operationalize each strategies. The alternative operationalizations and strategies themselves are not mutually exclusive. Each class of reductions can be applied repeatedly and in combination with others, in an order sensitive way. For example, it may not be possible to identify equivalence classes until the problem has been divided into independent subspaces. Once those equivalence classes are identified, it may then be possible to prune the problem spaces by only considering problems that fall into the most common classes.

Different problem reductions lead to quite different results and it appears to be difficult to predict ahead of time which combination will work. There is also a complex interaction between problem reduction method and the selection of a specific inference method, since different inference algorithms place differing restrictions on problem structure and representation. The question of how to select among and apply these abstract problem reduction strategies is an open research problem. One detailed example is given in the next section.

In short, the view of learning as a kind of planning provides an set of novel problems not previously addressed by machine discovery work. Leaving aside the question of how desires for knowledge arise, this framework demands answers to questions about how a desire for knowledge is translated into an executable plan for acquiring that knowledge. How are potentially relevant sources of data identified? How is data screened, transformed, and represented so that desired inferences can be made? How are alternative inferential approaches selected among and combined to best use the available data? How are the conclusions drawn by an inferential method evaluated? The central claim outlined in this section is that explicit, content-based representations of the characteristics of desired knowledge play a role in each of these processes. The next section describes an set of examples illustrating how that might happen.

3 Planning to Learn About Protein Structure

In this section, I will describe a coordinated set of activities in service of the goal of being able to predict protein tertiary structure from sequence, paying special attention to the processes of selecting and representing relevant information. The collection of programs described here is implemented in the INVESTIGATOR framework, developed at the National Library of Medicine [Hunter, 1990a]. Although not all of the decisions described below were made in a meaningful way by a program[2], I do endeavor to provide a theoretical framework that illuminates the choices that must be made and the factors that influence those choices, as a prolegomena to an implemented theory. In some areas, however, even the details of the possible transformations remain unclear. Nevertheless, in order to create sufficient computational theories of scientific discovery (or human learning), these questions will have to be addressed. This section explores these issues in the context of a real problem in molecular biology: predicting protein structure from sequence.

The task of predicting three dimensional structure from amino acid sequence is described in detail in the introductory chapter of this volume. In brief, the genome of an organism specifies the makeup of all of the proteins that constitute that organism. The genes specify a linear sequence of amino acids, which are assembled at the ribosome. Although the proteins are constructed as a linear sequence, they only become chemically active when they have folded up into a particular three-dimensional conformation. The positions of each atom in the protein in three-space is called its structure (or, more specifically, its tertiary structure). Proteins are very large molecules, and the folded shape can hide some regions, expose others, and bring elements of the protein that were at opposite ends of the sequence close together in space. These factors are important in determining what the function of the molecule is in the living system, and how it performs that function. Determining the structure of biomolecules is important in designing drugs, understanding key functions such as development or neuronal signaling, and in practically every area of biology. Technologically, it is now relatively easy to determine the sequence of proteins, but it remains very difficult to determine their structures. It is easy to demonstrate that all the information needed to determine structure must be present in the amino acid sequence alone. It has proved to be quite difficult to find the mapping from sequence to structure.

Much related work in the field takes similar approaches to the ones presented here to learning aspects of this mapping (e.g., Holbrook, Muskal and Kim; Zhang and Waltz; Lathrop, et al, all in this volume). However, the goal of this chapter is to elucidate some of the cognitive processes that go unstated (although not undone) in that work, and bring those processes into the realm of AI discovery research. For example, nearly all researchers applying learning algorithms to the problem of protein structure prediction screen their dataset for homologies, and use a sliding window to segment the problem. These choices make a tremendous difference in the outcome of the work; how are they made? What are the alternatives?

As is often the case in machine discovery work, it is easier to define the space through which a program must search than it is to describe an effective method for traversing that space. The space of possible data-gathering and inferential actions is rather different than the space of possible hypotheses (or formulae) for describing a dataset. The hope of this approach to automated discovery research is that it will be possible to characterize knowledge generating actions on the basis of their expected difficulty or cost, and to develop a set of methods for estimating the distribution of expected outcomes of the application of these actions, given some information about the knowledge desired and the characteristics of the available data. Several related efforts have been made, such as [Holder, 1991] which empirically characterizes the expected performance of a learning algorithm given a partial execution, or [Rendell & Cho, 1990] which makes estimates of the performance of various learning methods based on the true character of the concepts they are trying to learn.

A human scientist attacking a large problem develops a research plan, consisting of many constituent approaches to relevant subproblems. In the example explored below, this research plan is built by the instantiation of an abstractly stated discovery strategy. The first step in this process is to identify the specific knowledge goal. Then, the statement of the problem is used to select one of three high level discovery strategies. Once a strategy has been selected, the information in the representation of the strategy is used to determine what data is necessary. Knowledge of various data sources is used to select a source, and then to identify and extract an appropriate dataset from that source. The next step is to transform the available dataset to meet the requirements of the strategy. This transformation is a complex process, and, in this case, is the area where scientific creativity is most apparent. Then a particular inference method is selected. This selection may place additional requirements on the dataset. A representation is selected on the basis of the data and the inference method, and the dataset is transformed into that representation. Parameters of the inference method must be set, or the space of possible parameterizations explored, and the inferences made. Finally, the outcome of the inference process must be evaluated. As the example unfolds, several more general points about the process become apparent as well.

3.1 Characterizing the Desired Knowledge

The protein structure prediction problem is to find a mapping from a linear sequence of amino acids to a set of three dimensional coordinates for all the atoms in each amino acid. Typical proteins contain hundreds of amino acids, and thousands of atoms. Large proteins (e.g., Apolipoprotein B-100) are composed of more than 4500 amino acids. Spatial resolution of 2Å is about the level of accuracy of the training data available from crystal structures, and a large globular protein (like Apolipoprotein B) may be 150Å along its longest dimension. The largest version of the problem therefore involves a mapping from any of 20^{4500} ($\sim 10^{5850}$) strings to the positions of about 60,000 atoms in a lattice of 75^3 points (421,875 choose 60,000, or over $10^{46,000}$ possibilities). The number of possible mappings is proportional to the product of these two immense numbers! Fortunately, the problem is really much smaller than this. A vanishingly small portion of the large number of possible proteins is actually observed in nature. Most proteins are much smaller than 4500 amino acids and 150Å. A solution limited to proteins of 450 amino acids or less, using only 3 atoms per amino acid and 3Å resolution on a 90Å lattice would be a breakthrough. However, even this dramatically smaller problem has so many possible mappings to consider (merely 10^{585} strings and $\sim 10^{1700}$ possible structures!) that it is extremely unlikely to be discovered by a search through the space of possible mappings described in this way. However intractable, this characterization of the problem space is useful for reasoning about the data and possible representations. A significant aspect of the discovery process involves transforming this space to a more tractable approximation of it that retains its essential character.

Given the large number of possible solutions, why is this problem thought to be solvable at all? Nature does it all the time. Denatured (i.e. unfolded) proteins will fold into their native conformation (i.e. the shape they take in living systems) in aqueous environments of suitable temperature, pressure and pH [Anfinsen, 1973]. Cells solve this problem millions of times a minute. The mechanism that determines how proteins fold in the cell can be explained in the same terms as any other physical phenomenon. The forces acting on atoms in the protein can be accurately described by quantum mechanics, and the molecule's folded state minimizes its free energy in its environment. In a system with an accurate causal model such as this, it may be possible to computationally simulate the process, and achieve the goal. Unfortunately, finding the minimum energy conformation of even a much simpler system from an arbitrary starting state using quantum mechanics (called an *ab initio*—from first principles—calculation) is a computationally intractable problem. The use of approximations and other methods to increase the tractability of simulation is discussed below.

Despite the obvious insolubility of the problem in these terms, it is still important to be specific about what the general problem entails. This mapping is the knowledge goal. The subproblem decompositions and approximations we will make along the way are methods of attacking this original, insoluble problem. In order to select among and evaluate these simplifications, there must be a reference to which they can be compared. The full statement of the problem, no matter how computationally intractable, provides a baseline from which simplifying assumptions can be made, and by which the results can be evaluated.

3.2 The Knowledge Acquisition Strategy

Knowledge goals are addressed by taking actions that change knowledge state, that is, by making inferences. Unfortunately, means-ends analysis applied to the space of knowledge states using inferences as operators is unlikely to work. However, inference steps can be assembled into plans to acquire knowledge, and skeletons of these plans can form general templates for assembling novel plans without the need for additional reasoning from first principles. These skeletal plans for acquiring knowledge are termed *knowledge acquisition strategies* [Hunter, 1989a; Hunter, 1989b].

Discovering a mapping from one complex, high dimensional space to another is a common problem confronting intelligent agents, and there are several distinct general approaches for addressing it. These approaches can be divided into three broad categories:

- *Simulation* using an effective causal model of the phenomena that underlie the transformation, reasoning about the transformation analytically.
- *Induction* of an empirical mapping between the input and output spaces based on a sample of I/O pairs.
- *Case-based* methods also work from a sample of I/O pairs, but instead of trying to induce a mapping between them, case-based methods make predictions about an input by finding a stored example with a similar input, and using the matching stored output as the basis for the prediction.

An autonomous discovery system would decide among these (and perhaps other) alternative strategies when trying to discover such a mapping. Ideally, each of these broad classes of methods would be characterized by a function that would estimate the expected cost and utility of each method given the characteristics of the transformation space, the available data or examples, and the amount and usefulness of any background knowledge or bias. Unfortunately, there is as yet no known method of making such a calculation in a reasonable period of time. All three of these methods might be successfully applied to the protein structure prediction problem, and human scientists are pursuing research that can be classified into each category. These scientists make their decisions about which strategy to pursue based on a variety of factors, including personal or social ones such as the kind of academic training they have had, how an available resource might be used (e.g., a private database or parallel computer) or where they perceive the competition is the least strong. It is, however, possible for a program to embody heuristic, qualitative characterizations of the problem situations best suited to each of these classes of methods, and make a selection based on a characterization of the desired knowledge.

For each possible strategy, there are costs, in terms of how much computational effort the strategy is likely to require, and expected benefits, usually cast in terms of how likely the strategy is to succeed. It may be possible to easily eliminate a strategy on the basis of its intractability, or to easily select one on the basis of its probability of success. The first step in the selection process is to eliminate strategies that are intractable.

It appears to be possible to directly assess the computational demands of a simulation strategy for protein structure prediction. In simulation, there is a always a computational model of the causal factors underlying the desired transformation. The expected running time and other resource consumption of the simulation of a model can be assessed either analytically or empirically, generating an estimate the resources required to execute a model given a particular problem characterization. The simulation of the movement of a molecule the size of a protein can take hundreds of hours of supercomputer time to simulate nanoseconds of folding, even using heuristic energy functions rather than *ab initio* quantum calculations [Karplus & Petsko, 1990] The entire process of protein folding in the cell can take several seconds, indicating that a simulation of folding a single protein would take more than 30 years.

However, it is worth noting here that such a conclusion, based on simple extrapolation, can easily be incorrect. Variations on the parameters of the simulation (e.g., lattice size or time step), the underlying model, the implementation (e.g., parallelism or clever optimization techniques) or other factors offer potential speed-ups or tradeoffs that might some form of simulation appropriate for the problem at hand. The difficulty in making this decision is reflected in the fact that human scientists working on this problem are currently pursuing all three strategies, and there is a great deal of research in variations on the simulation strategy (e.g., [Skolnick & Kolinski, 1990]).

The difficulty in making correct high level strategic decisions for scientific discovery is a quite general problem. Making discoveries about phenomena of significance often requires taking a method that appeared intractable and finding a way to apply it. The mere fact that a method appears intractable on one analysis does not mean that it is not worth inferential effort to refine or recast the method. People seem to be able to develop intuitions about what approaches are genuinely intractable, and which are merely difficult open problems; of course, these intuitions are not always correct.

The selection of a knowledge acquisition strategy for an unsolved problem reflects the learner's assessment of its own inferential abilities, as well as an assessment of the problem characteristics. It is hard to accurately assess the cost of instantiating and executing a complex strategy, or its likelihood of its success, especially since the learner needs to assess alternative strategies without wasting inferential resources on evaluating strategies that will not be used. This is an issue, since as [Collins, 1987] pointed out, there can be significant inferential work to be done in just figuring out how to apply a potential planning strategy to the problem at hand. The estimates of difficulty and likelihood of success that people use to select among strategies may well be based on their observations of how well other people have done using those strategies, or own their own history, rather than on a deep analysis of how a particular strategy will apply to a current problem of interest.

Returning to the specific problem at hand, the alternative to the analytical approach of simulation are the two empirical approaches, induction and case-based reasoning. Both methods are potentially achievable within reasonable resource limits, so the question becomes which is more likely to succeed in accomplishing the goal? Until success is achieved, there is no direct way to make this decision. Both methods have significant potential, but no clear solution. Because the strategy and set of strategy instantiation and transformation methods are better developed for the inductive methods (including neural networks) in the current implementation of INVESTIGATOR than CBR methods are, the choice to use them can be made on the basis of the internal abilities of the learner. This decision criterion must be secondary to an assessment of how likely a strategy is to succeed, since otherwise a less well developed strategy will never be used, even if it is assessed as more likely to succeed on a given problem. In the general case, it is also worth exploring a less well developed strategy periodically if there are potential opportunities to improve it (or learn more about its applicability conditions) through experience. The question of how often to try a less well developed strategy is related to the more general problem of deciding when to gather more knowledge [Berry & Fristedt, 1985] .

After selecting a strategy, a learner must instantiate it, mapping the abstract components of the plan to the specifics of the current goal. The strategies describe the steps of an abstract plan and constraints on the concepts that can be used to fill variablized slots in the plan.

3.3 Selecting Relevant Data

The first step in most knowledge acquisition strategies is to find relevant data from which inferences can be drawn. Few machine learning or discovery programs address this issue. Almost universally, these programs use all of the data that is available to them. One of the design goals in building INVESTIGATOR is that it have potential access to a great deal of information by accessing remote databases over the Internet. The computational (and sometimes financial) expense of accessing this data is non-trivial, so INVESTIGATOR must make decisions about what data it will use. These decisions are made on the basis of (1) the content-specific knowledge-acquisition goals that drive the entire process, (2) the selection of a knowledge strategy, which specifies the kind of information need in order to make the desired inferences, and (3) characterizations of the knowledge sources that are available to the system.

In the case at hand, the inductive learning strategy requires a large number of pairs of problem statements and solutions. When applied to the current knowledge goal, that requirement becomes a need for protein sequences and the structures associated with them. INVESTIGATOR's internal representations of its available data sources show only one source of protein structures, and that data source also contains the related protein sequences: the Brookhaven Protein Data Bank (PDB) [Arbola, Bernstein, Bryant, Koetzle, & Weng, 1987] . Although in this case, the desired information can be found in a single location, this is not generally the case. Some knowledge goals may require using data from several different sources. Earlier work with IN-

VESTIGATOR explored using multiple sources of data to address a particular knowledge goal [Hunter, 1990a]. The representation of PDB contains information about where to find the database, how large it is and procedures to parse its entries. The general information in INVESTIGATOR about the database specifies that each structure in PDB contains three dimensional location data for each atom in the molecule; most structures have well over than 1000 atoms; that database entries also generally include information about the bonds between the atoms, other atoms in the structure (such as cofactors, water molecules, or substrates), data about the certainty of the each atomic position, and that there are currently about 900 structures in PDB. Generating representations of available data is currently done by hand, although information about the size of the databases is updated automatically whenever a database is accessed. The movement towards the adoption of the ASN.1 data description standard for biological databases raises the possibility of the automatic generation of parsers as well [Karp, 1991].

A selecting a source of data is only the first step. The next step in instantiating the induction strategy is to select the particular data items that it will use, and then select an appropriate representation. There are several reasons why an inductive learning strategy may want to use only a subset of available data. In order to make estimates of the confidence in a prediction method, a learner must put aside a test set that is not used in the training procedure, e.g., for cross validation. This test set must not be used in any aspect of training. Another reason to use only a subset of the available data is the possibility of errors in the training collection. Many datasets are annotated in some way with characterizations of the certainty or believability of the data. Since many inductive methods are sensitive to noise, it may be appropriate to remove uncertain items from the training data, assuming that they can be identified. A more complex consideration is matching the distribution of the data items in the training set with the expected distribution of similar items the universe. Information about the true distribution in the world is rarely available, but some partial characterizations can be used to select a subset of the training data that is likely to be closer to the true distribution than is the entire dataset.

These 900 structures in PDB include several that are merely theoretical predictions of structure (not empirically derived) and several of very poor resolution. These structures can be easily identified and removed from consideration. PDB also contains many variant structures of a given protein; e.g., bound to inhibitors. These variants are given easily identifiable names and it is possible to select only one representative from each set of related structures. Removing all of these redundant structures reduces the total set to 324 distinct, empirical structures.

The proteins with known structures are not a random sample of proteins; the selection process is biased in many ways, some of which are likely to be biochemically significant. One source of bias is that the proteins in the database are those that are interesting to biologists, and that are (relatively) easy to crystallize, and therefore obtain structures from. It is not clear if any correction can be made for this source of bias.

Another bias results from the fact that once a protein's structure has been determined, scientists become interested exploring the structures of similar proteins for comparison. Technical problems that were solved in the creation of one structure may generalize best to proteins of similar structure, increasing the incentive to investigate similar proteins. These are reasons that entries in PDB may have sequences that are much more similar to each other than a randomly selected collection of proteins would be. If present and uncorrected, this bias will have a significant adverse effect on both the inference process and on estimates of its accuracy.

In general, correcting a bias requires a characterization of the true distribution, and a method for resampling a dataset to reflect the true distribution. There are many possible biases that might be present in a sample, and unless a mechanism for drawing an unbiased sample exists, there is no general way to detect them. However, given a specification of a possible source of bias it may be possible to test for it. The knowledge that the excess-similarity bias might exist in PDB is socially derived, but testing and correcting for it can be done automatically.

A source of an unbiased sample of proteins is needed in order to correct for selection biases in the PDB dataset. The bias introduced by the requirement of crystalizability is easy to address, since there are many sources of protein sequences that are not derived from (or related to) crystals, e.g., the protein information resource (PIR) database. However, finding a collection of sequences that is not influenced by the same socio-scientific interestingness considerations is difficult. The sequences that appear in PIR are determined by those that scientist deemed worth expending the effort to acquire. However, there are datasets that exhaustively sample some naturally defined collection of proteins, such as those that appear on a particular chromosome, or are expressed in a particular cell (e.g., [Adams, Dubnick, Kerlavage, Moreno, Kelley, Utterback, et al., 1992]). These datasets are intended to reflect the true distribution of proteins.

The true distribution of sequence similarity can be estimated by using one of these unbiased datasets, or a sample of it. There are very effective computational tools for determining if a pair of proteins have a greater than random similarity (e.g., BLAST, [Altschul, Gish, Miller, Myers, & Lipman, 1990]). Using a (putatitively) unbiased sample, the expected number of hits is roughly 0.0006 per pair of proteins. The same test on PDB yields nearly 0.002 hits per pair, three times the expected number. The collection of proteins in PDB is biased to excessive similarity.

Since the number of similar sequences in a sample the size of PDB under the true distribution would be close to zero, the induction strategy needs to generate a resampling of PDB to identify a set of proteins that are not similar to each other. Although it is necessary to ignore some data for this reason, the chance of successful induction goes up with the size of the training set, so it is desirable to ignore as little as possible. Since a measure of similarity (BLAST) exists, it is possible to generate a maximum size subset of PDB by using the similarity measure to define equivalence classes, and selecting a single representative from each class.

Even the choice of selecting which member of a class ought to be used to represent the class is a nontrivial decision. If it is possible to determine a selection criterion that facilitates successful inference, it should be used. In this case, members were selected for high resolution, since induction is sensitive to noise in the features of the data. The final reduced dataset has 183 structures in it, none of which have any significant sequence homology to any other.

Although the method described above was generated manually in response to the specific demands of this particular problem, it suggests that a more general strategy for addressing biased data. Resampling a dataset to find a maximum sized subset of it that reflects a specified distribution is a well defined problem that recurs often in inductive inference. Likewise, methods of generating estimates of the true distribution of data along some dimension is also a recurring problem. Detecting that unrepresentative biases exist is a much harder problem. In this context, making that inference appears to require knowledge of the way scientists make decisions about what work do to.

3.4 Reducing the Size of the Problem Space

The problem of inducing a mapping from the entire amino acid sequence of a protein to the positions of each of the constituent atoms is intractable. The space of possible inputs and possible outputs is enormous, and the number of examples is quite small. The problem space must be transformed so that the mapping to be learned is smaller, and the number of examples of this mapping is larger. As described in above in section 2.3, this kind of problem transformation is a significant component of scientific creativity. In [Kass, 1990] Kass describes a theory of creative explanation that involves finding an partial match with a prior explanation and making small changes to the structure of the previous example to meet the requirements of the current case. The following section takes an analogous approach to finding a suitable problem transformation.

A method widely used in the inductive protein structure prediction is the translation of atomic positions into secondary structures [Cohen, Presnell, & Cohen, 1990; Holley & Karplus, 1989; Qian & Sejnowski, 1988; Zhang, Mesirov, & Waltz, 1992] . Secondary structure (for these purposes) is an assignment of each amino acid in the protein sequence to one of three classes, based on the hydrogen bonding characteristics of that element in the final structure. This process involves several kinds of transformations. First, a set of approximate equivalence classes (secondary structures) were created; they were devised by Linus Pauling in the 1950's to coarsely describe local aspects of protein structure, long before any 3D atomic structures of proteins were known. The classes were defined based on invariances found in early crystallographic experiments. The application of this set of equivalence classes dramatically decreases the resolution of the description of the structure, and discards a great deal of information about the original structure, making the problem much smaller. This move is an example of the "creating approximate equivalence classes" problem transformation described in section 2.3.

The next step in this approach involves pruning the space of secondary structures. The secondary structure assignments used by modern biochemists involve eight classes, defined on the basis of hydrogen bonds formed in the molecule. The six least common of these classes are combined into a catch-all category called random coil, focusing on the two most common secondary structures, helices and strands. This also reduces the size of the problem, and is an example of the "decrease the resolution of the distinctions made" problem transformation.

The final step in this structure prediction strategy is to segment the problem into predicting the secondary structure assignment of each amino acid separately, based on a local window of sequence neighbors. This move, taking a large problem and segmenting it into many smaller problems, is an example of the "find independent subproblems" transformation.

The composite transformation of the general problem makes the problem computationally tractable for existing induction algorithms. The size of the problem was reduced by thousands of orders of magnitude, to a matter of learning a mapping from a short string of amino acids to one of three classes. However, each of the transformations introduces an assumption which may or may not be justified: namely, that secondary structure is an appropriate definition of equivalence classes of structural segments; that helices and sheets are the important classes of secondary structure; and that predicting the secondary structure class each amino acid based on is sequence neighbors decomposes the overall problem into independent subproblems. The association of underlying assumptions with transformations is useful in both diagnosing failure (should the inference fail) or in directing the exploration of alternative decompositions.

The existing work on protein secondary structure prediction provides one path through the space. The planning framework outlined here identifies the decisions that were made in generating that path, and suggests where variations could be tried. Exploring a space of alternative conceptions of a problem is part of the scientific discovery process.

The variation explored here is the replacement of secondary structure with another equivalence class defined over the structures. Secondary structure divides a three dimensional protein structure in subregions, and then classifies the subregions. In order to find alternatives to secondary structure, the protein structures must be divided into regions and those regions assigned to classes. Finding such a classification is a new knowledge goal, and can be planned for recursively.

The data is given for this problem, so data source and selection issues do not arise. The specification of a desired knowledge identifies the general strategy required as classification. There are, however, several issues that must be addressed in the instantiation of this strategy.

AI classification methods, e.g., [Cheeseman, Kelly, Self, Stutz, Taylor, & Freeman, 1988; Fisher, 1987] require that the examples to be classified be described by a fixed-length vector of feature values, and one with a relatively small number of features. Available inference methods require the transformation of the supplied protein structures to fixed length segments.

Long, variable length sequences can be transformed into a large collection of short, fixed length sequences by segmentation, as in the final transformation step in the secondary structure method described above. The segments can be mutually exclusive (end to end) or overlapping (sliding window). The division of structures in to fixed length feature vectors is complicated by several factors. First, the "size" of a feature vector for a structure segment can be measured in two different ways, which are not proportional to each other. First is the number of amino acids in the structure segment, and second is the number of dimensions required to describe the positions of the atoms in the segment (which is three times the number of atoms). Since different amino acids have different numbers of atoms, a segment of a fixed number of amino acids will have a variable number of atom description dimensions, and a segment with a fixed number of atom description dimensions will have a variable (and non-integral) number of amino acids. This mismatch can be resolved by a problem transformation. The positions of the atoms in an amino acid are highly correlated with each other. Knowing the position of three particular atoms (which biochemists call the "backbone") in amino acid is generally enough to identify the location of the remaining atoms with a high degree of accuracy. The value of the positions of these atoms can be used as a proxy for the positions of all the others. Protein structures can be segmented into fixed length feature vectors containing three numbers representing the positions of each of three atoms for each amino acid in the segment.

Other problem reduction transformations can also be applied. The molecular segments (and the molecules themselves) are rigid bodies. Similarity of rigid bodies is invariant under positional translation and rotation;

that is, if a structure is similar to another, then it will still be similar if one or both of the objects is moved or rotated. This invariance allows for another reduction in the complexity of the classification problem transforming all objects that are identical under rotation or translation to a single class. Adopting a uniform coordinate frame with which to describe the segments accomplishes this. The protein structure fragments can be translated to a uniform coordinate frame by defining the frame relative to the moment of inertia of each fragment. Similar fragments have similar moments of inertia, and will be oriented so that their constituent atoms will have similar absolute positions.

Decisions remain to be about the number of amino acids per segment and whether the segmentation should be mutually exclusive or overlapping. Overlapping segments are a superset of all possible mutually exclusive divisions, and are preferable unless they produce too many examples for the inference method to handle. The size of the segments should be as large as the inference method can handle.

Selection of the classification method itself must also be made. The alternatives available during this work were k-nearest-neighbor clustering, conceptual clustering and Bayesian classification. Bayesian classification is preferable for several reasons. First, unlike much of the conceptual clustering work, it is explicitly suited to clustering real-numbered location data. Unlike k-nearest-neighbor classification, it uses the data to estimate how many classes there are as well as their content. Finally, unlike other methods, it can also generate classifications that have significantly differing within-class variances. This is valuable both because the natural classes may differ in this way, and because variance information is useful in trying to fit new data to the model defined by the classification. Both k-nearest neighbor classification and conceptual clustering have a strong tendency to minimize differences in variance between classes. Bayesian classification therefore appears to be the most appropriate of the clustering methods for this problem.

Once the data have been transformed to match the requirements of the goal and a specific clustering method has been selected, the inference can be done. In this case Autoclass III [Cheeseman, Stutz, Hanson, & Taylor, 1990] was used to do the Bayesian classification. Other details of this clustering process are described in [Hunter & States, 1991].

The final step in most learning strategies is to evaluate the results. In this case, since the goal was to find an alternative to an existing classification of a particular dataset, the results can be evaluated by correlating the original and induced class assignments for each element. The clustering generated a much larger number of classes than traditional secondary structure recognizes, 27 vs. 8. Some of the induced classes appeared to be more fine-grained variations on traditional secondary structure, but others showed very little correlation with secondary structure. The relationship between the induced

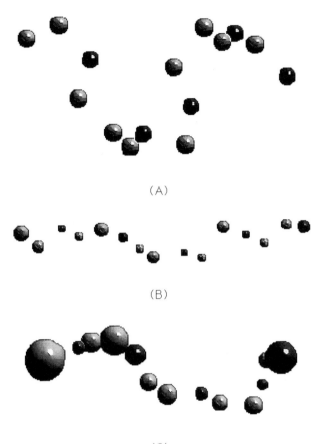

Figure 1. Three examples of the 27 protein structure classes used as an alternative to secondary structure. Two of the classes shown here (A & B) are similar to traditionally defined classes, and the other is not. The spheres depict the positions of the backbone atoms in five consecutive amino acids. The center of each sphere represents the mean position of the atom in the class; the size of the sphere represents the variation in position. Grey spheres are carbon atoms and black ones are nitrogen atoms. (A) is class 1 and is similar to alpha helix. (B) is class 8 and is similar to a beta strand. (C) is class 10, and structures placed in this class have secondary structure assignments in all eight secondary structure classes. Nevertheless, there are more than 800 examples of class 10 in the structure database. Table 1 completely describes the correlation between the induced classification and secondary structure..

class	β-bridge	β-strand	3_{10} helix	α-helix	bend	β-turn	none
1	23	1020	0	0	4	2	192
2	37	378	0	0	3	3	727
3	46	155	1	4	8	11	727
4	18	111	31	30	499	162	160
5	18	627	0	0	1	2	115
6	30	347	0	0	2	2	411
7	33	278	0	0	19	9	409
8	0	0	0	1077	0	1	1
9	0	0	0	1013	0	1	0
10	25	60	12	34	408	53	234
11	13	542	0	0	1	1	118
12	21	62	1	2	261	10	377
13	0	0	45	845	0	52	0
14	2	90	1	1	229	7	262
15	1	13	7	10	214	335	93
16	3	2	88	558	30	155	33
17	0	2	159	463	13	128	20
18	1	1	92	407	78	219	6
19	6	3	63	230	35	215	14
20	0	0	2	638	0	0	0
21	0	0	73	479	0	27	6
22	0	0	71	106	28	170	12
23	3	3	12	146	69	171	1
24	1	1	76	47	35	228	8
25	4	8	17	35	49	129	0
26	1	1	31	90	32	189	0

Table 1. The DSSP secondary structure assignments [Kabsch and Sander, 1983] for the amino acid in the center of the fragments placed into each class. So, for example, of the fragments assigned to class one, 1023 would be assigned to beta strand, and 221 would be assigned to random coil (not beta-strand or alpha-helix). Class ten, one of the most heterogeneous, would be assigned as 60 beta-strands, 34 alpha-helices and 732 random coils.

classification and the traditional one is shown in table 1. Some examples of the class definitions are shown in Figure 1.

This clustering provides an set of output classes which are an alternative to secondary structure classes. Many other alternatives to the original secondary structure plan are possible. The one described above provides one example, and illustrates the many decisions that a researcher must make in the course of addressing a knowledge goal. The actual classification itself is only a part of a much larger process.

The original method reduced the 8 secondary structure classes to three by identifying two classes as primary and combining the others into a single group. Since there is no equivalent identification in the new classification, and since induction methods can learn a mapping to 27 groups, this transformation was skipped. The final step in the original structure prediction strategy was to segment the problem into predicting the class assignment of each amino acid separately, based on a local window of sequence neighbors. This is straightforwardly applied to the new classifications, and no further transformations are necessary.

3.5 Choosing and Applying an Induction Method

The particular induction method used for a particular problem can be selected on the basis of either expected performance or on the cost of executing the method, or some combination. The identification of general methods for selecting appropriate inference methods for a particular problem is an open research problem. In the absence of an analytical method for distinguishing among alternative induction methods, running small scale comparison experiments on random samples of the data can provide justification for selecting one over the other.

The secondary structure prediction methods described above use feedforward neural networks trained with backpropagation to learn the mapping from the window of amino acids to the secondary structure class of the central amino acid in the window. The induction of decision trees based on expected information gain is the major alternative induction method used in machine learning [Quinlan, 1991] . In a set of sample runs on random subsets of the problem data, the accuracy of the two methods were statistically indistinguishable, and the decision tree learner runs several orders of magnitude faster than the neural network training. The neural network methods also require the setting of a free parameter, the number of hidden nodes. This parameter is usually set empirically, based on test performance, which requires a large amount of additional running time. On this basis, the decision tree learner was selected for the large scale induction run.

The fact that the radically different inference techniques of decision tree induction and backpropagation training of neural networks performed at nearly identical levels of accuracy may be somewhat surprising. It appears to be the case that in many circumstances the effectiveness of induction depends not so much on the particular inference method used, but on the data and representation of the data that it is applied to. Although algorithm development (and selection) is clearly an important component of machine learning, inference algorithms are not the sole factor involved in the satisfaction of a goal for knowledge. In particular, the selection and transformation of the data that the algorithms are applied to plays a central role in the outcome.

3.6 Evaluating the Outcome of Learning

The completed execution of a plan does not guarantee the success of the goal for which that plan was intended. The result of the learning strategy above is a decision tree that makes a mapping between amino acid sequence and the classification of protein structures induced before. How well does this tree address the original goal? At best, the resulting decision tree solves a transformed and dramatically simplified version of the original problem. Even if the tree were able to perfectly map from sequence to substructure class, it is not clear how to map from a set of substructure classes back to the positions of the constituent atoms. In particular, the segmentation of the structure lost information about the relationship of the segments which is difficult to reconstruct.

And the mapping from sequence to substructure class was far from perfect. The final application of the decision tree learner to the full dataset yields a decision tree that classifies an independent test set correctly slightly more than 36% of the time. In addition to this estimate of the absolute accuracy of this method, it is also possible to compare it to the accuracy of the secondary structure prediction strategy it was based on. Since the secondary structure method maps to one of three classes, and the variation maps to one of 27 classes, the accuracy statistics cannot be compared directly. The information content of the mappings can be measured, however, showing a slight edge for the variation: 0.9 bits per prediction for predicting one of three classes 63% of the time versus 1.68 bits per prediction for predicting one of 27 classes 36% of the time, under the observed class distributions. (The details of the this analysis, and a more specific description of the results can be found in [Hunter, 1992])

4 Conclusions

The purpose of this chapter was to illuminate the wide range of activities and decisions that go unstated in machine learning work, and to provide a framework for bringing these decisions into the realm of theories of learning and discovery. The process of getting from broadly stated problem to the final application of an inference method to a specific dataset contains many opportunities for machine learning research; this chapter is a preliminary attempt to explore those opportunities.

The exploration attempted to identify the decisions that had to be made in the pursuit of a particular strategy for making a discovery about protein structure prediction. Each decision point embodies alternative paths that might be taken towards the overall knowledge goal. The path actually taken above tried a variation on the previously described secondary structure prediction approach, generating an alternative classification of protein substructures. This alternative path produced only a minor gain in overall performance. However, the claim of this chapter is not that the particular alternative pursued solved the overall problem, but that it is one of many alternative plans for achieving the goal.

Machine discovery has generally been described as the search through a space of hypotheses for one that best fits a given collection of data. The task of this chapter was to make the collection of data seem less "given." Cast as a problem of selecting a potentially effective course of action in the service of an explicitly stated goal for knowledge, the question of what data to use (and in what form) becomes a central concern, not always part of the statement of the problem.

The many open questions and the plethora of on-line data, much of it symbolic, seems to make molecular biology an ideal domain for the testing of machine discovery tools. However, molecular biology offers too much of a good thing; the amount of data available is far too large for most existing machine learning methods, and is growing exponentially. The challenge posed by this domain to the machine learning and discovery community should now be clear. The task of making generalizable inferences about mappings between datasets, given a set of training examples, is not all there is to learning and discovery. A general theory of learning and discovery must also be able to figure out what mappings might be worth learning about, and what data might be relevant to learning them.

Notes

1. It is also worth noting that the metaphors used in science are not incidental to the research enterprise. They provide scaffolding for arguments, color the language used and guide inquiry (see, e.g., [Bloor, 1977; Hesse, 1966]).

2. It is always possible to write a computer program to make a particular choice. This decisionmaking is only meaningful if the program had alternative choices and a theoretically justifiable mechanism for making the choice. Arbitrary selection with backtracking in the case of errors, for example, is not an adequate mechanism for making complex choices.

References

Adams, M. D., Dubnick, M., Kerlavage, A. R., Moreno, R., Kelley, J. M., Utterback, T. R., Nagle, J. W., Fields, C., & Venter, J. C. (1992). Sequence Identification of 2,375 Brain Genes. *Nature*, 355(6361), 632-4.

Almuallim, H., & Dietterich, T. (1991). Learning with Many Irrelevant Features. In *Pro-

ceedings of Ninth National Conference on Artificial Intelligence, vol. 2 (pp. 547-552). Anahiem, CA: AAAI Press.

Altschul, S. F., Gish, W., Miller, W., Myers, E. W., & Lipman, D. J. (1990). A Basic Local Alignment Search Tool. *Journal of Molecular Biology,* 215, 403-310.

Anfinsen, C. B. (1973). Principles that Govern the Folding of Protein Chains. *Science,* 181, 223-230.

Arbola, E., Bernstein, F., Bryant, S., Koetzle, T., & Weng, J. (1987). Protein Data Bank. In F. Allen, G. Bergerhoff, & R. Sievers (Eds.), *Crystallographic Databases - Information Content, Software Systems, Scientific Applications* (pp. 107-132). Bonn: Data Commission of the International Union of Crystallography.

Berry, D., & Fristedt, B. (1985). *Bandit Problems: Sequential Allocation of Experiments.* NY, NY: Chapman and Hall.

Bloor, D. (1977). *Knowledge and Social Imagery.* London: Routledge and Kegan Paul.

Cheeseman, P., Kelly, J., Self, M., Stutz, J., Taylor, W., & Freeman, D. (1988). AutoClass: A Bayesian Classification System. In *Proceedings of Fifth International Conference on Machine Learning,* (pp. 54-64). Ann Arbor, MI: Morgan Kaufman.

Cheeseman, P., Stutz, J., Hanson, R., & Taylor, W. (1990). Autoclass III. Program available from NASA Ames Research Center: Research Institute for Advanced Computer Science.

Cohen, B., Presnell, S., & Cohen, F. (1990). Pattern Based Approaches to Protein Structure Prediction. *Methods in Enzymology,* (May 23, 1990).

Collins, G. (1987) *Plan Creation: Using Strategies as Blueprints.* PhD diss., Yale University, Report YALEU/CSD/RR#599.

Cox, M. T., & Ram, A. (1992). Multistrategy Learning with Introspective Meta-Explanations. In *Machine Learning: Proceedings of the Ninth International Conference,* (pp. 123-128). Aberdeen, Scotland: Morgan Kaufman

desJardins, M. (1992) *PAGODA: A Model for Autonomous Learning in Probabilistic Domains.* Ph.D. thesis, University of California, Berkeley, Computer Science Division (EECS), available as technical report UCB/CSD 92/678.

Dietterich, T. (1989). Limitations on Inductive Learning. In *Proceedings of Sixth International Workshop on Machine Learning,* (pp. 125-128). Ithaca, NY: Morgan Kaufman.

Fisher, D. (1987). Knowledge Acquisition Via Incremental Conceptual Clustering. *Machine Learning,* 2, 139-172.

Hesse, M. (1966). *Models and Analogies in Science.* South Bend, IN: University of Notre Dame Press.

Holder, L. B. (1991) *Maintaining the Utility of Learned Knowledge Using Model-based Adaptive Control.* PhD thesis, University of Illinois at Urbana-Champaign, Computer Science Department.

Holley, L. H., & Karplus, M. (1989). Protein Secondary Structure Prediction with a Neural Network. *Proceedings of the National Academy of Science USA* 86 (January), 152-156.

Horvitz, E., Cooper, G., & Heckerman, D. (1989). *Reflection and action under scarce resources: Theoretical Principles and Empirical Study* (Technical report no. KSL-89-1). Knowledge Systems Laboratory, Stanford Univ.

Hunter, L. (1989a) *Knowledge Acquisition Planning: Gaining Expertise Through Experience.* PhD thesis, Yale University, Available as YALEU/DCS/TR-678.

Hunter, L. (1989b). Knowledge Acquisition Planning: Results and Prospects. In *Proceedings of The Sixth International Workshop on Machine Learning,* (pp. 61-66). Ithaca, NY: Morgan Kaufman.

Hunter, L. (1990a). Knowledge Acquisition Planning for Inference from Large Datasets. In *Proceedings of The Twenty Third Annual Hawaii International Conference on System Sciences,* vol. 2, Software track (pp. 35-44). Kona, HI: IEEE Press.

Hunter, L. (1990b). Planning to Learn. In *Proceedings of The Twelveth Annual Conference of the Cogntive Science Society,* (pp. 26-34). Boston, MA: Erlbaum Associates

Hunter, L. (1992). Classifying for Prediction: A Multistrategy Approach to Predicting Protein Structure. In R. Michalski (Ed.), *Machine Learning IV: Multistrategy Learning* San Mateo, CA: Morgan Kaufman. Forthcoming.

Hunter, L., & States, D. (1991). Applying Bayesian Classification to Protein Structure. In *Proceedings of Seventh Conference on Artificial Intelligence Applications,* vol. 1 (pp. 10-16). Miami, FL: IEEE Computer Society Press.

Karp, P. (1991). *ASN.1 parser and Printer Documentation* (Technical report 5). National Center for Biotechnology Information.

Karplus, M., & Petsko, G. A. (1990). Molecular Dynamics Simulations in Biology. *Nature,* 347(October), 631-639.

Kass, A. (1990) *Developing Creative Hypotheses By Adapting Explanations.* Ph.D. thesis, Yale University, Available as Institute for the Learning Sciences Technical Report #6.

Langley, P., Simon, H. A., Bradshaw, G. L., & Zytkow, J. M. (1987). *Scientific Discovery: An Account of the Creative Process.* Cambridge, MA: MIT Press.

Lenat, D. (1979). On Automated Scientific Theory Formation: A Case Study Using the AM Program. In J. Hayes, D. Mitchie, & L. I. Mikulich (Eds.), *Machine Intelligence* New York, NY: Halstead Press.

Qian, N., & Sejnowski, T. (1988). Predicting the Secondary Structure of Globular Proteins Using Neural Network Models. *Journal of Molecular Biology,* 202, 865-884.

Quinlan, J. R. (1991). C4.5. Program available from the author: quinlan@cs.su.oz.au.

Ram, A. (1989) *Question-driven Understanding: An Integrated Theoryt of Story Understanding, Memory and Learning.* PhD thesis, Yale University, Report YALEU/CSD/RR#710.

Ram, A., & Hunter, L. (1992). A Goal-based Approach to Intelligent Information Retrieval. *Applied Intelligence,* to appear in vol. 2(1).

Rendell, L., & Cho, H. (1990). Empirical Learning as a Function of Concept Character. *Machine Learning,* 5(3), 267-298.

Rendell, L., & Seshu, R. (1990). Learning Hard Concepts through Constructive Induction: Framework and Rationale. *Computational Intelligence,* 6, 247-270.

Shrager, J., & Langley, P. (1990a). Computational Approaches to Scientific Discovery. In J. Shrager & P. Langley (Eds.), *Computational Models of Scientific Discovery and Theory Formation.* San Mateo, CA: Morgan Kaufmann.

Shrager, J., & Langley, P. (Ed.). (1990b). *Computational Models of Scientific Discovery and Theory Formation.* San Mateo, CA: Morgan Kaufmann.

Skolnick, J., & Kolinski, A. (1990). Simulations of the Folding of a Globular Protein. *Science,* 250(November 23), 1121-1125.

Tweney, R. D. (1990). Five Questions for Computationalists. In J. Shrager & P. Langley (Eds.), *Computational Models of Scientific Discovery and Theory Formation.* San Mateo, CA: Morgan Kaufmann.

Valient, L. (1984). A theory of the learnable. *Communications of the ACM* 27(11), 1134-1142.

Weinert, F. E. (1987). Introduction and Overview: Metacognition and Motivation as Determinants of Effective Learning and Understanding. In F. E. Weinert & R. H. Kluwe (Eds.), *Metacognition, Motivation and Understanding* Hillsdale, NJ: Lawrence Erlbaum Associates.

Zhang, X., Mesirov, J., & Waltz, D. (1992). Hybrid System for Protein Secondary Structure Prediction. *Journal of Molecular Biology*, 225, 1049-1063.

8

A Qualitative Biochemistry and Its Application to the Regulation of the Tryptophan Operon

Peter D. Karp

1 Introduction

This article is concerned with the general question of how to represent biological knowledge in computers such that it may be used in multiple problem solving tasks. In particular, I present a model of a bacterial gene regulation system that is used by a program that simulates gene regulation experiments, and by a second program that formulates hypotheses to account for errors in predicted experiment outcomes. This article focuses on the issues of representation and simulation; for more information on the hypothesis formation task see (Karp, 1989; Karp, 1990).

The bacterial gene regulation system of interest is the tryptophan *(trp)* operon of *E. coli* (Yanofsky, 1981). The genes that it contains code for enzymes that synthesize the amino acid tryptophan. My model of the trp operon—called GENSIM (genetic simulator)—describes the biochemical reactions that determine when the genes within the operon are expressed and when they are not, the reactions by which the genes direct the synthesis of the biosynthetic enzymes (transcription and translation), and the reactions catalyzed by these enzymes. Therefore my modeling techniques are specifically designed to represent enzymatically-catalyzed biochemical reactions whose substrates include macromolecules with complex internal structures, such as DNA and RNA. These techniques address such issues as: How might we represent the attributes and the structures of the objects that make up the trp operon? What is a suitable ontology for these objects—an appropriate level of abstraction at which to model them? How might we describe a gene regulation experiment, and how can we maintain a library of known experiments? How might we represent known biochemical reactions? How can we design a simulation program that predicts the outcome of a gene regulation experiment by correctly and efficiently simulating every reaction that occurs in that experiment, and only those reactions?

GENSIM embodies a *qualitative biochemistry* because it provides a framework for representing knowledge of biochemistry, and for performing qualitative simulations of biochemical systems. The specific features of this qualitative biochemistry are as follows.

I employ frames to represent biochemical objects that correspond to homogeneous populations of molecules. This representation describes the decomposition of complex objects into their component parts. I use frame knowledge bases to represent the objects present in the initial conditions of different experiments. Section 2 describes how instance frames represent chemical objects in simulation knowledge bases; Section 3 describes how class frames are used to represent general classes of biochemical objects, and presents a method for automatically instantiating these classes.

I employ frames called processes to represent biochemical reactions; reactions are arranged in an inheritance hierarchy and often inherit portions of their definitions from more general reaction classes. Section 4 discusses the GENSIM process knowledge base.

The GENSIM simulator uses information in the process knowledge base to determine what reactions occur among the objects in an experiment, and to predict what new objects will be present at the end of an experiment. Section 5 presents two different algorithms used by GENSIM to simulate process execution. Because biochemical reactions are probabilistic events that act on populations of molecules, when GENSIM simulates reactions it splits reacting populations of molecules into two subpopulations: those that do react and those that do not react (this operation is called *object forking*). Object forking is necessary to ensure simulation correctness, but it is a computationally expensive operation. Therefore, Section 5.5 presents methods for increasing simulation efficiency. For example, there are times when we can avoid object forking. Section 5.4 identifies a restriction on the syntax of biochemical reaction descriptions that is necessary to ensure simulation correctness.

Section 6 presents the results of several simulations that have been computed by GENSIM. Section 7 compares my model of the tryptophan operon to models of biochemical systems that have been created by other researchers.

I claim that the methods embodied by GENSIM are sufficient to represent qualitative scientific knowledge about objects and processes in molecular biology and biochemistry, such that the knowledge can be used to predict experimental outcomes, and such that other programs can reason about and modify this knowledge.

The mechanism of *transcription* will be used as an example throughout the remainder of this article. Transcription is a set of processes that are involved in the expression of genes, such as those within the trp operon. Transcription is somewhat analogous to copying a magnetic tape. An enzyme (called *RNA polymerase*) first attaches to the trp operon DNA at a *promoter* site, and then moves along the linear DNA strand, reading the message on the DNA and simultaneously synthesizing another long molecule called RNA that contains what is effectively a copy of the DNA message. When RNA polymerase recognizes a *terminator* DNA site, it releases both the DNA and RNA.

2 Representation of Biochemical Objects and Experiments

In the GENSIM framework, a user defines a gene regulation experiment by describing the objects present at the start of the experiment. I have used IntelliCorp's KEE frame knowledge representation system to represent all of GENSIM's knowledge (Kehler and Clemenson, 1984). To describe an experiment in which a particular strain of *E. coli* is grown in a particular medium, a user creates KEE instance frames that represent the bacterial DNA (wildtype or mutant), the proteins that are present within the cell (such as RNA polymerase and the regulatory trp-repressor protein), and small molecules that are present (such as glucose and tryptophan). Users do not create these frames "out of the blue," but by instantiating existing class frames (see Section 3).

In the ontology for this qualitative biochemistry, each "object" represents not a single molecule, but rather a homogeneous *population* of molecules. For example, all molecules of tryptophan in a experiment that are in a given state (such as those floating free in solution, as opposed to those bound to the trp-repressor protein) are represented by a single KEE frame. All molecules of tryptophan in a different single state (such as bound to the trp-repressor protein) are represented by a different single KEE frame.

These frames reside within a single KEE knowledge base for this particular experiment, called an *SKB* or *simulation knowledge base*. Other experiments could be described within other knowledge bases.[1] In the context of a

GENSIM simulation the SKB corresponds to the working memory of a production system. Since the facts it contains are represented using frames, all facts are literals and contain neither disjunction nor negation.

GENSIM does not represent temporal aspects of objects explicitly; the work of (Simmons and Mohammed, 1987) and (Williams, 1986) is relevant to this problem. GENSIM's task is to simulate the behavior of a biochemical system during a very short interval of time. Within such a short interval, new objects can come into existence because the creation of an arbitrarily small amount of an object is enough to change its concentration from zero to positive. However, we make the simplifying assumption that GENSIM simulations take place in a short enough interval that a population of molecules is never fully consumed; thus objects are never deleted from simulations. When an arbitrarily small amount of an object is destroyed, we cannot assume that its concentration has changed from positive to zero.

This assumption implies that the number of objects in a simulation must increase monotonically. In reality, biologists do perform experiments over intervals of time long enough that objects are completely consumed by reactions. However, this assumption simplifies the implementation of GENSIM significantly. Without it, GENSIM would have to reason about time and quantities. Yet the system is still able to make predictions for an interesting class of experiments. This assumption also simplified the implementation of the HYPGENE hypothesis formation program described in (Karp, 1989).

3 The Class Knowledge Base

GENSIM's *class knowledge base* (CKB) is a taxonomic hierarchy that describes classes of biochemical objects such as genes, proteins, and biochemical binding sites. The KB describes the properties and states of different classes of objects, and the decomposition of objects into their component parts. The CKB can be viewed as a library that records all known types of objects that could be present in experiments on the trp system (in practice, we have omitted many marginally relevant objects because bacteria are incredibly complex biochemical systems). Each object class is represented as a KEE class frame. The CKB is shown in Figures 1 and 2.

A central type of relationship among objects in this domain is the *containment* of one or more objects by a composite object. The example object structure in Figure 3 describes an experiment object that has two components: an enzyme (RNA-Polymerase) and a segment of DNA (Trp.Operon). The trp operon is in turn divided into a number of component regions. Several issues of interest arose in the representation of objects with complex component structures: how to represent different types of containment relationships, how to define classes of these objects, and how to instantiate these classes. The slots within the Trp.Operon class shown in

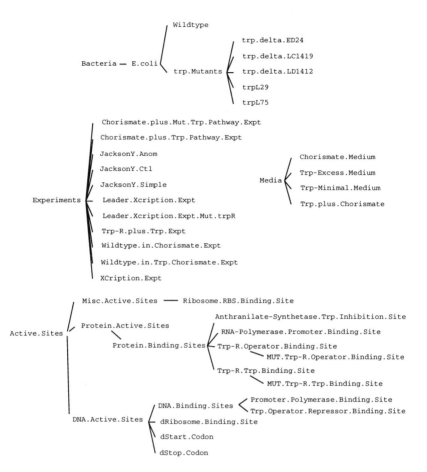

Figure 1. Object classes within the class knowledge base. The lines represent the class–subclass relation and connect object classes with the subclasses to their right. This figure shows objects that describe experiments, media, and bacterial strains, as well as active sites within proteins and DNA, and mutations.

Figure 4 are used to represent the component structure of this object (each slot has been truncated for brevity)

A user instantiates `Trp.Operon` by sending a `Create.Instance` message to the `Trp.Operon` frame. The LISP method invoked instantiates `Trp.Operon` and then recurses, sending the same message to each of the class frames listed in the `Component.Object.Classes` slot of `Trp.Operon`. Instantiating `Trp.Operon` itself involves creating a new instance of the class with a unique name, such as `Trp.Operon.1`. The

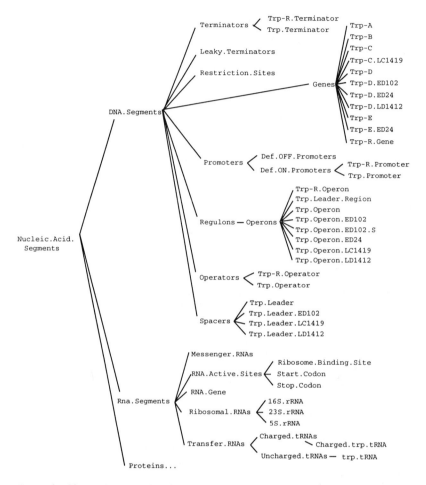

Figure 2. Object classes within the class knowledge base. This figure shows the "nucleic acid segment" objects that are used to describe various regions of DNA and RNA, as well as classes of proteins, which are shown in the continuation of figure 2 on the next page.

names of the created component objects are bound to the variables named in the `Component.Object.Bindings` slot of `Trp.Operon`.

A general problem that occurs when encoding class-level templates that are used to guide the creation of instance frames is how to encode relations among objects at the class level so that those relations can automatically be instantiated at the instance level. For example, every promoter object in an operon records what operator object in that operon controls the promoter. We wish to specify this general relationship in the operon class object, and

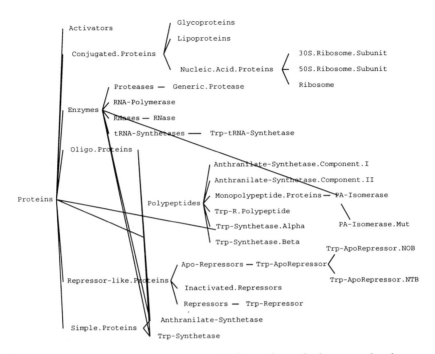

Figure 2 continued: The proteins are classified according to both structural and functional attributes.

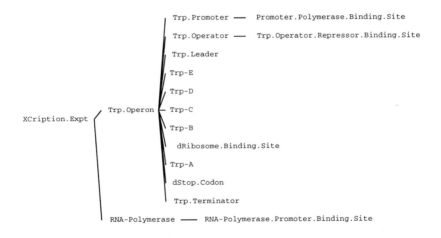

Figure 3. The objects in a transcription experiment. This experiment contains the trp operon and RNA polymerase, both of which have the internal structure shown. The lines in this figure represent the part-of relationship between a containing object and the parts to its right.

```
FRAME: Trp.Operon
         SLOT:                              VALUES
   Component.Object.Classes:     (Trp.Promoter Trp.Promoter
                                  Trp.Operator Trp.Leader
                                  dRibosome.Binding.Site
                                  Trp-E dStop.Codon ... )
   Component.Object.Bindings:    ($pro1 $pro2 $op1 $lead1
                                  $drbs1 $trpe $dsc1 ... )
   Component.Objects:
   Structural.Relations:         ((PUT.VALUE $Object
                                     'Regulated.Promoters $pro1)
                                   (PUT.VALUE $pro2
                                     'Regulator $op1))
```

Figure 4. The Trp.operon *class.*

whenever a user instantiates the operon class, the promoter within the newly instantiated operon should refer to the operator object within that operon object. GENSIM allows the user to list a set of variablized assertions within the Structural.Relations slot of an object class. These assertions are executed by Create.Instance using the variable bindings described in the previous paragraph. For example, the first PUT.VALUE expression asserts a relationship between a promoter and an object that regulates that promoter.

4 The Process Knowledge Base

The *process knowledge base* (*PKB*) describes the potential behaviors of the objects in the trp system such as biochemical binding, rearrangement, and dissociation events.

The sample process in Figure 5 describes a binding reaction between the activated trp-repressor protein and the trp operator. Table I gives the functions and predicates used in GENSIM processes. The process specifies that for any two molecules of type Trp.Operator and Trp-Repressor, if these objects contain complementary binding sites, and if these sites are empty and contain no mutations that interfere with this binding reaction, then new instances of these objects should be created and bound together as a new object.

Users represent processes using KEE frames. A process definition specifies actions that will be taken (listed in the Effects slot of the process) if certain conditions hold (listed in the Preconditions slot). In addition, since processes operate on objects, the Parameter.Object.Classes slot specifies the types of objects on which a process acts. Processes are executed by a *process interpreter*. The interpreter activates a process when at least one object is present from each class in the parameter-object classes of the process. The Parameter.Objects slot lists variables that are bound to the actual objects with which a process has been activated. In addition, an arbi-

```
Parameter.Object.Classes: Trp.Repressor Trp.Operator
Parameter.Objects:              $A              $B
Preconditions:  Check that $B contains an active site that
                interacts with objects of $A's type.
                [EXISTS $Bsite
                   (AND
                       (IS.PART.R $Bsite $B)
                       (OBJECT.EXISTS $Bsite Active.Sites)
                       (EXISTS $site.interaction.class
                           (AND
                               (MEMBER $site.interaction.class
                                   (GET.VALUES $Bsite
                                       Potential.Interacting.Objects))
                                   (OBJECT.EXISTS $A
                                       $site.interaction.class]
                Check that $Bsite is not occupied.
                [NOT (EXISTS $obj
                           (AND
                               (MEMBER $obj
                                   (GET.VALUES $Bsite
                                       Object.Interacting.With.Site))
                                   (OBJECT.EXISTS $obj
                                   (GET.VALUE $Bsite
                                       Potential.Interacting.Objects]
                Check that $Bsite does not contain a
                mutation that disables the current reaction.
                [NOT (EXISTS $mutation
                           (AND (IS.PART $mutation $Bsite)
                                (OBJECT.EXISTS $mutation
                                 Mutations)
                                (MEMBER $Current.Process
                                 (GET.VALUES $mutation
                                     Processes.Disabled]
Effects:        Create a new object that contains $A
                and $B as parts.
                (BINDV $Complex
                   (CREATE.COMPLEX RepOp.Complexes
                       (LIST $A $B) RBOUND))
                Record that $A is interacting with $Bsite.
                (PUT.VALUE $Bsite
                   Interacting.With.Site $A))
                Record that the promoters controlled by $B
                are no longer able to bind RNA Polymerase.
                (PUT.VALUE (GET.VALUE $B
                               Promoters.Controlled)
                   Receptive.To.Polymerase NO)
```

Figure 5. The definition of the process Trp-Repressor.Binds.Operator. *This process describes the binding of the activated trp-repressor protein to the trp operator. Comments that explain the process are given in italics.*

Predicate or Function	*Meaning*
(OBJECT.EXISTS X Y)	Object X exists within class Y
(IS.PART X Y)	Object X is part of object Y
(MEMB X Y)	Atom X is an element of list Y
(GET.VALUES X Y)	The value of slot X of object Y
(BINDV $X Y)	Binds variable $X to the value Y
(CREATE.COMPLEX X Y)	Creates an object of type X containing the objects in list Y as parts
(COPY.STRUCTURE X)	Creates a copy of object X
(PUT.VALUE X Y Z)	Stores Z into slot X of object Y
(EXISTS $X Y)	True if expression Y is true for one binding of $X
(FORALL $X Y)	True if expression Y is true for all bindings of $X

Table I. The predicates and functions used within GENSIM process definitions. OB-
JECT.EXISTS, IS.PART, *and* MEMB *are predicates. The symbols* AND, OR, *and* NOT
may also be used, and have their standard logical meanings.

trary list of variable bindings may be given in the Bindings slot.

Processes possess an additional type of precondition called Efficien-
cy.Preconditions. These preconditions prevent process invocations
that, although technically correct, are uninteresting. For example, the trp-repressor protein binds to the operator site at the start of the trp operon. It can
bind there during almost any of the 17 intermediate steps of the transcription
process that GENSIM generates to model the progression of RNA polymerase
along the DNA. These intermediate transcription-elongation complexes,
however, have no special functionality when bound to the repressor, and are
thus uninteresting. The Efficiency.Preconditions are used to prevent GENSIM from simulating these reactions—thereby increasing simulation
speed—and because expert biologists usually ignore these reactions. But by
putting these preconditions in a special slot, we make it easy to ignore them
during tasks such as hypothesis formation.

The process frames within the PKB are structured as an inheritance hierarchy, part of which is shown in Figure 6. At the top level is a general template for all processes. Its children are templates that provide descriptions of
general classes of events, such as chemical-binding and enzymatic-reaction
processes. In turn, the children of these templates either describe actual processes (such as the bindings of particular species of molecules), or define important subclasses of processes. An example of such a subclass is Mutual-
ly.Exclusive.Binding. This template defines preconditions for a
subclass of binding processes: for object A to bind to B, it cannot be the case

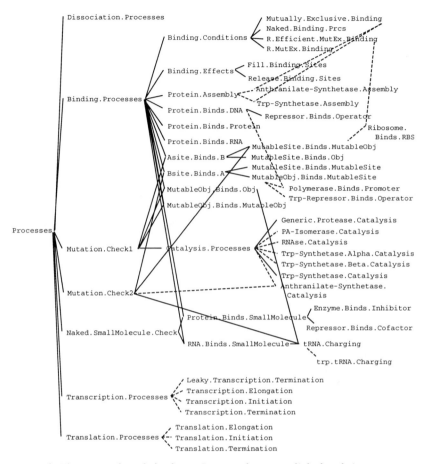

Figure 6. The process knowledge base. Process classes are linked to their super-classes by solid lines; executable process instances are linked to the classes of which they are members by dashed lines.

that A is already bound to an object of class B, or that B is already bound to an object of class A. A particular process instance can inherit slots from one or more template processes. For example, Trp-Repressor.Binds.Trp inherits most of its definition from the Repressor.Binds.Cofactor template, which specifies the behavior of the class of all repressor proteins. Trp-Repressor.Binds.Trp inherits additional preconditions from the process Mutually.Exclusive.Binding. Process classes often provide enough of the definition of a process instance that only the Parameter.Object.Classes slot must be modified in the instance, to define the actual classes of objects to which the process pertains.

I have created special machinery to facilitate the use of inheritance to modify process templates. Process preconditions, bindings, and effects are actually represented by *pairs* of slots—called for example, Effects.M and Effects.A. The values of the slot Effects.M (*main*) are inherited using KEE's *override* inheritance—new values for this slot override previous values. Values of Effects.A (*additional*) are inherited using *union* inheritance—new values for this slot are unioned with the previous values. The process interpreter executes the effects listed in both of these slots. The pairs of slots for preconditions and bindings are defined analogously.

This use of inheritance to define processes is similar to that used in object-oriented programming (OOP) systems (Goldberg and Robson, 1983; Stefik and Bobrow, 1986) (although GENSIM's process interpreter does not employ the message-sending control structure of OOP). Thus, our approach reaps many of the same benefits as OOP systems, such as facilitating the definition of new processes and the maintenance of existing processes. GENSIM's use of inheritance is novel in two ways. First is the use of inheritance in this particular type of language—a production-rule—like process-description language. Because GENSIM processes are so similar to the production rules used in expert systems, inheritance probably could be used in this way as a software-engineering tool in the construction of expert systems. The second novel aspect of this use of inheritance is the manner in which an individual process is dissected into pieces (preconditions, effects, parameter objects, bindings) that can be inherited and modified as required. OOP systems usually treat procedures as indivisible units that can only have additional code wrapped around them, rather than having their internals altered as desired.

The definition of a process inheritance hierarchy should have benefits in addition to those already defined. This approach should facilitate the definition of new processes by hypothesis formation programs such as HYPGENE. These programs could postulate new processes by instantiating process templates (see (Karp, 1989) for more details).

4.1 Alternative Reaction Representations

At least two other approaches could be used to represent biochemical reactions. One approach would eschew the use of processes, and would represent the behaviors of an object using slots within that object. For example, for an object O, one slot might list all objects that O can react with, and other slots might list other objects that inhibit or activate these reactions. Another slot might list the products of the reactions. This approach is problematic in several ways. First, a given object might participate in several reactions, each of which could involve different other reactants, and produce different products. Thus, the slot values must be encoded in a way that does not lose information about which reactants are associated with which products, activators, and inhibitors. Second, if five objects participate in a given reaction, presumably each object must describe the same reactants, products, activators, inhibitors, and so on, which is highly redundant. Third, as GENSIM processes illustrate, it usually is not sufficient simply to list the activators and inhibitors of a reaction; we usually must test for particular properties of these objects using complicated predicate-calculus formulae. Without the language of predicate calculus we could not express preconditions such as: the trp-repressor protein binds to the trp-operator region only if a specific binding site within the trp repressor is occupied by tryptophan. In summary, when reactions involve several reactants, it is clearer and more efficient to separate process definitions from object definitions. And when reactions involve complex preconditions and effects—as biochemical reactions often do—a special language is required to express this complexity.

A second approach would use processes that are somewhat more general than those most often used by GENSIM (in fact, GENSIM's representation of mutations uses this approach). If we were to model three different repressible operons using GENSIM—say, the trp, lac, and phe operons—we would have to create separate GENSIM processes to describe the binding of the trp-repressor to the trp operator, the lac-repressor to the lac operator, and the phe-repressor to the phe operator. GENSIM allows these processes to be constructed using inheritance from the general `Repressor.Binds.Operator` process, but we still might argue that this approach creates an excessive number of processes. The alternative would be to use a single general process, such as `Repressor.Binds.Operator`, to define a slot within each repressor object that specifies the operator(s) to which the repressor can bind, and to reference this slot from the `Repressor.Binds.Operator` process. Although this approach is considerably more compact, it has two disadvantages. First, it would force a proliferation of the slots that encode these object interactions—every general process (such as `Repressor.Binds.Operator`) would refer to such a slot. Second, this approach blurs the clean separation between structure and behavior that is inherent in the CKB and the PKB. The new specificity slot acts much like a process precondition, yet it resides within an object. If object behaviors are defined using processes only we have much more modular descriptions that will be easier to maintain and extend.

5   The Process Interpreter

GENSIM processes bear significant similarity to production rules, and the program that interprets processes is similar to a production system. The process interpreter uses processes to detect interactions among objects that exist in the current simulation, and computes the effects of these interactions. This section describes how the process interpreter activates and executes processes, and manages the existence of objects during a simulation. Since these is-

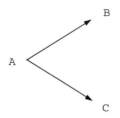

Figure 7. A simple reaction network in which an object A can cause two reactions; one produces B and the other produces C.

sues are so closely intertwined, this section alternates between the two. It begins with a brief description of object management, then presents a detailed description of process execution. It finishes by presenting points related to both issues.

Before proceeding, let us resolve the potential ambiguity of the term *process instance*. I use this term to mean the execution of a process on a given set of objects—an instance of process execution. Because processes are defined hierarchically in a KEE KB, the KB contains both class process frames and instance process frames; I use the term *leaf process* to refer to instance process frames.

5.1 Object Management

At least two possible approaches to the management of objects are conceivable in GENSIM. The term *object management* refers to the manner in which operations on objects (such as creation, deletion, and modification) are implemented. Consider the simple reactions in Figure 7, in which an object A is acted on by two processes: one converts A to object B, the other converts A to object C. A simulator might model the first reaction in one of two ways: it might modify A directly to produce B, or it might copy A to a new object, and then modify that new object to produce B.

GENSIM should produce correct and complete predictions: it must predict all and only all the correct reactions. Predictions should not depend on the order in which processes are executed; for example, care must be taken that the execution of the first reaction in Figure 7 does not prevent execution of the other by removing the A object, because both reactions would occur to some degree. In general, most chemical processes are probabilistic events that act on populations of molecules. Since objects A, B, and C represent populations of molecules, and reactions occur at some finite *rate*, it is likely that, at some time, members of all populations exist. Thus, when a biochemical reaction converts A to B, all members of population A do not disappear instantaneously.

We conclude that GENSIM should not destroy objects or modify their properties, because to do so would allow the possibility that the system would overlook some reaction. Rather than modifying A directly to create B, GEN-SIM copies A and modifies the copy to produce B. I call this operation *object forking*. The assumption that object populations are never fully consumed was discussed in Section 3.

This discussion also implies that, to predict both *what* reactions occur, and the *rates* of these reactions, requires a two-stage computation (GENSIM currently performs only the first stage):

1) Determine the complete set of reactions that will occur—that is, the complete set of objects that will be created and the set of processes that will fire. Forbus calls this task computing the "process and view structures" (Forbus, 1986).

2) Use information about reaction rates and molecular concentrations to compute *how much* of each object population forms. Forbus calls this task "resolving influences" (Forbus, 1986).

The intuition here is that to predict the rate of a reaction R that consumes reactants $I_1, \ldots, I_n$, we must know about all other reactions in which each I_i takes part, so that we can compute the relative rates of these competing reactions.

Most other qualitative-reasoning researchers have not used object forking. One reason for this may be that in their domains, objects do not represent populations of molecules, some of which probabilistically change to another state—they represent individual objects that change completely. Simmons and Mohammed (Simmons and Mohammed, 1987) use an explicit model of time to represent object properties as histories, so in effect, different versions of different objects exist at different points in time due to the different values their properties take on at these different points in time. The biochemistry domain does not allow this approach because the populations of molecules we model often coexist at a single time.

5.2 Reference Patching

One complication that arises during object forking is that the component objects of a complex object may refer to one another, and these references must be altered during the copy operation. This procedure is called *reference patching*. For example, a component of the `Trp.Operon` object—`Promoter.1`—contains a slot `Regulator` with value `Operator.1`. This slot indicates what operator object controls this promoter. The value of this slot must be altered in the object to which `Promoter.1` is copied, to name the object to which `Operator.1` is copied, since a promoter is regulated by only the operator in the same operon object.

Another complication is that there are some object slots for which reference patching should not be performed, such as slots that do not contain the names of objects. Thus, each slot in the system is described by a special frame that describes whether or not reference patching should be performed for that slot.

5.3 Implementation of the Process Interpreter

I constructed two different implementations of the process interpreter. The first uses a brute-force algorithm and is slow. It iterates through all processes in the PKB, and searches for objects in the simulation that are members of the parameter object classes of the current process. It then determines which combinations of these objects satisfy the preconditions of the process, and executes the effects of such processes, until no new reactions are detected. More precisely, the first interpreter cycles through the following steps until no new processes can be activated in Step 2.

1) **Process selection:** Select a member P from the set of all leaf processes that exist in the process knowledge base.

2) **Process activation (binding of processes to objects):** Consider each object class C_k, $k=1...N$ listed in the `Parameter.Object.Classes` of P. Let $\Im_k$ be the set of object instances within class C_k. If every set $\Im_k$ is nonempty, then create a new set A containing all possible tuples of the elements of each $\Im_k$. Each tuple contains an element of $\Im_1$, an element of $\Im_2$, and so on including an element of $\Im_N$. The set A is the set of possible bindings of the parameter-object variables of P, and is a list of all possible interactions of objects due to P. If any $\Im_k$ is empty, no activations of this process are generated.

3) **Filter process activations:** Remove from A every set of variable bindings for which process P has already been activated with that set of bindings in this simulation. Because objects never change, and because process preconditions can refer only to objects in the parameter objects of a process, the truth or falsity of the preconditions of a process as applied to a given set of objects will never change. Thus, it is never necessary to activate a process more than once on a given set of parameter objects.

4) **Process execution:** For each A_j remaining in A:
   a) Bind the variables in the `Parameter.Objects` slot of P to the objects in A_j
   b) Evaluate the variable bindings in the `Bindings` slot of P
   c) Evaluate the `Preconditions` of P. IF any are false, THEN continue to the next A_j; ELSE
   d) Execute the `Effects` of P

This approach is inefficient in two ways:

1) It repeatedly examines every process, even for processes for which no ob-

jects exist in some parameter-object class of the process

2) It repeatedly generates process activations that have been considered previously, which must be filtered out in Step 3 (at a cost) to avoid the larger cost of reevaluating the process preconditions.

The cost of these inefficiencies grows as more objects and processes exist in a simulation.

To improve what is essentially a generate-and-test algorithm, we move part of the test inside the generator. New process activations are generated only when the process interpreter first starts running, and when new objects are created. A given set of object bindings is never generated more than once for a process.

The second algorithm maintains two data structures. The first is the *process-activation queue*, which contains process variable-binding tuples—the variable bindings for which each process has not yet been executed. The interpreter repeatedly pops entries lists off this queue and executes the given process with the given variable bindings.

The second data structure is used to determine what process activations should be created when a new object is created. It is called the *live-objects list* and consists of a list of records of the form

$$(C\ (P_1 \ldots P_n)\ (O_1 \ldots O_n))$$

where

- C is the name of a class of objects that appears in the `Parameter.Object.Classes` slot of at least one process

- $(P_1 \ldots P_n)$ is the set of processes that contain C in their `Parameter.Object.Classes` slot—the processes that describe reactions involving this class of object

- $(O_1 \ldots O_n)$ is the list of objects within class C that exist in the simulation

When a new object O is created by the execution of a process, the following actions are taken:

1. Let C be the class of O.

2. Find the set $\mathfrak{R}$ of all records in the live-objects list such that record R_i describes a class that is equal to or a superclass of C. If none exist, exit.

3. Add O to the object list of each record in $\mathfrak{R}$.

4. For each R_i in $\mathfrak{R}$ do

    For each process P_j in R_i do

        Compute the new variable bindings for P_j. Imagine that P_j operates on two objects—one of class C, the other of class D. The activations of P_j consist of O paired with every object from class D

(as listed in the live-objects record for D). Append these activations to the process-activation queue.

Two properties of this approach are worth noting. First, new process activations are generated only when new objects are created. This approach is correct because new process activations must include at least one new object—since old objects are never modified, a group of old objects will never spontaneously activate an existing process that had not been activated previously. Similarly, because objects are forked and not deleted, process activations never have to be removed from the process-activation list.

An additional optimization is possible using a slightly different data structure. It may be the case that the interpreter could prove that an existing object O will always prevent process P from firing, because O will always cause a precondition of P to be violated (GENSIM could prove this by *partially evaluating* the preconditions of the process (Hsu, 1988)). In this case, the interpreter should never generate an activation of P that includes O. This information could be used in a similar approach that stored live objects within a class on a per-process basis, rather than with every process that acts on the class (the latter is done in the current live-objects structure). Objects would be removed from the list for a process when GENSIM proved that they could not fire that process.

5.4 A Restriction on Process Preconditions

The preceding approach to object management and process execution requires that we impose a restriction on the syntax of process preconditions to guarantee the correctness of our simulations. This restriction has an interesting biochemical interpretation.

The restriction is that a precondition of a process P may not check for the existence or nonexistence of an object D_1 unless D_1 either is a parameter object of P, or is part of an object that is a parameter object of P. For example, a process P_1 that describes the binding of object A_1 to B_1 may not check whether no objects exist in the simulation that belong to class D. Therefore, the following precondition is forbidden for process P:

```
(NOT (EXISTS $X (OBJECT.EXISTS $X D)))
```

But P may, however, check whether no objects of class D exist in the simulation as parts of B_1:

```
(NOT (EXISTS $X (AND (OBJECT.EXISTS $X D)
(IS.PART $X B1))))
```

Without this restriction the correctness of simulations is no longer guaranteed, because the truth of the shorter precondition will depend on *when* the process interpreter evaluates that precondition (which depends on when process P is executed). If evaluation occurs when no objects of type D exist, then the precondition will be true. But if it occurs after the execution of another process P_2 that creates an object of type D, then the precondition will be false. Thus, in this example the relative execution times of processes P_1 and P_2 (which times are undefined in GENSIM simulations because GENSIM has no model of time and assumes all reactions occur in a very brief interval) determines the truth of the precondition.

The value of the restriction is that by stipulating that D_1 must be part of B_1 it ensures that D_1 must exist at the time P_1 is activated. The second algorithm activates P_1 when, and only when, all of the parameter objects of P_1 exist. So, if P_2 created B_1, P_2 must have executed before P_1. Furthermore, given the framework of object forking, once created, B_1 cannot be modified. Thus, there is no possible ambiguity in the evaluation of the preconditions of P_1.

An important question to ask is: does this restriction have reasonable semantics in the biochemistry domain? The answer is yes. In general, biochemical reactions occur when a set of reactants is present in solution, and when each of the reactants is in a required state. Process preconditions examine the states of the reactants. In general, the only way one molecule can influence the state of another molecule is by physically attaching to the other molecule and altering its conformation. That is, there is no way for A_1 and B_1 to magically sense the presence or absence of D_1 in solution. To affect the reaction, D_1 must bind to A_1 or B_1 to alter that object's state, in which case D_1 is a reactant in this reaction, and should therefore be listed as a parameter object of the process. Thus, it makes no biochemical sense to write the type of precondition that we prohibit.

5.5 Optimizations

The reason we employ object forking is that this approach to managing simulation objects meets the correctness and completeness criteria described in Section 5.1. A drawback of object forking is that in the trp operon simulations are slower by roughly a factor of 20 than are simulations in which objects are modified directly. Object forking increases the computational resources required for simulation of the trp operon because some processes within this system generate many complex objects. During execution of the transcription process, for example, each movement of RNA polymerase along a DNA strand is accomplished by a different activation of a single process that generates a new copy of the transcription-elongation complex that contains DNA, mRNA, and RNA polymerase (each of which is a complex object). Object forking is costly both because the KEE frames that represent objects are expensive to create, and because the large numbers of created objects can later cause large numbers of additional reactions. Here we discuss methods for increasing the speed of simulations.

5.5.1 Avoidance of Object Forking. In the biochemical domain there is a specific case in which objects can be modified directly to avoid the cost of forking the object, without sacrificing the correctness of the simulation. The need to copy-then-modify objects rather than to modify them directly arose from the possibility that multiple processes might act on the original object. Modifying the original object could cause some of its behaviors to go undetected. However, if inspection of the PKB reveals that only a single process acts on a given object class (in which case the object class would be named in the `Parameter.Object.Classes` slot of a single process), the preceding consideration would appear to be nullified. Unfortunately, it is not completely nullified, because multiple activations of the process could act on the same object. For example, if we found that the only process acting on the class `RNA-Polymerase` is the `Polymerase.Binds.Promoter` process, the object `RNA-Polymerase.1` still could bind to two different instances of `Trp.Promoter`, such as `Trp.Promoter.1` and `Trp.Promoter.2`. Thus, we cannot avoid forking `RNA-Polymerase.1`. We can, however, avoid copy-then-modify when only a *single* known process acts on a given object class, and that process has only *one* parameter object. For example, the transcription-elongation process acts on a single `Transcription.Elongation.Complex` object (whose components are the DNA, enzyme, and RNA described earlier). This optimization has not been implemented within GENSIM.

Note that this optimization may cause problems for a program that must analyze a simulation-dependency trace, such as a hypothesis formation program. Such a program might try to understand why a final set of objects are predicted to be present in a given experiment by inspecting the intermediate objects that reacted to form those final objects. It is just those intermediates that this optimization destroys.

5.5.2 Object Merging. A procedure called *object merging* is used to detect when two different processes independently create the same object. When this event is detected, only one of the object descriptions is retained. This procedure produces a small economy by eliminating redundant storage of the merged objects. It produces a much larger savings by preventing processes from being invoked by the redundant objects, and by preventing the creation of the additional redundant objects that these duplicate reactions would produce.

5.5.3 Sharing Object Descriptions with an ATMS. It is possible to use an ATMS (DeKleer, 1986) to reduce the storage consumed by object forking. This approach was inspired by the ATMS property of allowing efficient exploration of alternative decisions through storing rather than recomputing elements of the problem-solving state that the alternatives share. For example, the ATMS has been used previously in qualitative physics to represent envisionments more efficiently (Forbus, 1984; deKleer and Brown, 1984). My hope was that an ATMS could be used in a similar way to provide efficient storage of different objects that have a large amount of common structure.

This use of the ATMS is novel because I propose using the ATMS to represent more efficiently common aspects of similar objects that coexist within a *single context* of the simulation. Previously, it has been used to represent more efficiently common aspects of similar objects that exist in *alternative* predictions of the state of the physical system (envisionments).

IntelliCorp's KEE contains an ATMS implementation (Intellicorp, 1986; Morris and Nado, 1986). In the following paragraphs, I describe this ATMS implementation, sketch how it might be used to solve this problem, discuss why this approach will fail, and then examine additional ATMS functionality that will solve the problem.

KEE's ATMS forms the basis for a facility called *KEEworlds*, which is well integrated with KEE's frame representation system. By default, any modification to a KEE frame (e.g. of a slot value) affects the *background* (the root world), and all slot-value queries access the background. New worlds are defined as children of the background and/or existing worlds. Users may explicitly direct assertions and queries to the background or to any existing world. By default, any fact true in the parent of a world W is also true in W. But W may override *some* of the facts defined in its parents: the values of existing slots in existing frames may be modified arbitrarily, however, it is possible to create, delete, or rename both frames and slots in the background only.

Figure 8 shows how the KEEworlds facility could be used to implement object forking. The background and the worlds W_1 and W_2 represent three consecutive states of the transcription process discussed earlier. In this process, a transcription-elongation complex object contains two other objects: an RNA whose length grows as the process executes repeatedly, and a DNA. Rather than create new versions of the elongation complex object for every step, the KEEworlds facility allows the core descriptions of each object to be inherited by the KEEworlds facility with only the changes to each object recorded explicitly, as shown in Figure 8. The substructure of the RNA.1 object changes the length of the RNA increases, and new objects A.1 and B.1 are created.[2]

The limitation of this mechanism arises in the following situation. Imagine the existence of a biological process that specifies that two RNA objects may bind together when they are components of a transcription-elongation complex. If this reaction were to occur between the two versions of the RNA.1 object in worlds W_1 and W_2, we would create a new world W_3 with parents W_1 and W_2. W_2 would inherit descriptions of RNA.1 from both W_1 and W_2. The problem is that the new world W_3 would contain only a single version of RNA.1, whose properties would result from merging the RNA.1 objects from W_1 and W_2. Chemically, two distinct RNA objects must exist in W_3, but KEE's approach to world inheritance causes the descriptions of

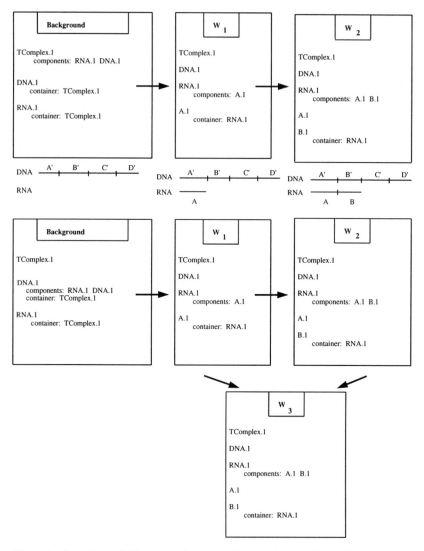

Figure 8. Use of an ATMS to share the descriptions of similar objects during a simulation.

RNA.1 from W_1 and W_2 to be merged, because both objects have the same name. Because object names are both the basis for sharing information between worlds and the source of the merging problem, the KEEworlds implementation is not able to reduce the space required to represent similar objects.

This limitation would not exist in a worlds mechanism that had the additional functionality of being able to rename objects from one world to another. That is, if we were able to rename RNA.1 to RNA.2 within W_2, no merging of the two RNA objects would occur in the child world W_3. GENSIM does not use this technique because we lack such an ATMS. (In KEEworlds, frames can be renamed only in the background.)

Other researchers employ an ATMS, but for different purposes: Forbus uses it to represent alternative envisionments more efficiently (Forbus, 1986), and Simmons and Mohammed use it to represent causal dependencies for later analysis by their diagnostic system (Simmons and Mohammed, 1987).

6 GENSIM Trials

I tested the GENSIM program in a number of trial runs. In each trial I used the program to predict the outcome of a different biological experiment. This section describes each trial by stating what objects were present in the initial conditions of the experiment whose outcome GENSIM predicts, and what reactions and new objects were predicted by GENSIM. For some trials, I show the internal structures of objects in the initial conditions or the prediction.

6.1 The Trp Biosynthetic Pathway

This simple trial models the trp biosynthetic pathway, in which a set of enzymes convert chorismate to tryptophan (the current model ignores the reactant serine). The initial conditions of the experiment are shown in Figure 9, the predicted outcome in Figure 10. Figure 11 shows the internal structure of every object in the prediction. GENSIM's prediction is correct in that it omits no reactions that should occur, it includes all reactions that do occur, and the objects produced by each reaction have the predicted parts and properties.

6.2 The Trp Biosynthetic Pathway with a Mutant Enzyme

This trial is a variation of the previous trial. In this trial, the enzyme tryptophan synthetase contains a mutation that prevents it from catalyzing the reaction that converts InGP to tryptophan. The mutation is represented as an object that is part of the tryptophan-synthetase object. GENSIM correctly predicts that the last two (rightmost) reactions in Figure 10 do not occur.

6.3 Transcription of the Trp Leader Region

The leader-region transcription trial focuses on another subset of the overall trp system: the transcription of DNA. Figure 12 shows the objects in the initial conditions of this experiment, which include a truncated version of the trp operon called Trp.Leader.Region.1 (I removed all the genes in the operon to make this trial easier to describe), the enzyme RNA polymerase, the trp-aporepressor protein, and tryptophan. The prediction generated by

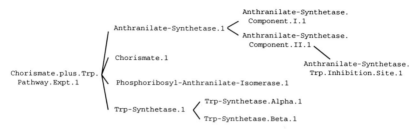

Figure 9. *The initial conditions of the trp biosynthetic-pathway experiment. Every object in this figure contains the objects to its right as parts. For example, the* Trp-Synthetase.1 *enzyme has two parts: the alpha and beta subunits of the protein. The experiment as a whole is represented by the object* Chorismate.plus.Trp.-Pathway.Expt.1, *which contains all the objects in the experiment as parts.*

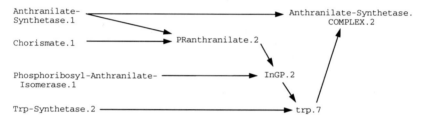

Figure 10. *The predicted outcome of the trp biosynthetic-pathway experiment. The lines in this figure indicate the process firings whereby objects react to create the objects to their right. For example,* Trp-Synthetase.2 *reacts with* InGP.2 *to form* trp.7.

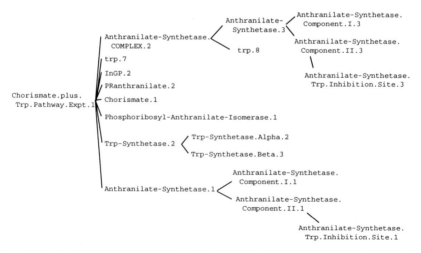

Figure 11. *The internal structures of the objects predicted to be present at the end of the trp biosynthetic-pathway experiment.*

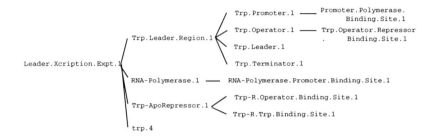

Figure 12. The objects in the initial conditions of the leader-region—transcription experiment.

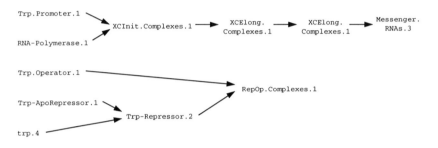

Figure 13. The outcome of the leader-region transcription experiment that was predicted by GENSIM.

GENSIM is shown in Figure 13. This prediction is correct. The two sequences of reactions in this experiment fork the population of trp operon leader-region DNA into two classes: those whose operator regions bind to the activated repressor protein Trp-Repressor.2, and those whose promoters bind to RNA-Polymerase.1 and undergo transcription to produce a messenger RNA.[3] The figures do not name Trp.Leader.1 as participating in these reactions, but rather name the components of the operon that react: the promoter Trp.Promoter.1 and the operator Trp.Operator.1.

The internal structure of one of the transcription-elongation complexes is shown in Figure 14. A transcription-elongation complex contains RNA polymerase, the DNA that RNA polymerase is transcribing, and the mRNA that RNA polymerase has synthesized thus far. The number of segments (parts) within the mRNA reflects the length of DNA that RNA polymerase has traversed. Since the mRNA contains two segments, we can infer that RNA polymerase traveled two segments along the DNA to produce this transcription-elongation complex. Figure 15 shows the internal structures of every object in this experiment.

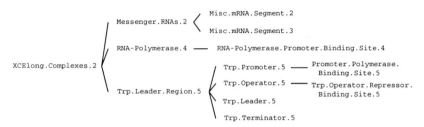

Figure 14. The internal structure of a transcription-elongation complex.

6.4 The Full Trp System

This trial simulates the entire trp system as it was known in the late 1960s. Figure 16 shows the initial conditions of this experiment. GENSIM's prediction is shown in Figures 17 and 18. Figure 17 shows the transcription of the trp operon by RNA polymerase, which yields a free mRNA (`Messenger.RNAs.18`). Some of this mRNA is degraded into its constituent bases by the enzyme `RNase.1`. The mRNA also reacts with ribosomes, as shown in Figure 18. `Messenger.RNAs.18` contains five ribosome-binding sites, including `Ribosome.Binding.Site.47`.[4] Each binding site attracts a ribosome, which translates the five different regions of mRNA into polypeptides such as `Trp-Synthetase.Beta.1` Some of these polypeptides bind together to form larger, functional proteins, such as `Trp-Synthetase.1`.

The enzymes produced from translation of the trp-operon mRNA react with chorismate to carry out the steps in the trp pathway. The trp thus produced enters into several reactions: It binds to and inhibits anthranilate synthetase, and it activates the trp aporepressor protein (the latter complex then binds to the trp operator). Finally, the trp-tRNA-synthetase enzyme catalyzes the binding of tRNA[trp] and trp to form charged tRNA[trp] (which is used in all protein synthesis).

Generation of this prediction required approximately 70 minutes of Dorado (Xerox 1132 LISP machine) CPU time. The prediction contained a total of 1050 objects (including components).

7 Related Work

Here I review the work of other AI researchers who have created models of biochemical systems, comparing and contrasting their techniques with those described in this article:

• Meyers' model of the life cycle of Lambda phage (Meyers, 1984)

• Round's model of the E. coli trp operon (Round, 1987)

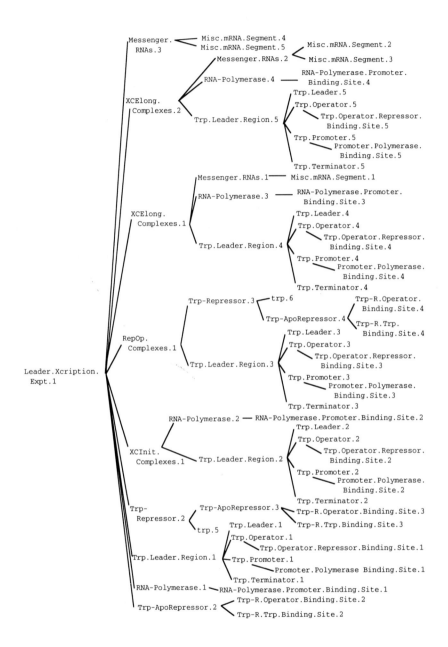

Figure 15. The objects in the predicted outcome of the leader-region-transcription experiment.

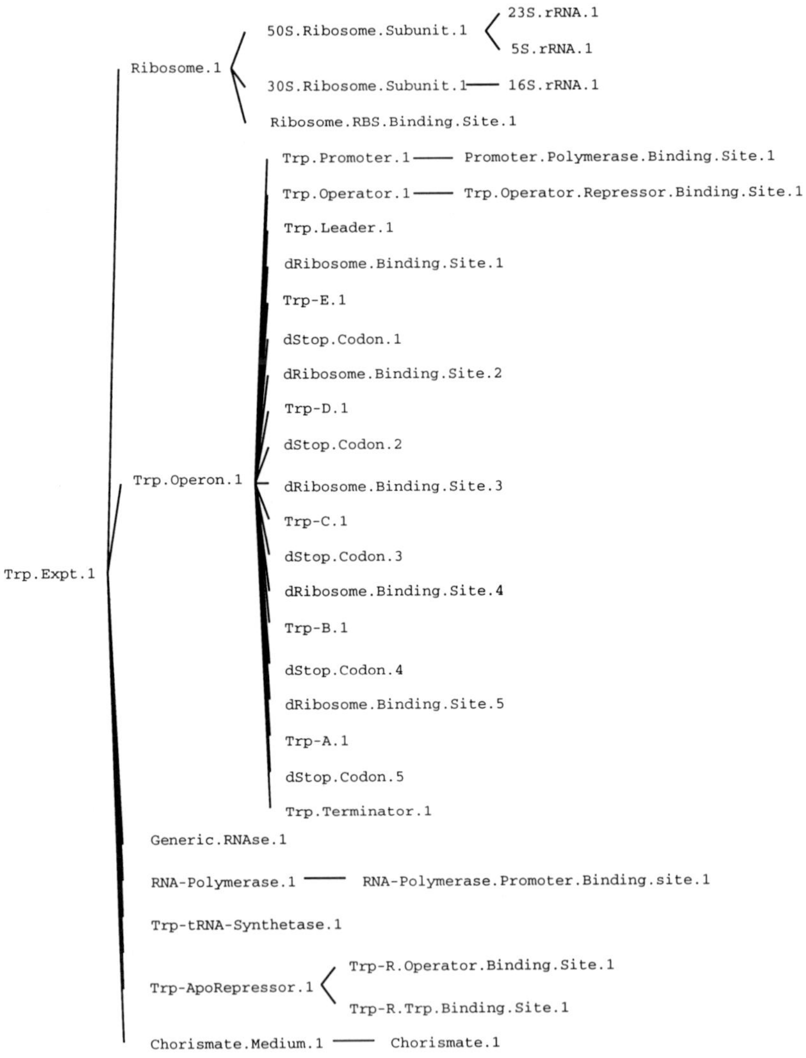

```
                                                    ┌── 23S.rRNA.1
                              50S.Ribosome.Subunit.1 ┤
                                                    └── 5S.rRNA.1
              Ribosome.1
                              30S.Ribosome.Subunit.1── 16S.rRNA.1

                              Ribosome.RBS.Binding.Site.1

                         Trp.Promoter.1──── Promoter.Polymerase.Binding.Site.1

                         Trp.Operator.1──── Trp.Operator.Repressor.Binding.Site.1

                         Trp.Leader.1

                         dRibosome.Binding.Site.1

                         Trp-E.1

                         dStop.Codon.1

                         dRibosome.Binding.Site.2

                         Trp-D.1

                         dStop.Codon.2

              Trp.Operon.1 dRibosome.Binding.Site.3

                         Trp-C.1

                         dStop.Codon.3
Trp.Expt.1
                         dRibosome.Binding.Site.4

                         Trp-B.1

                         dStop.Codon.4

                         dRibosome.Binding.Site.5

                         Trp-A.1

                         dStop.Codon.5

                         Trp.Terminator.1

         Generic.RNASe.1

         RNA-Polymerase.1 ──── RNA-Polymerase.Promoter.Binding.site.1

         Trp-tRNA-Synthetase.1

                              ┌── Trp-R.Operator.Binding.Site.1
         Trp-ApoRepressor.1   ┤
                              └── Trp-R.Trp.Binding.Site.1

         Chorismate.Medium.1 ──── Chorismate.1
```

Figure 16. The initial conditions of the experiment involving the full trp system.

- Weld's PEPTIDE model of biochemical reactions (Weld, 1984; Weld, 1986)

- Koton's GENEX model of gene expression (Koton, 1985)

- Karp's earlier model of the trp operon (Karp and Friedland, 1989)

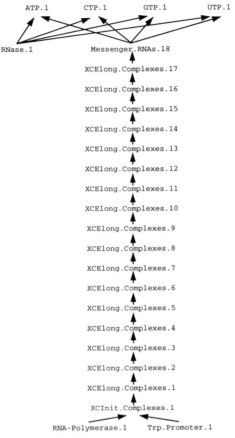

Figure 17. Simulation of the trp system, part 1. This figure shows a simulation of transcription of DNA and degradation of the resulting mRNA. The nodes of the graph are the names of objects (many objects in this figure contain 10 to 30 component objects). The links in the figure connect the reactants and products of each reaction; for example, Trp.Promoter.1 *and* RNA-Polymerase.1 *reacted to yield the transcription-initiation complex* XCInit.Complexes.1.

- Koile and Overton's model of the life cycle of the HIV virus (Koile and Overton, 1989)

- Brutlag *et al*'s model of DNA metabolism (Brutlag *et al.*, 1991)

- Mavrovouniotis' model of intermediary metabolism (Mavrovouniotis, 1990; see also Mavrovouniotis, this volume)

Virtually all of these researchers represent objects as frames that describe

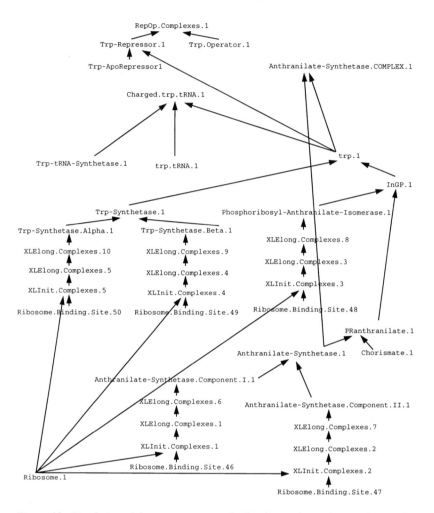

Figure 18. Simulation of the trp system, part 2. This figure shows the translation of the trp operon mRNA to produce the enzymes in the trp biosynthetic pathway, the reactions catalyzed by these enzymes, and the reactions involved in repression of the trp operon. Each ribosome-binding site named in this figure is a component of the Messenger.RNAs.18 *object in the previous figure.*

object properties and object part-whole structures. Exceptions are Koton, who used PROLOG clauses to represent this information, and Mavrovonioutis, who used Flavors. Although most workers represented object parts such as binding sites, none approached the complexity used for example in the GEN-SIM representation of a transcription-elongation complex (see Figure 14). In addition, none of the other programs represented classes of biological objects that were automatically instantiated to describe particular experiments, as described in Section 3. Koile and Overton represented little or no information about object properties or structures; their approach focuses on object quantities such as concentrations.

Only GENSIM and Weld's PEPTIDE perform object forking (in Weld's terminology he "splits the histories" of the "nodes" that represent populations of molecules—he also merges histories when identical nodes are produced by different reactions, which is identical to GENSIM's object merging). Koton states (p. 33) that her approach is to focus only on those binding reactions with the highest affinities, and not to simulate all possible competing reactions. Section 5 of this article provides the most thorough analysis of the reasons to perform object forking, and of ways to optimize this procedure.

The different researchers took varying approaches to representing quantitative information about the biological systems they modeled. Like GENSIM, Koton represented no quantitative information at all. Mavrovonioutis, Weld, Koile, and Karp (Karp and Friedland, 1989) applied techniques developed for qualitative physics (and developed new techniques) to their biological systems. They could represent very coarse quantitative information such as "the concentration of the HIV primary transcript is greater than zero" (Koile and Overton, 1989), or somewhat more precise order-of-magnitude information such as "the concentration of X is much greater than the concentration of Y" (Mavrovouniotis, 1990). Mavrovouniotis also used chemical theory to estimate values for kinetic and thermodynamic parameters of his system. Meyers represented reaction rates and protein concentrations as real numbers, but these numbers were not solidly grounded in experimental data. Brutlag is the only researcher to accurately represent and reason with experimental conditions such as temperature and pH.

All of the researchers represented reactions using some type of condition—action formalism. Meyers employed production rules. Round developed a process-description language that allows a user to decompose processes into their component subprocesses. Brutlag used KEE production rules. Koton used PROLOG rules containing *preconditions* and *postconditions* to represent reactions; Weld used a similar precondition-postcondition representation, but in addition each reaction had a *pattern* that was equivalent to GENSIM's parameter object classes. Section 5 shows that separating the parameter object classes from the rest of the preconditions facilitates the indexing of processes according to the objects whose behaviors they describe and leads to a more efficient simulation algorithm. Koile and Overton encode reactions using Forbus' qualitative process theory (see next paragraph). None of the systems except for GENSIM arrange reactions in an inheritance hierarchy, which is useful for describing complex reactions in a modular fashion. This approach may also be useful for hypothesis formation because by summarizing knowledge of known classes of reactions the taxonomy provides expectations for the types of unknown reactions we are likely to discover. Only this article and Weld's work describe simulation algorithms in any detail; Weld's algorithm is equivalent to the first GENSIM algorithm presented in Section 5. Only GENSIM and PEPTIDE allow quantification within reaction preconditions and postconditions, which provides the ability to express complex reactions.

Forbus (Forbus, 1984; Forbus, 1986) and Simmons and Mohammed (Simmons and Mohammed, 1987) use a notion of process in their process-modeling systems that is similar to that used by GENSIM; all include parameters, preconditions, and effects. GENSIM processes are most similar to what Forbus terms *individual views*, because both are concerned with creating and deleting objects, and with altering relations between objects. Those things that Forbus calls processes describe how quantities change in a physical system, whereas GENSIM has no notion of quantity. Forbus briefly discusses the use of an abstraction hierarchy to define processes, although he did not implement this idea (Forbus, 1984, p. 44). The main difference in our approaches is that for a process P_1 to be a specialization of another process P_2, Forbus requires that the parameter-object classes, preconditions, and quantity conditions of P_1 must be a subset of those of P_2. Since our `Preconditions.M` slot allows parent preconditions to be removed in a child process, we do not use this restriction. In addition, Forbus does not discuss inheritance from multiple parents. There are also differences between our process-definition languages. The preconditions of Forbus' processes must contain a conjunctive list of (possibly negated) predicates; the preconditions of GENSIM processes can include arbitrary predicate-calculus formulae, including disjunction and quantification. In addition, GENSIM and the system built by Simmons and Mohammed allow process effects to be conditionalized and universally quantified; Forbus does not allow this.

Weld addressed the problem of using a model of a given chemical reaction to predict the aggregate behavior of many molecules that undergo the same reaction. His technique is similar to mathematical induction. The *aggregation* technique allows him to predict the transcription of an entire gene by reasoning about an individual transcription-elongation event that advances RNA polymerase one base along a DNA strand. This technique reduces the execution time of simulations and produces simpler and more understandable causal explanations, but it has an important limitation: Weld's program cannot predict the final sequence of the transcribed RNA because the aggregation technique does not copy every base from the DNA to the RNA; in fact, PEPTIDE does not even know that the length of the mRNA is the same as the length as the DNA from which it was transcribed. For similar reasons, his program would be unable to predict what proteins would be translated from a given mRNA (as Weld notes on p. 52 of (Weld, 1984)).

8 Conclusions

This article has presented a qualitative biochemistry: an ontology for biochemical objects and reactions. It has also presented and analyzed methods for simulating biochemical systems. The ontology and the simulation methods provide a framework for representing theories of molecular biology, and for using these theories to predict outcomes of biological experiments. A user describes a theory by building a knowledge base of classes of objects that are relevant to the biochemical system (the CKB), and a knowledge base of processes that describe potential interactions among these objects (the PKB). A user describes the initial conditions of an experiment by constructing a knowledge base that describes the objects present at the start of the experiment. Predictions are computed by a process interpreter that uses the knowledge of reactions in the PKB to detect and simulate the interactions among the objects in the experiment.

The limitations of the GENSIM framework are that it does not allow us to represent quantitative aspects of the trp operon, nor does it allow us to represent temporal or complex spatial information. Although many interesting problems in this domain do not involve time, space, or quantities, many do. In addition, GENSIM incorporates the assumption that its predictions span a sufficiently short time interval that no population of objects within a simulation will be fully depleted. If we required GENSIM to reason about temporal aspects of the regulation of the trp operon, this assumption would be violated.

The contributions of this research include methods for representing the decomposition of objects into their component parts, and for instantiating structured objects from class descriptions. GENSIM processes are more expressive than are many production-rule languages because process preconditions can include negation, disjunction, and quantification. The PKB describes both particular chemical reactions and general classes of chemical reactions; it also uses KEE's frame inheritance to define processes in a novel way. This use of inheritance is applicable to traditional production-rule languages as well as to GENSIM's process-description language.

To produce correct simulations, GENSIM uses object forking to manage objects during a simulation, and restricts the syntax of process preconditions to eliminate process descriptions that have no valid chemical interpretation. I identified several optimizations to the simulator: under certain conditions we can modify objects directly rather than copying and then modifying (forking) them, we can merge the descriptions of identical objects that are created during a simulation, and we can share the descriptions of similar objects in a simulation using an ATMS. I also presented a novel algorithm that GENSIM uses to activate processes efficiently.

I tested GENSIM by predicting the outcomes of several experiments in the bacterial tryptophan operon from the history of attenuation. The program produced flawless predictions of the outcomes of experiments involving the trp biosynthetic pathway, the transcription of the trp operon, and the entire trp operon gene regulation system.

Acknowledgements

This work was supported by funding from NSF grant MCS83-10236, NIH grant RR-00785, DARPA contract N00039-83-C-0136, and by the National Library of Medicine. This work benefited greatly from many discussions with Peter Friedland, Charles Yanofsky, Bruce Buchanan, and Edward Feigenbaum. Dan Weld contributed comments on a draft of this article.

Notes

1. It is important to note that this is a simplified conception of experiments. Often experimenters both establish initial experimental conditions, and perturb the system at later times (often using a complex protocol) by adding reagents, applying heat or cold, etc.

2. For simplicity, we show the new objects A.1 and B.1 in W_1 and W_2 only, but as noted earlier, new objects must be created in the background.

3. Most bacteria contain only a single copy of the trp operon. Thus, when I refer to the population of operons, I assume that the experiment involves many cells, each of which has a trp operon.

4. I have modeled the trp operon as it was known before Platt's experiments revealed the presence of a ribosome-binding site in the leader region of the operon (Platt and Yanofsky, 1975).

References

D. G. Brutlag, A. R. Galper, and D. H. Millis. Knowledge-based Simulation of DNA Metabolism: Prediction of Enzyme Action. *Computer Applications in the Biosciences,* **7**(1):9-19, 1991.

J. DeKleer. An Assumption-based TMS. *Artificial Intelligence,* 28(1):127-162, 1986.

J. De Kleer and J. S. Brown. A Qualitative Physics Based on Confluences. *Artificial Intelligence,* 24(1-3):7-84, 1984.

K. Forbus. Qualitative Process Theory. Technical Report TR-789, Massachusetts Institute of Technology AI Laboratory, 1984.

K. Forbus. The Qualitative Process Engine. Technical Report UIUCDCS-R-86-1288, University of Illinois Computer Science Department, 1986.

A. Goldberg and D. Robson. *Smalltalk-80: The Language and Its Implementation.* Addison-Wesley, 1983.

J. Y. Hsu. On the Relationship Between Partial Evaluation and Explanation-based Learning. Technical Report Logic-88-10, Stanford University, 1988.

IntelliCorp. *KEEworlds Reference Manual,* 1986.

P.D. Karp. *Hypothesis Formation and Qualitative Reasoning in Molecular Biology.* PhD thesis, Stanford University Computer Science Department, June 1989. Technical reports STAN-CS-89-1263, KSL-89-52.

P.D. Karp. Hypothesis Formation as Design. In *Computational Models of Discovery and Theory Formation.* Morgan Kaufmann Publishers, 1990. (See also Stanford Knowledge Systems Laboratory report KSL-89-11.)

P. D. Karp and P. E. Friedland. Coordinating the Use of Qualitative and Quantitative Knowledge in Declarative Device Modeling. In *Artificial Intelligence, Modeling and Simulation,* pages 189-206. John Wiley and Sons, 1989. See also Stanford Knowledge Systems Laboratory report KSL-87-09.

T. P. Kehler and G. D. Clemenson. KEE, the Knowledge Engineering Environment for Industry. *Systems And Software,* 3(1):212-224, 1984.

K. Koile and G. C. Overton. A Qualitative Model for Gene Expression. In *Proceedings of the 1989 Summer Computer Simulation Conference,* 1989.

P. Koton. Towards a Problem Solving System for Molecular Genetics. Technical Report 338, Massachusetts Institute of Technology Laboratory for Computer Science, 1985.

M. Mavrovouniotis. Group Contributions for Estimating Standard Gibbs Energies of Formation of Biochemical Compounds in Aqueous Solution. *Biotechnology and Bioengineering,* 36:1070-1082, 1990.

S. Meyers. A Simulator for Regulatory Genetics and its Application to Bacteriophage Lambda. *Nucleic Acids Research,* 12(1):1-9, 1984. Also available as Stanford Heuristic Programming Project report HPP-83-12.

P. H. Morris and R. A. Nado. Representing Actions with an Assumption-based Truth Maintenance System. In *Proceedings of the 1986 National Conference on Artificial Intelligence,* pages 13-17. Morgan Kaufmann Publishers, 1986.

T. Platt and C. Yanofsky. An Intercistronic Region and Ribosome-binding Site in Bacterial Messenger RNA. *Proceedings of the National Academy of Sciences, USA,* 72(6):2399—2403, 1975.

A. D. Round. QSOPS: A Workbench Environment for the Qualitative Simulation of Physical Processes. Technical Report KSL-87-37, Stanford Knowledge Systems Laboratory, 1987. Also appears in Proceedings of the European Simulation Multiconference.

R. Simmons and J. Mohammed. Causal Modeling of Semiconductor Fabrication. Technical Report 65, Schlumberger Palo Alto Research, 1987.

M. Stefik and D. G. Bobrow. Object-oriented Programming: Themes and Variations. *AI Magazine,* 6(4):40-62, 1986.

D. S. Weld. Switching between Discrete and Continuous Process Models to Predict Molecular Genetic Activity. Technical Report TR-793, Massachusetts Institute of Technology AI Laboratory, 1984.

D. S. Weld. The Use of Aggregation in Causal Simulation. *Artificial Intelligence,* 30:1-34, 1986.

B. C. Williams. Doing Time: Putting Qualitative Reasoning on Firmer Ground. In *Proceed-*

ings of the 1986 National Conference on Artificial Intelligence, pages 105-112. Morgan Kaufmann Publishers, 1986.

C. Yanofsky. Attenuation in the Control of Expression of Bacterial Operons. *Nature,* 289:751-758, 1981.

9

Identification of Qualitatively Feasible Metabolic Pathways

Michael L. Mavrovouniotis

1 Introduction

Cells function as organized chemical engines carrying out a large number of transformations, called bioreactions or biochemical reactions, in a coordinated manner. These reactions are catalyzed by enzymes and exhibit great specificity and rates much higher than the rates of non-enzymatic reactions. Enzymes are neither transformed nor consumed, but that facilitate the underlying reactions by their presence. The coordination of the extensive network of biochemical reactions is achieved through regulation of the concentrations and the specific activities of enzymes. Single enzyme-catalyzed steps in succession form long chains, called biochemical pathways, achieving the overall transformation of substrates to far removed products.

Biochemical pathways are often described in symbolic terms, as a succession of transformations of one set of molecules (called reactants) into another set (called products); reactants and products are collectively referred to as metabolites.

In the construction of metabolic pathways one uses enzyme-catalyzed bioreactions as building blocks, to assemble pathways that meet imposed specifications. A class of specifications can be formulated by classifying each available building block, i.e., each metabolite and each bioreaction, according to the role it can play in the synthesized pathways. For example, a set of specifications may include some metabolites designated as required final products of the pathways, other metabolites as allowed reactants or by-products, and some bioreactions as prohibited from participating in the pathways.

Non-obvious alternative pathways, including those that are not known to be present in any single strain, are especially interesting, because they might prompt new discoveries. The complexity and density of intermediary metabolism generally permit a large number of pathways.

Many distinct pathways can be constructed to include the same bioreactions but achieve different transformations. For example, the reactions A→B+C and 2B+C→D can form the pathways 2A→→D+C and A+B→→D, depending on whether the reactions are combined in 2:1 or 1:1 proportions. Thus, a fully specified pathway must include a *coefficient* for each bioreaction, to indicate the proportions at which the constituents are combined.

Systematic synthesis of pathways that satisfy a set of such specifications is relevant in the early steps of the conception and design of a bioprocess, where a pathway must be chosen for the production of the desired product. For the synthesis of desired bioproducts, the operating pathway is a crucial factor in the feasibility of the process and the selection of appropriate cell lines and media

The synthesis of pathways can identify fundamental limitations in the e *anabolism* (synthesis of biomolecules) and *catabolism* (breakdown of biomolecules, e.g. for digestion) of any given cell, because the pathways determine what transformations are possible in principle. Consider, for example, the problem of identifying a mutant strain lacking a particular enzyme. One must define the set of combinations of substrates on which the mutant cell is able to grow by identifying suitable pathways (despite the lack of a particular enzyme) to consume the substrates in question. Such pathways may differ significantly from the standard routes. Thus, systematic generation of pathways is a more reliable way to predict the ability or inability of a mutant strain to grow on specified sets of substrates. Consequently, it can have a significant impact on the identification of mutant strains lacking a certain bioreaction. Conversely, if the target is not elimination of an enzyme but absence of growth on specific sets of substrates, one must pinpoint the enzymes that should be eliminated to *block* all the pathways for the catabolism of the substrates. The selection of an appropriate set of enzymes depends on the correct generation of all relevant pathways.

The rates of enzymatic reactions are influenced by factors such as the pH and the concentration of metabolites. Furthermore, the regulation of gene expression determines what enzymes are synthesized by a cell, and therefore what bioreactions are available to participate in pathways. Without detailed information on these phenomena, one cannot identify pathways that will definitely be active under given conditions. One can only identify *potential* metabolic pathways which are qualitatively feasible. The qualitative feasibility is confined here to two attributes. First, each bioreaction participating in a pathway must be feasible in the direction in which it is used. Second, the overall stoichiometry (the quantitative relationship between the metabolites involved, expressed as ratios) of the pathway, which derived from a linear combination of the stoichiometries of the constituent bioreactions, must satisfy imposed constraints.

In the following sections, I present an AI method for addressing both the question of judging whether a particular reaction is feasible and the process of taking a collection of reactions and set of constraints and then finding all of the feasible pathways. The next section focuses on thermodynamic feasibility and describes a group-contribution technique that allows the estimation of equilibrium constants of biochemical reactions. This method was implemented in Symbolics Lisp, but is not currently available in executable form; a future version will be implemented in Common Lisp. The remainder of the chapter describes a symbolic approach to the construction of pathways that satisfy stoichiometric constraints.

2 Thermodynamic Feasibility

The feasibility and reversibility of a bioreaction is determined by its equilibrium constant and the concentrations of its reactants (also called substrates) and products. Because intracellular concentrations vary within limited ranges (e.g., 1μM to 5mM), the equilibrium constant alone is sufficient for reaching a qualitative conclusion on a bioreaction's feasibility. In general, a feasible and irreversible reaction is characterized by an equilibrium constant, K, much larger than 1. A feasible and reversible (i.e., feasible in both the forward and reverse directions) reaction is characterized by an equilibrium constant of the order of 1. A reaction that is infeasible in the forward direction but feasible in the reverse direction is characterized by an equilibrium constant much smaller than 1. The quantitative interpretation of these criteria depends on the range of permissible intracellular concentrations for metabolites.

The thermodynamic analysis can also be carried out using the standard Gibbs energy of reaction, $\Delta G^{\circ\prime}$ which is closely related to the equilibrium constant, K:

$$\Delta G^{\circ\prime} = - RT \ln K \qquad (1)$$

Here, R is the ideal-gas constant and T the temperature. The standard state for $\Delta G^{\circ\prime}$ is a dilute aqueous solution at T =25°C, pH = 7, and concentrations of compounds (other than H^+, OH^-, and H_2O) equal to 1 M. The standard Gibbs energy of reaction is related to the standard Gibbs energies of formation of its reactants and products. Letting V_i be the stoichiometric coefficient of compound S_i, we can write a reaction (or any transformation with known stoichiometry) as:

$$\sum V_i S_i = 0 \qquad (2)$$

Here, V_i is positive for products and negative for reactants. Let $\Delta G_i^{\circ\prime}$ be the Gibbs energy of formation of S_i. The Gibbs energy of reaction, $\Delta G^{\circ\prime}$, is then given by the equation:

$$\Delta G^{\circ\prime} = \sum V_i \, \Delta G_i^{\circ\prime} \qquad (3)$$

From the Gibbs energies of formation of a set of compounds one can calculate the Gibbs energy for *any* biochemical transformation within this set of compounds.

Group-Contribution methods [Benson, 1968; Benson *et al.*, 1969; Domalski and Hearing, 1988; Joback and Reid, 1987; Mavrovouniotis *et al.*, 1988; Mavrovouniotis, 1990b; Reid *et al.*, 1977; Reid *et al.*, 1987] have been widely used to estimate numerical values of properties of pure compounds. To estimate a property, one views the compound as composed of functional groups and sums amounts contributed by each group to the overall value of the property.

A given group-contribution method must provide a set of functional groups, which serve as the building blocks for the compounds of interest. The contribution of each group to the thermodynamic property of interest must also be provided, along with the *origin*, a starting value that is used in the estimation (and is constant for all compounds). To estimate the property of a particular compound, one decomposes the compound into groups, and adds the contributions of the groups to the constant origin.

Let C_0 be the origin for the property C, and let C_i be the contribution of group g_i which is used N_i times in the compound. The property C for the whole compound is calculated as:

$$C = C_0 + \sum N_i \, C_i \qquad (4)$$

A group contribution method can be developed using data (i.e., the value of the property for several compounds), to estimate the contributions of the groups to the property of interest. In effect, if the data consist of values of C for a set of compounds, and the molecular structures (hence the N_is) of the compounds are known, then a number of equations of the form of Equation (4) are available, and the unknown origin C_0 and contributions C_i can be determined. It is generally desirable to have as many data points as possible and obtain values for the contributions by minimizing the sum of the square of the errors (multiple linear regression); the error is defined for each data point as the difference between the given value and the value estimated by Equation (4).

If C is a property applicable to reactions, in the linear manner suggested by Equation (3), then data on reactions and data on compounds can be treated uniformly. Reactions can be viewed as collections of groups by subtracting the number of occurrences of each group in reactants from its occurrences in products, because both Equation (3) and Equation (4) are linear. The same linear-combination treatment must also be applied for the contribution of the *origin* and all additional corrections.

We have recently developed a comprehensive group-contribution method [Mavrovouniotis, 1990b, 1991] for the estimation of the Gibbs energies of formation of biochemical compounds, and hence the Gibbs energies and equilibrium constants of biochemical reactions.

The data used in the regression were taken from several sources [Thauer et al.,1977, Barman, 1969, Barman, 1974, Hinz, 1986, Lehninger, 1975, Lehninger, 1986, Sober, 1970, Edsall, and Gutfreund, 1983] and were screened for gross errors. A large set of groups was used, to cover most biochemical compounds and achieve good accuracy. In addition, corrections were introduced to account for certain group-interactions.

Special groups were used for certain complex compounds with important metabolic roles. For example, the pair $NAD^+/NADH$ was represented by a single group, which represents the structural differences between the two compounds which are relevant for a large number of biochemical reactions. Finally, it should be noted that all compounds and groups were represented in their common state in aqueous solution. The determined contributions of groups have been presented by Mavrovouniotis [1990b, 1991].

Examples. A few example calculations will be provided here to illustrate the use of the group-contribution method. Consider the estimation of the Gibbs energy of formation of glutamate, whose syntactic formula is shown in Figure 1a. It can be broken down into groups in a straightforward manner, as shown in Figure 1b. The calculation entails the addition of the contributions (multiplied by the number of occurrences of each group) to the fixed contribution of the origin, as shown in Table 1. In this example, no special corrections are needed. The final result is -164.7 kcal/mol, which deviates by 2.4 kcal/mol from the literature value -167.1 kcal/mol [Thauer et al., 1977].

As an example involving a complex cyclic compound, consider next the estimation of the Gibbs energy of formation of ATP, whose structure is shown in Figure 2. Table 2 shows the calculation of the Gibbs energy from the contributions.

Another example is provided in Figure 3 and Table 3 for a biochemical reaction, catalyzed by *alcohol dehydrogenase*. The reaction is decomposed into

$$^{1-}O—CO—CH_2—CH_2—CH\underset{\textstyle NH_3^{1+}}{\overset{\textstyle CO—O^{1-}}{<}}$$

(a)

$$^{1-}OCO— \quad —CH_2— \quad —CH_2— \quad —CH< \quad \overset{\textstyle —COO^{1-}}{\underset{\textstyle —NH_3^{1+}}{}}$$

(b)

Figure 1. (a) The structure of glutamate. (b) Decomposition of the structure into groups

Group or Correction	Number of Occurrences	Contribution (kcal/mol)	Total Contribution
Origin	1	–23.6	–23.6
$-NH_3^{1+}$	1	4.3	4.3
$-COO^{1-}$	2	–72.0	–142.0
$-CH_2-$	2	1.7	3.4
$-CH<$	1	–4.8	–4.8
			–164.7

Table 1: Calculation of the Gibbs energy of formation of glutamate from contributions of groups. The contributions are those given by Mavrovouniotis (1991).

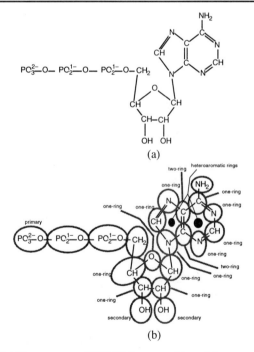

(a)

(b)

Figure 2. (a) The structure of ATP (b) Decomposition of the structure of ATP into groups

Group or Correction	Number of Occurrences	Contribution (kcal/mol)	Total Contribution
Origin	1	–23.6	-23.6
–NH$_2$	1	10.3	10.3
–OPO$_3$$^{1-}$ primary	1	–29.5	-29.5
–OH secondary	2	–32.0	-64.0
–CH$_2$–	1	1.7	1.7
–OPO$_2$$^{1-}$–	2	–5.2	-10.4
ring –O–	1	–24.3	-24.3
ring –CH<	4	–2.2	-8.8
ring –N<	1	7.6	7.6
ring –CH=	2	9.6	19.2
ring =N–	3	10.4	32.2
ring >C=	1	8.2	8.2
two-ring >C=	2	16.8	33.6
heteroaromatic ring	2	–5.9	-11.8
			–60.8

Table 2. Calculation of the Gibbs energy of formation of ATP from contributions of groups. The contributions are those given by Mavrovouniotis (1991).

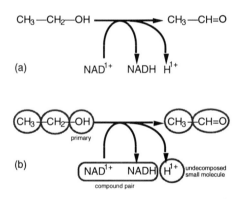

Figure 3 (a) The reaction catalyzed by alcohol dehydrogenase. (b) The reaction is decomposed into groups, so that its Gibbs energy can be estimated.

groups in Figure 3; note that the pair NADH / NAD$^+$ is considered a single group. The calculation in Table 3 ignores the contributions of the *origin* and the group –CH$_3$, because they are the same for ethanol and acetaldehyde, i.e., they have net number of occurrences equal to zero. The result is 4.8 kcal/mol, which compares well with literature values of 5.5 kcal/mol [Barman, 1969] and 5.9 kcal/mol [Hinz, 1986].

Group or Correction	Number of Occurrences	Contribution (kcal/mol)	Total Contribution
Origin	0		
H^{1+}	1	-9.5	-9.5
NADH *minus* NAD$^+$	1	4.7	4.7
$-CH_3$	0		
$-CH_2-$	-1	1.7	-1.7
-OH primary	-1	-28.6	28.6
-CH=O	1	-17.3	-17.3
			-4.8

Table 3. Calculation of the Gibbs energy of the reaction catalyzed by alcohol dehy-drogenase, from contributions of groups..   The contributions are those given by Mavrovouniotis (1991).

Discussion. Using the contributions and corrections of given by Mavrovouniotis [1990b, 1991], one can estimate the standard Gibbs energy of formation of a biochemical compound, provided that the molecular structure of the compound is known. The standard Gibbs energy and the equilibrium constant of any biochemical reaction can be estimated from the molecular structures of its reactants and products.

The method has broad applicability because it provides the contributions for a comprehensive set of groups. The error is usually less than 2 kcal/mol. Thus, the method provides an acceptable first approximation to the thermodynamics of biochemical systems. Mavrovouniotis [1990b, 1991] provides precomputed values for common metabolites. For compounds that have only small structural differences from the precomputed ones, only the contributions of groups describing the differences need be considered [Mavrovouniotis, 1990b].

A fundamental difficulty in the group-contribution methods for biochemical compounds is that there are often strong interactions among groups due to *conjugation*. The *conjugates* of a compound are alternative arrangements of the valence electrons; a compound that is strongly influenced by conjugation cannot be properly decomposed into groups.

We are currently investigating a new property-estimation framework, named ABC [Mavrovouniotis, 1990a], which is based on using contributions of Atoms and Bonds for properties of Conjugates of a compound. This approach has been enhanced by approximate quantum-chemical analysis and has been demonstrated for simple compounds in the ideal-gas state [Mavrovouniotis, 1990a]. It is expected that the ABC framework will be of great value in estimating their properties of biochemical compounds.

Information on Metabolites

- Set of groups that comprise the molecule
- Standard Gibbs Energy of formation in aqueous solution
- Typical concentrations (only for currency metabolites)
- List of reactions that consume the metabolite
- List of reactions that produce the metabolite

Information on Bioreactions

- Stoichiometry of the reaction
- Standard Gibbs Energy of reaction
- Physiological information on reversibility of the reaction
- List of metabolites the reaction consumes
- List of metabolites the reaction produces

Table 4: Information useful in the synthesis of biochemical pathways from the database of metabolites and bioreaction.

2 Synthesis of Pathways

An approach for the synthesis of biochemical pathway [Mavrovouniotis, *et al* 1990a] is presented here. This section gives the formulation of the problem and the developed algorithm, which is complete and sound. An example showing the step-by-step operation of the algorithm in a small abstract problem is provided, along with a discussion of computational issues. The next section in this chapter presents a case study on the biosynthesis of lysine from glucose and ammonia.

Biochemical pathway synthesis is here the construction of pathways which produce certain target bioproducts, under partial constraints on the available substrates (reactants), allowed by-products, etc. In connection with this formulation of the synthesis problem, it should be noted that:

- A pathway must include all reactions responsible for the conversion of initial substrates to final products, and not merely the steps leading from the intermediary metabolism to the product.

- The pathways sought are not restricted to the already known routes found in textbooks. New pathways are quite acceptable and present the most interest.

In order to construct pathways from bioreactions, one needs a database of metabolites and bioreactions. The information stored in the database for each bioreaction and each metabolite is shown in Table 4. The database included roughly 250 bioreactions and 400 metabolites..

Stoichiometric Constraints. A whole class of specifications in the synthesis of biochemical pathways can be formulated by classifying each building block (each metabolite and each reaction from the database) according to the role it is required or allowed to play in the synthesized pathways.

A given metabolite can participate in a pathway in any of three capacities: (a) as a net *reactant* or substrate of the pathway; (b) as a net *product* of the pathway; and (c) as an *intermediate* in the pathway, i.e., participating without *net* consumption or production. One can impose constraints on pathways by stating which metabolites are *required* and which are *prohibited* to participate in the synthesized pathways in each of the above three capacities. Not all metabolites need be strictly constrained as required or prohibited. Some may simply be *allowed* to participate in the pathways.

For example, metabolites (from a database of biochemical reactions and metabolic intermediates) can be classified according to whether they are allowed to be net reactants in the pathways:

1. *Required reactants* (or desired reactants) *must* be consumed by the pathway;

2. *Allowed reactants* may or may not be consumed by the pathway; and

3. *Excluded reactants* (or prohibited reactants) *must not* be consumed by the pathway.

In a realistic synthesis problem, the default characterization for each metabolite is specification (3): The bulk of the metabolites in the database are *excluded* from being net reactants of the synthesized pathways.

Specification (1) underlies a strict inequality, i.e., stoichiometric coefficient of the metabolite (in the pathway) less than zero, while specification (2) underlies a loose inequality, i.e., stoichiometric coefficient less than or equal to zero. Thus, the first constraint is strict, while the second one is loose. This distinction is relevant in the description of the algorithm, because strict constraints are initially satisfied only in their loose form.

The classification of metabolites as potential products or intermediates of the pathways is quite similar. For intermediates, however, the default characterization differs, as most of the metabolites would normally be classified as *allowed* intermediates. It should be noted that constraints on intermediates are generally not motivated by physiological considerations. They are usually a device for selecting a particular subset of the synthesized pathways.

The constraints on different roles of the same metabolite are not independent. For example, a metabolite that is required as a net product *must* be excluded as a reactant.

A given bioreaction can participate in pathways in either (a) its *forward,* or (b) its *backward* direction. Thus, one can impose constraints by stating which bioreactions are required, which are allowed, and which are prohibited to participate in the synthesized pathways in each of the two directions.

Many constraints designating bioreactions excluded in the backward direction will be present, stemming from knowledge about the (thermodynamic or mechanistic) irreversibility of bioreactions. To this end, one can introduce some kind of constraint on the equilibrium constants (or the Gibbs Energies) of the reactions that can be used; one possible constraint is a simple upper bound on the Gibbs Energy (or a lower bound on the equilibrium constant). Note that the same kind of constraint ought to apply to both the forward direction and reverse (backward) direction of the reaction, because the nominal direction of a reaction in the database is often arbitrary.

The constraints imposed on the two directions of a bioreaction are not completely independent. For example, it is not meaningful to specify a reaction as required in both the forward and reverse direction; a reaction that is required in one direction *must* be excluded in the other direction. Thus, there are in total 5 possible designations (out of a total of 3x3=9 simple-minded combinations) for a reversible reaction:

• Allowed in both directions

• Required in the forward direction and excluded in the backward direction

• Required in the backward direction and excluded in the forward direction

• Allowed in the forward direction and excluded in the backward direction

• Allowed in the backward direction and excluded in the forward direction

3 Description of the Algorithm.

The synthesis algorithm [Mavrovouniotis *et al* 1990a] is devoted to the satisfaction of the above kinds of constraints imposed on the participation of metabolites and bioreactions in biochemical pathways.

Given a set of stoichiometric constraints and a database of biochemical reactions, the developed algorithm synthesizes all biochemical pathways satisfying the stoichiometric constraints. The algorithm is based on the *iterative* satisfaction of constraints, and the stepwise transformation of the initial set of available bioreactions (which can be thought of as one-step pathways that, in general, do not satisfy the constraints), into a final set of pathways, which satisfy all imposed constraints.

To facilitate the description and analysis of the algorithm, some definitions are given here. A *combination* of a set of *constituent pathways* is a pathway whose coefficients are linear combinations of the coefficients of the constituent pathways. In order to retain the original direction of each constituent pathway, the linear combination may involve only *positive combination coefficients*. Let P and Q be pathways derived from the same reaction database. The pathway P is a *subpathway* of Q if and only if every reaction that has a positive coefficient in P also has a positive coefficient in Q. Equivalently Q is called a *superpathway* of P.

Reaction-Processing Phase. In order to account for the reversibility of reactions, each thermodynamically reversible reaction is decomposed into a forward and a backward reaction. From this point on, we prohibit the participation of both the forward and the reverse reaction in the same pathway, because such a pathway would be redundant.

The constraints placed on the original reactions are then easily transformed into constraints on the new reactions. For a reaction R_k, and its coefficient a_k:

- R_k may occur in the pathway, i.e., $a_k \geq 0$.

- R_k must occur in the pathway, i.e., $a_k > 0$.

- R_k must not occur in the pathway, i.e., $a_k = 0$.

Constraints dictating that certain reactions should not participate in the constructed pathways can be satisfied right from the start. Such reactions are simply eliminated and removed from the active database.

The remaining reactions can be thought of as *one-step pathways* which will be combined in subsequent phases of the algorithm to form longer and longer pathways satisfying more and more constraints.

Metabolite-Processing Phase. The main body of the algorithm tackles one constraint at a time, by transforming the set of particular pathways . Thus, at each iteration stage in the synthesis algorithm, the problem state, often called the *state of the design* [Mostow, 1983, Mostow, 1984] consists of the following elements:

- The set of constraints (on the stoichiometry) or metabolites that still remain to be processed.

- The set of incomplete pathways constructed so far. These are pathways that satisfy the already-processed constraints.

- Back-pointers which show, for each remaining metabolite, the pathways in which it participates. These data-structures must be initially created by passing over each of the initial one-step pathways.

At each pathway-expansion step, the set of active pathways is modified to satisfy a constraint. For example, if the constraint designates a metabolite as an excluded reactant and excluded product, all possible combination-pathways must be constructed by combining one pathway consuming the metabolite and one pathway producing it, such that the metabolite is eliminated from the overall net stoichiometry. Once the combinations are constructed, all pathways consuming or producing the metabolite are deleted.

More generally, the algorithm finds a modification of the set of pathways such that all surviving pathways satisfy the requirement. This involves the construction of new pathways as combinations of existing ones, as well as deletion of pathways. More specifically, for S the metabolite being processed and using the backward-pointers readily available in each metabolite, two subsets of the current pathway set, L, are assembled:

- The list of pathways that produce the metabolite: $L_p = \{P_i |$ S participates in P_i with a net stoichiometric coefficient $a_i > 0\}$.

- The list of pathways that consume the metabolite: $L_c = \{P_i |$ S participates in P_i with a net stoichiometric coefficient $a_i < 0\}$.

- The list of pathways in which the metabolite participates as an intermediate: $L_r = \{P_i |$ S participates in some reaction R with coefficient $r_i \neq 0$, but S does not participate in the net transformation of P_i, i.e., $a_i = 0\}$.

- The list of pathways in which the metabolite does not participate at all $L_n = \{P_i |$ the coefficient of S in each reaction R of P_i is $r_i = 0\}$.

The pathways that may, at this step of the algorithm, be deleted from the current set will be pathways from the lists L_p, L_c, and L_r, depending on the nature of the constraint. The pathways that may be constructed are linear combinations using exactly one pathway from L_c and exactly one pathway from L_p:

- Combination pathways: $L_e = \{a_k P_i - a_i P_k \mid P_i \in L_c;\ P_k \in L_p;\ P_i$ and P_k do not involve the same reaction in different directions; and a_i and a_k are the net coefficients with which S participates in P_i and $P_k\}$. Since $P_i \in L_c$, $a_i < 0$ and the combination $a_k P_i - a_i P_k$ has positive coefficients; thus, it is a legitimate combination of pathways. The net coefficient of S in $a_k P_i - a_i P_k$ is $a_k a_i - a_i a_k = 0$. Thus, for all pathways in L_e, S is only an intermediate; it is neither a net reactant nor a net product. As was noted earlier, we exclude combinations of two pathways that involve the same reaction in different directions.

For constraints on reactants and products, the construction of the new set of active pathways is delineated below. The different cases are listed by priority, i.e., in the order in which they should be applied. Once a particular case applies then the remaining cases are automatically excluded[1].

- If S is an excluded product and a required reactant (i.e., $a_k < 0$), all combination pathways are constructed, and the producing pathways are deleted. In effect: $L \leftarrow L \cup L_e - L_p$

- If S is an excluded reactant and a required product (i.e., $a_k > 0$), then: $L \leftarrow L \cup L_e - L_c$.

- If S is an excluded product and an allowed reactant (i.e., $a_k \leq 0$), then: $L \leftarrow L \cup L_e - L_p$

- If S is an excluded reactant and an allowed product (i.e., $a_k \geq 0$), then: $L \leftarrow L \cup L_e - L_c$

- If S is an excluded reactant and an excluded product (i.e., $a_k = 0$), then: $L \leftarrow L \cup L_e - L_c - L_p$

- If S is an excluded intermediate, then: $L \leftarrow L - L_c - L_p - L_r$, or, equivalently, $L \leftarrow L_n$

- If S is a required intermediate, then: $L \leftarrow L$.

- If S is an allowed reactant, an allowed product, and an allowed intermediate, then the set of active pathways is carried intact to the next iteration: $L \leftarrow L$

- If S is a required intermediate , then: $L \leftarrow L$.

After the processing of the constraint, there is a new set of active pathways which satisfy the constraint, with the exception that for strict-inequality constraints, i.e., required products ($a_k > 0$), required reactants ($a_k < 0$), and required intermediates, only the corresponding loose-inequality constraints are guaranteed to be satisfied. The strict-inequality constraints will receive additional consideration in the last phase of the algorithm.

In addition to the set of active pathways, L, the whole *state of the design* that was described earlier must also be properly updated after each constraint is processed. For example, to update the back-pointers that point from each metabolite to the pathways in which it participates, pointers corresponding to deleted pathways must be removed and pointers corresponding to new pathways must be added.

Pathway-Marking Phase. At the end of the metabolite-processing phase, there is a final set of active pathways satisfying all of the requirements, except the strict-inequality constraints for which only the corresponding loose inequalities are satisfied. Because of the linear nature of the requirements, all combinations of pathways also satisfy the constraints.

If each pathway is marked with the strict-inequality constraints it satisfies, the final answer to the synthesis problem can be obtained:

- The pathways satisfying the original stoichiometric constraints of the synthesis problem are all those combinations of pathways which include:

    ◊ at least one pathway consuming each required reactant,

    ◊ at least one pathway producing each required product,

    ◊ at least one pathway containing each required intermediate, and

    ◊ at least one pathway in which each required reaction participates.

Naturally, a single constituent pathway may possess many of the strict-inequality constraints and can serve to satisfy many of the above requirements.

Thus, if a pathway from the final active set satisfies all of the strict inequalities, then that pathway itself is acceptable as one solution to the overall synthesis problem; *any* combination of that pathway with other pathways from the final set is also acceptable. If, on the other hand, there is a strict-inequality requirement which is not satisfied by any of the pathways in the final set, then there is no solution to the original synthesis problem.

One may wonder whether there are, in the final set, pathways which do not satisfy any of the strict-inequality requirements, and whether there is any reason to construct or keep such pathways. There are indeed such pathways, called *neutral* pathways, generated by the algorithm. Since these pathways do not contribute to the satisfaction of any strict-inequality requirements, it is not *necessary* to use them in combinations constructed from the final set, but they may by freely included in such combinations as they neither prevent any requirements from being satisfied nor introduce additional requirements.

The algorithm that was presented above is correct (it generates *only* feasible pathways) and complete (it generates *all* pathways satisfying the requirements). The performance of the current implementation of the algorithm is quite efficient for well formulated problems. These mathematical and computational properties of the algorithm are discussed in detail below.

Correctness. If a combination of pathways from the final set (produced by the synthesis algorithm) contains at least one constituent pathway satisfying each of the strict inequality requirements (referring to required reactants, products, intermediates, or reactions), then the combination pathway satisfies all of the initial stoichiometric requirements.

The algorithm is correct because each of the original requirements is satisfied in one of the three phases (and after each constraint is satisfied it cannot be subsequently violated):

- Excluded reactions are removed during the reaction-processing phase.

- Excluded intermediates, reactants, or products are eliminated in the metabolite-processing phase. This happens because the pathways that violate the constraints are removed, and any new combination-pathways satisfy the constraints (by their construction).

- Constraints on required reactants or products are satisfied in two phases. In the metabolite-processing phase of the algorithm, after the processing of any particular metabolite, the current set of active pathways satisfies the stoichiometric constraints imposed on that metabolite at least in their loose inequality form. In the pathway-marking phase of the algorithm, a combination of pathways from the final set satisfies the union of the strict-inequality requirements satisfied by its constituent pathways, because the stoichiometries of a combination-pathway are linear combinations of its constituent pathways (with positive coefficients), and those constituent pathways that do not satisfy the strict inequalities satisfy the corresponding loose inequalities. Thus, acceptable final solutions will contain required reactants and products.

• Constraints on required intermediates and reactions are similarly satisfied in the pathway-marking phase.

Completeness. The synthesis algorithm creates a final set of pathways such that: Any pathway satisfying the original stoichiometry constraints is a combination of pathways from the final set, with one constituent pathway satisfying each strict-inequality constraint.

Incompleteness could only arise in the metabolite-processing phase. At the beginning of the phase, the algorithm has an initial set of (one-step) pathways. Since that set contains all the feasible reactions (unless they have been designated as excluded) any feasible pathway is (by definition) a combination of pathways from that set. The metabolite-processing phase processes each metabolite and its constraints, transforming the set of active pathways. Therefore, it must be shown that:

if *before* processing a particular metabolite there exists a pathway that: (a) Satisfies the constraints on the metabolite; and (b) can be constructed as a combination pathway from the current set of active pathways

then, *after* processing the metabolite, the pathway can still be constructed from the (changed) active set.

This holds because of the way each kind of requirement is handled. Consider, as an example, a metabolite S whose constraint is that it may not occur at all in the stoichiometry of the pathway (excluded reactant and excluded product). As defined in the description of the metabolite-processing phase, let L be the initial active set, L_c the set of the partial pathways (in the initial active set) that consume it, and L_p the set of partial pathways that produce it. Let $L_e=\{a_kP_i-a_iP_k \mid P_i\in L_c, P_k\in L_p,$ and a_i and a_k are the net coefficients with which S participates in P_i and $P_k\}$ be the set of new combination pathways created. The net coefficient of S in a pathway $P_e=a_kP_i-a_iP_k$ from L_e is $a_ka_i-a_ia_k=0$. Processing the metabolite will lead to a new set of active pathways: $L\cup L_e-L_c-L_p$. It will be shown that any pathway Q that can be constructed from L to satisfy the constraints on S can also be constructed from $L\cup L_e-L_c-L_p$.

If the composite pathway Q does not involve any pathways from L_c or L_p, then it can be constructed after the processing exactly the way it was constructed before, since its constituent pathways remain unaffected by the processing of the metabolite.

If Q involves constituent partial pathways from L_c and L_p, then for each of these partial pathways P_i let x_i be the coefficient of S in P_i and y_i the (non-negative) coefficient with which the constituent pathway P_i participates in Q. If the constraint on S is satisfied, its coefficient in Q must be zero. Thus:

$$\sum_i x_i y_i = 0 \tag{5}$$

Let Y be the total consumption and total production of the metabolite in Q:

$$Y = \sum_{(x_i>0)} x_i y_i = -\sum_{(x_i<0)} x_i y_i \tag{6}$$

By defining

$$f_i = |\, x_i\, y_i\, /\, Y\, | \tag{7}$$

The net stoichiometric coefficient of S in Q can be written as:

$$\sum_i x_i y_i = \sum_{i:(x_i>0)} \sum_{j:(x_j<0)} \left(x_i y_i f_j + x_j y_j f_i \right) \tag{8}$$

Note that, since $x_i>0$ and $x_j<0$ for each of the right-hand summation terms:

$$x_i y_i f_j + x_j y_j f_i = 0 \tag{9}$$

After the parameters f_i are determined, an equation similar to Equation (8) holds for any metabolite. Specifically, if a_i is the coefficient of another metabolite T in P_i, and a_Q is the coefficient of T in Q, then:

$$a_Q = \sum_i a_i y_i = \sum_{i:(x_i>0)} \sum_{j:(x_j<0)} \left(a_i y_i f_j + a_j y_j f_i \right) \tag{10}$$

where f_i and f_j are still derived from Equation (7), i.e., from the coefficients of S—the metabolite being processed. An identical equation holds for the coefficients of reactions in the pathways: If a_i is the coefficient of a reaction in pathway P_i and a_Q is the coefficient of the same reaction in Q, then Equation (10) holds.

Thus, the transformation in Equation (10) denotes that the composite pathway Q can be written as a sum of pairs of constituent partial pathways (with f_i and f_j the coefficients used in combining P_j and P_i), such that for each pair the metabolite has zero total coefficient, as Equation (9) states. To demonstrate that these pairs are exactly the combinations (i.e., the pathways of L_e) created by the algorithm, Equation (11) can be used to eliminate f_i and f_j from Equation (10):

$$a_Q = \sum_{i:(x_i>0)} \sum_{j:(x_j<0)} \left[y_i y_j \left(a_j x_i - a_i x_j \right) \right] Y^{-1} \tag{11}$$

The term $a_j x_i - a_i x_j$ refers precisely to a combination pathway from L_e, while the factor $y_i y_j Y^{-1}$ provides the coefficients of combination that construct Q from pathways in L_e. Hence, a composite pathway that satisfied the constraint *before* the metabolite was processed can still be constructed *after* the

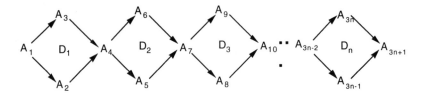

Figure 4. A set of reactions giving rise to an exponential number of pathways

metabolite is processed, using the combination-pair partial pathways created in the processing.

Computational Complexity Issues. The number of pathways that satisfy a set of stoichiometric constraints is, in the worst case, exponential in the number of reactions. Consider the reactions depicted in Figure 4. For each diamond (numbered as D_1, D_2, etc.) consisting of two parallel branches, a pathway can follow either the upper branch or the lower branch. If there are n diamonds (and $4n=m$ reactions), there are n junctions where these choices occur. Thus, there are $2^n=2^{m/4}$ distinct pathways. These are all genotypically independent: Since no two of them involve the same set of choices (at the junctions), it follows that no two of them involve the same set of enzymes.

Since the algorithm described here constructs all genotypically independent pathways, the algorithm would require time (and storage space) exponential in the number of reactions. Thus, the algorithm's worst-case complexity is at least exponential. In practice, however, the metabolism contains long sequences of reactions but few parallel branches of the type of Figure 4. Thus, with careful design of the computer programs it is possible to obtain results more efficiently than the worst-case complexity suggests.

It is useful to discuss, in the context of computational complexity, why the metabolite-processing phase of the pathway does not necessarily start from metabolites that are required reactants and may instead start from other intermediates. In the formulation of the problem, constraints are imposed on all metabolites. When the algorithm selects the next constraint to satisfy, it picks the one that appears easiest to process (an approach reminiscent of *greedy algorithms*); this would be the metabolite that participates in the smallest number of reactions, regardless of whether the metabolite is a required reactant or an excluded reactant.

The fact that the algorithm processes not only designated required reactants (or products) is an important factor in guaranteeing the completeness of the algorithm and guarding it against computational complexity. Consider the simple pathway of Figure 5, and suppose that the whole reaction database consists of the two reactions in the figure, and the objective is to convert pyruvate to oxaloacetate. An algorithm that searches from substrates towards

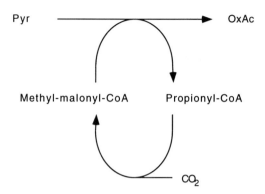

Figure 5. Carboxylation of pyruvate through an alternative pathway, involving Methyl-malonyl-CoA and Propionyl-CoA

products cannot start the construction of a pathway from the reaction:

PYRUVATE + METHYL-MALONYL-COA → OXALOACETATE + PROPIONYL-COA

because this reaction uses methyl-malonyl-CoA, which is not available as a reactant. Likewise, that algorithm can not start from:

PROPIONYL-COA → METHYL-MALONYL-COA + CO_2

because the reaction requires propionyl-CoA which is also not available. Thus, this type of algorithm fails to see that, taken as a cluster, these two reactions achieve the desired transformation. The algorithm presented here, on the other hand, considers the constraint that designates propionyl-CoA as an excluded reactant and excluded product, and immediately constructs the pathway of Figure 5 to satisfy the constraint.

Implementation. The algorithm was implemented in LISP, on Symbolics 3640 and 3650 computers. The performance of the implementation of the algorithm greatly varies with the exact formulation of the problem, but it is generally proportional to the cardinality of the final set of pathways.

- The requirements for setting up the initial data structures are proportional to the size of the database. Rough requirements per database object are 0.05 s of elapsed time (with garbage-collection suppressed), 70 list-words, and 70 structure-words[2].

- The requirements for the main body of the algorithm appear proportional to the number of solutions for those cases in which results were obtained. The program needs 0.15 seconds (elapsed time), 200 list-words, and 100 structure-words per synthesized pathway.

A typical problem requires 35s, 40k list words, and 40k structure words for the initial set-up, and 8 minutes, 1M list words, and 500k structure words for the construction of pathways (based on 5000 final pathways).

4 An Example of the Operation of the Algorithm.

A step-by-step application of the algorithm for a synthesis problem is presented here. The set of reactions under consideration is:

a. $A \rightarrow B$
b. $B \leftrightarrow C$
c. $C \leftrightarrow D$
d. $C + D \leftrightarrow F + K$
e. $F + K \leftrightarrow H + E$
f. $H + D \leftrightarrow E + F$
g. $A \leftrightarrow E$
h. $E \rightarrow F + G$
k. $F \leftrightarrow G$
m. $G \rightarrow L$

All metabolites are designated as excluded reactants and excluded products, with the exception of A, which is a required reactant, and L, which is a required product.

We first construct the reverse reactions, for reactions b, c, d, e, f, g, and k. We designate the reverse reactions as -b, -c, -d, -e, -f, -g, and -k respectively. We also list separately each metabolite and the pathways in which it participates. Representing only the reactions from which a pathway is constructed, an expression like [2a, 2-g, b] denotes a pathway that is constructed as a linear combination of the reactions a, -g, and b, with coefficients 2, 2, and 1, respectively. To represent instead the overall transformation accomplished by this pathway, the expression $2E \rightarrow \rightarrow B + C$ is used. The two expressions can be combined into $2E \rightarrow[2a, 2\text{-}g, b]\rightarrow B + C$. Using this notation the initial pathways are:

$A \rightarrow[a]\rightarrow B$
$B \rightarrow[b]\rightarrow C$
$C \rightarrow[\text{-}b]\rightarrow B$
$C \rightarrow[c]\rightarrow D$
$D \rightarrow[\text{-}c]\rightarrow C$
$C + D \rightarrow[d]\rightarrow F + K$
$F + K \rightarrow[\text{-}d]\rightarrow C + D$
$F + K \rightarrow[e]\rightarrow H + E$
$H + E \rightarrow[\text{-}e]\rightarrow F + K$
$H + D \rightarrow[f]\rightarrow E + F$
$E + F \rightarrow[\text{-}f]\rightarrow H + D$
$A \rightarrow[g]\rightarrow E$
$E \rightarrow[\text{-}g]\rightarrow A$

E →[h]→ F + G
F →[k]→ G
G →[-k]→ F
G →[m]→ L

The set of metabolites with the pathways in which they participate is:

A: [a], [g], [-g]
B: [b], [-b], [a]
C: [b], [-b], [c], [-c], [d], [-d]
D: [c], [-c], [d], [-d], [f], [-f]
E: [e], [-e], [f], [-f], [g], [-g], [h]
F: [d], [-d], [e], [-e], [f], [-f], [h], [k], [-k]
G: [h], [k], [-k], [m]
H: [e], [-e], [f], [-f]
K: [d], [-d], [e], [-e]
L: [m]

Following the algorithm, the metabolites that participate in fewer pathways must be processed first. L, which participates in only one pathway, is a required product (and an excluded reactant). Since L is produced by one partial pathway and is not consumed by any partial pathway, processing the constraints on this metabolite does not change any pathway.

The next metabolite that is processed must be either A or B; the order in which these two metabolites are processed does not affect the results and we arbitrarily choose B. One new pathway are constructed: [a,b] as a combination of [a] and [b]; this operation is denoted as [a]+[b]=[a,b]. Note that it is not permissible to construct the pathway [b]+[-b], because it would involve the same reaction in both the forward and reverse directions. The pathways [a], [b], and [-b] are then deleted. The set of active pathways is now:

A →[a, b]→ C
C →[c]→ D
D →[-c]→ C
C + D →[d]→ F + K
F + K →[-d]→ C + D
F + K →[e]→ H + E
H + E →[-e]→ F + K
H + D →[f]→ E + F
E + F →[-f]→ H + D
A →[g]→ E
E →[-g]→ A
E →[h]→ F + G
F →[k]→ G
G →[-k]→ F
G →[m]→ L

The updated set of metabolites becomes:

A: [a, b], [g], [-g]
C: [a, b], [c], [-c], [d], [-d]
D: [c], [-c], [d], [-d], [f], [-f]
E: [e], [-e], [f], [-f], [g], [-g], [h]
F: [d], [-d], [e], [-e], [f], [-f], [h], [k], [-k]
G: [h], [k], [-k], [m]
H: [e], [-e], [f], [-f]
K: [d], [-d], [e], [-e]

The metabolite A is processed next. Since A is a required reactant and excluded product, a new combination pathway are constructed as [-g]+[a,b]=[-g,a,b], and only pathway [-g] is deleted. For the next step G is selected arbitrarily among the metabolites G, H, and K (which participate in the same number of reactions). In processing G, there are two pathways consuming it ([-k] and [m]) and two pathways producing ([h] and [k]). Hence, four combinations would be constructed, except that [k] cannot be combined with [-k]. Three legitimate combinations remain, namely: [h]+[-k]=[h, -k]; [h]+[m]=[h, m]; [k]+[m]=[k, m]. The original four pathways in which G participated are deleted.

After the processing of A and G, the active pathways are:

A →[a, b]→ C
C →[c]→ D
D →[-c]→ C
C + D →[d]→ F + K
F + K →[-d]→ C + D
F + K →[e]→ H + E
H + E →[-e]→ F + K
H + D →[f]→ E + F
E + F →[-f]→ H + D
A →[g]→ E
E →[-g, a, b]→ C
E →[h, -k]→ 2 F
E →[h, m]→ F + L
F →[k, m]→ L

The set of metabolites becomes:

C: [a, b], [c], [-c], [d], [-d], [-g, a, b]
D: [c], [-c], [d], [-d], [f], [-f]
E: [e], [-e], [f], [-f], [g], [-g, a, b], [h, m], [h, -k]
F: [d], [-d], [e], [-e], [f], [-f], [h, m], [k, m], [h, -k]
H: [e], [-e], [f], [-f]
K: [d], [-d], [e], [-e]

The metabolite K, participating in four pathways, is processed next. The combinations [d]+[e]=[d, e], and [-e]+[-d]=[-e, -d] are created, and the pathways [d], [-d], [e], and [-e] are deleted. The set of active pathways becomes:

A →[a, b]→ C
C →[c]→ D
D →[-c]→ C
C + D →[d, e]→ H + E
H + E →[-e, -d]→ C + D
H + D →[f]→ E + F
E + F →[-f]→ H + D
A →[g]→ E
E →[-g, a, b]→ C
E →[h, -k]→ 2 F
E →[h, m]→ F + L
F →[k, m]→ L

The set of metabolites becomes:

C: [a, b], [c], [-c], [d, e], [-e, -d], [-g, a, b]
D: [c], [-c], [d, e], [-e, -d], [f], [-f]
E: [d, e], [-e, -d], [f], [-f], [g], [-g, a, b], [h, m], [h, -k]
F: [f], [-f], [h, m], [k, m], [h, -k]
H: [d, e], [-e, -d], [f], [-f]

Processing H in a very similar fashion, two combination pathways are constructed, namely [-f]+[-e,-d]=[-f,-e,-d] and [d,e]+[f]=[d,e,f]. The pathways now become:

A →[a, b]→ C
C →[c]→ D
D →[-c]→ C
C + 2 D →[d, e, f]→ 2 E + F
2 E + F →[-f, -e, -d]→ C + 2 D
A →[g]→ E
E →[-g, a, b]→ C
E →[h, -k]→ 2 F
E →[h, m]→ F + L
F →[k, m]→ L

The set of metabolites becomes:

C: [a, b], [c], [-c], [d, e, f], [-f, -e, -d], [-g, a, b]
D: [c], [-c], [d, e, f], [-f, -e, -d]
E: [d, e, f], [-f, -e, -d], [g], [-g, a, b], [h, m], [h, -k]
F: [d, e, f], [-f, -e, -d], [h, m], [k, m], [h, -k]

Since D involves now only 4 pathways, it is processed next. The fact that the coefficient of D in [d, e, f] and [-f, -e, -d] is 2 must be reflected in the construction of the combinations. The new pathways are constructed as 2[c]+[d,e,f]=[2c, d, e, f] and [-f,-e,-d]+2[-c]=[-f, -e, -d, 2 -c], and all four pathways that involved D are deleted. The set of active pathways is now significantly smaller:

A →[a, b]→ C

$3\ C \rightarrow [2c, d, e, f] \rightarrow 2\ E + F$

$2\ E + F \rightarrow [-f, -e, -d, 2\ -c] \rightarrow 3\ C$

$A \rightarrow [g] \rightarrow E$

$E \rightarrow [-g, a, b] \rightarrow C$

$E \rightarrow [h, -k] \rightarrow 2\ F$

$E \rightarrow [h, m] \rightarrow F + L$

$F \rightarrow [k, m] \rightarrow L$

Only three metabolites remain:

C: [a, b], [2c, d, e, f], [-f, -e, -d, 2 -c], [-g, a, b]

E: [2c, d, e, f], [-f, -e, -d, 2 -c], [g], [-g, a, b], [h, m]

F: [2c, d, e, f], [-f, -e, -d, 2 -c], [h, m], [k, m], [h, -k]

C is processed next and leads to two combinations, $3[a,b]+[2c,d,e,f]=[3a,$ $3b, 2c, d, e, f]$ and $3[-g, a,b]+[2c,d,e,f]=[3 -g, 3a, 3b, 2c, d, e, f]$. Then the active pathways are:

$3\ A \rightarrow [3a, 3b, 2c, d, e, f] \rightarrow 2\ E + F$

$A \rightarrow [g] \rightarrow E$

$E \rightarrow [3 -g, 3a, 3b, 2c, d, e, f] \rightarrow F$

$E \rightarrow [h, -k] \rightarrow 2\ F$

$E \rightarrow [h, m] \rightarrow F + L$

$F \rightarrow [k, m] \rightarrow L$

The two metabolites remaining are:

E: [3a, 3b, 2c, d, e, f], [g], [3 -g, 3a, 3b, 2c, d, e, f], [h, m], [h, -k]

F: [3a, 3b, 2c, d, e, f], [3 -g, 3a, 3b, 2c, d, e, f], [h, m], [k, m], [h, -k]

The two metabolites can be processed in either order to yield the final results. Processing F leads to three new combinations of pathways: [3a, 3b, 2c, d, e, f]+[k, m]=[3a, 3b, 2c, d, e, f, k, m]; [h, m] + [k, m] = [h, k, 2 m]; and finally [3 -g, 3a, 3b, 2c, d, e, f]+[k, m]=[3 -g, 3a, 3b, 2c, d, e, f, k, m]. After the original 5 pathways in which F participated are deleted, the remaining pathways are:

$3\ A \rightarrow [3a, 3b, 2c, d, e, f, k, m] \rightarrow 2\ E + L$

$A \rightarrow [g] \rightarrow E$

$E \rightarrow [3 -g, 3a, 3b, 2c, d, e, f, k, m] \rightarrow L$

$E \rightarrow [h, k, 2m] \rightarrow 2\ L$

Processing E (and omitting pathways that include the same reaction in opposing directions) leads to the combinations: $1/3[3a, 3b, 2c, d, e, f, k, m] + 2/3[3 -g, 3a, 3b, 2c, d, e, f, k, m] = [2 -g, 3a, 3b, 2c, d, e, f, k, m]^3$; [3a, 3b, 2c, d, e, f, k, m] + 2[h, k, 2m] = [3a, 3b, 2c, d, e, f, 3k, 5m, 2h]; and the much simpler [g]+[h, k, 2m]=[g, h, k, 2m]. Thus, the final pathways are:

$A \rightarrow [2 -g, 3a, 3b, 2c, d, e, f, k, m] \rightarrow L$

$3\ A \rightarrow [3a, 3b, 2c, d, e, f, 3k, 5m, 2h] \rightarrow 5\ L$

$A \rightarrow [g, h, k, 2m] \rightarrow 2\ L$

These three pathways are feasible solutions to the original synthesis problem. All other feasible pathways are linear combinations of pathways from this set, with positive coefficients.

When the algorithm is not permitted to run to completion (because of limited computational resources), it can provide useful *partial* results. Specifically, it will return a list of pathways that satisfy only *some* of the constraints involved; it will also return the list of *unprocessed constraints*. In the detailed example discussed in this section, if the algorithm must stop before the last step, it returns a list of four pathways that satisfy all constraints *except for the constraint designating E as an excluded reactant and excluded product;* the algorithm also indicates that the constraint on E has not been satisfied.

5 A Case Study: Lysine Pathways

We are going to perform, in this chapter, a case study on the synthesis and evaluation of biochemical pathways for the production of lysine from glucose and ammonia [Mavrovouniotis, *et al* 1990a].

It should be emphasized right from the start that the analysis we perform here is not exhaustive; our aim is merely to demonstrated the concerted application and utility of our methods in a real system and not to arrive to definitive answers on the synthesis of lysine.

The basic procedure we will follow in this case study is as follows:

- We synthesize a pathway as close as possible to the pathway believed to prevail

- We identify bottlenecks in the pathway by performing a maximum-rate analysis for each reaction

- We synthesize pathways that bypass bottlenecks

- We synthesize other pathways to explore alternatives that omit key enzymes

- We try to identify fundamental constraints on the structure and yield of the pathways

Note that this is a procedure suggested from the point of view of the goals of the analysis. The exact application of the methods may take place following a number of different structures. For example, one can generate *all* pathways producing the desired product from the substrates *a priori,* carry out all the maximum rate calculations for all pathways, and then perform all the tasks by appropriate search through this (potentially very big) set of pathways.

Table 5 shows the abbreviations that we will use for metabolic intermediates throughout this chapter. The core of the bioreaction network with which we will work is shown in Figure 6. It includes:

ABBREVIATION	METABOLITE
2PG	2-phosphoglycerate
3P-OH-Pyr	3-Phosphohydroxypyruvate
3P-Ser or P-Ser	3-Phospho-serine
3PG	3-phosphoglycerate
AcCoA (or Acetyl-CoA)	Acetyl-Coenzyme-A
αkG	α-ketoglutarate
Ala	Alanine
ASA	Aspartate-semialdehyde
Asp	Aspartate
Cit	Citrate
DHAP	Dihydroxyacetone-phosphate
Fru6P	Fructose-6-phosphate
FruDP	Fructose-1,6-diphosphate
Fum	Fumarate
GAP	Glyceraldehyde-3-phosphate
Glc	Glucose
Glc6P	Glucose-6-phosphate
Gln	Glutamine
Glt or Glu	Glutamate
Gly	Glycine
Glyox	Glyoxylate
i-Cit	Isocitrate
Lys	Lysine
Mal	Malate
OxAc	Oxaloacetate
PEP	Phosphoenolpyruvate
Pyr	Pyruvate
Suc	Succinate
SucCoA	Succinyl-Coenzyme-A

Table 14: Abbreviations of the names of metabolites

- Glycolysis

- *Lactate dehydrogenase*, converting pyruvate to lactate (a common anaerobic fate for pyruvate)

- The usual citric acid cycle (or tricarboxylic acid cycle, which will be referred to as TCA), with the exception of the bioreaction *α-ketoglutarate dehydrogenase* which will be assumed to be absent or non-functional

- The glyoxylate shunt to complement TCA and make up for the absence of

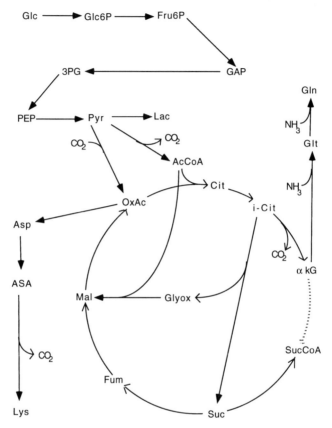

Figure 6: The basic bioreaction network for the synthesis of lysine

α-ketoglutarate dehydrogenase

- The bacterial pathway that leads from oxaloacetate to aspartate and on to lysine.

- *Glutamate dehydrogenase* and *glutamine synthetase* for the synthesis of glutamate and glutamine

Figure 6 was constructed to conform to the bioreaction network used in the analysis of experiments of lysine production. Note that the figure is substantially simplified, as:

- Many side-reactants and side-products are not shown.

- Many reactions are lumped together. In particular, the arrow drawn from aspartate-semialdehyde (ASA) to lysine represents 6 individual bioreac-

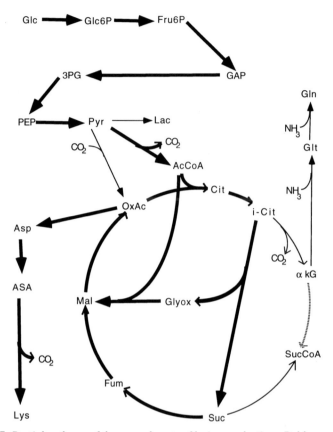

Figure 7: Partial pathway of the normal route of lysine production. Bold arrows in-dicate the reactions used in the pathway. Dotted arrow indicates a prohibited reac-tions.

tions.

One of the basic pathways believed to function in bacteria (such as *Bre-vibacterium Flavum*) for the conversion of glucose to lysine is shown in Fig-ure 7. The pathway uses the glyoxylate shunt to bypass α-*ketoglutarate de-hydrogenase*, which has not been included in the network.

The pathway of Figure 7 is actually only a partial one, because the path-way leading from aspartate to lysine requires succinyl-CoA and glutamate (at the same time producing succinate and α-ketoglutarate).

We can complete the pathway by looking for the smallest possible path-way which contains all the reactions already marked and additional reactions to balance the stoichiometries for succinyl-CoA, glutamate, succinate, and α-ketoglutarate. The stoichiometries of other metabolites (such as ATP or

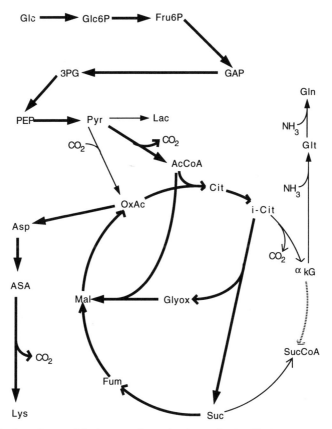

Figure 8. Completion of the basic pathway for the synthesis of lysine.

NAD) are also unbalanced, but we will consider them to be allowed reactants and allowed products.

The completed pathway is shown in Figure 8. The reactions added are *succinate kinase* and *glutamate dehydrogenase*, which, as might be expected, comprise the simplest alternative.

Maximum-rate analysis. We will calculate here the minimum enzyme requirement, which is a parameter related to the maximum rate of each bioreaction [Mavrovouniotis *et al.,* 1990b]. By comparing the rates of the bioreactions in the basic pathway of Figure 8 we will uncover kinetic bottlenecks. For the estimation of the maximum rate of a bioreaction, we need the equilibrium constant of the reaction, the concentrations of the reactants and products of the reaction, and the concentrations of enzymes:

• We would like to be as conservative as possible in choosing a value for the equilibrium constant, because it has a very strong effect on the maximum rate. We take the equilibrium constant of a bioreaction to be equal to the maximum value among:

◊ Any available data from the literature (residing in the database)

◊ The value estimated by the group-contribution method

- The concentrations of all metabolites are assumed to be in the default range we normally use for physiologically acceptable conditions. Thus, the concentrations of the products of each bioreaction are set to 5×10^{-6} and the concentrations of reactants are set to 5×10^{-3}.

- The concentration of the enzyme is not assumed to have any particular value. Since the maximum rate is proportional to the concentration of the enzyme, we can estimate [Mavrovouniotis, et al 1990b] the quantity r/E, i.e., maximum rate divided by the enzyme concentration, leaving the enzyme concentration unspecified.

Instead of using the ratio r/E, where the quantity E (in mol/l) refers to intracellular concentration and r (in mol/s l) refers to rate per unit cell volume, we can equivalently estimate the inverse of that ratio, i.e., E/r, which denotes the *minimum enzyme requirement* (per unit rate) for the bioreaction. The actual (i.e., experimental) E/r of a reaction must be higher than our estimate; since actual enzymes are less efficient it takes a higher (than ideally estimated) enzyme concentration to achieve a given rate. The minimum enzyme requirement, E/r, is a particularly convenient quantity because the minimum enzyme requirement of the whole pathway can be obtained simply by adding together the requirements of all the reactions.

In this context, it is convenient to take r not as the rate of the bioreaction examined, but rather as the rate of production of the final product. To achieve this transformation of reference-rate, we only need to multiply the initial enzyme requirement of each reaction by the corresponding coefficient of the reaction-stoichiometry of the pathway.

Note that, since a pathway involves many enzymes, the enzyme requirement of the pathway denotes the sum of the concentrations of different enzymes. This is not unreasonable considering that the different enzymes have to coexist and function in the same cell, and compete, in their synthesis, for same limited resources of the cell. Similarly, the pathway as a whole competes for resources for all of its enzymes, because it is functional only when sufficient quantities of all enzymes are present. Thus, in evaluating a pathway as a whole and comparing it to other pathways, it is useful to lump the concentrations of all the enzymes in the pathway and estimate the minimum enzyme requirement of the pathway.

The minimum enzyme requirement for each bioreaction in the basic pathway of Figure 8 is shown in Figure 9. For each reaction in Figure 9, the num-

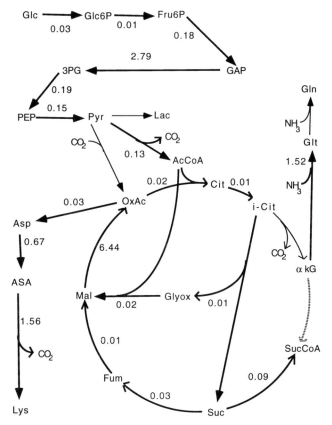

Figure 9. Calculation of minimum enzyme requirements for the basic pathway for lysine production

ber shown is the enzyme requirement of that reaction, in milliseconds. The total enzyme requirement for the whole pathway of Figure 9 is approximately 14 ms.

About half of the enzyme requirements of the pathway come from the bioreaction *malate dehydrogenase*, which has an enzyme requirement of 6.44 ms. The next larger contribution, equal to 2.7 ms, comes from *glyceraldehyde-phosphate dehydrogenase*. However, we have very little control over that enzyme since it belongs to glycolysis. Thus, *malate dehydrogenase* remains the main kinetic bottleneck of the pathway.

Bypassing the Potential Kinetic Bottleneck. We seek now new pathways that eliminate the kinetic bottleneck of malate dehydrogenase. In Figure 10 we show a first possibility, which has been already determined (experimentally) to function under certain conditions. This pathway involves the

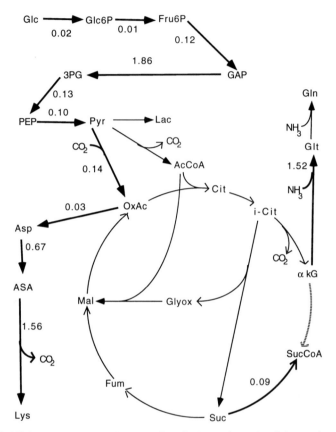

Figure 10. Minimum enzyme requirements for a lysine pathway involving carboxylation of pyruvate

carboxylation of pyruvate, bypassing the whole TCA cycle. This direct conversion of pyruvate to oxaloacetate can be achieved by two distinct bioreactions:

 • Pyruvate carboxylase
 • Oxaloacetate decarboxylase

The pathway of Figure 10 successfully bypasses the kinetic bottlenecks because its minimum enzyme requirement is only 6.4 ms, roughly equal to one half the requirement of the initial pathway. This pathway also has a higher maximum molar yield. Its yield is 100%, i.e., the pathway yields one mole of lysine per mole of glucose, as compared to a molar yield of 67% for the initial pathway of Figure 9.

If the original pathway has some good traits, we might prefer to bypass only the immediate vicinity of the bottleneck and retain much of the structure

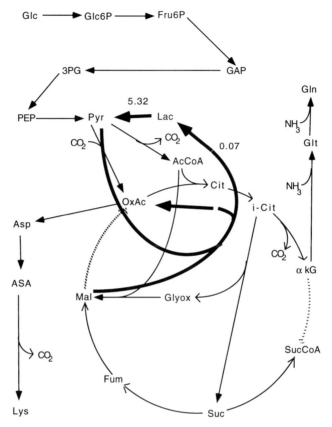

Figure 11. Pathway converting malate to oxaloacetate, with lactate and pyruvate as intermediates

of the original pathway intact, including the TCA cycle. A first alternative, shown in Figure 11, involves bypassing *malate dehydrogenase* with a set of just two reactions:

• *Lactate-Malate transhydrogenase* achieves the conversion:

MALATE + PYRUVATE → OXALOACETATE + LACTATE

• *Lactate dehydrogenase* achieves the conversion:

LACTATE → PYRUVATE

The combination of the two reactions converts malate to oxaloacetate. Unfortunately, the enzyme requirement of this bypass is approximately the same as that of *malate dehydrogenase*. Specifically, *lactate dehydrogenase* has a requirement of 5.32 ms (compared to 6.44 for *malate dehydrogenase*).

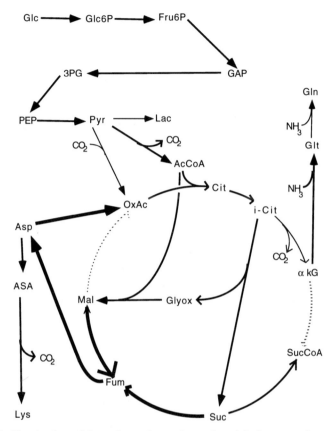

Figure 12. The simplest of the pathways bypassing malate dehydrogenase by converting fumarate to aspartate

Thus, this particular pathway offers little improvement over the original one. It is interesting to note that this pathway uses *lactate dehydrogenase* in the direction opposite to that originally drawn in Figure 6

Two more interesting alternatives are shown in Figures 12 and 13. They both involve:

• Conversion of malate to fumarate by using *Fumarase* in the direction opposite to that initially assumed in Figure 6

• Conversion of succinate to fumarate by *Succinate dehydrogenase* as in the original pathway

• Conversion of fumarate into aspartate through *Aspartate aminolyase*

  Since oxaloacetate is used in order to form citrate, half of the aspartate

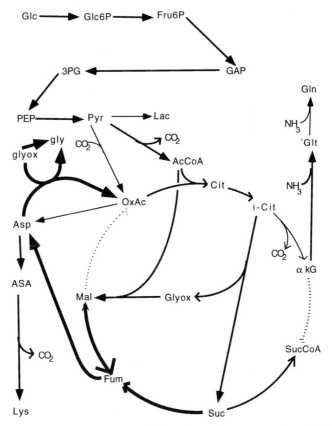

Figure 13. The kinetically most efficient of the pathways bypassing malate dehydrogenase by converting fumarate to aspartate

must be recycled back into oxaloacetate to close the TCA loop. The two pathways use different ways to achieve this:

- In the pathway of Figure 12 the reaction *aspartate glutamate transaminase* converts oxaloacetate to aspartate, by operating in the direction reverse to that assumed in the original bioreaction network (Figures 8 to 11).

- The pathway of Figure 13 uses a set of two reactions, *Glycine dehydrogenase* and *Glycine-oxaloacetate aminotransferase*, involving interconversion of glycine and glyoxylate.

The pathway of Figure 13 is longer, but it is actually the most efficient (kinetically) of all the pathways sharing the TCA structure of the original pathway. Its minimum enzyme requirement is 8 ms, i.e., almost half of the requirement of the original pathway.

Persistent Intermediates. In the two pathways discussed above, oxaloacetate is partly bypassed, in that it is needed only for the synthesis of citrate, and not directly for the synthesis of aspartate and lysine. An interesting question is whether we can bypass oxaloacetate *altogether* and produce aspartate directly from pyruvate or glucose.

With the reactions in our database, this turns out to be impossible. Thus, it appears that oxaloacetate is a key intermediate in the production of aspartate and lysine. The pathways we discuss in this chapter (and other pathways which were constructed but will not be discussed) indicate, in fact, that, the only *persistent* intermediates, i.e., intermediates that occur in all pathways are:

• The intermediates of glycolysis from glucose to phosphoenolpyruvate, with that section of the pathway fixed

• The intermediates of the pathway from aspartate to lysine, a pathway that is also fixed

• Oxaloacetate, for which no surrounding reaction is fixed, but the intermediate itself is always present (participating in different reactions)

One might argue that the conclusion that oxaloacetate is a necessary intermediate is obvious, because standard biochemistry textbooks classify lysine in the aspartate family [Mandelstam *et al.*, 1982, Rawn, 1983, Snyder *et al.*, 1985], and aspartate is commonly synthesized from oxaloacetate. However, the pathways discussed here involve several different bioreactions consuming or producing oxaloacetate; thus, the metabolism in the region of this intermediate can hardly be characterized as fixed. Our conclusion states that any lysine-producing pathway involves at least 2 of these reactions (hence there is no pathway that can avoid the intermediate altogether).

In the pathway of Figure 12 (and its variation suggested by Figure 13) aspartate and lysine are *not* directly derived from oxaloacetate, because fumarate is converted to aspartate by a single enzyme. In fact, aspartate is converted *into* oxaloacetate (rather than the reverse). Thus, the metabolism in the neighborhood of aspartate, fumarate, malate and oxaloacetate is quite different from what one would find in a standard biochemistry textbook. This portion of the metabolism suggests that it *is* possible to derive aspartate without the intervention of oxaloacetate. It turns out however that, within the enzyme database used here, the necessary TCA intermediates (malate or succinate) cannot be produced from glucose without the intervention of oxaloacetate; this constraint necessitates the presence of oxaloacetate in any pathway leading from glucose to lysine. In effect, the real obstacle is that production of fumarate from glucose requires the TCA cycle and hence oxaloacetate.

To illustrate this point better, assume that (in addition to glucose) we could use succinate as an allowed reactant. *A priori* biosynthetic classifications would still entail oxaloacetate as a required intermediate. Inspection of Figure 13 reveals, however, that succinate can be converted to fumarate and on to aspartate (by *aspartate aminolyase*), without the intervention of malate or oxaloacetate. Thus, with succinate as an additional substrate, it is entirely possible to synthesize lysine with a pathway that does not entail oxaloacetate.

If one rests with the preconceived pathways of biochemistry textbooks, one would draw a variety of conclusions about essential enzymes and intermediates. It would, for example, appear safe to assume that the carboxylation of pyruvate to oxaloacetate must involve either *pyruvate carboxylase* or *oxaloacetate decarboxylase*. This assumption would not be correct, because there are non-obvious alternatives, such as the pathway of Figure 12. Other pathways discussed here (e.g., Figures 11 or 13) contain other non-obvious possibilities for different biotransformations.

Fundamental Constraints. Some of the most interesting results of applying the synthesis algorithm involve not particular pathways found, but rather demonstrations that no pathways exist to meet certain sets of specifications.

We discussed already the fact that there is no pathway that will reach aspartate (and consequently lysine) from glucose without going through oxaloacetate. A second interesting constraint that was uncovered by the algorithm refers to the maximum yield of the pathway:

- The yield can exceed 67% only if carbon dioxide is recovered by some bioreaction.

In effect, if we eliminate reactions that consume carbon dioxide, the yield is restricted to be 67% or less. A point to keep in mind is that these constraints only hold for the set of reactions present in our database. It is entirely possible that inclusion of additional reactions will change these results.

5 Concluding Remarks

The problem of synthesizing qualitatively feasible biochemical pathways was discussed in this chapter. With respect to thermodynamic feasibility, a group contribution technique that allows the estimation of equilibrium constants of bioreactions was described. With respect to stoichiometric requirements, an algorithm for pathway synthesis was presented, based on the iterative satisfaction of constraints, and the transformation of the initial set of reactions (which can be thought of as one-step pathways) into a final set of pathways which satisfy all constraints. The algorithm generates all biochemical production routes that satisfy a set of linear stoichiometric constraints; these constraints designate bioreactions and metabolites (in their role as reactants, products, or intermediates of the pathways) as required, allowed, or prohibited. For the task of synthesis of biochemical pathways, this is the first algorithm that is formal and well-defined, with proven properties like completeness and correctness.

The algorithm is of significant value in the investigation of alternative biochemical pathways to achieve a given biotransformation (which is defined by a set of stoichiometric specifications). It can also produce pathways that bypass bottlenecks of a given pathway. A variety of alternative non-obvious routes for the synthesis of lysine demonstrates the utility of computer-based, systematic construction of pathways. Furthermore, the algorithm can identify fundamental limitations that govern the biochemical pathways and the process. In the case of lysine-producing pathways, it was shown that oxaloacetate is always present as an intermediate, and that in the absence of recovery of carbon dioxide by some bioreaction the yield of lysine over glucose is restricted to be 0.67 or less.

If the database of bioreactions is expanded to include a much larger number of bioreactions (and ultimately all known bioreactions), the computational performance of the algorithm would have to be drastically improved, in terms of both conceptual structure and actual implementation.

Notes

[1] The constraints are assumed to be consistent. For example, if S is a required product, it cannot be a required reactant.

[2] On Symbolics computers there are 36 bits in each word (32 bits for data and 4 bits for data-type). In LISP implementations on general-purpose hardware, one word might actually correspond to ~6 bytes. The distinction between list-words and structure-words is only important if one is recycling objects (and hence structure-words).

[3] To obtain smaller integer coefficients for the combination pathway, the fractions 1/3 and 2/3 were used instead of 1 and 2 in the construction of the combination. This has the same effect as dividing the resulting pathway by 3; clearly, the essence of the transformation and the overall significance of the pathway are not affected by multiplicative constants. Only the molar *proportions* of metabolites and reactions matter.

References

Barman, T. E. *Enzyme Handbook*, Supplement 1 (Springer-Verlag, New York, 1974).

Barman, T. E. *Enzyme Handbook*, Volume 1 (Springer-Verlag, New York, 1969).

Barman, T. E. *Enzyme Handbook*, Volume 2 (Springer-Verlag, New York, 1969).

Benson, S. W. *Thermochemical Kinetics* (Wiley, New York, 1968).

Benson, S. W., Cruickshank, F. R., Golden, D. M., Haugen, G. R., O'Neal, H. E., Rodgers, A. S., Shaw, R., and Walsh, R. *Chemical Rev.*, **69**, 279 (1969).

Domalski, E. S., and Hearing, E. D. "Estimation of the Thermodynamic Properties of Hydrocarbons at 298.15 K." *Journal of Physics and Chemistry Ref. Data,* **14**, 1637 (1988).

Edsall, J. T., and Gutfreund, H. *Biothermodynamics* (Wiley, New York, 1983).Hinz, H.-J. *Thermodynamic Data for Biochemistry and Biotechnology* (Springer-Verlag, New York, 1986).

Joback, K. G., and Reid, R. C. Estimation of Pure-Component Properties from Group Contributions. *Chem. Eng. Comm.,* **57**, 233 (1987).

Lehninger, A.E. *Biochemistry*, 2nd ed. (Worth, New York, 1975).

Lehninger, A.E. *Principles of Biochemistry* (Worth, New York, 1986).

Mandelstam, J., McQuillen, K., and Dawes, I. *Biochemistry of Bacterial Growth, 3rd edition*, pp. 163-165. Wiley, New York, 1982.

Mavrovouniotis, M. L, *Symbolic Computing in the Prediction of Properties of Organic Compounds*, Technical Report SRC TR 89-95 (Systems Research Center, University of Maryland, College Park, MD, 1989).

Mavrovouniotis, M. L. *Computer-Aided Design of Biochemical Pathways.* Ph.D. Thesis, Dept. of Chemical Engineering, Massachusetts Institute of Technology, 1989.

Mavrovouniotis, M. L. "Estimation of Properties from Conjugate Forms of Molecular Structures: The ABC Approach", 29: 1943-1953 *Industrial and Engineering Chemistry Research,* 1990a.

Mavrovouniotis, M. L. Group Contributions to the Gibbs Energy of Formation of Biochemical Compounds in Aqueous Solution. *Biotechnology and Bioengineering,* 36, 1070-1082, 1990b.

Mavrovouniotis, M. L. Estimation of Standard Gibbs Energy Changes of Biotransformations. *Journal of Biological Chemistry*, 266, 14440-14445, 1991.

Mavrovouniotis, M. L., Bayol, P., Lam, T.-K. M., Stephanopoulos, G., and Stephanopoulos, G. *Biotechnology Techniques,* **2**, 23 (1988).

Mavrovouniotis, M. L., Stephanopoulos, G., and Stephanopoulos, G. Computer-Aided Synthesis of Biochemical Pathways. *Biotechnology and Bioengineering*, 36, 1119-1132, 1990a.

Mavrovouniotis, M. L., Stephanopoulos, G., and Stephanopoulos, G. Estimation of Upper Bounds for the Rates of Enzymatic Reactions. *Chemical Engineering Communications,* 93, 211-236, 1990b.

Morrison, R. T., and Boyd, R. N. *Organic Chemistry, 3rd edition* (Allyn and Bacon, Boston 1973).

Mostow, J. "Rutgers Workshop on Knowledge-Based Design" *SIGART Newsletter* (90):19-32, October, 1984.

Mostow, J. "Toward Better Models of the Design Process" *AI Magazine* 6(1):44-56, Spring, 1985.

Old, R.W., and Primrose, S.B. *Principles of Gene Manipulation, 3rd edition.* Blackwell Scientific Publications, London, 1985.

Rawn, J. D. *Biochemistry*, pp. 883-888. Harper and Row, New York, 1983.

Reid, R. C., Prausnitz, J. M., and Poling, B. E. *The Properties of Gases and Liquids, 4th edition* (McGraw-Hill, New York, 1987).

Reid, R. C., Prausnitz, J. M., and Sherwood, T. K. *The Properties of Gases and Liquids, 3rd edition* (McGraw-Hill, New York, 1977).

Snyder, L.A., Freifelder, D., and Hartl, D.L. *General Genetics.* Jones and Bartlett Publishers, Boston, 1985.

Sober , H.A. (ed) *Handbook of Biochemistry* (CRC, Cleveland, Ohio, 1970).

Thauer, R. K., Jungermann, K., and Decker, K. *Bacteriological Reviews,* 41: 148 (1977).

10

Knowledge-Based Simulation of DNA Metabolism: Prediction of Action and Envisionment of Pathways

Adam R. Galper, Douglas L. Brutlag & David H. Millis

1 Introduction

Our understanding of any process can be measured by the extent to which a simulation we create mimics the real behavior of that process. Deviations of a simulation indicate either limitations or errors in our knowledge. In addition, these observed differences often suggest verifiable experimental hypotheses to extend our knowledge.

The biochemical approach to understanding biological processes is essentially one of simulation. A biochemist typically prepares a cell-free extract that can mediate a well-described physiological process. The extract is then fractionated to purify the components that catalyze individual reactions. Finally, the physiological process is reconstituted *in vitro*. The success of the biochemical approach is usually measured by how closely the reconstituted process matches physiological observations.

An automated simulation of metabolism can play a role analogous to that of the biochemist in using and extending knowledge. By carefully representing the principles and logic used for reasoning in the laboratory, we can simulate faithfully, on a computer, known biochemical behavior. The simulation can also serve as an interactive modeling tool for reasoning about metabolism in the design of experiments, in discovery, and in education.

1.1 Simulation Methods

Simulation is a modeling technique that represents the behavior of individual components of a system over time. There are two predominant approaches [Rothenberg, 1989]. The *analytic* approach to simulation uses mathematical analysis to represent the temporal behaviors of components, often in closed form. Analytic simulations capture aggregate system behavior by modeling small and relatively similar entities. *Discrete-event*, or discrete-state, simulation is used when the system's overall behavior is not understood well enough to permit formal mathematical analysis; instead, the low-level, pairwise interactions of components are encoded, the simulation is "run," and higher-level patterns of interaction are revealed.

Until recently, most simulations of metabolism were analytic. By metabolism, we mean a set of reactions, the members of which participate in the synthesis (anabolism), degradation (catabolism), or general maintenance of a substance. A typical reaction in a metabolic pathway may involve numerous reactants, intermediates, and products, and may be catalyzed by an enzyme and cofactors. Furthermore, each reaction may be characterized kinetically in terms of metabolite concentrations and reaction rates. The analytic approach to metabolic simulation typically requires the determination of steady-state rate equations for constituent reactions, followed by numerical integration of a set of differential equations describing fluxes in the metabolism [Bierbicher, Eigen, and Gardiner, 1983; Franco and Canela, 1984; Kohn and Garfinkel, 1983a; Kohn and Garfinkel, 1983b; Thomas, *et al.*, 1976; Waser, *et al.*, 1983].

For example, Franco and Canela present an analytic simulation of purine metabolism, including the salvage pathway and interconversion of purine mononucleotides, using information from the literature about the kinetic behavior of 14 metabolic enzymes [Franco and Canela, 1984]. They then simulate an increase or decrease in the concentration of any enzyme to approximate the metabolic changes observed in inborn errors of purine metabolism.

The feasibility of the analytic approach is limited by the extent to which the metabolic processes of interest have been characterized. For most metabolic pathways, either we are unaware of all the steps involved or we lack rate constants for each step. This lack of information precludes the use of the mathematical approach in describing the process. Even when reaction rates are known, differential equations incur great computational costs; numerical integration of Franco and Canela's set of 15 differential equations, implemented in FORTRAN 77, required almost 2 hours of CPU time on an IBM 4341 mainframe. Subsequent simulation of enzyme deficit and overproduction required an average of 275 seconds of CPU time per enzyme.

Although the closed-form solutions of analytic simulation are appealing, they are often cryptic and are difficult to use interactively. Differential equations model metabolites along only quantitative dimensions (e.g., concentrations, reaction rates); qualitative knowledge (e.g., structural properties of metabolites or enzymes) is often external to the simulation. If a reaction in a metabolic pathway is only partially characterized, a strict analytic approach to simulation may not work, for lack of quantitative data.

The discrete-event approach to simulation, on the other hand, can use all available data, both quantitative and qualitative, and can even incorporate analytic methods where applicable; semiquantitative models, which couple symbolic and numeric computing techniques, have been developed for a number of domains, including the human cardiovascular system and gene regulation in bacteria [Widman, 1989; Karp and Friedland, 1989; Meyer and Friedland, 1986].

The critical feature of discrete-event simulation is its natural support of qualitative representation and reasoning techniques, which offer explicit treatment of causality. Qualitative representations are thought to provide more insight into how physical systems function [deKleer and Brown, 1984]. The recent flurry of interest in qualitative reasoning has much to offer to both analytic and discrete-event simulations of physical systems [Bobrow, 1984].

Whereas the differential equation is the basic currency of analytic simulation, the rule is central to discrete-event simulation. Rule-based methods allow the representation of knowledge at multiple levels of detail [Buchanan and Shortliffe, 1984; Davis, Buchanan, and Shortliffe, 1977]. For example, in some instances, the actual catalytic mechanism and intermediates of a metabolic reaction are known and can be specified. In other instances, only substrates and products can be represented. Likewise, the regulation of a pathway can be represented at various levels of detail. For example, the feedback inhibition on the transcription process, which controls the overall level of activity of an enzyme, can be expressed in a few simple rules, without the entire process of gene expression being described. Other pathways may require a more detailed representation of all enzymes, activators, and inhibitors.

A rule-based, discrete-event simulation of metabolism can also be fast and highly interactive. Inference is commonly achieved through forward chaining, or deduction from an asserted fact, and through backward chaining, in which specific facts are inferred to support a hypothesis. Truth-maintenance mechanisms, which deduce and retract conclusions automatically when the underlying fact base changes, make the reasoning processes involved in rule-based simulations more robust and efficient [deKleer, 1986].

Most important, a discrete-event simulation, implemented with rules, can explain its predictions based on the known facts and on the rules relating those facts. Explanation graphs show the flow of logic, the relationships among stated facts, and the deduced conclusions. In comparison, analytic simulations often obscure the understanding being sought.

1.2 A Simulation of DNA Metabolism

We have built a rule-based, discrete-event simulation of DNA metabolism. In particular, we have focused on the pathways of DNA replication and repair in *Escherichia coli* (E. coli). The simulation relies on a panoply of artificial-intelligence (AI) techniques for representation, inference, and explanation; we refer to the simulation as *knowledge-based*. We have chosen initially to represent all domain knowledge qualitatively, because most biochemists reason about DNA metabolism in qualitative terms [Schaffner, 1987].

Unlike intermediary metabolism, in which the flow of substrates and cyclical reactions are critical, DNA metabolism is characterized by discrete, temporally ordered events, in which the concentration of substrate is assumed to be sufficient to support metabolic reactions. For example, when a nucleotide is present, we assume that its concentration is greater than K_m, the substrate concentration at which an enzyme-catalyzed reaction proceeds at half-maximal velocity. Thus, the reactions with which we are concerned either occur or do not occur; there are no partial reactions in our system.

With this commitment, we have little need for the precise quantitative measures that characterize enzyme kinetics. We map all continuous variables, such as substrate concentration, pH value, and temperature, into discrete ranges, in which enzymes either show activity or do not show activity, and we refer to these ranges within rules.

Currently, the simulation can predict the action an enzyme will take under a large number of experimental conditions, and can envision a subset of the possible metabolic pathways followed by substrates. In qualitative reasoning, envisionment is the determination of all possible behavioral sequences from an initial structural description. Ultimately, we hope to envision all possible pathways from an initial description of an experimental situation.

This chapter recounts our experience thus far in developing a knowledge-based simulation of DNA metabolism. Section 2 provides background information for computer scientists and biologists. In Section 3, we present our techniques in detail. Section 4 provides sample interactions with the simulation. Finally, Section 5 compares our techniques to related work on metabolic simulations, summarizes our conclusions, and discusses future research directions.

2 Background

We have begun a formal description, using AI techniques, of the replication and repair pathways of DNA metabolism in *E. coli*. In this section, we present, for computer scientists, a brief description of DNA metabolism, and, for biologists, an introduction to relevant symbolic processing techniques.

2.1. DNA Metabolism

The major mechanisms of DNA metabolism include replication, repair, transcription, and mutation. Genetic information is transferred from parent to progeny by the faithful replication of DNA, in which the nucleotide base sequence of the parent molecule is duplicated. Repair mechanisms preserve the integrity of DNA molecules by correcting occasional replication errors (mismatched base pairs) and eliminating damage caused by the environment (radiation, chemicals). The expression of genetic information begins with the transcription of DNA to RNA. Mutations of DNA molecules, which result in mutant phenotypes, can involve the substitution, addition, or deletion of one or more bases. These metabolic processes are not understood completely, but many of the implicated enzymes have been well characterized. In our simulation, we address the mechanisms of replication and repair in the common intestinal bacterium *E. Coli* by representing current knowledge about the critical enzymes.

DNA polymerase I from *E. coli* is one of the more complex enzymes of DNA metabolism, possessing at least five distinct enzymatic activities in a single polypeptide chain [Kornberg, 1980; Kornberg, 1982]. It is the central player in the major pathways of DNA replication and repair, and is one of the most highly characterized enzymes in DNA metabolism. The enzyme is able to synthesize DNA from the four precursor deoxynucleoside triphosphates—dATP, dGTP, dCTP, and dTTP—as long as a primer-template DNA molecule is present. The enzyme extends the 3'-hydroxyl terminus of a DNA primer, which is hydrogen-bonded to the template, by adding nucleotide residues one at a time, according to the Watson–Crick base-pairing rules—adenine with thymine and guanine with cytosine.

DNA polymerase I occasionally adds a nucleotide that cannot hydrogen-bond to the corresponding base in the template strand. When this happens, polymerization stops, because the primer is no longer correctly hydrogen-bonded. However, DNA polymerase I can remove the unpaired base using an endogenous 3' exonuclease activity and resume polymerization. This 3' exonuclease activity is known as proofreading. DNA polymerase I can also remove base-paired nucleotides from the 5' terminus; when polymerization oc-

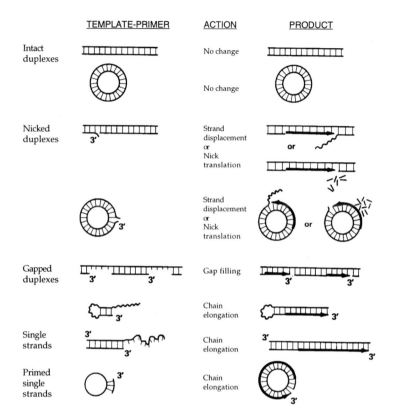

Figure 1. The activities of DNA polymerase I on various templates and primers. (Source: Adapted from Kornberg, 1980, with permission.)

curs simultaneously, nick translation may occur. Polymerization and exonucleolytic degradation are the primary activities of DNA polymerase I, as depicted in Figure 1.

E. coli DNA ligase performs an important function at the end of DNA repair, replication, and recombination—namely, sealing the remaining nicks. DNA ligase joins adjacent 3'-hydroxyl and 5'-phosphoryl termini in nicked duplex DNA by forming a phosphodiester bond. In E. coli, DNA ligase requires magnesium and nicotinamide adenine dinucleotide (NAD) as cofactors.

Phosphodiester bond synthesis occurs through three component reactions [Lehman, 1974], as depicted in Figure 2. First, the enzyme reacts with NAD to form ligase-adenylate, a complex in which an adenosine monophosphate (AMP) moiety is linked to a lysine residue of the enzyme through a phosphoamide bond. Nicotinamide mononucleotide (NMN) is released (see Figure

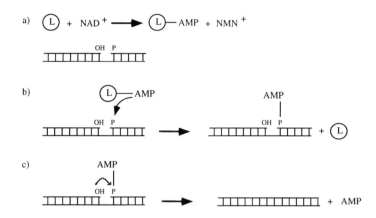

Figure 2. The activities mediated by DNA ligase. a) DNA ligase and nicotinamide adenine dinucleotide combine to form ligase adenylate. b) The adenyl group is transferred from the ligase-adenylate complex to the DNA at the site of the nick to generate a new pyrophosphate linkage. c) The 5' phosphate is attacked by the apposing 3'-hydroxyl group at the nick to form a phosphodiester bond, thus eliminating the AMP.

2a). Next, the adenyl group is transferred from the ligase-adenylate complex to the DNA at the site of the nick to generate a new pyrophosphate linkage, between the AMP group and the 5'-phosphoryl terminus at the nick (see Figure 2b). Finally, the 5' phosphate is attacked by the apposing 3'-hydroxyl group at the nick to form a phosphodiester bond, and AMP is eliminated (see Figure 2c).

Each of these component reactions is reversible; thus, DNA ligase is also able to catalyze an AMP-dependent endonuclease reaction. These nicking and sealing activities can be demonstrated through the AMP-dependent conversion of a closed superhelical circle via a nicked, adenylylated intermediate to a closed, relaxed circle [Modrich, Lehman, and Wang, 1972]. For a complete discussion of DNA metabolism, we refer the reader to any of several textbooks on molecular biology, including [Freifelder, 1985; Watson, 1988], and to reference texts on replication and repair [Kornberg, 1980; Friedberg, 1985].

The catalytic actions mediated by DNA polymerase I and DNA ligase depend on both the physiological conditions and the structure of the DNA substrate. For example, if conditions are not appropriate for binding free nucleotides, then polymerization by DNA polymerase I will not occur. Alternatively, if the 3' primer terminus of the DNA is not a hydroxyl group, then polymerase I will bind either too tightly or too loosely to the substrate, and synthesis of new DNA will be thwarted. If NAD is not present, then

DNA ligase will not seal a nick. Notice that these catalytic actions, as well as all those depicted in Figures 1 and 2, can be expressed succinctly as rules, with the appropriate descriptions of enzyme, substrate, and conditions.

2.2. Artificial Intelligence Methods

Artificial intelligence offers numerous methods for representing large amounts of knowledge and for reasoning with that knowledge to find solutions to problems. We use a common and very general framework known as a *production system*. A production system consists of a set of rules for drawing conclusions and performing actions, a working memory that structures the relevant information appropriately, and a control strategy for governing the use of the rule set on the working memory. Each of our production rules is expressed in an English-like if–then form. For example, to denote the requirement that a 3' terminus be paired and have a hydroxyl group for DNA polymerase I to extend a primer, we write

```
(IF (OR
     (AND (THE EXTERNAL-3P-GROUP OF DNA IS HYDROXYL)
          (THE EXTERNAL-3P-END OF DNA IS PAIRED))
     (AND (THE INTERNAL-3P-GROUP OF DNA IS HYDROXYL)
          (THE INTERNAL-3P-END OF DNA IS PAIRED)))
 THEN
 DEDUCE
     (A SPECIFICITY OF DNA-POLYMERASE-I IS PRIMER-EXTENSION))
```

We shall explain the representation of DNA and enzyme in Section 3.1; for now, notice that the premise and conclusion of this rule refer to objects in our simulated world (DNA, DNA-POLYMERASE-I). Each object, or *unit*, has various attributes, or *slots* (e.g., INTERNAL-3P-END, SPECIFICI-TY), each of which can take on a number of values (e.g., PAIRED, PRIMER-EXTENSION). Units correspond to real-world entities, and slots describe those entities; with these tools, we can build the second component of a production system—the working memory on which the rules act.

Unit representations, often referred to as *frame-based*, have several advantages over other representational methods [Fikes and Kehler, 1985; Minsky, 1975; Minsky, 1986; Stefik, 1979]. Frames can be organized into hierarchies, in which the most specific objects, called *instances*, inherit attributes from the more general objects, called *classes*. In addition, hierarchical frame-based representations are *object-oriented* and *modular* [Bobrow and Stefik, 1986; Brachman, Fikes, and Levesque, 1983; Levesque and Brachman, 1984; Stefik and Bobrow, 1986].

The final component of a production system is the control strategy, which is used to apply the production rules to the working memory. To determine the applicability of each rule, the production system can compare the premise of the rule to working memory; if the premise is true, the rule is "fired," and the actions prescribed by the rule are taken. The control strategy specifies the order in which rules will be compared to working memory and resolves conflicts that arise when several rules match at the same time. Two common control strategies are *breadth-first* and *depth-first* search.

The production-system framework can be used to reason in both the forward and backward directions. In the forward direction, we reason from the data available currently; the premises of rules are matched against working memory, and any actions are taken on the working memory. Then, the rule set is compared to the new working memory. This approach is often called *data-directed reasoning* or *forward chaining*. In the backward direction, we reason from our desired goals; the conclusions of rules are matched against working memory, and the premises become new goals to be achieved. We continue until the initial goal is achieved. This approach is known as *goal-directed reasoning* or *backward chaining*. Of course, the same rule set can be used for both forward and backward chaining.

In addition to a production system, we use a technique known as *truth maintenance*. A truth-maintenance system (TMS) supports *nonmonotonic reasoning*, in which the number of facts known to be true is not strictly increasing over time. Thus, the addition of a new piece of information to working memory may force the deletion of another. A TMS manages the dependencies among facts. A particular fact becomes true when one or more supporting facts becomes true. The same fact may become false during the course of a run through the simulation if new information causes the supporting facts to become false.

For example, a user may assert that DNA has a hydroxyl group at its 3' terminus, which is also paired. The system can conclude that DNA polymerase I could extend the primer from the 3' end, if the environmental conditions were appropriate (e.g., nucleotides are required). If the user now removes the fact that the 3' terminus is paired, the TMS retracts the earlier conclusion about DNA polymerase I's specificity for extending the primer. The TMS is similar to a forward chainer in that both examine facts that are currently true to determine whether new facts can become true. In addition, the TMS can withdraw a fact when there no longer are sufficient data to support that fact.

We refer the reader to any of several AI textbooks for a comprehensive introduction to the field [Nilsson, 1980; Rich, 1983; Charniak and McDermott, 1985; Schapiro, 1986].

3 Techniques

In this work, the domain-specific knowledge has been provided directly by the developers of the system and by readings from the literature

[Kornberg, 1980; Lehman, 1974]. In the future, we plan to simplify the process of knowledge acquisition, so that a biochemist will be able to enter new information without having to learn the details of the knowledge representation. We discuss some possibilities for knowledge-acquisition tools in Section 5.

The simulation currently resides in the Knowledge Engineering Environment (KEE), developed by Intellicorp, Inc. KEE provides a rich collection of knowledge-engineering tools in a Common LISP environment. A flexible and expressive frame system allows the representation of complex objects, relationships, and behaviors. KEE units can be organized logically into hierarchies to permit parsimonious representations. Rules are themselves units, and can be used for both forward and backward chaining. An assumption-based truth-maintenance system [deKleer, 1986] manages the dependencies among facts, as expressed by rules. Facts can thus be concluded automatically whenever existing evidence supports their inference; when justifications are retracted, all dependent facts are retracted as well. KEE's ActiveImages package provides a number of graphic displays for both viewing and modifying attribute values in KEE objects. The KeePictures package will permit us to develop graphic representations of metabolic objects, including intermediates and products.

In Sections 3.1 through 3.4, we distinguish between the representation of simulation objects and the representation of the interactions between these objects.

3.1. Representation of Objects

We have developed a modular and robust representation for the metabolites we wish to simulate. There are currently three major classes of objects: DNAS, ENVIRONMENTAL-CONDITIONS, and ENZYMES. An instance of each class requires specification of all possible attribute values; the rules describing an instance's behavior are described in Section 4.2. There are currently four major objects: DNA, an instance of the DNAS class; CONDITIONS, an instance of the ENVIRONMENTAL-CONDITIONS class; and two ENZYMES instances, DNA-POLYMERASE-I and DNA-LIGASE. All information regarding DNA—including class information, instances, active images, and rules—is contained in the DNA-KB knowledge base. Likewise, all information regarding the environmental conditions is contained in the CON-DITIONS-KB. All information regarding each enzyme instance is contained in the dedicated knowledge bases, POL-I-KB and LIGASE-KB. This design allows us to load units for selective testing, without the interference of knowledge from other objects in the simulation. This use of distributed knowledge bases also will eventually allow us to examine specific subsets of enzymes, much as a biochemist would mix reagents in the laboratory.

The descriptive information in the DNAS class is intentionally redundant.

Our goal is to provide methods for specifying the properties of DNA in as many ways as is natural for a scientist. For example, the biochemist can declare that the STRUCTURE of DNA is a NICKED-CIRCLE, or that the TOPOLOGY is CIRCULAR and the STRANDS are NICKED-DUPLEX. Either description will infer the other. The rules for reasoning about DNA are instances of the DNA-RULES class and refer only to attributes of a DNA unit. All 96 DNA-RULES instances are organized by the attribute of DNA referenced in the conclusion of the rule; thus, all rules that determine the TOPOLOGY of DNA are members of the TOPOLOGY-RULES subclass of DNA-RULES.

We use a hierarchy of four levels to describe DNA. At the lowest level, we describe a DNA molecule by characterizing the 5' and 3' termini at both external and internal positions. For example, a gapped, linear DNA molecule will have 3'-internal and 5'-internal termini at either end of the gap; in addition, there are 3' and 5' external termini at the ends of the molecule. We characterize each terminus by specifying the chemical group present (e.g., HYDROXYL, PHOSPHATE, DIDEOXY, ADENYL) and the nature of the terminus (e.g., PAIRED, UNPAIRED, RECESSED, PROTRUDING). At the next level, we summarize the information about the termini by filling the ENDS slot with values such as FLUSH and 3'-PROTRUDING. These values can be specified by the user or inferred by rules that consider the status of the component termini. At the next level, the user can fill slots that specify components of the overall structure of the molecule: The NICKS slot qualitatively describes the nicks present (NONE, SOME, ONE, MULTIPLE), the TOPOLOGY slot specifies the possible shapes (e.g., LINEAR, Y-FORM, CIRCULAR), the STRANDEDNESS slot can take on the values SINGLE-STRANDED and DOUBLE-STRANDED, and the STRANDS slot describes the strands independent of topology (e.g., INTACT-DUPLEX, NICKED-DUPLEX, PRIMED-SINGLE-STRAND). Finally, at the highest descriptive level, the overall STRUCTURE slot offers a list of common DNA structures (e.g., PRIMED-CIRCLE, NICKED-LINEAR, COVALENTLY-CLOSED-CIRCLE), from which the value of component slots can be inferred. The active image associated with the DNA unit is shown in Figure 3. We can conceive of multiple, independent DNA units in a simulation; if a reaction causes the generation of a new, independent DNA molecule (e.g., strand displacement followed by cleavage of the displaced strand), the simulation will contain two DNA instances, a duplex and a single-stranded molecule, each of which will interact differently with the enzymes present.

The CONDITIONS unit contains three quantitative attributes that describe the physical environment: TEMPERATURE, PH, and IONIC-STRENGTH (see Figure 4). Values of these slots have been mapped into discrete ranges to facilitate purely qualitative reasoning and to reduce the number of rules that cannot be handled by the TMS (see Section 4.3). Currently, the TEMPERA-

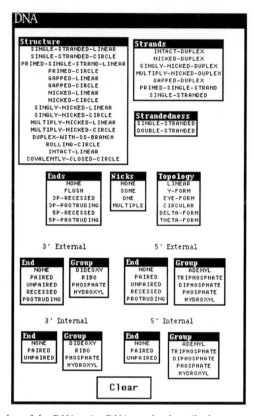

Figure 3. Display of the DNA unit. DNA can be described at several levels of detail. At the most detailed level, DNA can be characterized by the 5' and 3' termini at both external and internal positions; at the most abstract level, the substrate DNA can be one of 16 common structures. The goal is to provide methods for specifying the properties of DNA in as many ways as is natural for a scientist.

TURE-RANGE slot can take on values from among 0-TO-5, 5-TO-20, 20-TO-45, 30-TO-37, and 45-TO-100.

The significant PH-RANGE values are 6.0-TO-9.5 and 7.5-TO-8.0; the PH-RANGE slot value is unknown if the PH slot value is not within these ranges. The IONIC-STRENGTH-RANGE slot is handled in a similar fashion, with range values 0.001-TO-0.003 and 0.001-TO-0.3.

The CONDITIONS-RULES class manages the mapping of all quantitative variables into qualitative ranges, which are then referenced in the premises of rules that represent interactions between enzymes, substrates, and the environment. The other attributes in the CONDITIONS unit, including NUCLEOTIDES, MONOVALENT-CATIONS, DIVALENT-CATIONS,

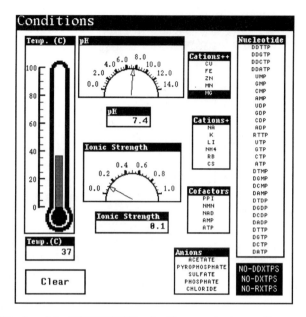

Figure 4. Display of the CONDITIONS unit. The quantitative attributes are mapped into range attributes (not shown). For example, when the TEMPERATURE is 37.5 degrees, the TEMPERATURE-RANGE attribute is 20-TO-45. All enzyme-activity rules that depend on temperature use this attribute to determine temperature.

ANIONS, and COFACTORS, represent physical objects, and could be modeled as units in the simulation. We have chosen not to do this, because we are interested in these objects only by virtue of their presence or absence; we have no use for structural descriptions of these objects. We thus consider these substances as attributes of the environment and assume that they are present in quantities that support the reactions simulated, if they are present at all.

We propose a general model for the qualitative representation of enzymes, embodied in the ENZYMES class. The ACTIVITY of an enzyme is determined by the environmental conditions; likewise, the SPECIFICITY of an enzyme depends solely on the substrate. In turn, the ACTION of the enzyme depends on the enzyme's specificity and activity. In many cases, an enzyme may exist in different STATEs—for example, free or bound to a substrate. The DNA-POLYMERASE-I and DNA-LIGASE units contain different lists of potential values for each of the ACTIVITY, SPECIFICITY, ACTION, and STATE slots. For example, DNA polymerase I can display binding activities (e.g., XMP-BINDING, XTP-BINDING, DNA-BINDING), synthetic activities (DIDEOXY-CHAIN-TERMINATION, STRAND-DISPLACE-

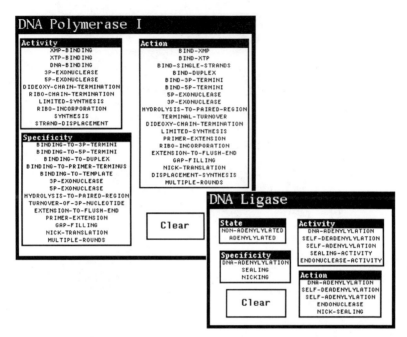

Figure 5. The DNA-POLYMERASE-I and DNA-LIGASE representations. Each sub-panel represents an enzyme attribute and contains all possible values of that attribute.

MENT), or degradative activities (3P-EXONUCLEASE, 5P-EXONUCLEASE). Similarly, ligase can bind (DNA-ADENYLYLATION, SELF-ADENYLYLATION), synthesize (SEALING-ACTIVITY), or degrade (ENDONUCLEASE-ACTIVITY). Recall that the ACTIVITY value depends solely on the environmental conditions; the SPECIFICITY slot for each enzyme has similar types of values, but depends on the substrate description. Slots describing an enzyme can take on multiple values at the same time; for example, in nick translation, the polymerization and 5' exonuclease activities of polymerase I are possible simultaneously. The active images for DNA-POLYMERASE-I and DNA-LIGASE, depicting all possible values for each slot, are displayed in Figure 5.

3.2. Representation of Interactions and Behaviors

The object representations described in Section 3.1 correspond to the working memory of a production system; the rule set, which operates on working memory, captures knowledge of the potential interactions between and behaviors of the simulation objects. Rules for simulating DNA-POLY-MERASE-I action are all instances of the DNA-POL-I-RULES class, contained in the POL-I-KB knowledge base. The LIGASE-RULE class is likewise independently contained in the LIGASE-KB knowledge base.

We structure enzyme rule hierarchies along the same lines as the representation of the enzyme; for example, there are POL-I-SPECIFICITY-RULES, POL-I-ACTIVITY-RULES, and POL-I-ACTION-RULES subclasses of the DNA-POL-I-RULES class. A typical instance of POL-I-ACTIVITY-RULES, describing the effect of the environment on the activity of an enzyme, is

```
(IF (OR   (A TEMPERATURE-RANGE OF CONDITIONS IS 0-TO-5)
          (A TEMPERATURE-RANGE OF CONDITIONS IS 5-TO-20)
          (A TEMPERATURE-RANGE OF CONDITIONS IS 20-TO-45))
      (A IONIC-STRENGTH-RANGE OF CONDITIONS IS .001-TO-.3)
      (A PH-RANGE OF CONDITIONS IS 6.0-TO-9.5)
   THEN
   DEDUCE
      (AN ACTIVITY OF DNA-POLYMERASE-I IS DNA-BINDING))
```

Another POL-I-ACTIVITY-RULES instance may reference previously deduced activities, in addition to other slots of the CONDITIONS unit.

To predict the action an enzyme mediates, we combine knowledge about the specificity and activity of the enzyme. If the ACTIVITY of DNA-POLYMERASE-I is DNA-BINDING, but there is no DNA present, then we cannot predict that DNA polymerase I actually will bind. A POL-I-SPECIFICITY-RULES instance asserts the readiness of the DNA substrate for action by an enzyme; an example can be found in Section 2.2. A POL-I-ACTION-RULES example follows:

```
(IF (AN ACTIVITY OF DNA-POLYMERASE-I IS SYNTHESIS)
    (A SPECIFICITY OF DNA-POLYMERASE-I IS PRIMER-EXTENSION)
  THEN
  DEDUCE
    (AN ACTION OF DNA-POLYMERASE-I IS PRIMER-EXTENSION))
```

Most rules for predicting enzyme action are fairly simple. However, there may be 15 to 20 underlying facts necessary to infer the required specificity and activity of the enzyme.

Prediction of enzyme action is only the first step in metabolic simulation; we also want to predict a sequence of different reactions that the enzymes may mediate as the substrate is altered by the actions of the enzyme. The KEEworlds facility is used to this end. The KEEworlds facility allows us to represent steps in a metabolic pathway as changes in the substrate or enzyme; rules can define new worlds (steps in a pathway) in which all information about metabolic objects is inherited from a parent world and only changes to these objects are stored explicitly in the child world. The KEEworlds facility is tightly coupled to the TMS; the TMS is used to predict what actions the enzyme would take in the altered environment. Multiple worlds can be linked together in a highly branched fashion typical of known pathways of DNA metabolism.

When an enzyme action is predicted, the simulation creates a new world in which the structure of the substrate DNA in the original world is modified by the enzyme's action; the new world inherits all information about the DNA from the original world, but modifies slot values accordingly. For example, if the ACTION of DNA-POLYMERASE-I is NICK-TRANSLATION on a nicked-linear structure, in a new world, the substrate DNA will now be an intact, duplex molecule. In addition, the enzyme structure may change as a result of its action. In the preceding example, the enzyme may begin bound to the nick; we describe this situation by filling the STATE slot of DNA-POLYMERASE-I with the value NICK-BOUND. In the new world, there is no longer a nick, and the enzyme is bound to a flush end.

Rules that generate new worlds are called new-world-action rules in KEE. The new-world-action rule for the example in the previous paragraph is

```
(IF  (THE STRUCTURE OF DNA IS NICKED-LINEAR)
     (THE STATE OF DNA-POLYMERASE-I IS NICK-BOUND)
     (THE ACTION OF DNA-POLYMERASE-I IS NICK-TRANSLATION)
     (THE INTERNAL-5P-ENDS OF DNA ARE ?Z)
THEN
IN.NEW.AND.WORLD
     (CHANGE.TO (THE STRUCTURE OF DNA IS INTACT-LINEAR))
     (DELETE (THE INTERNAL-3P-GROUP OF DNA IS HYDROXYL))
     (DELETE (THE INTERNAL-3P-ENDS OF DNA ARE PAIRED))
     (DELETE (THE INTERNAL-5P-ENDS OF DNA IS ?Z))
     (CHANGE.TO (THE STATE OF DNA-POLYMERASE-I IS FLUSH-BOUND))
```

This rule represents the *process* of nick translation in a nicked-linear molecule. The generated world has modified the DNA molecule—there are no longer internal 3' or 5' termini—and has changed the state of the enzyme. Nick translation is actually a process composed of similar, repeated steps; we lump these steps into one for this process. Other processes may require a finer granularity of representation.

3.3. Inference

We use an assortment of inference techniques in our simulation. The prediction of enzyme action involves a combination of forward chaining, backward chaining, and truth maintenance. In addition, the simulation of steps in a metabolic pathway requires forward chaining on new-world-action rules. Each of these rules generates a new world in a pathway, asserts new facts, and possibly retracts existing facts; the TMS then predicts enzyme actions in the newly generated world. Next, the new-world-action rules are fired in the new world, and the process repeats, until no new worlds can be generated.

Within each world, the TMS distinguishes between two types of facts. Primitive facts are added directly to working memory by the user. These facts do not depend on the truth of any other fact. The truth of deduced facts depends entirely on the truth of one or more other facts. Thus, only deduced facts can lose their support and be withdrawn by the TMS during a simulation. Primitive facts can be withdrawn by only the user.

The operation of the TMS is analogous to the activity of readjusting our belief in certain propositions based on a set containing contradictory evidence. Facts can become true through a cascading of evidence in which the consequent of one justification serves as one of the antecedents of another. If the facts asserted by the user lead to a contradiction, this contradiction is displayed to the user in a special window called a *worlds browser* and in the KEE message window. A menu item provides a complete explanation of the origin of the contradiction in terms of both the competing facts and the conclusions derived from those facts (see Section 3.4).

In our simulation, users can assert or retract facts via the graphical interface, or programmatically via a LISP expression. Using the mouse to point to a fact will assert that fact if it is unknown, or will retract that fact if it is known. Known facts are highlighted in inverse video. After a new primitive fact is asserted or retracted, the TMS adds facts that can now be deduced, and removes any deduced facts that are no longer true. All user-initiated assertions take place in the *background* world, from which all new worlds are spawned.

KEE restricts TMS justifications to purely monotonic rules; these rules are called *deduction* rules. For example, the following rule is monotonic; facts are added to only the current environment:

```
(IF   (OR    (THE EXTERNAL-5'-END OF DNA IS PAIRED)
             (THE INTERNAL-5'-END OF DNA IS PAIRED))
THEN
DEDUCE
      (A SPECIFICITY OF DNA-POLYMERASE-I IS 5'-EXONUCLEASE))
```

Assume, however, that we want to retract a fact explicitly, as in the following rule:

```
(IF   (AN ACTIVITY OF DNA-POLYMERASE-I IS DNA-BINDING)
      (OR    (A DIVALENT-CATIONS OF CONDITIONS IS MG)
             (A DIVALENT-CATIONS OF CONDITIONS IS MN))
      (A NUCLEOTIDES OF CONDITIONS IS DATP)
      (A NUCLEOTIDES OF CONDITIONS IS DTTP)
      (A NUCLEOTIDES OF CONDITIONS IS DGTP)
      (A NUCLEOTIDES OF CONDITIONS IS DCTP)
```

```
            (A NUCLEOTIDE-RANGE OF CONDITIONS IS NO-DDXTPS)
     THEN
     DO
            (AN ACTIVITY OF DNA-POLYMERASE-I IS SYNTHESIS)
            (DELETE (AN ACTIVITY OF DNA-POLYMERASE-I IS LIMITED-SYNTHE-
                    SIS))))
```

KEE cannot generate justifications for this rule, because the rule expresses explicit nonmonotonic reasoning. Likewise, rules with certain operators as premises, including LISP expressions, do not generate TMS justifications. These rules are expressed as *same-world-action* rules within KEE; we also refer to these same-world-action rules as *non-TMS* rules.

Since justifications are not generated for non-TMS rules, these rules are not invoked automatically when their premises become true, whereas TMS rules are. In addition, non-TMS rules cannot be included in explanation graphs. We group all non-TMS rules into a single class, and forward chain on this class whenever the value of a unit referenced in the antecedent of a non-TMS rule changes. Special functions called demons (or KEE *active values*) are attached to the attributes mentioned in the antecedents of non-TMS rules. These demons permit nonmonotonic reasoning with non-TMS rules.

To accommodate both standard production rules and the TMS representation of the same knowledge, we have modified the KEE rule parser. Whenever a new rule is entered into the knowledge system (whether via the standard user interface or via the KEE rule editor), the rule is parsed by KEE and the type, the premises, and the conclusions of the rule are determined. We have added a further rule-parsing function to the normal KEE rule parser that examines the rule type. If the rule is nonmonotonic, then the rule unit is added to the non-TMS rules class so that it will be invoked automatically whenever one of its premises changes, as described. If the rule is monotonic, then its premises are asserted into the TMS as justifiers for the conclusions of the rule. Thus, all monotonic rules have a double representation in the knowledge system. The fact that KEE is itself implemented as a series of knowledge bases allows us to modify KEE's action and to change its behavior.

3.4. Explanation

Our knowledge system has a mechanism by which it can explain its predictions for each step of a pathway. For any fact deduced by the TMS, an explanation graph displays the sequence of TMS justifications that were used to derive that fact. In Figure 6, the simulation has ascertained that, given the current state of the substrate, DNA polymerase I could translate a nick. If asked to explain this fact, the TMS would construct the explanation graph shown, based on the currently justifiable facts.

The explanation graph displays the following information. The user has stated that the DNA has some nicks and that it has an internal 3'-OH group.

```
                    A SPECIFICITY OF
                    DNA-POLYMERASE-I
                           IS
                    NICK-TRANSLATION
                           |
       DNA polymerase I can nick-translate any nick with a 3P hydroxyl group.


                THE              (THE STRANDS OF DNA IS NICKED-DUPLEX)
          INTERNAL-3P-GROUP           OR (THE STRANDS OF DNA IS
             OF DNA IS           SINGLY-NICKED-DUPLEX) OR (THE STRANDS
             HYDROXYL             OF DNA IS MULTIPLY-NICKED-DUPLEX)
                |                               |
       FROM.BACKGROUND.ONLY          DISJUNCTION.INTRODUCTION
                                                |


                                           THE STRANDS
                                           OF DNA IS
                                          NICKED-DUPLEX
                                                |
                        If there are SOME NICKS then the STRANDS are NICKED.


                                              THE
                                           NICKS OF
                                            DNA IS
                                             SOME
                                               |
                                    FROM.BACKGROUND.ONLY
```

Figure 6. An explanation graph depicting why (A SPECIFICITY OF DNA-POLY-MERASE-I IS NICK-TRANSLATION). The explanation graph uses TMS justifications to explain the system's reasoning.

These facts are labeled "FROM.BACKGROUND.ONLY." The TMS has invoked a rule by which it is able to deduce that any DNA with some nicks must be a nicked duplex. The firing of another rule allows the TMS to deduce, from the presence of the internal 3'-OH group in a nicked duplex DNA, that DNA polymerase I could perform nick translation on this DNA molecule.

The user can also ask the system about facts that have not been determined to be true by using the QUERY function. This function invokes the backward chainer and engages in a brief dialogue with the user, searching through the set of rules for ways to establish the given fact and asking the user for additional information that could serve to support this fact.

4 Sample Interactions

There are two modes of interaction with the simulation: prediction and envisionment. In the prediction mode, the user asserts known facts about an experimental system, by describing the DNA and environmental conditions via the corresponding active images; the TMS will conclude other facts automatically. The user can also reason backward from a desired enzyme action. In the envisionment mode, the user chooses to generate all possible metabolic pathways from initial conditions. We present brief examples of each mode, using DNA polymerase I in isolation.

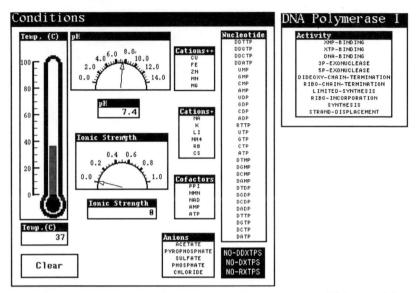

Figure 7. An initial experimental environment. The temperature is 37 degrees Celsius and the pH value is 7.4. No DNA polymerase I activity is possible.

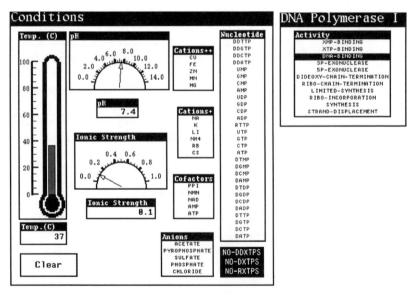

Figure 8. An increase in the ionic strength. DNA polymerase I is now able to bind to DNA. The display for the ACTIVITY of DNA-POLYMERASE-I now shows DNA-BINDING.

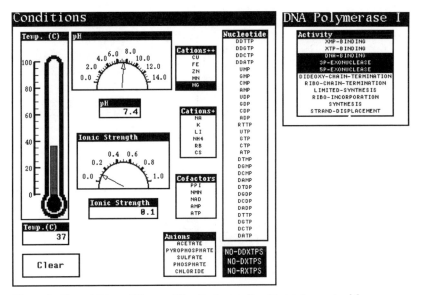

Figure 9. The addition of Mg++. The divalent cation Mg++ is required for exonuclease activities. 3P-EXONUCLEASE and 5P-EXONUCLEASE activities now appear in the ACTIVITY slot.

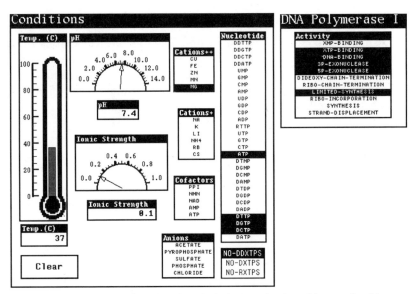

Figure 10. The addition of nucleotides. With the introduction of four nucleotides — ribo ATP, dTTP, dGTP, and dCTP — DNA shows limited synthetic activity due to the lack of dATP.

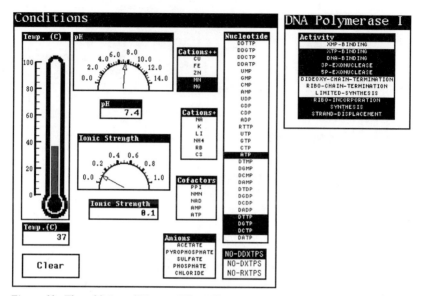

Figure 11. The addition of Mn++. Ribo ATP is incorporated into a growing strand, in the presence of Mn++. Three new activities are displayed: RIBO-INCORPORA-TION, SYNTHESIS, and STRAND-DISPLACEMENT.

4.1. Prediction of Enzyme Action

We begin with an experimental environment at 37 degrees Celsius and a pH value of 7.4 (Figure 7); notice that DNA polymerase I displays no activity. If we increase the ionic strength (Figure 8), polymerase I is able to bind to DNA. With the subsequent addition of the divalent cation Mg^{++} (Figure 9), DNA polymerase I now shows 3' and 5' exonuclease activities. In Figure 10, we add four nucleoside triphosphates—ribo ATP, dTTP, dGTP, and dCTP. Notice that DNA polymerase I can now bind to these triphosphates and incorporate some of them; the limited synthetic activity is due to the lack of dATP. In the presence of Mn^{++} (Figure 11), however, DNA polymerase I can incorporate ribo ATP into a growing strand; the activities RIBO-INCORPO-RATION, SYNTHESIS, and STRAND-DISPLACEMENT can now be concluded.

In Figure 12, we assert the presence of a GAPPED-LINEAR molecule, with paired 3' and 5' internal ends and a hydroxyl group at the 3'-internal terminus. The SPECIFICITY slot of DNA-POLYMERASE-I now indicates that DNA polymerase I can bind to three locations on the substrate (the 3' termini, the 5' termini, and the primer terminus), hydrolyze the molecule from either a 3' or a 5' terminus, or extend the primer, and, in doing so, fill the gap. In Figure 13, the simulation predicts seven actions for DNA poly-

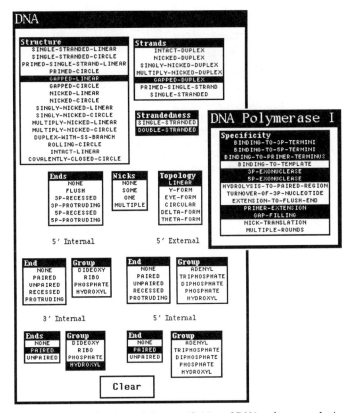

Figure 12. A description of DNA and the specificities of DNA polymerase I. A GAPPED-LINEAR structure is asserted; from this fact, the system concludes that the STRANDS are GAPPED-DUPLEX, the STRANDEDNESS is DOUBLE-STRANDED, the TOPOLOGY is LINEAR, and the 3' and 5' internal ENDs are PAIRED. The SPECIFICITY slot of DNA-POLYMERASE-I now indicates that DNA polymerase I can bind to three locations on the substrate (BINDING-TO-3P-TERMINI, BINDING-TO-5P-TERMINI, and BINDING-TO-PRIMER-TERMINUS), hydrolyze the molecule from either a 3' or a 5' terminus (3P-EXONUCLEASE and 5P-EXONUCLEASE), extend the primer (PRIMER-EXTENSION), and fill the gap (GAP-FILLING).

merase I, each of which can be explained graphically using TMS justifications. Other examples of the use of the system to predict enzyme action have been published elsewhere [Brutlag, 1988].

4.2. Envisionment of Metabolic Pathways

Figure 14 depicts a partial envisionment of the metabolic pathways that

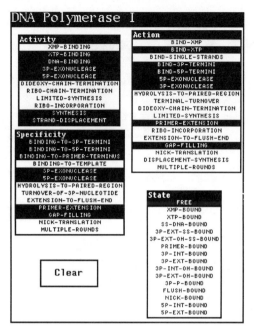

Figure 13. The predictions of ACTIVITY, SPECIFICITY, and ACTION for DNA-POLYMERASE-I.

originate with the gapped linear DNA molecule described in Section 4.1. KEE generates a graph of worlds; we have enhanced this graph to diagramatically depict changes in the structure and states of objects. In this example, DNA polymerase I is the only enzyme present. Each world is named for the action most recently taken by the enzyme; if the enzyme is free, the world is named after the structure of the DNA present in that world.

The system generates four new worlds based on the predicted actions of DNA polymerase I, as described in Section 4.1. Each of these worlds is the result of a binding process. In the first world (W_1), the enzyme is bound to the 3'-internal, or primer, terminus. Here, primer extension, or gap filling, is a predicted action; thus, a new world is generated in which the primer is extended, until the gap has become a nick. In this world, DNA polymerase I can nick translate; the system generates another new world in which the enzyme is now bound to the 3'-external terminus of an intact linear molecule. The only action possible in this world is the dissociation of DNA polymerase I from the substrate; a new world is generated to describe the result of this process. Finally, as depicted in the final world of this pathway, the free enzyme can bind to free nucleotides, but no further activity is observed.

The second world (W_2) contains the enzyme bound to the external 5' terminus of the gapped molecule. In this world, the enzyme can hydrolyze the

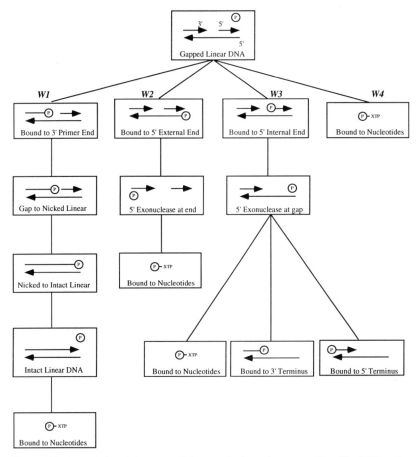

Figure 14. A partial envisionment of the metabolic pathways mediated by DNA polymerase I, beginning with a gapped, linear DNA molecule.

DNA from the external 5' position. The system generates a new world, corresponding to the result of exonuclease activity at the external end. In the world labelled, "5' exonuclease at end," DNA polymerase I has hydrolyzed the intact single strand of the substrate; as a result, the STATE of DNA-POLYMERASE-I has changed from 5P-EXT-BOUND to FREE, and the STRUCTURE of DNA has changed from GAPPED-LINEAR to SINGLE-STRANDED-LINEAR. Since the substrate no longer supports any enzymatic actions, the enzyme binds to free nucleotides in a new world, and the pathway is terminated.

In the third world (W_3), the enzyme is bound to the internal 5' terminus and 5' exonuclease is a predicated action. In the world labelled, "5' exonuclease at gap," the enzyme has hydrolyzed a segment of the gapped strand of the substrate; as a result, the STATE of DNA-POLYMERASE-I has changed from 5P-INT-BOUND to FREE, and the STRUCTURE of DNA has changed from GAPPED-LINEAR to PRIMED-LINEAR. The enzyme can now bind the primer and the 5' end of the molecule, as well as the free nucleotides present in the environment. New worlds are generated for each of these possibilities. Although not shown, the simulation continues with the extension of the primer in one pathway and the hydrolysis of the primer in another.

The final world (W_4) contains a situation encountered previously in the pathways originating From W_1, W_2, and W_3—namely, the enzyme has bound free nucleotides, and no further activity is observed.

5 Discussion

In recent years, several researchers have developed qualitative models of metabolic processes [Weld, 1986; Karp, this volume; Mavrovonioutis, this volume]. Weld's PEPTIDE system serves as the basis for his theory of aggregation, which detects repeating cycles of processes and creates a continuous process description of the cycle's behavior. We avoid many of the problems his theory addresses by representing continuous processes explicitly. For example, we do not model the polymerization process as a sequence of steps, each of which adds a nucleotide to a growing strand of DNA; instead, polymerization extends a primer as far as possible in one step, and then stops. Likewise, the exonuclease activities of DNA polymerase I are represented not as a sequence of discrete processes, but rather as one continuous process. Binding processes are modeled in a stepwise fashion; in discrete steps, polymerase I may bind to the end of a DNA substrate, then bind to a group at the end of the substrate, and then catalyze a polymerization or hydrolysis reaction. If an event can interrupt a continuous process, with qualitatively similar results at any point in time, we anticipate the event before the process has begun and generate two new worlds: one for the continuous process and one for the interrupted, continuous process. However, we do foresee that we will need aggregation and cycle detection techniques in the near future; the lack of cycle detection currently limits the envisionment capabilities of our system to those pathways that have no reversible reactions.

Karp's model of the regulation of the trp operon serves as the basis for a hypothesis-formation program, which can reproduce the discoveries made by biologists studying gene regulation over a 20-year period. Karp represents biochemical objects with KEE frames; these objects correspond to homogeneous populations of molecules. In our system, instances of the DNAS and ENZYMES classes represent single molecules. To illustrate the implications, suppose a DNA molecule has several spatially separated locations at which an enzyme can bind; in a real experiment, one DNA polymerase I molecule may bind at an internal nick, while another may bind at the external end of the same DNA molecule. Since we represent only a single enzyme molecule, our simulation generates pathways for only one enzyme action at a time. Thus, our system cannot envision all the pathways that may occur under experimental conditions; simultaneous combinations of actions may produce paths that are missing from our system. For this reason, we refer to our pathway generation technique as *partial* envisionment.

Karp's reactions are stored in KEE frames, and are organized into process knowledge bases. These processes are arranged in an inheritance hierarchy and can inherit attributes from more general reaction classes. Karp constructed a process interpreter to detect and permit interactions between objects. We store our reactions using KEE rule units, and use standard KEE reasoning mechanisms (forward chaining and truth maintenance) to generate pathways. Currently, none of our reactions dynamically generates simulation objects distinct from the original substrate; our new-world-action rules simply change the character of the original DNA molecule. Karp's system dynamically instantiates new objects; we foresee the need for a similar function, as we augment our representation of enzyme functions and add more enzymes to the system.

The goals of our system are different from those of Weld, Karp, and Mavrovonioutis. PEPTIDE's domain of DNA transcription was meant to test Weld's process aggregation methods; Karp's system contains a comprehensive model of bacterial gene regulation, but was developed to test theories of scientific discovery. Mavrovonioutis has developed a system for the computer-aided design of biochemical pathways. Our simulation has been developed for use by biochemists as an interactive reasoning tool. We believe that our representation of enzymes, substrates, and processes is natural and intuitive. The attributes both of the substrates and of the enzymes, as well as the rules relating them, are expressed in biochemical terms and phrases. Representing DNA metabolism in this way provides explanation and didactic capabilities that can be used readily by biochemists not involved in the development of the knowledge system. Knowledge of a metabolic step can be either detailed or sketchy and still can be represented by the rule-based methods we employ.

Currently, our representation paradigm requires that a user have an understanding of knowledge-representation techniques to change or add new information. For instance, to represent a new enzyme, the user must first create a new instance of the ENZYMES class. Then, he must specify all possible values of SPECIFICITY, ACTIVITY, ACTION, and STATE for the ENZYME, and write at least one rule to conclude each value of each attribute, following the general paradigm for enzyme representation described in section 3.1. To perform these operations, the user must know how to create a unit, how to specify the values allowed for attributes, what the syntax for writing a new rule is, and which semantics are allowed in the premises of those rules. KEE allows new units to be generated by simple menu selection and rules to be built in a context-sensitive text editor. In a future version of the knowledge system, we intend to provide a programmatically driven enzyme-acquisition function that, in conjunction with a tutorial, will greatly facilitate these steps.

Specifically, we would like to automate as much of the enzyme-representation process as possible. It is clear to us that many enzymes will share many of their rules with other enzymes of their class (e.g., all exonucleases hydrolyze DNA from the ends), and only a few of the rules are needed to specify uniquely any instance of an enzyme class. Hence, one method for automating the knowledge-acquisition process would be to write prototypical rules describing an enzyme class that refer to object types; these rules could then be inherited by specific instances of the enzymes, with references to object types replaced by specific objects. This approach is similar to Karp's use of process hierarchies. For example, the class of 3' exonucleases would have a set of general rules describing the binding and hydrolysis of 3' termini of DNA. Instances of 3' exonucleases would be represented by instantiated rules from the class level and by additional rules describing the specific behavior of the enzyme.

One advantage of this paradigm for enzyme representation is the ease with which knowledge can be validated. The steps we have outlined guarantee one form of completeness, in that every action of the enzyme can be concluded from at least one set of experimental conditions. Because of the natural modularity of the rules, it is easy for an expert to examine the premises of every rule, either manually or programmatically, to determine whether they cover every situation leading to the conclusion. In addition, consistency of the rule set is checked at the same time by the TMS, which constantly monitors contradictions or violations of cardinality in the frame system.

We are addressing three major limitations of our current representation of enzymes. First, there is no provision in our model for rules concerning interactions among enzymes. One enzyme influences the activity of the other enzyme only through its effects on substrates or cofactors. For example, DNA ligase inhibits nick translation by DNA polymerase I by sealing nicks in the substrate. There are no rules indicating that DNA ligase can limit the extent of nick translation by displacing the DNA polymerase I in a competitive fashion based on the processivity of the polymerase reaction. We are developing a framework for enzyme-interaction rules.

Second, the simulation predicts the action of only a normal, intact, and uninhibited enzyme. We might want to study an enzyme that was missing one of its activities or that had one activity inhibited (e.g., a mutant enzyme, a chemically modified enzyme, or a specific enzyme inhibitor). Although it is possible to do this manually by duplicating the enzyme and removing or altering specific rules, we would like to develop an automatic method for inhibiting any single activity of an enzyme. This method would allow the system to analyze, via backward chaining, experimental situations in which one or more activities may be missing. The system could then conclude from the results of an experiment which activities may be present or absent. Karp's system can simulate mutant enzymes.

The third limitation is the current lack of a communicative visual representation of the objects in the simulation. We would like to represent DNA molecules and enzymes with object-oriented graphics; we believe that we could summarize in small diagrams most of the information currently presented in lists of attribute values. A pathway could then be represented by a sequence of diagrams showing enzyme–substrate interactions; animation would be possible, as well.

Acknowledgments

We thank Lyn Dupré for her editorial comments. This work was supported by grant LM04957 from the National Library of Medicine. ARG and DHM are Training Fellows of the National Library of Medicine. The KEE Software was provided under the University Grant Program from IntelliCorp, Inc. We would also like to thank both IntelliCorp, Inc., and IntelliGenetics, Inc., for providing DLB with support for a sabbatical during which this work was initiated.

References

C. Bierbicher, M. Eigen, and W. Gardiner, "The Kinetics of RNA Replication," *Biochemistry* 22, 2544–2559 (1983).

D. Bobrow and M. Stefik, "Perspectives on Artificial Intelligence Programming," *Science* 231, 951–956 (1986).

D. Bobrow, ed., *Qualitative Reasoning About Physical Systems*, MIT Press, Cambridge, MA, 1988.

R. Brachman, R. Fikes, and H. Levesque, "KRYPTON: A Functional Approach to Knowledge Representation," *IEEE Computer* 16, 67–73 (1983).

D. Brutlag, "Expert System Simulations as Active Learning Environments," in R. Colwell, ed., *Biomolecular Data: A Resource in Transition*, Oxford University Press, Oxford, England, 1988.

B. Buchanan and E. Shortliffe, eds., *Rule-Based Expert Systems*, Addison-Wesley, Reading, MA, 1984.

E. Charniak and D. McDermott, *Introduction to Artificial Intelligence*, Addison-Wesley, Reading, MA, 1985.

R. Davis, B. Buchanan, and E. Shortliffe, "Production Rules as a Representation for a Knowledge-based Consultation Program," *Artificial Intelligence* 8, 15–45 (1977).

J. deKleer, "An Assumption-based TMS," *Artificial Intelligence* 28, 127–162 (1986).

J. deKleer and J. Brown, "A Qualitative Physics Based on Confluences," in D. Bobrow, ed., *Qualitative Reasoning About Physical Systems*, The MIT Press, Cambridge, MA, 1985.

R. Fikes and T. Kehler, "Control of Reasoning in Frame-based Representation Systems,"

Communications of the ACM 28, 904–920 (1985).

R. Franco and E. Canela, "Computer Simulation of Purine Metabolism," *European Journal of Biochemistry* 144, 305–315 (1985).

D. Freifelder, *Essentials of Molecular Biology*, Jones and Bartlett, Boston, 1985.

E. Friedberg, *DNA Repair*, W.H. Freeman, New York, 1985.

P. Karp and P Friedland, "Coordinating the Use of Qualitative and Quantitative Knowledge," in L. Widman, *et al.*, eds., *Artificial Intelligence, Simulation, and Modeling*, Wiley, New York, 1989.

P. Karp, "A Qualitative Biochemistry and its Application to the Regulation of the Tryptophan Operon," this volume.

M. Kohn and D. Garfinkel, "Computer Simulation of Metabolism in Palmitate-perfused Rat Heart. I. Palmitate oxidation," *Annals of Biomedical Engineering* 11, 361–384 (1983a).

M. Kohn and D. Garfinkel, "Computer Simulation of Metabolism in Palmitate-Perfused Rat Heart. II. Behavior of Complete Model," *Annals of Biomedical Enineering* 11, 511–532 (1983b).

A. Kornberg, *DNA Replication*, W. H. Freeman, New York, 1980.

A. Kornberg, *1982 Supplement to DNA Replication*, W. H. Freeman, New York, 1982.

I. Lehman, "DNA ligase: Structure, Mechanism and Function," *Science* 186, 790–797 (1974).

H. Levesque and R. Brachman, "A Fundamental Tradeoff in Knowledge Representation and Reasoning," in *Proceedings of the CSCI/SCEIO Conference 1984*, CSCI, London, Ontario, 1984.

M. Mavrovouniotis, "The Identification of Qualitatively Feasible Metabolic Pathways, this volume.

S. Meyers and P. Friedland, "Knowledge-based Aimulation of Genetic Regulation in Bacteriophage Lambda," *Nucleic Acid Research* 12, 1–9 (1984).

M. Minsky, "A Framework for Representing Knowledge," in P. Winston, ed., *The Psychology of Computer Vision*, McGraw-Hill, New York, NY, 1975.

M. Minsky, *The Society of Mind*, Simon and Schuster, New York, 1986.

P. Modrich, I. Lehman, and J. Wang, "Enzymatic Joining of Polynucleotides. XI. Reversal of Escherichia Coli Deoxyribonucleic Acid Ligase Reaction," *Journal of Biological Chemistry* 247, 6370–6372 (1972).

N. Nilsson, *Principles of Artificial Intelligence*, Tioga, Palo Alto, CA, 1980.

E. Rich, *Artificial Intelligence*, McGraw-Hill, New York, 1983.

J. Rothenberg, "The Nature of Modeling," in L. Widman *et al.*, eds., *Artificial Intelligence, Simulation, and Modeling,* Wiley, New York, 1989.

K. Schaffner, "Exemplar reasoning about biological models and diseases: A relationship between the philosophy of medicine and philosophy of science," *Journal of Medicine and Philosophy* 11, 63–80 (1986).

S. Schapiro, *The Encylcopedia of Artificial Intelligence*, Wiley, New York, 1986.

M. Stefik, "An Wxamination of a Frame-Structured Representation System," *Proceedings of the Sixth International Joint Conference on Artificial Intelligence*, 845–852 (1979).

M. Stefik and D. Bobrow, "Object-oriented Programming: Themes and variations," *Science* 6, 40–62 (1986).

R. Thomas, *et al.*, "A Complex Control Circuit: Regulation of Immunity in Temperate Bacteriophages," *European Journal of Biochemistry* 71, 211–227 (1976).

M. Waser, *et al.*, "Computer Modeling of Muscle Phosphofructokinase Kinetics,"*Journal of Theoretical Biology* 103, 295–312 (1983).

D. Weld, "The Use of Aggregation in Causal Simulation," *Artificial Intelligence* 30, 1–34, 1986.

J. Watson, *et al.*, *The Molecular Biology of the Gene*, Benjamin/Cummings, Menlo Park, CA, 1987.

L. Widman, "Semi-quantitative 'Close-enough' Systems Dynamics Models: An Alternative to Qualitative Simulation," in L. Widman, *et al.*, eds., *Artificial Intelligence, Simulation, and Modeling*, Wiley, New York, 1989.

11

An AI Approach to the Interpretation of the NMR Spectra of Proteins

Peter Edwards, Derek Sleeman,
Gordon C.K. Roberts & Lu Yun Lian

1 Introduction

The use of computers in chemistry and biochemistry has been widespread for many years, with machines performing many complex numerical calculations, e.g. solving quantum mechanical problems. However, some of the most interesting and challenging problems encountered in these domains are not numerical in nature. In particular, the interpretation or rationalization of many observed phenomena cannot be reduced to an equation or series of equations. Such problems are typically solved using intuition and experience and draw upon a great deal of empirical knowledge about the problem area. It is not surprising therefore, that these domains have proved such a fertile area for the application of artificial intelligence techniques. In this chapter we describe one such application, designed to assist a spectroscopist in the task of interpreting the Nuclear Magnetic Resonance (NMR) spectra of proteins [Edwards, 1989].

There are a number of scientific and medical applications of nuclear magnetic resonance spectroscopy and magnetic resonance imaging (MRI). The greatest impact of NMR in the chemical sciences has without doubt been in the elucidation of molecular structures. During the 1980s rapid developments in two-dimensional Fourier transform NMR made possible the determination of high quality structures of small proteins and nucleic acids. NMR spectrometers (in common with other laboratory experiments) invariably produce experimental data subject to noise, corrupted or missing data points, etc. User judgements in interactive processing of these data inevitably bias results, often unintentionally. The aim of the system currently under development is the automation of part of this task for NMR spectra of proteins. Our hope is that automation will limit the introduction of such user biases.

We now provide a brief introduction to proteins before describing the technique of nuclear magnetic resonance which can be used to elucidate the structure of such molecules.

2 Protein Chemistry

2.1 The Nature of Proteins

Proteins are probably the most diverse biological substances known. As enzymes and hormones, they catalyze and regulate the reactions that occur in the body; as muscles and tendons they provide the body with its means of movement; as skin and hair they give it an outer covering; in combination with other substances in bone they provide it with structural support, etc. Proteins come in all shapes and sizes and by the standard of most organic molecules, are of very high molecular weight. In spite of such diversity of size, shape and function, all proteins have common features that allow their structures to be deciphered and their properties understood. Proteins are biopolymers composed of amino acid building blocks or monomers. There are 20 common amino acids used to synthesize proteins; their structures and names are shown in Figure 1. The amide linkages that join amino acids in proteins are commonly called peptide linkages and amino acid polymers are called polypeptides. Figure 2 shows a piece of protein backbone with the peptide linkages labeled.

2.2 Protein Structure

The structure of a protein molecule is considered at three levels of detail: *primary*, *secondary* and *tertiary* structure. The primary structure describes the chemical composition of the protein; the secondary structure describes common structural arrangements of parts of the backbone; while the tertiary structure details the folding of these chains in three dimensional space.

Primary Structure The first stage in the process of protein structure pre-

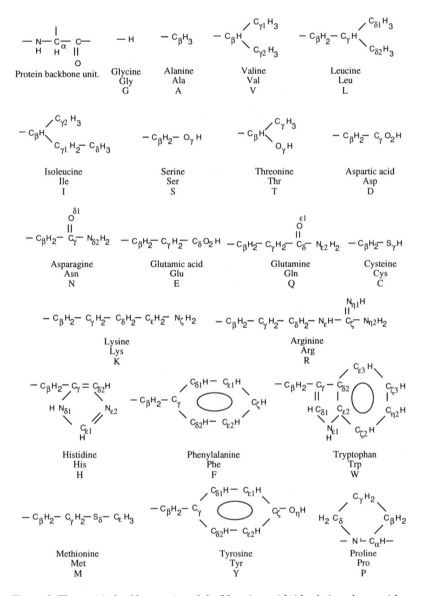

Figure 1. The protein backbone unit and the 20 amino acid side chains, shown with the three and one letter abbreviations for each. Proline is an imino acid, and its N and C_α backbone atoms are shown. Greek letters (α, β, γ, δ, ε, ζ, η) identify the distance (number of bonds) from the central (α) carbon atom. C=carbon, H=hydrogen, N=nitrogen, O=oxygen, S=sulphur atoms.

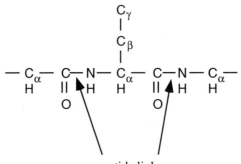

peptide linkages

Figure 2. Protein backbone with α, β *and* γ *carbons labeled. Peptide bonds link to-gether adjacent amino acids. When an amino acid forms a peptide bond, two hydro-gen atoms and one oxygen atom are released, and the remaining portion of the amino acid is called a* residue.

diction is the determination of its primary structure, i.e., the linear arrangement of the amino acid residues within the protein. This is determined by chemical means.

Secondary Structure The major experimental technique that has been used in the elucidation of secondary structure of proteins is X-ray crystallographic analysis. When X-rays pass through a crystalline substance they produce diffraction patterns. Analysis of these patterns indicates a regular repetition of particular structural units with certain specific distances between them. The complete X-ray analysis of a molecule as complex as a protein can take many months. Many such analyses have been performed and they have revealed that the polypeptide chain of a natural protein can assume a number of regular conformations. Rotations of groups attached to the amide nitrogen and the carbonyl carbon are relatively free, and it is this property that allows peptide chains to adopt different conformations. Two major forms are the β sheet and α helix.

The β sheet consists of extended polypeptide chain with backbone residues forming hydrogen bonds between the chains. The sheet is not flat, but rather is pleated, in order to overcome repulsive interactions between groups on the side chains. The α helix is a right-handed helix with 3.6 amino acid residues per turn. Each NH group in the chain has a hydrogen bond to the carbonyl group at a distance of three amino acid residues. The side chain groups extend away from the helix. Certain peptide chains assume what is called random coil arrangement, a structure that is flexible, changing and statistically random. The presence of proline or hydroxyproline residues in polypeptide chains produces another striking effect. Because the nitrogen atoms of these residues are part of five-membered rings, the groups attached by the N - Cα bond cannot rotate enough to allow an α helical structure.

Tertiary Structure The tertiary structure of a protein is the three dimensional shape which arises from foldings of its polypeptide chains. Such foldings do not occur randomly: under normal environmental conditions, the tertiary structure that a protein assumes will be its most stable arrangement, the so-called "native conformation." Two major molecular shapes occur naturally, fibrous and globular. Fibrous molecules have a large helical content and are essentially rigid molecules of rod-like shape. Globular proteins have a polypeptide chain which consists partly of helical sections which are folded about the random coil sections to give a "spherical" shape.

A variety of forces are involved in stabilizing tertiary structures including the formation of disulphide bonds between elements of the primary structure. One characteristic of most proteins is that the folding takes place in such a way as to expose the maximum number of polar groups to the aqueous environment and enclose a maximum number of nonpolar groups within its interior. Myoglobin (1957) and haemoglobin (1959) were the first proteins whose tertiary structures were determined by X-ray analyzes.

3 Protein NMR

The first NMR experiments with biopolymers were performed over thirty years ago. The potential of the method for structural studies of proteins was realized very early on. However, in practice, initial progress was slow because of limitations imposed by the instruments and the lack of suitable biological samples. In recent years there has been a huge increase in interest in the technique, primarily due to the development of two-dimensional NMR which makes the task of interpreting the data more straightforward [Jardetzky, 1981; Wüthrich, 1986; Cooke, 1988].

NMR techniques are complementary to X-ray crystallography in several ways:

- NMR studies use non-crystalline samples e.g. solutions in aqueous or non-aqueous solvents. If NMR assignments and spatial structure determination can be obtained without reference to a corresponding crystal structure, a meaningful comparison of the conformations in single crystals and non-crystalline states can be obtained.

- NMR can be applied to molecules for which no single crystals are available.

- Solution conditions for NMR experiments (pH, temperature, etc.) can be varied over a wide range. This allows studies to be carried out on interactions with other molecules in solution.

We shall now define a number of terms commonly used by NMR spectroscopists.

Chemical shift defines the location of an NMR signal. It is measured relative to a reference compound. The chemical shift is normally quoted in parts per million (ppm) units and is primarily related to the magnetic environment of the nucleus giving rise to the resonance.

Spin-spin coupling constants characterize through-bond interactions between nuclei linked by a small number of covalent bonds in a chemical structure.

NOEs (Nuclear Overhauser Enhancement/Effect) are due to through-space interactions between different nuclei and are correlated with the inverse sixth power of the internuclear distance.

3.1 Two Dimensional NMR

Conventional (one dimensional) NMR spectra of proteins are densely crowded with resonance lines. There is no straightforward correlation between the NMR spectrum of the simple, constituent amino acids and the macromolecules. This makes it difficult to detect individual residues within the spectrum. There are a number of reasons for this, including the spatial folding of proteins, which has an effect on chemical shift values; and physical side-effects due to the size of proteins. As a consequence of the difficulties involved in interpreting such data, spectroscopists choose to produce two dimensional spectra of proteins and other biopolymers[1].

With 2D NMR the natural limitations of 1D NMR can largely be overcome. The main advantages of 2D NMR relative to 1D NMR for proteins are that connectivities between distinct individual spins are delineated, and that resonance peaks are spread out in two dimensions leading to a substantial improvement in peak separation, thus making the spectra far easier to interpret.

Two main types of 2D experiment are important for proteins. One records through-bond interactions between ^1H nuclei (HOHAHA, COSY) while the other detects through-space interactions (NOESY). We shall not go into the details of how these different experiments are performed, suffice it to say that the first pair of techniques allow one to study interactions occurring within amino acid residues while the second illustrates longer-range interactions occurring between amino acids. Figure 3 shows a piece of protein backbone with selected through-bond and through-space interactions labeled.

The selection of techniques for the visualization of the data from a 2D experiment is of considerable practical importance. Spectral analysis relies primarily on contour plots of the type shown in Figure 4. Contour plots are suitable for extracting resonance frequencies and for delineating connectivities via cross peaks, but care must be taken when attempting to extract quantitative information from such a plot.

Limitations for the analysis of 2D NMR spectra may arise from a phe-

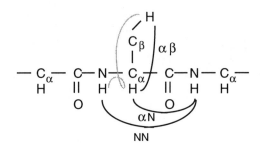

Figure 3. Protein backbone illustrating through-bond (dotted line) and through-space (solid line) ^1H - ^1H interactions.

nomenon termed "t_1 noise", i.e. bands of spurious signals running parallel to the ω_1 axis at the position of strong, sharp diagonal peaks. These signals may arise due to spectrometer instability or other sources of thermal noise. They may also be an artifact of inadequate data handling during the Fourier transform. Ideally, NOESY or HOHAHA spectra should be symmetrical with respect to the main diagonal. In practice, however, noise, instrumental artifacts and insufficient digitization tend to destroy perfect symmetry. A number of 2D NMR experiments, including COSY and NOESY are described by Morris [1986].

We shall now describe how NMR techniques may be used to determine protein structure.

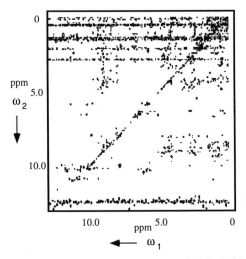

Figure 4. The two-dimensional HOHAHA spectrum of Nisin (a 34 amino-acid polypeptide)

4 Protein Structure Prediction

The process of determining the structure of a protein by NMR relies on a chemical sequence for the protein (assumed to be correct) being available. Each residue in the protein will give rise to a characteristic set of peaks in the HOHAHA and COSY spectra and interactions between residues will lead to cross peaks in the NOESY spectrum. The interpretation of these spectra involves detection of the residue spin-systems in the HOHAHA and COSY, followed by analysis of the NOESY in order to link these spin-systems together. The steps involved are:

1. The spin systems of individual amino acid residues are identified using through-bond ^{1}H - ^{1}H connectivities. Each spin system produces a pattern of signals within the HOHAHA and COSY spectra that is characteristic of one or more amino-acid residue. (Section 4.1)

2. Residues which are sequential neighbors are identified from observation of signals in the NOESY spectrum indicating sequential connectivities[2] αN, NN and possibly βN. (Section 4.2)

3. Steps (1) and (2) attempt to identify groups of peaks corresponding to peptide segments that are sufficiently long to be unique in the primary structure (sequence) of the protein. Sequence specific assignments are then obtained by matching the segments thus identified with the corresponding segments in the chemically determined amino acid sequence.[3] Note that for larger proteins, crystallographic data may also be used here. (Section 4.2)

4. The occurrence of certain patterns of NMR parameters along the polypeptide chain is indicative of particular features of secondary structure. NOESY signals are used to detect interactions between residues in the protein. (Section 4.3)

4.1 Assignment of Spin Systems

HOHAHA & COSY techniques A COSY spectrum consists of the conventional NMR signal along the diagonal and off-diagonal peaks (cross peaks) corresponding to ^{1}H - ^{1}H interactions. The peaks along the diagonal represent a normal spectrum of the system. Figure 5 is a schematic 2D plot showing the approximate positions of different types of protons along the diagonal.

With few exceptions COSY cross peaks are only observed between protons separated by three or less covalent bonds and thus are restricted to protons within individual amino-acid residues. Some of the 20 residues found in proteins give rise to unique patterns in the COSY spectrum. Not all residues

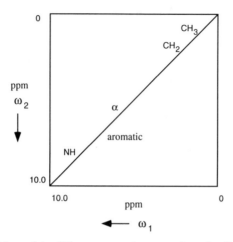

Figure 5. Positions of the different types of protons along the diagonal of a HOHA-HA or COSY spectrum.

produce unique patterns as a number of them have similar structures and thus give rise to very similar COSY cross peak patterns. Often one can only identify something as belonging to a class of residues. NH protons and aromatic protons are relatively easy to identify. However, multiple methylene (CH_2) groups often cause problems as it becomes difficult to ascertain their ordering.

In order to make the signals easier to analyze, a variation on the standard COSY technique is employed, HOHAHA. Whereas COSY only shows interactions occurring between neighboring protons, such as $\alpha\beta$, $\beta\gamma$ and so on, HOHAHA provides in principle, an overall picture by showing all ^1H - ^1H interactions occurring for each proton within the residue. Thus for a residue containing N, α, β and γ protons, the HOHAHA spectrum will contain a peak for each interaction with the N proton: $N\alpha$, $N\beta$, $N\gamma$; a peak for each interaction with the α proton: $\alpha\beta$, $\alpha\gamma$ and so on. This technique has only been in routine use relatively recently, and has largely superseded COSY as it provides *additional* information. However, as noted below in point (3) it is often necessary to use these two techniques together. Thus, in the NH region of the HOHAHA spectrum one sees cross peaks due to each of the protons in the residue. In the $C\alpha$ region one sees peaks caused by the $C\beta$, $C\gamma$ protons, etc. and in the $C\beta$ region peaks resulting from $C\gamma$, $C\delta$, etc. Figure 6a shows the HOHAHA spectrum for the threonine residue. Even with this technique we find that not all residues can be uniquely identified.

Correlations to δ protons are often not observed from the amide (NH) protons. The δ protons can however be observed in the $C\alpha$ and $C\beta$ regions and it is therefore quite common for different regions of the spectrum to be examined in order to detect the differing signals belonging to a spin system. In

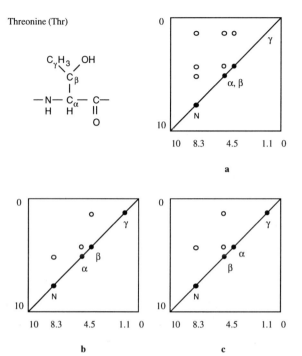

Figure 6. The HOHAHA spectrum (a) of threonine together with two possible forms of its COSY spectrum (b & c).

order to make the δ protons observable in the NH region it is necessary to adjust the experimental parameter known as the mixing time. Unfortunately, as this parameter is increased information starts to be lost from the spectrum due to relaxation processes.

For small proteins it is usually possible to pick out all of the spin systems despite there being many hundreds of protons contributing to the spectrum. The interpretation process begins with an attempt to assign the individual spin-systems within the HOHAHA spectrum. The region of the spectrum displaying peaks due to interaction between the N and Cα protons (approximately 3.8 - 5.5 / 7.6 - 9 ppm) is termed the "fingerprint" region and all interpretations begin in this area. Study of the HOHAHA spectrum of Nisin[4] shown in Figure 4 serves to illustrate the reason for this decision, as the resolution in this region is a great deal better than in the Cα or Cβ regions. Spin systems are detected by the following procedure:

1. Find a group of peaks which are aligned[5] along a vertical in the NH region.

2. As it is possible to have more than one set of spin system peaks on the

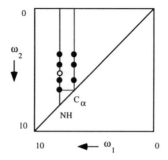

Figure 7. Detection of peaks belonging to the same spin-system. (The white circle indicates a peak that does not belong to the same spin-system as the others.)

same vertical, it is often necessary to resolve such overlapping systems. This is accomplished by the choice of a Cα signal in the NH region (Figure 7); a horizontal line is then traced to the diagonal; looking up the vertical from this point, all the Cβ, Cγ, etc. signals belonging to the same residue as the Cα are observed. If these signals are compared with the signals in the original part of the NH region, the group of peaks in that region belonging to the same spin-system should become obvious, as they will have a constant chemical shift value in the vertical direction.

3. For certain residues, the chemical shift values of the α, β, γ and other protons can be very similar, leading to the ordering of signals becoming confused (Table 1). From the HOHAHA spectrum it is impossible to say which signals are due to which protons and in such a situation it is necessary to resort to a COSY spectrum as this makes explicit the "adjacent" protons. Figures 6b and 6c show the COSY spectra for threonine with the chemical shift values of the α and β protons occurring in slightly different positions. As COSY only shows cross peaks for "one step" interactions it is quite easy to differentiate between the α and β protons, regardless of their chemical shift values; the α interacts with N and β, while the β interacts with α and γ. From the HOHAHA spectra in Figure 6a it is impossible to distinguish between these protons.

4. Often, all the signals for a particular spin system are not present, due to peak overlap and other effects. In such a situation the spectroscopist will often resort to "intelligent" guesswork based upon his knowledge of the technique to "fill the gaps." This knowledge is used to provide a plausible NMR reason why signals do not appear and may, for example, involve decisions based upon the similarities of chemical shift values for individual protons.

5. Once a pattern of signals has been detected within the spectrum, it is la-

Residue	Protons
Arg	H_β 1.63 (.43) H_β' 1.79 (.34) H_γ 1.52 (.34) H_γ' 1.56 (.34)
Gln	H_β 1.92 (.27) H_β' 2.10 (.20) H_γ 2.29 (.25) H_γ' 2.35 (.20)
Glu	H_β 1.97 (.20) H_β' 2.04 (.18) H_γ 2.27 (.20) H_γ' 2.34 (.21)
Ile	H_β 1.74 (.37) H_γ' 1.30 (.32)
Leu	H_β 1.60 (.37) H_β' 1.71 (.31) H_γ 1.51 (.30)
Lys	H_β 1.74 (.38) H_β' 1.84 (.34) H_γ 1.30 (.39) H_γ' 1.36 (.37) H_δ 1.54 (.24) H_δ' 1.57 (.23)
Met	H_β 1.89 (.19) H_β' 2.03 (.21) $H_{\epsilon 3}$ 1.98 (.21)
Pro	H_β 1.88 (.35) H_β' 2.18 (.40) H_γ 1.92 (.50) H_γ' 2.02 (.45)
Ser	H_α 4.50 (.47) H_β 3.72 (.44) H_β' 3.89 (.43)
Thr	H_α 4.53 (.43) H_β 4.17 (.31)
Trp	H_α 4.29 (.80) H_β' 3.42 (.22)

Table 1. Residues with protons which are difficult to identify. Each proton is followed by a mean chemical shift value, determined from a study performed on 20 proteins. The figure in parentheses is the standard deviation.

beled as having been produced by one or more of the 20 amino-acid residues. In the case of some patterns the spin system may only be labeled as belonging to a group of residues with similar structure, such as those with long side chains or aromatic groups.

Chemical shift values could be used to distinguish between the different residue types, but in practice such values are regarded as being too unreliable and are little used.

Thus, in order to perform a complete spin-system assignment, it is necessary to have both the HOHAHA and COSY spectra of the protein. The HOHAHA spectrum is used to identify the spin-systems while the COSY spectrum is used to identify troublesome α and sidechain protons prior to the sequential assignment process.

This entire process is currently performed using a ruler and pencil (to link signals in the spectrum together) and can take several days of a spectroscopists time.

4.2 Connecting the Spin Systems

NOESY technique Depending on the actual settings used during the experiment, NOESY cross peak signals (off-diagonal peaks) can be obtained for pairs of protons at varying distances apart. Figure 3 illustrates the interactions that can occur between 2 adjacent residues.

Which through-space interaction is prevalent will depend upon the geometric shape of the protein. It is possible to get non-sequential NOE interactions due to hydrogen-bonded interactions between adjacent sheets, etc. The NMR experiment may be "fine-tuned" to indicate only those interactions occurring within a certain distance. For example, those occurring between adjacent residues. This is achieved by use of the experimental parameter, mixing time (τ_m). It is usual to set τ_m initially to exclude all but the shortest range NOEs which are due to sequential interactions and very short through-space interactions[6]. This type of experiment is used during the sequential assignment process. For the determination of secondary structure it becomes necessary to alter τ_m to allow the longer range NOEs to give rise to signals. The region 3.8 - 5.5 / 7.6 - 9.0 ppm is the "fingerprint" region of a NOESY spectrum (c.f. HOHAHA).

It is possible to set τ_m in order to exclude all but *one* sequential neighbor of each residue and the shortest through-space interactions. This technique is particularly useful for sequence confirmation experiments when segments of polypeptide chain can be constructed based on the spectrum and checked against the chemically derived sequence.

The sequential assignment process requires that the chemical sequence of the protein be available.

Sequential assignment Using the three sequential connectivities αN, NN, βN it is possible to "walk" the entire length of the residue chain. Using just one of these types of connectivity is often not sufficient, due to absent or overlapping peaks, etc. The HOHAHA and NOESY spectra both possess diagonal peaks corresponding to correlations between protons from the residue. As these peaks occur in the same positions in both spectra, this gives us a means of relating cross peaks in the NOESY to the spin systems identified in the HOHAHA. Figure 8 illustrates the process of sequential assignment using these techniques. One begins by selecting a diagonal peak, such as a Cα peak, in the HOHAHA spectrum which belongs to a known spin system (*d1*). A is an off-diagonal peak within that spin-system. The corresponding diagonal peak in the NOESY is then detected (*d1'*) and a horizontal line drawn away from the diagonal to find the NOESY off-diagonal peak. (If more than one peak is present along the horizontal, then they are all treated as possibly being due to sequential connectivity.) A vertical line is then drawn back to the diagonal (*d2*). The corresponding diagonal peak in the HOHAHA spectrum is then identified (*d2'*) and the fact that the two residues are adjacent is noted. *B* is an off-diagonal peak in the adjacent spin-system[7]. This process is repeated until a peptide segment of perhaps five or six residues has been detected, e.g.

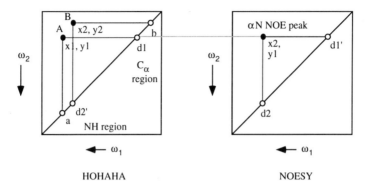

*Figure 8. Use of the HOHAHA and NOESY spectra to perform sequential assignments. HOHAHA peaks **a, d1** and **A** are due to residue R1, while peaks **b, d2'** and **B** are due to residue R2. NOESY peak **d1'** is due to R1 and peak **d2** to R2.*

GCA*L , where * indicates a residue which cannot be identified with absolute certainty from the HOHAHA/COSY spectra

The chemically determined amino acid sequence is then searched for peptide segments that will match the partial sequences identified by sequential NMR assignments. The sequence is needed at this stage to eliminate erroneous sequential assignment pathways, which may have resulted because non-sequential NOE connectivities have been interpreted as sequential ones[8]. In principle, all the information missing in incomplete spin system identifications can be obtained during the sequence specific assignment process. Patterns in the HOHAHA spectrum that have been labeled as one of a group of residues can be uniquely identified once their sequence positions are known. Once all the spin systems in the HOHAHA have been fully identified, they are labeled with their residue name and sequence position.

The sequence specific assignment technique described here works well for small proteins up to approximately 100 residues. If there are too many residues, signal overlap becomes a major problem. For larger proteins it is often necessary to use crystallographic data to help with NMR assignments.

4.3 Secondary Structure Prediction

We have already seen that the short range NOESY interactions allow us to determine which of the residues detected in the HOHAHA spectrum are adjacent. This same information can also be used to indicate some features of secondary structure. Non-sequential interactions also indicate secondary structure, e.g. interaction between the *ith* and *ith+3* residues is seen in α-helices. Accurate identification of the ends of a helix can be difficult. Table 2 summarizes the type of interactions seen in the NOESY spectrum for partic-

α helices			β sheet	
αN (i, i+4)	weak		NN (i, i+1)	weak
αβ (i, i+3)	strong		α N (i, i+1)	very strong
αN (i, i+3)	medium			
NN (i, i+2)	weak		**extended form**	
αN (i, i+2)	NONE		α N (i, i+1)	strong
NN (i, i+1)	strong			
α N (i, i+1)	medium			

Table 2. Common secondary structure NOESY interactions.

ular secondary structures, together with a guide to the peak intensity.

Coupling constant values (determined from the spectrum) can also be used to provide support for a particular structure.

4.4 3D Structure Determination

As we have seen, the NOESY spectrum can be used to indicate features of secondary structure. They can also be used to determine a tertiary (3D) structure for the protein.

The NOESY data is converted into a set of limits on the distances between pairs of interacting protons. Tables containing all internuclear distances in the protein are constructed with the spectroscopic information used to provide some of the entries and the geometry of common structural features used to provide others. Upper and lower limits are recorded for each distance. It should be noted that this is an approximate technique as there is no straightforward mapping from NOE to distance (as the general environment complicates the signal). Strong, medium and weak NOEs are taken to indicate upper distance limits of 2.5, 3.5 and 4.5Å respectively. Known molecular bond lengths, bond angles and standard geometries are used to provide interatomic distances for atoms separated by one or two bonds. Peptide dihedral angles obtained from coupling constants can also be recast as limits on distances between atoms separated by three bonds. A lower limit on interatomic distances is normally set as the sum of the van der Waals radii.

Generating a three dimensional structure from this data is not straightforward and a number of different approaches exist including Distance Geometry algorithms [Havel, 1983], Molecular Dynamics [Hermans, 1985] and systems employing geometric constraint satisfaction, such as the PROTEAN system (see below). Distance Geometry and Molecular Dynamics are examples of methods within the *adjustment paradigm* for interpretation of NMR data [Altman, 1988], i.e. they generate starting structures, usually at random, and then search the neighboring conformational space until the mismatch between the data predicted from the adjusted structure and the experimental data is minimized in terms of some chosen function. By contrast, methods within the *exclusion paradigm* generate starting structures in a systematic manner and test them for agreement with the given data set. All structures compatible with the data are retained as possible solutions, and all incompatible structures are excluded from further consideration.

Distance Geometry algorithms work with distances between points rather than Cartesian coordinates. They allow the choice of three mutually perpendicular axes to be made such that a "best fit" emerges as a 3D description of the structure. This fit usually contains some small incompatibilities with the distance information. These are minimized according to user supplied criteria, often some kind of energy relaxation calculation is required to relieve strain in the structure. Alternative solutions are generated by repeating the calculation with a random choice for the distances, each somewhere within its limits. The effect is to sample the conformation space. Confidence in a solution grows if repeated calculations arrive at a similar end point.

The input to Molecular Dynamics programs consists of the covalent structure of the molecule and a number of energetic terms, e.g. energy to stretch bonds, energy for van der Waal's repulsion. Other energy terms are linked to distance constraints. The program then solves Newton's equations of motion using the energy terms. Balance between the energy terms is important. There is no known test for uniqueness, but confidence increases if repeated simulations from different starting points converge to give a similar final result.

5 Computational Aspects of NMR

The earliest use of computers in NMR was for time-averaging of multiple scans in the mid-1960s. Systems for performing the first Fourier transforms in commercial NMR instrumentation appeared in 1969. From the early 1970s the majority of NMR instruments were interfaced to minicomputers which controlled data acquisition and performed FFT (Fast Fourier Transform) and standard post-FT processing. By the mid-1970s NMR instrumentation was designed around 16-20 bit word minicomputers with low resolution colour graphics and digital plotters used for output. In the early 1980s NMR instrument computers began to be replaced by modern microcomputer and minicomputer systems, augmented by array processors. The current generation of NMR instruments incorporate microcomputers performing tasks ranging from sample temperature control to data acquisition and supervision and control of the user interface. Most NMR instruments make use of high resolution graphics for data display. The current trend is to perform data reduction away from the spectrometer using general-purpose commercial workstations. Levy [1986] reviews some of the computational aspects of NMR.

The application of computers to NMR can be separated into two areas: 1) data acquisition and experiment control and 2) data reduction. The task of acquiring data and performing control over the spectrometer is handled by computers embedded in the instrumentation, usually through proprietary software that is not available to the user. The timing of experimental events, pulse programming and so on occurs on a rapid time scale. The data reduction task, on the other hand, has relatively light real-time constraints. Data reduction is usually performed using ex-spectrometer computers, which facilitate the use of new data reduction techniques and which remove lengthy processing from the instrument and thus lead to an increase in spectrometer throughput. The most common language in scientific computing remains FORTRAN, although recently C has begun to be widely used also. Artificial intelligence languages such as LISP, PROLOG and POP-11 are finding use in scientific software, but as yet only on a very small scale.

5.1 AI Applications & NMR

Chemistry was one of the first disciplines, aside from Computer Science, to actively engage in research involving AI techniques. The Dendral project [Carhart, 1977; Lindsay, 1980; Smith, 1981; Djerassi, 1982] is almost certainly the most well-known of these attempts to use AI for chemical applications, and aimed to develop computer programs to assist structural organic chemists in the process of structure elucidation. Dendral was the first major application of heuristic programming to experimental analysis in an empirical science, a practical problem of some importance. It was the first large scale program to embody the strategy of using detailed, task-specific knowledge about the problem domain as a source of heuristics, and to seek generality through automating the acquisition of such knowledge. The structure elucidation process involves a number of steps. First, chemical and spectroscopic data (including NMR data) are interpreted to provide a number of structural constraints. These constraints are substructures that must either be present, or absent from the molecule under investigation. All possible candidate structures consistent with these constraints are then generated. Additional discriminating experiments are then planned so that the one correct structure can be determined.

Heuristic Dendral was constructed from a simple acyclic structure generator and a planning module (the preliminary inference maker) that performed a classification based on mass spectral data. The early version of the system dealt only with ketone molecules while subsequent versions of the system were extended to handle additional classes of molecules such as ethers and amines [Schroll, 1969]. At the same time other spectral data were incorporated into the system in the form of one dimensional ^{1}H NMR spectra.

Another aspect of the Dendral project was the Meta-Dendral system [Buchanan,1971; Buchanan, 1973]. This arm of the project was concerned with the production of useful tools for chemists at a lower level than the complete structure elucidation system. The system was originally devised for the analysis of mass spectral data although it was extended by Mitchell and Schwenzer [Schwenzer, 1977; Mitchell, 1978] to the analysis of ^{13}C NMR data. The principles governing ^{13}C NMR are similar to those of ^{1}H spectroscopy, although the scale of observed shifts is greater for the former. Again, as in ^{1}H NMR, the precise chemical shift of a nucleus depends on the atom or atoms attached to it. The system generated rules which relate precise ^{13}C shift ranges to specific environments for the resonating carbon atom. The chemical shift range associated with a particular environment is found by matching the generated structure against a training set of molecules and their spectra. The minimum and maximum values of the shift corresponding to that environment are recorded and form the range used in the rules. Goal states can be characterized by various criteria such as requiring a rule to have a sufficiently narrow range or to be supported by a minimum number of examples in the training data. The system begins with a very primitive substructure (e.g. a simple carbon atom) and a correspondingly vague chemical shift range ($-\infty \rightarrow +\infty$). Operators modify this structure by adding hydrogen, carbon, and so on The generated rules are used to predict spectra for a set of candidate molecules and the structures ranked by comparison of the predicted spectrum with that of the unknown.

The use of a database of ^{1}H NMR data to eliminate incompatible candidates from the list of structures produced by exhaustive generation of isomers is described by Egli [1982]. Structures obtained by a generator program are evaluated by prediction of their ^{1}H NMR spectra. The predicted and observed spectra are then compared and the candidates ordered based on such comparisons. The approach to spectrum prediction is strictly empirical and involves the derivation of a set of expected chemical shifts for the protons in each candidate. Egli describes a suite of programs which allow a user to build and maintain a ^{1}H NMR database that correlates substructural environments with observed proton resonances; to predict the spectrum of one or more candidate structures for an unknown compound; to compare the predicted and observed spectra of the molecule and to order the candidates based upon this comparison.

A similar database of ^{13}C NMR correlations containing 10,350 distinct substructure/chemical shift pairs is described by Gray [1981]. This database is also used for prediction of spectra for generated structures. It is also used to perform the interpretation of the ^{13}C NMR spectra of unknown molecules (to arrive at a set of substructural fragments). This interpretation is performed so as to arrive at the minimal, internally consistent set of substructures.

The use of structural constraints provided by two-dimensional NMR is described by Lindley [1983]. Partial structures obtained from the two-dimensional NMR spectrum are combined with other spectral data in an effort to elucidate the correct structure of an unknown molecule. All the constraints are provided by a chemist, who is required to interpret the spectroscopic data.

A number of workers (other than those involved in the Dendral project) have addressed the problem of constructing computer programs to automate or semi-automate the task of structure elucidation. The use of a number of different techniques for computer-assisted structure elucidation is described in Hippe [1985]. These include library-search algorithms which perform the comparison of an unknown spectrum with those in a standard collection stored on disc. Such algorithms typically return a list of spectra and their associated structures ranked according to some matching function. Hippe also describes integrated methods of structure elucidation. Three major components are common to all systems which attempt the structure elucidation task. First, some interpretation of the chemical and spectral data is performed, in order to derive structural fragments. The next step involves molecule assembly, i.e. the generation of complete structures compatible with the fragments and constraints provided by the first phase. Finally, spectra of the generated structures are simulated and compared with the observed data. This allows structures to be ranked on the basis of the quality of the fit between predicted and observed data.

The CASE system [Shelley, 1977; Shelley, 1981; Munk, 1982] is a suite of programs designed to accelerate and make more reliable the entire process of structure elucidation.The task of reducing chemical and spectroscopic data to structural information is currently shared by the chemist and the system. Interpreters capable of detecting the presence of structural fragments based on infrared and ^{13}C NMR data [Shelley, 1982] exist. Two-dimensional NMR data may be used to provide information about the connectivity of atoms in a molecule. The INTERPRET2D module of the system [Christie, 1985] accepts 2D-NMR data input by the chemist and generates the structural conclusions consistent with this information as a set of alternative fragment sets. These sets describe all possible carbon-carbon atom connections consistent with the data and may also be used as input to a structure generator program.

CHEMICS [Sasaki, 1971; Yamasaki, 1977; Sasaki, 1981] uses ^{1}H NMR, ^{13}C NMR, infrared and ultra-violet data to decide which of a set of 150 structural fragments are present in an unknown molecule. The fragments believed to be present are arranged into sets which satisfy the molecular formula and ^{1}H and ^{13}C NMR spectra. A structure generator uses these sets as input to create molecular structures. CHEMICS analyzes the ^{1}H NMR data by first calculating the area of each group of signals in the spectrum. The number of protons associated with each group is thus assigned. Recognizable spin-system patterns are then identified. The most probable structural fragments are then inferred based on chemical shift values. The number of each of these fragments is estimated based on the peak area values. ^{13}C NMR data is interpreted as follows: first, the number of carbons associated with each peak in the spectrum is computed, based on signal intensities; next, the splitting of each peak is examined and individual signals are labeled as arising due to protonated or non-protonated carbons and the number of protons on each carbon recorded. Finally, based on the information already extracted together with the chemical shifts of the signals, a set of structural fragments consistent with the information are obtained.

The STREC system [Gribov, 1977; Gribov, 1980; Elyashberg, 1987] also uses the plan, generate and test approach. During the plan phase, infrared and ^{1}H NMR data are examined and a set of plausible fragments computed. A generator uses these fragments to generate all possible structural isomers. Each structure is then checked against a library of structural fragments for which spectroscopic data are available. The fragments detected have their characteristic spectral information compared with the experimental data for the unknown. If the experimental data do not confirm the presence of the fragment, analysis of that structure is terminated. Each fragment in the library has data for infrared, ^{1}H NMR, ultra-violet and mass spectra. STREC2 [Gribov, 1983] is an enhanced version of the original STREC system, capable of handling larger structures, which makes use of ^{13}C NMR data in addition to the techniques described above.

SEAC (Structure Elucidation Aided by Computer) uses infrared, ^{1}H NMR and ultraviolet data to infer the structure of an unknown molecule [Debska, 1981]. A system for the interpretation of infrared, ^{13}C NMR and mass spectral data, based on the idea of intersecting the interpretations of each of these techniques has been developed by Moldoveanu [1987]. Each of the three spectra is interpreted to generate three sets of plausible fragments; the intersection of these sets is then found and the resulting group of fragments is output to the user. The output also indicates the number of each of these functional groups present in the molecule and the possible positions of substitution of these groups in the unknown molecule.

Knowledge-based techniques have also been applied to the interpretation of other kinds of spectroscopy, including gamma ray activation spectra [Barstow, 1979; Barstow, 1980], ESCA (Electron Spectroscopy for Chemical Analysis) [Yamazaki, 1979], X-ray fluorescence spectroscopy [Janssens, 1986] and X-ray diffraction spectra [Ennis, 1982].

5.2 Computational Aids for Protein NMR

A number of attempts have been made to automate part of the protein structure determination process. One of these systems [Billeter, 1988] starts from a well-defined list of spin-systems which have been identified by the user. The program considers all possible assignments that are consistent with the data currently available. If new data are provided the program eliminates assignments that are inconsistent. It performs logical decision-making and bookkeeping functions and avoids making ambiguous decisions when multiple assignments are possible. Uncertain decisions, i.e. decisions based on NMR data that do not allow a unique interpretation are left to the user. Another system, developed by Cieslar [1988], identifies potential spin-systems within the HOHAHA spectrum by locating aligned peaks. However, attaching residue labels to these spin-systems is left to the user. Once spin-systems have been labeled, the program endeavors, through the use of NOESY signals, to identify sequential connectivities. Partial sequences are identified in this manner and then located within the chemical sequence. The system then constructs all possible assignments for all partial sequences that are consistent with the input data. In order to achieve consistency the partial sequences must not contain overlaps and no particular spin-system should be used in more than one position. All solutions for the assignment of the complete sequence are then generated and checked by the system. Eads [1989] describes a suite of programs which assist in the sequential assignment process and which use peak coordinates and intensity values directly as input. The programs trace spin-systems out to the β protons, look for NOESY cross peaks between relevant protons and create lists of sequential spin-systems. Tracing the spin-systems beyond the β protons and establishing correspondence with the primary sequence is left to the user.

The ABC system [Brugge, 1988] automates the process of determining secondary structure from NMR data. The program is able to identify α helical and β strand segments of chain by means of a set of qualitative criteria that are used in analyzing data derived from the NMR spectra. ABC is implemented within the BB1 architecture [Hayes-Roth, 1988]. Input to ABC consists of the primary sequence of the protein, lists of observed NOEs and residue information. The output of the program is a set of secondary structure elements, defined by their extent over the primary sequence. Each structure is also labeled with the evidence used to derive it and pointers to partial structures from which it was constructed. The output of ABC can be used as part of the input to programs for determining the tertiary structure of proteins. ABC has been tested using published data on nine different proteins and its ability to locate regions of secondary structure, and its precision in defining the extent of these regions have been measured. The system performs well and comes close to reproducing the results of expert analysis of NMR data.

The PROTEAN system [Lichtarge, 1986; Altman, 1988; Altman, 1989] is based on the exclusion paradigm described earlier. Its purpose is to sample the conformational space of a protein systematically and to determine the entire set of positions for each atom that is compatible with the given set of constraints. To maintain computational feasibility, PROTEAN solves the protein structure problem in a hierarchical fashion. The program uses knowledge of the protein sequence together with NMR data to determine the secondary structure. It next defines the coarse topology of the folded structure and then specifies the spatial distribution of atomic positions using a description of accessible volumes. From these values, the original data are predicted to verify the resulting family of structures.

The secondary structure of the protein is determined using the ABC system described above. The units of secondary structure and a set of experimental constraints (primary structure, NOE distances, surface and volume information) are then passed to the SOLID GS module. This computes the accessible volume for the units of secondary structure. SOLID GS uses abstract representations to reduce the number of objects whose positions need to be sampled. For example, helices are represented by cylinders. The next module, ATOMIC GS, refines the secondary structures and coils using discrete sampling for atoms. The output of this module is then processed by another (KALMAN) which employs a probabilistic refinement method[9] for determination of the uncertainty in each atom. The final component of the system, BLOCH, calculates NMR data and evaluates the match between observed and predicted values. The system has been used to investigate the tertiary structure of the *lac-repressor headpiece*, a protein with 51 amino acid residues. The structural solution proposed by PROTEAN closely matches that proposed by a manual interpretation of the data performed by an expert protein spectroscopist.

6 The Protein NMR Assistant

We are in the process of developing a Protein NMR Assistant (PNA) which will aid a spectroscopist in the identification of residue spin systems and the prediction of secondary structure. (We are not currently interested in the problem of tertiary structure prediction.) Previous systems which have addressed this problem, such as those described earlier, have tackled only part of the task and have left much of the interpretation to the spectroscopist. PNA aims to provide a complete system for the identification and assignment of spin-systems, leading to the prediction of secondary structure.

Two previous attempts at inferring protein structure using AI techniques are CRYSALIS [Engelmore, 1979; Terry, 1983] and PROTEAN [Hayes-Roth, 1986]. CRYSALIS attempted to infer the structure of a protein of known composition but unknown conformation using X-ray diffraction data. Both these systems made use of the blackboard architecture to integrate diverse sources of problem-solving knowledge and to partition the problem into manageable "chunks". We are currently investigating whether such an approach would be appropriate for the task of interpreting 2D NMR of proteins. The characteristics of this task are: a large solution space; noisy data; likelihood of multiple, competing solutions; and the use of a number of cooperating sources of knowledge. This would seem to make it suitable for the blackboard approach.

6.1 The Blackboard Architecture

A blackboard system consists of three main components: the blackboard, a set of problem-solving knowledge sources and a control mechanism. The blackboard serves to partition the solution space of the problem domain into one or more domain-specific hierarchies, representing partial solutions. Each level in the hierarchy possesses a unique vocabulary that serves to describe the information at that level. Objects on the blackboard can be input data, partial solutions as well as final solutions and possibly control information. Relationships between objects are denoted by named links. Domain knowledge is partitioned into separate modules which transform information at one level into information on the same or different levels. These modules are termed knowledge sources (KSs) and perform transformations using rules or procedures. The KSs are separate and independent. Each KS is responsible for knowing the conditions under which it can contribute to the solution and thus has a precondition which indicates the conditions on the blackboard that must exist before the main part of the KS can be activated. The choice of which KS to use is based on the state of the solution, the latest additions and modifications to the solution and on the existence of KSs capable of improving the state of the solution. A controller monitors the changes to the blackboard and decides what to do next. The solution evolves one step at a time with any type of reasoning step (data-driven, goal-driven and so on) being applied at each stage.

For a particular application it is necessary to define a solution space and the knowledge needed to find the solution. This space is divided into levels of analysis corresponding to partial solutions and the domain knowledge is divided into specialized KSs that perform the subtasks necessary to arrive at a final solution. How the problem is partitioned into subproblems makes a great deal of difference to the clarity of the approach, the resources required and even the ability to solve the problem at all. This discussion has been necessarily brief; a number of excellent articles on this subject exist [Hayes-Roth, 1983; Nii, 1986a; Nii, 1986b], together with two books [Engelmore, 1988; Jagannathan, 1989].

A blackboard system can serve as a powerful research tool, allowing the solution space and domain knowledge of an application problem to be partitioned in different ways and a variety of reasoning strategies to be evaluated. The robustness of blackboard systems stems primarily from the way in which they are organized which tends to localize changes. The answer produced by a blackboard system is often a complex datastructure, different parts of which may have been computed through different reasoning paths. A trace of the system's execution history is unlikely to prove very useful to the user. We are addressing the problem of visualization of results as part of the development of the current system.

The blackboard architecture has been used in a wide variety of applications, including speech understanding [Erman, 1980]; submarine detection [Nii, 1982]; image understanding [Nagao, 1979]; and computer controlled manufacturing [Ayel, 1988]. A number of generalized architectures have also been developed to allow blackboard application systems to be constructed more easily. Examples of such tools include: AGE [Nii, 1979], Hearsay-III [Balzer, 1980], BB1 [Hayes-Roth, 1988], GBB [Corkill, 1986], PCB [Edwards, 1990]. The PCB system is a problem-solving architecture designed to ease the construction of complex knowledge-based systems in chemical domains. Although the system we shall describe below is not built within this framework, its design and implementation owe much to the PCB system.

We shall discuss the Protein NMR Assistant in terms of the components of the blackboard architecture described above, i.e. the blackboard (its levels and objects), the knowledge sources (structure and function) and control. The system architecture is shown in Figure 9.

6.2 The PNA Blackboard

The blackboard is divided into five levels (as shown in Figure 9): data, spin-system, segment, labeled residue and secondary structure. The contents of each level are as follows:

data: Spectroscopic data (HOHAHA, COSY and NOESY) plus the chemical sequence.

spin-system: Hypotheses describing the identification of residue spin-systems within the HOHAHA spectrum.

segment: Partial sequences of 5 or 6 residues assembled from the spin- system hypotheses.

labeled residue: Fully labeled residue hypotheses each of which describes the sequence position of a residue, together with the spectroscopic data used to identify it.

secondary structure: Units of secondary structure identified through examination of the NOESY spectrum.

Objects on each of these levels are represented using a frame-based representation. The chemical sequence is represented by a frame containing a number of slots, the first of which contains the full sequence represented as a

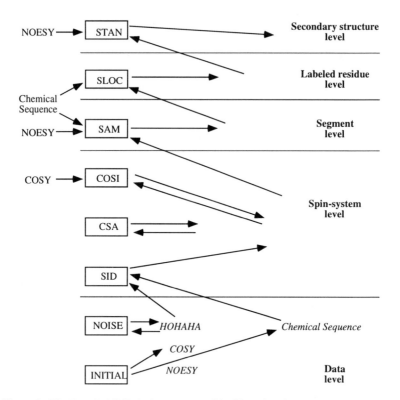

Figure 9. The Protein NMR Assistant system blackboard architecture.

list of the usual one letter abbreviations. Other slots contain the length of the sequence and the number of each of the twenty amino-acid residues present within the sequence. The spectroscopic data is represented on a peak-by-peak basis. Each peak in the HOHAHA spectrum is represented using the following slots: *id* (unique identification number for the peak); *xcoord* (x coordinate of the peak center); *ycoord* (y coordinate of the peak center); *xsize* ("width" of the peak in the x direction); *ysize* ("width" of the peak in the y direction); *peak-type* (label indicating whether or not the peak is noise); *infers* (list of the spin-system hypotheses which the peak is associated with).

Objects on the spin-system level define the nature of the residue spin-systems identified from the HOHAHA spectrum. Each hypothesis contains the following slots: *infers* (list of segment hypotheses supported by the spin-system); *supported-by* (list of HOHAHA peaks which make up the spin-system); *residue-type* (name of the amino-acid residue giving rise to the spin-system); *peak-list* (identification numbers and coordinates of the HOHAHA peaks which make up the spin-system); *diagonal-peaks* (positions of each of the diagonal peaks involved in the spin-system); *protons* (label indicating whether the COSY spectrum should be used o distinguish between peaks in the spin-system). If the system is unable to uniquely assign a spin-system to a particular residue, the *residue-type* slot contains a list of the possible residues associated with that spin-system, instead of an individual residue name.

Segment level hypotheses also contain *infers* and *supported-by* slots. *infers* is used to indicate which of the objects on the labeled residue level the segment hypothesis has provided evidence for, while *supported-by* lists those spin-systems which were connected to form the segment. Other slots within the segment hypotheses are: *segment-sequence* (the partial sequence stored as a list); *noesy-links* (peak data indicating the sequential connectivities for each of the residue pairs in the segment). In the event that a residue is not uniquely identified on the spin-system level, the *segment-sequence* slot will contain a list of possible residues in place of a single residue.

A fully labeled residue hypothesis contains all the information associated with the identification of a residue. As well as *infers* and *supported-by* slots (which indicate which secondary structure unit the residue is involved in and which segment supports it), objects on this level also contain the following: *residue-type* (residue name); *sequence-position* (position of the residue within the chemical sequence); *peak-list* (identification numbers and coordinates of the HOHAHA peaks which comprise the residue spin-system); *diagonal-peaks* (positions of each of the diagonal peaks involved in the residue spin-system); *noesy-links* (NOESY peak data used to assemble the segment in which the residue occurs).

The final level of the PNA blackboard contains the secondary structure hypotheses. These objects detail the exact nature and extent of any secondary structure unit identified within the protein. Structural hypotheses contain the following: *supported-by* (list of labeled residues which make up this unit); *structure-unit* (type of unit, i.e. α helix, β sheet); *start* (position in the chemical sequence at which the unit commences); *finish* (position in the sequence where the unit terminates); *spatial-noesy* (NOESY interactions used to infer the presence of the unit). In cases were there is uncertainty as to the exact point in the sequence where the structural unit begins or ends, the *start* and *finish* slots contain lists of residues, indicating a region of the protein sequence.

6.3 The PNA Knowledge Sources

The system currently consists of eight knowledge sources: INITIAL (Initialization) NOISE (Noise removal), SID (Spin-system identifier), CSA (Chemical shift analyzer), COSI (COSY interpreter), SAM (Sequential assignment module), SLOC (Sequence locator) and STAN (Structure analyzer). We shall now describe each of these KSs in turn.

INITIAL The first of the PNA KSs deals with the initialization of the blackboard and with the loading of spectroscopic and chemical sequence data. The coordinate data representing the HOHAHA, COSY and NOESY spectra are held in text files which are compiled by this KS into the internal representation described above. The chemical sequence is also compiled from a file containing the one letter residue symbols. In addition to loading the sequence, INITIAL also calculates its length and the number of each of the amino-acid residues that are present within it.

NOISE As described earlier (Section 3.1), the HOHAHA spectrum contains bands of noise (t_1 noise) which run parallel to the ω_1 axis. Before the system attempts to identify spin-systems within the spectrum, it first uses the NOISE KS to identify peaks which may be due to noise. NOISE examines the spectroscopic data and searches for groups of peaks which run parallel to the ω_1 axis, i.e. peaks which possess approximately the same y coordinate value. These peaks, once identified, have *noise* written to their peak-type slot. This information is then used by the other KSs during analysis of the spectrum.

SID This KS uses the coordinate representation of the HOHAHA spectrum[10] together with the chemical sequence of the protein and attempts to identify residue spin-systems. The chemical sequence is used in order to prevent residues absent from the protein being proposed. SID contains knowledge describing each of the twenty common amino acid residues and the approximate chemical shift values of each of their protons. Each of the residues is represented by a frame containing a description of the protons found in that residue, represented by a list. For example, isoleucine is represented by the list [N Ca Cb Cg1 Cg1 Cg2 Cg2 Cg2 Cd1 Cd1 Cd1], i.e. 1 amide proton, 1 Cα, 1 Cβ, etc. Another slot contains a list of the approximate chemical shift values of each proton. Thus, for isoleucine, the chemical shift list is: [8.26 4.13 1.74 1.30 1.01 0.78 0.78 0.78 0.69 0.69 0.69], i.e. the amide proton has a value of approximately 8.26, the Cβ a value of 1.74, etc. The approximate chemical shift values we are using were obtained from a statistical analysis of water soluble polypeptides and proteins [Groß, 1988]. It should be noted that the values are only approximate and are merely used as a guide to the likely nature of the spin-system.

The spin-system identification process proceeds as follows. Beginning at the limit of the amide proton region of the HOHAHA spectrum (9.0 ppm), a peak is selected that is close to the diagonal. All peaks with the same x coordinate as this peak (+/- some threshold value) are detected. SID then examines the spectrum for peaks in other regions with the same y coordinate as the peaks in this list. The set of peaks which are aligned in the NH region of the spectrum and which have companion peaks in other regions which are also aligned along a vertical, are then labeled as possibly belonging to the same spin-system. This list is then processed to remove all but one peak with any

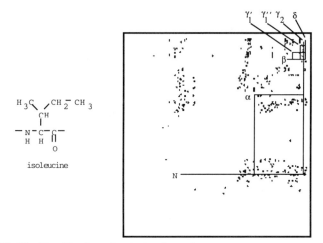

Figure 10. The identification of an isoleucine spin-system.

y coordinate value. The contents of this list correspond to the protons in an individual spin-system. This list is compared against the list of chemical shifts held by SID for each residue and all those residues which match the pattern of peaks are retained. By match here, we mean that the shift values for the spin-system peaks are equal to those in the residue chemical shift lists +/- some scatter parameter. We are assuming (for the moment) that the spectral data is complete, i.e that each residue in the protein gives rise to the correct number of cross peaks and that there are no missing or extraneous peaks.

All peaks in the spectrum that have been assigned to a spin-system are labeled as such and a spin-system hypothesis created. This hypothesis holds the identification numbers and coordinates of each peak involved in a spin-system together with the name of the residue. As we have already seen (Table 1), it can be difficult to detect the Cα and Cβ protons of certain residues due to very similar chemical shift values for different protons. It is important that the N, Cα and Cβ protons are clearly labeled as it is the positions of these protons that are used by the sequential assignment module (SAM). Figure 10 shows the alignment of cross-peaks in the Nisin spectrum corresponding to an isoleucine residue, while Figure 11 contains the spin-system hypothesis created by PNA to describe the identified isoleucine residue.

One of the problems to be solved within SID is a means of resolving peak overlap, i.e. how to distinguish between a number of peaks which occur in very close proximity. It is obvious that for spin-system identification to be successful, such peaks must be differentiated.

CSA This KS examines spin-system hypotheses which have been created

spin-system hypothesis 23:

infers :	[ ]
supported-by :	[peak835 peak1076 peak1082 peak1085 peak1086
	peak1153 peak1154 peak1285]
knowledge-source :	
	[spin-system-id]
residue type :	ile
protons :	[Cb Cg1]

peak list :   [835 310.8 712.34]   [1076 889.76 920.13]
               [1154 923.58 984.78]   [1085 890.7 974]
               [1285 310.7 976.6]   [1153 923.51 974.18]
               [1086 890.65 984.05]   [1082 890.6 957.56]

diagonals peaks: [310.8 N   712.34 a   890.7 b   923.58 g1   957.56 g1
                 974 g2   974 g2   974 g2   984.78 d   984.78 d
                 984.78 d]

Figure 11. The spin-system hypothesis corresponding to the isoleucine spin-system shown in Figure 10.

by the SID KS and uses knowledge of chemical shift data in order to check whether the residue has Cα and Cβ protons which may be confused with other protons. From an examination of Table 1, it is obvious that the residues listed there are likely to lead to just this kind of assignment difficulty. If such confusion occurs, the hypothesis is labeled accordingly. For example, in isoleucine residues, the Cβ and Cγ1' protons may easily be confused and thus [Cb Cg1] is placed in the protons slot of the spin-system hypothesis. If protons with difficult to assign resonances are not believed to occur in the residue, CSA writes *complete* to the protons slot.

COSI Using the COSY coordinate data, this KS attempts to distinguish between protons within spin-system hypotheses which have been labeled by the CSA KS. It performs this task using the list of coordinates of the protons within the spin-system together with the information provided by the CSA label. The *y* coordinates are used to detect the appropriate diagonal peaks in the COSY coordinate map. Cross peaks which occur between these diagonal peaks are then traced. The representation of the structure of the residue (described above) is then called upon and the system determines (based on knowledge about COSY interactions) which of the COSY cross peaks is due to each of the one step interactions. Thus, each of the important α, β and N protons is correctly labeled within the spin-system hypothesis and the value of the protons slot set as *complete*.

To illustrate the solution adopted by PNA to these problem assignments, consider Figure 6. From the HOHAHA spectrum of Threonine (6a) it is impossible to distinguish between the Cα and Cβ proton. However, as COSY only has cross peaks due to adjacent interactions (6b, 6c), the Cα - Cβ interaction can be seen, as can the N - Cα and Cβ - Cγ interactions. As the Cα proton gives rise to two cross peaks, one with N and the other with Cβ, while the Cβ proton is involved with Cα and Cγ, it is quite straightforward to differentiate between the α and β protons.

SAM This KS uses the chemical sequence and the spin-system hypotheses, together with a coordinate representation of the short τ_m NOESY spectrum with an additional descriptor for each peak to provide intensity information. The sequential assignment process then proceeds as follows. The chemical sequence is examined and either a unique residue, or unique dipeptide segment (pair of adjacent residues) is detected. In the case of a unique residue, the system then looks through the spin-system hypotheses for a hypothesis corresponding to this residue. For dipeptides, one of the residues in the pair is selected and the appropriate hypothesis retrieved. The coordinates of the Cα peak are extracted and the NOESY spectrum examined for a cross peak with the same y coordinate. The x coordinate of this peak is then retrieved and the spin-system hypotheses examined for a N proton with the same x coordinate. This group of connected peaks corresponds to a αN short range interaction. If the search for an interaction is unsuccessful, then the coordinates of the N proton peak in the starting residue are used and if this fails, the Cβ peak is used. If such an interaction is detected, SAM notes that the two residues are adjacent and the process is repeated using the spin-system hypothesis for the second residue. This continues until a 5 or 6 residue segment has been assembled at which point SAM creates a segment hypothesis. This hypothesis contains the partial sequence and the NOESY peak data used to construct it. SAM then selects another spin-system hypothesis and attempts to generate another 5 or 6 residue segment.

SLOC Once a peptide segment has been created by the SAM KS, the SLOC KS may be invoked. This KS attempts to locate the partial sequence defined by the segment hypothesis within the overall chemical sequence of the protein. The sequence is searched for a matching segment and the sequence position numbers of each of the residues are noted. At this stage, uncertainties as to the exact nature of a residue spin-system are resolved using the sequence. Each of the spin-system hypotheses used to generate the segment are then examined and the appropriate fully labeled residue hypotheses created.

STAN This KS uses the fully labeled residue hypotheses and a coordinate representation of the NOESY spectrum with an intensity descriptor for each peak. It contains information on the type of interactions expected for each secondary structure unit. This information is represented as a series of frames containing details of the type of protons involved, their relative positions in the sequence, the intensity of the signal and the secondary structure. For example, to represent that an αN (i, i+4) interaction with weak intensity indicates an α-helix, a frame would contain the following: [a n 4 weak alpha]. STAN examines the NOESY data for cross peaks indicating particular secondary structure units and creates structure hypotheses (described above) detailing the nature and extent of these structures. Table 3 contains a summary of the function of each of the PNA knowledge sources.

6.4 Control

The control component of PNA must integrate the performance of each of the domain knowledge sources described above with intervention by the spectroscopist during problem-solving. Unlike the KSs, each of which is a specialized problem-solving entity dealing with a small part of the overall task, the user is able to contribute at any stage of the process. The user may choose to interrupt the performance of the system and may, for example, create a new hypothesis or modify an existing one on any level of the blackboard. The control task faced by PNA is therefore a dynamic constantly changing one, with the system requiring a flexible control structure.

Rather than encoding a fixed control strategy into the system we are implementing a control framework which will allow the user to intervene during problem-solving. However, we have restricted the amount of user interaction which is allowed during the analysis of the data. For example, the SID knowledge source generates **all** potential spin-system hypotheses without any interruption by the user. One the spin-system identification process is complete the user is free to intervene and to inspect the hypotheses and if necessary to modify or even delete some of them. Other KSs, such as COSI or SAM modify or create only one hypothesis before allowing the user to intervene. This approach is, we feel, a useful compromise between no user interaction during problem-solving and allowing the user to intervene at any point during problem-solving - with all its inherent difficulties.

It should be noted that although Figure 9 indicates the flow of reasoning moving upwards from the data level, that the system also supports top-down reasoning. For example, the identification of a segment hypothesis within the chemical sequence may remove an uncertainty as to the nature of a residue spin-system, which will result in modifications to lower-level hypotheses.

7 Discussion

The Protein NMR Assistant aims to provide a spectroscopist with a powerful tool for the analysis of nuclear magnetic resonance spectra of proteins. Currently, much of this task is performed by hand and is extremely time consuming. By providing an interactive environment for the analysis of HOHA-

Knowledge Source	Function
INITIAL	Initialises the PNA blackboard by loading spectroscopic and sequence data.
NOISE	Identifies noise bands and other spurious peaks in the HOHAHA spectrum prior to the spin-system identification process.
SID	Attempts to identify residue spin-systems within the coordinate representation of the HOHAHA spectrum.
CSA	Using knowledge of approximate residue chemical shifts, examines spin-system hypotheses and labels those which contain "troublesome" protons.
COSI	Examines the COSY coordinate map in an effort to distinguish between troublesome signals identified by CSA.
SAM	Links spin-system hypotheses together to form segment hypotheses.
SLOC	Searches the chemical sequence for a segment generated by SAM and generates a residue hypothesis labeled with its sequence position.
STAN	Infers the presence of secondary structure units using residue hypotheses and the NOESY spectrum.

Table 3 Summary of the Protein NMR Assistant Knowledge Sources.

HA, COSY and NOESY spectra, it is hoped that the time required to perform the analysis of such data will be reduced and that the reliability of results will be increased.

A user interface, consisting of a series of windows displaying the spectra and allowing the user to interact during the interpretation process is under development. Such an interface is, we feel, a vital part of the overall architecture. We are investigating how the partial solutions created on the blackboard can be displayed in such a way that they are meaningful and assist the user in comprehending the actions of the system. Once fully implemented, PNA will be used to examine a number of proteins for which NMR data are available and the results and performance of the system evaluated.

We are currently investigating the application of machine learning techniques to the 2D NMR of Carbohydrates [Metaxas, 1991]. This study aims to generate an empirical theory relating the structural form of a molecule with its 2D NMR spectrum. It is hoped that the experience gained through this project will allow us to investigate the applicability of such methods to 2D NMR of Proteins. Empirical rules relating spectral features to protein structure could be used to assist in secondary structure prediction and perhaps during the sequential assignment process. The existence of some rules, such as those relating peaks in the NOESY spectrum to secondary structure, gives us confidence that this domain will prove suitable for the application of machine learning techniques. Any knowledge obtained using such techniques could be tested within the problem-solving environment provided by the Protein NMR Assistant.

Notes

1 It should be noted that three dimensional NMR experiments are also now possible.

2 Figure 3 illustrates these sequential NOE connectivities.

3 Proline residues can present a problem during the interpretation process, as they do not possess an amide proton and thus any residue adjacent to a proline will appear to be a terminal residue.

4 A 34 amino-acid peptide with molecular formula $C_{143}H_{230}N_{42}O_{37}$

5 By aligned we mean that the peak centers lie along the same vertical line allowing for some scatter value.

6 As some NOEs due to secondary structure features may appear in this experiment, it is necessary to refer to the chemical sequence during sequential assignment of spin systems.

7 If the NOE cross peak occurs between two protons within the same residue it is ignored.

8 We are of course assuming that the sequence is correct.

9 The double-iterated Kalman filter.

10 The transformation from the original HOHAHA spectrum to this coordinate representation is performed using a commercial 2D "peak picking" program.

References

R.B. Altman, B.S. Duncan, J.F. Brinkley, B.G. Buchanan and O. Jardetzky, Determination of the Spatial Distribution of Protein Structure Using Solution Data, in J. W. Jaroszewski, K. Schaumburg and H. Kofod (Eds.), *NMR Spectroscopy in Drug Research,* Munksgaard, Copenhagen, 1988, 209-232

R.B. Altman and O. Jardetzky, Heuristic Refinement Method for Determination of Solution Structure of Proteins from Nuclear Magnetic Resonance Data, *Methods in Enzymology,* 1989, 177, 218-246

J. Ayel, A Conceptual Supervision Model in Computer Integrated Manufacturing, in *Proceedings of the Eighth European Conference on Artificial Intelligence (ECAI88),* Munich, FRG, August 1-5, 1988, 427-432

R. Balzer, L.D. Erman, P.E. London and C. Williams, Hearsay-III : A Domain-Independent

Framework for Expert Systems, in *Proceedings of the First National Conference on Artificial Intelligence (AAAI80)*, Stanford, California, USA, August 18-21, 1980, 108-110

D.R. Barstow, Knowledge Engineering in Nuclear Physics, in *Proceedings of the Sixth International Joint Conference on Artificial Intelligence (IJCAI79)*, Tokyo, Japan, August 20-23, 1979, 1, 34-36

D.R. Barstow, Exploiting a Domain Model in an Expert Spectral Analysis Program, in *Proceedings of the First National Conference on Artificial Intelligence (AAAI80)*, Stanford, CA, USA, August 18-21, 1980, 276-279

M. Billeter, V.J. Basus & I.D. Kuntz, A Program for Semi-Automatic Sequential Resonance Assignments in Protein [1]H Nuclear Magnetic Resonance Spectra, *Journal of Magnetic Resonance*, 1988, 76: 400-415

J.A. Brugge, B.G. Buchanan and O. Jardetzky, Toward Automating the Process of Determining Polypeptide Secondary Structure from ^{1}H NMR Data, *Journal of Comput. Chemistry*, 188, 9 (6): 662-673

B.G. Buchanan, E.A. Feigenbaum and J. Lederberg, A Heuristic Programming Study of Theory Formation in Science, in *Advance Papers of the Second International Joint Conference on Artificial Intelligence (IJCAI71)*, London, September 1-3, 1971, 40-50

B.G. Buchanan and N.S. Sridharan, Analysis of Behaviour of Chemical Molecules: Rule Formation of Non-Homogeneous Classes of Objects, in *Advance Papers of the Third International Joint Conference on Artificial Intelligence (IJCAI73)*, Stanford, CA, USA, August 20-23, 1973, 67-76

R.E. Carhart, T.H. Varkony and D.H. Smith, Computer Assistance for the Structural Chemist, in D.H. Smith (Ed.), *Computer-Assisted Structure Elucidation*, ACS Symposium Series no. 54, ACS, Washington D.C., 1977, 126-145

B.D. Christie, Personal Communication, September 1985

C. Cieslar, G.M. Clore & A.M. Gronenborn, Computer-Aided Sequential Assignment of Protein ^{1}H NMR Spectra, *Journal of Magnetic Resonance*, 1988, 76, 119-127

R.M. Cooke & I.D. Campbell, Protein Structure Determination by Nuclear Magnetic Resonance, *BioEssays*, 1988, 8 (2), 52-56

D.D. Corkill, K.Q. Gallagher and K.E. Murray, GBB: A Generic Blackboard Development System, in *Proceedings of the Fifth National Conference on Artificial Intelligence (AAAI86)*, Philadelphia, PA, USA, August 11-15, 1986, 2, 1008-114

B. Debska, J. Duliban, B. Guzowska-Swider and Z. Hippe, Computer-Aided Structural Analysis of Organic Compounds by an Artificial Intelligence System, *Anal. Chim. Acta.*, 1981, 133: 303-318

C. Djerassi, D.H. Smith, C.W. Crandell, N.A.B. Gray, J.G. Nourse and M.R. Lindley, The Dendral Project: Computational Aids to Natural Products Structure Elucidation, *Pure & Applied Chem.*, 1982, 54 (12), 2425-2442

C.D. Eads & I.D. Kuntz, Programs for Computer-Assisted Sequential Assignment of Proteins, *Journal of Magnetic Resonance*, 1989, 82, 467-482

P. Edwards, D. Sleeman, G.C.K. Roberts & L.Y. Lian, *An Intelligent Assistant for Protein NMR*, Aberdeen University Computing Science Department Technical Report, AUCS/TR8910, 1989

P. Edwards, A Cooperative Expert System for Spectra Interpretation, PhD thesis, School of Chemistry, University of Leeds, 1990

H. Egli, D.H. Smith and C. Djerassi, Computer-Assisted Structural Interpretation of [1]H

NMR Spectral Data, *Helvetica Chimica Acta,* 1982, 65: 1898-1920

M.E. Elyashberg, V.V. Serov and L.A. Gribov, Artificial Intelligence Systems for Molecular Spectral Analysis, *Talanta,* 1987, 34 (1), 21-30

R.S. Engelmore and A. Terry, Structure and Function of the CRYSALIS System, in *Proceedings of the Sixth International Joint Conference on Artificial Intelligence (IJCAI79),* Tokyo, Japan, August 20-23,1979, 1: 250- 256

R.S. Engelmore and A.J. Morgan, *Blackboard Systems,* Addison-Wesley, Wokingham, England, 1988

S.P. Ennis, Expert Systems : A User's Perspective of Some Current Tools, in *Proceedings of the Second National Conference on Artificial Intelligence (AAAI82),* Carnegie-Mellon University, Pittsburgh, PA, USA, August 18-20 1982, 319-321

L.D. Erman, F. Hayes-Roth, V.R. Lesser and D.R. Reddy, The Hearsay-II Speech Understanding System: Integrating Knowledge to Resolve Uncertainty, *ACM Computing Surveys,* 1980, 12 (2), 213-253

N.A.B. Gray, C.W. Crandell, J.G. Nourse, D.H. Smith, M.L. Dageforde and C. Djerassi, Computer-Assisted Structural Interpretation of Carbon-13 Spectral Data, *J. Org. Chem.,* 1981, 46: 703-715

L.A. Gribov, M.E. Elyashberg and V.V. Serov, Computer System for Structure Recognition of Polyatomic Molecules by IR, NMR, UV and MS Methods, *Anal. Chim. Acta.,* 1977, 95: 75-96

L.A. Gribov, Application of Artificial Intelligence Systems in Molecular Spectroscopy, *Anal. Chim. Acta.,* 1980, 122: 249-256

L.A. Gribov, M.E. Elyashberg, V.N. Koldashov and I.V. Pletnjov, A Dialogue Computer Program System for Structure Recognition of Complex Molecules by Spectroscopic Methods, *Anal. Chim. Acta.,* 1983, 148: 159-170

K.H. Groß & H.R. Kalbitzer, Distribution of Chemical Shifts in [1]H Nuclear Magnetic Resonance Spectra of Proteins, *Journal of Magnetic Resonance,* 1988, 76: 87-99

T.F. Havel, I.D. Kuntz and G.M. Crippen, The Theory and Practice of Distance Geometry, *Bulletin of Mathematical Biology,* 1983, 45 (5), 665-720

B. Hayes-Roth, *The Blackboard Architecture: A General Framework for Problem Solving ?,* Stanford University, Computer Science Department, Heuristic Programming Project Report No. HPP-83-30, 1983

B. Hayes-Roth, B. Buchanan, O. Lichtarge, M. Hewett, R. Altman, J. Brinkley, C. Cornelius, B. Duncan and O. Jardetzky, PROTEAN: Deriving Protein Structure from Constraints, in *Proceedings of the Fifth National Conference on Artificial Intelligence (AAAI86),* Philadelphia, PA, USA, August 11-15, 1986, 2: 904-909

B. Hayes-Roth and M. Hewett, BB1: An Implementation of the Blackboard Control Architecture, in *Blackboard Systems,* Addison-Wesley, Wokingham, England, R.S. Engelmore and A.J. Morgan (Eds.), 1988, 297-313

J. Hermans (Ed.), *Molecular Dynamics and Protein Structure,* Polycrystal Book Service, 1985

Z. Hippe, Problem-Solving Methods in Computer-Aided Organic Structure Determination, *J. Chem. Inf. Comput. Sci.,* 1985, 25: 344-350

V. Jagannathan, R. Dodhiawala and L.S. Baum (Eds.), *Blackboard Architectures and Applications,* Academic Press: San Diego, CA, 1989

K. Janssens and P. Van Espen, Evaluation of Energy-Dispersive X-Ray Spectra with the Aid of Expert Systems, *Anal. Chim. Acta.,* 1986, 191: 169-180

O. Jardetzky and G.C.K. Roberts, *NMR in Molecular Biology,* Academic Press, New York, 1981

G.C. Levy, Current Trends in Computing: Hardware, Software and Nuclear Magnetic Resonance Research, *J. Molec. Graphics,* 1986, 4 (3),170-177

O. Lichtarge, C.W. Cornelius, B.G. Buchanan and O. Jardetzky, *Validation of the First Step of the Heuristic Refinement Method for the Derivation of Solution Structures of Proteins from NMR Data,* Knowledge Systems Laboratory, Computer Science Department, Stanford University, Report No. KSL-86-12

M.R. Lindley, J.N. Shoolery, D.H. Smith and C. Djerassi, Application of the Computer Program GENOA and Two-Dimensional NMR Spectroscopy to Structure Elucidation, *Organic Magnetic Resonance,* 1983, 21 (7), 405- 411

R.K. Lindsay, B.G. Buchanan, E.A. Feigenbaum and J. Lederberg, *Applications of Artificial Intelligence for Organic Chemistry: The Dendral Project,* McGraw-Hill, New York, 1980

S. Metaxas, P.Edwards and D. Sleeman, *The Interpretation of COSY ^1H NMR Spectra for Small Sugar Molecules,* Aberdeen University Computing Science Department Technical Report, AUCS/TR9109

T.M. Mitchell and G.M. Schwenzer, Application of Artificial Intelligence for Chemical Inference XXV. A Computer Program for Automated Empirical ^{13}C NMR Rule Formation, *Org. Mag. Res.,* 1978, 11 (8), 378-384

S. Moldoveanu and C.A. Rapson, Spectral Interpretation for Organic Analysis Using an Expert System, *Anal. Chem.,* 1987, 59: 1207-1212

G.A. Morris, Modern NMR Techniques for Structure Elucidation, *Magnetic Resonance in Chemistry,* 1986, 24: 371-403

M.E. Munk, C.A. Shelley, H.B. Woodruff and M.O. Trulson, Computer- Assisted Structure Elucidation, *Z. Anal. Chem.,* 1982, 313: 473-479

M. Nagao, T. Matsuyama and H. Mori, Structural Analysis of Complex Aerial Photographs, in *Proceedings of the Sixth International Joint Conference on Artificial Intelligence (IJCAI79),* Tokyo, Japan, August 20-23,1979, 2, 610-616

H.P. Nii and N. Aiello, AGE (Attempt to Generalize) : A Knowledge-Based Program for Building Knowledge-Based Programs, in *Proceedings of the Sixth International Joint Conference on Artificial Intelligence (IJCAI79),* Tokyo, Japan, August 20-23,1979, 2, 645-655

H.P. Nii, E.A. Feigenbaum, J.J. Anton and A.J. Rockmore, Signal-to-Symbol Transformation: HASP/SIAP Case Study, *AI Magazine,* 1982, 3 (2), 23-35

H.P. Nii, Blackboard Systems: The Blackboard Model of Problem Solving and the Evolution of Blackboard Architectures, *AI Magazine,* 1986, 7 (2), 38-53

H.P. Nii, Blackboard Systems: Blackboard Application Systems, Blackboard Systems from a Knowledge Engineering Perspective, *AI Magazine,* 1986, 7: (3), 82-106

S. Sasaki, Y. Kudo, S. Ochiai and H. Abe, Automated Chemical Structure Analysis of Organic Compounds: An Attempt to Structure Determination by the Use of NMR, Mikrochimica *Acta.,* 1971, 726-742

S. Sasaki, H. Abe, I. Fujiwara and T. Yamasaki, *The Application of ^{13}C NMR in CHEMICS, The Computer Program System for Structure Elucidation,* in Z. Hippe (Ed.), *Data Processing in Chemistry* (Studies in Physical and Theoretical Chemistry 16), Elsevier, 1981, 186-204

G. Schroll, A.M. Duffield, C. Djerassi, B.G. Buchanan, G.L. Sutherland, E.A. Feigenbaum and J. Lederberg, Applications of Artificial Intelligence for Chemical Inference III. Aliphatic

Ethers Diagnosed by their Low-Resolution Mass Spectra and Nuclear Magnetic Resonance Data, *Journal American Chemical. Society,* 1969, 91, 7440-7445

G.M. Schwenzer and T.M. Mitchell, Computer-Assisted Structure Elucidation Using Automatically Acquired ^{13}C NMR Rules, in D.H. Smith (Ed.), *Computer-Assisted Structure Elucidation,* ACS Symposium Series no. 54, ACS, Washington D.C., 1977, 58-76

C.A. Shelley, H.B. Woodruff, C.R. Snelling and M.E. Munk, Interactive Structure Elucidation, in D.H. Smith (Ed.), *Computer-Assisted Structure Elucidation,* ACS Symposium Series no. 54, ACS, Washington D.C., 1977, 92-107

C.A. Shelley and M.E. Munk, CASE, A Computer Model of the Structure Elucidation Process, *Anal. Chim. Acta.,* 1981, 133: 507-516

C.A. Shelley and M.E. Munk, Computer Prediction of Substructures from Carbon-13 Nuclear Magnetic Resonance Spectra, *Anal. Chem.,* 1982, 54: 516-521

D.H. Smith, N.A.B. Gray, J.G. Nourse and C.W. Crandell, The Dendral Project: Recent Advances in Computer-Assisted Structure Elucidation, *Anal. Chim. Acta.,* 1981, 133, 471-497

A. Terry, The CRYSALIS Project: Hierarchical Control of Production Systems, Stanford University Technical Report, HPP-83-19, 1983

K. Wüthrich, *NMR of Proteins and Nucleic Acids,* Wiley, New York, 1986

T. Yamasaki, H. Abe, Y. Kudo and S. Sasaki, CHEMICS: A Computer Program System for Structure Elucidation of Organic Compounds, in D.H. Smith (Ed.), *Computer- Assisted Structure Elucidation,* ACS Symposium Series no. 54, ACS, Washington D.C., 1977, 108-125

M. Yamazaki and H. Ihara, Knowledge-Driven Interpretation of ESCA Spectra, in *Proceedings of the Sixth International Joint Conference on Artificial Intelligence (IJCAI79),* Tokyo, Japan, August 20 - 23 1979, 2, 995 - 997

Molecular Scene Analysis: Crystal Structure Determination Through Imagery

Janice I. Glasgow, Suzanne Fortier & Frank H. Allen

1 Introduction

This chapter describes the design of a prototype knowledge-based system for crystal and molecular structure determination from diffraction data. This system enhances current methods for the determination and interpretation of protein structures by incorporating direct methods probabilistic strategies, experience accumulated in the crystallographic databases, and knowledge representation and reasoning techniques for machine imagery. The process of determining the structure of a crystal is likened to an iterative scene analysis,

This paper is based on "Crystal and Molecular Scene Analysis," by Glasgow, Fortier and Allen which appeared in the Proceedings of the Seventh IEEE Conference on Artificial Intelligence Applications, Miami Beach, Florida, Feb. 1991

which draws both from the long-term memory of structural motifs and the application of chemical and crystallographic rules.

A crystal consists of a regular three-dimensional arrangement of identical building blocks, termed the unit cell; a crystal structure is defined by the disposition of atoms and molecules within this fundamental repeating unit. A given structure is determined by interpretation of an electron-density image of the unit-cell contents which can be generated from the amplitudes and phases of the diffraction data. Normally, however, only the diffraction amplitudes can be measured experimentally: the necessary phase information must be obtained by other means. This is the classic *phase problem* of the crystallographic method.

The structure determination of small molecules (up to 150 or so independent non-hydrogen atoms) has become a routine process in the last fifteen years. This is best observed in the rapid growth of the Cambridge Structural Database which has seen its number of entries increase from 14,000 to 90,000 in that period of time. *Direct methods* have contributed much to this progress by providing a mathematical, computer oriented solution to the phase problem. By contrast, the determination of macromolecular structures remains a lengthy and difficult task in which the phase problem continues to be a major hurdle.

The initial electron-density images obtained for macromolecules are typically incomplete and noisy. Interpretation of these images often involves mental pattern recognition on the part of the crystallographer: the image is segmented into features which are then pattern matched against individual recollections of expected structural motifs. Once recognized, this partial structure information can be used to improve the phase estimates and hence the subsequent image. The success of this iterative approach to image reconstruction depends crucially on individual recall of existing structural knowledge and on the ability to recognize its presence in a noisy map.

Our proposed knowledge-based system incorporates databases of information on previously determined crystal structures from which templates for pattern matching can be derived. Clearly, this will enhance the memory capability of the individual crystallographer. Further, our approach to image reconstruction is influenced by some of the current cognitive theories for imagery. These theories suggest that an image is organized as a depiction of its meaningful parts and their spatial relationships. Based on this assumption, a schema has been designed and implemented in which an image is depicted as a multi-dimensional symbolic array. Here the symbols in the array correspond to the meaningful parts of the image. The schema also includes functions that correspond to the processes involved in mental imagery, functions which form the basis for effective pattern matching techniques.

In combination with the probabilistic direct methods, these concepts of knowledge-based imagery provide for a more fluid approach to crystal structure analysis: the phase determination is now guided by structural information established by a pattern recognition procedure which makes use of chemical and crystallographic reasoning. This allows the image reconstruction process to follow a hierarchical path and therefore take advantage of the structural organization of proteins.

In the next section we provide an overview of our symbolic array knowledge representation schema for imagery. In Section 3 we discuss how the crystallographic phase problem can be reduced to a search problem, and in Section 4 we describe the structural databases used in our system. Section 5 presents our iterative algorithm for crystal structure determination.

2 Imagery

Mental simulations can provide insights that contribute to effective problem solving techniques. James Watson reported visualizing "pairs of adenine residues whirling in front of my closed eyes" at a time when he and Crick were verging on solving the structure of DNA [Watson 1968]. Similarly, the chemist Kekulé reported that it was spontaneous imagery that led him to the discovery of the molecular structure of benzene [MacKenzie 1965].

In determining crystal structures, crystallographers also relate the use of mental visualization or imagery. The electron density representation of the unit cell contains features which must be interpreted in terms of the expected chemical constitution of the crystal. Additionally, the interpretation must conform to chemical and crystallographic rules, as established from earlier experiments. Thus, it is natural for crystallographers to use their own mental recall of known molecular structures, or of fragments thereof, to compare with and interpret the electron density features. Furthermore, since crystals are three-dimensional objects, this mental pattern recognition must involve the rotation and translation of images through space. Theories of cognition would support the view that humans do indeed perform these "mental rotation" functions [Shepard and Metzler 1971].

The schema we propose for crystal structure determination supports the functions of imagery and visualization by representing crystal structures using both descriptive and depictive knowledge representation techniques. A symbolic array data structure is used to denote the hierarchical and spatial structure of such an image. Information needed to construct a symbolic array as well as the chemical knowledge of a crystal are stored and manipulated as a frame structure.

In this section we describe a knowledge representation scheme for imagery that can be used to represent, manipulate and reason about crystal structures. Such a representation includes a data structure for storing an image and functions on the representation that correspond to the mental processes involved in imagery. Before presenting this scheme, we overview some of the research in cognitive psychology that has contributed to its design.

2.1 Mental Imagery

After many years of neglect, the topic of mental imagery has recently emerged as an active area of research in cognitive psychology. A debatable issue in this research concerns the underlying representation of images [Block 1981]: is an image represented as a *description* or as a *depiction* of its components?

Those who support the descriptive approach in the imagery debate suggest that images are not a distinct domain and thus are represented and manipulated as propositions [Pylyshyn 1981]. Contrary to this, supporters of the depictive approach state that imagery does involve a unique class phenomena and that images are organized into meaningful parts that are represented in terms of their spatial relations. The descriptive approach to representing images is appealing since it provides an abstract representation without significant loss of information. Although this representation is sufficient, it has been argued that it may not always be the most desirable. By studying the way people make inferences concerning spatial relationships, [Kosslyn 1980] has argued that mental imagery is used extensively. Further, he argues that both descriptive and depictive representations of images are involved in these mental processes.

As an alternative to defining a formal model for imagery, Finke has summarized much of the research in mental imagery by defining a set of "unifying principles" [Finke 1989]. The *implicit encoding* principle states that imagery is used to retrieve information that was not explicitly stored in memory. The principle of *perceptual equivalence* suggests that imagery is functionally equivalent to perception, in the sense that similar mechanisms are activated when objects or events are imagined as when the same objects or events are perceived. The *spatial equivalence* principle states that an image preserves, though sometimes distorts, the spatial relations of objects. The principle of *transformational equivalence* proposes a similarity relation between imagined and physical transformations. The final principle, the *structural principle*, states that the structure of an image is coherent, well organized and can be reinterpreted. These five principles allow the underlying intuitions of imagery to be expressed and further developed without restricting a model to the point where it applies to only a single task.

The primary goal of research in machine imagery is to develop representational tools for building programs that reason about and solve difficult problems using imagery. Similar to the cognitive approach of Finke, in developing computational tools for imagery we do not wish to restrict ourselves to a single model. Rather, we define a representation that allows the broad principles of imagery to be captured and expanded on.

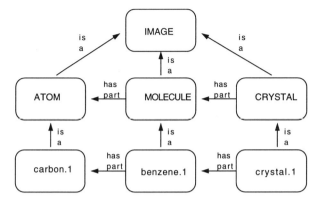

Figure 1. Semantic net for concepts and objects for crystallography domain

2.2 The Data Structure

The proposed representation schema for imagery is based on a formal theory of embedded, rectangular arrays [Jenkins and Glasgow 1989, More 1981]. Similar to set theory, array theory is concerned with the concepts of nesting, aggregation and membership. Array theory is also concerned with the concept of data objects having a spatial position relative to other objects in a collection. This theory strives to provide a universal recursive data structure that can be used effectively in a language that spans multiple programming paradigms. Such a language, Nial [Jenkins, Glasgow and McCrosky 1986], is being used to implement the computational processes for machine imagery as well as our knowledge-based system for crystal structure determination.

The array data structure provides a multi-dimensional realization of an image. The embedded nature of the array also allows for a parts-hierarchy depiction of an image. Detailed information (lower levels of the hierarchy) can either be hidden or made explicit in such a representation since hierarchical structure is expressed using embedded arrays. Thus the symbolic identification of meaningful parts of an image allows the depiction of a part to be suppressed unless attention is focused on that part.

Theories of cognition suggest that imagery involves both descriptive and depictive information [Kosslyn, 1980]. They have also suggested that in long-term memory depictive knowledge may be stored as a literal description of the locations of the parts within an image. Thus, the structure we propose is one which represents an image descriptively, yet allows a symbolic array depiction to be generated when needed [Glasgo and Papadias, 1992].

The important concepts in crystallography are: the periodically repeating motif in a unit cell of a crystal (CRYSTAL); the molecules and/or structural

FRAME: Dicyclohexano-18-crown-6 with potassium phenoxide and phenol	
class:	crystal
parts:	phenoxide-ring 0 0 0 DC-18-crown-6 1 1 1 phenol 2 2 2
molecular formula:	K-1 O-8 C-32 H-47
space group:	Pnca
unit cell dimensions:	14.15 23.794 9.491 90 90 90

Figure 2. Frame for a crystal structure

phenoxide ring		
	DC-18-crown-6	
		phenol

Figure 3. Two-dimensional projection of symbolic array for crystal structure

fragments (MOLECULE) and the atoms (ATOM). A semantic network that illustrates structural and hierarchical relationships between these concepts is presented in Figure 1. Instances of each of these concepts are also illustrated in the network.

A frame structure is used in our scheme to provide a descriptive representation of the concepts and objects for crystallography. An image frame has two required slots: a *parts* slot that provides a literal representation of the components of an image and their locations in Euclidean space; and a *depict* slot that contains a default function that generates the symbolic array representation of an image from the given parts and locations. An example of a frame that represents the depictive and descriptive knowledge of a crystal structure is illustrated in Figure 2.[1]

A symbolic array denotes the structural features of an image. This array may be depicted in one, two or three dimensions. Figure 3 illustrates a two-dimensional projection of the three-dimensional symbolic array data structure that would be generated using the depict slot of the image frame and the parts slot of the crystal frame.

Hierarchical organization is a fundamental aspect of imagery. Theories of selected attention suggest the need for an integrated spatial/hierarchical representation: when attention is focused on a particular feature, the brain is still

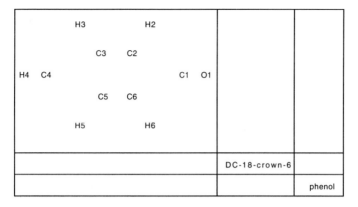

Figure 4. Embedded array representation of subimage phenoxide-ring, projected into two dimensions.

partially aware of other features and their spatial relation to the considered feature. Our symbolic array representation supports such theories by considering an image as a *recursive* data structure. A symbolic element of an array can itself denote a subimage. Consider the image of the crystal structure depicted in Figure 3. The symbols in this structured representation can denote structured subimages. Figure 4 illustrates the symbolic array depiction of the crystal structure when attention is focused on the subimage of phenoxide-ring. As with the image of the crystal, this embedded array would be generated using the depict slot of the image frame for the phenoxide-ring.

The primary goal of the knowledge-based system for crystal structure determination is to obtain a detailed and precise three-dimensional picture of the atomic arrangement in the crystal. In Section 5 we describe an algorithm that reconstructs such an image of a crystal in the form of a symbolic array.

A computational model for mental imagery has previously been proposed [Kosslyn 1980]. In his theory, images have two components: a surface representation (a quasi-pictorial representation that occurs in a visual buffer) and a descriptive representation for information stored in long-term memory. The two-dimensional surface representation of his theory is fundamentally different from the symbolic array representation described in our chapter. However, the design of the frame representation and the functions defined on images in our representation were greatly influenced by Kosslyn's empirical studies and model.

2.3 Functions on Images

The effectiveness of a scheme for knowledge representation is measured primarily by how well it facilitates the processes that operate on the representation. Larkin and Simon argue that diagrams are computationally prefer-

NAME	OPERATION
Retrieve	Retrieve an image representation from long-term memory.
Construct	Construct a symbolic array depiction of an image from a descriptive literal representation.
Compose	Compose two images into a single complex image with a given spatial relationship.
Symop	Use symmetry information to retrieve regularities in an image.
Resolve	Use pattern matching information and world knowledge to transform an image into one of higher resolution.
Compare	Compare images and determine similarity measure.
Consistent	Determine if an image is consistent with world knowledge.

Figure 5. Functions for constructing images

able to propositional representations, not because they contain more information but because the indexing of the information supports efficient computations [Larkin and Simon 1987]. In this subsection we propose a set of primitive functions that were designed to support the cognitive inferences involved in imagery. These functions on symbolic arrays are considered in three categories: functions for *constructing* images, functions for *transforming* images and functions for *accessing* images.

The first class of functions we consider are those involved in constructing an image. These functions are summarized in Figure 5.

Theories of cognition support three distinct memory systems: sensory storage, working or short-term memory and long-term memory [Baddeley 1986]. When considering machine imagery, we are mainly concerned with representation in working memory. One way to construct an image in working memory is to *retrieve* an instance of this image from long-term memory. Computationally, we interpret long-term memory as a database of frames that provide a propositional and a literal representation of an image. The creation of an image from such a representation is on an "if-needed" basis. An invocation of the function specified in the depict slot results in the *construction* of a symbolic array representation of the image from the literal representation of its parts.

A basic process of thought is the creation of new concepts from old. Imagery involves constructing and manipulating images in unique ways. Our model supports processes for imagery by allowing complex images to be constructed as a composition of simpler images. For example, we may store images of a ball and a box, but the image of a ball sitting on top of a box is created from the two subimages and the desired spatial relation. The hierarchical representation of images permits us to *compose* two or more images

NAME	OPERATION
Rotate	Rotate array depiction of an image a specified number of degrees around one of the axes.
Translate	Translate position of component within a symbolic array.
Zoom	Increase or decrease the apparent size of a depiction of an image.
Project	Project a three dimensional array onto two dimensions.

Figure 6. Functions for transforming images

into a single image in which the components are spatially related.

Images can also be constructed through the processes involved in perception and recognition. In this case the initial representation of an image comes from sensory store, which holds information impinging on the sense organs. As suggested in [Marr and Nishihara 1978], an image may go through several stages of representation going from perception to recognition. The processes involved in these transformations are complex and dependent on the domain. One such process is the ability to *compare* two images and determine a measurement of closeness. This measurement can depend on both spatial and non-spatial features of an image. We also consider the function *resolve* that takes the results of pattern matching and refines the image. Resolving an image may result from reconstructing recognized features into a new image. Once this has been done, the resulting image can be checked for consistency with world knowledge. In the crystallographic domain, for example, a complex image may be constructed that depicts molecules at too close a distance. Such an image could be evaluated as impossible by the *consistent* operator given this domain of interpretation.

Images are often constructed using incomplete knowledge. This is particularly true when considering three dimensional images where perception may be in two dimensions. In cognition, missing information can be provided by considering regularities such as symmetry in an image [Pentland 1986]. The function *symop* is used to retrieve regularities through symmetry operations such as reflection and rotation.

As suggested by empirical experiments in cognitive psychology [Shepard and Metzler 1971], mental imagery also involves processes for manipulating objects in space. Figure 6 summarizes the proposed functions for transforming images.

Note that the functions for transforming a symbolic array representation of an image are typically not meant as an alternative form of representation, but as a means of viewing an image from a variety of perspectives. These functions are necessary in developing a theory of recognition based on pattern matching of spatial images. For example, we may need to *rotate* and

NAME	OPERATION
Find	Scan a depiction of an image to determine the location of a component.
Focus	Shift attention to a particular component of an image.
Query	Retrieve propositional information from an array depiction of an image.

Figure 7. Functions for accessing images

translate a perceived image before it can be pattern matched with an image reconstructed from long-term memory.

The final class of functions corresponds to processes for accessing an image. These functions are particularly useful when reasoning about images. Figure 7 summarizes these functions.

The *focus* function is a mapping from an image and a symbolic feature of the image to a new image such that attention is concentrated on the specified feature. If the designated feature is not an atomic array, then the new image will be the old image with the feature replaced by its symbolic array representation. Knowledge involving the spatial relations of an image can be retrieved using the *query* operation.

2.4 Otherapplications of this work

The research in machine imagery underlying the crystallography system has impact beyond the molecular recognition application. Since the knowledge representation schema was designed to capture fundamental properties of mental imagery, its implementation provides a basis for the computational modeling of cognitive theories that involve processes related to imagery. These include the sequential and parallel processes involved in memory retrieval of images, attention, recognition, learning and classification [Glasgow 1990a, Glasgow 1990b]. As well, the scheme provides a framework for developing other knowledge-based applications. Currently, we are considering additional applications in the areas of haptic perception, game playing, medical imaging and robotic motion planning.

3 The Crystallographic Phase Problem

Even though the diffraction experiment yields several hundred to thousands of observations, and normally a relatively high ratio of observations to unknown parameters, the information sought - a three-dimensional picture of the atomic arrangement in the crystal - cannot be calculated directly from the measured data. This is because such a calculation requires knowledge of both

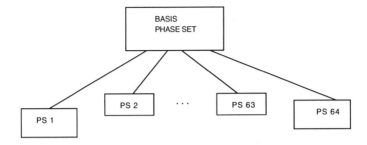

Figure 8. Phase Search Tree

the amplitude and the phase of each diffracted ray and the latter cannot be measured experimentally. This is a basic problem in any crystal structure determination, and it cannot be easily circumvented, despite the mathematical overdeterminacy, because of the Fourier transform relationship between the crystal structure and its diffraction pattern.

The most successful and straightforward approach to the solution of the phase problem are the so-called *direct methods* [Hauptman 1986]. This approach uses probability theory to retrieve phase information from the amplitude data. It essentially predicts the value of certain linear combinations of the phases and provides a way, through the variance of the distributions, of ranking the information according to reliability. The process evaluates several thousand of such linear equations and yields a redundant system of equations from which the values of the individual phases will then be extracted. Phasing is initiated from a basis set of, typically, four phases whose values can be selected (for origin and enantiomorph specification), together with a number of further selected phases whose values are permuted. This yields several possible solutions corresponding to the several possible phase permutation combinations, and indeed the method is referred to as the *multisolution approach*. Figures of merit are then calculated and used to assess which of the solutions appears to be the best one. The last, and finally the only important test, is whether or not any of the phase sets will produce an interpretable image of the structure.

The crystallographic phase problem can be thought of as a general search problem [Fortier, Glasgow and Allen 1991]. In this context, the multisolution approach can be described as a simple generate-and-test search procedure as illustrated in Figure 8. The morphology of the search tree is unusual, though. The tree has a single depth level with a large branching factor; the number of nodes in such a tree is usually between 32 and 128. What characterizes and limits the search is the fact that the heuristic evaluation functions used (the

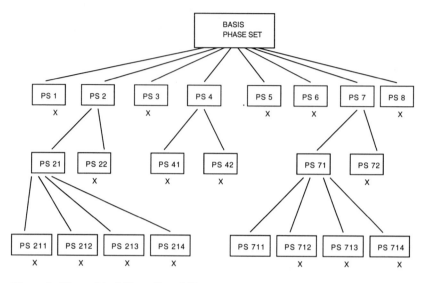

Figure 9. Hierarchical Phase Search Tree

figures of merit) are not effective in pruning partially developed solutions. This is because these heuristic functions do not test the actual goal of the search: the interpretability of the reconstructed image. Rather, they provide ranking numbers that are derived from the underlying probabilistic model. They depend, thus, on how well the actual structure fits the statistical model. The *a priori* model, assumed by direct methods, is that the repeating atomic motif in the crystal can be represented by a collection of atoms uniformly and randomly distributed through space.

Traditional direct methods explore the phase space and evaluate phasing paths by using only very general chemical constraints—the electron density distribution must be everywhere nonnegative and its peaks must correspond to atoms—and the constraints imposed by the amplitude data. While these constraints have proven sufficiently limiting for applications to small molecules, they are not adequate for tackling the more complex structures such as those of proteins.

Several additional chemical constraints, such as limits on bond lengths and angles or expected conformations, are usually available at the outset of a structure determination project. In a direct methods procedure, these additional constraints are supplied by crystallographers, who use their recall of existing results to reconstruct structural templates, and their visual abilities to match these templates with the developing electron density image. Recent theoretical results have shown, however, that information from partial structure identification, together with diffraction data, can be incorporated in a general direct methods joint probability distribution framework [Bricogne 1988, Fortier and Nigam 1989]. These results open the way for AI contributions to direct methods for solving protein structures by allowing for a flexible, context driven solution procedure which can automatically take advantage of all available information. In particular, the image reconstruction can be modeled as an iterative resolution process in which any structure recognition can be used to evaluate the phasing paths as well as guide the phasing exploration through the incorporation of further chemical constraints. A phase search tree that reflects this hierarchical strategy is illustrated in Figure 9. Furthermore, this work has provided the theoretical basis needed for the computer generation of the phasing distributions. It thus becomes possible to consider dynamic systems in which distributions, tailored to the knowledge base, are generated as needed.

4 The Structural Databases

Crystallographers, perhaps mindful of the intrinsic importance of their results, have a long and successful history of documentation. Early printed indexes and compendia have now been replaced by computer-based information banks. Complete three-dimensional structural data for some 140,000 compounds, from simple metals to proteins and viruses, are now stored in four crystallographic databases [Allen, Bergerhoff and Sievers 1987]. All of the databases are regularly updated with new material and the long-term memory of existing crystal structures increases by about 10% per year. The Cambridge Structural Database [Allen, Kennard and Taylor 1983] (CSD:90,000 + organo-carbon compounds) and the Protein Data Bank [Bernstein, Koetzle, Williams, Meyer, Brice, Rodgers, Kennard, Shimanouchi and Tasumi 1977] (PDB: 550 + macromolecules) contain the vast bulk of available experimental knowledge of three-dimensional molecular structures.

The systematic recall of three-dimensional structural knowledge from the databases is essential to our imagery approach to crystal and molecular structure determination. However, this knowledge is not explicit in the plethora of three-dimensional crystallographic facts, e.g. coordinates, cell dimensions, symmetry operators, etc., that dominate the information content of the databases. Rather, it must be derived from the stored facts via mechanisms for search, retrieval, classification, reasoning and rule generation. These activities are made possible by the rule-based two-dimensional representations of formal chemistry (structural diagrams or sequence data) that are also included in the databases. This is knowledge that can be searched using the syntactic language of chemistry and which underpins the interpretation of the three-dimensional structural facts.

A new crystal structure determination is seldom undertaken without some prior knowledge of the expected two-dimensional chemistry of the compound. This knowledge forms the basis for a database search to locate the key chemical fragments of the molecule, e.g. helices, rings, ring systems, acyclic functional groups, etc. In three-dimensions these fragments may occur in a number of different conformations, each of which represents a potential template for pattern matching with the electron density maps. Methods for machine learning, embodied in cluster analyzes based on suitable shape descriptors, serve to classify the database fragments into conformational subgroups. [Allen, Doyle and Taylor 1991]. The derivation of syntactic rules, which describe the conformational relationships of fragments one with another, provides a linguistic framework which permits larger templates to be built. Template generation and model building are active research areas for both small and large molecules (see e.g. [Dolata, Leach and Prout 1987; Wippke and Hahn 1988; Blundell, Sibanda, Sternberg and Thornton 1987]). The results, apart from their use in crystallography, are extensively used in rational drug design projects.

A systematic and comprehensive knowledge of the weak hydrogen-bonded and non-bonded interactions is also crucial to image reconstruction and validation from electron-density maps. These interactions not only govern the limiting contact distances between molecules in the crystal structure, but also play a key role in stabilizing the molecular structures of large molecules such as proteins and nucleic acids.

Crystallographic data have always been the primary source of information on the dimensions and directional preferences of hydrogen-bonded systems [Taylor and Kennard 1984]. The use of statistical analysis, decision theory, and the classification of H-bonded motifs observed in crystal structures, suggest rules that govern H-bond formation [Etter, MacDonald and Bernstein 1990]. Application of these rules provide knowledge of the environmentally dependent limiting geometries and motif templates that are relevant to crystal structure determination (see e.g., [Sawyer and James, 1982]).

The study of limiting contact distances between non-bonded atoms has a similar dependence on crystal structure results. Even today, most chemists use the non-bonded radii of Pauling [Pauling 1939] which are based on limited experimental data and assume that (a) non-bonded atoms are effectively spherical in shape and (b) the radii are additive and transferable from one chemical environment to another. Database analyzes (e.g. [Taylor and Kennard 1984, Allen, Bergerhoff and Sievers 1987]) indicate that these assumptions are inexact, i.e. the limiting contact distance between two atoms depends on their chemical environments and on their direction of mutual approach. Interest now focuses on geometries and motifs which are stabilized by even these weak intermolecular forces, both in small molecules [Desiraju 1989] and in proteins [Rowland, Allen, Carson and Bugg 1990]. The knowledge of non-bonded atomic shapes defines not only the limiting contact distances between atoms, but also the spatial shape and size of both fragments and molecules. Further, the motifs formed by non-bonded interactions provide additional templates for use at all stages of a crystal structure determination.

In addition to statistical techniques, concepts from machine imagery research are being used for motif classification. Research in this area includes determining methods for developing classification schemes for images based on symbolic representations of both the conformation and configuration of molecules. Such a classification scheme will be used to extract syntactic rules of three-dimensional molecular structures from the crystallographic databases.

5 Crystal Structure Recognition

The problem of determining the structure of a crystal from diffraction data belongs to the general class of image reconstruction problems. The goal of the reconstruction is to produce a complete image which contains both depictive and descriptive knowledge of the three-dimensional atomic arrangement in the crystal. This image is built from information on the unit cell, the symmetry operators within the unit cell and finally the unique asymmetric portion of the repeating atomic motif. Determining a crystal structure is therefore analogous to a scene analysis in which the structural atomic motif enclosed in the unit cell is recognized by using a memory of previously determined structural templates and is understood through the application of chemical and crystallographic rules.

Thus our approach borrows partially from research in the area of vision. In particular, we incorporate existing segmentation algorithms that decompose an image into its meaningful parts. The technique used for recognizing a fragment of a crystal structure involves comparing its image to a stored representation of a previously recognized structure and evaluating the fit. This template matching approach is a simple and relatively old technique that has been used in vision applications. Recognition in our model also assumes constructed shape and volume descriptions, as in the approach of Marr [Marr 1982].

The crystallographic application differs from vision applications in a number of ways. First, the image for a crystal is perceived and depicted in three dimensions. This eliminates many of the problems of feature segmentation and recognition involved in vision applications: features in three dimensions do not overlap and we can utilize three-dimensional segmentation and pattern matching techniques. As well, we are not concerned with factors such as light sources, surface material or atmospheric conditions that may distort the appearance of a visual image. The complexity that does exist in the crystallographic application relates to the incompleteness of data due to

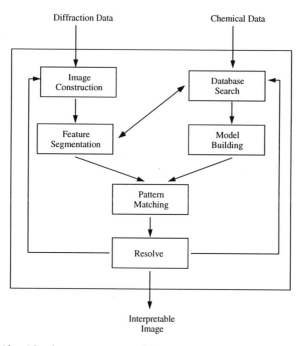

Figure 10. Algorithm for structure recognition

the phase problem.

In our approach, the process of crystal structure determination is modeled as *resolving* the three-dimensional image of the atomic arrangement within the crystal. By using a hierarchical approach, the phasing search space is expanded to a multilevel search tree. At each level of the search tree, any partial structure determined through pattern matching is used to update the probability distribution so as to provide higher resolution images. Thus, the identification process is an iterative one. Once an image of the crystal has been constructed, we focus on particular regions of the structure and try to pattern match them with structural templates from the database. Good matches serve not only to guide the identification search, but also to refine our image of these substructures and iteratively refine our complete structure.

Figure 10 illustrates the processes involved in structure recognition. Initially, an image of the structure, in the form of an electron density map, is constructed using the measured amplitudes and a given phase set. The known chemical information for the crystal is used to do a preliminary database search for fragments that could be anticipated in the structure. Simultaneously, the current image is segmented into distinct three-dimensional "blobs" or subimages that correspond to the structural features of the image. These fea-

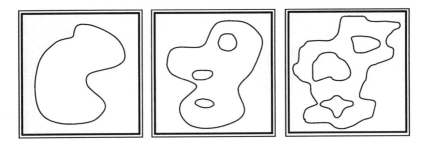

Figure 11. Resolution stages of molecular image

tures are then compared with images of the fragments retrieved from the database. Heuristics, based on the results of this three-dimensional pattern matching, are used to prune the search tree. In addition, matched images provide the necessary information for improving and expanding the phases and thereby resolving the image. These processes are repeated until the resolution of the image matches that of the diffraction data. Figure 11 illustrates a two-dimensional projection of images going through several stages of resolution, where the higher resolution images correspond to utilizing an increased phase set in their construction.

We now present a brief discussion of each of the steps in the crystallographic image reconstruction algorithm.

• **Image Construction.** Just as in vision, the image of a crystal may go through several stages of representation. At this step of the algorithm, the image of the crystal is represented as a three-dimensional electron density map resulting from the diffraction experiment and the current phase set. Figure 12(a) illustrates a two dimensional projection of a three-dimensional array representation of an electron density map, where the values in the array denote the electron density at the corresponding locations within the unit cell of a crystal.

Initially the electron density map is constructed using low resolution phases from the basis set expanded by selecting a small number of additional phases. Such a map will correspond to a low-resolution, noisy image of the crystal but, as additional phases are determined in successive iterations of the algorithm, the maps will reveal clearer and clearer (higher-resolution) images as illustrated in Figure 11.

• **Feature Segmentation.** In this process we partition the electron density map into distinct, three dimensional structural features. Standard image preprocessing techniques, such as noise reduction, local averaging, ensemble averaging, etc. are applied prior to segmentation. These techniques are used to enhance features of an image by establishing regions that either contain or

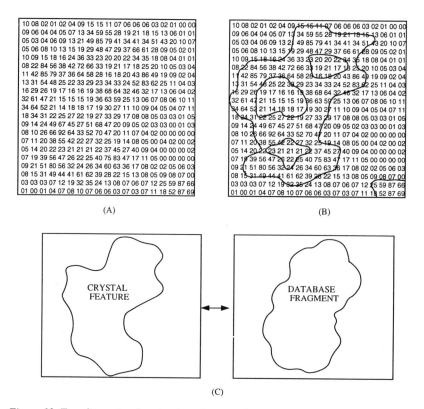

Figure 12. Two-dimensional projection of stages of image recognition: (a) Electron Density Map (b) Segmented Electron Density Map (c) Pattern matching step

do not contain electron density. A technique for determining distinct blobs/regions is then used to segment the map into features. World knowledge about anticipated shapes is used to determine whether these features are consistent with the chemical knowledge of the structure. Output from the process consists of a set of distinct blobs/regions that correspond to the structural features of the image; these may now be used to pattern match with anticipated patterns retrieved from the database. Figure 12(b) illustrates the blobs resulting from a segmentation process on an electron density map.

A library of segmentation functions for three-dimensional images is being implemented and tested on the images of crystal. Included in this library are functions that correspond to boundary detection, region growing, hierarchical and boundary melting techniques.[2]

We are also considering techniques that incorporate knowledge of the crystallographic domain. The selection of appropriate segmentation functions, to be used at each iteration of the algorithm, depends on the level of resolution of the image being considered.

At this stage, we also determine some descriptive information about the segmented feature. This includes volume and shape information that can be used to assist in the pattern matching process.

• **Database Search.** The knowledge-based system is designed to incorporate information from the crystallographic databases described in Section 4. Prior knowledge of the two-dimensional chemistry of each new crystal structure defines a 'query' domain for a chemical search of the databases. This query is partitioned (a) to generate bonded chemical fragments for which likely three-dimensional templates are required for pattern matching, (b) to identify hydrogen-bond donors and acceptors present in the molecule, and (c) to identify atoms or functional groups which are likely to play a key role in the non-bonded interactions that stabilize the crystal and molecular structure. In (b) and (c) the databases are searched and analyzed to retrieve limiting geometries and likely three-dimensional motifs for use in pattern matching and image resolution.

• **Model Building.** Once an anticipated fragment has been retrieved from the database, a symbolic array image for the fragment is reconstructed. From this image of the fragment we can generate a blob-like depiction at a resolution level corresponding to the current resolution of the features of the crystal.

• **Pattern Matching.** The input to this process is the set of unidentified features derived from the segmentation step and the set of anticipated fragments selected from the database using chemical and structural information. The goal of the process is to compare each of the unidentified features with database fragments to determine the best three-dimensional structural matches. Both iterative and parallel algorithms for carrying out these comparisons are currently being considered [Lewis, 1990].

To facilitate a pairwise comparison, the three-dimensional representation of the known molecular structure is oriented within the cell of the unknown structure. Techniques from molecular pattern recognition are being used to achieve the correct position through rotation and translation [Rossman, 1990]. Patterson-based techniques are used to focus attention on the most promising regions of the electron density map. A template matching approach is then applied and the degree of fit assessed. Figure 12(c) illustrates a pair of subimages considered for pattern matching.

• **Resolve.** Information gathered from successful pattern matches (those with a high degree of fit) is used to update the phase set and subsequently generate a new electron density map for the crystal. This information is first checked for consistency with other knowledge for the domain; for example the image composition is checked against packing constraints for the crystal. The structural information, which is kept at a resolution level matching that of the current image, is then incorporated in the direct methods phasing tools.

This provides additional chemical constraints which serve in the improvement of the current phases and the expansion to higher resolution phases and therefore higher resolution images. Note that keeping the structure recognition information at the current image resolution level ensures that this information guides rather than drives the structure determination process.

The resolve process also controls the search space for the algorithm. Recall that we are attempting to reach a goal state in which enough phase information is available to construct an interpretable image. Incorrect pattern matches may lead to paths in the search tree (Figure 9) in which the expansion to higher resolution phases does not contribute to forming a clearer image. Intermediate evaluation functions applied to the evolving images allow us to prune such paths and only consider those that lead towards a goal state.

The processes described above are repeated until a fully interpretable image of the structure has been resolved. At this stage we can combine the *where* information, derived from the segmentation process, with the *what* information, derived from the pattern matching process, to construct a symbolic array representation for the crystal. The "where" information provides the exact location of each of the distinct features within the unit cell of the crystal; the "what" information gives the chemical identity of these features. By combining the "where" and "what" information in a symbolic array, we are able to reconstruct a precise and complete picture of the atomic arrangement for the crystal. Using the symbolic array representation and the known chemical data for the crystal, a frame representation can be constructed and added to the database of known structures.

Each individual module described above is being implemented and tested in an independent manner to establish an initial working prototype for each subtask. Once this preliminary, but extensive, work has been completed, the modules will be integrated and the system tested in its entirety. Currently, three-dimensional electron density maps are obtained by use of existing crystallographic software. A library of functions for the preprocessing and segmentation of these images at various levels or resolution is under development. As well, routines for the extraction of meaningful features (size, shape, centre of mass, etc.) from the derived segments are being developed. A prototype for the semantic network memory model has been established. The network incorporates the customory "chemical structure" hierarchy of protein structures (atom, residue, secondary structure,etc.) as well as the "classification" hierarchy that allows for the inheritance of properties. Routines for the construction of symbolic array and electron density map representations from the frame representations have been tested for selected cases. Work has begun on the pattern matching module and on the implementation of a direct space pattern matching function. The resolve module is still at the design stage, although several of the direct methods algorithms in its core have already been implemented and tested.

Although the initial implementation of the algorithm is sequential, the algorithm and the individual processes are being designed to incorporate any potential parallelism for later re-implementation. For example, we can concurrently process the pairwise pattern matching of fragments from the database with features from the crystal. Further, the hierarchical phase search tree (Figure 9) can be considered as an "OR" search tree. That is, if any path can be generated from an initial state to a goal state then a solution is found. Since these paths are independent, they can be generated in parallel.

In the reconstruction algorithm described above, imagery plays an important role in identifying crystal structures. The spatial/hierarchical structure of a crystal is represented as a symbolic array image. Such a representation can be transformed into three-dimensional depictions for pattern matching. Image transformation functions are then used to pattern match features of a crystal with the depictions of molecular structures reconstructed from the symbolic arrays. Ultimately, the image reconstruction process results in a symbolic array depiction for the initially unidentified crystal structure.

The programming language Nial, which is based on the theory of arrays, is being used to implement the prototype system. The array data structure and primitive functions of Nial allow for simple manipulations of the crystal lattice. Furthermore, the Nial Frame Language [Hache, 1986] provides an implementation for the frame structures used in the imagery model. Nial also provides the syntax to allow us to express the parallel computations inherent in our reconstruction algorithm [Glasgow, Jenkins, McCrosky and Meijer, 1989].

6 Related Work

Computer-assisted structure elucidation by use of knowledge-based reasoning techniques is one of the most active application areas of artificial intelligence in chemistry. When applied to two-dimensional structural chemistry, the goal is the interpretation of chemical spectra (mass spectra, IR, NMR data) in terms of candidate two-dimensional chemical structure(s). A number of systems have been developed, of which the DENDRAL project is by far the best known [Gray, 1986]. Some of the fundamental methodologies used in DENDRAL - for example, mechanisms and algorithms for knowledge representation, pattern matching, machine learning, rule generation and reasoning - have had a lasting impact on the computer handling of two-dimensional chemical structures. They have also contributed significantly to the development of chemical database systems and of tools for computer-assisted synthesis planning and reaction design (see e.g., [Hendrickson, 1990]).

Applications to three-dimensional structural chemistry and crystallography are still relatively new and comparatively more fragmentary. They can be broadly divided into two interrelated categories, depending on whether their main purpose is the classification or the prediction of three-dimensional molecular structures. For small molecules, the primary application area is that of molecular modeling in relation to projects in rational drug design [Dolata,Leach and Prout,1987; Wippke and Hahn, 1988] For macromolecules, artificial intelligence tools have also been used extensively in the computer-assisted classification of structural subunits, an essential precursor to structure prediction. Numerous studies of protein structure classification and prediction, aimed at various levels of the protein structural hierarchy, have been reported (e.g., [Blundell, Sibanda, Sternberg and Thornton,1987; Clark,Barton and Rawlings,1990; Hunter and States,1991; Rawlings, Taylor, Nyakairu,Fox and Sternberg, 1985; Rooman and Wodak,1988]). In addition, promising work in application of artificial inteligence methods to the interpretation of NMR spectra of macromolecules has begun (e.g. Edwards, *et al*, this volume).

The use of artificial intelligence techniques to assist crystal structure determination, particularly in the interpretation of electron density maps, was suggested early on by Feigenbaum, Engelmore and Johnson [1977] and pursued in the CRYSALIS project [Terry,1983]. This project has not yet resulted, however, in a fully implemented and distributed system. More recently, several groups (e.g. [Finzel et al., 1990, Jones et al., 1991, and Holn and Sander, 1991] have reported the use of highly efficient algorithms for the automated interpretation of medium to high resolution electron density maps using templates derived from the Protein Data Bank [Bernstein et al.,1977] Our project, however, is concerned with the full image reconstruction process and, in particular, the ab initio phasing of diffraction data. Primarily it is the low to medium resolution region of the image reconstruction problem that is being addressed here. Clearly, our approach can draw from the many important results mentioned above.

7 Conclusion

The knowledge-based system described in this chapter offers a comprehensive approach to crystal structure determination, which accommodates a variety of phasing tools and takes advantage of the structural knowledge and experience already accumulated in the crystallographic databases. Intrinsic to our approach is the use of imagery to represent and reason about the structure of a crystal. Artificial intelligence tools that capture the processes involved in mental imagery allow us to mimic the visualization techniques used by crystallographers when solving crystal structures.

The problem of structure determination is essentially reformulated as the determination of an appropriate number of sufficiently accurate phases so as to generate a fully interpretable image of the crystal. In other words, we reduce the overall problem to a search problem in phase space. The search is guided by the continual refinement of an image through the use of partial structure information. This information is generated by matching the salient features of the developing image with anticipated structural patterns established in previous experiments.

The process of determining the structure of a crystal is likened to an iterative scene analysis which draws both from the long-term memory of structural motifs and the application of chemical and crystallographic rules. In this analysis, the molecular scene is reconstructed and interpreted in a fluid procedure which establishes a continuum between the initially uninterpreted image and the fully resolved one. The artificial intelligence infrastructure, with its machine imagery model, allows for a coherent and efficient reconstruction. Indeed, it provides a data abstraction mechanism that can be used to reason about images and, in particular, to depict and reason with relevant configurational, conformational and topological information at a symbolic level. Thus our approach builds upon the current methodology used for protein crystal structure determination by setting a framework in which reasoning tasks as well as numerical calculations can be invoked. In this integrated approach, the process of crystal structure determination becomes one of molecular scene analysis. Taken individually, such analyzes result in the recognition and understanding of a specific chemical scene. Put together, they provide insight into the three-dimensional grammar of chemistry and the rules of molecular recognition.

Acknowledgements

Financial assistance from the Natural Science and Engineering Research Council of Canada, Queen's University and the IRIS Federal Network Center of Excellence is gratefully acknowledged.

Notes

1. The depict slot is not illustrated in the frame in Figure 2 since this function is constant for all images. For a detailed description of the frame representation for imagery and the implementation of the depict function see [Papadias 1990].

2. See [Baddeley, 1986] for an overview of algorithms for two-dimensional segmentation.

References

F. H. Allen, G. Bergerhoff, and R. Sievers, *Crystallographic Databases.* IUCr, Chester, 1987.

F. H. Allen, M. J. Doyle, and R. Taylor. Automated Conformational Analysis from Crystallographic Data. 1. A Symmetry-modified Single-linkage Clustering Algorithm for 3D Pattern

Recognition. *Acta Crystallographica,* B 47: 29-40, 1991.

F. H. Allen, O. Kennard, and R. Taylor. Systematic Analysis of Structural Data as a Research Tool in Organic Chemistry. *Accounts of Chemical Research,* 16: 146-153, 1983.

Alan Baddeley. *Working Memory.* Oxford Science Publications, 1986.

D. H. Ballard and C. M. Brown. *Computer Vision.* Prentice Hall Inc,. 1982.

F. C. Bernstein, F. F. Koetzle, G. J. B. Williams, E. F. Meyer Jr. , M. D. Brice, J. R. Rodgers, O. Kennard, T. Shimanouchi and M. Tasumi, The Protein Data Bank: A Computer Archival File for Macromolecular structures. *Journal of Molecular Biology.* 112: 535-542, 1977.

N. Block, ed. *Imagery,* MIT Press, 1981.

T. L. Blundell, B. L. Sibanda, M. J. E. Sternberg and J. M. Thornton. Knowledge-based prediction of protein structures and the design of novel molecules. *Nature,* 326:347-352, 1987.

G. Bricogne. A Bayesian Statistical Theory of the Phase Problem. A Multi-channel Maximum-entropy Formalism for Constructing Joint Probability Distribution Factors. *Acta Crystallographica,* A44:517-545, 1988.

D. A. Clark, G. J. Barton and C. J. Rawlings. A Knowledge-based Architecture for Protein Sequence Analysis and Structure Prediction. *Journal of Molecular Graphics,* 8:94-107, 1990.

G. R. Desiraju, *Crystal Engineering.* Elsevier, London, 1989.

D. P. Dolata, A. R. Leach and C. K. Prout. WIZARD: Artificial Intelligence in Conformational Analysis. *Journal of Computer-Aided Molecular Design,* 1:73-86, 1987.

M. C. Etter, J. C. MacDonald and J. Bernstein. Graph-set Analysis of Hydrogen-bond Patterns in Organic Crystals. *Acta Crystallographica,* B46: 256-262, 1990.

E. A. Feigenbaum, R. S. Engelmore and C. K. Johnson. A Correlation Between Crystallographic Computing and Artificial Intelligence Research. *Acta Crystallographica,* A33:13-18, 1977.

R. A. Finke. *Principles of Mental Imagery.* MIT Press, 1989.

B. C. Finzel, S. Kimatian, D. H. Ohlendorf, J. J. Wendoloski, M. Levitt and F. R. Salemme. Molecular Modeling with Substructure Libraries Derived from Known Protein Structures. In *Crystallographic and Modelling Methods in Molecular Design,* C. E. Bugg and S. E. Ealick, eds. Springer-Verlag, New York, 1990.

S. Fortier, J. I. Glasgow, and F. H. Allen. The Design of a Knowledge-based System for Crystal Structure Determination. In H. Schenk, editor, *Direct Methods of Solving Crystal Structures.* Plenum Press, London, 1991.

S. Fortier and G. D. Nigam. On the Probabilistic Theory of Isomorphous Data Sets: General Joint Distributions for the SIR, SAS, and Partial/Complete Structure Cases. *Acta Crystallographica,* A45:247-254, 1989

J. I. Glasgow. Artificial Intelligence and Imagery. In *Proceedings of Tools for Artificial Intelligence,* Washington, 1990.

J. I. Glasgow. Imagery and Classification. In *Proceedings of the 1st ASIS SIG/CR Classification Research Workshop,* Toronto, 1990

J. I. Glasgow and D. Papadias. Computational Imagery, *Cognitive Science,* In press, 1992.

J. I. Glasgow, M. A. Jenkins, C. McCrosky and H. Meijer. Expressing Parallel Algorithms in Nial. *Parallel Computing ,* 11,3:46-55 1989.

N. A. B. Gray. *Computer-Assisted Structure Elucidation.* John Wiley, New York, 1986.

L. Hache. The Nial Frame Language. Master's thesis Queen's University, Kingston, 1986

H. Hauptman. The Direct Methods of X-ray Crystallography. *Science,* 233:178 - 183, 1986.

J. B. Hendrickson. The Use of Computers for Synthetic Planning. *Angewandte Chemie International Edition (English).* , 29:1286-1295, 1990.

L. Holn and C. Sander, Database Algorithm for Generating Protein Backbone and Side-chain Coordinates from a Cα Trace: Application to model building and detection of co-ordinate errors. *Journal of Molecular Biology,* 218:183-194,1991.

L. Hunter and D. J. States, Applying Bayesian Classification to Protein Structure. in *Proceedings of the Seventh IEEE Conference on Artificial Intelligence Applications*, IEEE Computer Society Press, 1991.

M. A. Jenkins and J. I. Glasgow. A Logical Basis for Nested Array Data Structures. *Programming Languages Journal* 14 (1): 35-49, 1989.

M. A. Jenkins, J. I. Glasgow, and C. McCrosky. Programming Styles in Nial. *IEEE Software.* 86:46-55, January 1986.

T. A. Jones, J-Y. Zou, S. W. Cowan and M. Kjeldgaard. Improved Methods for Building Protein Models in Electron-density Maps and the Location of Errors in Those Models. *Acta Crystallographica*, A47:110-119, 1991.

S. M. Kosslyn. *Image and Mind.* Harvard University Press, 1980.

J. H. Larkin and H. A. Simon. Why a Diagram Is (Sometimes) Worth Ten Thousand Words. *Cognitive Science 11*: 65-99, 1987.

S. Lewis. Pattern Matching through Imagery. Master's thesis, Queen's University, Kingston, 1990.

N. MacKenzie. *Dreams and Dreaming.* Aldus Books, London, 1965.

D. Marr and H. K. Nishihara. Representation and Recognition of the Spatial Organization of Three-dimensional Shapes. In *Proc. of the Royal Society of London,* B200: 269-294, 1978.

D. Marr. *Vision.* W. H. Freeman and Company, San Francisco, 1982.

T. More. Notes on the Diagrams, Logic and Operations of Array Theory. In Bjorke and Franksen, editors, *Structures and Operations in Engineering and Management Systems.* Tapir Pub. , Norway, 1981.

D. Papadias. A Knowledge Representation Scheme for Imagery. Master's thesis, Queen's University, Kingston, 1990.

L. Pauling. *The Nature of the Chemical Bond.* Cornell University Press, Ithaca, 1939.

A. P. Pentland. Perceptual Organization and Representation of Natural Form. *Artificial Intelligence, 28* :295-331, 1986.

Z. W. Pylyshyn. The Imagery Debate: Analog Media Versus Tacit Knowledge. In N. Block, editor, *Imagery,* 151-206. MIT Press, 1981.

C. J. Rawlings, W. R. Taylor, J. Nyakairu, J. Fox and M. J. E. Sternberg. Reasoning about Protein Topology Using the Logic Programming Language PROLOG. *Journal of Molecular Graphics,* 3:151-157,1985.

M. J. Rooman and S. J. Wodak. Identification of Predictive Sequence Motifs Limited by Protein Structure Data Base Size. *Nature*, 335:45-49 1988.

M. G. Rossman. The Molecular Replacement Method. *Acta Crystallographica* A46:73-82, 1990.

R. S. Rowland, F. H. Allen, W . M. Carson, and C. E. Bugg. Preferred Interaction Patterns from Crystallographic Databases, In S. E. Ealick and C. E. Bugg, editors, *Crystallographic and Modeling Methods in Molecular Design.* Springer, New York, 1990.

L. Sawyer and M. N. G. James. Carboxyl-carboxylate Interactions in Proteins. *Nature,* 295:79-80, 1982.

R. N. Shepard and J. Metzler. Mental Rotation of Three-dimensional Objects. *Science,* 171:701-703, 1971.

R. Taylor and O. Kennard. Hydrogen-bond Geometry in Organic Crystals. *Accounts of Chemical Research,* 17:320-326, 1984.

A. Terry. The CRYSALIS Project: Hierarchical Control of Production Systems. Technical Report HPP-83-19, Stanford University, Palo Alto, CA, 1983.

J. D. Watson. *The Double Helix.* Wiley, New York, 1968.

W. T. Wippke and M. A. Hahn. AIMB: Analogy and Intelligence in Model Building. *Tetrahedron Computer Methodology,* 1:141-153, 1988.

The Anti-Expert System: Hypotheses an AI Program Should Have Seen Through

Joshua Lederberg

One of the most difficult steps in the development of an expert system is the recruitment and exploitation of the domain wizards. Almost always it is necessary to establish teams of specialists to deal with the programming issues and the user interfaces as well as the incorporation of domain specific knowledge. Experts will communicate how they read a gel, or what is the canonical biological interpretation of DNA sequences conserved over phyletically diverse organisms. The computer scientist will rarely have an independent base of knowledge and experience for critical judgments about the wisdom thus received.

Therein may lie the greatest hazards from the proliferation of expert systems; for much of that expertise is fallible.

It is 14 years since I have been actively involved in the collaborations that led to the DENDRAL and MOLGEN projects; and I am just now at an early stage of planning a resumption of research on theory formation and validation, as applied to molecular biology. But I recall how easily the most primitive errors could become locked into firm rules – which would sometimes persist for a long time until revealed by lucky accident. For example, we had what we called a *badlist* in DENDRAL, intended to filter out substructures that experience told were unstable or otherwise untenable. This can give enormous economy in pruning back a combinatorial explosion. One such rule was quite plausible: *badlist* included a proscription against substructures with 2 -NH_2 (amino) groups pendant on a single carbon; $C..(NH_2)^2$ can be expected to split off ammonia. But one of us overlooked two outstanding exceptions, namely urea (NH_2)-C=O-(NH_2) and guanidine, (NH_2)-C=NH-(NH_2). We were too fixated on prohibitions that would apply successfully to much larger molecules.

I intend, however, to put that self-skepticism to a larger, constructive purpose. My first target is an examination of many of the central doctrines in the history of micro- and molecular biology, especially those that we have learned to have led us to egregious error. I call those the "Myths we have lived and died by." By and large they are half-truths whose domain of veracity and application was perceived to go far beyond the evidentiary basis that led to their adoption. And we cannot live with prolonged suspension of disbelief in these myths, or we would be practicing nothing but an unremitting nihilism.

I will examine the logical structures that founded the adoption of these beliefs, and again the data and reconstructions that led to their demise. This will require a system of knowledge representation that will enable a more formal examination of these theories, and in turn a computer based system for critical scrutiny (theorem-proving) and new hypothesis generation. All of this work is a direct extrapolation of the DENDRAL effort, which used essentially the same approach for "theories" (postulated chemical structures) in the more readily formalizable domain of organic chemical analysis. There the data came originally from mass spectrometry and NMR; later we developed a more flexible interactive system (CONGEN) that enabled all source inputs. One of the interesting uses of CONGEN was as a theorem-prover, namely to reexamine the purported proofs of structure that had been published in a leading journal of organic chemistry. You guessed it, many of those proofs were at least formally defective; and in at least one case that had eluded the human reviewer, substantively so.

My intention is to review the principal doctrinal themes of molecular biology from a similar perspective. But armed with an easy retrospectroscope, I thought it only fair to be put on the line for some as yet unsubstantiated future revulsions of thought. These are to illustrate objectives. As yet I have done no explicit programming on this issue. Nevertheless, I have found great value in the style of thinking that is evoked in the context of designing the computer systems. (Harking back to DENDRAL, it also led to a style of crit-

ical mental chemistry that matches in importance the first order assistance
from the machine.)

So here are two intended *bona fides*—Contradictions to the existing
regime of thought that, I believe, will be experimentally tested in the near future. Both of them are deeply embedded in the conventional wisdom!

1. The 3-dimensional shape and functionality of (folded) proteins is fully
   determined by the primary amino-acid sequence, and this in turn by the
   nucleotide sequence of the gene. [The latter part of this statement is already eroded by knowledge of messenger RNA splicing, and further by
   some remarkable examples of post-transcriptional editing of RNA]. This
   doctrine has been essential for the development of mechanistic ideas of
   cell and organelle assembly, and especially for our modern views of antibody formation.

   But this is probably an overstatement. My counter-prediction is that we
   will discover examples where ambiguous and divergent patterns of folding
   will enable a given primary protein sequence to fold into two or more well
   defined, and biologically distinctive final conformations. It is hard for me
   to imagine that evolution has not exploited this potentiality for flexibility
   in use of a given blueprint. Evidence for this has been counter-selected,
   and often discarded as precipitates or "noise". A number of experts of
   folding have agreed, that "yes", this should be more carefully considered.

2. The germ line in multicellular animals is completely segregated from the
   soma. This Weismann's doctrine is the foundation of the refutation of
   lamarckian and lysenkoist ideas, and perhaps for that reason has never
   been critically examined, except with the crude anatomical methods of the
   last century. It is certainly very nearly true! However exceptions could be
   of critical importance, for evolution, pathology, and biotechnology.

I am seeking a still more systematic way to discover issues where a computer-aided custodian could be a help, not of mere incremental advance, but
of further scientific and technological revolutions. The following list is a
brief history of biological myths that took substantial effort to overthrow.
Could a computer program help us overthrow today's myths faster?

1. *Bacteria are Schizomycetes* i.e., divide only by fission. But Lederberg
   [1946] showed they had sex.

2. *Bacteria reproduce sexually* was a radical revision, but Lederberg
   [1951] took it too literally and missed the unique mechanisms of progressive DNA transfer (takes 100 minutes!) discovered by Jacob.

3. *Toxins kill* is an important paradigm in history of infectious disease. But
   the world (and Koch in particular) was misled for 80 years in searching
   for the "cholera toxin" as an agent lethal by parenteral assay. That toxin

"merely" promotes the secretion of water into the gut. The misunderstanding has cost tens of millions of lives that could have been saved by feeding salt water.

4. DNA → RNA. True enough, but it overlooked the reverse transcriptase (DNA ← RNA), which earned a Nobel Prize for Baltimore and Temin.

5. *Colinearity of DNA with protein* (1:1 theory) and *enzymes are proteins* were the key ideas in the classic work of Beadle and Tatum; Benzer; and Yanofsky. However, they overlooked mRNA processing and introns, which earned Cech a Nobel prize (for ribozymes).

6. *Only germ cells mate.* But somatic cells can be fused too [Lederberg 1955], and enable somatic cell genetic analysis; see the second "future myth," above.

7. *Mutations are deleterious.* This was long believed, but based on entirely circular reasoning, namely: most visible mutations are visible. But 99% of nucleotide substitutions are invisible. This myth delayed the evolutionary theory of drift [Kimura, 1991] and engendered gross miscalculations of the genetic disease load attributable to mutation.

8. *Mutations are spontaneous.* But they are chemical changes in DNA, and this is by no means homogeneous in molecular structure throughout the genome. In addition, DNA is deformed in a wide variety of ways as part of the mechanisms of regulation of gene expression. There is abundant chemical evidence that "activated" DNA is more accessible to reagents like dimethyl sulfate and DNAse-1; but the biological consequences of this differential reactivity have scarcely been examined.

9. *Genes have a fixed locus and segregate 1:1* (Mendel onward) But some genes jump! (McClintock) Segregation is not so rarely perturbed by "gene conversion"

10. *Infinitude of antibodies* and Pauling's instructionist theories. These ideas slowed the development of clonal selection theory, which is now the accepted explanation of antibody formation.

11. *Tetranucleotide DNA* - P.A. Levene's model was at most a tentative recapitulation of primitive data, but it was taken too rigidly, and greatly delayed the recognition of DNA as the genetic material

12. *Chemicals cause cancer.* Some do, but this idea greatly oversimplifies the multifactorial basis of carcinogenesis, and leads to enormous misfocus in managing environmental hazards.

13. *Life evolved on earth* - (Oparin, Miller-Urey). but chemical evolution probably started with cosmic condensation. Open possibility: all organic

material on earth is derived from cometary and meteoritic infall, may now be leading hypothesis.

With a few exceptions I have been personally involved in these bifurcations. At least once (2, above) to my chagrin!!

References

Detailed accounts and bibliographies of the cases mentioned can be found in the following sources:

Brock, T.D. 1990 *The Emergence of Bacterial Genetics*. Cold Spring Harbor Laboratory Press.

Buss, L.W. 1987. *The Evolution of Individuality*. Princeton University Press.

Friedland, P. and Kedes, L. 1985. Discovering the Secrets of DNA. *Comm. ACM* 28:1164-1186.

Kimura, Motoo, 1991 Recent Development of the Neutral Theory Viewed from the Wrightian Tradition of Theoretical Population Genetics. *Proc. Natl. Acad. Sci. USA* 88: 5969-5973.

Lederberg J. 1956. Prospects for the Genetics of Somatic and Tumor cells. *Ann. N.Y. Acad. Sci.* 63: 662-665.

Lederberg J., Cowie D.B. 1958. Moondust. *Science* 127: 1473-1475

Lederberg, J. 1987. How DENDRAL was Conceived and Born. In *ACM Conference on the History of Medical Informatics*. pp. 5-24. Association for Computing Machinery, N.Y., 1987.

Lederberg, J. 1988. The Ontogeny of the Clonal Selection Theory of Antibody Formation: Reflections on Darwin and Ehrlich: *Ann. NYAS* 546:175-187. 1988

Lederberg, J. 1991. The Gene (H. J. Muller 1947). *Genetics* 129:313-316.

Lindsay, R.K., B.G. Buchanan, E. A. Feigenbaum and J. Lederberg *Applications of Artificial Intelligence for Organic Chemistry: The Dendral Project*. McGraw-Hill Book Co., (1980).

McClintock, 1983. *The Significance of Responses of the Genome to Challenge*. Les Prix Nobel. Stockholm: Almqvist & Wiksell.

Stefik, M. 1981. Planning with Constraints MOLGEN .1. *Artificial Intelligence* 16: 111-139

Stryer, L. 1988. *Biochemistry* (3d. ed.) New York: W. H. Freeman.

Index

acid springs, 7

active conformation, 22

active site of an enzyme, 22

active site, 22, 31, 244, 297

adaptive optimization, 121, 157

adenine, 17, 23-24, 123, 369-371, 435

adenosine triphosphate, 16-18

AI techniques, 39, 210, 219, 368-369, 412, 417

alanine, 20-21, 25, 181, 350

algorithm, 60, 65, 112, 117, 122, 129-132, 134-137, 140, 146, 150-153, 155-159, 161, 201, 209, 217-219, 225-226, 230, 237, 243, 246-247, 254-258, 263, 270, 283, 304-305, 307, 319-321, 333-345, 349, 361-362, 435, 439, 448-450, 453-453, 455, 457

Allen, Frank H., 433

allosteric control, 22

allosteric regulation, 31

alphabet, 4, 22, 49-52, 58-59, 69, 73, 81, 103-105, 107, 216, 223

ambiguity, 55, 75-78, 98-100, 302, 307

ambiphilic residues, 181-182

amino acid, 0, 13, 18-23, 25, 27, 69, 92, 101, 104, 159, 161-163, 168-179, 182-185, 187-191, 193-194, 197-198, 200-201, 204-206, 210, 212-214, 216-217, 223-224, 228, 243-244, 246, 254, 269-270, 277-279, 282-284, 289, 397-399, 401, 403, 409, 417, 422
    residue, 178, 200
    sequence, 0, 13, 20, 22-23, 161, 169-170, 172, 174-175, 182, 184, 189-191, 194, 212-213, 216-217, 223-224, 254, 269, 277, 284, 403, 409
    See also amino acids

amino acids, 13, 17-23, 25-28, 66, 101, 149, 156, 159, 162, 164, 170-173, 176, 178-180, 182, 184-186, 188-189, 192-193, 197-198, 204-205, 207, 212, 214, 217-218, 220, 224, 227, 236-237, 239-240, 243, 254, 269-270, 278-281, 283, 397, 399, 401
    See also amino acid

amino group, 18

anticodon, 92-93

antisense message, 26

archaea, 6-7, 12, 14, 17, 41

archebacteria, 7

ARIADNE, 101, 119, 213, 219-221, 223-228, 236, 251, 255
    pattern language of, 224
    protein representation of, 223

ARIEL, 213, 219, 228-229, 231, 234, 236, 239, 242-243, 247, 251, 255

Aristotle, 5

ATMS, 308-311, 321

atoms, 13, 17, 19-23, 30-31, 42, 66, 162, 168, 188, 190, 197, 215-216, 270-271, 275, 277, 279-281, 284, 332, 398-399, 410, 413-414, 417, 434, 438, 444, 446-447, 451

ATP, 16-18, 252, 329-331, 352, 385-386
    see also adenosine triphosphate

Autoclass III, 280, 286

automata, 44, 52, 54-55, 57, 60, 62, 111, 119, 196, 205, 208

backbone, 20, 170, 198, 214, 279, 281, 397-399, 401-402, 457

backpropagation, 160, 165-166, 179, 189, 192, 200-202, 283

backward chaining, 367, 373-374, 380, 392

bacteria, 5-10, 12-14, 25-26, 34, 37-38, 40, 46, 292, 322, 352, 367, 461

bacteriophages, 7

behaviors, 31, 35, 119, 296, 300-301, 308, 319, 366, 374, 378

benzene, 21, 435

binary model, 140, 179-180, 182-183

biochemical pathways, 325, 333-335, 349, 361-363, 391

biochemical process, 15

biochemical reaction, 291, 302, 329, 332

biochemistry, 7, 11, 30, 34-35, 45, 127, 160, 209, 253, 256, 258, 289-291, 303, 307, 321, 360-361, 363-364, 393-395, 396, 463

biological knowledge, 1, 33, 289

biological sequence, 50, 119, 252, 256
    See also biological sequences

biological sequences, 47-49, 69, 82, 96-98, 115, 216, 218, 257

biomolecules, 12, 15-17, 269, 326

bioreaction, 326-327, 333-335, 349-351, 353-355, 359, 361-362

bioreactions, 325-327, 333-335, 353, 356, 360-362

blackboard system, 418-419

blood, 10-12, 15

Boltzmann machines, 122, 139-140, 158

bonding state, 183-184, 187, 191

bonds, chemical, 18

bones, 11

bottlenecks, 238, 349, 353, 355-356, 362

brain function, 137

brewer's yeast, 34

Brutlag, Douglas L., 365

cancer, 11, 33, 38, 43, 216, 462

canonical representations, 200

carbohydrates, 15, 18, 30, 43, 427

carbon atoms, 18-19, 21, 30, 281, 398, 413

carboxyl group, 19

cardiovascular tissue, 11

CASE system, 414

case-based methods, 272

catalysts, 13, 30, 123

catalyzed reactions, 30-31

cell membranes, 7, 12, 17

cells, 2, 4-15, 21, 29, 31, 33, 35, 37-38, 101, 123, 151, 211, 256, 271, 322, 325, 462-463
  types of, 11-12, 33, 100-101

chaining, 367, 373-374, 380, 391-392

chaining, backward, *see* backward chaining

chaperones, 22

characters, 16, 49, 193, 217, 224, 243-244, 246-247

chemical reactions, 13, 15, 17-18, 22, 31, 321

chemistry, 15-17, 22, 30, 101, 209, 363, 394, 396-397, 412, 429, 431, 445-446, 451, 453, 455-456, 460-461, 463

Chomsky hierarchy, 54, 57-59, 61-63, 69, 81, 85, 100, 105

chroloplasts, 14

chromosomes, 13, 18, 24-25, 29, 34, 37, 39-40, 85, 96, 107, 276

CKB, 292, 301, 321
  See also class knowledge base

class knowledge base, 292-294

closure properties, 58-59, 82, 87, 96

clustering, 177, 201-204, 207, 244, 247, 250, 253, 267, 280, 282, 286, 455
  algorithm, 201, 247, 455

codons, 25, 27-28, 32, 65, 67-68, 92-93, 104, 296

cognition, 2, 137, 159, 194, 260, 435, 437, 440-441

collaborative research, 44

compartments, 11, 16

computational biology, 42, 44, 48

computational linguistics, 47-49, 60, 120

computer languages, 63

conformation, 14, 20-22, 24, 27, 48, 102, 123, 162, 186, 191-192, 194, 196-197, 209, 214, 252-253, 269, 271, 307, 400, 412, 417, 447

connection machine, 201, 228, 236, 238, 240, 255

connection weights, 136, 138-139, 144-145, 147, 150, 152-153, 155, 174

connectionist research, 137, 158

connective tissue, 11

context-free languages, 51-52, 99, 118, 120

context-sensitive languages, 53

control regions, 29, 102

control signals, 27

copia, 94

COSI, 421, 424, 426

CRYSALIS, 417, 430, 432, 454, 458

crystal structure, 161, 191, 252, 400, 433-435, 437-439, 443, 446-448, 451, 453-456
  recognition, 447

crystallographers, 208, 435, 444-445, 454

crystallographic application, 447

crystallographic phase problem, 435, 442-443

crystallography, 42, 123, 161, 168, 286, 400, 437-438, 442, 446, 453, 456

crystals, 2, 162, 191, 214, 276, 400, 435, 456, 458

CSA, 421, 423-424

currency metabolite, 18

cysteine, 21, 183-188, 193, 244, 256

cytoplasm, 12, 14, 27, 41

cytosine, 23, 123, 369

cytosines, 24

data structure, 68, 236, 305-306, 435, 437-439, 453

decarboxylases, 30

decidability properties, 59

degeneracy of the code, 25

dehydrogenases, 30

DENDRAL, 225, 256, 412-414, 429, 431-432, 453, 459-460, 463

deoxyribose, 23, 160

developmental grammars, 64

developmental pathways, 5

diploids, 24, 25, 32, 107

discovery system, 263-266, 272

discovery, 5, 7, 47, 97, 115, 211, 218, 259-266, 268-274, 279, 284-285, 287, 323, 366, 391, 435

discovery, AI approaches, 261

discrete-event simulation, 367-368

disulphide bonds, 21, 400

diversity of living things, 4-5, 11

DNA Database, 43

DNA metabolism, 317, 322, 365, 368-369, 371, 380, 391

DNA sequence, mapping from, 26

DNA sequences, 8, 24, 26, 39, 61, 118-120, 216, 254-256, 459
coding of, 26
DNA, 0, 3, 8, 12-14, 16-17, 19, 23-29, 32, 34, 36-41, 43, 46-48, 61, 63, 65, 67, 69-72, 75, 77-82, 85-87, 93, 96-99, 101-104, 106-107, 109, 115, 118-120, 123, 158, 161, 163, 212, 216, 235, 254-258, 290-294, 298, 307-309, 311, 313, 317, 320, 322, 365, 368-377, 379-394, 435, 459, 461-463
double bonds, 21
drug testing, 33
dyad symmetry, 51, 70, 104
E. coli, 7, 34, 38, 92, 115, 221-222, 289, 291, 314, 368-370
Earley parsers, 60
Edwards, Peter, 396
egg cell, 14
electron density, 435, 444, 446, 448-453, 454
embryological development, 2
endocrine tissue, 11
endoplasmic reticulum, 15
energy assumption, minimal free, 128
energy, 2-3, 6, 10, 13-19, 22, 30-31, 117, 123-125, 127-131, 134-135, 137-144, 146-147, 150, 162-163, 191, 194, 214-215, 271, 273, 327-333, 335, 363, 412
entropy, 17
enzymes, 13, 18, 22, 30-31, 38-40, 85, 117, 123, 289-290, 311, 314, 318, 325-327, 342, 349, 353-354, 361, 366-369, 374-377, 379, 390-393, 397, 462
epithelium, 11
escherichia coli, 7, 34, 368, 394
escherichia coli, see also E. coli
eubacteria, 7
eucarya, 6-9, 14, 46
eucaryotes, 6, 11, 13-14, 25-26, 29, 33-34
eucaryotic cells, 6, 11-14, 29, 31, 34
eukaryotes, 5, 106, 114, 254
European Molecular Biology Laboratory, 43
evolution, 2-5, 8-9, 11, 16, 25, 29, 31-32, 45, 85, 87, 93, 96, 102, 105-109, 116, 257, 431, 461-463
evolutionary linguistics, 105
evolutionary process, 2-3
evolutionary theories, 8, 462
evolutionary variation, 4
exhaustive search, 130-132, 134, 162
exons, 26-28, 68
fats, 12, 18, 30
feedforward networks, 165-166
folded protein, 20, 22-23, 26, 101, 162, 178, 179, 192, 461
formal language theory, 48, 57, 61, 79, 85, 117, 119
Fortier, Suzanne, 433

forward chaining, 367, 373, 380, 391
frame structure, 435, 438
functional languages, 102-104
Galper, Adam R., 365
gel electrophoresis, 36-37, 39
Genbank, 43, 46, 68, 169
gene duplication, 32
gene expression, 12, 47, 99-100, 116-118, 316, 323, 327, 367, 462
gene grammars, 65, 68-69, 97, 100
genetic code, 12, 21-22, 24, 32, 47, 120, 161, 213, 255
genetic expression, 24, 35
genetic material, 2, 4-7, 9-10, 12-15, 19, 32, 462
genetic messages, 12
genetic regulation, 29, 394
genetic simulator, 290
GENEX, 316
genotype, 3-4
GENSIM, 290-292, 296, 298, 300-303, 306-308, 311, 313-314, 318-321
See also genetic simulator
Glasgow, Janice I., 433
glutamate dehydrogenase, 351, 353
glutamine synthetase, 351
glycine, 20-21, 181-182, 350, 359
glycogen, 18-19
glycolysis, 14, 350, 355, 360
Golgi apparatus, 15
grammar derivation, 116
grammar rules, 53, 65, 116
grammars, 48, 50-57, 59-60, 64-66, 68-69, 71-72, 75-76, 81, 87-90, 94-97, 99-101, 103, 105-106, 108, 110-120, 219
grammatical inference, 60, 114-115
greedy algorithms, 132, 342
guanine, 23, 123, 369
helices, 23, 28, 163, 197, 205-207, 224, 249, 278, 417, 446
helix-turn-helix motif, 23
helper molecules, 22
See also chaperones
heme, 13, 23, 177, 183, 187
heuristic algorithms, 131-132
hierarchical pattern-matching, 218
hierarchical representations, 195
histidine, 21-22, 181, 226
HOHAHA, 401-409, 416, 419-422, 425, 428
Holbrook, Stephen R., 161
human language, 48, 61, 120
Hunter, Lawrence, 1, 259
hydrogen atom, 20
hydrogen bonds, 23-24, 41, 127-128, 278, 399

hydrophillic, 12

hydrophobic sidechains, 21

image construction, 449

imagery, 286, 433-442, 445, 447, 453-457

indexed languages, 56, 81

inference, 60, 101, 114-115, 119, 199, 213, 215, 219-220, 225-226, 254-255, 258, 260, 262-268, 270-271, 276-280, 283-284, 287, 367-368, 374, 380, 412, 431

inferences, 9, 31, 195, 225, 262, 265, 268, 270-271, 274, 285, 436, 440

information processing, 16

inheritance, 2-3, 5, 9, 32, 35, 39, 290, 298, 300-301, 309, 319-321, 391, 453

INITIAL, 79, 83, 111-112, 134, 145, 151-154, 162, 166, 208, 212-213, 215, 218-219, 228, 231, 239, 290, 311-314, 316, 321-322, 333, 335-336, 339-340, 343-344, 354, 356, 361, 368, 373, 383-384, 400, 421-422, 434, 441, 453-453

IntelliCorp, 291, 309, 323, 374, 393

interactions, 15-16, 29, 31, 102, 116, 123, 127-128, 149, 164, 172, 175, 178, 191, 194, 207, 217, 242, 301, 304, 321, 332, 366, 368, 374, 376, 378, 383, 391-393, 399-404, 406, 408-410, 421, 424-425, 446-447, 451, 457

intermediary metabolism, 30, 44, 317, 326, 333, 368

intestines, 7

intra-molecular interactions, 116

introns, 26-28, 32, 41, 91, 102, 462

INVESTIGATOR, 268, 274-275

ionization, 20

ionize, 20-21

Karp, Peter, 44, 289

KEE, 44, 291-292, 296, 300, 302, 307, 309, 319, 321, 323, 374, 380-382, 388, 390-391, 393

Kim, Sung-Hou, 161

kinases, 30, 244

kinetic bottleneck, 355

knowledge acquisition strategies, 271, 274

knowledge goals, 265-266, 271, 274

knowledge-based systems, 29, 419

L-system, 57, 64,118
  See also Lindenmayer system

language families, 54, 57-59, 82, 84-85, 99

language theory, 48, 57, 61, 79, 85, 97, 117, 119

language, 2, 5, 16, 47-52, 54-63, 65-66, 69-73, 75-86, 95-101, 103-108, 111, 113-114, 116-120, 209, 213, 219, 224, 226, 228, 236, 239, 257, 285, 300-301, 319, 321, 323, 412, 437, 445, 453, 456-457

Lathrop, Richard H., 211

law of thermodynamics, 17

Lederberg, Joshua, 459

Lian, Lu Yun, 396

life, 2-4, 7-9, 11-12, 15-18, 26, 29, 34, 36, 45, 48, 84, 97-98, 106, 314, 317, 462

life, building blocks of, 16

ligaments, 11

Lindenmayer systems, 57, 120

linguistic tools, 63, 97, 117

linguistics, mathematical, 48-49

lipids, 12, 15, 17

LISP, 44, 236, 293, 314, 327, 343, 362, 374, 381-382, 412

living parts, 11

logic grammar formalisms, 48

lymphatic tissue, 11

lysine pathways, 349

lysosomes, 15

machine imagery, 433, 436-437, 440, 442, 447, 455

machine learning system, 263-264

macromolecules, 15, 48, 119, 137, 160, 257, 290, 401, 434, 445, 454

Mavrovouniotis, Michael L., 325

mechanisms of evolution, 31

membrane, 12-13, 15, 17, 34, 191, 193

mental imagery, 434, 436, 439, 441-442, 454, 456

metabolic pathways, 5, 30-31, 325-327, 366-368, 379-380, 383, 387, 389, 394

metabolite-processing phase, 336, 338-340, 342

metabolites, 30, 326-327, 332-336, 342, 344-348, 350, 352, 354, 361-362, 367, 374

methionine, 21, 181

MFT machine, 136, 141

MFT networks, 122, 132, 139-140, 156

Millis, David H., 365

mitochondria, 6, 14, 25, 34

model building, 193-194, 446, 451, 457-458

model organisms, 33, 35, 44

models, binary *see* binary model

modern organisms, 9, 14

molecular scene analysis, 433, 455

molecular segments, 279

MOLGEN, 459, 463

morphology, 5, 118, 443

mucus, 11

multicellular organisms, 5-6, 9-11, 13

muscles, 11, 13, 18, 397

Muskal, Steven M., 161

mutation, 3-4, 8-9, 32, 35, 48, 93, 108-109, 111, 116, 168, 212, 216, 297, 311, 369, 462

mutations, 9, 32, 35, 37, 68, 93, 106, 108, 112, 212, 216-217, 226, 293, 296-297, 301, 369, 462

natural language, 49, 61-63, 65, 82, 98, 116, 118, 120

natural selection, 3

nature, 9, 36, 45, 55, 66, 68-69, 74, 77, 88, 94, 96-97, 99, 101-102, 104, 115, 137, 148, 160, 192,

194, 208-209, 216, 218, 249, 251-258, 270-271, 285, 287, 324, 337-338, 375, 394, 396-397, 420-422, 425-426, 437, 456-457

nerves, 11

network optimization, 165, 167

network performance, 138, 167, 176, 184-185

network weights, 166, 173, 178, 182-183

neural networks, 44, 121-122, 136-138, 147, 149, 154, 156-161, 163-164, 168, 170, 173, 175, 177-179, 189, 192-193, 209, 252, 256, 258, 261, 264, 274, 283
  analysis in, 180
  applications, 137
  models, 138, 150

neural networks, learning in, 138

New York Times, 16

NMR spectra of proteins, 396-397, 401

NMR spectrum, 401, 414, 427

NMR, 42-43, 162, 168, 191, 214-215, 396-397, 400-403, 406, 408-409, 412-420, 426-432, 453-454, 460
  See also nuclear magnetic resonance

node weights, 144

NOESY, 401-403, 407-410, 416, 419, 421-422, 425-427
  technique, 407

NOISE, 171, 212, 217, 275, 277, 397, 402, 420-422, 449, 461

noncoding sequences, 26
  See also introns

nondeterministic languages, 55

nuclear magnetic resonance, 42, 46, 214, 396-397, 426, 428-432

nuclei, 6-8, 13, 401

nucleic acid, 17, 23, 46, 69, 72, 84, 103, 105, 117, 133, 160, 169, 257-258, 294, 394

nucleic acids, 17, 23-26, 45, 69-71, 73, 75, 77-78, 81-82, 84, 87, 96, 101-103, 105, 107, 118, 120, 123, 159-160, 168, 194, 251, 253, 258, 323, 397, 432, 446

nucleotides, 16, 23-25, 27, 32, 90, 106-107, 127, 369, 371, 373, 376, 381, 385, 388-390

nutrients, 4, 11-12, 17

object descriptions, 308

object forking, 290, 303, 307-309, 319, 321

object management, 302, 306

object merging, 308, 319

object representations, 378

oils, 12, 17

oligonucleotides, 40

oligos *see* oligonucleotides

ontology, 249, 290-291, 321

organelles, 6-8, 11, 14

organisms, 0, 2-15, 17, 20, 24-25, 30-35, 38-39, 44, 46, 97-98, 108, 113, 459

oxidative phosphorylation, 14

oxygen, 6, 13-14, 19, 183, 398-399

PAGODA, 264, 286

parallelism, 122, 129, 137, 157, 273, 453

parse tree, 63-66, 68, 111

parsers, 60-61, 78, 97, 112, 275

parsing, 25, 60-61, 63, 65, 78, 88, 92-94, 98, 100, 110, 112-113, 117

pathway, 156, 311-312, 314, 318, 322, 326-327, 333-346, 349, 351-362, 366-367, 379-380, 382, 388-391, 393

pathways, 5, 30-31, 33, 225, 325-327, 333-349, 352, 354-355, 358-363, 365-369, 380, 383, 387, 389-391, 394, 409

pathways, biochemical, *see* biochemical pathways

pattern construction, 218, 225, 228, 231, 235-236, 243, 246-247, 249

pattern recognition, 63, 97, 116, 119-120, 149, 193, 209-210, 225, 253, 434-435, 451, 455

patterns, 35, 42, 63, 85, 90-91, 101, 138, 165-167, 169, 180, 190, 204-206, 210-214, 217-220, 222, 224-225, 227-231, 233-234, 236-243, 246-252, 254, 257, 366, 399, 403-404, 407, 409, 415, 450, 455-457, 461

PCR *see* polymerase chain reaction

people, 2, 5-6, 9-11, 22, 33-35, 38, 261, 273, 436

PEPTIDE, 19-20, 27-28, 183, 194, 198, 252, 316, 319-320, 390-391, 397, 399, 403, 408-410, 425, 428
  bonds, 19, 20, 27-28, 198, 399

phages, *see* .bacteriophages

phenotype, 3-5

phenylalanine, 21

phosphatases, 30

phospholipid cell membrane, 12

phospholipids, 12

photosynthesis, 17

phylogeny of languages, 113

physical maps, 40

physics, 1, 17, 20, 77, 129, 159, 308, 319, 322, 363, 393, 429

physiology, 5, 15, 35, 107

PKB *see* process knowledge base

polarity, 20

poly-A tail, 27

polymerase chain reaction, 7, 40-42

polymerase, 26-28, 40-41, 76, 95, 119, 291, 295, 297-298, 307-308, 311, 313-314, 320, 369-373, 377-379, 382-384, 386-390, 392

polymers, 19, 23, 397

polypeptides, 19-20, 194, 255, 314, 397, 422

prediction, 21-22, 97, 118-119, 121-123, 126, 128, 130, 133, 136-137, 144-146, 148-151, 153, 155-164, 167-168, 170-183, 187, 189-194, 197, 206-207, 209, 212, 214-215, 221, 226, 249, 252-258, 260-261, 269-270, 272, 275, 277-278, 283-288, 311, 313-314, 322, 363, 365, 379-380, 383, 386,

403, 409, 413, 417, 427, 432, 453-454, 456

predictions, 143, 153, 162, 170, 173, 175-178, 180-186, 192-193, 196, 218, 221, 223, 226-227, 252-253, 261, 272, 275, 292, 302, 309, 321-322, 368, 382, 388

primary sequences, 212, 215-218, 220, 231

primary structure, 19-20, 23, 25, 122-123, 161, 191, 212, 397, 399-400, 403, 417

primary transcript, 27-28, 319

primitives, 150, 196, 199, 201, 208, 224-225, 236

problem space, 271, 277

process activation, 304

process execution, 290, 302, 304, 306

process interpreter, 296, 300-301, 304-306, 321, 391

process knowledge base, 290, 296, 298, 299, 301, 304, 308, 321

process preconditions, 300, 304-307, 321

process selection, 304

prokaryotes, 5, 7, 114, 254

PROLOG, 66, 68, 88-89, 93, 110-112, 119, 257, 318-319, 412, 457

promoter, 28, 62, 95, 115, 291, 294, 296, 303, 308, 313, 317

promoters, 27, 29, 95, 296-297, 313

PROTEAN, 254, 410, 416-417, 430
    system, 410, 416

proteases, 30, 183, 193, 244

Protein NMR Assistant, 417, 419-420, 426-428

protein chemistry, 209, 397

protein folding problem, 22, 195

protein NMR, 400, 415, 417, 419-420, 426-429

protein sequences, 24, 43, 48, 119, 161, 169, 175, 179, 205, 208, 212-213, 216-219, 223, 228, 236, 246-247, 252, 254-255, 257, 274, 276

protein structures, 21, 42-43, 102, 116, 119, 122, 159-164, 167-170, 178, 183-184, 189, 191-192, 193, 194-201, 204, 206-209, 212, 214-216, 219, 224, 252, 253-255, 257-260, 268-270, 272, 274, 277-281, 284, 286-287, 397, 402-403, 415, 417, 427-430, 433, 445, 453, 454, 456, 457
    features of, 161, 192

protein, 0, 7, 12-13, 19-29, 31-32, 37-39, 42-43, 45-46, 48, 101-102, 106, 109, 116, 119, 122, 145, 149, 157-164, 167-170, 172, 175, 177-180, 182-184, 189-201, 204-220, 222-225, 228, 231, 236-237, 244-248, 250-261, 265, 268-281, 284-288, 291, 296-298, 301, 311-314, 319, 397-403, 407-408, 410, 415-417, 419-423, 425-430, 433, 445, 453, 454-457, 461-462

pseudogenes, 32, 68

qualitative biochemistry, 289-291, 321, 394

quaternary structure, 23

reaction representations, 300

recombination, 3-4, 9, 48, 84-85, 107, 109, 117, 370

reference patching, 303-304

replication, 78, 82-83, 109, 117, 368-371, 393-394

representation, 0, 47, 65, 77, 93-94, 102, 118, 122, 124, 128, 136, 141-142, 144-151, 155, 157, 162, 167, 181, 189-190, 195-201, 205, 207-209, 217, 219, 223-224, 227, 234, 236, 257, 260, 264-268, 270, 275, 283, 289-292, 301, 309, 318-319, 367-368, 372, 374, 377-380, 382, 391-394, 419, 422, 424-425, 428, 433, 435-442, 447, 449, 451-453, 455, 457, 460

repressors, 29

reproduction, 2, 4, 9, 16, 32, 34-35

residue state classes, 204

respiration, 6, 14, 17

reverse complementarity, 69

reverse transcriptase, 41, 462

ribose, 23

ribosomes, 7, 14, 123, 314

rings, 21, 188, 399, 446

RNA structure, 26, 70, 128, 130, 145, 148, 156

RNA, 13-14, 16-17, 23-24, 26-28, 69-70, 74, 76-77, 79, 87, 90, 92-93, 95, 97, 100, 104, 107, 118-137, 139, 141-157, 159-160, 256, 290-291, 294-295, 297-298, 307-311, 313-314, 320, 323, 369, 393, 461-462

Roberts, Gordon C. K., 396

rule extraction, 165

rule-based expert systems, 225, 393

saccharomyces cervesiae, 34

SAM, 421, 423, 425-426

scientists, 0-2, 24, 33, 36, 43-44, 192, 259-260, 262-263, 267, 272-273, 276-277, 368-369

SEAC, 415

search algorithms, 122, 129-130, 132

search space, 3, 9, 129-131, 134-137, 145, 225, 262, 448, 453

Searls, David B., 47

secondary metabolism, 30

secondary structure, 23, 71-81, 88-92, 94, 96-97, 99, 101-105, 116, 118, 121-125, 127-136, 141-145, 147-151, 153, 155, 157-160, 169-173, 175, 177-178, 182, 186-187, 190-194, 197, 199, 207, 209, 212, 218, 221-223, 227, 253-256, 258, 261, 265, 277-288, 397, 399, 403, 408-410, 416-417, 419, 421, 425-429, 453

selection, 2-5, 10, 32-33, 97, 107, 109, 163, 226, 228, 251, 260, 262, 264, 266-268, 270, 272-277, 279-280, 283, 285, 304, 326-327, 391, 401, 450, 462-463
    process, 4, 272, 275

sequence analysis, 48, 97, 119, 210, 213, 216, 219, 252, 255, 456

sequence databases, 0, 24, 168, 248, 250, 252, 257

sequence tagged sites, 41

serial algorithms, 128, 149

serine, 21, 244, 256, 311

sexual recombination, 3-4, 9

SID, 421-424, 426

sidechains, 20-22

simulation, 117-118, 133, 152, 156, 162, 167, 194, 261, 271-273, 289-292, 298, 301, 304-310, 317-323, 365-369, 373-375, 377-383, 386, 390-395

skin, 10-11, 397

Sleeman, Derek, 395

SLOC, 421, 425

small molecules, 15-17, 162, 291, 434, 444, 446, 454

Smith, Randall F., 211

Smith, Temple F., 210

spin systems, 403, 405, 407-409, 417, 428

spliceosome, 27

splicing, 26-27, 32, 68, 73, 85, 87, 98, 461

STAN, 421, 425-426

state vector, 199-201, 206

Steeg, Evan W., 121

stoichiometric constraints, 327, 334-335, 338-339, 342, 361

STREC system, 415

string variable grammars, 89

structural linguistics, 69

structure determination, 161-163, 169, 209, 400, 410, 415, 429-431, 433-435, 437, 439, 443-448, 453, 454-456

STSs *see* sequence tagged sites

subpathway, 335

substrates, 30-31, 191, 214, 275, 290, 325-327, 333, 342, 349, 367-368, 376, 391-392

sulfur compounds, 17

sulphur vents, 7

sunlight, 6, 14, 17

super-secondary structure, 23, 169, 197, 206, 209, 218, 258

superpositional grammars, 94

symbolic array, 434-435, 437-442, 451-453

symbols, 22, 49-50, 52, 54, 56, 59, 62, 96, 124, 205, 208, 298, 422, 434, 439

synthesis algorithm, 335-336, 339-340, 361

synthetases, 30, 211, 258

tendons, 11, 397

ternary model, 179-181

tertiary structure prediction, 156, 164, 175, 189-190, 215, 417

tertiary structure, 23, 122-123, 149, 156, 158, 163-164, 175, 189-191, 193, 212, 215, 268-269, 397, 400, 416-417

thermodynamic feasibility, 327, 361

threonine, 21, 181, 226, 244, 404-406, 425

thymine, 23-24, 369

Tinoco model, 129

Tinoco-Uhlenbeck Theory, 127

tissue types, 11

tissues, 11, 15, 45, 100

topoisomerases, 29

transferases, 30

translation, 3, 25-27, 30, 98-100, 161, 169, 277, 279-280, 290, 314, 318, 370, 378, 380, 383, 392, 435, 451

transmembrane potential, 18

trp biosynthetic pathway, 311, 318, 322

trp system, 292, 296, 311, 314, 316-318

tryptophan operon, 289, 291, 322, 394

tryptophan, 21, 289, 291, 301, 311, 322, 394

two-dimensional NMR, 401-402, 418, 427

tyrosine, 21, 245

vacuoles, 15

vertebrates, 12

virus, 2, 5, 7, 13, 34, 37, 40, 90, 175, 184, 192, 211, 252-254, 257, 317

viruses, 2-4, 7, 13, 26, 68, 99, 247, 257, 445

vision applications, 447

Waltz, David, 195

water, 12, 16, 18-19, 21, 169, 178, 199, 208, 275, 422, 462

Webster, Tereas A., 211

Winston, Patrick H., 210

X-ray crystallography, 42, 123, 161, 168, 400, 456

X-ray, 42, 121, 123, 161-162, 168, 191, 214-215, 222, 399-400, 415, 417, 430, 456

yeasts, 5-6, 11, 34, 40, 250, 255

Zhang, Xiru, 195